Detecting Women

D1520900

Detecting Women

Gender and the Hollywood Detective Film

PHILIPPA GATES

Published by State University of New York Press, Albany

Printed in the United States of America

For information, contact State University of New York Press, Albany, NY
www.sunypress.edu

Production by Kelli W. LeRoux
Marketing by Anne M. Valentine

Library of Congress Cataloging-in-Publication Data

Gates, Philippa, 1973–
    Detecting women : gender and the Hollywood detective film / Philippa Gates.
        p. cm.
    Includes bibliographical references and index.
    ISBN 978-1-4384-3405-6 (hardcover : alk. paper)
    ISBN 978-1-4384-3404-9 (pbk. : alk. paper)
    1. Detective and mystery films—United States—History and criticism.   2. Women
detectives in motion pictures.   3. Women in motion pictures.   I. Title.

    PN1995.9.D4G385 2011
    791.43'6556—dc22   2010023363

10 9 8 7 6 5 4 3 2 1

Contents

List of Illustrations   vii

Acknowledgments   ix

PART I

The Crime Lab
Gender and the Detective Genre

1 INTRODUCTION: The Case   3

2 DETECTING CRITICISM: Theorizing Gender and the Detective Genre   17

PART II

The Rise and Demise of the Classical Female Detective
1929 to 1950

3 MOVIE MODERNIZATION: The Film Industry and Working Women
   in the Depression   43

4 DETECTING AS A HOBBY: Amateur and Professional Detectives
   in the 1930s   69

5 SOB SISTERS DON'T CRY: The Girl Reporter as Detective in the 1930s 93

6 IN NAME ONLY: The Transformation of the Female Detective
   in the 1940s   135

7 THE MARITORIOUS MELODRAMA: The Female Detective in 1940s
   Film Noir   163

PART III

From Crime-Fighter to Crime Scene Investigator
1970 to Today

8 FEMME MIGHT MAKES RIGHT: The 1970s Blaxploitation Vigilante
    Crime-Fighter   191

9 DETECTING THE BOUNDS OF THE LAW: The Female Lawyer
   Thriller of the 1980s   221

10 DETECTING IDENTITY: From Investigative Thrillers to Crime Scene
   Investigators   257

Appendix I   299

Appendix II   301

Appendix III   331

Notes   333

Selected Filmography   353

Works Cited   361

Index   375

List of Illustrations

Figure 1.1   Angela Lansbury as Jessica Fletcher   5

Figure 1.2   Rebecca De Mornay in *Guilty as Sin*   16

Figure 2.1   Bonita Granville in *Nancy Drew, Trouble Shooter*   28

Figure 2.2   Pam Grier in *Foxy Brown*   37

Figure 3.1   Fay Wray and Glenda Farrell in *Mystery of the Wax Museum*   58

Figure 3.2   Claire Trevor in *Career Woman*   65

Figure 4.1   Lola Lane in *Girl from Havana*   74

Figure 4.2   Edna May Oliver as Hildegarde Withers   83

Figure 5.1   Carole Lombard and Robert Armstrong in *Big News*   100

Figure 5.2   Glenda Farrell as Torchy Blane and Barton MacLane as
              Steve McBride   120

Figure 6.1   Rosalind Russell and Cary Grant in *His Girl Friday*   142

Figure 6.2   Florence Rice in *Girl in 313*   155

Figure 7.1   June Vincent and Dan Duryea in *Black Angel*   176

Figure 7.2   Ann Sheridan in *Woman on the Run*   181

Figure 8.1   Tamara Dobson in *Cleopatra Jones*   201

Figure 8.2   Pam Grier in *Friday Foster*   209

Figure 9.1   Glenn Close and Jeff Bridges in *Jagged Edge*   230

Figure 9.2   Cher in *Suspect*   245

Figure 10.1   Jodie Foster in *The Silence of the Lambs*   272

Figure 10.2   Holly Hunter in *Copycat*   279

Acknowledgments

The author gratefully acknowledges that financial support for this research was received from a grant partly funded by Wilfrid Laurier University Operating funds and partly by the SSHRC Institutional Grant awarded to Wilfrid Laurier University.

The author would like to thank Jenny Romero of the *Margaret Herrick Library*, Mark Quigley of the *UCLA Film and Television Archive*, Eve Goldin and Kristen MacDonald of *The Film Reference Library* in Toronto, and Heidi Rubenstein of *Special Collections* at Georgetown University for their assistance during my research trips to their archives. I would like to acknowledge the wonderful contribution that Joe Saltzman has made to documenting the history of the female reporter with the *Image of the Journalist in Popular Culture* online resource. I would also like to thank Larin McLaughlin for her support of this project at SUNY Press and Kelli LeRoux for all of her hard work through the production stages.

On a more personal note, I would like to thank my friends and colleagues at Laurier—Andrea Austin, Madelaine Hron, Russell Kilbourn, Ute Lischke, Tanis McDonald, Mariam Pirbhai, Katherine Spring, Paul Tiessen, Eleanor Ty, and Jim Weldon—for their friendship and support. I would like to thank my doctoral student Elizabeth Clarke for sharing with me her own research on Hollywood's male detectives of the 1950s and 60s, and my colleague Paul Heyer and former undergraduate student Ashley Bell for bringing to my attention even more *noir* films with female detectives. I would especially like to thank my research assistant Lisa Funnell who discovered the female reporter in the B-western and did so much digging for me that one summer in the initial stages of the project. Lastly, thank you to my parents—Philip and Micaela Gates—who initiated and continue to share my passion for detective films—from Warren William in the 1930s to Clint Eastwood in the 1970s to Ashley Judd in the 2000s. This book is for you!

The author is grateful for the kind permission to reproduce selections from the following copyrighted material:

An earlier version of Chapter 7—The Maritorious Melodrama: The Female Detective in 1940s *Film Noir*—appeared as "The Maritorious Melodrama: *Film Noir* with a Female Detective" in the *Journal of Film and Video* 61.3 (Fall 2009) by Philippa Gates. Copyright © 2009 by the Board of Trustees of the University of Illinois. Used with permission of the University of Illinois Press.

An earlier version of Chapter 10—Detecting Identity: From Investigative Thrillers to Crime Scene Investigators—appeared as "Manhunting: The Female Detective in the Contemporary Serial Killer Film" in *Post Script: Essays in Film and the Humanities* 24.1 (Fall 2004) by Philippa Gates. Copyright © 2004 by Post Script, Inc. Used with permission of Post Script, Commerce, TX.

Part I

The Crime Lab

Gender and the Detective Genre

1

Introduction

The Case

In *All about Eve* (Mankiewicz, 1950), Margo Channing (Bette Davis) explains her dilemma as a woman with a career as a star of the stage:

> Funny business—a woman's career. The things you drop on your way up the ladder so you can move faster; you forget you'll need them again when you get back to being a woman. It's the one career all females have in common whether we like it or not: being a woman. Sooner or later we've got to work at it, no matter how many other careers we've had or wanted. And in the last analysis, nothing's any good unless you can look up just before dinner or turn around in bed—and there he is! Without that you're not a woman. You're something with a French provincial office or a book full of clippings . . . but you are not a woman.

Although Margo is speaking for the woman in postwar America, she sums up the fears of all career women in Hollywood film—from the 1930s to today. According to Hollywood, a career and marriage do not mix and without the latter, "you are not a woman." In order to succeed at a career, a woman must abandon many of her softer, "feminine" traits and embrace the more "masculine" ones of ambition, drive, and independence; however, being too masculine drives away male suitors and—as is implied in the majority of Hollywood films—life without marriage and a family cannot be considered a successful one. Thus, if a woman in a Hollywood film chooses to have a career, then she must at least demonstrate the willingness to abandon it at some point for a man. This is the product of the assumption that there is something "unnatural" (read: masculine or lesbian) about the woman who denies the socially prescribed—but perceived as natural—roles of wife and mother. The Hollywood heroine is ultimately faced with the "problem" of finding a balance between her professional ambitions and personal happiness and of how to avoid "dropping"—on her way up the career ladder—those feminine charms she will need later to catch a husband.

"Can a woman have it all—a husband, a family, and a career? The question is hardly new, but it was back then," Mick LaSalle notes in regard to Depression-era Hollywood film (184). Films of the 1930s offered a space for the exploration of changing women's roles. Just as Ben Singer has reminded us of the existence and popularity of female heroines in the action serials of the 1910s that were since forgotten ("Female," 91) and books on pre-Code film, like LaSalle's, that remind us that female stars dominated the box office in the 1930s, so too is one aim of *Detecting Women* to recover a decade of strong female protagonists and stars all but forgotten today. The proliferation of feminist film theory and gender studies has encouraged the re-examination of women's presence and contributions to classical Hollywood film, but only certain kinds of recovery work have been undertaken. Discussions of women in the 1930s and 40s tend to focus on the "bad girls" of pre-Code "fallen women" films or of *film noir*, or the "good girls" of the woman's film. I am interested, however, in exploring the "good girls"—women who were the center and driving force behind narratives and presented as positive models of womanhood—at the center of the traditionally male genre of the detective film.

From her first appearance in nineteenth-century fiction to the contemporary criminalist film, the female detective has struggled to be both a successful detective and a successful woman. As Kathleen Gregory Klein indicates, this was the practice from the earliest of the British detective stories and American dime novels: the female detective—whether American or British, working or upper class—was never allowed to blend effectively the two roles of woman and detective (35). The only female detectives who seem to have avoided this dilemma are those who are either too old—e.g., spinster Jane Marple and widow Jessica Fletcher—or too young—e.g., teenager Nancy Drew—for romantic relationships and thus elude the complications that arise when career and romance compete. The vast majority of fictional female detectives from 1864 to today, however, have been forced to make a decision to pursue either love or detection because the two are seen as mutually exclusive—the former requiring the detective to be feminine and the latter masculine. In terms of feminist criticism, this exclusivity has incited debate amongst scholars whether the female detective is merely an impossible fantasy as embodying both feminine and masculine traits or a realistic advancement of female empowerment. In terms of popular debate, it is often assumed that it took the Women's Movement beginning in the 1960s to spark empowered representations of women in Hollywood film and that classical Hollywood tended to construct female characters in keeping with old-fashioned (read: Victorian) values and gender roles. In the new millennium, we assume that we have made progress in terms of equal rights and opportunities across the lines of class, race, sexuality, and especially gender; however, contemporary mainstream film does not necessarily advance themes any more progressive than those touted in classical Hollywood films more than half a century ago. In fact, in *Detecting Women*, I will demonstrate how, before World War II,

Hollywood did offer progressive and transgressive (proto-)feminist role models who resisted their socially prescribed roles. Ironically, in a decade characterized by the economic and social upheaval of the Great Depression, Hollywood presented surprisingly sophisticated and complex debates surrounding working women. My interest in Hollywood's working women is not in those women who engaged in only what were regarded as female occupations—e.g., secretary, teacher, and nurse—but those who also engaged in the assumed male profession of criminal investigation. The prolific female detective of 1930s Hollywood film was an independent woman who put her career ahead of the traditionally female pursuits of marriage and a family and who chased crime as actively as—and most often with greater success than—the official male investigators who populated the police department.

Most importantly, the female detective did so and was not punished for her transgressions of traditional female roles—as she would be in subsequent decades. Some films concluded with the female detective rejecting marriage in

Fig. 1.1 Everybody's Favorite Aunt: Angela Lansbury as schoolteacher-turned-writer-turned-sleuth, Jessica Fletcher, in television's long-running series "Murder, She Wrote" (1984–96). Photo from author's collection.

order to pursue her career; even though more concluded with her accepting a proposal in the final scene, the female detective was allowed—throughout the course of the story—a freedom and voice as the film's protagonist rarely offered to women in film—then and now. Indeed, the female detective was more concerned with proving her abilities as an intelligent and competent detective and "getting her man"—in terms of catching the criminal—rather than "getting a man"—in terms of matrimony. In other words, these heroines were possessed by what female detective author Mary Roberts Rinehart describes as "[a] sort of lust of investigation" (572). These women were not "something with a French provincial office or a book full of clippings;" they were strong, intelligent, exciting women who managed to balance what Margo Channing knew was impossible by 1950 and perhaps even in the new millennium—simultaneous success in their professional ("masculine") and personal ("feminine") lives. As such, these female detectives are exciting gender-benders that challenge the assumption that femininity and masculinity are fixed categories aligned with opposite sexes. In a decade when the Great Depression was undermining men's assumed natural place at the top of the patriarchal order through unemployment, these working women embodied an active defiance of their socially prescribed passive position and, in effect, pursued the American Dream as self-made women.

The Crime Scene Kit

For a group of films to constitute a genre they must share a common topic and a common structure (Altman, 23). The detective film has the common topic of the investigation of a crime and the common structure of the detective as protagonist driving the narrative forward to a resolution of the investigation. A genre is a body of films that have narratives, structures, settings, conventions and/or characters in common and that are readily recognizable to audiences and promotable by producers. For example, a film with a hardboiled hero sporting a fedora, trench coat, gun, and cigarette, operating in the shadows of city streets at night or in the rain, and faced with the temptation of a sultry but potentially dangerous woman is likely a *film noir*. A genre is the product of popularity: the box-office success of one type of film leads to imitators and, once a critical number of films sharing similar tropes and structures appears, a genre is declared. A film's popularity may, of course, be influenced by a variety of factors: a star's appeal, a director's name, an effective advertising campaign, positive word-of-mouth, or a specific release date, etc. I would assert, however, that films that offer protagonists, narratives, issues, or themes that seem outdated in terms of contemporary social attitudes will be unlikely to prove popular with audiences and inspire imitation. Correspondingly, while audiences like to see the same *kind* of film over and over again, they do not want to see the *same film*: innovation and change are as much a part of a genre film as its familiar conventions. As

Rick Altman argues, change must occur within a genre otherwise it would go sterile (21). Genre hybridity (blending conventions) and parody (sending up established conventions) make genre films appear fresh to audiences.

The focus of *Detecting Women* is the detective film that offers a female protagonist at the center of the narrative and who actively—physically (i.e., as a crime-fighter) and/or mentally (i.e., as a sleuth)—investigates a mystery surrounding a crime or a criminal racket. Many mystery-comedy films and series focused on married detective couples—inspired by the popularity of MGM's Nick and Nora Charles (William Powell and Myrna Loy) in *The Thin Man* (Van Dyke, 1934). MGM made five additional "Thin Man" films (1936–47) and started a new series featuring Joel and Garda Sloane (1938–39).[1] Columbia tried to compete with MGM's sparring couples with their own, William and Sally Reardon (1938).[2] The couple-detective film sees the married twosome work together on a case with the male detective as the lead investigator and his wife as his assistant in a Sherlock Holmes/Dr. Watson dynamic. However, *Detecting Women* excludes the popular detective-couple film as it deviates from the core theme explored in films with a central female detective; namely the struggle of a single woman in pursuing a career in a male world. The female detective can be an amateur—a schoolteacher, nurse, or reporter who investigates the murders that occur in the course of her day job—or a professional of which there are far fewer until the 1990s—a policewoman or private investigator who investigates crime for a living.

I concede that for many people the term "detective" can evoke ideas of the classical sleuth rather than necessarily other kinds of investigative protagonists.[3] In the broadest sense, there are two types of detective-hero (male or female): the criminologist (the popular term in the 1930s)/criminalist (the popular term today)—better known as the sleuth—and the undercover agent (professional)/crime-fighter (amateur).[4] These two types are distinguished by their relationship to the community they investigate and their skill set as investigators of crime. In the case of the criminologist/criminalist, the criminal typically works alone and his or her crime is murder rather than a drugs or prostitution racket; the detective occupies a position as an outsider with specialized knowledge—whether deductive reasoning, behavioral profiling, forensics analysis, crime scene investigation, or personal familiarity—that can be utilized to investigate a crime. Rather than being on hand to witness criminal acts, the criminologist/criminalist arrives after the crime has been committed and must "read" the evidence to identify "whodunit." This type of detective does not necessarily have to possess fighting or weaponry skills in order to defeat the criminal physically but, instead, requires a degree of intelligence and/or experience to unravel the mystery or outsmart the criminal. While the investigation of the criminologist/criminalist includes analyzing clues, questioning witnesses, and drawing conclusions from the information gathered, that of the undercover agent/crime-fighter involves being on hand to witness the criminal activities. The undercover agent/crime-fighter has specialized knowledge and/or skills that allow her to infiltrate a specific criminal community, pass effectively as one of them, and ultimately expose the ring from the inside. It is in this undercover mode that the female detective employs the masquerade of femininity to disguise her more "masculine" (i.e., crime-fighting) abilities from the criminal ring and the threat they imply. In other words, her femininity functions as a decoy—as the television series "Decoy" (1957–59) starring Beverly Garland as an undercover cop confirms. Lastly, in the case of the undercover investigator, rather than the identity of the criminal(s) being a mystery—i.e., whodunit?—the aim of the investigator and the conclusion of the investigation are to see the criminals brought to justice. While sleuthing is mainly a mental process that can be undertaken *in absentia* of the crime scene (thus the idea of the "armchair detective" who can solve the mystery without leaving her own living room), crime-fighting is a physical process involving both being present during the criminal activities and in terms of the method by which the criminals will be defeated.[5]

Whatever the ability of films to reflect social reality, it is imperative to bear in mind that Hollywood's is, using Richard Maltby's term, a "commercial aesthetic": the primary function of a Hollywood film is to entertain in order to attract audiences and make a profit (*Hollywood*, 14–15). Therefore, Hollywood narratives and characters are likely to be more exciting and dramatic than the reality that generates them. The number of star "girl reporters" investigating headlining stories in Hollywood films of the 1930s was not representative of the reality of women's experiences in journalism with the vast majority of them relegated to the society column; however, Hollywood is quite accurate in its omission of female police officers and federal agents from its narratives until the 1990s as there were few in reality. Instead, the vast majority of Hollywood's female detectives are amateur sleuths or undercover crime-fighters who investigate out of personal interest rather than as a career detective. Whether or not the representation of female detectives is grounded in reality is less the issue than what those representations and their alteration over time indicate about changing social attitudes toward women and heroism.

The male detective has appeared consistently in Hollywood film since the coming of sound in the late 1920s, which made possible the cinematic rendering of the convoluted plots and dialogue-heavy explanations of the classical detective story. As I have explored previously in *Detecting Men: Masculinity and the Hollywood Detective Film* (2006), the British classical sleuth and the softboiled versions of American fiction's hardboiled detectives dominated the screen in the 1930s; the 1940s saw both replaced by the American hardboiled private eye in *film noir*; the private eye was replaced by the police detective who shifted from conservative and stable in the late 1940s, to neurotic and often corrupt during the 1950s, to almost absent from the screen in the 1960s, to a violent vigilante by the early 1970s. The hardboiled private eye returned in the late 1970s and early 80s but was overshadowed by the dominance of the cop as action-hero by the mid-80s. The 1990s and 2000s, however, saw the return of the sleuth in the educated, intelligent, middle-class criminalist. Although other kinds of detectives existed during each of these decades, these were the dominant trends within the genre of the detective film and each represents a shift in social attitudes toward law and order and the type of masculinity that society deems heroic. This is the history of the male detective, however, and I have been as remiss as other scholars for all but ignoring women in my research and writing about the detective film.

The aim of *Detecting Women* is to redress the exclusion of women from discussions of the genre as central heroes. As such, this study delineates the popular trends in terms of the female detective in film, the social issues that each trend explores, and the social attitudes toward women that each espouses. Surprisingly, the female detective appears alongside her male counterpart early in both detective fiction and film and, in the 1930s, tended to be an amateur sleuth, an undercover agent, or a girl reporter. The "masculinity" that defined the character in the 1930s gave way to her feminization in the early 1940s, and her pervasiveness during the Depression was succeeded by her gradual disappearance in the immediate post-World War II period. In marked contrast to her independence, fast-talk, and career success of the 1930s, the female detective—in her handful of outings in 1940s *film noir*—wanted to be a dutiful wife rather than an independent career woman, and her only motive to unravel the mystery was to save the man she loves. After 1950, the white female detective left the big screen, except for a couple of rare outings, until the 1980s. In the early 1970s, however, there was a cluster of black female investigators in blaxploitation films and, just as the white male detective had become a vigilante hero at the time, so too was this female detective a crime-fighting avenger. In the 1980s, the female detective exploded in popularity—on television with cops Cagney and Lacey and sleuth Jessica Fletcher; in fiction with hardboiled private eye V.I. Warshawski and FBI profiler Clarice Starling; and in film with the prolific female lawyer. The female detective continued in popularity in the 1990s and 2000s and, just as the male detective had become a criminalist, so too did the female detective become an expert in crime scene investigation, behavioral science, and forensics.

My interest in the figure of the female detective is manifold. Although there have been many studies produced in recent years exploring the role of women in the detective genre (as authors and protagonists), few offer a broad history of the female detective and fewer still look at her history in film. The aim of the first part of the book is to recuperate the classical Hollywood female detective of the 1930s and 40s—since she has been all but ignored. The critical interrogation of the classical detective film has tended to focus on *film noir* in which there are few female detectives and, instead, independent women tend to be demonized as the lethal *femme fatale*. Related to that is the concern that contemporary film audiences seem to regard classical Hollywood as a less sophisticated and progressive version of contemporary film. *Detecting Women* thus offers a re-evaluation of today's popular conception that classical Hollywood contained few strong and/or transgressive models of "good girls." Critics have explored the impact of the Production Code on the representation of women, sex, and violence in Hollywood film; nevertheless, the representation of the female detective transcends the pre- and post-Code division of 1934 and, instead, is indicative of the effects of the Depression and World War II on society's prescribed sex roles.

The representation of the female detective altered greatly between the early and late 1930s as I will explore in subsequent chapters, but 1934 was not the decisive moment of change. When I began my research into female detectives of the 1930s, I assumed that the Code would account for the arrival and proliferation of the girl reporter. After all, as Andrea Walsh suggests, "Code-prescribed limits on sexuality inadvertently promoted the 'career heroine' " (138). Perhaps the Code can account for the female reporter's increased presence by the mid-30s but her appearance in late silent and early sound film was the result of broader socioeconomic influences, including the Depression and the shift in gender roles the crisis initiated. Similarly, although many critics have noted the shift in gender roles in postwar film (i.e., *film noir*), the return to a more traditional gender dichotomy coincided with the *beginning* of World War II. The representation of women in Hollywood film seems to be the most transgressive between 1929 and 1933 in that working women were generally presented as "hardboiled" by their experiences in the Depression-era city and most likely to choose independence and a career over marriage. During the mid-30s, the working woman seemed to want both—a career and romance—and was, surprisingly, sometimes able to achieve both. However, by 1939 the tide had turned and Hollywood women were usually more desirous of love than a career, and those who chose otherwise were derided or punished. Thus, one of the aims of *Detecting Women* is to look past the pre-Code-era division and instead focus on that of the Depression/World War II in order to understand trends in the representation of independent and career-minded women; another is to explore how and why it was in the lower level B-picture mystery-comedies that these women thrived.

Hollywood had benefitted from the "leisure revolution" of the 1920s. As Steven Ross documents, motion pictures earned $720 million in box-office receipts in 1929—a figure almost four times the combined receipts for all spectator sports and live theatrical entertainments (181). The impact of the Depression meant that money was tight for moviegoers, but theater and studio pockets were just as empty. Exhibitors tried to attract audiences back to the cinema with the institutionalization of the double feature (a B-film preceding the headlining, and typically more prestigious, A-feature). Studios resisted the practice as it meant a twofold increase in output but soon discovered that the B-picture afforded the opportunity for testing out new talent at reduced risk. As

New York Times' critic Leonard Spinrad suggests, after the success of series like the "Charlie Chan" films in the 1930s, "The mystery story became honey for the B's" (4 Sept 1948). And it is the B-picture in which, I argue, the exciting and positive representations of independent women—women who challenged social discourses about gender—appeared. The Depression affected not only the film industry as a business, facilitating the proliferation and dominance of the B-picture throughout the decade, but also Hollywood's narratives, characters, and themes whether through an exploration of the impact of the crisis on American national identity or its disavowal.

Similarly, I found that, in discussions of the female detective, another decade and series of films has been ignored: blaxploitation films of the early 1970s. While film criticism has acknowledged the alternative representations of raced masculinity that blaxploitation offered, feminist film critics have only recently explored African-American women in roles that were unavailable to white women in mainstream film at the time. The short-lived but prolific movement (approximately 1971–75) saw a shift from white, conservatively heterosexual women to black, self-determined sexual women and the female detective shift from a sleuth to a woman of action, echoing the male crime-fighters of the period (e.g., Dirty Harry and Shaft). Just as the economic crisis of the Depression created a social climate amenable to women who transgressed traditional social roles, so too did the social upheavals of the late 1960s caused by the Women's and Civil Rights Movements see many Americans desirous of films that challenged the status quo. As Maltby suggests, the early 1970s—just as in the early 1930s—was a period when a combination of economic conditions and technological developments destabilized the established patterns of audience preference, creating opportunities for greater experimentation and variation from Hollywood's established norms ("More"). The economic changes Maltby is referring to included the collapse of the studio system and the replacement of the system of self-censorship (the Production Code) with the system of ratings (i.e., G for general, R for restricted). Blaxploitation films were regarded as B-grade films, thus it would seem that the space for the experimentation is often in the lower levels of production—the series of the 1930s and the blaxploitation films of the early 1970s. As Maltby qualifies, however, the experimentation was not necessarily subversive nor did it entail complete deviations from social attitudes and mores; instead, these variations "occurred within strict limits and existed, in large part, to test, negotiate and reconfigure the boundaries of Hollywood's conventions" rather than to supplant them (ibid.).

Thus, *Detecting Women* explores how often the most interesting and challenging representations of the female detective occur on the margins—in 1930s B-mystery comedies and 1970s exploitation films—rather than in big-budget and award-winning films. Eventually familiarity may breed parody or contempt, but initially popularity breeds imitation: the large number of B-detective series in the 1930s is a case in point. Even when imitation has occurred in what have been perceived traditionally as the lesser strata of motion pictures—e.g., B-pictures, comedies, exploitation films—it nevertheless denotes popularity and popularity suggests that a cultural nerve has been struck. Audiences vote with their box-office dollars to see more of the same—whether that is an interrogation of relevant social, economic, or political issues or an escape from them. Despite the cultural turn in academic scholarship from the reification of high culture over mass culture (as with the influential Frankfurt School) to the embracement of popular culture because of its mass appeal and consumption (as with the later Birmingham School of Cultural Studies), there remains a hierarchy of texts worthy of study and praise. While the terms "popular" and "mainstream" may persist in carrying with them derogatory connotations, a lack of prestige does not necessarily mean a lack of relevance when studying culture and its products.

The female detectives of 1930s B-pictures and 1970s blaxploitation films offer representations and models of femininity not necessarily available in more prestigious and serious dramas. In contrast, the female detective in Hollywood's dramas has—whether in the 1940s in a reaction to World War II or in the 1980s in response to the gender war—mainly offered a reflection of masculine backlash as much as feminist gain. As John Thompson suggests in his "Note" for *The Trouble with Women* (Lanfield, 1947) for the *Toronto Film Society*,

> Like all films, *The Trouble with Women* must be viewed in the context
> of the time in which it was made, given then-prevailing attitudes and
> conventions. It is a lighthearted look at the subject—the equality
> of the sexes—which, oddly enough, is seldom explored currently
> in a serious manner by Hollywood. (11 Aug 1981)

Indeed, the aim of *Detecting Women* is to analyze the female detective film in the context by which and for which it is produced, informed by a cultural studies and new historicist approach. Part of my goal in this research project was to bring to light the sheer number of female detectives that have been overlooked in previous studies of the genre, especially those of the 1930s and 40s.[6] I screened as many of the films as I could find available as commercial copies, in archives, or on specialty television channels. Although there is not enough space in this book to discuss them all, I have tried to include as many in my discussion as possible in order to demonstrate the pervasiveness of certain narratives, characters, and themes as well as the shift in emphasis that occurs between certain trends and have included the rest in Appendix II.

Lastly, my interest in the female detective was aroused because so many of them, especially in the 1930s and 1990s, were gender-benders—at the very least highlighting, and often critiquing, the socially prescribed roles available to them. The detective narrative is driven by the goal of the detective to solve the mystery of "whodunit" and that pursuit demands an active protagonist who ventures into the public realm to discover the truth. These three ideas of being active, operating in public, and seeking the truth are associated with masculinity. The films with which this study is concerned substitute a woman in that male role and thus can open up a space for a debate about gender since the sex of the protagonist can see her at odds with the expectations of the role she attempts to fulfill. The figure of the female detective varies in terms of what she represents from being merely a novel kind of detective in the traditionally male genre to being a feminist interrogation of the myths of socially-assigned sex roles. The biological idea of sex—i.e., being born male or female—does not predetermine one's gender—i.e., that one should be masculine or feminine. Feminist scholars, notably Judith Butler, have exposed gender identity as a cultural construct employed to enforce heterosexuality and defined by a set of oppositional conceptions: masculinity is associated with being strong, dominating, rational, and active—and feminine with being weak, submissive, emotional, and passive (*Gender*, 17). Butler argues that gender is performative—that all social subjects, whether male or female, perform their gender rather than their gender stemming from some essential sense of identity.

While the female detective of the 1930s and 40s often exposed and/or challenged those sex roles, she was always white and always heterosexual. It was not until the 1970s that Hollywood offered non-white female detectives—for example, those played by Pam Grier in blaxploitation films—but they were also Hollywood's last notable female African-American detectives. The exceptions are Whoopi Goldberg's roles in *Fatal Beauty* (Holland, 1987) and *The Deep End of the Ocean* (Grosbard, 1999); however, I do not discuss these films as the former is an isolated comic occurrence not in keeping with the themes of the millennial comedies on which I focus and the latter (despite the fact that the character is not only black but also a lesbian) because she is only a secondary character in the film. Jennifer Lopez has played the only Latina detectives in high-profile films, including *Out of Sight* (Soderbergh, 1998) and *The Cell* (Singh, 2000); however, I do not discuss the former as it is less a film about investigation as it is a romance between a thief and the detective (in the vein of *The Thomas Crown Affair* [Jewison, 1968 and McTiernan, 1999] nor the latter as it is a film more concerned with the relegation of the detective to the role of *femme fatale*. And neither film highlights her ethnicity as an issue or potential skill. In contrast, the blaxploitation heroine is empowered as a crime-fighter *because* of her race—because she has specialized knowledge of the black community—and *because* of her sex—because she can infiltrate a criminal organization unsuspected. And here the female detective uses female stereotypes against men: after all, no one ever suspects that a beautiful woman can have the brains and brawn to see justice served. Thus, rather than being women playing a male role, these female detectives offer a range of femininities and masculinities—in effect, blurring the lines of gender.

And many female detectives in the 1990s and 2000s, in a response to the growing visibility of lesbian culture especially in the detective genre, represent the blurring of the lines of sexuality as well. While the "dyke dicks" of lesbian fiction may not have made it to the big screen, they did influence their Hollywood sisters by encouraging, or capitalizing on, a queering of the female detective's identity. Bobbie Robinson sums up the critical discourse surrounding the contemporary female criminalist:

> [Ruby Rich] characterizes female dicks as "crisscrossing the bodies of sex and gender" (24). Glenwood Irons calls their work "gender bending," and Pricilla Walton and Manina Jones say, more simply, that the female dick "performs gender" (102). (95–96)

Robinson addresses the concerns that critics have had regarding the contemporary female detective of fiction, notably Patricia Cornwell's Kay Scarpetta, in terms of gender identity. While Eluned Summers-Bremner sees Scarpetta as a hardboiled detective in a skirt and that "inevitably it's her femininity that's in doubt" (134), Sabine Vanacker suggests that the female detective is divorced from her traditional role of life giving (i.e., as a potential mother) and, instead, is reinscribed as a "dealer in death, who aggressively 'manhandles' the corpses of victims and gruesomely thrives on decaying and decomposing bodies" (66). Robinson suggests that critics such as Summers-Bremner and Vanacker fail to consider the entirety of the female detective's identity and that Scarpetta (and I would add other contemporary detectives such as Clarice in *The Silence of the Lambs* [Demme, 1991] and M. J. in *Copycat* [Amiel, 1995]) identify with those corpses as victims—and, importantly, they are typically female victims (99). This "tenderness" and humanism that Robinson identifies is what I argue is a specifically female approach to homicide investigation that empowers the female detective and sees her succeed where often the male investigators in the narrative fail. Just as Robinson suggests, "With mixed images, Cornwell forces her readers to examine their assumptions about constructing femininity and masculinity" (106), I suggest that so too does the female criminalist film.

The Case Log

The first part of the book focuses on the female detectives of classical Hollywood film. Chapter 2 explores the history and key conventions of the female detective as established in nineteenth-century detective fiction. The "problem" with having a female heroine at the center of the detective story at the end of the nineteenth century was how to reconcile traditional notions of femininity with the perceived masculine demands of the detective plot—a problem that seems to plague the fictional female detective in contemporary film. Chapter 3 details how the detective film emerged during early sound film and how the codes and conventions of the genre were rapidly established and solidified in a reaction to the economic and social impact of the Depression—especially the representation of the modern, urban, working woman. Chapter 4 examines why the amateur detective—including schoolmarm Hildegarde Withers, teenager Nancy Drew, and nurse Sarah Keate—were afforded more success and freedom in the 1930s than the few examples of professional female detectives who attempted to make a career out of detecting. While many of these series heroines were drawn from literary sources—Mary Roberts Rinehart's Nurse Adams, Mignon G. Eberhart's Nurse Keate, and Stuart Palmer's Hildegarde Withers—Hollywood was producing its own kind of female detective who was an independent, brash, and outspoken working girl: the "girl reporter." Thus, Chapter 5 explores how Hollywood's prolific girl reporter embodied a deliberation on gender roles in the 1930s as a female protagonist who could be independent and successful in the assumed male world of work and one that was not necessarily punished for her transgression of the borders between male/female and public/private space. Chapter 6 focuses on the demise of the girl reporter in 1940s Hollywood film and the transformation of the female detective in general to a figure of parody, passivity, or—by the 1950s—questionable sanity. Chapter 7 examines how, in *film noir*, the sex of the investigating protagonist results in a hybridization of generic conventions with the narrative being driven forward as much by the female protagonist's personal desires (as with a melodrama) as by her investigation (as in a male-centered *noir* film).

The last part of the book focuses on the female detective of postclassical film. Chapter 8 considers the female crime-fighters of 1970s blaxploitation films—representing the few examples of non-white female detectives in American film—to date. Chapter 9 details how the only prominent female detective-figure in the 1980s was the lawyer and how she was the product of male anxieties resulting in a seemingly feminist, while simultaneously reactionary, image of female empowerment. Chapter 10 concludes the study with a look at the rise of the criminalist investigator who specializes in behavorial, crime scene, and forensic science—as well as the popularity of the chick flick detective-comedy.

Nick Browne argues that film genre criticism has often tended to focus on the regulation, classification, and explanation of film through the lens of genre and, instead, should explore film genres as gravitating toward "specific assemblages of local coherencies—discreet, heterotopic instances of a complex cultural politics" (xi). More recently, scholars have explored film genres as products of specific socioeconomic and industrial moments rather than as a cohesive body of films over a long period of time. The detective genre as a term, then, does connote consistency over the decades as it identifies a group of texts with the common topic of the investigation of a crime and the common structure of the detective as protagonist; however, the genre is not cohesive in terms of its representation of female detectives. *Detecting Women* investigates the dominant trends within that overarching genre that, in themselves, offer a cohesive investigation of women in the male world of criminal investigation but, in contrast with one another, illuminate the changes in the social conception of gender

Fig. 1.2. Guilty as Charged: Rebecca De Mornay as a female lawyer in *Guilty as Sin* (1993) juggling her career and romance (although not with Don Johnson pictured here). Photo from author's collection.

over time. Rather than search for generic cohesion, I explore the individual trends that were popular in specific decades in order to demonstrate that the thematic concerns of films are determined less by generic convention and more by socioeconomic change. The detective film—whether featuring a sleuth or a criminalist, and crime in the Depression-era metropolis or twenty-first-century cyberspace—presents a fantasy of resolution for social anxieties concerning crime—and, more interestingly, gender. Through an investigation of the evolution of the detective film—and its relationship to changing social conceptions of gender—we can recover the history of detecting women in film.

2

Detecting Criticism

Theorizing Gender and the Detective Genre

Part I: Detecting the Genre

The classical male detective of nineteenth-century fiction was the product of, and intended as the antidote for, the anxieties of the upper classes in regards to the perceived threat to social order that was posed by the lower classes. As such, the classical detective was, as Robert Reiner suggests, a "rational and unfailing resourceful individual symbolising a superior ideal of self-disciplined initiative, who is symbiotically related to a well-ordered social organisation" (147). Generally, it is agreed that American author Edgar Allan Poe is the "father of the detective story" with his short story "Murders in the Rue Morgue" (1841) featuring Auguste Dupin as a sleuth who employed observation and deduction to solve the mystery. Poe's "tales of ratiocination," as they were termed at the time, established the pattern for the detective genre, including the hermetically sealed room, the wrongly accused man, the solution by unexpected means, the trail of false clues, and the criminal being the least likely person. These conventions continued to dominate the genre from Sir Arthur Conan Doyle's "A Study in Scarlet" (1887) featuring Sherlock Holmes to the Golden Age fiction of authors such as Agatha Christie and Dorothy L. Sayers written between the two World Wars. At the same time, a new kind of hero was emerging in the U.S.: a tough, hardboiled, working-class private investigator as the urban evocation of the hero of the Wild West. This history, however, has incorrectly divided the genre into two distinct national types: the intellectual and bloodless British story set in the domestic sphere (e.g., the old manor house), and the realistic and violent American story set in the public sphere (e.g., the mean city streets). Also this is the history of the male detective and it has overshadowed that of the female detective and her place in both detective fiction and film. After all, Anna Katharine Green was the most famous writer of detective fiction in America before Dashiell Hammett and her first novel, *The Leavenworth Case*, was the best-selling novel of 1878. Green also created the first female detectives in American fiction, including Amelia Butterworth who starred in three novels and established the character of the amateur spinster sleuth.

In reality, women only appeared on the police force in the UK in 1914 with the creation of the uniformed Women's Police Service, and the Metropolitan Women Police Patrols were approved in 1918. Even then, the first "policewoman" was not appointed until 1921 and no others followed in her footsteps until 1932 (Kestner, 5–6). In the U.S., women matrons were hired by the New York City Police Department to tend to the increasing number of women being arrested in 1891; Isabella Goodwin was hired as a matron in 1896 and went on to become the first female police "detective" in 1912.[1] The first woman to be classified as a "policeman"—in other words, meaning she could exercise the powers of arrest—was Mary Owens, appointed to the Chicago Police Department in 1893; and the first woman to be classified as a "policewoman" was Alice Stebbin Wells, hired by the Los Angeles Police Department in 1910. Wells pioneered prevention and protection principles related to youth, including enforcing laws in places of recreation frequented by women and children like movie theaters; note, however, that her role did not include detective work. Kate Warne was the first female private detective, employed by the Pinkerton National Detective Agency from 1856; she was also, perhaps, the first female secret service agent as she performed such duties while in the employ of the Pinkerton's. Mary Sullivan receives the honor of being the first woman homicide detective (1918) and the first Director of Policewomen (1926) in New York. It is, perhaps, surprising then that the first fictional female detectives appear early in the genre's history—in the 1860s—in both American and British detective fiction.

Gothic and Domestic Precursors

Catherine Ross Nickerson sees multiple sources as facilitating the appearance of women's detective fiction: Poe's tales of ratiocination, the sensational story-paper, popular nonfiction crime and trial stories, the domestic novel, and the socially critical examples of the gothic novel (xiii). These influences facilitated the first fully-fledged American detective novel, *The Dead Letter* (1866) by Metta Victor (as Seeley Regester), and later Green's *The Leavenworth Case* (1878)—both of which integrated detective and domestic novel structures, as would be typical of the detective fiction written by women that followed. In other words, in early women's detective fiction, the question of "whodunit" is often inextricably tied to the question "who will marry whom?" (ibid., 39). Not all detective stories written by women featured female detectives, especially in the early days of the genre; however, detective stories featuring female detectives tended to be—as they still are today—written by women.

Nickerson suggests that detective fiction is a "blood relative" of the gothic (45). William Patrick Day argues that Poe's stories and the detective genre develop out of the inner logic of the gothic novel that sees the supernatural confront the human world: "The detective challenges the encroachment of its terrors, the disorder brought on by crime and the monster in the shape of the criminal, returning the world to order and stability" (52). There is, however, an even closer connection between the gothic and women's detective fiction: the tradition of the "female gothic," established by Ann Radcliffe's *The Mysteries of Udolpho* (1794), features a female protagonist faced with a secret or mystery. This connection between the gothic and the detective narrative is not confined to this period either. Just as Nickerson suggests that early detective stories retain the moments of emotional terror of the gothic, so too does Tania Modleski see *film noir* of the 1940s as a descendent of the same tradition. I would add that many of the detective films of the 1930s cross over into the horror genre (notably, *Mystery of the Wax Museum* [Curtiz 1933])—with the heroine in the role of a monster's potential victim as much as in the role of the detective who will identify and stop him. Maureen Reddy also sites the sensation novel—the originators of which include Mrs. Henry Wood, Wilkie Collins, and Mary Elizabeth Braddon—as another antecedent to the female detective story and a close relative of the female gothic. Reddy argues that the criminality of the female villain of the sensation novel "stems from the same sources" as the victimization of the gothic heroine (7–8). Joseph Kestner notes other antecedents in the novels of George Elliot, Mary Elizabeth Braddon, and Thomas Hardy, offering models of female independence in British fiction even if not in detective fiction: "Intelligence, self-assertion, daring and defiance marked a range of female protagonists in English fiction before the creation of Sherlock Holmes" (3).

Kathleen Gregory Klein regards the detective genre as a fundamentally anti-feminist or even misogynist genre: after all, the victim is almost always female, the criminal and the detective are both typically male, and—when the detective is a woman—the anticipated success of the detective to solve the crime suddenly comes into question (1). However, other scholars have found examples of women's detective fiction that offer a critique of paternalist power and/or a celebration of a female hero. For example, Nickerson celebrates the fiction of Metta Victor, Anna Katherine Green, and Mary Roberts Rinehart, suggesting that it is their combination of the seemingly opposed realist-based domestic tradition and the fantasy-based female gothic that allows for their work to "have a certain bite, especially on questions of gender expectations" (12). The female gothic, in the tradition of *The Mysteries of Udolpho*, offers a heroine who must assert self-control and rely on her intelligence and moral strength to overcome the tests, confrontations, or entrapment she faces.[2] In a similar vein, the domestic novel of nineteenth-century American fiction offers a heroine who, motherless, must find her own way in the world—physically, morally, and emotionally. Nickerson suggests that the difference between the two traditions is mainly in the conclusions: that the domestic heroine achieves a level of serenity unavailable to her gothic counterpart, but that both traditions "valorize intelligence in women" and "that all serious learning involves self-knowledge" (14). Lisa Dresner qualifies that there are limitations imposed on the heroine in the female gothic novel in terms of her abilities as a detective and that she can be regarded as an "almost-detective": "No matter how strong her desire to investigate, and no matter how strong her linguistic and interpretive mastery, she is never allowed to bring her investigation to a successful conclusion through her own efforts" (39). Therefore, despite her antecedents in the female gothic novel, the female detective, in terms of how we define the character today, did not appear until the 1860s in British fiction and the 1880s in American. As Nickerson explains, "we can call them detectives (as we do Agatha Christie's Jane Marple) when they compete with, supplant, supplement, or correct a more official, male-headed investigation" (x).

Early British Detective Fiction

The first female detectives were W. Stephens Hayward's Mrs. Paschal in *The Experiences of a Lady Detective* and Andrew Forrester Junior's Mrs. Gladden in *The Female Detective* both published in 1864.[3] These female detectives, however, were anomalies: Forrester and Hayward wrote no sequels and Mrs. Paschal and Gladden had no immediate successors. The female detective appeared in greater numbers by the 1890s in an attempt to capitalize on female readership with the female detective's novelty during the Sherlock Holmes "boom" (Panek, 106–7). Periodicals such as *Strand Magazine*, *Ludgate Monthly*, and *Harmsworth Magazine* were a vital source for Victorian female detectives before they reached novel form. Notable books based on initial series and starring female detectives included Catherine Louisa Pirkis's *The Experiences of Loveday Brooke, Lady Detective* (1893), Grant Allen's *Miss Cayley's Adventures* (1899) and *Hilda Wade* (1900), and Richard Marsh's *Judith Lee, Some Pages from Her Life* (1912), and *The Adventures of Judith Lee* (1916).

The proliferation of the female detective at the end of the century may have occurred as part of the mythologizing of the "New Woman": certainly the new millennium saw shifts in gender roles for both men and women, and the New Woman—perhaps best symbolized riding a bicycle—rebelled against restrictive Victorian conceptions of womanhood and offered a redefinition of femininity that could be strived for. As Michele Slung notes, "Though these early female characters represented in varying degrees the then emerging 'modern' woman, they were all alike in eschewing domesticity in favor of detection, if only long enough to give them a recordable career" (xv–xvi). Being a detective meant operating beyond the socially prescribed role of homemaker; however, it also meant rejecting an assumed role of passivity in regards to social realities, politics, and crime and taking up the active role of social observer and investigator. Thus, the female detective did offer an alternative to popular conceptions of gender roles at the time and this was no doubt her appeal—even if only as a novelty.

And it is here, from the start, that the "problem"—as identified by feminist critics—with having a female investigator at the center of the detective story appears. At the end of the nineteenth century, how could traditional notions of femininity be reconciled with the more "masculine" demands of the detective plot—domesticity vs. action, emotionality vs. logic, the private vs. public sphere, etc.? It is no doubt because of the irreconcilability of these conflicting discourses that these early female detectives were, as Slung suggests, "*over*endowed with feminine charms to compensate for their mannish profession" (xix).[4] Ironically, the skill that makes these women successful detectives is linked to the fact that they are women and is identified as "feminine intuition." While the male detective of this period utilizes keen observation and deductive reasoning to identify the criminal, the female detective relies on her tenacity, energy, and instincts to facilitate her solution of the mystery. And it is in this aspect that the sex of the detective perhaps has the greatest impact on the story by affecting the method of investigation: science, logic, and reason remain firmly aligned with masculinity even into the twentieth century and across the Atlantic in American fiction as well.

Early American Detective Fiction

The dime novel was a popular form of mass entertainment in the U.S. from approximately 1860 to 1912: while frontier stories about America's expansion West dominated the medium in the 1860s and 1870s, crime and detective stories proved more popular in the 1880s and 1890s (Roberts et al., 1). The significance of the dime novel as the mass entertainment of the second half of the nineteenth century cannot be overlooked as it was a medium widely available to a large percentage of the population; nevertheless, it has tended to be derided by critics as a lesser form of the genre and only recently is receiving due critical attention. As E. F. Bleiler argues, the dime novel was the "first mass-produced entertainment industry of importance, it stood in the same relation to the average young American as television does today" (viii). The first dime novel detective was "Old Sleuth, the Detective," the creation of Harlan P. Halsey, published in 1872.[5] It was the Old Sleuth's publishers, George Munro's Sons and Munro's Publishing House, who copyrighted the term "sleuth"—at least, they successfully sued rival publisher, Beadle and Adams, for using the term (Klein, 31).

Nick Carter is perhaps the best known of the dime novel detectives and the hero of the longest running series; however, the dime novel also featured women detectives. As Garyn Roberts et al. note, publishers needed quantity and one of the key gimmicks that writers had to exploit was repetition—and innovation:

During the height of the detective dime novel era, from about
1880 to 1900, the variety of detective heroes was staggering. They
came in all shapes and sizes, from all types of ethnic, economic
and social backgrounds, and yet they were all cut from the same
basic whole cloth. Each detective tended to be superior in strength
and intelligence and each detective represented the highest moral
values of that era. In no time, female detectives were added to
this fictional legion, and their particular adventures provide some
revealing insights into the technique of formula construction in
early popular literature, and in the socially proscribed roles of men
and women in late Victorian/American society. (5)

Although it is difficult to pinpoint the first female detective of the dime novel,
we do know that the *Old Sleuth Library* series introduced different female sleuths
in *The Great Bond Robbery, or Tracked by a Female Detective* (1885); *Lady Kate,
The Dashing Female Detective* (1886); *Gypsy Rose, the Female Detective* (1898);
and *Madge The Society Detective* (1911).[6] The attitude espoused in the *Old
Sleuth* detective stories was that work for women was a temporary necessity and
that marriage was regarded as the "natural" occupation for any eligible young
woman. Rather than altering the detective narrative to accommodate themes
and issues specific to these female protagonists, these women might be regarded
as, using Klein's term, "honorary men"—essentially substituting a female hero
for a male one with little alteration to the kind of detective story being told.
In these stories, the female detective had the exact same skills, intelligence, and
strength of her male counterparts.

Whereas in twentieth-century pulp detective stories masculinity and femininity are firmly opposed and embodied by the tough hero in the first instance
and the sultry *femme fatale* in the second, Roberts et al. argue that in the nineteenth-century dime story the male/female dichotomy is embodied within the
single character of the female detective (6). For example, Kate Edwards of *Lady
Kate, The Dashing Female Detective* is proficient at disguises—convincingly passing
as an old woman and a male sailor—and physical action—handling a pistol and
sword with equal dexterity. As her author writes, "The woman in her nature
had been put aside. At once she was the cool, cunning, level-headed detective"
(Sleuth, 13). However, at other points in the story, the author highlights the
anxiety that the heroine might be somehow masculinized by her activities as a
detective when one of her suitors declares, "I love Kate Edwards, despite the
fact of her being engaged in the unwomanly profession of a detective!" (ibid.,
53). More interesting perhaps, is the revelation that Kate loathes herself when
she succumbs to her feminine side. When she realizes that she has let herself
fall in love with a criminal, "[b]itterness and mortification filled her soul; she
despised herself for her weakness" (ibid., 31). In the end, appropriate gender
roles are reasserted as Kate retires from her career as a detective to marry the

criminal she was hired to pursue and he, in turn, is inspired by Kate's love to give up his life of thievery.

The turn of the century saw the appearance of a stronger and also respectable female sleuth in the more respectable form of the hardbound novel. While the dime novel was aimed at pubescent male readers of all classes, the hardbound novel was intended for middle- and upper-class adults. Green's Amelia Butterworth first appeared in *That Affair Next Door* (1897) and set the mould for the spinster sleuth as a strong-minded woman and one who chose to pursue detecting out of interest as her wealth afforded her the possibility of a life of leisure. The 1910s saw a proliferation of women detectives in American fiction: Hugh C. Weir's *Miss Madelyn Mack, Detective* (1914); Green's other notable female detective, socialite Violet Strange from *The Golden Slipper and Other Problems* (1915); Arthur B. Reeves's criminal-turned-sleuth *Constance Dunlap: Woman Detective* (1916); and Jeanette Lee's Millicent Newberry from *The Green Jacket* and sequels (1917, 1922, and 1925). Mary Roberts Rinehart's first novel, *The Circular Staircase* (1907), featured a middle-aged spinster, Rachel Innes, and Rinehart also created many other women sleuths; only Hilda Adams, a nurse who does undercover work for the police, however, appeared in a series—beginning with the novelettes "The Buckled Bag" (1914) and "Locked Doors" (1914) and later in the novels *Miss Pinkerton* (1932) and *The Haunted Lady* (1942).[7] Unlike the dime novel stories that echoed male detective story formulas and re-established conventional gender roles for their adolescent male readers, the stories written by respected women writers were intended for women readers and challenged established gender roles. Nickerson sees Rinehart's detective stories as continuing in the vein of those of Victor and Green, using the female gothic in the female detective story to critique the structure of modern women's lives though the heroine's rebellion and disillusionment: as such, her stories were dubbed the "Had-I-But-Known" variety (119–20).

Silent Film

The dime novel as a form died out slowly between the turn of the century and World War I for a variety of reasons: formulas had become worn, the profit margin had decreased, and the single novel format was supplanted by the story collection format of the pulp magazine (Roberts et al., 3). The hardboiled detective story was coming into vogue in the 1920s and by the early 30s had supplanted the British classical detective tradition and the American domestic/gothic tradition—at least in the U.S. While the male detective made the successful transfer to pulp stories, the female detective disappeared from American fiction with the death of the dime novel and, by the Depression, she had vanished. This, however, is when she starts to appear on the big screen. Detective fiction had "justified" the masculine activities of the female detective by a handful of different strategies: (1) that she employed her skills only to clear the name of a loved one; (2) by making her the assistant of a male relative; (3) by reuniting her with a male love interest at the end of the adventure; or (4) by suggesting that her crime-fighting career is over with the solution of this sole case (J. Roberts, 4). These women tended to work only until marriage was proposed and their foray into the public and male sphere of detective work was seen as far from respectable; it was aligned with occupations like prostitution because of the detective's association with criminals and the lower classes. This long established tradition in fiction made its way onto the silent screen with little deviation, along with the donning of disguises, solving a straightforward mystery, and—in the case of the young and eligible detective—falling in love with the main suspect.

In 1908, the French Éclair film company made a film series based on dime novel detective, Nick Carter, which prompted a contemporaneous critic to say, "Detective stories are perfectly suited to the cinema. With their brisk and simple plots, an absence of complex psychology, their logical development of events, their rapid jumps, their crimes, waylayings, kidnappings and chases they are fundamentally cinematographic;" according to French historians Maurice Bardèche and Robert Brasillach, however, the series was more of an adventure saga with cliff-hanger endings rather than a series of stories with a mystery at their center (Qtd. in Spinrad, X5). And the "Nick Carter" series is an indicator of the trend of crime films through to the late 1920s: such series offered action as the solution to the mystery rather than observation and deduction—and this was as true for the female detective as her male contemporary. By 1915, the film industry began to move from one (10–15 minutes) and two (20–25 minutes) reelers to "feature length" films (50+ minutes), offering the possibility of greater character development and plot elaboration with the increased running time. As Larry Langman and Daniel Finn note, at the same time, the industry successfully broadened its audience base from immigrants and the working class by attracting middle-class viewers to the theater: many films were adaptations of classical pieces of literature or popular stage plays, thus aligning the formerly derided entertainment with more established modes of higher culture (*Silent*, xiv).

In 1942, Hedda Hopper in her column for the *L.A. Times* talked about an alternative model of femininity offered in the 1910s: "Back in the dear, dead days when woman's place was in the home and she was plenty burned up about it, we had quite a sizable escape literature in the form of the serial queen" (Hopper). In film, the silent film serial queen—including "Lucille Love: The Girl of Mystery" (1914) starring Grace Cunard, and "The Perils of Pauline" (1914) and "The Exploits of Elaine" (1914–15) starring Pearl White—fired guns, rode horses, was stalked by wild creatures, and fought off the villains successfully. These action adventuresses inspired similar kinds of heroines in detective mysteries. Michael R. Pitts cites Laura Sawyer playing Kate Kirby in *Chelsea 7750* (1913), *An Hour before Dawn* (1913), and *The Port of Doom* (1913) as the first female detective in film (*III*, 133); however, Langman and Finn note that two shorts by the independent Yankee Film Company—*The Monogrammed Cigarette* (1910) and *The Woman Who Dared* (1911)—each featuring a young woman who follows in her detective father's footsteps when he is murdered (*Silent*, 183 and 307).[8] In *The Rogues of Paris* (1913) directed by Alice Guy Blaché, a female detective and her criminologist father deal with a gang of crooks who try to swindle a woman out of her inheritance. Action-oriented, serial queen Pearl White starred as a detective in *Pearl as a Detective* (1913). In *Trapped in the Great Metropolis* (1914), a reporter (Rose Austin) teams up with her detective boyfriend to infiltrate a white slave operation. In *The Mystery of Richmond Castle* (1914), a female detective (Grace Carter) helps a young man prevent an unscrupulous secret society from seizing his inheritance. *The Floor Above* (1914) features a couple (Henry Walthall and Estelle Coffin) who have a falling out over his inheritance but find their way back together over a murder. Ruth Roland starred as *The Girl Detective* in a series of short films (1914–15) as a society girl who works as a special investigator for the police. In *Kinkaid, Gambler* (1916), a female detective (Ruth Stonehouse) initially investigates and later proves the innocence of a gambler in Mexico accused of stealing from a real estate magnate. In *The Dazzling Miss Davison* (1917), a detective (Marjorie Rambeau) infiltrates a gang of international crooks who have been stealing from the wealthy. In *The Mysterious Mr. Tiller* (1917), a detective (Ruth Clifford) goes undercover to investigate a series of robberies from police headquarters. In *Sylvia of the Secret Service* (1917), a Washington Secret Service agent (Irene Castle) proves the innocence of the young man entrusted with the famous Kimberly diamond when it goes missing on a sea voyage. In *The Web of Chance* (1919), a detective agency boss's niece and secretary (Peggy Hyland) clears her lover of stealing a million-dollar contract from his employer. *Madame Sphinx* (1918) sees a young sleuth (Alma Rubens) investigate the murder of her guardian, proving her lover innocent of the crime. In *Cheating Cheaters* (1919), a detective (Clara Kimball Young) goes undercover to thwart two gangs who wish to steal a valuable jewel collection and she reform one of the thieves with whom she has fallen in love. And, lastly, in *Counterfeit* (1919), a young woman (Elsie Ferguson) joins the Secret Service in order to catch a gang of counterfeiters for the reward money.[9] As one can see from these descriptions, there was a standardized set of characters, plots, and themes in the silent film featuring a female detective-protagonist.

   The 1920s saw the continuation of the female detective onscreen although less often in comedies and action serials and increasingly in dramas with requisite happy endings (i.e., she falls in love). In *The Invisible Web* (1921), a female sleuth (casting unknown) is one of the suspects in a murder case. In *Amazing Lovers* (1921), a French secret service agent (Diana Allen) goes undercover to expose a gang of counterfeiters. In *The Bedroom Window* (1924), a writer of detective fiction (Ethel Wales) investigates the death of her brother-in-law and falls in love with the main suspect. *The Great Jewel Robbery* (1925) sees a detective (Grace Darmond) on the trail of stolen jewels and kidnapped along with her childhood sweetheart, leaving it up to the police to save them both. In *Wild, Wild Susan* (1925), a bored socialite (Bebe Daniels) goes to work for a detective agency, but her harrowing adventures prove to be fabricated by her lover in order to cure her wanderlust. In *Before Midnight* (1925), the heroine (Barbara Bedford) helps a wealthy young man clear his name when he is falsely accused of smuggling a valuable emerald into the country. *Fair Play* (1925) sees a devoted secretary (Edith Thornton) scouring the underworld for evidence to exonerate her boss from a murder charge. *The Danger Girl* (1926) features a sleuth (Priscilla Dean) who masquerades as a bride running away from a bad marriage in order to protect a gem collection from thieves. In *The Jazz Girl* (1926), a bored socialite (Edith Roberts) turns detective along with a newspaper-man in order to capture rum runners. In *The Girl from Chicago* (1927), a young woman (Myrna Loy) infiltrates a New York gang to find out who committed the murder for which her brother is being charged and, in the process, falls in love with the main suspect who is revealed to be an undercover detective. The romantic ex-thief became a popular character and saw female variations with *Cheating Cheaters* (1927) in which a jewel thief (Betty Compson) is revealed to be an undercover agent; similarly, in *Lady Raffles* (1928), a society crook (Estelle Taylor) is revealed at the end to be an undercover agent for Scotland Yard. *Beware of Blondes* (1928) sees an undercover detective (Dorothy Revier) mistaken for, but also apprehend, a jewel thief called Blonde Mary while falling in love with the store clerk entrusted with the transport of a valuable emerald. In *The Leopard Lady* (1928), a leopard trainer (Jacqueline Logan) goes under-cover in a circus to investigate a series of thefts and murders but is hesitant to expose the perpetrator because he saved her life. And in *Blockade* (1928), Anna Q. Nilsson plays a U.S. revenue agent who goes undercover to smash a rum-running racket.[10] The arrival of sound in the late 1920s may have changed the film industry but generic plots remained the same during the transition-to-sound period between 1927 and 1930.

This list is not meant to be exhaustive (as I am sure that there are many films featuring female detectives that have been lost or remain undiscovered) but is representative of how prolific the woman as a heroic detective was in silent film. A couple of predominant narrative and thematic patterns are evident from the plot synopses of these early films. First, the crime at the center of the mystery is often bloodless theft rather than violent murder; however, this is unrelated to the fact that the detective is female but is a feature of the genre in silent film. Second, often the female detective investigates only because a relative has been murdered or a relative or lover accused of murder. The presence of a lover allows for a focus on romance as much as on investigation and facilitates a "happy" resolution with the heroine's retiring from detective work to marry. Third, the female sleuth is often undercover and her true identity is not revealed (to the audience or her lover) until the end of the film. This no doubt allows, as I will discuss more thoroughly in the case of later sound films that often rely on this trope, for the heroine to act like a typical young woman (i.e., feminine) rather than a competent detective (i.e., masculine) and attract the attentions of a young man intent on marrying. This initial disguise, and later revelation, of her true identity in the final reel allows these films to offer a less potentially problematic image of a woman in the starring role as it presents the heroine in a predominantly feminized role.[11] Lastly, there is a sense of mobility in regards to identity in silent film: heroines and villains don disguises of different sexes and classes; female detectives operate undercover; and criminals can be revealed to be other detectives or reformed into husbands. Despite this seeming flexibility of identity, these films—likely in a reflection of the social discourse regarding gender roles at the time—insist on reassigning her femininity by the conclusion of the film. As Ben Singer suggests, the serial queen represented a paradox as she embodied "an oscillation between contradictory extremes of female prowess and distress, empowerment and imperilment" (*Melodrama*, 222). Similarly, the female detective of the 1910s and 20s embodied female power through her displays of heroic action but was also subjected to victimization.

Detective Fiction's Golden Age

Detective fiction became increasingly popular during the Depression, according to James Hart, because of people's desire to relax without having to confront their lowered expectations due to the national crisis and also because mystery stories had become more respectable with the polished and sophisticated works produced during the 1920s (257–58). By the early 1930s, the hardboiled trend was firmly established in American fiction with the middle- or upper-class, suave sleuth being replaced by a tough working-class private eye. In terms of female detectives, the hardboiled tradition all but excluded the possibility of a female hero; instead, women were relegated to the role of the dangerous *femme fatale*. There were a couple of isolated hardboiled female detectives: Erle Stanley Gardner (as A. A. Fair) created Bertha Cool (1939) and Sam Merwin created Amy Brewster (1945). Both women were tough, large, and behaved like men—using profanity, in the case of the former, and smoking cigars, in the case of the latter. In other words, they were women cut from the cloth of the male hardboiled private eye and as such are anomalies that did not produce successors or imitators. The popularity of the female hardboiled private eye would not come until the 1980s with the protagonists of writers such as Sue Grafton and Sarah Paretsky.

While the Depression would redefine detective fiction in America in the 1930s, it was World War I that affected British. American fiction moved toward an urban, tough, and morally questionable private eye as detective-hero in a reaction to the socioeconomic crisis of the Depression; on the other hand,

British writers retained their stable, reliable, and infallible classical sleuths in a seeming desire to forget the Great War's horrors and impact on British culture and confidence. The result was the "Golden Age" of British detective fiction and one of its most famous female sleuths—Miss Marple—appears. Although Amelia Butterworth may have started a trend in American fiction of spinster sleuths, Agatha Christie's Jane Marple was the first in British fiction in 1927.[12] Like Christie, the other important women authors of the Golden Age created at least one female sleuth along with their often more famous male sleuths: Dorothy Sayers created Harriet Vane (who ultimately marries Sayers's more famous male sleuth, Lord Peter Wimsey) and Margery Allingham produced Amanda Fitton. The spinster sleuth also proved popular still in American fiction with Stuart Palmer's Hildegarde Withers who featured in fourteen novels and three short story collections (1931–69). American detective fiction of the 1930s also saw the creation of teenage sleuth, Nancy Drew, in 1930 authored by Carolyn Keene (a *nom de plume* for a syndicate of outliners, writers, and editors).[13]

Frances DellaCava and Madeline Engel note that the female detective did not alter much from her origins until after World War II:

Fig. 2.1. In a Man's World: Bonita Granville is the teenaged sleuth that solves the mystery in *Nancy Drew, Trouble Shooter* (1939). Photo from author's collection.

> This pre-1945 group of women investigators represents a common
> persona—ladylike, respectable, and untrained yet successful sleuths.
> Many were unemployed, portrayed as financially independent middle-
> and upper-class society matrons. Those who were employed other
> than as detectives had occupations acceptable for women of the
> time, such as teacher, nurse, and shop assistant. (3)

While she may not have deviated from the nineteenth-century model in regards
to these aspects, the spinster sleuth like Britain's Marple and America's Withers
did deviate in important ways. No longer was the reliance on disguises—male
and female—to infiltrate different social spaces; instead, the sleuth appeared
consistently as herself—even if she did use people's preconceptions about an
older woman against them, disarming witnesses and suspects into revealing valuable information with a masquerade of feeblemindedness. Also the emphasis on
the exciting physical exploits that had defined the female detective of the dime
novel and serial silent film was abandoned in favor of more "armchair-detective"
ratiocination. Importantly, a key feature of the early tradition—the "excuse" for
why the sleuth becomes involved in the case—is also discarded. Rather than
investigating to clear the name of a man whom she loves or the assistant of a
male relative, the 1930s sleuth investigates because she derives pleasure from,
and is proved adept at, solving mysteries. In other words, these heroines were
possessed by what Mary Roberts Rinehart describes in the Nurse Adams story
"The Buckled Bag" as "[a] sort of lust of investigation" (572). Lastly, by making
the sleuth of the 1930s too young (the teenager) or too old (the spinster) for
marriage, the issue of the female detective choosing to detect until receiving a
marriage proposal or having to choose between a career and marriage is eliminated. Of course, the spinster sleuth was not the only type of female detective
to appear in this period, but Jane Marple remains the best-known and one of
the most influential female detectives—even though she never appeared in a
Hollywood-produced film.[14]

Sound Film

Sound arrived in Hollywood in 1927 and meant that detective film plots and
characters could become more complex with the added dimension of dialogue.
Films in the 1930s still offered female undercover crime-fighters like those of
silent film in the 1910s and 20s; however, they also offered adaptations of
some of detective fictions most popular American sleuths—including nurse
Hilda Adams (1932), schoolteacher Hildegarde Withers (1932–37), nurse Sarah
Keate (1935–38), and teenager Nancy Drew (1938–39)—and a similar shift
in themes and structures. Exclusive to Hollywood film, however, was an entire
breed of female detective that never appeared in detective fiction: the modern,
outspoken, and active "girl reporter" as a product of the modern American city.

It is with these three trends of female detectives in classical Hollywood film that I will begin my investigation in the subsequent chapters. First, however, I will explore the debates that have arisen in the feminist criticism of the genre before embarking on my own examination of the filmic female detective.

Part II: Detecting Feminist Criticism

Second-wave feminism is the woman's movement that emerged in most Western countries in the 1960s and is seen as an extension of the first wave. The first wave of feminism occurred in the late nineteenth and early twentieth centuries in the U.S. and the U.K. in a response to nineteenth-century medical discourse that claimed that biology is destiny and, therefore, that sexual difference (and resulting gender hierarchy) was natural. First-wave feminism had its origins in *A Vindication of the Rights of Woman* (1792) in which author Mary Wollstonecraft argued that women only appeared inferior to men because of their lack of access to education and that women should be treated as rational beings—just like men. The first-wave movement culminated in women gaining the right to vote (suffrage) in the U.S. in 1920. Simone de Beauvoir's *The Second Sex* (1949) predates the second-wave movement but is the starting point for second-wave feminists and their writings, including Betty Friedan's *The Feminine Mystique* (1963) that applied de Beauvoir's insights into the oppression of women in France to postwar Anglo-America (Chaudhuri, 4). Annette Kuhn identifies second-wave feminism as

> a set of political practices founded in analyses of the social/historical position of women as subordinated, oppressed or exploited either within dominant modes of production (such as capitalism) and/or by the social relations of patriarchy or male domination. (*Pictures*, 4)

Key publications of the movement—including Kate Millet's *Sexual Politics* (1969), and Germaine Greer's *The Female Eunuch* (1971)—represented the rise of a militant feminism in reaction to the virulent antifeminism that had thrived from the end of World War II through the 1950s, and the domestic role it prescribed for women. Friedan regards the 1930s as a period in which women had more freedom and independence than the "claustrophobic world of the suburban housewife of the 1950s" (Ware, 16). Ruth Schwartz Cowan in her study of the impact of technology on women's role in the household disagrees with Friedan's assessment of the decade and argues that the 1920s and 30s laid the foundation for the 1950s. Cowan insists,

> The mystique makers of the 20's and 30's believed that women were purely domestic creatures, that the goal of each normal woman's life

was the acquisition of a husband, a family and a home, that women who worked outside their homes did so only under duress or because they were "odd" (for which read "ugly," "frustrated," "compulsive," or "single") and that this state of affairs was sanctioned by the tenets of religion, biology, psychology and patriotism. (178)

There were two related but different strands to second-wave feminism: an activist movement and an academic one. The "Women's Liberation Movement" that began in the 1960s enacted social change over the following two decades with a movement of women out of the home and into the workplace—a sphere that had been seen as predominantly the domain of men. Incited by second-wave feminism, feminist theory appeared in academia by the 1970s both in the feminist critique of texts—e.g., exposing patriarchal ideology implicit in the literary "classics"—and in the texts produced by women—e.g., gynocriticism and the female aesthetic. In terms of film, feminist theory generated two distinct lines of inquiry. Marjorie Rosen's *Popcorn Venus* (1973) and Molly Haskell's *From Reverence to Rape* (1974) took an historical studies approach to studying film and represented the American "images of women" or "reflection theory" strand of feminist film studies in which they regarded the representation of women on-screen as the product of patriarchal culture. Haskell describes movies as "one of the clearest and most accessible looking glasses into the past" (xii) and this approach to film—as a direct and undistorted reflection of society—was criticized in later decades for being too simplistic. In a more sociological vein, Joan Mellen's *Women and their Sexuality in the New Film* (1974) explored sexist structures in European film. British theorists, Pam Cook, Claire Johnston, and Laura Mulvey rejected the sociological and historical approaches to cinema in favor of one informed by psychoanalysis, structuralism, and semiotics as part of the broader movement of "screen theory," named after the influential British film studies journal, *Screen*. American feminist theorists soon followed suit in journals such as *Jump Cut* (founded in 1974) and *Camera Obscura* (founded in 1976) and, by the 1980s, "queer theory"—a term coined by Teresa de Lauretis to describe gay and lesbian criticism—was also proliferating. While psychoanalytic film theory laid the foundations for film theory of the 1980s and 90s, more recently there has had been a revisioning of feminist film theory with the historicist and cultural turn. Christine Gledhill argues that theories that focus on women as a textual sign are too abstract and ahistoricist; they ignore individual film's social and industrial context ("Pleasurable," 67).

The interest in cultural context sparked a new branch of theory associated with the Birmingham School of Cultural Studies and theorists like Stuart Hall and Raymond Williams. Stuart Hall's "preferred reading" model explored how meanings are "encoded" by producers, "decoded" by readers/viewers, and how dominant ideology structures "preferred" readings that audiences can then accept, negotiate, or oppose depending on their social background. Film theorists began to move past the hypothetical spectator implied by psychoanalytic film theory and consider, instead, what Annette Kuhn distinguishes as the "social audience" and the sociocultural implications of going to the movies ("Genres," 305). The critical movement of New Historicism has also seen a concern with how historical reality has an impact on cultural texts. In terms of film, new historicists question the reductive binary established in film theory between texts that embody dominant ideology and those that subvert it (Lucia, *Framing*, 153). The cultural and historicist turn in film criticism meant that, by the 1990s, there was an increased interest in film as a social and economic institution, the ethnography of audiences, the cultural relevance of texts, and a more historicist approach. Indeed, *Detecting Women* grew out of a desire to map the history of the female detective in relation to changing social, economic, historical, and industrial contexts.

Identifying the "Problem"

In terms of the detective genre, feminist criticism evolved out of an interest in women's detective fiction writers and the degree of feminism represented by their female detective characters. While critics like Patricia Craig and Mary Cadogan [*The Lady Investigates* (1981)] and Kathleen Gregory Klein [*The Woman Detective* (1988)] focus on detective fiction, their debates regarding female detectives as characters have often been adopted into discussions of the genre in film without necessarily taking into account the specificity of the medium, its production, and its consumption. Much of the focus of feminist criticism addressing the female detective until recently has identified the "problem" as the discontinuity that arises when a female protagonist is placed in the central position of a male genre. Klein argues, in detective fiction, the "anticipated pattern of successful crime solving" of a male detective "suddenly collapses" when he is replaced with a female protagonist (1). Indeed, the two most prevalent debates—commencing in the 1980s but often continuing today—have been, first, whether casting a woman in a male role results in a feminist representation and, second, whether the narrative and themes of the detective genre must accommodate female concerns with the sex-change of the protagonist. As Maureen Reddy asserts,

> If women, because of their socialization, read the work rather differently than men, as feminist theorists like [Carol] Gilligan and [Nancy] Chodorow assert, then it stands to reason that a woman detective might read clues differently than a male detective would and that her relationship to the problem presented would differ from the male detective's. (10)

The detective is a reader—a semiotician reading the signs to determine the pattern of the "writing" (murder) of an "author" (the killer) and, thus, the identity of that author—but does the female detective "read" the crime scene differently from the male?

The "problem" of the female detective film is most often worked out along the lines of, borrowing Andrea Walsh's term, the "femininity-achievement conflict" (139). In other words, the female detective's "feminine" success is determined through her ability to acquire a proposal of marriage, while her "masculine" success is determined by her ability to discover "whodunit." As Carla Kungl notes, in early detective fiction, not to be married signalled the failure of the female detective as a woman (88). Similarly, in the 1980s and early 1990s, the "problem" of the female detective's appropriation of a male position was, as Linda Mizejewski argues,

> most easily resolved through familiar heterosexual strategies: the excessive fetishization and domesticization of the female detective [. . .]; the imposition of a romantic subplot [. . .]; the glamorization [. . .]; the heterosexual partnership [. . .]. An alternative resolution of the female dick problem in cinema has been to represent her as a Hollywood version of the lesbian, thereby associating her with another kind of "illegitimacy." ("Picturing," 6–7)

Klein echoes Mizejewski's notion of "illegitimacy" as she notes that none of the early female detectives of the American dime novel "was portrayed as a complete detective and a complete woman simultaneously; in particular, each was set up to prove her femininity—or be branded unnatural" (50). In many ways, this accounts for the "failure" of the female detective as a woman; her ability, ambition, and success as a detective are "unnatural" (i.e., masculinized or lesbian) traits and are incompatible with the female qualities of being domesticated, nurturing, subservient, and attractive to men that would lead to the prescribed female roles of wife and mother. The female detective could not win. On the one hand, she possessed masculine traits of rational thinking and/or tough action, as well as ambition in her career, but she had to prove her femininity in order to be socially acceptable. On the other hand, she was a woman and, therefore, it was deemed problematic for her to be able to do a man's job without some kind of justification or negotiation first. Hence, the "problem" posed by the presence of a woman at the center of the male detective genre.

New Ways of Looking

In general (excluding *film noir*), the detective genre is a conservative one, ultimately upholding societal values and reassuring readers/viewers that the society spun into chaos by a crime can always see order restored—including gender roles through heterosexual coupling. I would like to suggest two shifts in the critical approach to the detective film: first, rather than adopting the debates of detective fiction scholarship wholesale into film, we consider the specificity of film, its mode of production, questions of stardom, etc.—as Elizabeth Cowie, in her reading of the female detective film *Coma* (Crichton, 1978), suggests ("Popular," 63); and second, rather than judging the female detective of the past by contemporary expectations of feminism, we should evaluate these films as a product of their time—not ours. For example, Kungl criticizes the tradition in feminist criticism that finds the female detective wanting as a feminist role model because of the question of matrimony:

> To posit, therefore, that women detectives are either failures as women (because they do not marry but have careers as detectives) or as detectives (because they marry and end their careers as detectives), represents not only circular logic but a rejection of the ways women writers were coming to terms with the important debate about women and work in their society. (85)

Thus, in the critique of the female detective film, there must be a recognition of the social realities of the period and a consideration of how these texts can offer an examination or questioning of those realities through a representation of women within the confines of socially acceptable generic conventions.

Todd Davis and Kenneth Womack explain that postmodern theorists such as Jean-François Lyotard believed that "a proliferation of narratives would flourish"—an increase in the range of discourses with which human beings could define themselves; instead, we have seen "a reduction of narratives based upon the premise of polarization and an economic model—which Fredric Jameson anticipated in his writing about late capitalism—that 'sells' the goods of duality" (xvi). In other words, theorization has tended to see issues only in terms of opposites—a black-and-white approach that identifies texts and meanings as positive/negative, feminist/misogynist, and progressive/regressive—with little possibility of a middle ground or—more radical still—of a text espousing *both* polarities in different moments. For example, in early feminist film criticism, a feminist reading often included identifying a text as either positive or negative in its representation of gender. Such assumptions have proven reductive and contemporary critics have attempted to expand feminist criticism beyond the positive/negative binary. As Tania Modleski suggests, there is a problem in attempting to determine the *degree* of feminism of texts:

> . . . even contemporary mass-produced narratives for women contain elements of protest and resistance underneath highly "orthodox" plots. This is *not* to say that the tensions, anxieties, and anger which pervade these works are solved in ways that would please modern feminists: far from it. [. . .] If the popular-culture heroine and the

feminist chose utterly different ways of overcoming their dissatisfaction, they at least have in common the dissatisfaction.[15] (25)

I would argue then that the majority of films that offer a female heroine must, to some degree, explore her dissatisfaction with the social roles with which she finds herself in conflict and elucidate which gender roles were considered socially acceptable at the time. Obviously, some detective films offer a greater critique and/or rejection of women's prescribed social roles than others, but the fact that these films explore other options for women outside of social convention is impressive when one notes the scarcity of real-life female detectives before the 1990s. And, lastly, whatever the shortcomings of the female detectives in terms of a feminist statement or a critique of female roles during their period, their representation must be considered in comparison to the alternative: omission. That is why certain decades are excluded from this study because, except for the rare exception, the 1950s, 1960s, and 1970s offered few such heroines or narratives. Therefore, when those heroines are present and especially predominant, they must be acknowledged as important.

In terms of detective fiction criticism, critics like Kimberly Dilley have criticized Klein's assumption that masculine models are universal in the genre and Klein's reduction of the female detective to an "inadequate woman"/"inadequate detective" debate (xviii). In contrast, Dilley praises Reddy's feminist approach to the detective fiction that emphasizes women's voices—from those of women writers to women characters—and the subjective nature of language and truth (xix). Reddy's reading of the genre identifies the female detective as a reader of clues and the creator of narrative by reconstructing the story of the crime from the clues. Of course, it may be easier to locate a feminist voice in the detective fiction of women writers—as the majority of scholars writing on female detectives have done—rather than mainstream texts produced by a predominantly male team of screenwriter, producer, and director—as in the case of a Hollywood film. Few of the many examples of filmic female detectives are adapted from women's detective fiction or produced by women filmmakers, and the aim of this study is to analyze mainstream narratives featuring a female detective for how they negotiate and explore the debates about women in traditionally male professions, roles, and narratives. While mainstream films rarely preach feminism, they are pro-feminist to a degree by having women in the position of central protagonist and detective. From this starting point, the films then tend to explore the gender-related issues that can arise from having a woman as the focus of the film, operating in a predominantly male world. Indeed, Mulvey has established that mainstream film most often presents the female body as object of the "male gaze" ("Visual"); however, as Mizejewski notes, in the case of filmic female detectives, "Their job isn't to look good, but to do the looking" (*Hardboiled*, 4).

And this is why the female detective is regarded as problematic—because she defies her prescribed gender role. According to Judith Butler, gender identity is a construct determined by culture to enforce the heterosexualization of desire through the establishment of oppositional conceptions of masculine—i.e., strong, dominating, rational, and active—and feminine—i.e., weak, submissive, emotional, and passive (*Gender*, 17). Gender can be understood as performative as individuals are expected to suppress their individuality in favor of exhibiting socially prescribed behavior; nevertheless, gender is not perceived as performative but natural. Acts, gestures, and desires are enacted by the individual in an effort to convince others that the demonstrated and perceived gender identity is authentic. As gender is a "performance" then it becomes evident that that performance can be a false one—a masquerade—whereby individuals pretend to adhere to their gender while simultaneously being other. The performance of drag fully subverts the distinction between the inner and outer psychic space by assuming the gender performance of the opposite sex, and exposes the three contingent dimensions of gender as read through the body: anatomical sex, gender identity, and gender performance (ibid., 137). Butler suggests that hegemonic heterosexuality, in its constant and repeated effort to imitate its own idealizations, is then as much an imitation as drag and, therefore, holds no claim to being natural (*Bodies*, 125).

The female detective's engagement in sleuthing—e.g., observation, logical reasoning, and questioning suspects—and/or crime-fighting—e.g., chasing, attacking, or shooting the criminals—is oppositional to socially accepted female behavior. Some films attempt to contain the female detective's "masculinity" through her enacting a masquerade of femininity. In terms of the film's diegesis, the masquerade is justified by the detective's need to operate undercover: she presents herself as more traditionally feminine—e.g., attractive, ditzy, submissive, or passive—in order to investigate the crime unrecognized as an investigator. The masquerade presents femininity as a mask that can be worn or removed and, according to Mary Ann Doane, offers the female protagonist a recourse by which to maintain the power and "maleness" of the active gaze of a male character—yet conceal it—as her possession of it would be deemed threatening by the male (25). Many classical Hollywood films did not reveal the heroine's status as a detective until the end of the film, thus, deluding the audience as well to the protagonist's "true" nature. The masquerade is a strategy that is as common in films of the 1930s (e.g., *The Woman Condemned* [Davenport, 1934]) as it is in the 1970s (e.g., *Foxy Brown* [Hill, 1974]) and the 2000s (e.g., *Miss Congeniality* [Petrie, 2000]).

The critical debates incited by the female detective can be restricted by their presupposition that the detective genre, its protagonist, and audience are intended to be male. Importantly, the detective films and novels of the twentieth and certainly the twenty-first century featuring a female detective-hero were/are intended to be consumed by a female audience (even if also by a male). As Klein notes, the detective genre has always attracted both male and female audiences,

Fig. 2.2. Femme Masquerade: Pam Grier's heroine uses the masquerade of femininity to disarm the bad guys in *Foxy Brown* (1974). Photo from author's collection.

unlike other popular genres that cater specifically to one audience (e.g., romances to women) or the other (e.g., westerns to men) (8). Today we are told that since the birth of the blockbuster in the mid-70s, the majority of mainstream films have been aimed at the 19-year-old male viewer and we believe that classical Hollywood films, before the introduction of the ratings system in 1968, were created for a general audience. It is true that they were *exhibited* to a general audience in the sense that all ages were permitted to see the film, but Richard Maltby discredits the myth that producers were unaware of, or uninterested in catering to, different kinds of audiences. As he explains,

> Rather than Hollywood maintaining a view of the audience as an undifferentiated mass, the industry sought to provide a range of

> products that would appeal to different fractions of the audience,
> and to include a set of ingredients that, between them, would appeal
> to the entire range of different audience fractions. ("Sticks," 25)

In the exhibition sector, binary terms—mass/class, unsophisticated/sophisticated, and Main Street/Broadway—were used in differentiating small town and big city audiences; sex, however, was as significant an audience divider as class in the 1930s and Hollywood made films especially to exploit that fraction. As Tino Balio suggests in the case of *Gone with the Wind* (Fleming, 1939), "That the era's most successful production was targeted at women and employed a women's perspective provides a starting point for an understanding of production trends during the thirties" (1). In the same vein, Melvyn Stokes explains, whether or not women represented the majority of the film audience in the 1920s and 30s, the industry believed that they did and that gave women box-office power that the film industry catered to (43–44). Similarly, Mick LaSalle reminds us, "Since 1960, female stars have been second-class citizens, but in the twenties and early thirties, women dominated at the box office. The biggest stars were women, and it was a rare month indeed when a male face turned up on the cover of a fan magazine" (4). And the importance of female stars, as well as the female audience, in the 1930s should not be overlooked. In 1935, movie star Mae West earned $480,833—an income second only to newspaper magnate William Randolph Hearst in America (Allen, 173). As LaSalle suggests about Norma Shearer, and I would argue the same is true for the majority of female stars in the 1930s, "She could not and did not make movies that challenged the sexual double standard. But she did make pictures that explored the anxieties relating to the new woman" (27). Today when Hollywood places a woman at the center of a film and offers a plot propelled by her goals and desires, it is to attract female filmgoers (even if along with the male ones). The widespread presence of female detectives and the female audience they invite allow us to question the "maleness" of the detective genre.

The Investigation

Detecting Women will demonstrate that the themes of the detective genre do alter with the sex of the detective-hero. From the first appearance of the female detective in nineteenth-century fiction, some dominant and gender-specific conventions and themes were established and do reappear in later decades in film. While the male detective almost always appears as himself and trades on his name/reputation, the female detective is typically unknown as a detective and often goes undercover, using a masquerade of femininity to conceal her masculinity (as an empowered detective) from the villains and the audience. The male detective is often a professional and undertakes a case for remuneration while the female detective tends to become involved for personal reasons, often to clear the name of the man whom she loves. And while the male detective is the hero who comes to the rescue of the potential victim (often a woman), the female detective often mistakenly bestows her trust on the real killer, unbeknownst to her, and needs to be rescued by the man she loves or the official male investigator. And all films featuring a female detective engage with concerns related to the sex of the protagonist in terms of her struggle with being a woman and a detective, even if they are not necessarily positive in their conclusion of that debate. While one might argue that this concern with the incompatibility of femininity and masculine professional work results in a criticism of women who attempt to do so, I would argue that the very address of the issue highlights the problems that women face within patriarchal culture. Reddy defines "feminism" as

> . . . a way of looking at the world that places women's experiences at the center. It sees women as capable of intelligence, moral reasoning, and independent action, while also giving attention to the multivarious social, legal, and psychological limitations placed on women by the patriarchal societies in which most live. (9)

In this sense, Hollywood films with female detectives at their center offer space for feminism.

The Rise and Demise of the Classical Female Detective

1929 to 1950

3

Movie Modernization

The Film Industry and Working Women in the Depression

When I first began this project, I felt that the 1930s were the forgotten decade in the study of the detective genre in general. Scholars had explored *film noir* of the 1940s and 50s and neo-*noir* of the 1970s, 80s, and 90s, but the 1930s were written off as the decade before *noir*—in other words, before the detective genre became interesting, as it were. What preceded *noir* was a kind of narrative regarded as boring, staid, and predictable—the British classical detective story. However, scholars have ignored the vast range of types of detective films and characters that proliferated during the decade and, more importantly, the great number of popular series. While it is true that some British detective characters appeared in Hollywood films of the 1930s, including Sherlock Holmes and the Saint, the majority of the detectives were adapted from American fiction. One key aim of this project was a recovery of the 1930s and the kinds of images that Hollywood offered to American audiences during the Depression; however, in recent years, it would seem that Hollywood too is fascinated with inter-war America. *Seabiscuit* (Ross, 2003) and *Cinderella Man* (Howard, 2005) offer heroes faced with national and personal crises and yet triumphant in an era marked by socioeconomic failure—and the similarity between the films' messages did not go unnoticed by critics at the time of their release. As Scott Feschuk quips in his review of *Cinderella Man*,

> In the summer of 2003, Hollywood made the case that, during the dark years of the Great Depression, it was a plucky, underdog horse named Seabiscuit that lifted to its feet a nation on its knees. But scratch that—now apparently it was a plucky, underdog boxer named James L. Braddock. (8 June 2005)

Notably, 2005 also saw Peter Jackson's remake of the Depression-era classic, *King Kong*—another tale of human triumph in the face of adversity in unparalleled proportions. Several films of 2008 were set during the Depression, including the British films aimed at international audiences like *Mrs. Henderson Presents* (Frears, 2005) starring Dame Judi Dench and *Miss Pettigrew Lives for a Day* (Nalluri, 2008) starring American actor Amy Adams, and Hollywood films *Kit Kittredge: An American Girl* (Rozema, 2008) starring child-actor Abigail Breslin. Hollywood has also been casting its glance further back in history with *Changeling* (Eastwood, 2008) starring Angelina Jolie about a kidnapping in the Prohibition-era 1920s, and *Leatherheads* (Clooney, 2008) starring Renée Zellweger (notably as a girl reporter) and George Clooney about the birth of pro-football in the mid-20s. It would seem that in the 2000s, Hollywood perceives a nostalgia for the era of the Depression—no doubt because the impact of the socioeconomic crisis on American society and the American spirit seems to mirror the current situation in the U.S. Unlike Vietnam, which saw the country divided, 9/11—and the subsequent conflicts in Afghanistan and Iraq and the economic downturn of the late 2000s—is the first major widespread social crisis since the Depression that has united the nation in a common vision. In light of this, a consideration of Hollywood's reaction to the impact of the Depression on American society seems especially fitting.

Part I: Hollywood's Industry

Classical Hollywood and the Code

The term "classical Hollywood" is often used interchangeably with the "studio era" when delineating a certain time period: most critics agree that the classical Hollywood era began to form in the 1910s, was in place by the 1920s, and was defunct by the 1960s. The "Big Five" studios—Loew's (later MGM), Paramount, RKO, Fox (later 20th Century Fox), and Warner Bros.—and the "Little Three"—Columbia, United Artists, and Universal—collectively were called "the Majors" and controlled the industry from the late 1920s to the mid-50s. The Big Five were the most powerful, being vertically integrated companies, controlling all three aspects of the business: manufacturing (production), wholesaling (distribution), and retailing (exhibition). Of the Little Three, Columbia and Universal lacked their own theaters for exhibition and United Artists was a distributor for independent producers; nevertheless, all three had an arrangement with the Big Five for exhibiting their films and thus the Majors benefitted from each other's successes. Those who did not benefit were independent exhibitors and producers from "the Minors"—Hollywood's smaller but respectable studios like Monogram and Republic—and "the Poverty Row" studios. The term "classical Hollywood," however, does not just refer to a mode of production and industrial organization (i.e., "the studio system") but also the specific film style and visual "language" that were the standard during this period. The editing style of classical Hollywood film is called "continuity" or "invisible" editing as the goal is to clarify narrative, character motivation, and theme without drawing attention to the film style itself.[1] In terms of narrative, classical Hollywood films tend to offer goal-oriented, motivated protagonists who drive a narrative characterized by cause-and-effect logic, and enjoy mainly happy—but always moral—endings. While content was determined by generic and Hollywood's broader ideological conventions, it was also dictated by the institution of the Production Code.

In 1915, the Supreme Court's decision in the case of *Mutual Film Corporation vs. Ohio Industrial Commission* declared that motion pictures, as entertainment, were not protected by the First Amendment, which affords the right to free speech and the freedom of the press. The complaints of civic groups about salacious content in a number of films released in 1923–24 caused the MPPDA (Motion Picture Producers and Distributors of America)[2] to take action: President Will Hays created a self-regulatory initiative called "The Formula" and expanded it as the "Don'ts and Be Carefuls" in 1927 administered by the Studio Relations Committee (SRC). The goal of these self-regulatory censorship initiatives was to stave off federal censorship, but increased concerns with Hollywood's salacious content resulted in the establishment of the "Production Code" in 1930 to ensure that "No picture shall be produced which will lower the moral standards of those who see it," as the first general principle of the Code declared. Critics felt that the Code was not enforced strictly enough and, by 1934, Hollywood was "[f]aced with an alliance of small exhibitors, small-town Protestant conservatives, and Progressive reformers" who wanted to see federal regulation of the movies (Maltby, "More"). Why did Hollywood incur the wrath of social interest groups with sex and violence in its films? As Sid Silverman notes in a 1930 article in *Variety*, "As figures at the box office dwindled the boys underline the sex angle more. And who's to blame them" (7). As Thomas Doherty notes, experience had taught the industry that "the 'immorally suggestive twist' led audiences in a straight line to the box office" (107). So, as Maltby suggests, with the negative impact of the Depression on attendance, "producers returned to their old sinful ways, exploiting their audiences' baser instincts with a flood of sexually suggestive and violent films" ("More").[3] In the pre-Code era (i.e., before 1934), actress Mae West saved Paramount financially just as *King Kong* had saved RKO, but she would fall victim to the more rigorous application of the Code under Joseph Breen beginning in 1934.

As Maltby suggests, there are two versions of the myth regarding the Code. The popular conception of Hollywood film from 1930 to 1934 today is, using Robert Sklar's description, that these years were Hollywood's "Golden Age of Turbulence"—a period of subversion and challenge in representation. In this version of Hollywood's history, the Production Code was not enforced *at all* until 1934 (hence the misnomer "pre-Code" film) and its enforcement in 1934 should be regarded as the unfortunate demise of an innovative period of filmmaking.[4] Maltby, however, asks why would the fourth largest capitalist enterprise in the U.S., with its commercially driven product, attempt something *radical* "at the very moment of perhaps the greatest social and political instability the U.S. had experienced?" Thus, in the other version of the myth, as Maltby explains, Hollywood was regarded as "the fallen woman being rescued from sin and federal censorship by virtuous hero Joe Breen riding at the head of the Legion of Decency" ("More"). Indeed, pre-Code film has, in the last few decades, been repackaged by television networks and video distributors as a critics' genre unrelated to industry practice. In other words, Hollywood producers did not intend to produce a specific kind of film (i.e., genre) now known as "pre-Code" or "Forbidden Hollywood" film—including the girl reporter film *Dance, Fools, Dance* (Beaumont, 1931). Maltby argues that the convening of specific factors—namely, the economic collapse of the leisure market during the Depression and the technological development of sound films in the late 1920s—were responsible for Hollywood's first Golden Age of Turbulence—*not* a lack of censorship. Nevertheless, as a result of the rising social pressure and to avoid the institution of federal censorship, the SRC was replaced with the Production Code Administration (PCA) and placed under the leadership of Breen. There were no substantive changes to the 1930 Code in 1934 and Breen was given no additional powers; instead he refined the definition of what was acceptable under the Code. Thus, while the popular conception is that these administrative changes in 1934 meant a remarkable shift in representation in classical Hollywood film, scholars suggest that the shifts in representation were more gradual than dramatic.[5]

Hollywood film did change between the first recession of the Depression (1929–33) and the second (1937–38): from a glamorization of the gangster who broke the law to that of the G-Man who upheld it; from the double entendres of Mae West in the early 30s to the sexual innocence of Shirley Temple (the number one box-office draw from 1935–38). Roosevelt's Presidential Administration and its series of economic stimulus programs known collectively as "The New Deal" (1933–38) ushered in an era of reform and the restoration of cultural equilibrium—and Hollywood films after 1934 reflected it. As Charles Eckert suggests, films such as *42nd Street* (Bacon, 1933) embodied "the New Deal philosophy of pulling together to whip the depression" (3). In the Code-era (i.e., after 1934), the flavor *du jour* was no longer sex and violence but instead films with a more positive spin on American society. As Hollywood discovered, such films offered more profit and less trouble if only because Breen's enforcement of the Code during production reduced the amount of reshooting after and the number of films irreparably damaged by the cuts that the state and national censor boards would demand (Doherty, 335).

B-Pictures and Comedies

The term "B-picture" can refer to both a film with a low-budget and to a film that fills the lower half of an evening's film bill. As Brian Taves notes, with each Hollywood studio releasing on average one feature a week, B-pictures were the norm and the big-budget film the exception (313). Roughly 75 percent of films made during the 1930s (over 4000 films) fall under the B-classification, and, therefore, their sheer number indicates their importance in understanding the 1930s. Also it was at the B-level that studios often spun individual films into series: series kept production costs down and guaranteed an audience when a theme or character struck the right chord. As Tino Balio has documented, there was a drop in admissions in 1931 of 12 percent to 70 million and a drop in the price of tickets from 30 cents to 20 cents while the cost of talkies saw production costs double and revenue from foreign markets dwindle; by 1932, admissions dropped to 55 million (13–14). In the early 1930s, several studios—RKO followed by Paramount, Fox, and Universal—went into receivership and the others—Loew's, Warners, Columbia, and United Artists—saw huge deficits. Despite the popular assumption that only wealthier patrons could afford to go to the movies during the Depression, research suggests that everyone went to the movies as an escape from harsh realities (Muscio, 65). The Hoover administration regarded the cinema as a necessity, and free tickets were distributed along with food and clothing. By mid-1936, the major studios made a profit for the first time since 1931 but, a year later, the second recession of the 1930s would be felt. Between 1937 and 1938, the net earnings of the seven major studios declined 41.6 percent and another 11.4 percent by 1939 (Ohmer, 147). And outbreak of the war in Europe in 1939 also affected Hollywood negatively as 30 percent to 40 percent of Hollywood's total income came from overseas. The 1930s saw both film producers and exhibitors strain to survive the economic hit of the Depression, and the double bill was a key component of that struggle.

By mid-1932, 40 percent of theaters had adopted the double feature and 60 percent by the end of the decade. Exhibitors blamed the studios for having to resort to the double feature because the poor quality of the films they purchased meant that they had to offer audiences two films in order to make an evening's bill more attractive. In turn, the studios regarded the practice of the double bill as the problem since it meant that they had to produce twice as many films and, of course, that meant that the films could not always be of the highest quality. Certainly, the public perception voiced by critics in forums like the *Harvard Business Review* and *New York Times* blamed the double bill for the falling quality of Hollywood films (Ohmer, 148). Critics, however, also blamed audiences: their patronage facilitated the continuance of the practice. The independent producers and exhibitors convinced the National Recovery Administration to legalize dual billing in August 1934, and the double feature helped bolster production for the independent producers (Balio, 29). By 1935, all the Majors had opened B-units but they relied on the smaller but well-respected independent studios—including Republic, Monogram, Grand National, Mascot, and Tiffany—to meet the demand for the 700 features a year that *Variety* estimated was required.[6] All studios wanted to minimize the financial risk that filmmaking entailed, and both the Majors' B-units and minor studios adopted various practices that worked within their budgets: they focused on genre films and series minimizing the costs of sets; they imitated genres, characters, and plots with proven popularity; and they used original stories and screenplays produced by contract screenwriters or recycled former stories that did poorly at the box-office rather than purchasing the rights to popular novels and plays. Certainly, the "old manor" type of classical detective story was perfect for the low-budget Bs since most of the action required minimal set changes and relied heavily on dialogue for plot development.

Although B-pictures have tended to be critically neglected, as Taves argues, B-pictures were not only important financially to the industry but also stylistically and culturally (331). As Wheeler Winston Dixon suggests, however,

> While many "B" films were simply designed to fulfill a programming need, [. . .] many other "B" movies were the works of serious artists who saw that only by working in the depths of poverty row could they hope to accomplish the sort of films the majors would never let them make. (2)

For example, Edgar G. Ulmer left Universal Pictures for Producers Releasing Corporation (PCR) where, as long as he finished a film for around $40,000, "he could do whatever he wanted and tackle subjects that no major would let him touch" (ibid., 2). Few B-level directors, however, had much say in casting, crew, script, or editing and this had nothing to do with a lack of talent. As Taves argues, it "required rare abilities" to excel at low-budget filmmaking—to know exactly what shots were necessary, editing in the camera without wasting footage on more than a few takes, arranging lighting and camera angles to conceal the cheapness of the sets, and eliciting an effective performance with few rehearsals (329–30). Taves also notes that while studio moguls and the Hays Office were concerned with A-films, "many B's contain surprising deviations from archetypal plots, concentrating on unconventional themes and offbeat or bizarre elements that almost certainly would have been shunned in the big-budget arena" (337). In the same vein, Dixon argues,

> "B" films often offered a much more realistic glimpse of American life in the 1930s and 1940s than the majors would allow. With millions of dollars in an "A" budget, the major studios would usually stick to safe escapist entertainment, while those "B" directors who wished to do so could tackle subjects like juvenile delinquency [. . .] or social inequities [. . .] long before the majors thought it fashionable. (3)

It is no doubt for this reason that the strong and sometimes transgressive figure of the female detective was solely the product of programmers or B's as it was here that she was considered beneath notice and able to proliferate.

The fact that the majority of the classical Hollywood films that I examine in this study were B-pictures, rather than necessarily artistic triumphs, award winners, or social problem films, does not invalidate their worth in terms of understanding the social moment in which they were produced. Indeed, the mere fact that many B-picture protagonists were spun into series attests to their popularity and relevance to the contemporaneous audience. I would suggest that the other reason why the films I examine in this study are less respected is their tendency to include comedy in measures often equal to mystery. Andrew Bergman argues that film comedies of the early 1930s including those of the Marx Brothers and Ernst Lubitsch "had blown things apart" while comedies by the mid-30s were "warm and healing" if "off-beat and airy" like the screwball comedy (132). In other words, the early 1930s comedy was concerned with the divisiveness and alienation experienced by its protagonists in their society while those of the mid-30s were concerned with their unification, thus echoing the Depression/New Deal divide. As Bergman suggests, in the midst of the Depression, comedies "created an America of perfect unity: all classes as one, the rural-urban divide breached, love and decency and neighborliness ascendant" (133). Depression-era comedies became progressively less critical and more placating to audiences feeling the effects of the economic crisis and a similar pattern appears in the detective genre: early 1930s films interrogated the myths of law/order and gender binaries that are realigned with traditional values later in the decade.

Elizabeth Kendall argues that the shift in the 1930s from serious drama—and the stars associated with it such as Greta Garbo and Marlene Dietrich who embodied "a fatal languor or obsessive ferocity"—to comedy—and the stars associated with that impulse such as Ginger Rogers and Barbara Stanwyck who demonstrated a "vibrant strength of character"—was the product of the poverty and uncertainty resulting from the Depression (xiv). It would seem that the best medicine for the Depression—and its impact on the economy, crime, and women—was to treat it as a laughing matter. As Geoff King notes, film comedy is popular but not prestigious, critically acclaimed, or award-winning: "Comedy, by definition, is not usually taken seriously" (2). It may not be taken seriously, however, comedy can be critical—and not just in the more obvious cases of political satire and black comedy. The very fact that comedy is *not* taken seriously can be liberating; as King argues that "sometimes gives it license to tread in areas that might otherwise be off-limits" (2)—for example, facilitating the representation of the tough and wise-cracking female detective.

Part II: Women and Work

The Great Depression was the worst and longest economic depression in modern history—to date. Beginning in the U.S. with the Stock Market Crash ("Black Tuesday") on October 29, 1929, and spreading to most of the world's industrialized countries, the Depression lasted in the U.S. until the economic upturn afforded by World War II in the early 1940s. It was a serious weakness in the economy that sparked the Depression, arising from personal debt amongst average Americans to the war debts owed by European nations. The Depression affected banks, international trade, personal income, goods prices, construction, and farming and sparked a rapid decline in production and sales and a rapid increase in unemployment: in short, the U.S. was producing more goods than its citizens could buy. The lowest point of the Depression was 1933 with more than 15 million Americans (25 percent of the nation's workforce) out of work. For the first time, the American Dream was seemingly impossible to achieve: hard work and determination in the face of adversity no longer guaranteed reward and success. The ideal of the American Dream, however, was one traditionally aimed at men, and it was not until the Depression highlighted women's entry into the workforce that Hollywood film began to interrogate its myths in regards to women.

The rapid development of industrialization and mass production's dramatic increase in productivity led to lower prices, making consumer goods (like radios) more accessible to more of the population. The work week had decreased from 47.4 hours at the beginning of the decade to 42.1 hours by the end of it, giving Americans more time at leisure to find pleasure outside of their alienating and unfulfilling labor—and this was true of the white-collar "business" class as much as for the blue-collar "working" class. The composition of the labor force changed quickly between 1900 and 1930 with the total labor force expanding by 68 percent and the white-collar sector more than doubling; similarly, the number of women workers doubled from 5.3 million to 10.8 million, typically in the clerical and service sectors. It was in this period that the concept of a "consumer society" was born and that class identity could be determined by consumption instead of occupation. Similarly, the 1920s saw the housewife recast from producer to consumer—a "professional" buyer of new household electrical appliances and gadgets—and that, through cosmetics, women could literally buy their happiness (Cowan, 181–82). The ability to "buy" into a social identity becomes particularly poignant during the economic downturn of the Depression.

Women in the 1930s benefitted from the political and social rights that first-wave feminists had fought hard for in the previous decades. By 1935, the Depression had crippled the feminist movement and some wondered, as Genevieve Parkhurst's 1935 *Harper's* article asked, "Is Feminism Dead?" Parkhurst, along with other feminists of the time, felt that, since suffrage had been attained in 1920, there was no clear path, symbol, or goal for women to pursue (Ware, 87). The 1930s saw the movement slow down as women's issues seemed less relevant in the face of widespread economic strife in the Depression. As Lois Scharf notes, "The debate over the 'new woman' of the previous decade, who combined work and family, was completely subsumed by anxiety over the 'forgotten man' who combined no work with a possibly demoralized and disintegrating family" (137).

Scharf argues that while the Depression affected all, it had the greatest long-term effect on women: "When prosperity returned, the occupational (and related educational) levels attained by women around 1930 had dissipated and were not recovered" (xi). The number of women working in the female-dominated professional category (e.g., as teachers, nurses, social workers, librarians, etc.) in 1940 was barely higher than it had been in 1920. Frank Stricker argues that it is not accidental that the greatest decline in the number of female professionals (half of whom were schoolteachers) occurred—not during the sexual revolution of the 1920s when feminism was seen as unfashionable by the younger generation—but in the Depression when "school boards, state governments, and male teachers exerted terrific pressure against women teachers" (6). The Depression saw a backlash against working women who were often regarded as taking positions away from men—especially married women who presumably had husbands who could support them; however, notably, there was an increase in married women who joined the workforce during the Depression. Ironically, the fact that certain jobs were sex-typed—i.e., regarded as only women's work—protected women from losing their jobs and made it easier for them to find work during the Depression (Ware, 37). While many men found themselves part of the 25 percent of the workforce unemployed during the worst years of the Depression, the number of women entering the workforce increased, if only slightly, and while some female professions were hard hit (e.g., teachers and physicians) others (e.g., nurses, librarians, and social workers) experienced progress (Stricker, 5–6). Most working women, however, did see their earnings fall during the first five years of the Depression.

Although it was intended to help save the economy and the average American from the Depression, Roosevelt's New Deal was ultimately more of a morale booster than an economic one, and it would be World War II that would save the U.S. economy from its decade-long slump. The initial phase of the New Deal during the first 100 days of Roosevelt's administration in 1933 included the Triple-A farm program, planned crop reduction, new laws regulating Wall Street and banking, and the end of Prohibition.[7] The second phase of the New Deal (1934–35) included undertaking social security legislation and expanded relief under the Works Progress Administration. In 1936, the New Deal reached its "high tide" and Roosevelt had a stunning electoral victory, taking all but two states; however, in 1937, the tide turned when Roosevelt cut back on government spending, which in turn precipitated a second recession almost as severe as that of 1932–33. The New Deal did see the National Recovery Administration codes specifically benefit women by shortening work hours, raising their wages, and increasing their employment; however, these gains affected only the half of the female workforce that worked in manufacturing or trade, not those in domestic service, clerical work, or professional positions.

During the 1920s and 30s there was a pervasive backlash against working women—especially working wives who were seen as abandoning their social responsibilities and competing economically with men. In other words, women were transgressing the established division of labor: a woman's true work role was in the home, and the man's was in the workplace as family breadwinner. Women entered the workforce out of economic need while public sentiment discouraged it; and this debate was played out in the films of the time even if not always realistically. In 1932, *The Office Economist* ran a photograph of a young office worker Dorothy Wilson who was trading in her day job for one in the movies. The photo featured Wilson surrounded by fellow clerks from the *Stenographers and Secretaries' Club of Los Angeles* and the caption explained how the women wanted the movie studios "to tell them how they can dress like the stenographers depicted in the films on their salaries" (Qtd. in Strom, 2). Similarly, a reviewer for *Variety* notes for *The Daring Young Man* (Seiter, 1935), "[Mae] Clarke wears some hotsy-totsy costumes for just a working press girl, but maybe it doesn't matter" (24 July 1935). Both the photo and review reflect the disparity between Hollywood's representation of office workers and their reality. The Hollywood version was infinitely more glamorous; however, it was also somewhat transgressive, even if superficially and based in fantasy.

Sharon Hartman Strom argues that by 1930 "the gender and class hierarchy of the office was securely in place" (367). That may have been true in the real-life office but, in Hollywood, that hierarchy was being turned on its ear. As Robert McElvaine suggests, the Depression effected a "feminization" of American society with the "self-centered, aggressive, competitive, 'male' ethic of the 1920s" discredited (340). Being male no longer guaranteed independence or success and a new gender "balance" was created. Hollywood's films of the time then explored how women took on more masculine social roles in order to subsist as there was no longer an assurance that a dominant male could offer economic and social security. As John Bodnar argues,

> Hollywood did a better job than the New Deal or the CIO in acknowledging the outlook of women in American society during hard times. [. . .] In some instances, such as the "fallen women" films of the early thirties, females [. . .] almost always reminded audiences of two fundamental points: there was no future worth living in the working class, and the path to upward mobility invariably depended on a man. (26–27)

As Philip Hanson suggests, "No decade ever made clearer the relationship between identity and economics" (*This*, 17). Female identity became inextricably linked to the body and the body was tied to the economic situation of the 1930s. The Depression saw the rise of the "fallen woman" cycle of films in which women were forced by circumstance, rather than moral failing, to prostitute themselves for economic survival. As Bergman suggests, the fallen woman film arose in response to the Depression just as the gangster film but was "the obverse of gangsterism. The male character chose a mobster's life as a means to success; the female opted for prostitution as a result of continued failure" (50). In the figure of Mae West, there was at least a partial challenge to the idea of the fallen woman as failure and victim, and what West did for love, the girl reporter did for work. Just as West's characters argued that women could derive sexual gratification in love (and promiscuity), so too did the girl reporter playing detective prove that having to work for a living did not have to be a chore but could be a thrill. Notably, both types of woman were defined as spirited and plucky but specifically working class with their outspoken and brash ways.

Women had to economize during the Depression: for married women, this meant maximizing the family budget; for single women, this meant delaying family life. The Depression saw a decrease in marriage, divorce, and birth rates and, by 1938, according to one estimate, 1.5 million people had postponed getting married because of economic hard times (Ware, 6). This perhaps explains why so many working women on screen in the 1930s were shown pursuing a career rather than marriage; however, it also explains why birth control became increasingly acceptable and how it helped to redefine marriage—at least for middle-class, urban, white women. Birth control became more widely available during the 1920s and a 1936 Gallup poll revealed that 63 percent were in favor of the teaching and practice of birth control.[8] Kathleen Gregory Klein argues that this availability of birth control and more importantly its social acceptance, including popular marriage manuals encouraging its use, helped to redefine the wife's role in marriage as "companionate" rather than necessarily maternal (97). This shift of women's marital role to companionate was reflected in 1930s films with a new equality in heterosexual relationships. As Hanson notes,

> . . . approved heterosexual male and female romantic equality becomes the desired ideal. Especially in an economic period when positing an alternative ideal in place of the perceived failed dynamics of the Hoover era was bankable with mass audiences, a new romantic equilibrium materialized on the screen. ("Feminine," 132)

Hollywood's working women protagonists had been hardened by their experiences of the Depression and the necessity to support themselves like men—and the newspaper world offered the ideal space for such gender-benders. As film historian Deac Rossell notes,

> By the 1920s, newspapering was firmly established as a genre where women could take the leading roles. [. . .] Where women had been typically the love object, or the dramatic and emotional

catalyst between male leads in most films, here she could have a job, move independently through society, be a leader. All without necessarily endangering her femininity or being typed as man-less. ("Hollywood," 17)

The Depression allowed for a working woman with non-traditional desires: in other words, a modern woman.

Part III: Sex and the City

What characterizes films of the late 1920s and early 30s was the exploitation of the new technology of sound and a fascination with "modern," urban America. Indeed, while some detective films of the 1930s borrowed the old country manor setting from the classical British detective story, the majority exploits and indulges in the specifically American setting of the big city—usually New York and Chicago (in the 1930s) and later Los Angeles and San Francisco (in the 1940s). Stories set in the eastern metropolises often focus on crime resulting from Prohibition and gangland activities and, those set in the west, with crime related to Chinatown and immigration. The term "modern" can evoke a specific period in time ("modernity"), an artistic sensibility ("Style Moderne"), technological development ("modernization"), among other associations from rationality and individuality to social mobility.[9] In films of the 1920s and 30s, the modern is often presented visually in opposition to, and as a replacement for, the Victorian. My aim here is not to attempt to pin down its various associations but to explore how those associations were processed through American culture at the time in film. Sound cinema appears in the period of modernity and represents a modernizing technology; however, it is the visual and aural space that the "talkies" provided for the exploration of modern ideas that the following chapters explore. America was redefining itself, differentiating itself from the "Old World," and it did so by embracing a new mode of speaking ("modern talk"), new kinds of settings ("modern style"), and a new mode of dress ("modern look"). And the female detective—as independent, socially mobile, stylish, and fast-talking—embodied all things American and modern.

Modern Talk

Until 1927, film was silent—and sophisticated. A visual "language" had been solidified by the 1920s and late silent film had attained a high level of artistry and expression. Sound came to motion pictures in 1927, but it was not until 1930 that all American film production and exhibition was in sound. This period of transition saw a temporary disruption of the fluidity of silent film with the new technology requiring cumbersome equipment; however, within two years, innovations in sound technology meant quieter and more portable equipment and the opportunity to recover from the restrictive mode of filmmaking of the early "talkies." The revolution in sound was not just a technological one, however, but also a cultural one. The nature of comedy altered in Hollywood with the coming of sound: the talkies required "voiced verbal humor" and the silent comedians—with their reliance on physical comedy and slapstick—found themselves replaced by wise-cracking comedians from vaudeville and burlesque (Balio, 256). And, with the screwball comedies that sound made possible, came a defining of American culture through language and a differentiation from the language and culture from which America had emerged—e.g., British. As Maria DiBattista argues, the early 1930s to the mid-40s was "a time when America's image both at home and abroad was being refashioned and then tested in a loud theater of an economically unsettled, politically boisterous, and finally bellicose world" (39). The specifically American language offered by the movies was modern—defined by speed, crime, Prohibition, gangsterism, the underclass, and the urban. Other aspects of American culture reflected this shift also: for example, the hardboiled detective stories of Dashiell Hammett and Raymond Chandler were differentiated from the British classical detective story by their gritty realism, choppy style, and colloquial phrasing. As DiBattista demonstrates, the growing divergence between British and American English and America's redefinition of culture through language was commented on—on both sides of the Atlantic—from writers like F. Scott Fitzgerald and Virginia Woolf to literary critics Edmund Wilson to H. L. Mencken (42–44). America's national character was tied up in American gangland slang and a specific attitude and style of delivery: being blunt. I would add that there was also a shift in class in terms of who shaped national culture. In Britain, it was the aristocracy and upper-middle class that defined "proper" diction and delivery but, in America, it was from the working class that the nation borrowed its colloquialisms and directness.

Although the twentieth century saw a redefinition of American society and values as middle-class or even classless, Americans talked about belonging to a broadly defined working class in the nineteenth century (Ross, xi). In the movies, only snooty aristocratic types couched their meaning in politically correct phrasing; conversely, American English was defined by plain-speaking. As Dennis Broe notes,

> The private detective was not directly of the working class (he does not punch a clock, has his own office and business, and works for multiple clients). Yet, he has multiple affinities in the directness of his language, especially when speaking to wealth and power. (Broe)

For example, in *The Dark Corner* (Hathaway, 1946), upper-class Hardy Cathcart (Clifton Webb) instructs his hired heavy to ask the private detective (Mark

Stevens) on the other end of the phone for "200 dollars to leave town." The heavy (William Bendix), speaking the same language as the private eye, translates that into "two yards' powder money." In the 1941 film version of *The Maltese Falcon* (directed by John Huston), the leader of the villainous gang, Kasper Gutman (played by Sydney Greenstreet) is a refined, if self-indulgent, European established in direct contrast to the hero, private detective Sam Spade (played by Humphrey Bogart). In the first film adaptation of the novel directed by Roy Del Ruth in 1931), however, Gutman (here played by Dudley Digges) is American and the distinction made between him and Spade (played by Ricardo Cortez) is based on class—not nationality—and is established mainly through their choice of diction. So, while Digges's Gutman refers to "the immense" and "immeasurable wealth of the Order of St. John of Malta," Cortez's Spade suggests that they were "pretty well-fixed" and that "the Holy War was a great racket!"

I am not arguing that Hollywood film presented a specifically working-class centered world—in fact, the world of Hollywood from early on is predominantly middle class in terms of what values are upheld and praised (Muscio, 66). Instead, I am proposing that Hollywood helped to define American national identity as distinct from British by adopting the language and behavior of its lower classes. As Steven Ross suggests, Hollywood films did not explore the divisions or shifts in class so much as offer cross-class fantasies to appeal to the broadest audience possible (194). Cortez's Spade—rather than confirming himself as working class—is classless: his diction suggests a working-class past while his taste for finery suggests he has attained a comfortably bourgeois lifestyle through working for a living. In the early 1930s, the idea of class based on wealth was fragile in the face of the Depression, and the heroes (and villains) of Hollywood film demonstrated the mobility of class identity. In the case of the working woman, this mobility of class was coupled with one of gender.

It is out of this redefinition of American cultural identity that Hollywood's girl reporter and amateur detective is born. She is a product of the modern, urban, working- or middle-class America—and talks like it. As Kaja Silverman asserts in *The Acoustic Mirror*, feminist criticism has mainly focused on the visual aspect of female representation (e.g., Laura Mulvey's influential theory of the male gaze) and yet, classical Hollywood film is centrally concerned with the voice. Despite this concern, Silverman argues that women in mainstream film rarely have an authoritative voice. I am not contesting Silverman's point that women in experimental feminist film have a greater voice; however, I do want to suggest that women in Hollywood film had a more pronounced and respected voice in the 1930s than perhaps any other decade. The blonde goddess of the early 1930s—exemplified by Mae West and Jean Harlow—embodied a contradiction: her coarse talk did not deliver the same connotations that her heavenly body promised. With Harlow, it was her lower-class diction that defined her speech; with West, it was her sexual suggestiveness and slow drawl. On the other hand, the girl reporter is quick-witted and her sarcasm is all too apparent.

For example, Florence Dempsey (Glenda Farrell) in *Mystery of the Wax Museum* (Curtiz, 1933) calls her editor with the scoop that a corpse has been stolen from the morgue. When he asks her if there were any witnesses, the girl reporter is quick to explain over the phone, "Yeah, there were nine or ten witnesses. No, they didn't talk. They were pretty stiff. No, dope! Not drunk—dead!"[10] As Elizabeth Dalton notes, Florence's "gutsy dialogue" is "perfectly complimented by her staccato delivery—a remarkable 390 wpm" ("Meet," 37)—while the ideal rate of speech is closer to 190 wpm. Using American slang and talking at the speed of a New York minute, the girl reporter is—using DiBattista's term—"a fast-talking dame." DiBattista chooses the word "dame" because it is a prime example of Hollywood's differentiation of American culture from British: the British dame of the aristocracy becomes the American "dame" of gangland. As DiBattista suggests, the fast-talking dames "offer the most exhilarating and—to use a much abused but in this instance indispensible word—*empowering* model for American womanhood" (x).[11]

And modern America was all about speed, mobility, and talking. Hollywood's image of the big city in the 1930s was replete with subways, trains, cars, elevators for skyscrapers, phones, wires, speed of talking—even music. In *Dance, Fools, Dance*, socialite-turned-girl-reporter Bonnie Jordan (Joan Crawford) plays the piano for gangster Jake Luva (Clark Gable). "There's your 'Moonlight Sonata,' only *not* as it was written," she explains after playing the classical piece at a brisk pace, making it sound more current. The modern city is identified not just as a place for social mobility but also "automobility;" the female detective of the 1930s not only could pass in different classed spaces (e.g., Bonnie Jordan is just as much at home on a yacht as in the newsroom or a nightclub), but also tended to move rapidly from one space to another using an automobile. In *Hold that Girl* (MacFadden, 1934), girl reporter Tony Bellamy (Claire Trevor) always hitches a ride by flagging down a passing car, hopping on the running board, and demanding of the driver to "Follow that taxi!" Many of the girl reporters and female detectives own their own cars (including teenager Nancy Drew) or drive other people's with great skill while chasing down the story. Modes of communication also advanced with modernity: the telephone meant the expedited relaying of information, and the girl reporter was constantly hunting down a phone to give her editor the scoop—or to cut the phone line in order to prevent her rivals from doing the same. As Tom Gunning suggests, modernity can, in part, be regarded as "a collapsing system of previous experiences of space and time through speed" ("Tracing," 16).

The screwball comedy offered two types of modern woman: the mad-cap heiress who rebelled from upper-crust stagnation and the self-defined working girl; in other words at "the extremes of the social order where fluctuations in fortune and in identity tend to be quite pronounced" (DiBattista, 86). In Hollywood films of the 1930s, there is an association between the upper-class, the Old World, and effeminacy—whereas America's rugged individualism allowed

Fig. 3.1. Fast-Talking Dame: Glenda Farrell's brash girl reporter (right) is contrasted to her more feminine roommate, played by Fay Wray (left), in *Mystery of the Wax Museum* (1933). Photo from author's collection.

for a new kind of masculinization of men. The ideal of this period—being one's own man—was as applicable for women as it was for men. It is for this reason that the women of the 1930s were fast talkers—loud, brash, confident, independent, and outspoken—and why witty repartee comes into play: verbal jousting identified sexual attraction in a way other than physical intimacy (and avoided Code-related sexuality). A lot of Hollywood's fast-talking dames were working girls and often they worked with words as a writer or a reporter; however, not all of these characters saw their day job turn into detective work. Hollywood's most famous female reporters—"Babe" Bennett (Jean Arthur) in *Mr. Deeds Goes to Town* (Capra, 1936), Ann Mitchell (Barbara Stanwyck) in *Meet John Doe* (Capra, 1941), Hildy Johnson (Rosalind Russell) in *His Girl Friday* (Hawks, 1940), and Tess Harding (Katharine Hepburn) in *Woman of the Year* (Stevens, 1942)—did not appear until later in the newspaper film genre and did not investigate a crime. The films that leaned the furthest toward the comedy end of the spectrum—including the Capra and Hawks films—tended to focus on screwball relations while those that leant to the more serious end of the scale had more murder than mayhem; however, fast-talking and witty banter were common in both types. As DiBattista suggests, the girl reporter and fast-talking dame like Hildy in *His Girl Friday*

. . . makes us aware of how "talking pictures" gave women the chance to speak up, speak out, and speak to their own desires, dreams, and ambitions. Presented with this opportunity, they made the most of it. They spoke fast and furiously, as if their survival depended on their doing so. As, indeed it did. [. . .] The comedies of the thirties and early forties teach us nothing if they don't impress upon us that slow-witted, reticent, or inarticulate women had little chance for sexual happiness, still less for professional success. (270)

Although it might seem to be a product of the Code with talk replacing sex, the woman's ability to compete with men at the level of language and articulation was facilitated by the introduction of sound film. It even predates that, however, as is apparent in the silent version of *The Office Scandal* (Stein, 1929). In an exchange reported to the audience through intertitle cards, girl reporter Jerry Cullen (Phyllis Haver) talks back to her editor:

Jerry:	Police baffled! *And* you're the little *guy* who's all conceited over the great Male Sex!
Pearson:	I suppose your women's intuition tells you who the killer is?
Jerry:	Oh, no—I'm not supposed to have any brains. I'm only a wallflower.

Even though this exchange is silent, Jerry's sarcasm is not lost in translation. Jerry is just one example that the fast-talking dame actually predates the talkies and that she was a product of modern, urban America rather than sound film, specifically.[12]

Modern Style

Just as Hollywood's fast-talk, slang, and directness defined America's national identity in terms of language, so too did film's Art Deco architecture, décor, and star's costumes distinguish America's urban, modern identity through the image. The studio system allowed for the construction of costly sets that could be redressed and reused for multiple films and this led to the development of a "studio look" or "house style" and association with specific kinds of film. For example, Warner Bros. was known for its gritty, ripped-from-the-headlines, urban films in the first half of the 1930s; thus, when the studio took a horror film script based on the 1925 fire at Madame Tussaud's in London, it transformed it into a film about American Depression-era urban life. With *Mystery of the Wax Museum*, as Scott MacQueen explains,

> The locale was switched to New York City and the narrative thread was grafted onto a more typical [Darryl] Zanuck storyline of news gathering in the big city. All of the working class, tabloid sensations that distinguished the Warners product were added: tough gum-cracking reporters, city newsrooms, antagonism between the sexes, Irish cops, bootlegging, drug addiction, slum life and raucous off-color dialogue. (42)

A studio's style was determined not by camera-work, as different films had different directors and cinematographers, but by *mise en scène* (everything placed in front of the camera including sets, props, and costumes). Studio art departments included unit art directors, illustrators, modelers, set dressers, and architects under the supervision of art directors like Cedric Gibbons at MGM, Van Nest Polglase at RKO, and Hans Dreier at Paramount. While the most ambitious sets and costumes were those designed for prestige, period A-pictures, the most interesting ones were those of the late 1920s and early 30s used for films addressing female sexuality.

Films that focused on the flapper and the "fallen woman" were the epitome of modernistic in terms of design.[13] "Art Deco" is a label that has come to signify a popular trend in design (1910–35); the term itself, however, was not coined until the 1960s and, at the time, was known as "modernism" or "Style Moderne" (Fischer, 11). The Art Deco movement is regarded as the product of the machine age and many elements evoked or referred to the mechanical—notably its simplified geometric and symmetrical patterns—and its color palette was often reduced to black, white, and silver. While the style was met with disdain from art critics in the U.S., it impacted every level of design in Hollywood film and was popularized with the 60 to 90 million moviegoers that, by the 1930s, were frequenting the cinema each week (Fischer, 22–25). As Balio explains,

> Since modernism became associated with luxury, glamor, and affluence, it became the perfect visual style to complement [Irving] Thalberg's urban strategy of producing pictures based on contemporary sources and themes. MGM's most famous modernistic set is undoubtedly the stunning art deco lobby of *Grand Hotel* (1932), which Gibbons designed in collaboration with Alexander Toluboff. (88)

Gibbons had brought the innovative new design trends he had seen at the influential "Exposition Internationale des Arts Décoratifs et Industriels Modernes" (1925) in Paris to American film as art director on MGM's trilogy about the sexual mores of young women starring Joan Crawford: *Our Dancing Daughters*

(Beaumont, 1928), *Our Modern Maidens* (Conway, 1929), and *Our Blushing Brides* (Beaumont [uncredited], 1930). In the early 1930s, it was Polglase, heading up RKO's art department who made an impact with innovative modernistic designs, including what was nicknamed the "Big White Set" in films such as the Ginger Rogers/Fred Astaire musical *Top Hat* (Sandrich, 1935).

While the art department's job was to create an "illusion of reality," as Gabrielle Esperdy explains, Hollywood was helping to establish that reality:

> Quite often, however, audiences recognized the stylish world of penthouses, nightclubs, hotels, and ocean liners depicted on screen only because they had already seen it in another picture. In this way movie sets exposed many Americans to a wide range of contemporary design, much of which was simultaneously on display in the pages of shelter and decorating magazines and the showrooms of department and home furnishing stores. (201)

Thus, Hollywood shaped social attitudes and aspirations not only by the kinds of characters, plots, dialogue, and values—i.e., narrative elements—but also sets, costumes, and settings—i.e., visual elements. America's national identity was being constructed by Hollywood through Art Deco objects and sleek glass and chrome interiors in contrast to the coziness and clutter of the Victorian home associated with the nineteenth century, the rural, and the Old World. The contrast of American Modern to British Victorian is highlighted at the beginning of *Mystery of the Wax Museum*, when the narrative shifts abruptly from the gothic museum in early 1920s London to the Art Deco morgue in 1930s New York City.

As Lea Jacobs suggests, by the early 1930s, the association between the fallen woman and art moderne was well established; however, as the decade progressed, set designs—in keeping with the trends—became sparser and more streamlined (53). It was not just sleek, modern interiors that signaled wealth and success but specifically American architecture—after all, Art Deco was often referred to as "skyscraper style." While Art Deco was a product of Europe, the skyscraper was associated with urban America. In *Baby Face* (Green, 1933), the upward mobility of Lily Powers (Barbara Stanwyck)—from walking the streets to making it to the top—is indicated in a series of shots of the exterior of the building showing her promotion from one department (and corresponding building storey) at a time. The skyscraper, as Donald Albrecht notes, became "the quintessential expression of modern American architecture" (149) or, as Esperdy notes, "the era's preeminent symbol of modernity" (202)—from William Van Alen's Chrysler Building (completed in 1930) to Shreve, Lamb, and Harmon's Empire State Building (completed in 1931). Vojislava Filipcevic argues that the image of the skyline vs. that of the slum identified the two extremes of the

Depression-era metropolis—the highlife and poverty; importantly, the image of the skyscraper could embody a tribute to man's accomplishments in the modern era or a critique of urban society (278–79).

For example, in *King Kong* (Cooper, 1933), the Empire State Building is the emblem of monumental architecture, and the site of the battle between the primitive (gorilla) and the modern (airplanes). While New York offers a glamorous contrast to the wilderness of Skull Island, the film depicts the metropolis as eerily parallel to the world of the island. Just as the wall represents the island's monumental architecture, which towers over the islanders, so too does the Empire State Building rise above ant-sized New Yorkers. And, just as Kong had to defeat predators in the jungle to protect Ann, so too does he attack the train that slithers like the snake lizard and the planes that buzz overhead like the pteranodon.[14] In the end, New Yorkers are presented as no more sophisticated than the superstitious islanders when they panic at Kong's escape.

Similarly, while the city is sleek and glamorous in the "Lullaby of Broadway" sequence in *Gold Diggers of 1935* (Berkeley, 1935), it ultimately proves destructive—at least for the urban woman. As Bita Mahdaviani suggests, from the turn of the century onwards, popular texts—from illustrated postcards to early films—linked the modern skyscraper and the modern woman: common images included ankles of women passing by the foot of the skyscraper and/or as the wind tunnels produced by the tall buildings blew women's skirts up.[15] The lyrics of the "Lullaby of Broadway" explain that the Broadway and Manhattan "babies" (i.e., young women) stay out all night and live in luxury provided by their fathers; they are also linked to symbols of big city life—the subway train, the taxi, and the night club.[16] In the first part of the "Lullaby" sequence, the only thing that is visible is the female singer's face in close-up. The camera tracks around behind her and pans down until her face is on the horizontal and she is looking up; she then places a lit cigarette in her mouth (another symbol of the modern woman) and her face is replaced by a miniature of the city. The almost 15-minute sequence that follows contrasts commuters heading off to work with a "Broadway baby" coming home and then the same Broadway baby getting up in the evening to begin her "day" when the commuters are coming home. Her life of leisure and pleasure, however, is brought to a dramatic and tragic end when she plummets to her death from a skyscraper balcony when the crowd of nightclub dancers pushes open the balcony door. Although the camera offers us her point of view with a shot of the ground spiraling towards us, there is no sense of loss with her death. Even the crowd that watches her fall looks more thrilled than horrified and the only one who misses her is the cat who waits by her apartment door for its morning milk. In *Skyscraper Souls* (Selwyn, 1932), a secretary (Verree Teasdale)—who has killed her boss and former lover—throws herself off the top floor of the office building and falls to her death. Similarly, in *Three Wise Girls* (Beaudine, 1932) one of the film's heroines, Gladys (Mae Clarke), contemplates committing suicide by leaping from her high-rise apartment (provided by her married lover). Modernistic architecture may have been the symbol of urban America's advancements but it was often employed to suggest the erosion of America's morality.

Modern Look

Not only did the girl reporter as a working girl mark a shift in terms of how women spoke, but she also represented how the modern woman dressed. As Charles Eckert has demonstrated, Hollywood was selling American women an image of modern femininity through consumer tie-ins for clothes, accessories, and cosmetics. Such cross-industry pollination meant that moviegoers could purchase the kinds of identities they were visually consuming in the theater. In 1930, *Motion Picture* ran a story that opened: "The modern woman is a screen shopper. You, being modern, are a screen shopper" (Donnell, 70). And one of the key ideas that Hollywood sold during the Depression was that identity could be purchased (although the price was often moral as well as monetary). Fashion functions as a marker of class and, thus, through the exchange of clothing, a character could alter her class identity. As Sarah Berry notes, filmmakers recognized "the significance of clothing to American dreams of self-invention and class transgression"—both on and behind the screen: "the mythology of the 'makeover' became synonymous with the Hollywood star's rise from obscurity to fame" (xviii). Hollywood suggests that mobility is possible by dressing the part.[17] The fallen woman's moral decline in the early 1930s was inversely proportional to her rise through society and was indicated through a change in wardrobe: from sensible shoes to delicate heels, from woolen jackets to fur coats, from tweed suits to silk gowns, and from naked necklines to bejeweled décolletages, moral decline never looked so tempting.

As Jacobs notes, "the display of clothes became highly conventionalized within the fallen woman film, and was accorded a prominent narrative function" (57). In a similar manner—although for opposite effect—the female detective was firmly distinguished as a specific kind of woman by her clothing. Rather than the silken shifts, fur coats, and decadent jewels of the Art Deco woman, the fast-talking dame was marked as an urban, working woman in clothes adapted from the male wardrobe: tailored suits, mannish hats, sensible shoes, and fur only as a coat collar or stole. The three most popular outfits for Hollywood working girls were the structured dress with a belt, pockets, or detail marking the waist; a suit jacket and calf-length skirt; or the suit skirt paired with a blouse. The outfit is completed with a hat, often styled on a man's fedora or panama, and something at the neck (a scarf, tie, or bow) as the female version of the man's tie. As Lucy Fischer suggests, "the economic slide of the 1930s had a chilling effect on the popularity of modernism—a mode identified with the energy of the Roaring Twenties and the post-World War I business boom" (87). By the mid-30s, Deco-inspired clothes and surroundings evoked negative associations with the lost highlife of the flapper and the immoral desires of the fallen woman. Instead, the "good" working girl of the 1930s was associated with a modern style rather than the Style Moderne. While studio photo stills, lobby cards, and other visual advertising for fallen women films sold the glamorous gowns that Stanwyck and Crawford wore in their films, so too did those for the female detective films sell the sensible but stylish uniform of the career-minded woman.

There was a conscious attempt by Hollywood producers and studio designers to capture the combination of masculinity and femininity that the female detective embodied. As the caption of a publicity still for *Human Cargo* (Dwan, 1936) suggests about star Claire Trevor's tweed suit,

> Utterly tailored, yet utterly feminine is this distinctive three piece suit for travelling or daytime wear . . . . Made of a mannish fabric, brown and tan herringbone tweed in one of the softer weaves, the suit is distinguished by four slot pockets on the jacket, a girlish wide collar worn over the collarless top-coat, and a trim front closing that buttons all the way from the throat to the waistline.[18]

Similarly, the caption for another still, this time for Trevor's pin-striped suit in the film, states:

> William Lambert, studio designer, relieves the severity of the suit by a lingerie blouse trimmed in fine, handmade lace, and the brightness of patent leather twinkles in the pumps, handbag, and the bunched leaf trimming at the front of the hat.[19]

Thus, the female detective—and by extension the star who played her—attained a balance of gender roles in her wardrobe.

And it was a particular kind of star that was associated with these gender-bending women. The great stars of the 1930s—including Norma Shearer, Greta Garbo, Irene Dunne, and Jean Harlow—never played the female detective; others associated with dramatic roles, like Bette Davis and Joan Crawford, did play female detectives but only on one or two occasions; alternatively, the women who played the female detectives were character actors or B-film stars—including Glenda Farrell, Claire Trevor, and Joan Blondell. It was these actresses' association with the working class—with a history of playing golddiggers and working girls who talked back—that embodied the spirit of modern and urban America. And, in the final analysis, not only did these women play modern women but they embodied the same values themselves as women who chose to pursue a career—only as Hollywood stars rather than female detectives.

Fig. 3.2. The Modern Look: Claire Trevor sports the typical working woman's attire as a lawyer in *Career Woman* (1936). Photo from author's collection.

A Flâneuse?

Although other women may be presented as virtue-in-danger or dangerous temptress, the girl reporter—as a hardboiled and masculine woman—is not threatened by the city but is, instead, its master or at least its explorer. While amateur female detectives other than the reporter—for example, teenager Nancy Drew, schoolteacher Hildegarde Withers, and nurse Sarah Keate—investigate crimes in a small town (Drew) and isolated "old manor" type spaces (Withers and Keate), the girl reporter as detective investigated crime in the urban metropolis. While critics have noted that women tended to be a part of the spectacle of the city for the male gaze (Wilson, *Sphinx*, 16), in the films with which I am concerned, the heroine often reverses the assumed relationship of the woman with the gaze. First, as less feminine in her dress and demeanor than the typical leading lady, the girl reporter does deflect the gaze: she is treated by the men in the film as a colleague or rival rather than as a love object. Second, because she takes up the role of detective in the film, the girl reporter possesses the gaze herself and utilizes it to observe and investigate crime scenes and suspects. This empowered gaze of the detective-figure utilized in city spaces is associated with what Anne Friedberg refers to as the "fundamental paradigm of the subject in modernity, the *flâneur*" (3).

Walter Benjamin saw the rise of the detective story as a response to the redefinition of the body and the mobile transformation of identity in modernity. As Gunning notes, both real-life policing and detective fiction are driven by the need to pin an identity (i.e., the criminal's) down to a specific body ("Tracing," 20). Indeed, Benjamin saw a correlation between Poe's detective-hero and the *flâneur*. As James V. Werner notes, "In Poe's formulation the *flâneur* and detective are closely aligned in characteristics and methodology," including an experience of observation based more on intuition than science (9–10). *Flânerie* suggests a mobile but passive viewer; however, the Hollywood detective (male and female) does not merely observe the city but utilizes the gaze to identify criminals and bring them to justice, thus restoring society to a state of order. As Gunning notes, the detective of early popular American detective fiction—like that of Anna Katharine Green—operated mainly in interior spaces ("Exterior," 114); instead, the girl reporter in 1930s film, walks and drives down the city streets with unexpected confidence. Janice Mouton suggests that the definition of *flânerie* implies walking only—i.e., "aimless strolling" (8); however, as Ruth Iskin notes, bicycling and driving constitute "modern forms of *flânerie*" (339).

Feminist critics have debated the possibility of a similar position of subjectivity for women. As Elizabeth Wilson notes,

> It is this *flâneur*, the *flâneur* as a man of pleasure, as a man who takes visual possession of the city, who has emerged in postmodern feminist discourse as the embodiment of the "male gaze." He represents men's visual and voyeuristic mastery over women. According to this view, the *flâneur*'s freedom to wander at will through the city is essentially a masculine freedom. Thus, the very idea of the *flâneur* reveals to be a gendered concept. ("Invisible," 65)

It seems necessary then to question the assumed masculinity of this privileged position of observation and surveillance, and explore the possibility of a *flâneuse*. As Deborah Parsons notes,

> *Flânerie* has thus also become a metaphor for the gendered scopic hierarchy in observation of urban space. Despite defining modernism away from canonical versions towards a recognition of less dominant modes, notably a "female" modernism, however, feminist literary criticism and cultural sociology has tended to support the masculine definition of the urban observer. (4)

To regard the perception of the city as an exclusively male privilege ignores a female subjectivity and relegates the urban woman to being merely a part of the city spectacle rather than its consumer. Indeed, Mulvey's conception of cinematic spectatorship through the lens of psychoanalysis assumes an empowered male gaze and the female body as its object, a binary that would be disrupted by a *flâneuse*. Critics such as Griselda Pollock, Elizabeth Wilson, and Janet Wolff have argued against the possibility of a female *flâneur* because real women operated within the domestic, as opposed to the public, sphere. Friedberg, however, argues that with shopping came a licensed freedom to roam the city and a gaze imbued with power as a consumer, facilitating female *flânerie* (36–37). The *flâneur*, as conceived of by Benjamin, had to preserve a liminal perspective in order to interpret the city objectively. Friedberg suggests that, like the window-shopper, the *flâneur* is "just looking" (34).

According to Edward Dimendberg, *film noir* of the 1940s and 50s illustrates a shift in the conception of the city. Early *noir* (1940s) focused on centripetal ("center-seeking") space through elevated or aerial views of the city and through street-level scenes with a fascination for urban density and the visible (e.g., the skyline, recognizable places, public monuments). On the other hand, later *noir* (1950s)—focused more on centrifugal ("center-fleeing") space and the impact of the automobile, highway, and mass media on urban space—was concerned with invisibility and speed. Dimendberg explains that in early *film noir*, protagonists stroll through the densely populated city on the street and experience meetings and conflicts in that public space as a kind of "walking cure" for urban malaise and an attempt "to connect parts of the city into a coherent environmental image" (120 and 149).[20] But, in the 1930s, there is no need for the hero to perform a walking cure; as Dimendberg notes, the image of the city in the 1920s and 30s is of a cohesive and organized unity (82–83). In the 1930s detective films, the modern metropolis (usually New York) is presented as unproblematic in terms of space: it is recognizable, cohesive, and knowable—and the protagonist is not intimidated by the space but is rather its master.

The girl reporter's independence at exploring the modern city spaces alone marked a transgression of traditional gendered behavior—i.e., being a respectable "lady" as opposed to a "dame" or a "streetwalker." Bergman notes that there was a distinct increase in the number of prostitutes in the U.S. in the early 1930s (50), a reality that was echoed in "fallen woman" films in which women were seen as victims of the city. Critics have noted, however, that the *flâneur*, the reporter, and the prostitute are all the products of the modern city and have similar relationships to its public spaces. Helen Richards suggests that, as modern society came under the influence of mass culture and mass consumption, the *flâneur* had to adapt in order to survive: "This adjustment can be seen in the evolution of the *flâneur* into a journalist, and the appearance of the *flâneuse*" (150). The girl reporter is like the streetwalker in that she walks the city streets but unlike her in that the reporter is allowed to "sell her wares" (i.e., her stories) without being regarded as a social disease or criminal. While the first critics of female *flânerie* suggested it was an impossibility for women to occupy this urban role (Pollock, Wilson, Wolff), later ones argued for a kind of female *flânerie* facilitated by the roles offered to women in the modern city—as consumer (Friedberg) or rag-picker (Parsons)—and the most recent have assumed that female *flânerie* existed in some form both in historical practice and in literary representations (Iskin, Nesci, Nord). As Deborah Epstein Nord argues, "rather than assume the absence of female spectatorship, we might ask instead what circumstances and discourses shaped it and what typified its forms and contradictions" (12). Therefore, I posit that Hollywood's girl reporter as detective challenges the idea of urban perception as specifically masculine as an empowered observer who investigates crime scenes, suspects, and the city while operating within the male world of work, politics, and urban life as a reporter.

Detecting as a Hobby

Amateur and Professional Detectives in the 1930s

Inspector Piper:	How many men have you seen?
Hildegarde Withers:	Plenty of them . . . that is . . . I . . . !
Inspector Piper:	Well, maybe if you'd seen more men, Hildegarde Withers . . .
Hildegarde Withers:	I've seen enough men today, Oscar Piper, to know that if this murder is going to be solved, a woman's got to do it.

—Edna May Oliver and James Gleason in *Penguin Pool Murder* (1932)

Softboiled Detectives

Although the hardboiled detective story had superseded the classical detective story in American fiction by the 1930s, it did not do so on film. It would not be until America's entry into World War II that Hollywood would embrace the darker themes and characters of the hardboiled variety in *film noir*. Instead, Hollywood had a Golden Age of its own with dozens of detective series based on detectives that fell somewhere between Britain's armchair sleuth and America's tough private eye. There were a few British imports: most memorably, Basil Rathbone played Sherlock Holmes accompanied by Nigel Bruce's Dr. Watson in 14 films and on broadcast radio (1939–46). Although one of the few imports to Hollywood from the British classical tradition, even Holmes was updated from operating in the nineteenth century to the mid-twentieth. RKO produced the other two series with a British detective but both were set in the U.S.: George Sanders played Leslie Charteris's The Saint in five films (1939–41)

and then Michael Arlen's The Falcon in four films (1941–42) before his real-
life brother, Tom Conway, took over as *The Falcon's Brother* (Logan, 1942) for
10 films (1942–46). American writers produced popular detective heroes who
also sustained series. S. S. Van Dine's detective-hero Philo Vance was played by
William Powell in 27 films (1926–36) and Perry Mason, the Lone Wolf, The
Crime Doctor, Michael Shayne, Dick Tracy, and Boston Blackie all appeared
in series at different studios. As well, the Asian detective was also popular in
this period: Earl Derr Biggers's detective Charlie Chan played most memorably
by Warner Oland appeared in 47 films (1925–49); John Marquand's Kentaro
Moto, in eight films (1937–39); and James Lee Wong, in six films (1939–40).
The B-film detective series that proved so popular in the 1930s and 40s all
but disappeared in the 1950s as low-budget genres—like the mystery and
western—moved to television.

   Rather than tough and hardboiled detectives that would dominate
the cultural imagination in the 1940s in Hollywood's *film noir*, the B-series
detectives—even those who were adapted from hardboiled stories—e.g., Nick
Charles from Hammett's *The Thin Man*—were recast as suave, debonair
men-about-town: in other words, they were soft rather than hardboiled.[1] In
this sense, the male detective was a gender-bender. The stars who played the
1930s detectives—George Sanders, Tom Conway, William Powell, and Warner
Oland—all began their careers playing cads and/or downright villains. With
"real" Americanness associated with the working class, being an Englishmen or
an upper-class American became indistinguishable in Hollywood films, and this
conflation was exacerbated by the Depression when living well was regarded as
the out-dated privilege of the few. For audiences affected by the Depression,
the debonair detective afforded a glimpse of the modern life of luxury. What
James Parish and Don Stanke describe as the Hollywood "debonair," Drew Todd
calls the "Art Deco dandy"—an American character that, as an "emblem of the
modern age," was slim, well-dressed, witty, suave, and could handle the new
woman of the age (Todd). Todd notes that while the character of the dandy
from the nineteenth century carried homosexual overtones, such implications
were erased from the twentieth-century American dandy who used his somewhat feminized masculinity to charm the ladies. According to Todd, the Deco
dandy is interesting and empowered by his liminality: he is not European nor
typically American; he is not of the aristocracy, nor is he of the working class;
he is not effeminate, nor is he the traditional American tough guy. Todd does
not discuss the professions of the dandies to which he refers, but Hollywood's
softboiled detectives engaged in traditionally manly pursuits—investigating
crime, confronting villains in physical conflicts, seducing women, and finding
adventure in general. Moreover, they were often compared with more physical
and less cerebral men—i.e., typical American tough guys—who were portrayed
as "dumb lugs" in comparison.

   And from the same cultural moment that facilitated the softboiled male
detective came the female detective as a similar kind of gender-bender. While

the female detectives of 1930s fiction may have remained firmly entrenched in the classical sleuth tradition, on screen a different kind of model was emerging. The screen female detective defies social assumptions of "proper" feminine roles and behavior by stepping out of the domestic sphere and taking on the presumed male pursuit of detecting. And these female detectives proved fashionable: Hildegarde Withers, Torchy Blane, Nancy Drew, Sarah Keate, and Kitty O'Day were all popular enough to sustain series. In *A Guide to American Crime Films of the Thirties*, Larry Langman and Daniel Finn differentiate two categories of crime film: the detective film—the category to which the films featuring Nancy Drew, Sarah Keate, and Hildegarde Withers belong—and the newspaper-crime film—the category to which Torchy Blane belongs. Although all of these female characters engage in detective work in the course of the narrative and the questions of crime and its solution are similar across both types of film, the themes related to social issues including women, work, and marriage differ. In the newspaper-crime film, the female reporter like Torchy is a hardboiled woman of the city, whereas amateur sleuths like Nancy, Sarah, and Hidegarde are more closely associated with the classical sleuth, solving crimes in small towns and isolated old manor houses. More importantly, the girl reporters of the city represented what Andrea Walsh has termed the "femininity-achievement" conflict in that their sex was an issue in the male sphere of investigating and reporting crime, and they were faced with the question of marriage *or* a career. The female amateur detectives, on the other hand, often side-stepped this debate by being either too old—in the case of Hildegarde Withers—or too young—in the case of Nancy Drew—for marriage and because their sleuthing was considered a hobby rather than a career.

These cinematic female detectives did not exist in a vacuum but were illustrative of a popular trend that extended to broadcast radio. As Jack French details, there were about a dozen radio series in the 1930s and 40s that focused on female detectives, whether private eyes, reporters, or G-women and almost another dozen that offered detective-couple teams. Series with a primary female detective, although not related to any film series, included "The Affairs of Ann Scotland" (1946–47, ABC) with Arlene Francis; "Candy Matson, Yukon 2-8209" (1949–51, NBC) with Natalie Parks-Masters; and "Kitty Keene, Inc." (1937–41, CBS) with Beverly Younger (followed by Gail Henshaw and Fran Carlon). There was some intersection between film detectives and their stars with radio programs like "Big Town" (1937–1942, CBS; 1943–48, CBS; 1948–51, NBC; 1952, CBS) starring Claire Trevor (1937–40) as Lorelei Kilbourne (followed by Ona Munson and then Fran Carlon) and "Miss Pinkerton" (1941, NBC) starring then-husband and-wife team of Joan Blondell and Dick Powell.

There were two types of female detective in 1930s film: professionals who investigated for a living and amateurs who sleuthed out of interest. Female private investigators and police detectives were rare but, following in the tradition of the dime novel and silent film, the female detective working undercover (as I discussed in Chapter 2) was still a popular trope. In terms of the amateur sleuth, while those of early detective fiction tended to be middle- to upper-class women of leisure—i.e., with the time to pursue criminals as a hobby—Hollywood's female detectives tended to be working women who investigated crime on the side or as a result of their job as teacher, nurse, or reporter. The amateur female detective had a nose for sleuthing, sought the opportunity to use it, and wanted to do what the professional female detectives did do—make a career of it. Ironically, the women who did attempt to make a career out of sleuthing are those who tended to give it up by the end of the film. There seemed to be a reluctance on the part of Hollywood producers to see a woman *make a living* as a detective; however, there was apparently a freedom allowed the amateur sleuth to pursue detective work instead of matrimony—as long as they only engage in the activity as a hobby.

Professionals Undercover

The professional detective is one whose day job is to detect. As one might imagine, the professional female detective was far less common than the amateur in fiction and film in the 1930s, most likely because she was a rare occurrence in reality. It was also likely due to the pressure exerted by official law enforcement agencies on Hollywood producers in pre-production consultation or post-release criticism to portray their on-screen representatives in specific ways. Detective stories and films were not always kind in terms of their presentation of official investigators. For example, a reviewer for *Variety* for the first "Torchy Blane" film, *Smart Blonde* (McDonald, 1937), notes that "Three types of cops are offered: (a) the bawling chief of detectives and dumb; (b) a half-wit desk sergeant; (c) a balmy flatfoot chauffeur" (13 Jan 1937). There is evidence that Hollywood was under the scrutiny of law enforcement agencies in terms of the industry's presentation of those agencies as a *Motion Picture Herald* review for the third "Torchy Blane" film, *The Adventurous Blonde* (McDonald, 1937), notes:

> The New York and other police departments currently are irritated by the manner in which policemen, of all strata, are portrayed on the screen. Producers don't want to incur the ire of any police department any more than they desire to go out of their way to satisfy their vanity. [. . .] They are making pictures which they assume will provide the maximum amount of amusement and satisfy the maximum number of persons. They also have an eye to financial returns. Spokesmen for New York's "finest" are quite wrought up because screen writers, producers and directors prefer to have some handsome hero, heroine, or even nitwit, solve a crime in a manner that makes the arms of the law look stupid. Whether or not anybody else is, they probably will be quite interested in "The

Adventurous Blonde." All the picture does is do what the police quite evidently don't want pictures to do. In ways customary to the screen, a run of the mill plainclothes cop is made to look silly while a blonde newspaper woman outdoes all the real sleuths of factual history and visionary imagination in solving a complicated crime. [. . .] Not concerned with ethics, the patrons were not only interested in how "Torchy Blane" proved herself a better detective than "Steve McBride," but also in the ways in which she outhoaxed a bunch of jealous newspaper rivals who tried to hoax her out of a wedding, and in the manner in which she hoaxed an unsuspected culprit into confessing himself a murderer. (11 Sept 1937)

As the reviewer suggests, audiences are not concerned with the realism of the narrative or representation of criminal investigations: they are concerned only with seeing the film's heroine accomplish her crime-fighting goals. Hollywood was also expected to consult those law enforcement agencies on developing characters for films. For example, as Charles R. Metzger notes in a memo, it was pointed out to the producers of *Sealed Lips* (Waggner, 1942) "that their script would have to be approved by the F.B.I. if, as now present, hero was a G-man and the story purported to deal with the actual methods of the F.B.I." (25 March 1941). There was a suggestion made to the producers to change the hero to a private detective or unidentified state police department to avoid having to seek approval from the FBI. This might go some ways to explaining why private eyes and amateur detectives were so much more pervasive at the time than official investigators.

Private Detectives

There were a handful of female private detectives: Kate Kirby (played by Laura Sawyer) in *Chelsea 7750*, *An Hour before Dawn*, and *The Port of Doom* (Dawley, 1913), and films like *The Mystery of Richmond Castle* (1914), *The Girl from Havana* (Stoloff, 1929), *Are You There?* (MacFadden, 1931),[2] *Murder at the Vanities* (Leisen, 1934),[3] *The Woman Condemned* (Davenport, 1934), and *Private Detective* (Smith, 1939).[4] Although unable to locate a copy of *The Girl from Havana* for screening, I was able to read a copy of the script (29 April 1929) by Edwin Burke (dialogue) and John Stone (scenario). In the script, Joan Anders (Lola Lane) is an undercover agent for the Jeweler's Detective Agency, and she is called in to work on a robbery from a store in Los Angeles when the thieves flee for Havana on a ship. Joan is upset that she is falling in love with one of the thieves, Allan (Paul Page), and is not looking forward to closing the case. When the captain asks her if she likes her job, she replies, "Not this time" and tells him that his job is "cleaner and nicer." Both Allan and Joan are masquerading as something they are not: Allan is pretending to be a thief pretending to be a ship's steward; Joan is pretending to be a thief pretending to be a chorus girl. Luckily, Allan is actually the son of a man murdered by the villains and he joined them only to bring them to justice. When Joan's real identity is discovered, one of the villains, Spike (Warren Hymer), kidnaps her and threatens to rape her before killing her. Spike says menacingly, "You've been stalling for three days. We'll settle that first." As the script details, "He starts for her. She screams." Allan comes to her rescue and fights Spike but, interestingly, when Spike is about to shoot Allan, it is Joan who comes to *his* rescue. The script does not offer a sense of whether or not Joan will marry Allan or give up her career, but it does confirm that they are in love.

In *The Woman Condemned*, a popular singer, Jane Merrick (Lola Lane), goes missing and an undercover private eye, Barbara Hammond (Claudia Dell), is arrested for snooping around Jane's apartment. When she is brought before the judge, a young reporter and practical joker, Jerry Beal (Richard Hemingway), rescues her by claiming she is his fiancée. The judge agrees to let her go as long as she is released "into the protective custody of her husband"—in other words, they have to be married right then and there. With her identity as a detective still unknown to him, Barbara and Jerry investigate the disappearance of the singer; however, Barbara is arrested, interrogated, and confesses to the murder of Jane's twin sister. At first Barbara seems inept—getting arrested twice—and a little too soft for the game—she does scream and confess to a crime she did not commit under interrogation; however, it all turns out to be part of her covert operation for the police and she helps solve the mystery surrounding

Fig. 4.1. Unusual for Such a Girl: Lola Lane plays an undercover agent for the Jeweler's Detective Agency in *The Girl from Havana* (1929). She falls in love with Paul Page's thief (right) who, it turns out, is also working undercover. Photo from author's collection.

the murder by tricking the real killer into revealing himself. Having said that I would point out that, except for the last minute revelation that her seemingly incompetent behavior has just been a cover, Barbara does come across as somewhat ineffectual and the ending seems an unlikely resolution to the case. Just as the few outings of these private professional detectives is undercover, so too are the handful of "official" female detectives.

Undercover Agents

There are a few female agents who are crime-fighters but not necessarily sleuths; they unravel the mystery because they infiltrate criminal rings rather than employing investigative or deductive skills. These films include *Unknown Woman* (Rogell, 1935) in which Marian Marsh plays a federal agent posing undercover to smash a ring of racketeers; *15 Maiden Lane* (Dwan, 1936) in which Claire Trevor plays an insurance investigator undercover as a thief;[5] *The Girl from Scotland Yard* (Vignola, 1937) in which Karen Morley plays a Scotland Yard detective who is asked to act as an international agent to uncover a ring of sabateours; and *China Passage* (Killy, 1937) in which Constance Worth plays a U.S. government agent who goes undercover to investigate a diamond smuggling ring. Eleanor Hunt played Bobbie Reynolds opposite Conrad Nagel's Allan O'Connor in the "Federal Agent" series: *Yellow Cargo* (Wilbur, 1936), *Navy Spy* (Wilbur, 1937) *The Gold Racket* (Gasnier, 1937), and *Bank Alarm* (Gasnier, 1937). While Bobbie was a Department of Justice agent in the first two films, she is downgraded to O'Connor's assistant by the last two; however, she is notable as the only female federal agent who is featured in a series.

Similarly, there were few female police detectives in Hollywood films of the time. Many films feature the figure of the police matron—i.e., a woman who deals with female prisoners or social welfare cases—however, few Hollywood films of the 1930s featured a woman who was employed as a detective by the police department. An exception is *Woman Unafraid* (Cowan, 1934), starring Lucile Gleason as Augusta Winthrop, a female cop whose job is to police decorum at a dance hall. She also takes "delinquent girls" into her home to help them straighten out their lives. The film follows Augusta's investigation into the murder of a young woman who comes to Augusta to help protect her and her baby. Ultimately, Augusta elicits a confession out of a gangster while recording their conversation on a Dictaphone for the police to use as evidence. Older and wiser, Augusta is a very positive and rare representation of middle-aged womanhood as confident, kind, tolerant, and strong.

The rest of the women who worked undercover for law-enforcement agencies tended to do so because of an expertise related to their day job, for example Nurse Adams (Joan Blondell) in *Miss Pinkerton* (Bacon, 1932). Nurse Adams is an interesting anomaly: she is a nurse but not a spinster; she is working undercover but is not a professional; and she faces the same dilemma as the girl reporter as a working woman—career or marriage. Thus, the film *Miss Pinkerton* brings together the themes of the two different types of female detective film popular in the 1930s—the amateur detective film and the newspaper-crime film—that otherwise remain firmly disparate in their character types, storylines, and themes. In the original stories by Mary Roberts Rinehart, Miss Adams is in her late twenties (and late thirties by the last installment) and an "autumnal romance" with middle-aged Inspector George Patten is hinted at but never conclusive. In the film, Joan Blondell is cast as a young, vibrant, and sexualized Nurse Adams (indeed, several censor boards objected to the scene in which Blondell takes off her uniform and reclines on her bed wearing only a slip). Nurse Adams is bored with her career and asks a fellow nurse, "So this is romance? Three pairs of tonsils and a break-away kidney all in one day!" Her boredom and desire for romance are cured when she is sent by the police to the Mitchell manor house to take care of matriarch Julia (Elizabeth Patterson) after the untimely demise of her nephew. Adams asks Inspector Patten (George Brent) what her rank is and he gives her the title "Miss Pinkerton," after the well-known Pinkertons private detective agency. Blondell was often cast as the golddigger in films of the early 1930s and brings with her to Adams that set of associations. Rather than being a quiet, comforting angel type of nurse, Adams is instead a tough and brash wisecracker (like the girl reporter).

Adams observes the suspects and comes up with the correct conclusions as the pieces of the mystery puzzle come together. This is fortunate since Inspector Patten does not seem as capable: Adams first has to correct his wrongful assumption that the nephew committed suicide, then his suspicions of the nephew's rival in love. "Wrong again, Sherlock Holmes!" she retorts. When she realizes that Patten is on the wrong track, she decides to investigate herself. As she notes, "I can't make any more mistakes than the detectives!" While most female detectives tend to be eager investigators who plunge head first into a case without weighing the possible consequences, Nurse Adams desires to abandon her "career" as a detective after she accidentally kills her patient with a lethal injection. Adams, however, proves her determination when she fights valiantly against an attack by the murderer. After apprehending the murderer (who is revealed to be the family lawyer), Patten renews his romantic attentions on Adams and moves in for a kiss when the phone rings: it is headquarters reporting another murder has occurred. Patten invites Adams to join him on the case and, despite her success on this one, she declines. She tells Patten that she wishes to return to her "peaceful and calm" (i.e., boring) life at the hospital and the final shot of the film is of her running up the stairs with Patten chasing her to propose. Ironically, the film ends with the female detective declining detective work *and* marriage (although one suspects that she might agree to the latter eventually) and returning to her day job.

These female detectives repeated the pattern established in nineteenth-century American and British detective fiction and continued in silent film narratives: the detective embodies the image of femininity in her undercover role as innocent by-stander or thief and her "masculinity"—her job as an agent investigating crime—is often only revealed at the end of the film. The majority of these films starring a "professional" female detective managed to avoid the "problem" of the female detective by foregrounding her femininity and all but ignoring her masculinity. Far more prolific and competent than the professional female detective, however, was the amateur female sleuth. And, as was the case with the male detective series, it is the *amateur* sleuth who found herself popular enough to return to the screen in a series of films.

Amateur Sleuths

Since one would assume that having a career as a professional detective demands a certain level of proficiency and achievement, it seems ironic that the more successful and pervasive female detectives were amateur sleuths. This is most likely due to the fact that the amateur is not trying to make a career out of her hobby; instead it remains just that—a hobby—and, thus, appears less threatening or problematic in terms of reconciling a career with contemporaneous conceptions of femininity. The idea of a female detective pursuing crimes related to her profession as a nurse, schoolteacher, or reporter seemed more acceptable in an era where the reality was that more women were seeking work because of the Depression. While Hildegarde Withers and Nancy Drew may have avoided the question of marriage due to their age, this was not true in classical Hollywood film—even films that are adapted from stories featuring well-known spinster detectives. A middle-aged Nurse Sarah Keate is recast by Hollywood as an attractive young woman and even the spinster Hildegarde Withers finds romance with police Inspector Piper.

While the girl reporter of the newspaper-crime film represents a shift to the modern and the urban, the amateur sleuth is firmly entrenched in the tradition established by early and Golden Age detective fiction: notably, solving crimes committed in "old manor" situations. In other words, a murder is committed in an isolated and sometimes spooky building—whether a country house, a hospital, a school, or a theater's backstage—and the investigation involves interviewing and surveying the small group of suspects present at the time of the murder. Films featuring the amateur female detective focused on the pleasure of seeing undervalued women—e.g., spinsters, socialites, and teens—beat men at their own game but most often ignored the pressing social debate about working women and marriage that plagued the girl reporter.

Socialites

Nancy Drew is not a modern working woman investigating crime in the city; she is a teenager—the daughter of a successful lawyer—and sleuths the crimes that are committed in her seemingly wholesome small town purely out of interest. The "Nancy Drew" series—*Nancy Drew, Detective* (Clemens, 1938), *Nancy Drew, Reporter* (Clemens, 1939), *Nancy Drew, Trouble Shooter* (Clemens, 1939), *Nancy Drew and the Hidden Staircase* (Clemens, 1939)—stars Bonita Granville and, no doubt, was developed for the screen because of the character's huge popularity in children's fiction. They were popular films and the series only came to an end because Granville left Warner Bros.

In the first installment, *Nancy Drew, Detective*, Nancy vows to find the elderly alumna of her school who promises to donate money for a new pool and then abruptly disappears. Nancy is excited at the prospect of detective work and greets it with girlish enthusiasm. As she says to her father (John Litel), "I'll find Miss Eldridge if it takes a hundred million years!" Despite her youth, Nancy proves to be a much more competent detective than any of the men in her world. Following a couple of leads, Nancy goes to police Captain Tweedy (Frank Orth) with the last two digits of a license plate. Tweedy assures her he will be able to discover the owner of the car "just like that" (snapping his fingers); Nancy expresses amazement at his abilities as she quickly calculates that there could be half a million cars with plates ending in those numbers. Although her father is a noted lawyer, it is Nancy who notices that a car is following them. Interestingly, Nancy not only owns her own car but, even when she is with her father, she is still the one who does the driving. When her father curtails her investigation, she enlists the assistance of her neighbor, Ted Nickerson (Frankie Thomas). They are both relatively brave: they spy a man trying to break in to her house and Ted tackles him while Nancy aims to strike him with a wrench from her car's glove compartment—but the "intruder" turns out to be her father. Later, when the gang of villains attempts to kidnap her and Ted for ransom, Ted knocks a gun out of one of the kidnapper's hands and Nancy picks it up. Although she shoots wild with her eyes closed, Nancy does force the criminals to abandon her and Ted.

The rest of the films in the series follow a similar pattern: a crime is committed; Nancy is the only one who pursues the investigation; she enlists Ted's unwilling assistance; she often engages in a car chase and/or they find themselves the prisoners of the villains; and, in the end, Nancy convinces the authorities of the criminals' guilt. In Nancy's case, her problem with gaining the respect of male authority figures has less to do with her sex and more to do with her age, but the film shows that the problems that plagued the teenager—save the marriage question—were universal for the female detective. Like the other female detectives, Nancy struggles to gain the respect of her father and other figures of male authority and she also wants to pursue a career—as a lawyer (like her father). As she explains to her teacher in *Nancy Drew, Detective*, "I think every intelligent woman should have a career." Certainly, Nancy's life is free from romance: her relationship with her Ted is platonic and innocent despite occasional stabs of jealousy on Nancy's part. There is a suggestion that someday Ted and Nancy will fall in love with each other—when they are older—and, in *Nancy Drew, Trouble Shooter*, it is her father who contemplates marriage when he falls in love with their comely neighbor (although he remains unmarried in the next film). In her discussion of the Nancy Drew books, Bobbie Ann Mason explains, "The series is purposely mum about sex, as any girl's premarital life is supposed to be. [. . .] Mysteries are a substitute for sex, since sex is the greatest mystery of all for adolescents" (84).

Whereas many of the 1930s female detectives investigated crime in old manors and urban settings, Nancy's sphere of reference is the small town of River Heights and the nearby holiday community of Sylvan Lake. *Nancy Drew, Reporter* differs from the other films in the series in that a few urban street scenes are offered when Nancy attempts to turn in evidence to the police; however, the crowded streets serve mainly to provide the opportunity for the guilty party to steal the evidence from Nancy more than to comment on urban life. Unlike her more hardboiled and cynical urban counterparts, this female detective investigates crime out of a sense of innocent curiosity. The films are less gruesome than other mysteries of the time with characters tending to be kidnapped and threatened rather than murdered and this was obviously in keeping with the intended audiences of the films. Many reviewers of the series stressed that the "Nancy Drew" films were juvenile and not adult fare; however, the pressbook for *Nancy Drew, Detective* stressed Nancy's place in the female detective tradition—especially the Warner Bros. detective tradition—with the following on the inside cover: "Warner Bros. bring you another popular-story series to your screen. *First* . . . S. S. Van Dine's Philo Vance *And* . . . Perry Mason—Clue Club Series *Then* . . . Torchy Blane Adventure." Nancy was presented as a girl growing up—as the tagline on one poster suggests: "Nancy's through playing with dolls! . . . She'd rather play with danger!" Ilana Nash argues that Warner's Nancy is "markedly younger, more inept, and generally less admirable than her literary counterpart" and that she was altered for the screen to "provide a model of girlhood that conforms almost exclusively to traditional gender expectations, reassuring consumers of the ultimately harmless frivolity of youth, and tacitly instructing girl viewers in how to personify a patriarchally sanctioned version of femininity" (72–73). Admittedly, Nancy is not as tough, independent, or outspoken as the other female detectives of the decade; however, she is a far more proactive, brave, and intelligent girl than most of Hollywood's young heroines at the time. Nancy is an impressive character as an intelligent and adept sleuth—despite her age—who solves complicated criminal mysteries through observation and ratiocination before the official investigators do so.

The socialite appeared in a handful of other films with varying degrees of centrality and agency. In *Moonlight Murder* (Marin, 1936), Steve Farrell (Chester Morris) is the police detective sent to investigate a murder that occurs during a performance at the Hollywood Bowl. Dr. Adams (Grant Mitchell) assists the police in the lab but his niece, Toni Adams (Madge Evans), is a college graduate with a science degree, and she helps Steve by running tests on samples and evidence taken from the scene. Toni is an unusual sight in the detective film of the 1930s as a young, beautiful woman with a science degree from highly respected John Hopkins University, sporting a lab coat and shown actually performing laboratory tests.[6] However, she acts only as an assistant to the male lead, Steve, and is not much of a presence in the investigation as a whole. In *15 Maiden Lane* (1936), the *Jewelers' Indemnity and Protective Corporation* must pay out a great deal of money when the Montagne Diamond is stolen. However, the niece of the Corporation's president, Jane Martin (Claire Trevor), goes undercover as a thief to recover the jewel. *International Crime* (Lamont, 1938) is one film in "The Shadow" series and finds the hero (Rod La Rocque) saddled (at least, as far as he is concerned) with socialite Phoebe Lane (Astrid Allwyn). She is the boss's niece and a journalism student who wants to be a real reporter. Although she initially seems more of a hindrance than a help to the Shadow, she has seen the villain they seek and proves useful in identifying him and helping to bring him to justice. In *The Mad Miss Manton* (Leigh, 1938), socialite Melsa Manton (Barbara Stanwyck) discovers a murder but the police do not believe her when the body disappears. Engaging the assistance of her socialite cohort, Melsa begins to investigate the case and discovers a second body. Initially male reporter, Peter Ames (Henry Fonda), is critical of Melsa because of her wealth and social status but, as he begins to fall in love with her, he assists in her investigation. The main suspect is initially cleared in the case because his alibi establishes him as being across the city at the time of the murder. Melsa, however, proves herself an intelligent sleuth when she figures out that the murderer used the subway lines under construction to get across town in the small time frame and commit the murder.

The amateur detective of leisure most often becomes involved in a case only because she is the niece of an important man somehow involved in the case—e.g., Toni, Jane, and Phoebe—and she tends to give up detecting at the end of the film. Her attention also tends to be diverted away from sleuthing by a romance with a young man involved in the case—e.g., Melsa with reporter Peter Ames, and Jane with Detective Walsh (Lloyd Nolan). Although, Melsa proves to be a very competent sleuth and, without her investigation the murderer would have escaped punishment, the pattern of the socialite-turned-detective—as it is in *Human Cargo* (Dwan, 1936), *The Girl on the Front Page* (Beaumont, 1936), and *International Crime*—is to enjoy the disjunction of a carefree socialite proving that she is capable of working for a living. Indeed, the pleasure of *Human Cargo*, *The Girl on the Front Page*, and *The Mad Miss*

Manton is—not unlike the screwball comedy—to see the class divide crossed and the upper-class socialite heroine abandoning her snobbishness to fall in love with the working-class newspaperman.

Spinsters

The spinster sleuth was a product of the late nineteenth and early twentieth centuries in a period that Barbara Miller Solomon has described as the "golden age for spinsters" (Qtd. in Ware, 64). During this period, many women chose to remain single and instead focus on a professional career or social reform; their emotional fulfillment was found through their homosocial relationships with other women. As Susan Ware notes, at the time, this was not only a fulfilling lifestyle for women to choose but it was also considered socially respectable: spinsters were often regarded as role models (64–65). Conversely, by the 1920s, the spinster was the object of pity or ridicule and regarded as neurotic and unfulfilled because she chose to opt out of heterosexual relations (like the lesbian).

In terms of detective fiction, Patricia Craig and Mary Cadogan identify Anna Katharine Green's Miss Amelia Butterworth as establishing the model of the unmarried "elderly busybody" (11)—or the spinster sleuth. This older female figure, it is implied or assumed, becomes a sleuth because she is not married and, without her own affairs to consume her time and energy, she turns her attentions to other people's. It is worth remembering that in the detective fiction of the late nineteenth and early twentieth century, a spinster could be much younger than we would assume today: in the 1890s, a woman not married by 30 could be called a spinster, and to be socially acceptable she had to remain celibate. As Carla Kungl notes, many of the first female detectives of fiction fit into this group, including Catherine Louisa Pirkis's female sleuth Loveday Brooke (85–86). In terms of 1930s film series, schoolteacher Hildegarde Withers was the only middle-aged female sleuth, and she was created in the mould of Green's spinster sleuth, Amelia Butterworth. Catherine Ross Nickerson's description of Amelia could readily describe Hildegarde: she "prides herself on being orderly, straightforward, energetic, dignified, and unsentimental, but she reports to us that she overhears others call her 'a meddlesome old maid' " (100). And, like Amelia, Hildegarde also uses her status to her advantage by playing into people's assumptions about spinsterhood: both perform "the doughty Victorian" or "the absentminded spinster" (ibid., 100).

As Elizabeth Dalton notes, Warner Bros. was known as "the workingman's studio" and specialized in topical films that reflected the contemporary scene; it is no surprise then that it was at this studio that working women were most often depicted ("Women," 267). Warner Bros. certainly produced the majority of female detective series in the 1930s, including the "Torchy Blane," "Nancy Drew," and "Nurse Sarah Keate" films; in fact, the only female detective series of the 1930s that Warner Bros. did not produce was the "Hildegarde Withers" series. Hildegarde was the heroine of six films produced by RKO. Edna May Oliver may not have been the last actor to play Hildegarde, but she is the one best remembered and most closely associated with the role. In *Penguin Pool Murder* (Archainbaud, 1932), we are introduced to the heroine as she escorts her class of young pupils around the New York City Aquarium. Like many of the older detectives—Jessica Fletcher, Miss Marple, Hercule Poirot, and Columbo—Hildegarde Withers does not look like a danger to criminals with her disarming appearance. Tall, prim, and stern, Hildegarde is the very image of the proper schoolmarm with her preference for Victorian blouses, ill-fitting coats, long skirts, odd hats, and fur stoles. Using her signature umbrella with silver-knobbed handle, she thwarts a thief's getaway attempt by thrusting it between his legs as he runs past. A little later, she is also one of the people who discovers a body in the aquarium's penguin pool. Inspector Oscar Piper (James Gleason) is called in to head up the investigation, and he and Hildegarde seem immediately at odds. As she begins to "interfere" in his investigation, Oscar says, "You seem to have authority over everyone but your own pupils" who have run amok at the aquarium. She strikes back by calling him "young man" and saying that if she had got him young enough as a pupil there might have been something she could have done for him—suggesting that he did not turn out all right.[7] After Oscar has interrogated the suspects, drawn incorrect conclusions, revisited the scene of the crime, and ignored most of Hildegarde's theories, he finds himself stymied about the case.

> Oscar: If that penguin could talk, I'll bet he'd tell us who did it.
>
> Hildegarde: And, um . . . if he could laugh, I know whom he'd be laughing at.
>
> Oscar: You know, I can't quite make you out, Miss Withers.
>
> Hildegarde: Ah! This is a busy day for you, Inspector. Now you have *two* mysteries to solve.

The next day, Hildegarde makes him breakfast at her home, discusses the case with him, and presents him with a typed transcript of the notes she made the day before regarding case details and suspect testimony. Oscar is surprised by, and mocks, the meticulousness of her notes.

> Oscar: You know, you oughtena be a schoolteacher, Miss Withers. You oughta be a . . .

Hildegarde: Detective!?!

Oscar: Well, no, I wouldn't say a detective. You see, it takes
               a certain type to be a detective.

Hildegarde: I've noticed *that*.

When it is revealed that the murder weapon was likely Hildegarde's own hatpin and that she is a suspect, she is incensed: "Now, I'm riled. I started in this affair because . . . it was exciting. Now that I'm in it, I'm going to stay in it until we find out who *did* kill him." And by the end of the film, it is she who solves the mystery surrounding the murder before Oscar does. And, even though in *Murder on a Honeymoon* (Corrigan, 1935), Oscar tells Hildegarde, "After our luck turns over, I'll probably work the case all out for you as usual. Like that . . ." and he snaps his fingers, Hildegarde is accurate when she retorts, "You're really remarkable, Oscar . . . I mean with your fingers." It is, after all, Hildegarde who always figures out the case and "whodunit" and not the official investigator on the case.

Hildegarde's role as schoolteacher is cited in the early films as her best qualification for being a successful detective. As Hildegarde tells Oscar in *Penguin Pool Murder*, "I've taught school long enough, Inspector, to know when

Fig. 4.2. Spinster Sleuth: James Gleason's Inspector Piper meets his match in Edna May Oliver's Hildegarde Withers. Photo from author's collection.

someone is telling the truth or not." Similarly, when Oscar is frustrated by the D.A.'s criticism of the police department's efforts and he fears that he will be ordered to quit the case, Hildegarde retorts, "Well, nobody can order me to quit! My business is giving orders. If I can handle a classroom of children, one district attorney ought to be easy!" In *Murder on the Blackboard* (Archainbaud, 1932), Hildegarde investigates the murder of a colleague at her school and exposes the romantic (and murderous) intrigues occurring amongst the school's faculty. Hildegarde is known for both her strength of character but also her verbal agility. When someone throws a hatchet at her head and narrowly misses, Oscar expresses his admiration:

Oscar: I've got to admit you can take it.

Hildegarde: Well, and don't forget, when necessary, I can dish it
              out too.

Oscar: I wish you'd let me forget it!

Hildegarde may be made of sterner stuff—at least when it comes to reprimanding school boys and police detectives—but she does have some humorous moments of weakness. In *Penguin Pool Murder*, she faints when the villain pulls out a gun and almost shoots her in the courtroom; in *Murder on the Blackboard*, she takes a tipple from another teacher's stash to steady her nerves; and in *Murder on a Honeymoon*, she struggles to climb out a window as her long legs and awkward skirt get in the way. Rather than undermine the audiences appreciation for her character, these moments help to temper her severity as a schoolmarm and make her more likable.

   Although Hildegarde is the more astute observer and the better detective, Oscar is surprisingly more on the mark when it comes to romance. Hildegarde assumes the young couple in *Penguin Pool Murder* will be reunited at the end of the film, but Oscar is proven correct when the young woman rejects her suitor. Similarly, in *Murder on the Blackboard*, Hildegarde thinks the young lady will be pining away when her lover is thrown in prison for killing his wife; however, Oscar is right when he says, "Don't worry. She'll get over it. Dames always do." Indeed, when Hildegarde calls up to see how she is doing, she is busy feeding a young police detective breakfast. In these early films in the series, Hildegarde looks outdated in her frumpy outfits and seems old-fashioned in her opinions as she chastises an insolent young receptionist in *Penguin Pool Murder* for wearing too much make-up and a "vulgar" shade of lipstick; however, by the third film, she seems quite progressive. In *Murder on a Honeymoon*, she comforts working girl Phyllis La Font (Lola Lane) who laments that she cannot be "goofy and cockeyed with love" with the young man she desires.

Hildegarde: Well, can't you still be?

Phyllis: What? A tramp like me?

Hildegarde: You're wrong, young lady. This isn't 1900. If I had
               your youth and looks . . . I'd pick out the nicest and
               nearest unattached man and marry him.

It may not be 1900 and the rules may be different for young people in the
1930s, but the film suggests that the old rules still apply for the middle-aged.
The spinster is too old for romance—or so it is assumed by scholars of the
genre. In the series, there is a solid relationship formed between Hildegarde
and Oscar, and he comes out to California to make sure she is not in danger
when she is in the thick of *Murder on a Honeymoon*. Notably, at the end of
the first film, *Penguin Pool Murder*, Oscar's initial dislike of Hildegarde's assistance is replaced with a grudging and then growing respect of her abilities as a
sleuth—but also as a woman. He thinks a young couple is guilty because they
are the most obvious suspects but she thinks he is wrong.

Hildegarde: And you're willing to send them to the chair on the
               evidence you have?

Oscar: Loving couples are not always reunited in the last
               chapter, Miss Withers. You've taught too much Sir
               Walter Scott.

Hildegarde: Well, if I've taught too much Sir Walter Scott, you've
               read too many detective stories. All you're after is a
               conviction . . . anybody's conviction. I never saw such
               a man!

Oscar: How many men have you seen?

Hildegarde: Plenty of them . . . that is . . . I . . . !

Oscar: Well, maybe if you'd seen more men, Hildegarde
               Withers . . .

Hildegarde: I've seen enough men today, Oscar Piper, to know
               that if this murder is going to be solved, a woman's
               go to do it.

As the door closes Oscar is impressed. He sits down and says, "Boy . . . and she can cook too!" The film concludes with Oscar's proposing to Hildegarde and the two of them marching down to the marriage license bureau together. Perhaps, RKO did not initially have plans to continue Hildegarde's adventures past the first film but, whatever the reason, the proposal is ignored in subsequent films in the series.

After three films, Hildegarde underwent a transformation when Edna May Oliver left RKO for a contract with MGM and Helen Broderick replaced her as the schoolteacher sleuth. Whereas Oliver's schoolteacher could be unfashionable, bumbling, and awkward (for comic effect), in *Murder on a Bridle Path* (Killy, 1936), Broderick's is more stylish and sophisticated and decidedly humorless—both as a character and for the audience. She also has less agency in terms of investigating on her own or her theories alone being the correct ones. In the same vein, Gleason's Oscar is shown to be more competent than he was in his initial outings alongside Oliver's Hidegarde. In fact, the film concludes with Broderick's main clue—a pipe smoked by a man with false teeth—proven to be not a clue at all: the medical examiner dropped his pipe at the scene of the crime. For the first time, Oscar has the last laugh over Hildegarde in terms of her sleuthing abilities.

Each star offered a very different rendition of the female sleuth and Oliver's acid humor was very different from Broderick's firm resolve and ZaSu Pitts's decided daffiness. However, what Pitts's Hildegarde does receive that Oliver's struggled for was continuous respect from the official investigator. Unlike Oliver's, Pitts's Hildegarde is established as an officially recognized asset to the police department in *The Plot Thickens* (Holmes, 1936): she has a courtesy badge and, when she is wrongfully arrested, all she has to do is mention her name and the officers apologize profusely. Also her status as a schoolteacher is altered by the later films: whereas Oliver's was seen at work with her pupils in the first two films, by the fifth film it is only mentioned once and she is never seen at work. Indeed, not in keeping with the idea of a schoolteacher, Pitts's Hildegarde lives in a chic apartment and retains a French maid whereas Oliver's kept her own house in the first film. By the last film in the series, *Forty Naughty Girls* (Cline, 1937), Hildegarde's occupation is not even mentioned and, instead, she and Oscar stumble upon a murder at a theater while taking in the show. As noted in the *Variety* review, Pitts's Hildegarde follows "the not-too-bright cop around and annoying him by her more deft but accidental evidence-uncoverings. The expected happens when she finally solves the shootings" (8 Sept 1937). As in the previous films, Oscar initially doubts her investigative abilities but, when she reveals the identity of the murderer, he admits, "Hildegarde, I gotta hand it to you. You certainly know your stuff."

Pitts's Hildegarde does prove herself a competent detective in *The Plot Thickens* and *Forty Naughty Girls* but her characterization as a clever detective is more difficult to believe than Oliver's. Part of the comedy of the last two films derives from the disjunction between Pitts's daffy demeanor and her superior mental aptitude. While Oliver's Hildegarde was a cerebral superior to the Inspector, Pitts's is a little too ditzy to be believed as a sharp intellect. In terms of romance, Oliver's Hildegarde is the only one to receive a proposal from Oscar; however, it is implied in the last two films that Oscar is Hildegarde's boyfriend. In *The Plot Thickens*, Oscar calls her at home to cancel their golf date because of a murder and, in *Forty Naughty Girls*, the murder occurs at the theater while they are on a date. Their romance is confirmed in the last film when Hildegarde stumbles in her row and ends up sitting in a man's lap. She comments, "I'm sorry. I've never met you before. The Inspector wouldn't like that." Although displays of affection are absent, Hildegarde is notable for being one of the few spinsters not considered too old for romance, thanks to Hollywood: Oliver was around 50 years old when she played Hildegarde and Pitts around 43. Successful at both detective work and romance in middle age and popular enough to sustain a series, Hildegarde Withers is one of the 1930s most significant female detectives.

Nurses

Warner Bros. offered a spinster sleuth series of their own, most likely in the hopes of rivaling the success of RKO's "Hildegarde Withers" series. The original Sarah Keate of Mignon G. Eberhart's stories was an unmarried, middle-aged nurse more of, as Craig and Cadogan note, "the nitty-gritty type rather than a hand-holding administering angel" (136). Technically, Sarah Keate was only allowed to keep her name in the first film (*While the Patient Slept* [Enright, 1935]) and the last (*Mystery House* [Smith, 1938]), otherwise she was known as Sally Keating (*The Murder of Dr. Harrigan* [McDonald, 1936] and *Murder by an Aristocrat* [McDonald, 1936]), as Miss Keats (*The Great Hospital Mystery* [Tinling, 1937]), and as Sara Keate (*The Patient in Room 18* [Connolly, 1938])—but the heroine in each film is based on Eberhart's sleuthing nurse. Along with her changing name, Eberhart's spinster was recast in various guises by Warner Bros. (or Twentieth Century-Fox in the case of *The Great Hospital Mystery*). The series trajectory suggests that the mature female sleuth with strength of character and intelligence of mind seems to have only been popular in the early 1930s while more attractive working-girls were the fashion by the later 1930s.

In *While the Patient Slept* (1935), Aline MacMahon portrays Nurse Sarah Keate, not unlike Oliver's Hildegarde, as stately, stuffily dressed, and possessing good posture, strong opinions, and a slightly skittish side when frightened. Although MacMahon was in her mid-30s when she played the character, her Nurse Keate seems more middle-aged. The Warner Bros. pressbook implies that this was a conscious effort—e.g., it comments on the fact that MacMahon wore "grandma's age nurse's uniform" which differs from the day's more modern uniforms. And certainly the only romantic attentions she attracted were those of the middle-aged and portly, Lieutenant Lance O'Leary (Guy Kibbee was in his mid-50s at the time). And, like Hildegarde (at least in her later adventures), Nurse Keate has the respect of the official investigators as a competent detective. We are told that she and Lance have met on previous cases and that she helped him find the solution to the mysteries. The case in *While the Patient Slept* proves no different when a family gathers at Mr. Federie's deathbed in order to make one last attempt to win his favor for an inheritance; however, one of them is shot to death. Although the official investigators—Lance and Jackson (Allen Jenkins)—dominate the sleuthing for the first half of the film, eventually Lance asks for Sarah's theories on the case when a second murder occurs.

> Lance: Do you realize this case would have been over if you'd hung on to that elephant?
>
> Sarah: Well, after this, do your own detecting. I'm going to stick to nursing.
>
> Lance: Oh Sarah, you wouldn't turn me down now, would you? Why, every clue I've gotten so far, I've gotten from you.

Later, in the film, Lance uses her as bait to draw out the murderer. And like Hildegarde (at least in her first film), the middle-aged spinster nurse is proposed to by the male detective, and it seems likely she might be about to accept when they are interrupted. The romantic conclusion may have had more to do with the pairing of MacMahon and Kibbee for the film: the pressbook refers to their status as a "screen team," having starred in eight other films together between 1932 and 1935.

The posters for the film referred to Nurse Keate as the "famous female detective," "the most amazing character in modern detective fiction," and "the favorite sleuth of a million mystery readers"—and, yet, Warner Bros. struggled to find a solid niche for the series. Although considered popular enough to sustain a series, Nurse Keate proved problematic and was subsequently recast from spinster to young, attractive, and of marriageable age and played by a different actor in almost every film of the series. Kay Linaker (in her mid-20s) played the nurse in *The Murder of Dr. Harrigan* with more feminine charm. Linaker's Sally Keating insists on getting involved in the case when Dr. Harrigan is found murdered and Mr. Melady missing because, as she says, "it is my responsibility. My entire career, my reputation as a nurse is in jeopardy. Mr. Melady is my patient." Although she proves competent and driven, it is her boyfriend, intern George Lambert (Ricardo Cortez), who soon supplants her as the main detective and presents the solution of the case to the official investigators. The film ends with her agreeing to give up nursing to marry Lambert. Similarly,

Marguerite Churchill (in her mid-20s) played the nurse (here Sally Keating) in *Murder by an Aristocrat* and ended her sleuthing adventure with agreeing to marry Dr. Allen Carick (Lyle Talbot). Warner Bros. halted the series after a lukewarm reception to the first three films and Twentieth Century-Fox took over, making *The Great Hospital Mystery*. The film starred Jane Darwell (in her late 50s) as an appropriately older, rounder, and brusque head nurse, barking orders at her staff and proving her superior intelligence as a detective. We are introduced to Darwell's Nurse Keats reprimanding a young and inept probationary nurse (Joan Davis) who, in turn, marvels at Keats's skills at observation and deduction: "Gee, Miss Keats. You're sure a *born* detective." Like Oliver's Hildegarde and MacMahon's Nurse Keate, Darwell's has a sharp wit and snaps many a comeback to the short-sighted police investigators. It is also she who deduces the identity of the murderer and sets the successful trap that exposes the killer in the end.

Darwell's Keats is much more self-assured as a detective than MacMahon's earlier portrayal of the spinster and this is likely due to the associations with Darwell's star persona as a tough and brusque older woman. For example, in *Laughing at Trouble* (Strayer, 1936), Darwell plays a similar kind of detective: Glory Bradford is the publisher of a small-town paper and takes it upon herself to prove that John Campbell (Allan Lane), her niece's fiancé, is innocent of murdering his uncle. The majority of the film revolves around the antics of various characters spending the evening at Glory's home after John escapes from jail and hides out there. In the course of the evening, however, Glory proves a clever sleuth, deducing who the real murderer is and tricking him into confessing his crime. In terms of romance, Glory explains to her niece that she too was in love once but her fiancé died of pneumonia: "They think I'm just some sort of an institution, mixing up in men's business. Tough old chicken—too strong minded to put with a husband . . . and children. Oh well, I don't think so." The film highlights the fact that people assume that a strong woman pursues a career because she cannot pursue romance. Interestingly, the film debunks this myth and presents Glory as capable of attracting male attention—the town sheriff's—in middle-age as well as being the only person intelligent enough to identify the real murderer. The starring of Darwell in both *Laughing at Trouble* and *The Great Hospital Mystery* was most likely an attempt to cash in on the popularity of Hildegarde Withers by offering a similar kind of spinster sleuth.

Back at Warner Bros. a year later, Nurse Keate was once again a young and comely nurse, this time played by Ann Sheridan (in her early 20s) in *The Patient in Room 18* and *Mystery House*. And, as in the first film, she is once again teamed up with Lance O'Leary—although this time, he is also younger and more handsome (as he was in Eberhart's stories). While Lance was a policeman in both Eberhart's stories and *While the Patient Slept*, in the last two films, he is recast as a private detective. He is also clearly the main detective of both films rather than Nurse Keate. In *The Patient in Room 18*, Lance (Patric Knowles) is a dapper, British gentleman, formerly of Harvard, Oxford, and Scotland Yard—as his book's dust jacket informs us. He suffered a nervous breakdown when he failed on a case for the first time and is hospitalized; however, the murders at Keate's hospital soon cure him with a new investigatory success. In *Mystery House*, Nurse Keate is played again by Sheridan while Dick Purcell replaces Patric Knowles as Lance, but Sarah also undergoes a transformation. In *The Patient in Room 18*, Sheridan's nurse is strong-willed, feisty, and self-possessed and her relationship with Lance is established as combative in a battle of the wills. On a previous case, Lance (Knowles) had her subpoenaed and, on the witness stand, subjected her to an interrogation of her personal life; now, as her patient, Sara has the upper hand. When he disobeys her orders, she puts her hand on his head and literally thrusts him back into bed and later scolds him for smoking and reading detective magazines against doctor's orders. In *Mystery House*, on the other hand, Sarah welcomes him with open arms and eager kisses when the niece of a private patient of hers wants to hire a detective. Romance, however, must take a backseat, Sarah insists, when a murder is committed. Lance (Purcell) asks Sarah, "When murder flies in the window, love staggers out, is that it?" And, lastly, in *The Patient in Room 18*, Sara has some investigative agency (although less than in *While the Patient Slept* and *The Great Hospital Mystery*) and tells Inspector Foley (Cliff Clark) that he has misidentified the guilty man. On the other hand, in *Mystery House*, Sarah is merely Lance's sounding board as he does all the investigating. In regards to murder, Lance tells her in all seriousness, "Don't worry your pretty little head about it." Sarah assists in Lance's investigation, but she does not come up with any of her own theories. In fact, when she is stumped by a murder victim's note that the "key" to the mystery is hidden in his toupee, Lance explains that it could be a figurative, rather than a literal, key—i.e., a number written in the toupee's lining. Sarah says in earnest, "I never thought of that. My, aren't you clever?"

Nurse Keate's uneven portrayals suggest that there is an equation that determines her agency as a detective: her abilities as a sleuth are proportional to her age and inversely so to her looks. She helps to solve the cases in *While the Patient Slept* and *The Great Hospital Mystery* when she is portrayed as older, and it is the male detective who solves the cases in *The Murder of Dr. Harrigan*, *The Patient in Room 18*, and *Mystery House* when she is younger and more attractive. However, it would seem that this had less to do with the nurse's looks and more to do with Warner Bros. trying to find a winning formula that appealed to audiences. The studio first attempted an older, stern, and witty female sleuth not unlike Hildegarde Withers paired with an older police detective (Guy Kibbee) not unlike Oscar Piper; then an attractive but career-hardened young woman not unlike Torchy Blane; lastly, an attractive young woman gradually replaced by her boyfriend as the central sleuth in the story. Lance was the new focus of the series by 1938, as a write-up by I. A. Fein at Warner Bros. states, Warner

Bros. have "high hopes for their new detective hero, Lance O'Leary" and that he "will follow in the footsteps of their former sleuths, Philo Vance and Perry Mason."[8] As I will discuss further in a later chapter, this last shift—to the female detective-hero with a male love interest abandoned in favor of a male detective-hero with a working-girl love interest—became the dominant trend by 1940 and seems to have been a product of a broader shift in social attitudes towards independent-minded women by the end of the decade.

Amateur Freedoms

Perhaps the most unusual aspect of the film reviews at the time is how many did *not* comment on how unusual it was to see a woman in the role of detective—especially an official investigator. Indeed, very few of the dozens of reviews from the trade papers or newspapers that I looked at over the course of my own investigation commented on the fact that these characters were not ones commonly found in real life. One that did was a *Variety* reviewer for *The Girl from Havana*: "Lola Lane plays a detective, which, offscreen, would be unusual for such a girl" (4 September 1929). Similarly, a *Variety* reviewer comments that the novelty of *Unknown Woman* is having an undercover G-woman as the protagonist (26 Jun 1935). Some later films sparked comments of incredulity in regards to the female detective but usually not from her role as a detective but from the implausible situations the film plunges her into. For example, a reviewer for *Variety* suggests, in response to *There Goes My Girl*, "One situation which cannot get by anyone over 12 is that wherein Miss Sothern is shot, solves a double murder at the same time, and, because of her sleuthing, is given every type of protection by the police on the exclusiveness of her story" (16 June 1937). While in reality, official female investigators may have been rare in the 1930s, in Hollywood film the amateur female sleuth was common.

　　Unlike detective fiction at the time that offered tough, hardboiled, male heroes or—when it featured female detective-heroes at all—spinsters and teenagers, Hollywood film was an equal opportunist and centered films around a range of female detectives that could be young or old, spinsters or lovers, feminine or masculine—at least in the 1930s. Some were professional private detectives and others were amateur investigators, but all of them pursued their passion to sleuth no matter whether it was their boyfriends, the police, or the villains who tried to stop them. And they were, in general, successful—bringing the villain to justice. Because the Depression had made working women a reality and also shifted gender roles toward a model of equality, the female detective as an independent or career woman (i.e., a more masculine type of femininity) was a dominant and widely exploited trend in Hollywood film of the 1930s. Nevertheless, a clear distinction was made between professionals and amateurs. As the case of Nurse Keate evinces, when women were more focused on their career—i.e., masculine in ambition—they were usually more masculinized in appearance and manner, and it was these detectives who were the most successful at beating the male investigators to the solution of the mystery. However, in the case of the protagonist who was more feminine in appearance and manner, her success at detecting was dependent on whether she was an amateur or a professional. When the more feminine detectives *work* as an investigator—as professional private eyes—they tend to have to share the glory of pursuing and solving the case and/or give up the job at the end of the story—i.e., their professional success is undermined. Conversely, when these women *play* at being detective—i.e., as amateurs who pursue it as a hobby—they prove themselves better than their male rivals and often return for more adventures in other installments.

The vast majority of Hollywood's female detectives in the 1930s were amateurs who did something else as their day job—including, nursing and teaching. As I will explore in the next chapter, the most prolific of the working-girl detectives was the girl reporter but, unlike the femme detectives above, the girl reporter was a more masculinized figure. She was hardboiled by her experiences of trying to work and survive in the city and, unlike the more femme detectives of this chapter, she was cynical about love and marriage rather than desirous of it. The girl reporter is allowed much more success and independence than the professional female detectives, but this can perhaps be put down to volume and social realities. While there were few real-life (and on-screen) female private investigators, lawyers, and police detectives, there were thousands of female reporters in real life (even if most of them were working on the society column instead of the front page). The girl reporter is an ambitious career woman who is cynical not romantic, brash not demure, and competitive not supportive. And the only man who is attracted to her—typically a fellow newspaperman or police detective—is similarly hardboiled. It is also necessary to take into account stardom when discussing these roles because stars or actors who were associated with more feminine roles (e.g., the love interest and good girl)—such as Jane Wyman and Ann Sheridan—played female detectives that were more naïve, pretty, and romantic; those associated with playing tougher roles (e.g., the golddigger and working girl)—such as Glenda Farrell and Joan Blondell—brought with them a sense of being jaded, disillusioned, and cynical about people—and especially love. And it tends to be the stars associated with hardboiled roles that played the girl reporter throughout the 1930s, stars like Farrell, Blondell, and Claire Trevor.

5

Sob Sisters Don't Cry

The Girl Reporter as Detective in the 1930s

Detective Steve McBride: This rat hole is no place for a woman.

Reporter Torchy Blane: But I'm a newspaperman.

Detective Steve McBride: Well, you just sit quiet and maybe nobody will notice.

—Barton MacLane and Glenda Farrell in *Smart Blonde* (1937)

As Roger Dooley notes, "journalism was by far the most popular occupation for "30s screen heroes" with two types of newspaper film: those critical of "yellow journalism" in the vein of *Five Star Final* (LeRoy, 1931) and the cynical comedy-melodrama newspaper in imitation of *The Front Page* (Milestone, 1931) (256).[1] Popular consensus, both at the time and now, is that *The Front Page* is regarded as the birth of the newspaper film. As a reviewer for the *Motion Picture Herald* notes in a review for the girl reporter film *Back in Circulation*, "About six years ago United Artists released *The Front Page*. Since then in a cycle of newspaper melodramas, practically every studio has experimented with the idea" (7 Aug 1937). However, some film historians, including Dooley, point out that films like *Big News* (La Cava, 1929)—featuring not one, but two, female reporters—can be regarded as important precursors to the male-centered *Five Star Final* and *The Front Page*. I would also add that silent films like *The Office Scandal* (Stein, 1929), also starring a female reporter, offered the same character types and themes as the sound films that followed them.

Not only was journalism, in general, a popular occupation for Hollywood's Depression-era heroes, but also its heroines: the one profession in which women thrived and succeeded during the Depression—on and off the screen—was journalism. The number of real-life women editors and reporters had more than doubled from just over 7,000 in 1920 to almost 15,000 by 1930 (Ware, 75). As Laura Hapke notes, for women in the 1930s,

The schoolmarm or the nun of business was not the decade's only permissible model for achievement, as the career of the stylish foreign correspondent Dorothy Thompson flamboyantly demonstrated. [. . .] Thompson, however, was breaking the boundaries between the male and female worlds without incurring the wrath of the fourth-estate establishment.[2] (190–91)

Thompson was the exception to the rule in real-life journalism, and Hollywood's representation of female reporters on the screen was not necessarily an accurate portrayal of the real-life newspaper business. Real-life female reporters were all but confined to covering "social" news or "women's page" features; if they were used for a main story, it was to cover the human angle or play up the emotional aspect of the story—i.e., "sob stories." Female reporters were, thus, often referred to by the derogatory appellation "sob sister." Film critic Pauline Kael argues that Hollywood's female reporters were all based on the most highly publicized real-life female reporter of the time—Adela Rogers St. Johns—including *His Girl Friday*'s Hildy (Rosalind Russell), right down to her imitation of St. Johns's striped suit (48). The "girl reporter," using Howard Good's term, was popular in classical Hollywood films of the 1930s and early 40s, perhaps most memorably embodied by Glenda Farrell as Torchy Blane who continually avoided marriage (for nine films between 1937 and 1939) to chase another story. Hollywood's most prolific girl reporter heroine, however, was perhaps based more on fantasy than reality as the reviewer for *Variety* notes with her first outing in *Smart Blonde* (1937): "She plays the kind of sob sister who does all that newspaper girls never do. Her act is to prove how useless cops are and she succeeds" (13 Jan 1937). Indeed, the girl reporter did most often function as a detective since her pursuit of the scoop on a story—usually a murder—inevitably leads her to figure out "whodunit" before the police or her rival newspapermen.

    Film historians and scholars have noted that the number of films of the 1930s that feature a girl reporter (although not always as a detective) are significant. As Deac Rossell notes,

> . . . the newspaper film genre was the only place where an actress could portray a role that stood on equal footing with men. Reduced to a symbol of power in the gangster film cycle, and to a symbol of civilization in the schoolteachers and reformers of the western genre, in the newspaper film a woman could take the lead, be an accomplisher, catch the crooks, save the day, scheme for power, find success. ("Fourth," 244)

Similarly, Larry Langman and Daniel Finn note that, although women in Hollywood film were often relegated to the role of love interest for the male detective,

... at least one area predominated in which they were able to demonstrate their sexual freedom. Some female reporters were models of independence for women when independence was the least admired attribute in a wife or mother. Many newspaper-crime dramas featured a strong-willed female reporter, a role coveted by actresses and doubtlessly appreciated by numerous movie fans. (*Thirties*, xx)

As Dooley suggests, "Though girl reporters were never, to be sure, as popular as courtesans, Cinderellas or heiresses, among the heroines who worked at all they ran second only to entertainers (including singers and dancers), figuring prominently in more than forty films of the 1930s" (263). My research suggests that the number is closer to 70 films in the 1930s, including (in order of release) *A Woman against the World* (Archainbaud, 1928), *The Office Scandal* (Stein, 1929), *House of Horror* (Christensen, 1929), *In the Headlines* (Adolfi, 1929), *Big News* (La Cava, 1929), *Dance, Fools, Dance* (Beaumont, 1931), *Up for Murder* (Bell, 1931), *Sob Sister* (Santell, 1931), *Platinum Blonde* (Capra, 1931), *Anybody's Blonde* (Strayer, 1931), *The Final Edition* (Higgin, 1932), *Strange Adventure* (Del Ruth and Whitman, 1932), *The Secrets of Wu Sin* (Thorpe, 1932), *Mystery of the Wax Museum* (Curtiz, 1933), *High Gear* (Jason, 1933), *A Shriek in the Night* (Ray, 1933), *The Famous Ferguson Case* (Bacon, 1932), *The Sphinx* (Rosen, 1933), *Headline Shooter* (Brower, 1933), *Devil's Mate* (Rosen, 1933), *The Mad Game* (Cummings, 1933), *Orient Express* (Martin, 1934), *Hi, Nellie!* (LeRoy, 1934), *Hold that Girl* (MacFadden, 1934), *Back Page* (Lorenze, 1934), *After Office Hours* (Leonard, 1935), *Death from a Distance* (Strayer, 1935), *The Daring Young Man* (Seiter, 1935), *Front Page Woman* (Curtiz, 1935), *Too Tough to Kill* (Lederman, 1935), *We're Only Human* (Flood, 1935), *Big Brown Eyes* (Walsh, 1936), *Mr. Deeds Goes to Town* (Capra, 1936), *Human Cargo* (Dwan, 1936), *36 Hours to Kill* (Forde, 1936), *Women are Trouble* (Taggart, 1936), *The Girl on the Front Page* (Beaumont, 1936), *Wedding Present* (Wallace, 1936), *Beware of Ladies* (Pichel, 1936), *Espionage* (Neumann, 1937), *Parole Racket* (Coleman Jr., 1937), *Smart Blonde* (McDonald, 1937), *Woman in Distress* (Shores, 1937), *Behind the Headlines* (Rosson, 1937), *There Goes My Girl* (Holmes, 1937), *Fly Away Baby* (McDonald, 1937), *It Can't Last Forever* (MacFadden, 1937), *Exclusive* (Hall, 1937), *One Mile from Heaven* (Dwan, 1937), *My Dear Miss Aldrich* (Seitz, 1937), *Back in Circulation* (Enright, 1937), *The Adventurous Blonde* (McDonald, 1937), *No Time to Marry* (Lachman, 1938), *Blondes at Work* (McDonald, 1938), *Arson Gang Busters* (Kane, 1938), *International Crime* (Lamont, 1938), *Torchy Blane in Panama* (Clemens, 1938), *One Wild Night* (Forde, 1938), *Four's a Crowd* (Curtiz, 1938), *Personal Secretary* (Garnett, 1938), *Five of a Kind* (Leeds, 1938), *Torchy Gets Her Man* (Beaudine, 1938), *Off the Record* (Flood, 1938), *The Phantom Creeps* (Beebe and Goodkind, 1939), *Torchy Blane in Chinatown* (Beaudine, 1939), *The Adventures of Jane Arden* (Morse, 1939), *Torchy Runs for*

Mayor (McCarey, 1939), *News is Made at Night* (Werker, 1939), *Mr. Wong in Chinatown* (Nigh, 1939), *Torchy Blane . . . Playing with Dynamite* (Smith, 1939), and *The Invisible Killer* (Newfield, 1939).[3] While not every girl reporter played detective, the vast majority of them did. As female reporter/federal agent Bobbie Reynolds (Eleanor Hunt) explains in *Yellow Cargo* (Wilbur, 1936), "where there's a mystery, there's always a story."

Although Torchy Blane may be a long forgotten heroine of classical Hollywood now, at the time, the intrepid reporter was enormously popular and Farrell had quite a following. The "Torchy Blane" films were notably—other than any films starring Superman's alter ego Clark Kent—the only series to star a reporter (Good, 1). A reviewer for the *Hollywood Reporter* remarked in reference to *Fly Away Baby* that "Miss Farrell's Torchy is about the most authentic of all newspaper girl characters" (2 Jun 1937). This is perhaps due to the fact that the story of the film was suggested by the book penned by real-life girl reporter Dorothy Kilgallen who had entered in a similar flight race around the world. Or it may have been because, as Torchy in seven of the nine films (1937–39), Farrell represented a strong-minded but kind-hearted woman with plenty of drive and guts. With his book *Girl Reporter*, Howard Good offered a revisioning of the girl reporter as a character-type because what little scholarship had discussed Torchy tended to treat her "as a somewhat exceptional figure—exceptionally attractive, exceptionally energetic, exceptionally tough" (7). Good argues that Torchy's uniqueness was inferred by critics who noted that all of the female reporters that came before her were masculinized, unattractive, and sour. However, as I will explore in this chapter, Torchy was not the only girl reporter and her representation certainly was not exceptional: her character and traits were established years before her arrival on-screen in 1937 and, in some ways, by Farrell herself through previous roles.[4]

Why was the girl reporter so pervasive and popular in the 1930s? According to film scholars, newspaper stories in general were popular as a result of a number of factors: they provided witty conversationalists for the new talkies; many Hollywood producers, writers, and other key figures in the studios were ex-"newsies" themselves; the genre allows a wide range of storylines; and people have always had a fascination with hardened crusty reporters and the press (Good, 5). Andrea Walsh suggests that changes within the industry (e.g., the arrival of sound and the stricter enforcement of the Code) were at least partly responsible for the proliferation of the working woman: "Spoken dialogue facilitated the depiction of a more complex interpersonal world, while Code-prescribed limits on sexuality inadvertently promoted the 'career heroine' " (138). The girl reporter is a career woman, working in the male dominated world of journalism; however, she is trying to prove her "masculinity" not only as a successful "newspaperman"[5] but also as a detective. Debates have raged amongst feminist critics whether the parachuting of women into traditionally male roles (like that of the detective) represents a feminist representation.[6] I argue that the 1930s girl reporter as detective can be seen to offer a decidedly feminist hero in that she defies the stereotype of the masculine (i.e., unnatural) woman: she is presented as a successful detective—catching the criminal—*and* a successful woman—attracting her investigative competition. Uncovering a criminal plot or bringing a criminal to justice did not preclude a marriage proposal from the rival male reporter or police detective on the case. While feminist critics will likely argue that getting the man, in terms of marriage, is not a feminist message, it is important to note that such conclusions tended to be tacked on, most likely to appease the Production Code Administration. The girl reporter did not always feel inclined to accept the proposal because it might mean the end of her career as a detective and, in the case of a series, she found herself still unmarried at the beginning of the next film. As I noted earlier, Carla Kungl has criticized the tradition in feminist criticism that finds the female detective wanting as a woman if she chooses her career and lacking as a detective if she chooses matrimony. Just as this presupposition in relation to detective fiction represents "a rejection of the ways women writers were coming to terms with the important debate about women and work in their society" (Kungl, 85), a similar approach to detective films short-circuits a consideration of how these films were attempting to explore women's experiences in the modern urban America. The girl reporter was ambitious, driven, tough, and often beat the men at their own game; however, unlike the majority of moments in Hollywood's history (including now), she was not punished for her transgression of the borders between male/female and public/private territories.

Part I: Masculine Women

While all of the films discussed here and in the subsequent chapter share a common element—a girl reporter as the protagonist—there were different trends within the genre, including the one with which this chapter is concerned: the newspaper-crime film. Not all girl reporters functioned first and foremost as detectives (although the trend in the 1930s was increasingly just this) and the films that featured a girl reporter as protagonist varied from social problem films (e.g., *One Mile from Heaven* [Dwan, 1937]) to horror films (e.g., *The Corpse Vanishes* [Fox, 1942]). Also, while the girl reporter at the beginning of the decade wanted to be more feminine and desired marriage over her career, the majority in the mid-30s enjoyed their masculine lifestyle and chose to chase the story rather than men. I distinguish between these two types as "sob sisters" and "newspapermen," respectively: a sob sister writes a society column and is presented in the film as lacking in terms of the drive to be a career reporter, while a newspaperman is a girl reporter who has a reputation for being as active, driven, and competent as any male on the paper.

Jim Collins explains that the normal trajectory for a genre includes three phases: consolidation, "a Golden Age," and the period of decline, which includes self-parody (246). The first phase—consolidation—of the girl reporter film (1929–32) was more concerned with gender and work during the darkest days of the Depression than with seeing its heroine prove herself a competent reporter and detective. In fact, only a few of them played sleuths and many of them did not desire a career as a front-page reporter: these are the films with sob sister heroines. The focus of the sob sister film was on the negative impact that the Depression, working, and city life had on its heroine and the conclusion they came to is that it made women hardboiled. During these years, the girl reporter appeared in a variety of types of narrative: *Up for Murder* (1931) and *Sob Sister* (1931) debated whether the woman—and her femininity—could be recovered through romance and marriage; *Big News* (1929) focused on the heroine's marital problems with her reporter husband; and *The Office Scandal* (1929) was more like the Golden Age newspaperman film in which the girl reporter proves her abilities as a reporter and detective by solving a murder mystery. By 1933, the trend had consolidated into the standardized newspaper-crime formula: the girl reporter is usually an inexperienced (cub) reporter or under-appreciated society columnist who desires to prove herself worthy of the appellation "newspaperman" and a front-page byline; she is usually pitted against male competition from a rival paper or the police department; sometimes she finds herself the captive of the criminals and requires rescuing by the male rival with whom she has fallen in love; nonetheless, she always figures out the mystery before the official male investigators and gets the scoop over her rival reporters. Using Mary Roberts Rinehart's expression, these women were possessed by "[a] sort of lust of investigation" (572). The genre's phase of self-parody in the 1940s will be addressed in the following chapter.

The female reporter had to face chauvinism and scrutiny in the male-dominated world of the newspaper office and indicative of her ability to compete with her male rivals at their level was her masculinized nickname and appearance. Some were known by masculinized versions of their names like Timmy in *Back in Circulation*, Tony in *Hold that Girl*, Pat in *Espionage*, *Mystery Ship*, and *The Corpse Vanishes*, and Jerry/Gerry/Geri in *The Office Scandal, The Sphinx, Hi, Nellie!, Back Page,* and *I Killed that Man*; others by nicknames that evoked their personalities from Nosey Toodles in *Strange Adventure* to Torchy in the "Torchy Blane" films; and still others were referred to by their last name like Gallagher in *Platinum Blonde* and *Midnight Manhunt* or their home state such as Tex in *One Mile from Heaven*.[7] In the same vein, they rejected slinky gowns and fur coats for more masculine attire—always a hat usually paired with a tailored suit, belted dress, or sensible skirt and blouse or cardigan, but sometimes even trousers. As Anne Hollander notes, in American society, emancipated women of the time sported a modern look that imitated male fashions (151). While they may be less feminine than a leading lady was expected to be, the female reporters are firmly differentiated from the type of newspaperwomen that had preceded them—what were described as "masculine women" who typically sported short hair and a man's suit and, it was implied, were lesbians. This is made explicit in films like *Big News*, *Orient Express*, and *Front Page Woman*.

Although unable to locate a print of *Orient Express* to view, I was able to find the "Revised Final Shooting Script" by Carl Hovey and Oscar Levant (screenplay) and William Conselman (dialog) (20 Sept 1933). In the script, Mabel Warren is introduced as "a masculine woman [. . .] tossing off a glass of gin. Beside her is Janet Pardoe, young and pretty. Mabel shoves her glass at the attendant and smiles affectionately at Janet." The conversation that follows suggests that Mabel (Dorothy Burgess) is in love with Janet (Irene Ware) and upset that she is going away, but Janet does not seem to return her affections. Mabel recognizes a man, Dr. Czinner (Ralph Morgan), believed to be dead for five years—and smells a story. When Mabel exclaims, "I know that man—I know him well," Janet's comment "How unusual" confirms that Mabel is a lesbian.[8] Certainly, the representation of Mabel as lesbian was significant enough to see the PCA Code-enforcers object. In a letter to Colonel S. Joy, James Wingate comments, "The definite indication of lesbianism on the part of Mabel Warren should be deleted entirely under the Code. [. . .] We suggest toning down the intimacy between Mabel and Janet" (2 Oct 1932). Although a key figure in the film, the girl reporter is only one of a large ensemble cast and, two fifths of the way through the script, Mabel gets off the train and exits the narrative.

In *Big News*, reporter Margaret Banks (Carole Lombard) reportedly scoops her husband, Steve (Robert Armstrong) while he was out getting drunk—but the film never shows her at work. The film is instead concerned with the male reporter's career and his struggle with drink and marriage. Tired of being "miscast" (as one of Steve's colleagues suggests) in the role of Steve's mother rather than his wife, Margaret informs Steve that she wants a divorce. When Steve is the main suspect in the murder of the paper's editor-in-chief, however, Margaret comes to his defense and falsely confesses to the murder in order to save her husband. This model—namely, that the woman must prove her love for her man and faith in their relationship in order to see him declared innocent of murder—is one that the murder-mystery film in general will come back to in the 1940s. Margaret may be a newspaperman but she is presented as very feminine in comparison to the society editor, Vera (Cupid Ainsworth), who is a large woman with short hair and masculine attire including a pocket square and a signet ring (read: a lesbian). Although Vera is the butt of many jokes for her male colleagues at the paper, she does give as good as she gets. For example, Vera tells Steve that she saw his wife waiting for him in the hall. He asks if she is sure it was his wife and she replies, "It is . . . if I know my women!" and then laughs uproariously. At another point, Vera reads the paper, drinking and mocking what she reads. Her editor, Addison (Charles Sellon), orders her to get back to work and explains, "Certainly I want you to be gay . . . but you're not going to be gay on my time!" There is disagreement amongst scholars over

whether or not the term "gay" had attained its current connotation of homosexuality in the late 1920s but some sources report that the term was used by
homosexuals in the 1920s, if not in the mainstream.[9] Indeed, this film suggests
that the sophisticated viewer would have got the joke.

In *Front Page Woman*, Curt Devlin (George Brent) remarks that Nell (Grace
Hayle)—a female reporter similar in appearance to Vera in *Big News*—makes him
"feel effeminate." Ellen (Bette Davis), his girl reporter rival, is thus differentiated
from Nell as feminine. This representation of the hardboiled female reporter and
her embodiment of "unnatural" femininity did not go unnoticed at the time
by Joseph Breen at the PCA. In a letter, Breen voices his objection to a line
in the script for *Front Page Woman*: "the appearance of a 'masculine woman'
should not suggest any characteristics of perversion" (10 April 1935)—"perversion" connoting homosexuality in the terms of the Code. And yet the finished
scene in the film did offer this "masculine woman." Nell, however, is only a
minor character, and no leading lady in any of the girl reporter films is ever
presented as—or accused of—being a "masculine woman." Whereas the girl
reporter would most often be defined as brash and brave, sassy and independent—in other words, masculine *and* feminine—in *Big News* and *Front Page
Woman*, there are two female reporters: one femme and one butch. And both
films are adamant that the former is appealing and the latter unnatural. They

Fig. 5.1. Interesting Precursor: *Big News* (1929) features not one, but two, female
reporters, including Carole Lombard's who compromises her career to save her husband
(Robert Armstrong). Photo from author's collection.

also suggest that, if the girl reporter stays too long in the newspaper racket instead of marrying, the former will become the latter.

Sob Sisters: 1929–32

In *Female* (Curtiz, 1933), Alison Drake (Ruth Chatterton), the owner and manager of an automobile factory, receives a visit from an old school friend, Harriet (Lois Wilson). Their conversation leads to a discussion of marriage vs. sexual freedom.

> Harriet: Aren't you ever going to marry?
>
> Alison: No thanks, not for me. You know, a long time ago I decided to travel the same open road that men travel. So I treat men exactly the way they've always treated women.
>
> Harriet: You evidently don't have much respect for men.
>
> Alison: Of course, I know that for some women, men are a household necessary. Myself, I'd rather have a canary.
>
> Harriet: My, but you've changed, Alison. You're not the same girl I knew in school. Why—you used to be so romantic and so . . . well . . . so different.
>
> Alison: You mean, I've grown hard and cynical.
>
> Harriet: Something like that.
>
> Alison: Oh well! Perhaps you are right. But darling, you can't work with men for fourteen hours a day for five years and not lose your girlish illusions.
>
> Harriet: Well, if it does all that to you, why did you go into the business in the first place.
>
> Alison: Necessity.

Many of Hollywood's career-women protagonists in the early 1930s cite financial necessity as the reason for their foray into the male sphere of work. And Harriet is not the only character who is concerned that the result of women becoming successful in a career is their becoming hardboiled. Nevertheless, becoming hardboiled is regarded as a necessary defense mechanism required to survive the male world of work, the tough city environment, and the economic hardship of the Depression. For many Depression-era career women—and the men who loved them—the question was not whether women became masculinized if they pursued a career in the city: this was established as fact. The burning question—at least in the early films featuring a girl reporter—was whether or not becoming masculinized precluded the ability to be re-feminized if the woman desired a future "career" as a housewife. Not all of the films I discuss in this first section place the girl reporter at the head of the criminal investigation; I include a handful of others in order to define the parameters of the girl reporter film in its formative years—as generic patterns were being developed and refined. The legacy of these early films is their highlighting of the marriage-career debate and the impact of the Depression on working women.

Ernest R. Groves summed up the social assumptions of the time in a 1929 article entitled "The Personality Results of the Wage Employment of Women outside the Home and Their Social Consequences:" "The woman who has been coarsened or hard boiled by her business contacts is seriously handicapped in the winning of a mate. The qualities she has acquired repel a man" (Qtd. in Hapke, 190). In *Dance, Fools, Dance* (1931), the heroine, Bonnie Jordan (Joan Crawford), becomes a sob sister only because she needs the money to support herself and her alcoholic brother after their father loses everything in the stock market crash. Bonnie is willing to marry her playboy boyfriend, Bob Townsend (Lester Vail), but she is upset that he proposes out of an old-fashioned sense of duty rather than for love—so she rejects his proposal. Her brother Rodney (William Bakewell) asks her what kind of work a girl like her can get: run a tea shoppe, model clothes, or open a beauty parlor. But she tells him that,

> No, I'm not going to do any of those stupid, silly, conventional things. You'd be surprised what a young girl can earn when she sets her mind to it; I'm no dud. [. . .] That's your idea of me, huh? Beautiful but dumb. Alright, I'll show you. I'm going out and get myself a man-sized job. You can do exactly as you please.

While her brother gets drunk, Bonnie finds herself a job on a newspaper. She encourages him to find a job as well, explaining, "You don't know the thrill of trying to make good on your own—not just trading on your name and running around at parties all the time." Bonnie struggles at first to become a good writer at the paper but does come to enjoy her job; however, her pleasure in her career is short-lived when a fellow writer is murdered while investigating a mob massacre. In order to find out who is responsible, Bonnie takes a job undercover at the mob's nightclub and discovers that the killer is her brother and that he has been running booze for mob boss, Jake Luva (Clark Gable). Bonnie proves herself a newspaperman: she calls in the scoop only moments after her brother dies in her arms following a shootout with Luva. Just as her career is taking off, Bonnie decides to quit the newspaper business to marry Bob, and the film concludes with her being in the news instead of writing it. While *Dance, Fools, Dance* does have a mystery surrounding a murder, the focus of the film is the effect of the Depression on socialite Bonnie, transforming her from a pleasure-seeking socialite to a hard-working sob sister.

The plot of *Anybody's Blonde* (1931), is similar to that of *Dance, Fools, Dance* in that a reporter (Dorothy Revier) goes undercover at a nightclub in order to investigate the murder of her brother (here a boxer rather than a rum runner). By 1931 the girl reporter theme was familiar. As a reviewer for *Variety* notes, "Leaves nothing for the imagination once the audience knows that Dorothy Revier, sob sister on the newspaper, is the sister of the slain fighter, Jack Dorgan" (24 Nov 1931). She ends up attracting the unwanted attention of club owner, Steve Crane (Lloyd Whitlock), and falling in love with fighter, Don O'Hara (Reed Howes). O'Hara is jealous of Janet's flirtation with Crane, not aware that she is only trying to get close to Crane to prove her brother was murdered. In the end, she is able to extract the truth from Crane's girlfriend and bring him to justice and get a proposal out of O'Hara.

Sob Sister (1931) offers no mystery for the heroine, Jane Ray (Linda Watkins), to solve other than how to win the love of her reporter rival, Garry Webster (James Dunn); nevertheless, the film is one of the most explicit in setting up the femininity-achievement conflict. A series of stories bring Jane and Garry closer together at first and then further apart as their rivalry outweighs their romance. In a scene possible only in the pre-Code era, Garry accuses Jane of spending the night with him just to get a scoop for her paper. Jane does have a reputation for being tough as a newspaperman: early in the film she gets a story in to her editor on the only available phone for miles and then cuts the line to prevent her rivals from doing the same. Garry wonders, "You're not getting hardboiled, are you?" Later, for a party, Jane trades in her tailored suit (i.e., masculine clothes) for an evening gown (i.e., feminine) and Garry is forced to admit that she has "a certain amount of charm" and looks "almost like a human being." He tells her he dislikes women "who eat men," including sports women and sob sisters—in other words, women who do enter traditionally male spheres of endeavor. He is unconvinced that she is good marriage material and that, now she has felt the "drug" of being a "newspaperman," she will never be satisfied being "just" a housewife. But she explains to him that she is not a sob sister by choice but by necessity and, rather than have to prove herself a good newspaperman as will be typical in the mid-30s, here, Jane must prove herself a good homemaker. She prepares breakfast for Garry every morning in her apartment, which he comes to refer to as "the American home," and the film concludes with her acceptance of his proposal.

Up for Murder (1931) centers on a female reporter, society columnist Myra Deane (Genevieve Tobin), and her relationship that forms with cub reporter

Robert Marshall (Lew Ayres). The film is a remake of a 1927 film *Man, Woman and Sin* (also written and directed by Monta Bell) and is a moral tale of extramarital relations rather than a murder mystery. Here the female reporter inspires a murder rather than investigates one. I mention the film only because it offers a glimpse of the other path that the female reporter could take; namely, allowing a rich, older, married man to take care of her instead of marrying for love or focusing on her career as a reporter. The film suggests that immoral love leads to destruction. Myra came to the paper as innocent girl and a talented writer; however, her affair with the paper's older publisher, William Winter (Purnell Pratt), makes her cynical about life and love. More surprising is that it affects her ability to be a good reporter.

> Winter: It's getting stale. [. . .] Look here, Myra, I wish you would write me a good yarn about this affair tonight—one of those *bright* stories you used to turn in. [. . .] You haven't written anything hot in about . . .
>
> Myra: Quite a few years, isn't it, since a bright-eyed, little schoolgirl all full of ambition began writing on *The World*. But I was lucky—I found a nice, kind publisher who took an interest in my *career*. Tell me something, that first day I came in here, which were you looking at—my writing or my knees?

The film suggests that it is the desire to be a good reporter that makes her interesting and exciting and her alternative of being a kept woman, makes her cynical.

Furthermore, it was not just the girl reporter who could not survive the Depression as a "keptie" but also the male.[10] *Platinum Blonde* (1931) suggests that the male reporter cannot live like "a Cinderella man" or "a bird in a gilded cage," as male reporter Stew Smith (Robert Williams) describes being married to socialite Ann Schuyler (Jean Harlow). Although very much in love, their marriage falls apart because of their class differences. At the beginning of the film, Stew regards his colleague Gallagher (Loretta Young) as "just one of the boys." When Gallagher betrays some jealousy toward Ann, Stew complains, "They're you go—talking like a woman. Well, you're my pal, aren't you? And don't turn female on me!" However, after seeing Gallagher dressed in a gown for a party and later in an apron to make him breakfast, Stew sees her as a woman. The film ends with Stew seeking a divorce from Ann and marriage with Gallagher—and getting back to his career as a newspaperman.

In *The Final Edition* (1932), city editor Sam "Brad" Bradshaw (Pat O'Brien) says that he is firing Anne Woodman (Mae Clarke) because she is "a rotten newspaperwoman;" however, she retorts it is because she refused his proposal. Ignoring his decision, Ann pursues leads in a case and ultimately exposes racketeer, Sid Malvern (Bradley Page), as the murderer of the police commissioner. Despite her cleverness and bravery as a detective throughout the majority of the film, she tells Brad that she is quitting reporting and detecting.

> Brad: You're a cinch. I'll make a newspaperwoman out of you yet.
>
> Anne: Oh, no you won't. I'm through. I'm quitting!
>
> Brad: You're kidding. What for?
>
> Anne: Oh, it's too hard on the nerves.
>
> Brad: Well, I made you a proposition.
>
> Anne: I beg your pardon. It was a proposal. [. . .]
>
> Brad: Well, what do you say?
>
> Anne: A word of two syllables: uh-huh. [they kiss]

Although she seemed to enjoy the "lust of investigation" as a detective and getting the scoop as a newspaperman, Anne chooses to abandon her career for marriage to a newspaperman (even though she knows that Brad will never be as devoted to his wife as much as he is to the paper).

Similarly, in *The Secrets of Wu Sin* (Thorpe, 1932), Nona Gould (Lois Wilson) gives up her career for marriage despite her sleuthing skills. Jim Manning (Grant Withers), editor for *The Tribune*, offers Nona a job and a new lease on life after he prevents her from committing suicide. She soon is frustrated with the "sob sister" assignments that Jim gives her and asks to be allowed to work on the illegal alien smuggling story; however, Jim says, "It's no job for a girl." Ignoring his orders, Nona follows Eddie Morgan, the reporter assigned to the case, into Chinatown—where Nona used to live and where she retains connections with the Chinese American community. Nona surveys the neighborhood, trails Eddie, and then demonstrates superior sleuthing skills when she beats Eddie to call in to the paper what she learned about the next "delivery". Nona questions Jim's ethical stance in terms of hurting people for the sake of a story:

> Nona: No, no I was just thinking. That Chinese story; those men who may be sent to prison. A scoop for you means disgrace for their families.
>
> Jim: You've got to be hardboiled in this game, Nona. "All the news that is news"—that's been my policy ever since they

stuck me in this office, to give this rag some pep. And
our circulation proves that it's a pretty good motto.

Nona: You'll print everything? No matter who it hits?

Jim: Certainly. That's my job.

Unfortunately, what Jim does not know is that the person it is going to hit is
him when his fiancée's father is shown to be linked to the smuggling racket.
Jim proves as good as his word when he prints the story even though his
fiancée breaks off their engagement because of it. Jim, however, has realized
his feelings for Nona and the film concludes with their marriage. As Nona
explained to Jim earlier, "Life doesn't mean much unless you have someone to
love and plan for, does it?" Their marriage most likely concludes Nona's career
as a reporter even though she proved a superior newspaperman and detective
because, as Jim's reply to Nona suggests, "No, I guess you're right. Even an
interesting job is secondary."

The goal of these early girl reporters was to marry and they were content
with being sob sisters until they found love; conversely, the goal of their successors by the mid-30s was to become a respected "newspaperman" or career-
reporter. This second type of reporter appears as early as 1929 with *The Office
Scandal* but is not the norm until 1933. As Robert McElvaine notes, 1933
was a turning point in Hollywood film because of the New Deal: "the nation
moved from a passive acceptance of the Depression's effects to active attempts
to overcome them" (340). Correspondingly, the women in Hollywood film
decided to be no longer victims of social circumstance. The pre-1933 focus
on marriage appears in post-1933 films only in a few cases, mainly in those
where the conflict is based on class as much as gender. For example, in *The
Girl on the Front Page* (1936), socialite Joan Langford (Gloria Stuart) inherits
The Chronicle when her father dies. Managing editor, Hank Gilman (Edmund
Lowe), is skeptical of Joan's interest in the paper and threatens to quit if she
comes to the paper's office. He explains that "she's probably one of those half-
wit females who thinks 'It might be amusing to run *The Chronicle* between
cocktails.'" Joan thus trades in her stylish look as a socialite for a bookish look
(with her hair pinned back, glasses, and a practical suit) to go undercover on
the paper. Hank, however, is a good newspaperman and his observation skills
and research allow him to see through her disguise immediately. He attempts
to curb her interest in newspapering by sending her first on false stories and,
when that does not deter her, on tough stories involving death and personal
danger. She does well as a cub reporter until a murder is committed in her
neighborhood—a socialite neighbor is accused of shooting his butler. Then Joan
proves to be an incompetent newspaperman: she is too soft and more interested
in keeping up appearances than she is in chasing a story. She misses the fact

that the big story is "right under her nose:" her butler is the president of "The Thursday Club," a group of servants who blackmail their upper-class employers. Instead, it is Hank who figures out the story and sets up the blackmailers in order to expose them. Joan, however, is allowed to report the story and have it run under her byline. As Hank explains, "Yeah, I'm going to make a newspaperman out of her . . . even if I have to marry her." Joan sighs in response, "Oh, darling!" and the audience is assured that she will leave the newspapering to Hank and she will happily take up the role of his wife. The triumph of the film—and others like it, including *The Mad Miss Manton* (Jason 1938) and *Human Cargo* (1936)—is not seeing the heroine become a hardboiled newspaperman but to have an upper-class socialite abandon her snobbishness and fall for the uneducated, working-class newspaperman.

    Front Page Woman seems to have been the last gasp of the sob sister and certainly an anomaly by 1935, with heroine Ellen Garfield (Bette Davis) as the butt of the male reporter's jokes. The film opens with Ellen unable to complete her story of a death-row execution, because she faints, and her colleagues make fun of her writing, calling it "literature" instead of "real" reporting. Her boyfriend and rival reporter Curt Devlin (George Brent) encourages her to quit the newspaper business and marry him because he believes that "women make rotten newspapermen." I would suggest that Ellen's representation has less to do with ignoring a trend and more to do with the star status of Brent and Davis at the time: the two starred together as the romantic leads in about a dozen films (1932–42) and *Front Page Woman* seems more interested in the two being brought together using the popular girl reporter narrative rather than in exploring the femininity-achievement themes of the genre. Indeed, unlike any other female reporter film in the 1930s, *Front Page Woman* spends as much time showing Curt's individual investigation as Ellen's. While Curt scoops her by planting a false set of jury votes so that she reports the wrong verdict before it is made public, Ellen is able to get the final scoop by encouraging a female suspect to confess. In the end, Curt has to admit that she is a good newspaperman but Ellen agrees with him that "it isn't any job for a woman." Like Jane in *Sob Sister*, Ellen does not really want to be a career woman; she just wanted Curt to admit that she was as good as any man at the job and is happy to marry him. Indeed, *Front Page Woman* does seem to have been an anomaly and is remade—and, in a sense, recuperated—as *Blondes at Work* (1938) with the iconic newspaperman heroine—Torchy Blane.

Newspapermen: 1933–40

Torchy Blane may be the epitome of the girl reporter of the 1930s as the only one to star in her own series, but she was not the first. The female newspaperman dominated the genre from 1933 to 1940 and offered a gender-bending heroine that successfully integrated masculinity into womanhood and incurred mainly praise from male authority, adoration from male rivalry, and popularity with Depression-era audiences. The girl reporter did not appear in Hollywood film out of a vacuum but was already an established character in comics of the late 1920s. The comic-strip character Connie, created by illustrator Frank Godwin and appearing in the Ledger Syndicate (1927–44), was originally depicted as a debutante, but in 1934—seeking work because of the Depression—she became a reporter and later a private detective. Similarly, Jane Arden, who appeared in an internationally syndicated daily newspaper comic strip (1928–68), was a girl reporter.[11] In the same vein as the plucky girl reporter of a comic strip of the time, Jerry Cullen (Phyllis Haver) in the silent film *The Office Scandal* (1929) is the unappreciated sob sister of the *Globe Dispatch* who wants to prove herself a newspaperman.[12] She is the modern woman: she works, smokes, takes charge, and talks back. The film is a little heavy-handed with its delivery of the femininity-achievement conflict but does readily sum up the debates that would dominate the genre for over a decade. In the film, a famous horseman, Champ Tracy, has been murdered and the *Globe Dispatch*'s editor, Pearson (Raymond Hatton), cannot find a reporter to send out to cover the story. He says to Jerry, "You *would* be the only one in the office—when I need a man to slam into a murder!"[13] Jerry is incensed and retorts:

Jerry: How is it one of your delightful sex always gets the chance over me when anything big happens?

Pearson: A big yarn like this is no job for a woman.

Jerry: If I'm not as good a newspaperman as any bozo in this shop, I'll roll a peanut down Broadway!

When she threatens to quit and work for another paper, her boss gives her a raise and she stays—but Jerry is sent to cover night court instead of the Tracy murder. Andrew Corbin (Leslie Fenton), a former star reporter brought low by gambling, is presented to the court charged with vagrancy. Jerry defends Andrew to the judge based on his past reputation and then gets him a job on her paper. When the headlines read that the Tracy case is still unsolved, Jerry argues with Pearson.

Jerry: Police baffled! And you're the little guy who's all conceited over the great Male Sex!

Pearson: I suppose your women's intuition tells you who the killer is.

Jerry: Oh, no—I'm not supposed to have any brains! I'm only a wallflower.

And, of course, that is the film's point—she defies the stereotype that women should be for decoration only and, instead, proves she does have brains.

Andrew and Jerry become close working on the paper together. At a party, Andrew makes a pass at her but she is hardboiled and jaded. She says, "Yeh, I know! I'm a wonderful little woman and knowing me is going to make a new man of you! [. . .] Now don't be a sap and fall in love with me." He tries again and finds her more receptive to his kisses; however, her feelings for him are affected by the clue she uncovers on the Tracy case. Lillian Tracy (Margaret Livingston) confides in Jerry that her lover bears whip marks on his wrist from when her husband caught them in bed together; later, Jerry sees the telltale marks on Andrew's wrist, she suspects that he is Lillian's lover and Tracy's murderer. But, rather than being a "sap" over the disappointing news, Jerry gets tough. She drags Lillian into the bathroom while the police wait in the room next door and barks, "I'm going to make you talk if I have to smash the truth out of you!" She moves menacingly toward Lillian and shakes her roughly. Her shaking reveals whip marks across Lillian's back and, suddenly, Jerry realizes that Lillian—not her husband—has been the victim. Lillian agrees to tell the police the truth, that she killed her husband after years of abuse. Pearson realizes that Jerry is a great newspaperman, and the film makes no too fine a point about it.

Pearson: Well, why don't you shove off and get your story going?

Jerry: You mean, you want me to write it?

Pearson: Sure—if you think you're man enough.

Jerry: Man enough! Say, I'll be the head man of your office yet.

Jerry has finally received the respect she has earned and has achieved her goal of being a feature writer. It is here that the film ends rather than on a romantic climax with Andrew.

Several girl reporter films present their heroine not only as a successful reporter-detective but also as a woman-of-action who is proactive in coming to her own rescue rather than being a damsel-in-distress. In *A Shriek in the Night* (1933), Pat Morgan (Ginger Rogers) tries to out-scoop her competition on the rival paper, Ted Rand (Lyle Talbot), on the story of her wealthy boss's murder (she was working undercover as his secretary). Her character is afforded a position of respect in terms of authority as the detective on the case, Inspector Russell (Purnell Pratt), appreciates Pat's intelligence; and she is regarded as a significant threat by Mr. Harker's murderer who attempts to dispose of her in the building's basement incinerator. Left unconscious to die,

Pat awakens—although unbeknownst to the audience in order to generate suspense—and saves herself before the murderer is able to light the incinerator. Similarly, in *Behind the Headlines* (1937), Mary Bradley (Diana Gibson) is identified as "one of the boys" in visual terms—seated at a desk with her arms crossed across her chest and her feet up on a chair (despite her wearing a skirt)—and in terms of her behavior—as she is the one who suggests taking away the microphone of "Rambling Radio Reporter" Eddie Haines (Lee Tracy) who is trying to scoop all the print reporters. Unfortunately, Mary finds herself the victim of a kidnapping; however, Mary is resourceful and attempts to alert others of her whereabouts, leaving the watch that Eddie gave her at the scene of the crime and then using Eddie's broadcasting equipment to try and get a message to radio listeners. When the villains discover what she is doing, she hides herself and the radio pack in the armored car from the robbery in order to help the police track the signal. Resourceful and brave, Mary elicits a proposal from Eddie but concludes the film trying to scoop him on the story, suggesting that Mary is still Eddie's equal and not necessarily ready to abandon her career for matrimony. Lastly, in *Personal Secretary* (1938), "The Comet" Gale Rodgers (Joy Hodges) and her rival Mike Farrell (William Gargan), battle over the outcome of the court case of Flo Sampson (Kay Linkaer): Mike believes she is guilty of killing her husband while Gale thinks she is innocent. Again and again, Gale proves herself the superior reporter and detective, single-handedly figuring out who killed Sampson and attempted to kill Mike. She tracks down the killer but finds herself in a predicament when he traps her in his shop. Although Mike and the police eventually arrive, Gale is prepared to deal with the killer herself: she positions herself with large bell jar to smash over the killer's head if he does attempt to harm her. Although Gale, like many other girl reporters, agrees to quit her job and marry Mike, she is presented by the film unequivocally as a skilled sleuth and newspaperman but also a woman of strength and action.

And, it would seem that strong women were not only admirable during the Depression, but necessary. Many girl reporter films suggested that the only match for the hardboiled man of the modern American metropolis was a hardboiled woman and *Headline Shooter* (1933) is perhaps the film that is most obvious in highlighting this assumption. Jane Mallory (Frances Dee) writes the news and cameraman Bill Allen (William Gargan) shoots it. Jane is tough: she cadges cigarettes off Bill; she holds her own in their biting repartee; and, when her car is crushed in the aftermath of the earthquake they are covering, she steals his—kissing him only to pick the keys from his pocket. Later, when kidnapped by gangsters, Jane happily plays cards with her captors rather than play the victim. Jane is engaged to boring but reliable, Hal (Ralph Bellamy, playing a character not unlike the one he plays in *His Girl Friday* [Hawks 1940]). Bill asks a receptionist how girls—like Jane—get so hardboiled; she replies that it is their brushes with hardboiled guys—like Bill—that make them that way.

Bill admits that he's a "hit and run"—inspiring women to break engagements but never getting engaged himself—but Jane is the first girl he has met that he has wanted to take home. The girl reporter can soften the heart of the hardest man because she is tough, resourceful, independent—in other words, his equal. Jane tries to convince herself to marry Hal in order to escape from the "racket" that involves selling other people's emotions instead of having one's own. Rather than being scared off the job by the kidnapping incident, however, Jane realizes that she cannot quit the business. Hal pleads with her, "This is no place for a woman." Jane replies, "Oh Hal, can't you see? This is something that's a part of me. I can't help it." Although she consents to marry Bill at the end of the film, sirens tell them that another story is breaking and the two take off to chase the scoop as rivals, rather than lovers.

Part II: Case Studies

Star persona had a significant impact on the girl reporter film. As Richard Dyer explains, film stars are differentiated from actors or performers by their extra-filmic dimension—public appearances, interviews, studio publicity, biographies, and coverage of the star's private life in the press—through which audiences know of her beyond her film roles (*Heavenly*, 2–3). Under the Studio System, the majority of stars had long-term contracts with one studio and their roles and public image were controlled by the studio even if they were big box-office draws: names, hair color, clothes, and roles were altered until a performer found a persona popular with audiences and could be cultivated as a star. Although most of the actors who played the girl reporter were not the most famous stars of their studio, they were often B-level stars and they carried with them the associations of their previous roles. For example, both Joan Blondell and Glenda Farrell played golddiggers in the early 1930s and that association with being hardboiled, working girls of the city carried them through to girl reporter roles. Indeed, both stars were associated less with glamour and more with spunk and/or comedic abilities. Blondell as Timmy Blake in *Back in Circulation* (1937) is upset when told by her boss and boyfriend, Bill (Pat O'Brien) that she looks "like something that came out of the faucet" after a job covering a train crash; and when she spies the beautiful Mrs. Wade (Margaret Lindsay) at a nightclub, Timmy sighs that if she had a face like that then Bill would not stand her up for a date. Similarly, Farrell as Florence Dempsey in *Mystery of the Wax Museum* (1933) is supposed to be less attractive than her roommate, Charlotte (Fay Wray); however, Charlotte's femininity also makes her attractive and vulnerable to the evil Igor (Lionel Atwill). According to Dyer, a star embodies a specific social type and this can lead to various "fits" with the character that the star plays, from a perfect fit to a problematic one (*Stars*, 142–46). It was rare for a star during the Studio System to be cast against type when they had proved popular in a certain kind of role and two stars that proved continually popular in the role of the assertive and out-spoken girl reporter were Claire Trevor and Glenda Farrell.

Claire Trevor

Claire Trevor played the girl reporter several times, including Jane Lee in *The Mad Game* (1933), Tony Bellamy in *Hold that Girl* (1934), Bonnie Brewster in *Human Cargo* (1936), Lucy "Tex" Warren in *One Mile from Heaven* (1937), and Christine Nelson in *Five of a Kind* (1938). While *One Mile from Heaven* is more of a social problem film than a mystery and *Five of a Kind* is about new technologies and formats for journalism, both films share a focus on a girl reporter as the main character and a concern with journalism ethics. *The Mad Game*, *Hold that Girl*, and *Human Cargo*, however, offer girl reporters who investigate crimes as detectives. In *The Mad Game*, Trevor helped to establish not only her own tough-girl persona that would pave the way to her most acclaimed role—i.e., good bad-girl Dallas in *Stagecoach* (Ford, 1939)—but also that of the girl reporter. Jane is hardboiled and tough: she practically swaggers with confidence when she walks and uses slang when she talks; she also drinks and rolls her own cigarettes; and she claims to have covered over a hundred murders. In other words, she is just one of the guys. Her interest in racketeer Eddie Carson (Spencer Tracy) is to write his biography, but she begins to fall for him as she gets to know him personally. With Prohibition nearing an end, Carson's second in command, Chopper (J. Carrol Naish), tries to convince his boss to take up a new and more profitable racket—kidnapping; however, Carson is against the idea because his own daughter was once the victim of kidnapping and murder. Carson agrees with his attorney to plead guilty to an income tax charge so that he will receive only a small fine and a suspended sentence, but the judge takes a bribe from Chopper to lock Carson up for five years. In prison, Carson promises to help the law using his knowledge of the racket to break Chopper's stranglehold on the city and undergoes plastic surgery in order to go undercover. Jane's sleuthing leads her to discover the undercover plan and she tries to help Carson rescue Chopper's kidnapped victims and, later, comfort Carson as he dies in her arms after a shootout with Chopper. The film concludes with Jane toasting Carson as "a pretty swell guy" with a mug of beer rather than getting married to the man she loves.

Hold that Girl sees its independent and feisty heroine, Tony, also acting like one of the boys, sporting tailored suits, smoking cigarettes, and dating whomever she likes—even a gangster, Tom Mallory (Alan Edwards)—much to policeman Barney Sullivan's (James Dunn's) chagrin. Tony's favored mode of transport is to flag down a car and hop on the running board with only one hand on the door to steady herself and a cry of "Follow that taxi!" Her outgoing—and masculine—behavior also attracts the attention and affection of the two men on opposite sides of the law: the dashing Mallory and the upstanding Sullivan. In retaliation for her refusing a date, Sullivan has her arrested for "indecent exposure" (she tossed her underwear out of a high-rise window to attract attention when being held by a madman) and for "resisting an officer" (she refused his romantic overtures). Although she confesses to her family that she is falling in love with Sullivan, she does not stop dating Mallory and spends the weekend on his yacht, but assures Sullivan that Mallory is "not going to get away with anything" (i.e., sex with her). Interestingly, it is not only the high-living bachelor (Mallory) who must be convinced of the pleasures of marital bliss but also the independent woman (Tony): Tony teaches Mallory that marriage and fidelity should be respected, and Sullivan shows Tony that the more traditional role as wife is preferable to her chaotic life as a newspaperman. The film, nevertheless, is critical of the double standard that marriage represents for women at the time. Tony chastises Mallory for covering for his friend's marital infidelity:

> You men are all alike. You think you can marry a woman and then do anything you please. Everything's fair as long as she doesn't find out. You want your home, security, children, and then when you build a big, high fence around your wife you think it's a great joke to go out and play around. But just let your wife try your game and what a howl you raise. [. . .] Well any woman would feel that way about it.

Although the film concludes with Tony and Sullivan's marriage, it is Sullivan who sees the appeal of settling down and the last line of the film—"Gee, ain't it great being married?"—is Sullivan's and not Tony's.

Bonnie Brewster in *Human Cargo* is the weakest of Trevor's girl reporters but this is most likely due to the fact that Bonnie is a socialite-turned-reporter—a character type that brings with it the debate about class as we saw earlier in *The Girl on the Front Page*. The pleasure for the audience with the socialite who dabbles in reporting is to see a spoiled girl of the elite exposed to the harsh realities of an honest day's work, and, typically, she chooses to quit the business and leave it to the professionals. Bonnie wants to put her journalism degree to use to prove to her father that she is not "nothing but a useless consumer" who cannot even buy her "own lipstick and spinach." She is assigned to the fashion editor but the paper's star reporter, "Packy" Campbell (Brian Donlevy), decides to use her as cover to attend a nightclub and to get information on the club's owner, Baretto, and his alien smuggling racket. Bonnie is present when the cops kill Baretto and later when Carmen (Rita Hayworth), an illegal alien with information, is murdered. At first, Bonnie is upset by the violence but she quickly learns to put the story ahead of her personal feelings and heads to Vancouver to infiltrate the smuggling ring. Packy joins her and, when the story starts to break, he tells her, "End of the line, kid. This is where you get off. [. . .] You're the greatest little woman in the world but this is my party. Now you go home and get a good night's sleep." In retaliation, Bonnie decides to go over Packy's head to the district attorney; however, at the D.A.'s house, she discusses the case with "public citizen No. 1," Gilbert Fender (Morgan Wallace), who—it turns out—is public enemy No. 1 and the head of the racket. Bonnie, thus, finds herself in trouble (the chauffeur is ordered to "take care" of her) and Packy must come to her rescue. The ending of the version of the film I watched at UCLA was missing; however, according to a review of the film by Charles R. Metzger for Joseph Breen at the PCA, the film ends with "Bonnie telephon[ing] her story in, but says she is tired of being a newspaper woman, so is going to marry Packy" (20 March 1936).

Like Tony in *Hold that Girl*, Trevor's roles in *The Mad Game*, *Human Cargo*, *One Mile from Heaven*, and *Five of a Kind* were successful girl reporters; however, unlike Tony, Jane in *The Mad Game* and Tex in *One Mile from Heaven* do not settle down to get married at the end of the film. Jane's love interest is killed in a shootout and Tex goes home to Texas to be the society editor for the *Cattleman's Daily Bugle*. Interestingly, trade paper reviewers of *One Mile from Heaven* made particular note of the lack of romance—seeing it as a negative. For example, the reviewer for the *Motion Picture Herald* notes,

> Exhibitors who attempt to arouse popular interest in this picture will find themselves facing quite a task. Departing radically from the customary production formula in that it entirely ignores love interest, it caused the preview audience to laugh in several places where the objective sought was presumably to stir the more sentimental emotions. (24 July 1937)

However, the lack of romance was not missed by everyone and the reviewer for The *Motion Picture Daily* writes, "Unusually, there is no romantic interest, but to the credit of the picture, it is not missed, and in fact, probably would detract from the story as it stands" (17 July 1937). The lack of romance keeps the film firmly focused on its social issues—black life in Harlem and the ethics of newspaper reporters—and, thus, feels more like a social problem film than a lighthearted comedy. Trevor played several of the tough, independent, working women who could, and did, take care of themselves in the 1930s; Glenda Farrell was another.

Glenda Farrell

The shift in representation of the female reporter from sob sister to newspaperman is perhaps best highlighted by the remake of *Front Page Woman* as the "Torchy Blane" film *Blondes at Work* (1938). As Elizabeth Dalton notes, *Blondes at Work* was almost a carbon copy of *Front Page Woman* from the sets to the camera angles to the dialogue ("Meet," 39).[14] However, what is key about this remake *is* the difference: Davis's sob sister is replaced by Farrell's hardboiled newspaperman. As one poster for *Smart Blonde* suggests, Torchy is "A hard-boiled reporter with a soft-boiled heart!" Torchy (Glenda Farrell) is far more competent than Ellen (Davis) and the majority of the jokes of which Ellen is the butt in *Front Page Woman*, are ones that Torchy plays on her rivals. Whereas, the first film had Ellen faint at the execution and submit the wrong story, the second excises this whole segment. And, whereas, in the first, Ellen is tricked by Curt (Brent) into reporting the wrong jury's verdict to her paper, in the second, it is Torchy who tricks her male colleagues and scoops the right one. Similarly, while the first undermines Ellen's competence with a focus on Curt's investigation, the second confirms the girl reporter's place at the center of the film by reducing the amount of time spent on Steve's (Barton MacLane's) investigation and increases that on Torchy's. Just as *Blondes at Work* takes some of Curt's role and gives it to Torchy rather than having her follow in Ellen's footsteps, so too does the film offer Torchy as a sort of hybrid of Curt and Ellen—more newspaperman than sob sister.

Torchy Blane appears in nine films (seven of which starred Glenda Farrell) and embodies this successful integration of masculinity into Depression-era femininity. Torchy is introduced at the beginning of *Smart Blonde* (1937) as an action woman and the equal to any male hero: she chases a train down the tracks only to leap onto the end car. More interesting, perhaps, is that with a quick straightening of her jacket and skirt, she arouses no suspicion in the train car and is readily accepted as a respectable lady. Torchy is the quintessential fast-talking dame of the 1930s. David Zinman suggests that, while Farrell "stood head and shoulders above any of the other leading ladies in machine-gun style delivery," her skill was that she "could race along a mile a minute and still get dramatic inflection into her voice" (38). Credit for Torchy cannot be given to the author of the story—"No Hard Feelings"—on which the film's script was based as Frederick Nebel's original story was about a male reporter, Pete Kennedy. Although Farrell told an interviewer that Torchy was the product of her visit to New York to watch female reporters in action and to make "Torchy true to life" (Qtd. in Saltzman), Farrell had already all but established the character three years before in *Mystery of the Wax Museum* (1933) as Florence Dempsey and again in *Hi, Nellie* (1934).

Like Torchy, Florence is a fast-talking female reporter who argues her own way—or, as a reviewer from *Film Daily* described her, "a wisecracking sob sister" (18 Feb 1933). As Dalton notes, before she played Torchy, Farrell "had already given the definitive sob-sister performance" as Florence with "her gutsy dialogue [. . .] perfectly complimented by her staccato delivery—a remarkable 390 wpm" ("Meet," 37). On New Year's Eve, Florence stumbles into the office tipsy to talk to her editor Jimmy (Frank McHugh) about the front-page news of socialite Joan Gale's suicide. Jimmy is angry that Florence does not take her job seriously enough, for example, enjoying the ringing in the New Year rather than getting the scoop.

Jimmy: Consider yourself crippled—financially! See if you can jar your charming friends loose from enough to eat on.

Florence: Meaning what?

Jimmy: That you're a sure bet to place in the breadline. There's no room on this rag for the purely ornamental! You're easy on the eyes and pretty conceited about it.

Florence: Is momma's little dumpling getting tough?

Jimmy: I'm through clowning, Florence. You're all washed up. Get out!

Florence: What do you mean, you poor ham? It's New Years!

Jimmy: We get out a newspaper just the same. Did you ever stop to think about that?

Florence: Is it my fault if nothing happens.

Jimmy: What do you mean "nothing happens"? Look down there. Now, out of that insane mob you say nothing happens. There is a story in every person down there.

So Florence heads out in search of a story and discovers that Gale's body has been stolen from the morgue. Jimmy wants her to pursue the story that Gale's boyfriend, playboy millionaire George Winton (Gavin Gordon), murdered her; however, Florence is more interested in the angle that Gale's body is not the first to go missing from the morgue. Jimmy tells her to do what he tells her, but a bout of fake tears and bull-headed stubbornness gets Florence her own way; her masquerade as a "typical" woman is an asset for manipulating her tough editor. In the end, Florence is proved right: not only was Gale's body stolen by Ivan Igor (Lionel Atwill) of the wax museum but all the exhibits feature wax-coated corpses rather than wax figures.

The film is explicit in its debate about gender but not in terms of whether Florence's sex is an impediment to being a good reporter. The film assumes that, because of the Depression, unmarried women need to work and, instead, it questions traditional notions of gender by drawing lines across class. Florence and Jimmy are working class and, therefore, presented as tough while Florence's roommate, middle-class Charlotte (Fay Wray), and upper-class playboy, Winton, are presented as feminine. Florence explains to Charlotte how they differ as women: "Alright, alright! You raise the kids; I'll raise the roof! I'd rather die with an athletic heart from shaking cocktails and bankers than expire in a pan of dirty dishwater." Similarly, when they arrive for the opening of the wax museum, Florence demonstrates her lack of interest in traditional courtship and femininity when Charlotte's boyfriend, Ralph (Allen Vincent), greets her.

Ralph: Gee, that's a pretty dress. Have I seen it before?

Charlotte: Yes, I think so.

Florence: [with biting sarcasm] Thank goodness that's settled.

And it is Charlotte's love for Ralph that makes her vulnerable; when she goes to the museum in search of him after a lover's quarrel, Igor takes the opportunity to kidnap her and attempt to "transform" her with a coating of wax into Marie Antoinette.

Similarly, while wealthy Winton tends to—for lack of a better word—wimp out when things look dangerous, hardboiled Florence is the one who investigates the basement of an eerie townhouse. When the police want to open the coffin that Florence believes contains Gale's body, Winton is scared and tries to leave; when they do open it and reveal that it is filled with bootlegger's whisky, Florence collects as many bottles as she can carry—as her "percentage" for notifying the police. Fascinatingly, it is precisely Florence's masculinity that attracts her suitors. As they drive back to the paper in his car, Winton confesses his admiration of her bravery and brashness.

Winton: You like taking chances, don't you?

Florence: Why?

Winton: You go in for dangerous things.

Florence: Darned if I don't. Slow down to ninety! I said the office
            not the cemetery.

Winton: I never believed that there were women like you in the
            world—you have game and decency.

Florence: And so determined to live that I'm going to get out and take a taxi if you don't watch where you're going.

Winton: I've only known you 24 hours, but I'm in love with you.

Florence: It doesn't usually take that long. I'll forgive you—you were in a tough spot when I met you.

Winton: No, I'm . . . I'm crazy about you!

Florence: *That's* what caused it, huh?

Winton: You don't believe me. You think I'm just talking. Will you marry me?

Florence: How much money have you got?

Winton: [laughs] Heaven knows! A lot.

Florence: [laughs] That being the case, I'll take it up with the board of directors.

In the end, Florence refuses Winton's proposal, although she seems very tempted by it. She may talk tough to Charlotte about her cutthroat attitude toward men and money but, in the end, she accepts Jimmy's proposal. Standing in Jimmy's office, Florence looks out the window to Winton waiting for her below in his car.

Florence: Listen, stupid! Could I possibly ever do anything that would meet with your approval?

Jimmy: Yes, you could. Cut out this crazy business. Act like a lady. Marry me.

Florence: Marry you? [she looks out the window to see Winton waiting for her] I'm gonna get even with you, you dirty stiff! I'll do it!

She shakes his hand and they move in for a kiss as the romantic music swells. This ending does, however, seem to be tacked on—especially as the film spent more time developing a romantic relationship between her and Winton and a totally combative one between her and Jimmy. There has been no romance between the two characters and Jimmy seems more of a father-figure to Florence than a lover. It seems likely that she accepts his proposal because she perceives it as a challenge or a dare—or because Winton has proven too much of a wimp—rather than out of a romantic desire for Jimmy.

In *Hi, Nellie!* Farrell's Gerry Krale takes a back seat to managing editor Samuel "Brad" Bradshaw (Paul Muni) as the protagonist of the film; nevertheless, Gerry is very similar to Florence as a wisecracking girl reporter.[15] Gerry is "Nellie Nelson," the lovelorn column writer, but when Brad (her former fiancé) angers the paper's owner, he is demoted to the column and Gerry promoted to staff writer. Interestingly, Gerry's lovelorn column has been less than a success: she receives very few letters and writes half-hearted responses; Brad, on the other hand, makes the column a major attraction and increases the paper's readership. The film suggests that Gerry is too hardboiled and cynical about romance whereas Brad believes in love and puts his heart into the job—again offering an interesting gender reversal. Despite the fact that the majority of women reporters in real life worked on the social pages, the girl reporter films of the mid-30s suggest she is too disillusioned to be a good sob sister (i.e., feminine); she is more newspaperman than most of the men on the paper (i.e., masculine).

Torchy (as played by Farrell) is very similar to Florence and Gerry, except perhaps even more confident—in terms of her faith in her own hunches—and even more independent—in terms of her evasion of marriage. In *Smart Blonde*, we are introduced to Torchy interviewing "Tiny" Torgensen (Joseph Crehan) who has just made news for buying the business enterprises of Fitz Mularkay. When Torgensen is shot next to her in the taxi, Torchy utters a short scream but quickly regains her composure and runs to the nearest phone to report the story excitedly to her editor at the paper. In this first film, Torchy and Lieutenant Steve McBride (MacLane) are not yet a couple and, instead, are rivals in that Torchy always wants the story and Steve always wants her off the case. In his office, they discuss Torgensen's murder and Torchy explains that Steve's plan to round up the usual suspects is not going to work and that his theory about the case is all wrong; she then shares with him her theories and ends up being correct. The character of Torchy is very much set in the first film: she always calls Steve "Skipper" (although one assumes in irony); she is always hungry, especially for steak; and she always is thrilled by death rather than horrified.[16] Lastly, Torchy always sets her quick mind to figuring out theories on the mysterious murders they encounter, pursuing those theories as a sleuth, and successfully identifying the criminals responsible while Steve—as the official investigator—fails to.

Torchy does change depending on which star plays her and the associations that that star brings with them, in effect overriding some of Torchy's own characteristics with the star's own. For example, in *Torchy Blane in Panama* (the fifth film in the series), Lola Lane's Torchy becomes more action-oriented and

Fig. 5.2. The Quintessential Girl Reporter: As is typical in the series, Glenda Farrell's Torchy Blane ponders the mystery at hand while Barton MacLane's Lieutenant Steve McBride merely looks on. Photo from author's collection.

somehow also more feminine.[17] *Smart Blonde* begins with Farrell's jumping on board a moving train from the side of the tracks wearing a long, tight skirt in a rare display of physical action; and in *Blondes at Work*, Farrell disarms a woman holding her hostage by burning her hand with a cigarette and turning the gun on her captor with a "Now, you shut up and sit down!" In *Torchy Blane in Panama*, however, Lane's Torchy parachutes out of a plane into the Atlantic Ocean just to catch up with Steve (Paul Kelly) who is on a ship to Panama. Later, she punches Steve in the stomach for leaving her out on the story, climbs nimbly down a rope to sneak off the cruise ship, and wears trousers regularly (much to Steve's dismay). Lane was associated with working-girl roles—for example, she played the struggling actress in the Hildegarde Withers's film *Murder on a Honeymoon* (Corrigan, 1935)—but she had also played the female reporter—for example, Kay Palmer in *Death from a Distance* (1935). Although many reviewers saw Lane as adding something to the role, the public reacted differently and could not accept the newcomer in a role that had been well-established over four films. And while MacLane's Steve was always initially skeptical but ultimately appreciative of Farrell's Torchy's playing detective because she always cracks the case, Kelly's Steve is serious when he tells Lane's Torchy to "leave detecting to the detective."

Also demonstrative of a shift in characterization is Torchy's presentation as feminized. In *Torchy Blane in Chinatown* (1939), no man in the film is impressed when Farrell's Torchy wears a revealing and slinky gown to the engagement party but, in *Torchy Blane in Panama*, Lane's Torchy receives appreciative comments from various men.

Canby:	Miss America of the fourth estate. Hey, looking at her now I can almost forget she's a reporter.
Steve:	Hey, that's my girl you're talking about.
Canby:	Huh? So it is, so it is. Excuse me.
Steve:	Hiya Torchy. Gee, you look like a million.
Torchy:	Why, thank you, Mr. McBride.
Canby:	Sit down and join us, Torchy. I was just telling Steve nobody'd dream you're a newshound in that get up.
Torchy:	Thank you Mr. Canby. I could say the same for you in any get up. The reverse is true with you, Mr. McBride—you positively reek of flatfoot since you've been away from my refining feminine influence.

Although more of an action-hero than Farrell's Torchy, Lane's is also supposed to be more traditionally—as she says—feminine. For example, when Torchy suggests that Panama may be the destination of the bank robber, Steve leaves without her, explaining in a note that being "around guys who knock over bank tellers is no business for a woman." Similarly, when the police prevent Torchy from entering the scene of the crime, Torchy has to convince them that she is "man" enough to be there.

Officer:	Hold it! You can't go in there, lady. There's been a hold-up and a murder.
Torchy:	You're wrong, boys. Hold-ups and murder are my meat. Here's the open sesame that swings wide all portals—my press pass: "Torchy Blane of *The Star*."

Significantly, whether a woman of action (as played by Lane) or a cerebral sleuth (as played by Farrell), Torchy evades marriage for nine films. At the beginning of *Smart Blonde*, Torchy sees Steve merely as rival. At the Millionaire Club, the hatcheck girl (Jane Wyman who plays Torchy herself in 1939) comments to Torchy, "Ain't he masterful?" But Torchy fails to appreciate Steve's masculine charms and retorts, "Yeah, all he needs is a leopard skin!" Halfway through the film, Torchy has fallen for Steve's charms and her editor, angry that she is helping Steve solve the case instead of giving the paper an exclusive, asks why she doesn't just marry the guy. Torchy replies, that is one of the angles she is working on. *Smart Blonde* ends with Steve proposing to Torchy, but *Fly Away Baby* begins with Steve standing her up at the marriage license bureau because he is on a case. *The Adventurous Blonde* begins with their intention to get married but a story (fabricated by other reporters to keep them apart) intervenes; the film ends with Steve arriving at the airport too late to stop Torchy from flying away on another story. *Blondes at Work* begins with Captain McTavish (Frank Shannon) complaining about Torchy's access to stories through Steve and suggests that Steve, "Muzzle that girl or marry her!" When Steve tells Torchy, "after we get married, you're going to chuck your job on the newspaper and you're gonna stay home where you belong" Torchy replies, "Look, we've been all over this a thousand times. I've got ink in my blood and a nose for news that needs something besides powder." In *Torchy Blane in Panama*, the relationship between Lane's Torchy and Kelly's Steve is based more on rivalry and antagonism: Torchy finds a clue at the scene that Steve missed and exclaims, "Why you're so dumb that all our kids, if we had any, would probably turn out to be morons!"

Unlike the majority of girl reporter films, the "Torchy" films regard the combination of marriage and a career as relatively unproblematic (at least in the first seven films). In *The Adventurous Blonde*, Torchy tells Steve, "Wedding bells and mysteries don't mix. When we start our honeymoon, the mystery's going to be over." However, she does not mean that she will give up her career as a reporter, just that she wants the case closed before they get married. Captain McTavish hopes that Torchy will give up reporting when Steve and she are finally married; however, Steve replies, "She'd rather give up on me!" He knows that Torchy cannot quit being a reporter and be happy; their marriage will not be the end of her reporting career, nor does he seem to wish it were. At the end of *The Adventurous Blonde*, Torchy is angry at Steve for standing her up yet again for a case and allows her editor, Maxie (Raymond Hatton), to send her to Cleveland to chase a new story.

Maxie: I'll never forget you for this, Torchy.

Torchy: Now, Maxie. Don't give me any of that I'll-never-forget-you-for-this-little-girl stuff. I'm only on this trip because I was a bride who was left . . . at the police station.

Maxie:	You won't be sorry for this. You'll be the belle of the air races and come back to a big fat bonus for *this* [he indicates the front page]—"Torchy Blane traps publisher into Hammond confession"—and your own office marked "Feature Writer."
Torchy:	With flowers, and a fence, and the patter of little typewriters. I'll bet that big flatfoot would like to choke me.

She conflates images of a wedding (flowers), married life (fence), and her career (typewriters) suggesting that she will not give up her career just because she is getting married. Occasionally, Torchy is tempted by the idea of being a housewife. For example, when she is held captive by the villains in *Torchy Gets Her Man*, Torchy mutters, "Maybe I should have married Steve and had babies." And, by the last film of the series starring Farrell, Torchy contemplates family over career. In *Torchy Runs for Mayor*, Steve nominates Torchy for mayor as a joke, but Torchy decides to run.

Steve:	Ah, go on! Can't you take a joke? You can't do that!
Torchy:	Why not?
Steve:	Because you're going to marry me.
Torchy:	If there's any law that says a mayor can't get married, we'll have it changed.
Steve:	Nah! What kind of nincompoop do you think I'd be married to a mayor? What do you want me to do—stay home and peel the potatoes while you run the city?
Torchy:	Oh, you won't have to do that! I'll be getting a very good salary—we'll hire a cook.
Steve:	Listen, if we're going to hire a cook, I'll pay for it with my own dough. And, what's more, is you're going to stay home where you belong and take care of my babies.

In the end, she is elected mayor; however, when someone hands her a baby for a photo op, Torchy looks at the baby, gets a far away look in her eyes, and says, "Oh, Steve, I don't want to be mayor; I want to get married." The film, in general, has a different tone than the previous film as it deals with more serious topics such as political corruption. Perhaps then, another delaying of Torchy and Steve's marriage is seen as too flippant and unrealistic a conclusion for the film. Despite the proposal and the marriage license, the girl reporter concludes the series in *Torchy Blane . . . Playing with Dynamite*, this time played by Jane Wyman, unmarried and pursuing her career as a girl reporter. The turning of the tide had begun, though, and even Farrell would quit the business and settle down as Susan (another girl reporter) in *A Night for Crime* (Thurn-Taxis, 1943), which I will explore in the following chapter.

Part III: The Feminine Touch

Reporting Feminine Ethics

Gender is a key issue in the majority of girl reporter films and not only because of the marriage-career conflict. For example, *My Dear Miss Aldrich* (1937) begins in Lower Platte, Nebraska, with Miss "Lou" Atherton (Edna May Oliver) suggesting that her school-teacher niece, Martha Aldrich (Maureen O'Sullivan), has yet to attract a husband because she is "pro-women's rights." Similarly, managing editor of the New York paper, *The Globe-Leader*, Ken Morley (Walter Pidgeon), is accused of being a "woman-hater." It is not unexpected then that, when Martha inherits *The Globe-Leader*, she runs into a difference of opinion with Ken.

Ken:	You'd be amazed at how many papers have a circulation made up of nothing but *that* kind of people.
Martha:	*That* kind of people?
Ken:	Yes, people that just look at the pictures, just turn to the comics, and . . . and crossword puzzles, and advice to the lovelorn.
Martha:	I'm sorry, Mr. Morley, I don't understand you. Aren't they supposed to have newspapers . . . they're the people?
Ken:	*That* isn't what I mean. Now *The Globe-Leader* isn't read only by university professors but we go on the theory that every man who buys the paper is an intelligent, interested citizen.
Martha:	Every *man* that buys the paper.

Ken: Yes.

Martha: But don't women buy the paper too?

Ken: Certainly they do! We carry more department store
            advertising than any other paper in town but, when a
            man picks up *The Globe-Leader*...

Martha: [interrupting] I'm afraid I have to go in.

Martha proves Ken wrong about women in the newspaper business: she gets
the scoop on the pregnancy of a visiting royal when every male reporter on
the paper—including Ken—has been thrown out of the Queen's hotel room.
Martha explains to Ken with much sarcasm how she obtained the story.

Martha: Well, I don't know if you'd approve, Mr. Morley.
            They tell me you don't think very highly of women in
            newspaperwork.

Ken: Never mind about that! What do you know about the
            Queen?

Martha: You must promise to tell me if I did wrong. I wouldn't
            want to violate any rules established by men for newspaper
            reporting.

Ken: Are you going to tell me, or are you not?

Martha: Well, I . . . I'm just a silly woman so I walked into your
            outer office and I called up the Queen and I asked if she
            was going to have a baby and she said "Yes, in August,"
            and she promised not to tell any other paper. What did
            I do wrong, Mr. Morley?

Her scoop gains her Ken's respect and, when she asks for it, a job on the paper
as a newspaperman. However, when she fails to report the secret marriage of
her friends on moral grounds, Ken fires her for being "unprofessional."

In many of these girl reporter films it is precisely *because* of her sex that
the female reporter gets the scoop and because she has—it is assumed—a different, more human approach to reporting as a woman that includes caring about
people. In films like *The Office Scandal, Headline Shooter,* and *Front Page Woman,*
this assumption is confirmed when the girl reporter is able to get a female
suspect to open up and tell the truth about a crime—and that gives them the

scoop over their male rivals. Being in touch with one's feminine side did not just mean getting the scoop, however, but being a better kind of reporter in a world of yellow journalism. And the *Motion Picture Association* warned studios that they were under scrutiny by the newspaper world for its representation of reporters and editors. For example, in a letter to Mr. S. J. Briskin at RKO regarding the film *Behind the Headlines*, Breen wrote:

> In addition, the material is questionable as reflecting *unfavorably on newspapers*, and we most earnestly recommend that you give serious thought to this phase of the story before proceeding further with its production. [. . .] Mr. Hays urged me at that time to keep a sharp lookout for pictures dealing, in any way, with newspapers, and to advise our studios of the quite definite purpose of the organized publishers to resist, and aggressively oppose, pictures which place newspapers in an unfavorable light.[18] (8 March 1937)

A comparable letter was sent to Warner Bros. regarding *Back in Circulation*;[19] however, the majority of reviews of the film laud its similarity to *The Front Page* because of its revival of themes of ethics and newspapermen getting the story regardless of the cost. The reviewer for *Variety* notes, "Yarn gives the women reporter's role much more depth and substance than the usual fourth-estate film figment" (27 July 1937). While Breen and the *Motion Picture Association* were concerned with the backlash against these films, critics were praising them for delving into socially relevant debates about crime and the media. And these debates became increasingly frequent in regards to the girl reporter film as the genre evolved, and the line between ethics and exploitation often ran parallel to the gender divide. Ethics, these films suggest, are aligned with the feminine and, even if the girl reporter would do just about anything to get the scoop at the beginning of the film, she had learned the value of humanity over sensationalism by the end of it.

Despite the seeming levity of the girl reporter film with a focus on rivals, scoops, and romance, these films did also tackle issues of the media and reporting crime seriously. The ethics of reporting the news was a topic of debate from early on in the girl reporter film following in the tradition of *Five Star Final* and *The Front Page*.[20] In *The Final Edition*, the moral stance is embodied by the girl reporter, Ann (Clarke), who got the scoop from the grieving widow when her male rivals failed to. As she explains to them, "Say, anybody with an ounce of gray matter could see that poor woman couldn't have given out a statement on the weather the way she felt then. You should really teach your boys better manners. You'd get a lot more out of people." In *The Adventurous Blonde*, *The Globe*'s editor chastises his male reporters for faking a murder story to prevent Torchy and Steve from getting married. He warns them that it was not ethical and that "if you boys can't compete with Torchy Blane fairly you might as well turn in your cards and go back to want ads." Mary Bradley in *Behind the Headlines* accuses Eddie of being unethical: "Eddie, you haven't a business principle or an ethic. You'd lie, double-cross, cheat or steal to get a story. You're an utter cockroach. And we did the world a good turn today by stepping on you."[21]

In *Back in Circulation*, Timmy (Joan Blondell) is just as guilty as her male rivals at the start of the film: she wants the scoop at any cost. To gain access to the scene of a train wreck, she pretends that her reporters are actually local medics. Once they gain entry, Timmy instructs them,

> Alright, Buck, you get down to the relief train and get a list of the dead. Murphy, you find a good spot for a picture and hold it 'til we're all ready to go. One boom of that flashlight of yours and we'll have every railroad cop around here on our necks.

She tricks her rival "Snoop" Davis (Craig Reynolds) into giving her the scoop and then strands him in the mud rather than giving him a lift back to the city to report his story. Although her editor and boyfriend, Bill Morgan (Pat O'Brien), is happy with her gruesome photo from the scene of the wreck and admires her willingness to do anything for the paper (including lying for him on the stand in a libel case), he criticizes her story for lacking something important—"human interest." In other words, Timmy is too hardboiled. What her editor seems to misunderstand, however, is that—what makes her too masculine to cater to the human interest angle—is exactly what makes her an unscoopable newspaperman (at least according to the logic of the film). Another story materializes—the suspected poisoning of motor baron, Spencer Wade—and Timmy's male colleagues argue that this job requires "finesse." In other words, it needs "a woman's touch"—or at least a woman who can effect the woman's touch—and Timmy is sent out to investigate. Timmy has the funeral stopped, an autopsy ordered, and gets the scoop. When the other reporters arrive in town, one asks her, "How do you do it, Timmy? With a crystal?" and Snoop asks, "Are you sure you didn't poison the old boy yourself—just to get a scoop?" Timmy is not afraid to use violence either: when a suspect makes an inappropriate pass at her, she punches him in the face. And, a few minutes later, when he tries to stop Bill from calling in the story, Bill asks Timmy to punch him again and she is happy to oblige.

Timmy's demonstration of a lack of ethics in terms of how she treats the widow, Arline Wade (Margaret Lindsay), earns her a lecture from Dr. Forde (John Litel) about the sensationalism of the press; yet, on the other hand, when she does get in touch with her feelings and begins to believe in Arline's innocence, Timmy receives one from Bill that she has gone soft and is relying on "feminine intuition." In the end, it is her sympathy for Arline that results in a confession that clears both Arline and Dr. Forde of her husband's murder.

As the reviewer for *Variety* notes, "it is these scenes that the professional hard-ness of the news folks concerned only to the get the story is softened with human and compassionate motives" (27 July 1937). In other words, *Back in Circulation* asserts that, for the girl reporter to be heralded as a hero, she must not become too hardboiled by the business but must keep in touch with her feminine side. It also reassures her that doing the job ethically (i.e., femininely) will pay off with the scoop.

Other films offered similar conclusions: namely that the girl reporter must be "softened" (i.e., feminized) to be heroic. In *One Mile from Heaven*, it would appear that there is little room for ethics in the world of journalism.[22] Tex (Claire Trevor) discovers that the white girl being raised by a black woman, Flora Jackson (Fredi Washington), is actually the daughter of white socialite Barbara Harrison (Sally Blane), who had been told by the baby's father that the baby had died. Tex has the exclusive on the story and wants to print it but the judge threatens to hold her in contempt of court if she does; regardless, she starts to write the story until her emotions get the "better" of her. She writes a fake story for the other newshawks to find so that the Harrisons and Flora will be left alone. This costs her her job with her paper; however, the film assures us this was the right thing to do, and Tex is rewarded with the position of society editor on a paper back in Texas.

It Can't Last Forever (1937) is focused mainly on Russ Mathews (Ralph Bellamy), a theatrical agent who pulls a con: he stages incidents that convince the public and companies looking for a radio show to sponsor that he is "The Master Mind"—a man who can predict the future. The editor of *The Chronicle* assigns Carole Wilson (Betty Furness) to do a series of stories on the Master Mind—"the inside stuff, the woman's angle;" however, Carole has become hardboiled by her experiences and seems tired of a business that would rather publish what is popular than the truth. For example, she sees through Matthews' con and presents her exposé story to her editor, but he refuses to publish it when all of the other papers are singing the Master Mind's praises. Carole is presented as very intelligent, resourceful, and ethical; she is certainly the only reporter in New York City that sees the truth about the Master Mind and, in the end, she decides to leave the business to run away with Mathews.

Many of these films use the girl reporter film as a means to critique the fourth estate while, simultaneously, offering an alternative to yellow journal-ism. As McElvaine suggests, women in Depression-era films did not escape their social situation "through 'male,' 'self-centered,' 'rugged' individualism, but through cooperation and compassion" (341). The girl reporter is, at once, masculine and feminine—possessing the assumed male drive to be independent and successful as a career newspaperman, while, at the same time, possessing the assumed female emotionality that may "betray" her sex but actually makes her a better, and more ethical, reporter. She brings "feminine" values to the male-dominated world of journalism and, in doing so, makes it a more principled and accountable medium; in other words, being a sob sister is precisely what makes these women the best newspapermen. Interestingly, it is that femininity that also makes them superior detectives.

Detecting Female Knowledge

In the girl reporter films of the 1930s, skilled sleuthing is identified as specifically feminine—and not because of "female intuition." In some films, the sleuthing skill aligned specifically with the sex of the girl reporter is the possession of "female knowledge"—the knowledge of things that women learn about being feminine. In other films, female-specific sleuthing is aligned with female thinking, which is differentiated from the male tendency to fight crime solely with action. Female knowledge always comes into play when a suspect in a case is a woman. In *My Dear Miss Aldrich*, although Martha's perceived "feminine" impulse to keep a female friend's secret results in her losing her job, Martha's femininity is precisely what lands her the next scoop. Upset over being fired, Martha goes shopping for a new hat where she overhears a woman (Janet Beecher) explain that she needs a hat delivered by six o'clock that evening. Martha knows that the woman is Mrs. Sinclair and that the Sinclairs are important labor leaders who have refused to come to a deal with industrialist Mr. Talbot. As a woman, Martha knows that the only reason that Mrs. Sinclair would need a new hat by that evening is if she has an important meeting that night—likely with Talbot. This leads Martha to follow the Sinclairs to a secret meeting place at an inn upstate and to eavesdrop on the meeting. While her feminine knowledge gains her the scoop, her being feminine betrays her identity: Mrs. Sinclair is able to discover Martha's affiliation to the paper through the contents of her purse. Later, however, the feminine contents of her purse save the day: first, Martha is able to free herself, her rival, and her aunt with her broken compact mirror; and, second, she uses her red nail polish to give her aunt (Oliver) pox-like spots, resulting in the inn being quarantined and thus preventing the Sinclairs from escaping.

In *Blondes at Work*, Lieutenant Steve McBride (MacLane) goes in search of "female knowledge" by asking a cosmetics' sales girl what kind of woman would wear that particular shade of lipstick (the answer is a dark brunette). As a woman, Torchy (Farrell) does not need any such assistance and picks up on a clue ignored by the male detective: the laundry mark on the woman's slip. By tracing the mark to the correct laundry, Torchy is able to identify the woman in question when she picks up her order. In *Adventures of Jane Arden* (1939), debutante Martha Blanton has been travelling and shopping extravagantly despite the fact that her family lost its money during the Depression. It is girl reporter, Jane Arden (Rosella Towne), who deduces that Martha has been smuggling jewels for a racket and was killed when she felt compelled to report the racket to the district attorney. In *The Corpse Vanishes* (Fox, 1942), girl reporter Pat Hunter (Luana Walters) pursues a lead that the police have ignored: the orchids that each dead bride in the case was given to wear to her wedding. Following the lead takes Pat to the mansion of the creepy Dr. Lorenz (Bela Lugosi) where she discovers that he extracts hormones from the glands of each bride to keep his wife looking young. Lastly, in *A Night for Crime* (Thurn-Taxis, 1943), reporter Susan Cooper (Farrell) figures out the whereabouts of missing movie star, Mona Harrison, when she recognizes the location used in Mona's last film as Reno, Nevada. This is defined in the film explicitly as feminine knowledge because over half of the women who get a divorce in the U.S. travel to Reno to get it.

Action is defined as a masculine trait in these films and mental machinations as more feminine—and this is, indeed, in keeping with the tradition of detecting in Hollywood films. The pioneering sleuths—Poe's Dupin, Conan Doyle's Holmes, and Christie's Poirot—were European gentlemen. Refined, cultured, and intellectual, these gentlemen solved crime through observation, ratiocination, logic, and deduction and were differentiated from the often inept and uneducated working-class policemen who invariably failed to solve the case before the amateur sleuth. The gentleman is a central type of hero in British popular culture; on the other hand, in America, it is the urban tough guy as the twentieth-century incarnation of the frontier hero. In America's Wild West and on its mean city streets, the successful defeat of one's enemies most often required the courage to use violence. In American popular culture, physical action to fight crime is associated with American and masculine heroism; the decidedly non-physical mental process of ratiocination is associated with an Old World, feminized kind of masculinity. By extension then, the female detective is more likely to combat crime cerebrally than physically—and this is certainly the case with the girl reporter.

Certainly, Ann (Clarke) in *The Final Edition* is reprimanded by her editor when she begins chasing a new story by doing research in the paper's archives first. Brad (O'Brien) comments scathingly, "I thought you were working here? [. . .] Well, it would be a good idea to get on the job instead of looking at pictures." Her impulse to research her facts is in contradiction to the man-of-action's impulse. This sentiment to act rather than think is echoed in other female detective films (not just the girl reporter films) of the time. In *The Plot Thickens* (Holmes, 1936), Inspector Oscar Piper (James Gleason) interrogates the murder victim's butler. When the butler explains to the Inspector what he thought when he discovered his master's body in the library, Oscar quips, "Never mind what you thought. What you'd do?" Similarly, Torchy Blane's impulse to ratiocinate when confronted with a mystery is derided by Steve as "just paper figuring" in *Smart Blonde*. He accuses her of being "just one of these destructive critics: you say everything a guy does is rotten but you don't build up anything yourself"; however, she proves him wrong when she presents him with a theory that turns out to be correct.

The girl reporter defies the stereotype of women in classical Hollywood film as mere objects for the male gaze because she also possesses an empowered gaze—as the detective. As Linda Mizejewski suggests, her "job isn't to look good, but to do the looking" (*Hardboiled*, 4). For example, in *The Office Scandal*, Jerry (Haver) visits Lillian (Livingston) in her luxurious apartment to ascertain her guilt or innocence in the murder of her husband. While the police detective has a word alone with the widow, Jerry sneaks a drink from Lillian's bar and then listens in on their conversation. Rather than offering the typical shot of someone eavesdropping around the corner of a door slightly ajar, *The Office Scandal* presents a dramatic extreme close-up of Jerry's eye peering between the two halves of the sliding doors. This shot is intercut with a point of view shot of Lillian and the detective through the door. Jerry does not behave "like a lady" and await the return of her hostess but, instead, exhibits the masculine trait of possessing a powerful and penetrating gaze, highlighted by the shot composition and editing of the scene.[23] In *Women are Trouble* (1936), aspiring newspaperman Ruth Nolan (Florence Rice) is hired by the paper's editor, Blaine (Paul Kelly), but is not allowed to pursue any stories; instead, she is told by Blaine that her value to the paper is to make the office "brighter" (i.e., be eye candy for the male reporters). However, she counters this role by exercising her own gaze—taking photographs of the men working in the office and her exercise of the gaze brings the next break in a big story. The male reporter, Casey (Stuart Erwin), tells Ruth to drive around to the back alley behind the courthouse to keep her out of the way while he gets the scoop inside; however, it is Ruth who catches the villains on film with her camera while Casey misses out on the scoop.

Similarly, in *International Crime* (1938), Phoebe Lane (Astrid Allwyn) defies the stereotype of the socialite (as the niece of the paper's owner) and proves herself a proficient reporter and detective to Lamont Cranston (Rob La Rocque)—the famed radio detective known as "The Shadow." Phoebe is the only person who can identify the criminal in a case and their search of city nightclubs becomes a minute-long montage sequence of Phoebe scanning the nightspots—with her powerful and investigative gaze—for the face they seek. Once Phoebe identifies the man, Lamont wants her to go home; however, Phoebe retorts, "Go home the very minute the fun begins? Gee, I am not going to do all the hunting and miss the shooting." *Mystery of the Wax Museum* also thematizes looking: Florence's (Farrell's) ability to see the truth is compared with the powerful gaze of the evil Igor (Atwill). Igor's original wax museum burned to the ground and he was too badly injured in the blaze to sculpt; instead, he steals corpses who resemble famous historical figures, embalms them in wax, and displays them as wax figures in his new museum in New York. His powerful gaze is literalized: he looks at Charlotte (Wray) and, on screen, her image dissolves—in a reflection of his perception of her—into that of her as Marie Antoinette. Florence is the only person who is observant enough to see literally the truth behind Igor's wax creations and recognize the figures' resemblances to real people who have disappeared. Comparing the figures to the newspaper's "art" (photos), Florence makes positive identifications and uncovers Igor's evil plot in time to save Charlotte from a fiendish fate. Armed with a knowledge of the feminine and the empowered gaze of the masculine, the girl reporter proves to be a superior and prolific detective for the Depression.

Depressing Success

The girl reporter film offered a space for the debate about women, work, and marriage, but did it offer a proto-feminist role model? Philip Hanson suggests many 1930s films do not really put forth feminist messages despite appearances because they use a "slippery strategy of backing away from the feminist issues it has raised" by the end of the film with a conventional, moralizing ending. He explains, "Films of the 1930s remained unwilling to pursue questions they had uncovered which might lead to the conclusion that gender relations are fundamentally unfair" ("Feminine," 131). Critics such as Hanson might argue that the abrupt marriage proposals (and often acceptances) that concluded many of these films negate the possibility of a feminist message. As Dalton notes in relation to *Mystery of the Wax Museum*, "Farrell's surprise capitulation is typical. A woman could be resourceful, intelligent, even cynical, for fifty-nine minutes, but in the last two she would realize that it was love and marriage that she really wanted" ("Women," 272). I would argue, however, that tacked-on endings do not necessarily reverse the entire narrative that has preceded it. Even reviewers at the time did not appreciate the tacked-on romances. For example, the *Variety* reviewer for *The Girl on the Front Page* suggests that the love angle is "no match for what's gone before," specifically the film's "racy situations and comedy sequences" (11 November 1936). As this review suggests, if a film has a great story and/or quality comedy, then romance seems an unnecessary element to tack on at the end—even though Hollywood most often did.

Certainly, those interested in the effects of films on audiences recognized the impotence of tacked-on morals at the end of a film. As Professor Kimball Young noted, in his address at the *Motion Picture Conference* at the University of Wisconsin–Madison in October 1934,

> . . . the mere tacking on of a moral at the end of a film may mean nothing to the child or adult who sees it. In other words, those interested in reforming the movies must not imagine that the mere addition of a moral story at the end of a film would serve to counteract the possible evil of specific episodes in the story itself.[24] (10)

Similarly, one of the most significant shifts in the implementation of the Code under Breen's leadership was that toward tacked-on endings. In the annual report for 1936 devoted to the Code, Breen noted the inadequacy of marrying off the lead characters in the final scene to make amends for their life of sin throughout the film or "the subterfuge of attempting to wipe out a protracted wrong by one last line of dialogue affirming the right" (Qtd. in Jacobs, 114–15). What Breen considers a negative issue, I suggest is a positive: the addition of a socially prescribed conclusion need not necessarily devalue the independence of the heroine in the rest of the narrative. And, after all, many of the heroines of these films did not settle down at the end of the film, for example in *The Office Scandal, International Crime, One Mile from Heaven*, and the "Torchy Blane" films.

Considering the social context of these films and the representation of women that has succeeded them (including those of contemporary film), these films offered remarkable role models with independent, career-minded women who did not need to negotiate or apologize for their ambitions. The reality was that for many female filmgoers, marriage was one of the few options to attain a better standard of living because of women's lack of access to higher education and/or career opportunities—especially during the Depression. What these films put forth is the idea that *if* these women are to marry then at least they are marrying on their own terms—i.e., because they want to rather than have to. With that in mind, what is most interesting about the girl reporter is that she attracted her man, not because of her potential to be feminized (as is the case of the female detective in the majority of other periods of Hollywood film including today), but because of her *masculinity*—her outspoken nature, her independence, and her careerist ambition, drive, and success. In other words, she is a woman who could be masculine *and* valued, respected *and* desired. As *Headline Shooter* articulates clearly, only the hardboiled woman can be a match for the hardboiled man—because she is his equal.

Thus, it was in this period of social upheaval in reality that a generous space for the representation of female independence and careerist ambition was afforded in film. In the 1930s, the feminist-achievement conflict that has dominated the history of the female detective narrative may have been a conflict, but it was one of personal choice and certainly not a "problem" that needed to be resolved. Female aggression in the 1920s was, as Hanson notes, "consistently contained by being enfolded in male authority" ("Feminine," 132n39); worse, in the 1940s, it was punishable by death as in the case of the *femme fatale*. In the 1930s, however, it was often celebrated and *always allowed*. Rather than being punished for her independence and transgression of traditional social roles, the girl reporter of the 1930s was rewarded for her careerist ambitions and success—i.e., precisely for being masculine—and that is why these sob sisters didn't cry.

6

In Name Only

The Transformation of the Female Detective in the 1940s

Bill: You know, I still don't get it. You tell me, now, what better ambition than to find a happy marriage, have children, and a home.

Kathy: Propaganda—not for me. For marriage, I read life sentence. A home life; I read TV nights, beer in the fridge, second mortgage. Uh-uh. Not for me. For me life has to be something more than that.

—Sterling Hayden and Barbara Stanwyck in *Crime of Passion* (1957)

The New Deal was a series of economic planning programs initiated by the Roosevelt administration in 1933 in an attempt to offer relief in terms of creating work for the unemployed, reform in terms of business practices, and recovery in terms of the economy during the Depression. In 1936, the New Deal reached its "high tide" and Franklin D. Roosevelt had a stunning electoral victory, taking all but two states; however, in 1937, the tide turned when Roosevelt cut back on government spending, which in turn precipitated a second recession almost as severe as that of 1932–33. In the end, scholars suggest that the New Deal was more of a morale booster than an economic one. As Susan Ware comments, "However much of the New Deal had restored hope to the American people, it utterly failed to curtail the Depression" (xv–xvi). Instead, it was World War II that was responsible for pulling the U.S. out of what effectively had been a decade-long slump. The upturn in the economy, conversely, saw a downturn in popular attitudes toward women and their place in wartime society. Books like Philip Wylie's *Generation of Vipers* (1942) warned of the consequences of female empowerment, namely its deleterious effects on masculinity or what Wylie termed "Momism" (i.e., over-mothering). Although public familiarity with psychoanalysis had been growing since Sigmund Freud's visit to America in 1908, the war popularized its practice—e.g., draftee psychiatric evaluations—and saw many of its problems—e.g., "GI cowardice"—attributed to "overprotection" by mothers (Walker, 201). And this shift in social attitudes toward women was echoed in Hollywood's representation of "positive" female role models in 1940s film.

In his introduction for *The Mad Miss Manton* (Jason, 1938) on the *Turner Classic Movies* channel, Robert Osborne suggests that the mystery-comedy featuring a madcap heiress (Barbara Stanwyck) and newspaperman (Henry Fonda) was produced to capitalize on the detective-couple trend inspired by the popular "Thin Man" series (1934–47). Osborne notes that 1938 was the peak of popularity for screwball heroine films and "Thin Man" imitations. In terms of the female detective, however, 1938 saw the turning of the tide in terms of her independence. The popularity of "Thin Man" detective-couples saw more female detectives working with their male love interests rather than attempting to beat them as rivals. By 1938, the female detective was more inclined to "share" the investigation with the male but, by 1940, she was increasingly cast as "secondary"—merely a sidekick to the male detective. And while the female reporter or amateur detective melted into the background of the mystery-comedy, a new kind of film appeared—the darker, more dramatic *film noir*—which pushed women either out of the investigation altogether or recast them as self-sacrificing wives devoted to saving their men wrongly accused of murder (the latter will be explored in the following chapter).

In the early 1940s, the girl reporter came to be regarded as a potential disruption to dominant masculinity. In *Woman of the Year* (Stevens, 1942), a man comments that star reporter Tess Harding (Katharine Hepburn) is regarded as "the number two dame in the county—right next to Mrs. Roosevelt." His friend retorts, "So they're giving them numbers now—like public enemies." Kathleen Gregory Klein suggests that the female detective, like the criminal, must be put in her "proper"—i.e., secondary—place: "Like the criminal, she is a member of society who does not conform to the status quo. Her presence pushes off-center the whole male/female, public/private, intellect/emotion [. . .] dichotomy" (4). Although, during the Depression, Hollywood had not seemed to mind the disruption of that dichotomy, with the coming of war Hollywood reset gender polarities. For example, while Torchy Blane and other girl reporters of the 1930s were celebrated for their masculinity, Tess Harding is criticized for it—despite Hepburn's association with feminist ideals and her portrayal of strong women on screen. In *Woman of the Year*, Tess's husband Sam (Spencer Tracy) exclaims that the joke is that "the *Outstanding Woman of the Year* isn't a woman at all!" Rather than making concessions (as supposedly Sam has) to accommodate both of their careers as newspapermen with marriage, Tess has proven herself a lousy wife to Sam and a worse mother to the young refugee she adopted. While real-life foreign correspondent Dorothy Thompson (on whom the character of Tess is based) was celebrated, Laura Hapke suggests that Tess is "the butt" of the "misogynist satire" (191). Except for the opening sequence of the film that celebrates her fame as a foreign correspondent, the majority of the film details Tess's failings as a woman. These are highlighted in an excruciating (to watch) scene at the end of the film in which she attempts to "play house" to save her marriage: Sam watches with pleasure as batter oozes out of the waffle maker, toast flies out of the toaster, coffee boils over on the stove, and Tess dissolves into tears. The film's anti-feminist message is tempered only with Sam's final speech of the film in which he asks Tess to stop going from one extreme (pure career woman—"Miss Harding") to another (pure housewife—"Mrs. Craig") and aim for halfway ("Tess Harding-Craig"). However, as Andrea Walsh notes, "Whereas one might argue that the portrayal of Tess merely critiques workaholism and not feminism, one must ask why Tess, and not Sam, is depicted so negatively" (147).

During the war, the majority of film viewers were women and Hollywood catered to the needs of its audience with film narratives that centered on female characters and desires. The war required the employment of millions of female workers, but social convention had previously discouraged women from entering the workforce. As Bilge Yesil explains, wartime propaganda agencies like the War Manpower Commission (WMC) and the Office of War Information (OWI) had to advertise war work to women as laudatory, glamorous, and—above all—patriotic in order to attract them to it (103). Hollywood, to help the war effort and under advisement from the OWI, saw its heroines join the WAVES in *Here Come the Waves* (Sandrich, 1945), the WACS in *Keep Your Powder Dry* (Buzzell, 1945), the Red Cross in *So Proudly We Hail!* (Sandrich, 1943), and the defense plant in *Swing Shift Maisie* (McLeod, 1943). These films, along with the OWI's propaganda, attracted women to specific kinds of work that, before the war, would have been unthinkable for "respectable" women but, during the war, were recast as necessary, patriotic, and appealing. While the war meant that women could pursue opportunities beyond the traditional and socially sanctioned roles of wife and mother, Susan Hartmann notes that popular discourse set limits on the possibility of social change with three key themes conveyed: first, that women were replacing men in the workforce *only* for the duration of the war; second, that women would retain their femininity even as they performed masculine labor; and, third, that there were "feminine" motivations behind women's willingness to work—they did so in support of their men (23).

And America's women did flock to the workforce during the war, filling the void that enlisted men left behind. As M. Joyce Baker explains,

> As jobs opened in the wartime marketplace, women responded to the patriotic flourish of government posters, radio broadcasts, magazine articles and film footage by attempting to keep both the home fires and the furnaces of production burning. The female

labor force increased by 6.5 million or 57 percent during the war years, boosting the number of women workers to nearly 20 million by 1945. (3)

And this entry into the workforce was not necessarily temporary. As Lois Scharf notes, "In spite of the post-1945 demobilization and economic dislocation, women did retain, regain, or discover new areas of employment" (159). However, there was a widespread social backlash against female independence at the end of the war as men returned from the war to the workplace; women were expected to leave their newly-won independence and return once more to the home while men reestablished themselves in the role of breadwinner. Hollywood reflected the backlash offering two types of representation: positive portrayals of women who returned to their traditional roles in the home and were re-feminized; and negative portrayals of women who attempted to maintain their independent lifestyles and were defeated or destroyed. It is no coincidence then, Jack Boozer argues, that the emergence of Hollywood's lethal siren, the *femme fatale*, occurred simultaneously with postwar readjustment (23). By 1940, as Europe was in the thick of World War II, we see the waning of the tough girl reporter and independent amateur detective. Suddenly, being brash, fast-talking, and masculine seemed out of style for a woman, and Hollywood's female detectives became more feminine in appearance, less ambitious in their careers, more desirous of marriage, less prominent in terms of screen time, and less respected by the male law enforcers.

Part I: Girl Reporters

That does not mean, however, that there were no girl reporters in the decade. The girl reporter continued to be a popular character type in the 1940s, appearing in films like *Emergency Squad* (Dmytryk, 1940), *City of Chance* (Cortez, 1940), *The Fatal Hour* (Nigh, 1940), *His Girl Friday* (Hawks, 1940), *Doomed to Die* (Nigh, 1940), *Phantom Submarine* (Barton, 1940), *Double Alibi* (Rosen, 1941), *Sleepers West* (Forde, 1941), *City of Missing Girls* (Clifton, 1941), *Mr. District Attorney* (Morgan, 1941), *Meet John Doe* (Capra, 1941), *The Saint's Vacation* (Fenton, 1941), *The Bride Wore Crutches* (Trauble, 1941), *Mystery Ship* (Landers, 1941), *Lady Scarface* (Woodruff, 1941), *Man at Large* (Forde, 1941), *I Killed that Man* (Rosen, 1941), *Borrowed Hearts* (Collins, 1941), *Sealed Lips* (Waggner, 1942), *Woman of the Year* (Stevens, 1942), *Pardon My Stripes* (Auer, 1942), *Who is Hope Schuyler?* (Loring, 1942), *The Corpse Vanishes* (Fox, 1942), *Just off Broadway* (Leeds, 1942), *You Can't Escape Forever* (Graham, 1942), *The Boss of Big Town* (Dreiffus, 1942), *Secrets of the Underground* (Morgan, 1942), *A Night for Crime* (Thurn-Taxis, 1943), *Criminals Within* (Lewis, 1943), *Rogues' Gallery* (Herman, 1944), *Midnight Manhunt* (Thomas, 1945), *Big Town* (Thomas, 1947), *Traffic in Crime* (Lesander, 1946), *The Corpse Came C.O.D.* (Levin, 1947),

I Cover Big Town (Thomas, 1947), *The Trouble with Women* (Lanfield, 1947), *Deadline for Murder* (Tinling, 1946), *Big Town after Dark* (Thomas, 1947), *Big Town Scandal* (Thomas, 1948), *Behind Locked Doors* (Boetticher, 1948), *Follow Me Quietly* (Fleisher, 1949), *The Lone Wolf and His Lady* (Hoffman, 1949), and *The House Across the Street* (Bare, 1949). However, the majority of these girl reporters had less agency and were often "newspapermen" in name only. They are rarely seen at their papers, talking to their editors, or writing a story—let alone investigating one. Whereas approximately three-quarters of the films starring girl reporters in the 1930s saw their heroines as lead investigators, only a handful did so in the 1940s and, in those few cases, the girl reporter was only a parody of her Depression-era predecessors. The majority of the films in the 1940s featuring a girl reporter saw her pushed from the center of the criminal investigation and relegated to the secondary position of love interest to the male detective.

The reduction of the girl reporter's agency did vary by degree, depending on the type of film. One trend, as apparent in films such as *His Girl Friday* (1940), *Meet John Doe* (1941), *Woman of the Year* (1942), and *The Trouble with Women* (1947), was to retain the girl reporter as a lead character but retract her role as detective by offering a narrative without a mystery to investigate—only a scoop to chase. Another trend was to retain the mystery narrative but offer the girl reporter merely as a sidekick to a well-known male detective, usually within a series, for example with Mr. Wong (*Doomed to Die* [1940] and *Fatal Hour* [1940]),[1] Michael Shayne (*Sleeper's West* [1941] and *Just off Broadway* [1942]), The Saint (*The Saint's Vacation* [1941]), The Falcon (*The Falcon Takes Over* [1942], *The Falcon's Brother* [1943], and *The Falcon Strikes Back* [1943]), and the Lone Wolf (*The Lone Wolf and His Lady* [1949]). The girl reporter plays a larger role as an investigator in films such as *Criminals Within* (1943) and *The Corpse Came C.O.D.* (1947) but is still secondary in screen time (appearing a third to halfway through the film) and agency to the male detective. While the girl reporter film of the 1930s had often suggested that the heroine is a thorn in the side of the male detective or editor, films like *City of Missing Girls* (1941) suggested that she was damaging the male's career and should give up her's to support his. Lastly, there were a handful of 1940s films with girl reporters in strong and lead investigative roles—for example, *The Corpse Vanishes* (Fox, 1942), *A Night for Crime* (1943), and *Rogues' Gallery* (1944)—however, these films and their heroines border on the parodic and could not be taken as seriously as their 1930s predecessors. The 1940s saw the girl reporter-detective recast in reduced roles and reassigned to more traditional gender roles.

Parodic Decline

As Jim Collins notes, the period of decline for a genre includes self-parody (246) and, certainly, 1940 marked the beginning of the decline of the girl reporter film. It is difficult to pinpoint the moment that the comedy of the girl reporter film shifted into parody; however, *His Girl Friday* confirmed that the final phase of the genre had commenced. I will briefly examine *His Girl Friday* here despite the fact that its girl reporter is not a detective because the film is perhaps the best-known example of the girl reporter film and parodies the trend that I identified in the previous decade.

Like Torchy Blane, Hildy Johnson (Rosalind Russell) was originally supposed to be a male reporter: the film is a remake of one of the first notable newspaper films, *The Front Page* (Milestone, 1931), based on the stage play of the same name penned by Ben Hecht and Charles MacArthur: both the play and film feature Hildy as a male reporter who wants to quit the business and get married. Director Howard Hawks decided to alter the sex of the character upon hearing a woman read the character's lines. Hawks's female Hildy follows in the footsteps of her girl reporter predecessors and, in many ways, the story is very similar to that of *Headline Shooter* (Brower, 1933), including starring Ralph Bellamy as the stable, solid, but eventually rejected fiancé. *His Girl Friday*, however, takes this familiar narrative of the girl reporter film and begins about three years after the majority of the films conclude. While other girl reporter films focus on their early days as a reporter when they are trying to further their career and find themselves falling in love with the male rival, *His Girl Friday* begins with Hildy having just finalized her divorce from the male rival, editor Walter Burns (Cary Grant), and trying to quit the newspaper business to marry a "normal" man, Bruce Baldwin (Bellamy).

The film is conscious of its origins as a narrative about the early 1930s (as *The Front Page*) and opens with the written prologue:

> It all happened in the "dark ages" of the newspaper game—when to a reporter "getting the story" justified anything short of murder. Incidentally you will see in this picture no resemblance to the men and women of the press today. Ready? Once upon a time . . .

The prologue suggests an attempt to distance its biting criticism of the fourth estate, local politics, and the justice system to a different time and place. Rather than offering a serious contemplation of the feminine-achievement struggle of the heroine, the corruption of city officials and politicians, or the ethics of the pressroom journalists, the film exploits all of the above as fodder for laughs. While comic moments arose in the 1930s from the girl reporter and her beau never making it to the church, crime and corruption were never things to be laughed at. The Depression-era girl reporter cared very much for the well-being of the innocent she tried to defend even if a lesson in ethics was one that she had to learn. Hildy, on the other hand, uses both death-row convict Earl Williams and his girlfriend, Molly Malloy, for information and a scoop. Most telling perhaps is that Molly's suicide is barely even paused over—let alone mourned—in the film. With political corruption and yellow journalism assigned to the past by the film's prologue and played for laughs in the course of the film, *His Girl Friday* abandons the concerns of the Depression-era newspaper film.

The film begins with Hildy's being adamant about quitting the business in the hopes of leading a normal "feminine" life, as an exchange with Walter suggests.

Walter: I know ya, Hildy. I know what quitting would mean to you!

Hildy: What it would mean?

Walter: It would kill ya!

Hildy: [she laughs] You can't sell me that, Walter Burns.

Walter: Who says I can't? You're a newspaperman!

Hildy: That's why I'm quitting. I wanna go someplace where I can be a woman.

Walter: You mean be a traitor!

Hildy: A traitor? A traitor to what?

Walter: A traitor to journalism. You're a journalist, Hildy!

Hildy: A journalist? Now what does that mean? Peeking through keyholes? Chasing after fire engines? Waking people up in the middle of the night to ask them if they think Hitler is going to start another war? Stealing pictures off old ladies?!? I know all about reporters, Walter. A lot of daffy buttinskis running around without a nickel in their pockets and for what? So a million hired girls and motormen's wives'll know what's going on. Why . . . Ah, what's the use? Walter, you . . . you wouldn't know what it means to . . . well, want to be respectable and live a half-way normal life. The point is, I . . . I'm through.

Later, in the pressroom, Hildy gives her rival newspaperman a similar speech as she is on her way out the door to join Bruce.

And, that, my friends, is my farewell to the newspaper game. I'm going to be a woman, not a news-getting machine. I'm going to

have babies and take care of them, and give them cod liver oil and
watch their teeth grow, and . . . and . . . Oh dear! If I ever see one
of them look at a newspaper again, I'll brain them!

However, Earl Williams then escapes from jail and Hildy forgets all about her
promises to Bruce. Her speeches are the very opposite of the sentiments of the
majority of the girl reporters who preceded her: indeed, women like Florence,
Torchy, and all the various Jerry/Gerry/Geri's tended to declare that the business
is in their blood. Of course, *His Girl Friday* suggests that Hildy doth protest
too much and that she too has, like Torchy, "ink in [her] blood and a nose for
news that needs something besides powder." Hildy's struggle, however, is not that
of the Depression-era reporter who was trying to prove herself in a male world
inhospitable to working women; instead, Hildy is an established newspaperman
and respected by her cohorts at the paper and rivals in the courthouse pressroom.
Hildy's sex is *not* an issue in terms of her career, only in terms of what kind of
marriage she will have. She can marry Bruce and retire to Albany for a life of
normalcy or she can re-marry Walter and return to her life as a newspaperman.
Hildy may talk fast but she is not hardboiled and her fast talk, once indicative

Fig. 6.1. All Talk and No Hardboil: Rosalind Russell's *His Girl Friday* (1940) is a wartime
parody of her Depression-era predecessors. Photo from author's collection.

of modern American identity, is played merely for laughs. Indeed, the content of the rapid-fire dialogue of the film was considered by director Hawks to be secondary to its delivery, who allowed Grant to ad lib many of his lines and Russell to have hers rewritten by a writer that she hired on the side.

The film concludes with Hildy back where she began, in a sense—ready to marry Walter but knowing that a breaking story in Albany is more than likely to prevent their honeymooning in Niagara Falls. It is this circularity as much as the humor and stereotyped characters that indicate the parodic decline of the girl reporter film. For example, in *The Corpse Vanishes* (1942), the young and handsome Dr. Foster (Tris Coffin) asks Pat Hunter (Luana Walters) whether she is "one of those hardboiled reporters that we read about or see in the movies." In the same vein, the continual postponement of marriage that in the "Torchy Blane" films was merely a device to keep her single and sleuthing for nine films, became a running joke in the 1940s. In *Mystery Ship* (1941) the couple have tried 12 times to get married and even some of the male-centered detective series, including the "Bulldog Drummond" and "Mr. District Attorney" series, capitalize on the joke.[2] The parody was not just in the overdetermination of specific elements or the repetition of certain gags but also the film's own consciousness of the genre's circularity: both *Mystery Ship* and *Rogues' Gallery* (1944) conclude with a new story breaking and the protagonists turning to one another and saying in unison "Well, here we go again!"

Mystery Ship offered a reuniting of *Torchy Blane in Panama*'s pairing of Lola Lane and Paul Kelly, this time as girl reporter Pat Marshall and Inspector Allan Harper, respectively. It also reunited them in the same setting—a ship at sea. Despite the name of the film, there is no mystery on the ship for the girl reporter to investigate; instead, it is an operation to deport convicts. And, rather than being portrayed as a competent and useful investigator or even assistant, Pat is regarded as an annoyance rather than an asset. Bobbie Logan in the "Mr. Wong" films is portrayed in a very similar way. While Pat and Bobbie are presented as less than competent as crime-fighters, Patsy Clark (Robin Raymond) of *Rogues' Gallery* is presented as more than capable. Although partnered with her paper's photographer, Eddie Porter (Frank Jenks), Patsy is clearly the lead detective: she is far more intelligent and capable than he is, and he is present as comedic, rather than investigative, assistance. Indeed, her competence is noted by the official investigator, Lieutenant O'Day (Bob Homans), who says, "The way that she digs up stuff, she must have a strain of bloodhound in her. [. . .] Anytime she wants to be a cop, I've got a job for her." Similarly, in *Mr. Wong in Chinatown* the police Commissioner tells Bobbie, "If you ever decide to quit the newspaper game, we can use brains like yours." These girl reporters represent the two types of girl reporter that came to dominate the 1940s: Pat and Bobbie are well-meaning but interfering and Patsy is smart and brash; however, all are played for laughs and are some of the most heavy-handed parodies of the girl reporter of the decade.

The girl reporter—as a character type that evoked specific debates and connotations in the 1930s—is, in the 1940s, a signifier detached from its origins in the Depression. In the 1930s, the girl reporter represented the working woman's struggle between her career in a man's world and her life as a woman; in the 1940s, she was an empty stereotype, a comic character that the audience was encouraged to laugh *at* rather than *with*. As Jack D. Grant suggests in his *Hollywood Reporter* review for *Deadline for Murder*, the girl reporter had worn out her welcome by the mid-40s:

> Some parts of the investigation are annoyingly complicated by an interfering newspaper woman. Now this news girl didn't have to be quite so annoying. It is apparent that her role was slanted for comedy, but under the direction of James Tinling, the character goes too far overboard. (17 June 1946)

Decidedly Secondary

When there was detecting to be done in the 1940s, it was done by men. With World War II, Hollywood realigned detective work with male knowledge. For example, in *Mildred Pierce* (Curtiz, 1945), Inspector Petersen (Moroni Olsen) explains to Mildred (Joan Crawford), "You know, Mrs. Beragon, being a detective's like . . . well, like making an automobile. You just take all the pieces and put them together, one by one . . . First thing you know, you have an automobile . . . or a murderer!" In the detective films of the 1940s, the female detective was replaced by a male investigator and the only roles open to women were at the sidelines. Indeed in the "Mr. Wong" films, *The Saint's Vacation* (1941), *The Falcon Takes Over* (1942), *Boss of Big Town* (1942), *Midnight Manhunt* (1945), and the "Big Town" films, the girl reporter takes a backseat to the male detective in terms of investigating the mystery and the romance is most often downplayed, with few kisses or marriage proposals.

For example, in *Emergency Squad* (Dmytryk, 1940), Betty Bryant (Louise Campbell) is a recent journalism graduate looking for a job on a paper. An editor tells her that, if she can find a story worthy of the front page, then she can have a job. She ends up writing a story about the brave policemen of the "emergency squad," and it is at this point that the film focuses more on the heroism of the male police as heroes than the goals of its girl reporter. Indeed, the film foreshadows the postwar police procedural—such as *The House on 92nd Street* (Hathaway, 1945), *Call Northside 777* (Hathaway, 1948), and *The Naked City* (Dassin, 1948)—with its detailing of police procedures and its uniform praise for the police force. In *The Bride Wore Crutches* (1941), Midge Lambert (Lynne Roberts) is described as "about the best newspaper woman in town" but her role in the film is to train cub John "Dizzy" Dixon (Ted North) to be a newspaperman rather than investigating the mystery alongside him. Her reward, as it were, is for Johnny accidently to shoot her in the leg (thus explaining the title of the film when the film concludes with their wedding). Florence Rice, who played Ruth in *Women are Trouble* (Taggart, 1936), appears twice in the early 1940s as the girl reporter, including as Terry Parker in *Mr. District Attorney* (1941).[3] Terry is smart, determined, and successful as a reporter, however, the film's focus in on the career of "socialite lawyer" (Dennis O'Keefe), attempting to prove himself worthy of the position his uncle attained for him at the D.A.'s office. Rice also features in *The Boss of Big Town* (1942)—not to be confused with the later "Big Town" series. Linda Gregory (Rice), as is typical of the girl reporter in the 1940s, is never seen at her paper or talking to her editor. Her position on the paper is not established, and the only "writing" of hers seen is her final stories in the headlines.

Although June Clyde played one of the gutsy girl reporters of the early 1930s—Nosey Toodles in *Strange Adventure* (Del Ruth and Whitman, 1932)—in the 1940s, her "newspaperman" Lois Grant of *Sealed Lips* (1942) is decidedly different. The publicity material for the film issued by John Joseph, describes Lois as a role model,

> . . . who proves that brains and beauty can be contained in one package; that blonde hair doesn't necessarily mean an absence of grey matter; that a saucy nose also be a nose for news. In other words, she's a crackerjack newspaperwoman. On the trail of a big story she lands her man. (3 May 1941)

Despite this ringing endorsement, Lois does not investigate herself and instead, she asks that California Bureau of Investigation agent, Lee Davis (William Gargan), give her the scoop when he has wrapped up his case. For a character that was known for speaking up, out, and often in the 1930s, here the girl reporter is suspiciously quiet. For example, when the authorities arrive to free Lee from capture and arrest the gangsters, it is Lee's valet (Ralf Harolde) who speaks on Lois's behalf. Similarly, in the final scene, Lois is about to call in the scoop to her publisher, but Lee begs her not to unless she wants "the man you're going to marry to lose his job." She drops the phone and kisses him instead.

And this pattern continued into the late 1940s with girl reporters playing second fiddle to more competent male reporters and investigating to a lesser and lesser degree. In *Criminals Within* (1943), girl reporter Linda (Ann Doran) assists Corporal Greg Carroll (Eric Linden) identify and capture a ring of saboteurs operating on an army base. She is proven not only a competent sleuth but also a brave crime-fighter: when trapped in a steam room set to kill her, Linda does not wait to be rescued but smashes a window with a chair to escape. What detracts from Linda's agency as a detective is that she is introduced halfway through the film and as Greg's assistant. In *Traffic in Crime* (1946), Sam Wire (Kane Richmond) is the main focus of the story while reporter Ann Marlowe

(Anne Nagel) is there merely to inspire Sam as a potential love interest and is not even shown chasing a story. The "Big Town" series—*Big Town* (1947), *I Cover Big Town* (1947), *Big Town after Dark* (1947), and *Big Town Scandal* (1948)—all feature girl reporter, Lorelei Kilbourne (Hillary Brooke); however, she does not complete much sleuthing or writing in the series in comparison to her editor and boyfriend, Steve Wilson (Philip Reed). In *Behind Locked Doors* (1948), reporter Kathy Lawrence (Lucy Bremer), has uncovered the fact that a criminal is hiding out from the police in a sanitarium; however, it is the private detective, Ross Stewart (Richard Carlson), who does the majority of the investigating by going undercover.

While many girl reporters of the 1930s promised their men that they would marry and give up their careers, many of them—including Frances in *Headline Shooter*, Maddy in *The Daring Young Man*, Torchy in *Fly Away Baby* and *The Adventurous Blonde*—ended their films by abandoning their men to chase another story. Indeed, in the 1940s, the girl reporter—like Lois in *Sealed Lips* and Kathy in *Behind Locked Doors*—does not even get to call in the big story (supplied to her by the male detective) because the male detective silences her with a kiss. The 1940s girl reporter did not seem to mind being pushed to the background of interesting stories, and seemed all too happy to give up her career as a newspaperman for domestic bliss.

Desiring Domesticity

A handful of girl reporters did occupy stronger and more central roles in 1940s films as investigators but, when they did, they were typically recouped and returned to a subordinate role by the end of the film by exchanging their job as reporter and detective for that of wife to a reporter or detective. Returning to the themes of the earliest films featuring girl reporters (1929–32), these 1940s films suggest that these women pursue reporting only to occupy them and pay the bills until the right man comes along. Interestingly, although being a girl reporter did not equip her with the skills of a housewife, the male detective desired her anyway, as this exchange from *The Boss of Big Town* implies.

Michael: You heard what she said. She won't marry me.

Linda: I will.

Michael: Can you cook?

Linda: Nope.

Michael: Can you wash?

Linda: Hate it.

Michael: Well, what can you do?

Linda: Love you.

Michael: You'll do.

While Linda may not be that domestically inclined, in the 1940s more girl reporters were shown at home and completing domestic tasks. While it was unusual to even see the 1930s girl reporter in her place of residence because she was always at the paper, in *The Bride Wore Crutches*, we see Midge vacuuming her living room in her bathrobe and offering to make Johnny lunch in her kitchen. The 1940s girl reporter was driven out of the office and into the home.

In *Double Alibi* (1941), Sue Carey (Margaret Lindsay) is a sob sister working on the "guide to health" column but she wants a chance at working on the murder story. Her editor (William Gargan) turns down her request saying, "Look, Sue, this is a man's work." She is well aware that her sex denies her many opportunities and complains, "Just because I'm a girl I never get a break." Similarly, at a crime scene, Sue is refused access as the police officer explains, because "[a] young girl like you shouldn't be worrying your head about a career. You should be home bringing up babies." When her editor subsequently proposes, Sue protests, "I don't want to be domestic, Giff. I want to be a newspaperman!" Sue is one of the few strong reporter-detectives of the 1940s as she investigates a mystery alongside the murder victim's ex-husband, Stephen Wayne (Wayne Morris), in order to clear his name. In the end, they prove him innocent and Sue gets the story; however, when she calls in to her editor, she says, "Remember when you said I would never make a newspaperman? Well, you were right!" Instead of giving him the scoop, Sue puts the phone down and kisses Stephen. Even though *Double Alibi* is one of the few films of the 1940s that offers a competent girl reporter-detective, it differs from its 1930s predecessors in that Sue puts romance ahead of the story.

In *I Killed that Man* (1941), assistant District Attorney, Roger Phillips (Ricardo Cortez), relies on his reporter girlfriend, Geri Reynolds (Joan Woodbury), to investigate because she has had more success in the past than the D.A.'s office. She chases many leads and does a good job of recognizing the significance of certain facts and clues; however, she makes a mistake when she confronts Lowell King for information, unaware that he is the real villain. Roger comes to her rescue and bursts into King's place without backup; interestingly, however, Geri has to save him right back and strikes King with a vase to prevent him from shooting Roger. Geri is seldom shown at the paper or writing her stories but she is a good investigator and, even if her boyfriend has to rescue her from the villain, she is brave and quick-thinking enough to save him too. However, while in the girl reporter films of the 1930s, it is the man who convinces the jaded heroine to give love a try and marry him; in *I Killed that Man*, it is Geri who continually pressures Roger to marry her. And, after she saves his life, Roger agrees to marry Geri.

In *The Corpse Came C.O.D.* (1947), *The Daily Register*'s "sob sister" Rosemary Durant (Joan Blondell) is a competent investigator but she does not appear in the first third of the film. Instead the film focuses on her rival Joe Medford (George Brent) and his infatuation with the glamorous movie star Mona Harrison to whom a corpse is delivered. Rosemary is well aware that she is not as feminine as other women when she sees Joe flirting with the studio receptionist. She asks, "What have I got that makes men avoid me so eagerly?" It would seem that it is masculinity as Joe calls her "butch" later in the film. Rosemary is physically capable: when Joe manages to lock her in a closet to get her out of the way, she bashes her way out. She then steals the photo plates from his photographer, forcing Joe to chase and then tackle her. And it is her femininity that proves Rosemary's weakness: Joe steals the plates back by distracting her with a kiss. In the end, they decide to work as a team to solve the mystery together and Joe proposes to her. Rosemary excitedly explains that the bonuses they received from their respective papers for their stories will buy them a home in the San Fernando Valley. Whereas it was the girl reporter's masculine behavior and ambitious drive that attracted male adoration in the 1930s, by the 1940s, she must rediscover her femininity and domestic drive to have a "happy ending."

Girl Reporters Gone Bad

As a review in the *Motion Picture Herald* for *Follow Me Quietly* suggests, the girl reporter "in the accepted fashion tries to trail the killer and succeeds only in getting in the way of the detective" (16 July 1949). Varying from incompetent to downright lethal, the girl reporter was developing a bad reputation in the 1940s. In *City of Missing Girls* (1941), Astrid Allwyn (who played Phoebe Lane in *International Crime* [1938]) is girl reporter Nora Page but gets second billing behind H. B. Warner (who plays police detective Captain McVeigh), and the film is more concerned with the career of her love interest—assistant D.A. Jimmy Horner (John Archer). Nora's stories may be on the mark but they make Jimmy look like a fool when she scoops him. McVeigh tells Nora "a story" about a girl and a boy who were brought together by the city. He says, "The girl interfered with his success at every turn. [. . .] She was just an ambitious little . . . newspaper reporter. She never stopped to think of the harm that she might be doing." What McVeigh's talk insinuates—and convinces Nora and the audience—is that she is more a menace than assistance to the real (read: male) crime-fighting hero.

Although occasionally the Depression-era girl reporter had found herself needing to be rescued from the criminals, in the 1940s, trusting the wrong man became a common theme in both the girl reporter film and *noir* films with female detectives. Indeed, this theme would be resurrected in the erotic thrillers of the 1980s (as I will explore in a later chapter). Poor judgment in men, it would seem, was the shortcoming of the female detective and an increasingly significant problem by the 1940s. And, while the 1930s girl reporter demonstrated strength of character, bravery, and clear thinking when faced with the enemy, her wartime counterpart was often reduced to stereotypically feminine behavior including screaming and fainting. *Man at Large* (1941) sees its girl reporter, "Dallas" Gilmartin (Marjorie Weaver) determined and clever enough to figure out that a man is a Nazi agent; however, she is ultimately proven incompetent by misunderstanding the situation and giving information to the enemy. Although nicknamed by undercover FBI agent, Bob Grayson (George Reeves) as "Dallas" after her hometown, she is nothing like "Tex" (Claire Trevor), in *One Mile from Heaven* (Dwan, 1937). World War II sees the girl reporter leaving the city to chase scoops on international spy rings, but it is her male rival who solves the case and exposes the ring while Dallas is relegated to the role of a screaming, hysterical female who leaps into his arms out of fear at the end of the film. In *The Corpse Vanishes* (1942), Pat (Walters) sounds hardboiled when a bride dies at the wedding she is covering and she cries out excitedly, "It's sensational! Another kidnapping of a dead bride. What a story!" However, at the ominous mansion of Dr. Lorenz (Bela Lugosi), she misses the final showdown with the villain because she screams and faints at the critical moment. Her editor is impressed with the scoop and Pat is rewarded professionally with her own byline and, atypically for a 1940s heroine, turns down young Dr. Foster's proposal.

While some girl reporters are reduced to hysterical females or interfering annoyances in the 1940s, in *noir* films like *Blonde Ice* (Bernhard, 1948), she is portrayed as downright lethal to the male. Claire Cummings (Leslie Brooks) is a society reporter who marries a rich businessman and quits the reporting racket. At her wedding, she flirts with her male colleague with whom she had had a romance and tells sports writer Les Burns (Robert Paige) that she is really in love with him. She proceeds to kill her husband on her honeymoon and uses Les to help establish an alibi. She then returns to work on the paper after deciding that she cannot survive on widow's compensation, but soon realizes that pursuing another rich man would be more rewarding than pursuing a story. Eventually the truth comes out about her crimes and a doctor psychoanalyzes her. He explains that her need for attention and wealth is the result of her childhood, growing up with a mother who had to work because her father left with another woman. Films like *Blonde Ice* in the late 1940s suggest that women who work are dangerous—not only to the men they hunt, but also to their offspring. Claire is shot in a struggle over a gun and a cop makes the most damning comment of all—and one never heard in the 1930s—"She wasn't even a good newspaperwoman."

CASE STUDIES

The attitude in the 1940s toward independent, working women was no more apparent than in the alterations that Glenda Farrell's roles—and the characters that she had played in the 1930s—underwent. Farrell herself was recast as the "new" kind of girl reporter in *A Night for Crime* (1943) as were her 1930s characters Torchy Blane in *Torchy Blane . . . Playing with Dynamite* (Smith, 1939) and *Private Detective* (Smith, 1939), and Gerry Krale in *You Can't Escape Forever* (1942) and *The House across the Street* (1949).

From Torchy to Susan

A Night for Crime demonstrates what happened to the girl reporter character that Glenda Farrell had helped establish in *Mystery of the Wax Museum* (Curtiz, 1933) and *Hi, Nellie!* (LeRoy, 1934) and exemplified in the "Torchy Blane" films. In *A Night for Crime*, Farrell plays girl reporter Susan Cooper whose boyfriend, film publicity director Joe Powell (Lyle Talbot), has been trying to marry her for seven years. When a murder is committed in the apartment next door, Detective Hoffman (Ralph Sanford) accuses Susan and Joe of the crime. Susan investigates the murder of her neighbor and the subsequent disappearance of the movie star, Mona; however, she is not a strong character or significant investigator until about halfway through the film. Although at one point she nearly becomes the victim of the killer who attempts to strangle her, Susan does prove herself an able sleuth when she recognizes the location in the film footage of Mona that they are watching and they find the killer. At the end of the film, Joe has given up on the idea of Susan ever marrying him and enlists in the army. Susan suddenly changes her mind because, as she explains, she is "crazy about a man in uniform." *A Night for Crime* demonstrated that the star who had helped to define the trend in 1933 and then dominated it between 1937 and 1939 was not immune to the changing trends: Susan is shown in her apartment and never at work on the paper; the male detective dominates the investigation for the first half of the film; and Susan is desirous of marriage at the end of the film.

From Torchy to Torch Singer

While Torchy Blane is most closely associated with Glenda Farrell, in the last film in the series—*Torchy Blane . . . Playing with Dynamite*—Torchy is transformed into a different kind of woman, as embodied by Jane Wyman. Elizabeth Dalton suggests that Wyman had "evidently watched Glenda Farrell very carefully. She mimics Glenda's style right down to the fingertips. She even manages to capture the tilt of Glenda's head and the way she charges out of a room—but still, that extra something is missing" ("Meet," 41). Even the pressbook for the film notes that Torchy has changed and places emphasis on her new look; the advertising notes her "chicness" and how her suits may be tailored but are softened with touches like hand-stitching. The most telling shift in her representation, however, is one poster that seemed shockingly different from the ones used for Farrell's Torchy: Wyman is shown in high heels and a silk robe falling off her shoulder with the title "Danger!" Compared to the posters for the previous "Torchy" films, this looks like it is advertising a *film noir* with a *femme fatale*. This promise of a sultry heroine is not fulfilled in the film as Wyman's Torchy sticks to the tailored suit rather than sporting the slinky robe of the poster. By 1939, however—whether because of the shift is social attitudes towards women or change in star from hardboiled Farrell to softboiled Wyman—Torchy became more feminine. Interestingly, *Playing with Dynamite* does not see Wyman's Torchy hunt for clues, chase up leads, or produce theories on a criminal mystery as Farrell's always did; instead her Torchy is more of a crime-fighter figure as she goes undercover in a prison to expose a group of bank robbers. The emphasis is less on sleuthing and more on successfully masquerading as a criminal. And, for Torchy's "final" film—*Private Detective*—the heroine leaves newspapering altogether.

Originally written as the next Torchy film, *Private Detective* saw Wyman—and Torchy—recast as Myrna "Jinx" Winslow.[4] By the 1940s, the female detective seemed to forget that she had once enjoyed "a lust of investigation" and, instead, regarded her career—whether as full- or part-time sleuth—as a necessity until a man came along. A reviewer for *Variety* stated that the reason for the end of the Torchy series, according to producer Bryan Foy, was because of "difficulty in finding material to maintain it on a level with its initialer, so he's switched his heroine from a crime-probing newspaperwoman to a private detective" (30 Nov 1939). However, *Private Detective* might as well be a "Torchy" film and the similarities were certainly not lost on those familiar with the series. As another reviewer for *Variety* stated, "Warners put the 'Torchy Blane' series into the garage for an overhauling and repaint job. 'Private Detective' has a new finish, but underneath it is plainly the 'Torchy' formula, with wider cruising range apparent than was the case in the girl reporter series" (6 Dec 1939). As Doris Arden in her review for *The Chicago Times* states,

> Torchy Blane and Myrna Winslow [. . .] are sisters under the skin. Jane Wyman, who stepped into the Torchy role after Glenda Farrell resigned from it, appears here as Jinx, and the roles are so much alike they're practically duplicates. Both heroines, in case you want evidence, are nosey, pert and vivacious young women; both of them are forever on the verge of marrying a policeman boy friend

and forever changing their minds, and both go poking into police business, stirring up confusion and excitement and uncovering clues like mad. The one point of distinction as far as the script writers are concerned, is Miss Blane is a reporter and Miss Winslow is a private detective. (22)

Nevertheless, I would argue that the character *is* different—not so much perhaps from Wyman's Torchy but certainly from Farrell's. A poster describes Jinx as the "sweetest sleuth" and the "cutest clue-chaser," terms that were the antithesis of Farrell's girl reporter. The pressbook for *Smart Blonde* (McDonald, 1937), describes Farrell's Torchy as outspoken, strong-willed, and tough: "Softly like a herd of elephants . . . Torchy Blane will tip-toe to your heart! Take equal parts bloodhound, wrecking crew, encyclopedia, perpetual motion . . . and you've got Torchy Blane, America's best-loved . . . Smart Blonde." Also the replacement of Farrell with Wyman saw a shift in terms of her relationship with her fiancé. Torchy and Steve's marriage was postponed by the announcement of new mysteries to investigate but Farrell's ink in her veins made it seem unlikely that Farrell's Torchy would give up reporting when married; however, at the end of *Private Detective*, Jinx says that she has had enough detecting and would rather be married.

The last Torchy-related transformation of the 1940s occurs with *A Shot in the Dark* (McGann, 1941). Frederick Nebel's story "No Hard Feelings," which had been the basis for Torchy's first outing in *Smart Blonde*, was used again as the basis for *A Shot in the Dark*. The film, however, turns the girl reporter back into a male newspaperman and Torchy's female equivalent in the film is literally a "torch singer" at a club. These transformations of both the character of Torchy Blane and the star, who most memorably embodied her, demonstrate the alterations that the girl reporter film underwent in the changing cultural climate of wartime.

From Nellie to Dolly

Roy Chanslor wrote the story on which *Hi, Nellie!* (1934), *Love is on the Air* (Grinde 1937), *You Can't Escape Forever* (1942), and *The House across the Street* (1949) were all based. In *Hi Nellie!* Farrell had played Gerry Krale as a hardboiled heroine in the vein of Farrell's other girl reporters, Florence and Torchy; however, Gerry's incarnation in *You Can't Escape Forever*—Laurie Abbott (Brenda Marshall)—is much less empowered. The film nods to the accomplishments of women in male spheres of work: Meeker (Dick Elliott) exclaims, "What an age we live in! My wife builds battleships and I write a lovelorn column." But the film does not value female independence and sees Chanslor's girl reporter transformed from gutsy to girlie. The film begins with Laurie trying to be tough by going to an execution but, once there, she faints.

Rather than admit her failure, she reports the wrong story, assuming that the execution went ahead when it was actually stayed, and receives a demotion to the lovelorn column. The film suggests, on the one hand, that women are not competent enough to do a man's job because of "female" weaknesses (i.e., fainting), and, on the other, that men have a "natural" flair at the job. Steve "Mitch" Mitchell (George Brent) gets an itchy ear every time he has a hunch and, in the case of the Varney execution, his hunch is correct: Varney is given an eleventh-hour pardon. After three days on the job, it is evident that Laurie is not a good "newspaperman," and Mitch tells her that she will have to quit the business and marry him. In the end, she agrees to but insists, "I'm not giving up my career. I'm not going to stay home and take care of any kiddies." Steve's ear begins to itch, however, and the audience knows that motherhood and domesticity are Laurie's future rather than a career.

The House across the Street offers a similar 1940s style girl reporter. A witness for a federal case is murdered and Dave Joslin (Wayne Morris) of *The Star Chronicle* writes a hard-hitting story about it. Lovelorn columnist Kit Williams (Janis Paige) begs Dave, her sweetheart, for another chance at a front-page story even though she "muffed" the last chance. She exclaims that if she has to do one more month of being "Dolly Trent" (this film's name for "Nellie"), she will become "a gibbering idiot." When he says quit the job and marry him instead, she says that she would still end up a gibbering idiot. Dave is demoted by his editor to the lovelorn column after he writes and prints a story against local racketeer Keever (Bruce Bennett). When Dave gets a new lead for the case against Keever, Kit reads his notes and begins to investigate it herself. She proves to be a more skilled and successful detective: she extracts important information from a witness (a girl) and later figures out its significance; she also knows they are being watched and plants her purse on a suspect in order to arrest him. Interestingly, this initial burst of investigative interest in the case is short-lived and Dave ends up completing the investigation while Kit complains that all she wants to do is go home to bed. With his investigation leading to Keever's arrest, Dave is promoted to Managing Editor, which leaves the lovelorn editor position free. Dave gives Kit two choices—to be "Dolly Trent" or "Mrs. Dave Joslin." She chooses the latter. While *Hi, Nellie!* concluded with Farrell's girl reporter remaining single and pursuing her career, both the 1940s versions end—as did the majority of girl reporter films in the 1940s—with her choosing matrimony over reporting.

Part II: Still Detecting

Female detectives who were not reporters were fewer in number in the 1940s compared to the 1930s—especially in terms of series characters. Although the themes of these films differed from the focus on the marriage vs. career of the girl reporter film, the professional and amateur detectives underwent a transformation by 1940 that echoed that of their reporting counterpart. Like the girl reporter, female undercover police detectives and amateur sleuths became increasingly secondary, minor, or absent—and often a parody of her former self. Instead of femininity being a disguise utilized by the female detective for undercover work as it was in the 1930s, it became her predominant characteristic, melded in an uncomfortable—and usually unsuccessful—marriage with the strength of character and drive that were necessary to engage in crime-fighting and criminal investigation. And it is because of this uncomfortable marriage that the element of parody becomes predominant: the female detective became an impossibility—or a fantasy—being simultaneously hardboiled, brave, and independent as a crime-fighter and yet hysterical, glamorous, and desirous of a man to rescue her when the case gets too tough. And whereas the amateur detective (who investigated as a hobby) was allowed greater success and agency in the 1930s than the professional detectives (who investigated for a living), in the 1940s the female detective became two conflicting character types rolled into one—and her status as a professional or an amateur made little difference.

The Professionals

A couple of films featured female private investigators, including *Private Detective* (1939) with Jane Wyman, *The Undercover Woman* (Carr, 1946) with Stephanie Bachelor, and *Exposed* (Blair, 1947) with Adele Mara.[5] As I noted in the last section, *Private Detective* was originally intended to be the next in the "Torchy" series but instead sees Wyman's heroine renamed "Jinx," recast from a girl reporter to a private detective, offered a new male rival/fiancé Lieutenant Jim Rickey (Dick Foran), and reporting to her Nationwide Detective agency boss, Simmy Sanger (Selmar Jackson), instead of a newspaper editor. The film begins with Jinx quitting her job at the Nationwide Detective Agency and informing Jim that, after five years' postponement, she is ready to marry him. A case, however, distracts them when Millard Lannon is shot and his ex-wife and her new fiancé are suspected. Jinx does put together all the clues and figures out who is responsible for Lannon's murder; moreover, it is evident that without her sleuthing the official detectives would not have identified the killer. Nevertheless, after being knocked unconscious, kidnapped, and left to die by carbon monoxide poisoning, Jinx confesses to Jim, "I don't want to be a detective anymore. Is it too late to get married?" It would seem that as the new decade dawned (*Private Detective* was released in December 1939) that the female detective was not as tough as she had been and was no longer determined to pursue her career at the expense of being married.

Although rare in the 1930s, women as police detectives became a popular trope in the 1940s. In *Girl in 313* (Cortez, 1940), Joan Matthews (Florence Rice) is a jewelry expert working undercover for the police (rather than a police detective) in order to infiltrate a suspected gang of thieves. Her real identity is hidden until halfway through the film for the audience and until the end to the thieves—including Gregg Dunn (Kent Taylor) with whom Joan falls in love. Gregg is killed in his attempt to escape the police and Joan is upset; she abandons detecting and runs away to Mexico. On the train heading south, she orders a double martini (as she used to do with Gregg) and looks forlornly out the window as she commences her travels (as she once planned to do with Gregg). Although she does not get married, she does abandon her career because of a broken heart.

More typical, as the decade wore on, was the police trainee or recent graduate of the police academy working undercover, for example in *Undercover Maisie* (Beaumont, 1947) with Ann Sothern, *Mary Ryan, Detective* (Berlin, 1950) with Marsha Hunt, *Women from Headquarters* (Blair, 1950) with Virginia Huston, and *Undercover Girl* (Pevney, 1950) with Alexis Smith. *Undercover Maisie* is an interesting conclusion to the "Maisie" series of ten films (1939–47).[6] Much of

Fig. 6.2. Undercover Agent: Florence Rice abandons her career as an undercover agent when the thief she loves is killed in *Girl in 313* (1940). Photo from author's collection.

the humor of the series is the result of the dissonance between the heroine's feminine looks and her outspokenness and often cluelessness. Brooklyn showgirl Maisie Ravier (Ann Sothern) found herself in a different outrageous situation in each film—from being stranded in an African village to joining a circus to being an undercover police agent. *Undercover Maisie* begins with Maisie trying to make her way to New York City for a job; however, when a woman cons her out of all her money, jewels, and clothes, Maisie finds herself back in L.A. at the police station. Lieutenant Paul Scott (Barry Nelson) is impressed with her observation skills:

> Paul: Miss Ravier, have you ever had special training in observation?
>
> Maisie: Well, I just observed I got robbed, didn't I?
>
> Paul: The description of the suspect. Brief, clear, all the pertinent details, the best I ever heard. In fact, so good I've decided that you must have had special training along those lines.

Paul convinces the police chief to take Maisie on as a policewoman to work "bunko," investigating confidence rackets. Because she proves too "distracting" in the academy for the male trainees, Maisie is put into private training, then attracts the romantic interests of both her tutor and Paul.

Although her feminine appearance is disarming and a great cover for an undercover policewoman, her first case does not go well when she accidentally reveals her identity as a detective and is kidnapped by the racketeers. She does eventually prove to be physically capable, proactive, and intelligent: for example, when kidnapped by con artists who intend to kill her, Maisie sends messages written in lipstick (a specifically female innovation) on her dinner plates so that the dishwasher will see them and hopefully inform the police of her whereabouts. And when her kidnappers take her to the countryside to shoot her, she uses her judo skills, learned at the police academy, to keep them at bay. Her combination of feminine looks with intelligence and physical abilities attract the attentions of Paul. She agrees to marry him and, with surprising frankness, Paul refers to her judo moves when he says, "Oh, Maisie, what a wonderful honeymoon we're gonna have!"

MGM's publicity slip entitled "Heroine of 'Maisie' Reconverts" suggests that Maisie is different in this last installment:

> The familiar and popular screen character has come out of a post-war reconversion program with a brand new personality, a stylish new wardrobe, a new hair-do and a new job. [. . .] For her role

as a policewoman, Ann Sothern is making several changes in the
character of Maisie. She's far more serious minded, for one thing.
For another, she deserts her customary frilly wardrobe for the tailored
suits of a policewoman, in much of the picture. (1 Nov 1946)

Despite Maisie's seemingly positive embodiment of masculine and feminine qualities and being an official investigator as an undercover police officer, however,
there is a sense of incredulity and a lack of seriousness to her representation.
As in the other films of the series, the pleasure is to see bubbly Maisie thrown
into impossible situations. It is hard to believe that pretty, petite Maisie could
be an expert at judo and, with such little training, single-handedly defeat two
opponents, especially with one armed with a gun. However, with her appearance being in a period where there are few strong women, comical Maisie is
somewhat of a delight.

In *Undercover Girl* (1950), Chris Miller (Alexis Smith) is a rookie just
finishing up her training at the police academy when her father is killed in
the line of duty. As she explains to her boyfriend, Jess (Richard Egan), Chris
feels guilty that her father went into debt to pay for her education, and she is
pursuing a career in order to repay him. In fact, his need for money pushed
her father to turn dirty at the end of his career. Jess thinks that Chris should
settle down and comments sarcastically on the fact that the jujitsu she is learning at the academy will "come in handy when keeping house," but Chris insists
emphatically, "I'm not giving up my uniform for an apron." Her sex may seem
incompatible with her career to Jess, but Lieutenant Mike Trent (Scott Brady)
sees it as an asset for infiltrating the narcotics gang. Part of her successful infiltration is Chris's subsuming of her own identity to that of her criminal alter
ego "Sal Willis." While at the academy, Chris sported the more gender-neutral
garb of shorts, T-shirt, and runners; conversely, to pass for a moll from Chicago,
Chris wears more feminine and sultry outfits. In order to maintain her cover,
she has to break up with Jess and, to disguise her true feelings, she dons her
tough, gang moll persona of "Sal." At first, Chris struggles to deal with the
dirty world of organized crime, but later finds herself struggling to retain her
moral center when she has the opportunity to kill the man responsible for her
father's death. She holds the gun to his head, but Mike arrives just in time to
convince her that she is a better person if she arrests the villain rather than
kill him. The film concludes with their kiss and little sense of Chris's pursuing
her career as a police woman.

The Amateurs

By the 1940s, the "old manor" type of detective story seemed decidedly out-
dated and there were far fewer amateur sleuths than in the decade previous.
However, Mary Roberts Rinehart's Nurse Adams appeared in a remake of *Miss*

Pinkerton (Bacon, 1932). *The Nurse's Secret* (Smith, 1941) is a carbon copy of the original's plot—except for one important detail. Whereas Joan Blondell's Adams had attempted to flee from George Brent's proposal, in the remake, Nurse Ruth Adams (Lee Patrick) accepts that of Regis Toomey. Interestingly, the attempt to return Nurse Adams to the screen nine years after her first outing with little alteration is precisely what is problematic about the film. When Inspector Patten (Toomey) needs a nurse to take up residence at the Mitchell manor, he explains that, "Well, now, it can't be just any girl, Doctor. She's got to be able to use her head and have a lot of nerve too." Ruth does have a brain and nerve but she is more reserved, stern, and experienced than Blondell's brash nurse of a decade earlier. Although not as much a wisecracker, Ruth does, however, inherit many of the original script's witticisms. While Blondell's 20-something nurse screamed and became flustered out of inexperience, the same behavior in Patrick's nurse seems out of character for a 40-year-old. And it is because of this characterization of the female detective and other elements adopted wholesale from the original film that make this 1941 version feel uneven and dated. The 1940s witnessed two trends: female detectives in dark *films noirs* or female detectives as sidekicks to male love interests in mystery-comedies. In this light, *The Nurse's Secret* seems to lack currency and the only element that betrays its contemporaneousness is the male detective's treatment of the female detective. Just as Lance O'Leary suggested in *Mystery House* (Smith, 1938) to Nurse Sarah Keate, so too does Tom tell Ruth, "So stop worrying your pretty little head and get a good night's sleep."

Not only did the 1940s amateur detective give up on her career, but also she was far fewer in number—especially in series. As Michael Pitts suggests, "By the mid-1940s the popularity of female detectives had ebbed following the 1930s series. [. . .] Kitty O'Day was the only female detective with a sustained series, and she lasted for only three entries" (*II*, 247).[7] In *Detective Kitty O'Day* (Beaudine, 1944), Kitty is a secretary who likes to read detective magazines and listen in on her boss's telephone conversations. Her boyfriend, Johnny Jones (Peter Cookson), resents the extra hours Kitty has to work for Mr. Wentworth—especially, when that work is at his suburban mansion. Kitty is an interesting character: she behaves in a stereotypically feminine fashion sometimes—for example, she screams and faints when she discovers the body of her employer hanging in his bathroom—but then is brave and self confident at other moments—for example, she listens at the door to hear what Chief Clancy (Tim Ryan) has to say about the case and makes no attempt to pretend she was doing anything else when caught doing so. From the start, Kitty interferes with the Inspector's investigation: she tells the butler to go back to his duties when the Inspector has told him to stay where he is; she interrupts and takes over the interrogation of the suspects, leaving the Inspector to say exasperatedly, "Will you please let me ask the questions?"; and she pokes fun at the police's efforts on the case and forces Johnny to investigate alongside her to uncover the truth. In the climax of the film, the villains threaten to torture Johnny and, at first, Kitty screams—but then she helps fight back and gets in a couple of good blows using her purse as a weapon. Kitty and Johnny are saved by the arrival of the Inspector, but they have won his respect by solving the case.

In the sequel, *The Adventures of Kitty O'Day* (Beaudine, 1944), Johnny and Kitty (having lost their jobs when their boss was killed in the last film) now work in the Townley Hotel: Kitty at the telephone switchboard and Johnny at the travel desk. Kitty still listens in on people's conversations and, this time, overhears the owner of the hotel being shot. Again in this film, Kitty demonstrates bravado as she fights back when the villain attempts to silence her permanently, but then she faints when the police come to her rescue. In the final scene, Chief Clancy (Ryan again) attempts to relate the whole story to the room of suspects, but Kitty—as usual—steals his thunder. Despite the fact that Kitty figures out the identity of the villains and that Johnny calls her "Miss Sherlock Holmes," it is worth noting that it takes her a while to arrive at the correct conclusion and, in the meantime, she accuses every other suspect of the crime. The film ends with Kitty promising to give up sleuthing; however, when the Chief announces a new murder case, Kitty gets excited. Kitty is not necessarily a great detective but, unlike her professional counterparts in the mid-40s, Kitty shows no sign of giving up her "hobby" to marry her beau.

The third film of the series, *Fashion Model* (Beaudine, 1945), saw Marjorie Weaver replace Jean Parker as the heroine and her name change from Kitty O'Day to Peggy Rooney.[8] I was unable to find a copy of the film but, according to the script, the heroine is working as a model when one of her colleagues is murdered, and she ends up investigating the case. Like her previous incarnations, the female sleuth is proactive and smart, but she also confides her suspicions to the real killer and finds herself in need of rescuing. Unfortunately, one must assume that the second film did not do well since the third saw alterations to the cast and that a fourth was not produced. Unlike those of her 1930s counterparts—Kitty's series is cancelled after only a couple of installments and is the only female detective series of the decade. Despite the presence of her boyfriend in each film, Kitty does not struggle with the femininity-achievement debates that her 1930s counterparts did since she is not planning to get married nor pursue a career as a detective. As a police detective says in the second film, "You know, you'd make a pretty good detective. Well . . . pretty anyway." Chief Clancy then chimes in, "Miss O'Day, for my sake, please don't take up detective work seriously." And it would appear that she honored his wishes.

Part III: Absent from the 1950s

The female detective—whether amateur sleuth, professional detective, or girl reporter—was all but absent from the screen in the 1950s (the few examples will be discussed in the following chapter on *noir*). I wanted to conclude this chapter with an example of what did become of the gutsy girl reporter in the decade defined by the "feminine mystique" as Betty Friedan terms it. The drive to push women back into the home and into nurturing nurses for returning soldiers had begun during the war but was dramatically intensified by the end of the decade. The image of woman as domestic goddess was so pervasive in popular culture in the 1950s that it became perceived as natural and any women who defied the stereotype in film were punished—including the girl reporter.

In *Crime of Passion* (Oswald, 1957), Kathy Ferguson (Barbara Stanwyck) is a sob sister popular with her readers for supplying them with, as her editor suggests, "a regular dose of Ferguson schmaltz." Her editor does not respect her work and, when she explains that she cannot go chasing after a new story because she has not finished her next day's column, her editor says they can reprint some "cornball" from last month and no one will notice. Nor do the police respect her when her editor sends her down to the department press-room to get the woman's angle on a story. Captain Alidos (Royal Dano) tells the reporters in the pressroom to stop pestering the police for a story and let them do their job first. Kathy retorts, "Just a minute, you have your work to do, we have ours!" He shoots back, "Your work should be raising a family, having dinner ready for your husband when he gets home." When she locates a wanted woman by writing an open letter plea in her column, Kathy earns the respect of Alidos's partner, Lieutenant Bill Doyle (Sterling Hayden): they go out for dinner. At first, she insists that marriage is not for her.

> Bill: You know, I still don't get it. You tell me, now, what better ambition than to find a happy marriage, have children, and a home.
>
> Kathy: Propaganda—not for me. For marriage, I read life sentence. A home life; I read TV nights, beer in the fridge, second mortgage. Uh-uh. Not for me. For me life has to be something more than that.

Kathy soon changes her mind and, upon arriving at her new home as Mrs. Bill Doyle, Kathy is singing a very different tune:

> Here I am with only one ambition left—to make you happy. And I will, darling, I will. I . . . I just want to be a good wife and do things for you and I . . . I hope . . . well, I hope all your socks have holes in them and I can sit for hours and hours darning them.

But Bill tells her that he has "other plans" for her and Kathy is invited to enjoy her other wifely role—as his lover.

Married life, however, proves to be stifling for Kathy with dinner party conversation revolving around social gossip, new appliances, and diets. At one party, Kathy snaps: she slams down a pot to silence everyone and runs into the bathroom explaining, "I'm sick." Little does anyone realize that she is not physically sick but becoming mentally ill. Later, she explains to Bill,

> I can't stand another night of it . . . not another minute. Sarah, Alidos, and the Captain. Iridescent beads and lavender chiffon. The Inspector and Mrs. Pope, that's Tommy and Alice, you know? "Oh, Sarah, you will look stunning. Oh, Sarah, the men adore the Captain. Oh, Sarah, the Captain is such a brilliant man!" Well, I despise all of them. I despise all that crawls around them. I won't be one and I won't let my husband be one! Is this what you have to look forward to? This . . . this mediocrity? This waiting to be wrapped away in mothballs of a pension—2 percent up and 2 percent down? Don't you have any vision? Don't you want to . . . [she breaks off sobbing]

Bill says that the job is only important because it provides them a living that keeps them together and Kathy decides to make an effort.

Since success in the suburbs is measured by social connections, Kathy decides to social climb—by any means necessary. She begins to tail Alice Pope (Fay Wray) and, once she has learned her routine, pretends to almost crash her car into Alice's—in order to make her acquaintance. Alice's husband, Inspector Tony Pope (Raymond Burr), is aware of what Kathy was trying to do, suggesting that she cut the corner with her car to "cut corners" in her social life. Tony, more so than Kathy's own husband, respects her as a driven career woman.

Tony: You doing anything now?

Kathy: Only what every other wife does.

Tony: No, not you. Not a woman like you. There must be something more.

Kathy: I used to think so too . . . until I met Bill.

Tony: I'm stubborn. I can't buy that.

Kathy: Why not? Why isn't it enough for me now just to be a . . .

Tony: Yes. I know you love your husband. But whatever it was that drove you along in your newspaper work, whipped

you into doing the things you did, you were "you"
then—you're the same "you" now. That "you" isn't going
to make a very easy settlement with life.

Kathy, however, manages to channel her former ambitions for her own career
into Bill's and, through her relationship with Tony, she assists Bill's rise through
the ranks. When Tony announces to her that he is going to retire, Kathy takes
the opportunity to suggest Bill as his replacement and murmurs, "Inspector
William Doyle." The thought of Bill's promotion to top rank fuels Kathy's
passion and she seduces Tony. Later, however, Kathy's plans fall apart when
Tony dismisses what he promised her as "pillow talk" and explains, "I've got a
responsibility to the department. I won't sell that out for something we both
stole. Bill's not good enough for the job, he just isn't." Kathy tries to reason
with him but, when he refuses to change his mind, Kathy steals a gun from
the police station and shoots Tony. Ironically, it is her husband who heads up
the investigation and figures out that she is guilty of the crime.

   The film's warning is as much to women as to men: men should think
twice about trying to change the ambitious career woman into a housewife—and
women should think twice about aspiring to be an independent woman. The
very skills that had been regarded as positive in the 1930s for chasing down a
scoop or figuring out "whodunit" are considered not only negative but dangerous by the 1950s. In the 1950s, the only permissible model of womanhood
in Hollywood film is the nurturing housewife, and careerist ambition and a
happy home life cannot co-exist. The female detective could no longer be a
part of the happy world vision of the mystery-comedy and, instead, when she
did appear in films in the 1940s and 50s, it was in dark dramas like *Crime
of Passion* and Hollywood's *film noir*. With independence and femininity seen
as mutually exclusive by the time of America's entry into World War II, the
female detective was no longer a strong and central Hollywood heroine but—at
best—a secondary character and a love interest to the male detective and—
at worst—a joke or a criminal. And throughout the majority of the 1950s—just
as she would in the 1960s and 70s—she just was not there at all.

7

The Maritorious Melodrama

The Female Detective in 1940s Film Noir

Inspector Ferris: If I had a husband I wanted to get rid of, I'd do exactly what you did.

Eleanor Johnson: If he wants to run away, that's his business.

Inspector Ferris: And your business too, Mrs. Johnson!

—Ann Sheridan and Robert Keith in *Woman on the Run* (1950)

World War II, and especially its aftermath, saw a change in the representation of the female detective, as the independent woman came to be depicted as all but the criminal herself. While the perceived threat the female detective represented to masculinity in the 1930s was to replace the man as crime-solver, in the 1940s it was to replace him as breadwinner. Women who desired a career, wanted to maintain their economic independence, and prove their worth against men on equal terms were the real menace, it would seem. Certainly by the late 1940s, female characters who attempted to take charge in their relationships with men were punished—like the *femme fatale*—or restored to their appropriate place in the home as subordinate to their husbands. And, perhaps, for this reason the debate regarding gender that the female detective raised is relocated in the 1940s from the mystery-comedy to the darker and more sinister *film noir*.

Critics of *film noir* have discussed at length the figure of the *femme fatale* as dangerous femininity, but *noir*'s female investigative protagonists have been all but ignored. As Elizabeth Cowie notes, there are female characters in *film noir* who function as the investigator, as defined by Frank Krutnik, as one who "seeks to restore order" ("*Film*," 133). The gender of the female detective complicates the traditionally male *noir* detective narrative, resulting in a hybridization of generic conventions. The narrative is driven forward as

163

much by the female protagonist's personal desires (as in the woman's film) as by her investigation (as in the detective film); however, at the same time, the heroine's independence as a detective poses an undesirable challenge to the masculinity of her husband (as does the *femme fatale* in *film noir*). Just as the woman's film dubbed a "maternal melodrama" by scholars demands a woman make personal sacrifices to facilitate her daughter's success in the world, so too do these *noir* films with female detectives demand the sacrifice on the part of the female protagonist to see the man she loves returned to his "proper" place as head of the household. Thus, I term these films "maritorious melodramas" as opposed to "maternal" because they see the female protagonist "excessively devoted" to her husband rather than her daughter.[1] I say "excessively" because the *noir* female detective is expected to make numerous sacrifices—from giving up her career to prostituting herself—in order to save the man she loves; on the other hand, her husband is not expected to make any concessions and, instead, is often guilty of neglecting her or committing adultery. In the *noir* films featuring a female detective, the heroine is simultaneously empowered—because she occupies the center of, and drives forward, the investigative narrative—and contained—because ultimately she is proven incompetent as a detective and is returned to the prescribed social role of devoted and sacrificing wife.

Part I: *Film Noir*

Film noir arose in a rebellion against the classical Hollywood mode of film-making and storytelling, with a darker look and critique of American society. *Film noir* is argued by most critics to be a film style or movement (rather than a genre) defined by darker themes, characters, and visual style, beginning with John Huston's *The Maltese Falcon* in 1941, enjoying its heyday around 1944, and ending with Orson Welles' *Touch of Evil* in 1958.[2] Unlike classical Hollywood films in general, which tended to take an optimistic view of American society, the *noir* detective film interrogates the myths that films like the classical detective films propagated. Many *noir* films were adaptations of hardboiled stories by American authors like Dashiell Hammett, Raymond Chandler, and Cornell Woolrich—stories that Hollywood had largely avoided in the 1930s because of their vicarious treatment of sex and violence that challenged the restrictions of the Production Code. The adaptation of hardboiled fiction to the screen began with *The Maltese Falcon* based on Hammett's 1930 novel,[3] and Krutnik attributes this shift in Hollywood's embracing of hardboiled fiction as related to the popularization of Freudian psychoanalysis in American society: the psychoanalytic framework was used by filmmakers to circumvent some of the restrictions of the Code by "enabling a more elliptical and displaced mode of representation which could be 'decoded' by audiences familiar with the popularised psychoanalysis" (xii). Psychoanalysis had been increasingly accepted in American culture since World War I but it would be World War II and the visibility of the effects of posttraumatic stress disorder—or what was known at the time as "shell shock"—in returning veterans that would see its popularity cemented.

Noir films—especially as the war came to a close—were often centered on the problems facing returning veterans: unemployment, alienation, degradation, disablement, and broken homes. Many of these problems were regarded as the result of increased female independence and changing gender roles. In reality, many women had left the home to take up employment and pursued sexual gratification in the absence of their husbands; in *film noir*, these women were branded as evil—competing with men in the workplace for jobs, at home as breadwinners, and in bed by challenging their husband's masculinity. As Tania Modleski argues, *film noir* "possesses the greatest sociological importance (in addition to its aesthetic importance) because it reveals male paranoid fears, developed during the war years, about the independence of women on the homefront" (21). When men had gone off to war, women had stepped up to take over their jobs in the name of the war effort; however, upon the return of those men, women were encouraged back into the home. In other words, women were needed to nurture the physically or mentally wounded veterans and not compete with them in the workplace. This led to a bifurcation of roles for women in *film noir*—nurturer or *femme fatale*. For example, in *Out of the Past* (Tourneur, 1947), *femme fatale* Kathie Moffet (Jane Greer) is presented as more exciting but also more deadly compared to Ann Miller (Virginia Huston); similarly, in *Double Indemnity* (Wilder, 1944), lethal Phyllis Dietrichson (Barbara Stanwyck) is contrasted with her innocent daughter Lola (Jean Heather). Janey Place suggests that for the *noir* hero, the *femme fatale* is "the psychological expression of his own internal fears of sexuality, and his need to control and repress it" (53).

The female detective in *film noir* is, at heart, a nurturer but is often forced by circumstance to masquerade as the *femme fatale*. It is her determination to prove her lover's innocence that wins his heart—*not* the masquerade of dangerous and exciting sexuality—since they are not there to see it. So this masquerade functions for a different reason: first, to demonstrate just how far the heroine is willing to go to prove her love and, second, to allow her a brief escape from the proprietary confines of her role as "good" woman. She does ideally want to return to a nurturing role as wife, but she is changed and strengthened by her outings as a *femme fatale* and, in that sense, perhaps offers a third type of *noir* female model. These films show her only in the process and the narrative concludes just as she solidifies her new identity; therefore, they suggest that the perfect woman is the nurturer who is strong and resourceful and that those qualities are linked to the darker side of female sexuality. In other words, these films potentially challenge the *film noir* gender binary by offering something in between the feminine nurturer (mother) and the masculine *femme fatale* (lover).

The heroine takes up the role of detective only to save the man that she loves and returns to the role of dutiful wife upon the conclusion of the case—but she is not the same woman as the innocent one she was initially (at least, sexually). As Michael Renov suggests, the ideal woman presented in postwar films like *The Best Years of Our Lives* (Wyler, 1946), "can be a sexy mother figure, for the twin attributes of the rehabilitating female are seduction and nurture—the former to revitalize the sexual identity, the latter to soothe the traumas to mind and body" (132). The *noir* female detective is similarly a sexualized mother figure for the hero who, although absent for the duration of the film, will return needing her comfort after his ordeal of being falsely accused. Her experiences as detective lead her on a journey through the seedy underbelly of urban America; in the course of that journey, she must rediscover her sexuality through interactions with other men; and the result is that she returns to the man she loves as a more sexually exciting but still nurturing woman.

One of the first films that was identified by critics at the time as (what would later be labeled) *film noir* was *Stranger on the Third Floor* (Ingster, 1940). Reviewers at the time noted how the film echoed the cinematography and *mise en scène* of the German Expressionist film *The Cabinet of Dr. Caligari* (Weine, 1920) and brought, with that style, a dark and foreboding tone to the film.[4] As a *noir* detective film, *Stranger on the Third Floor* offers a shift in tone from the mystery-comedies of the 1930s and their assurance that murder and crime were only temporary disruptions to what could be regarded as an inherently stable and good society. The *noir* detective film, on the other hand, suggests that society is neither stable nor good, that evil is in the heart of all human beings, and that anyone—under the right circumstances—is capable of murder. The dark vision of American society that *noir*'s cinematography and *mise en scène* presents is matched by more sinister characters, crimes, and themes than the detective films of the previous decade. And, in this new darker world, the female detective could not wisecrack her way to a happy ending nor necessarily find the solution to "whodunit" without making some personal sacrifices.

As Krutnik comments, the female investigator is rare in *film noir* and he argues that the "detective activity" of the heroines like Jane in *The Stranger on the Third Floor* and Carol in *Phantom Lady* (Siodmak, 1944) is "compromised by her femininity." Krutnik dismisses the agency of these women as detectives because "the woman's placement in the conventional masculine role as detective is motivated by, and ultimately bound within, her love for the wrongly-convicted hero" (194). I disagree that such a motivation should negate the agency that such female detectives demonstrate as investigators since several male detectives in *noir* films—most famously *Laura* (Preminger, 1944)—are also motivated to investigate out of love/desire. However, other than *The Stranger on the Third Floor* and *Phantom Lady*, Krutnik does not discuss any other *noir* female detectives. Angela Martin identifies nine such films but her article is concerned with the broader project of exploring all types of central female protagonists in *film noir* and, rather than offering an analysis of the female investigator: to this end, she only lists them (218–19). Helen Hanson does offer an analysis of the female detective in four films and regards them as *an extension* of the female detective tradition established in the mystery-comedies of the 1930s (27). In response to Krutnik's assertions, Hanson suggests that the romantic strand is as necessary to the female detective narrative as the crime strand: "The 'woman's angle' and her investigative quest, with the question of her male counterpart's innocence at its centre, allows her to 'test' her male counterpart before the film closes in marriage" (30). I see the *noir* films with a female detective less as an extension of the mystery-comedies of the 1930s (since those also continued throughout the 1940s, as I outlined in the last chapter) and more as a deviation. Although the narratives of these films are driven by the investigation of a mystery just like the mystery-comedies, the mystery is not the central focus; rather these films are concerned with how far these female detectives are willing to go for the man they love.

Investigating for Love

I found over a dozen *noir* films with a female detective made in the 1940s: five offer her in a minor investigative role; five offer her as a secondary investigator to a male; and five offer her as a primary investigator. Several of these dozen films—including *The Leopard Man* (Tourneur, 1943), *Phantom Lady* (Siodmak, 1944), *Deadline at Dawn* (Clurman, 1946), *Black Angel* (Neill, 1946), and *I Wouldn't Be in Your Shoes* (Nigh, 1948)—are based on short stories or novels written by Cornell Woolrich (sometimes as William Irish). Woolrich appears to have been fascinated by the notion of a woman willing to investigate the darker side of humanity in order to prove that the man she loves is innocent, even if only in a minor capacity; for example, in *The Leopard Man*, nightclub performer Kiki Walker (Jean Brooks) investigates alongside her manager, Jerry (Dennis O'Keefe); and, in *I Wouldn't Be in Your Shoes*, Ann Quinn (Elyse Knox) inspires Inspector Clint Judd (Regis Toomey) to reopen the case and to save her husband Tom (Don Castle) from the electric chair. Although the main protagonist of *Stranger on the Third Floor* is reporter Michael Ward (John McGuire), his fiancée (Margaret Tallichet) also ends up playing detective in the last third of the film in order to clear his name. Similarly, when her boss—private eye Bradford Galt (Mark Stevens)—is framed for murder in *The Dark Corner* (Hathaway, 1946), secretary Kathleen Stuart (Lucille Ball) assists in his investigation to clear his name.

Other films offered their heroines centrality as the film's main protagonist and more agency as a detective. For example, in *I Wake up Screaming* (Humberstone, 1941), Frankie Christopher (Victor Mature) is accused of murdering Vicky Lynn (Carole Landis)—the "hash slinger" he turned into a "lady"—and her sister, Jill (Betty Grable), investigates. At first, Jill pursues Frankie in order to question him, but then finds herself falling for him. Notably, when Inspector Cornell (Laird Cregar) turns up to arrest Frankie, Jill displays an unusual amount of coolness and strength for a heroine in the 1940s: she cracks Cornell over the head, traps another officer in the bed wall-unit, and then files off Frankie's handcuffs. Together Frankie and Jill follow the clues, but it is Frankie who takes over the investigation and confronts both Vicky's killer—Harry, the apartment switchboard operator (Elisha Cook Jr.)—and her stalker—Cornell. The film ends with Harry arrested, Cornell dead, and Jill married to Frankie.

Similarly, in *The Lady Confesses* (Newfield, 1945), Vicki McGuire (Mary Beth Hughes) investigates to clear the name of her fiancé, Larry Craig (Hugh Beaumont), of his wife's murder. Although the film does its best to convince the audience that nightclub owner Lucky Brandon (Edmund MacDonald) is guilty of the crime, Larry is ultimately revealed to be the murderer when he kills again to protect his alibi. Although Vicki proves very brave and competent in terms of following a suspected murderer, gathering clues, and providing the police with leads, she—like many of her fellow *noir* female detectives—remains ignorant of the fact that she is working alongside the real murderer. At the end of the film, however, Vicki is provided a new—and more positive—romantic interest in Lucky when the police captain asks him to see that Vicki gets home safely.

Deadline at Dawn (Clurman, 1946), also based on a Woolrich novel, sees June Goth (Susan Hayward)—a bitter, cold-hearted, and disillusioned dancehall girl—help a sailor, Alex Winkley (Bill Williams), clear his name of the suspicion of murder. Alex cannot remember what happened except that he accompanied a woman, Edna (Lola Lane), home to fix her radio and he wakes up to find her dead.[5] June does not want to get involved: as she debates what to do, a woman's dog barks at June but the owner reassures her, "Oh, he won't hurt you. He's just a puppy . . . a baby. He wouldn't hurt a flea. Make up your mind now." Although the woman's last comment is addressed to the dog, it is as applicable to Alex and June repeats absently, ". . . a baby." Suddenly the tough and cynical working girl finds her nurturing side aroused by Alex's guileless nature and she tells him that she will help him.[6] Although June discovers some of the key clues, ultimately her agency is limited since she investigates alongside three others—including the murderer. June realizes that the big city and life as an independent woman cannot bring her happiness and tells Alex that she will go back home with him to Norfolk and marry him.

In *Undercurrent* (Minnelli, 1946), Ann Hamilton (Katharine Hepburn)—the tomboyish daughter of a famous chemistry professor—is in danger of becoming a spinster when she meets industrialist Alan Garroway (Robert Taylor). Their honeymoon is over in more senses than one as dowdy Ann is catapulted into Washington D.C.'s high society. Ann is able to overcome her lack of sophistication by sporting fine clothes and by hosting successful parties, but she has to play detective in order to fix her marriage. Her husband's emotional problems are causing a strain and Ann begins investigating his past—especially the rumor that he may have killed his brother, Michael (Robert Mitchum).

When Michael turns up alive at the Middleburg farm, however, Ann gratefully gives up her investigation and ignores the evidence she has discovered against her husband. In this sense Ann fails as a detective and it is Michael who must explain that Alan suffers from a deep-seated feeling of insecurity and, as a result, killed a German engineer to pass off his invention as his own, gaining acclaim and wealth for it. When Alan is killed, Ann is left free to fall in love with Michael and the film concludes with them, literally, making beautiful music together on the piano.

The Second Woman (Kern, 1950) also sees the female detective investigate the mystery of her lover's past. Ellen Foster (Betsy Drake) is a secretary for an insurance company in Minnesota visiting her aunt in California when she meets architect Jeff Cohalan (Robert Young). A variety of "accidents" have occurred on Jeff's property, and Ellen, knowing the statistical unlikelihood of so much "bad luck" happening to one person, investigates. Like Alan in *Undercurrent*, Jeff is haunted by his past: he and his fiancée were in a car accident that claimed her life. Like the heroine of *Rebecca* (Hitchcock, 1940), Ellen worries that the man she loves is obsessed with his former love because he is still in love with her; however, the truth is that the former love was not a "good" woman but one free with her sexuality and, therefore, not deserving of the hero's love.[7] Eventually Jeff confesses that he was not the one driving the night Vivian died; instead, she was running away with her lover—Jeff's married business partner. The revelation of the truth allows Jeff and Ellen to marry and live happily ever after.

Adolescent Detectives

While Nancy Drew could investigate criminal activities and maintain her innocent view of the world in the 1930s, the adolescent detective in the 1940s found herself confronted with the dark knowledge of adulthood. In *The Seventh Victim* (Robson, 1943), schoolgirl Mary Gibson (Kim Hunter) is told that her sister, Jacqueline (Jean Brooks), has disappeared and Mary leaves for New York at once to investigate. Mary hunts for information at her sister's company, the place where she rented a room, the Missing Persons Bureau, and the morgue. Lastly, she tracks down Jacqueline's lawyer (who is later revealed to be her husband), Gregory Ward (Hugh Beaumont). Mary is dismissed as an investigator because of her tender age. When Mary seeks solace from Greg after witnessing a murder, he treats her like a child:

Greg: Drink your milk.

Mary: I don't like to be ordered to do anything.

Greg: Oh, I'm sorry. I didn't intend to treat you like a child.

Mary: But you have treated me that way.

Although Mary wants to be treated as an adult, she becomes less determined as a detective—at one point giving up with her investigation—and increasingly reliant on men—including Greg, Jacqueline's psychiatrist, and a poet—to do the detective work for her as the case unravels. While they do find Jacqueline in the end, the satanic cult that she has joined drives her to suicide for "betraying" their identity to her psychiatrist in the course of her therapy. The search for Jacqueline brings Greg and Mary together and the film suggests that the appropriate role for Mary is not schoolteacher or detective, but Greg's wife.

Unlike Mary in *The Seventh Victim*, the teenaged heroine of *Shadow of a Doubt* (Hitchcock, 1943), Charlie (Teresa Wright), is firmly the primary investigator in the film. Charles Oakley (Joseph Cotten) finds himself the object of a manhunt and so decides to surprise his family in Santa Rosa with a visit, knowing that the small town is the ideal hiding place because life there is so "ordinary." At the same moment that he decides to wire his family of his visit, his young niece Charlie (named after him) feels the desire to wire him. Charlie is bored with the "rut" (i.e., ordinariness) her family seems to have settled into and knows that her uncle's visit would "shake things up." Young Charlie remarks on the strange, almost telepathic, connection that the two of them share,

> Because we're not just an uncle and a niece. It's something else. I know you. I know you don't tell people a lot of things. I don't either. I have a feeling that inside you somewhere there's something nobody knows about. [. . .] Something secret and wonderful and . . . I'll find it out.

Her uncle's secret, however, is not something "wonderful": it is that he is a serial killer. Charlie certainly proves herself a better detective than the case's official investigator, Jack Graham (MacDonald Carey). When another suspect is taken into custody, Jack believes that Charles is innocent. Charlie, however, puts together the clues and figures out that Charles is, in fact, the "Merry Widow Murderer"—and this knowledge makes her her uncle's next target.

Charlie warns her uncle "Go away, or I'll kill you myself!" so he decides to do away with her first. The first attempt on her life—when a stair breaks and Charlie falls—seems like an accident; it is only when her mother exclaims that she "might have been killed!" that Charlie suspects foul play. Then Charles traps Charlie in the garage with the car's motor running; luckily, a family friend hears Charlie's cries for help. When Charlie recovers evidence from her uncle's room (a ring with someone else's initials engraved inside it), Charles concedes defeat to his worthy adversary—and agrees to leave town. Relieved that her uncle is boarding the train, Charlie allows her guard to drop and he takes the opportunity to kidnap her and to try to kill her. As the train picks up speed, Charles attempts to throw Charlie off the train; however, she has the strength to stand her ground, and it is Charles who falls under the wheels of a passing train. Justice is done and Charlie has saved her family from the horror of knowing that there was a murderer among them.

Although *The Seventh Victim* capitalizes on the fear that powerful and seemingly upstanding members of a community may belong to a secret cult, *Shadow of a Doubt* is more disturbing in its implication that your most trusted loved ones could be evil and that the ideal of "small town America" may also be just a façade. Uncle Charles challenges Charlie's preconceived notions about the world:

> You think you know something, don't you? You think you're the clever little girl who knows something. There's so much you don't know, so much. What do you know, really? You're just an ordinary little girl, living in an ordinary little town. You wake up every morning of your life and you know perfectly well that there's nothing in the world to trouble you. You go through your ordinary little day, and at night you sleep your untroubled ordinary little sleep, filled with peaceful stupid dreams. And I brought you nightmares. Or did I? Or was it a silly, inexpert little lie? You live in a dream. You're a sleepwalker, blind. How do you know what the world is like? Do you know the world is a foul sty? Do you know, if you rip off the fronts of houses, you'd find swine? The world's a hell. What does it matter what happens in it? Wake up, Charlie. Use your wits. Learn something.

At her uncle's funeral, Charlie tells Jack that her uncle tried to make her see the world as he did: he "hated the whole world." Jack, however, assures Charlie that the world is "not quite as bad as that. Sometimes it needs a lot of watching. It seems to go crazy every now and then . . . like your Uncle Charlie." Unlike Nancy Drew, the adolescent detective in the 1940s is changed by her experiences of investigating murder and of questioning her seemingly stable world. And, once the mystery is solved and the transition to adulthood is complete, it is assumed that—unlike Nancy Drew—the young women will give up detecting for marriage. Charlie's last step in growing up is to give up her childish notion of Uncle Charles as her ideal man and accept the reality of Jack as her future husband.

Charlie was not the only female detective in *film noir* to fulfill the role of central and successful investigator; however, I have not included *Shadow of a Doubt* in the section following because the film differs from the established pattern in three important ways and likely due to the age of its protagonist: first, Charlie does not investigate to save the innocent man that she loves (he is guilty); second, she does not masquerade as a *femme fatale* or have to make the "ultimate sacrifice" (i.e., have sexual relations with another man) to save him; and, third, the moments of melodramatic excess are used to create tension rather than disrupt the conservative ending.

Part II: Melodrama-Noir

Phantom Lady (Siodmak, 1944), *Black Angel* (Neill, 1946), and *Woman on the Run* (Foster, 1950) have all been identified as *film noir* by critics, the Internet Movie Database, and/or distribution companies that have released these titles as part of *noir* DVD collections.[8] I will, therefore, not spend time establishing how these films can be regarded as *noir* but begin with that assumption and, instead, explore how they are also melodramas. There is something about the focus on a female protagonist that changes the themes of a *film noir*. As Donald Phelps notes, "the best of the Woolrich adaptations—epitomized by Roy William Neill's *Black Angel*—express something virtually alien to *noir* mood and *noir* ethos: a lingering, faintly nostalgic sensitivity, a persistent albeit wistful humanism" (64)—leading Phelps to define such films as "cinema *gris*" rather than *noir*. I would argue that *Phantom Lady* (another Woolrich adaptation) and *Woman on the Run* possess a similar "nostalgic sensitivity;" however, it is not just a female protagonist and a sense of nostalgia or humanism that complicate the identification of these films as *noir*, but also their moments of excess in terms of representation.

Films are identified as belonging to a specific genre based on their emotional effect (e.g., the horror film), content (e.g., the musical), themes (e.g., the social problem film), setting (e.g., the Western), or protagonist (e.g., the gangster film). Both melodrama and *film noir*, however, are examples of categories that have been constructed by critics rather than the film industry itself and have resisted a clear delineation as genres. The label *film noir* was applied retrospectively by French critics to describe a body of Hollywood films that first appeared during World War II, while, at the time, these films were released as detective films, crime melodramas, or thrillers. As James Naremore argues, the use of the term *film noir* was not widespread until the 1970s and was a creation of a belated rereading of classical Hollywood by scholars and critics (14)—as was the case with melodrama. Today, the term melodrama is most often associated with films featuring heightened emotionality and female protagonists, aimed at an assumed female audience. As Ben Singer argues, however, melodrama was initially a term used by the film industry during the silent era to describe films with "action, thrilling sensationalism, and physical violence" ("Female," 95). Similarly, Steve Neale suggests that in classical Hollywood film, the term was used by studios to describe "war films, adventure films, horror films, and thrillers, genres tradition-ally thought of as, if anything, 'male' " ("Melo," 69)—rather than the woman's film. The term's association with narratives driven by female desire has been the result of psychoanalytic critical discourse of the 1980s that applied the term to classical Hollywood films that, at the time of their release, were labeled—and often dismissed as—woman's films or "weepies."[9]

Critics identify visual style as a key component of *film noir*. Hollywood directors and cinematographers developed a dark and ominous tone by opting for a *chiaroscuro* visual style—with contrasting light and dark shadows—versus Hollywood's dominant style of three- and often high-key lighting. Echoing German Expressionism, *film noir* offered a highly stylized visual design that drew attention to itself and suggested an exteriorization—or expression—of a character's internal state of mind. Neale argues that the elements regarded "as exclusive to *noir*" and "its principal hallmarks" are "the visual and aural rhetoric—the use of extreme *chiaroscuro*, discordant sounds and music, and other expressive and 'expressionistic' devices" (*Genre*, 169–70); however, I would note that such "visual and aural rhetoric" have also been identified as the hallmarks of melodrama. As Laura Mulvey notes, "the melodrama is characterized by the presence of a protagonist whose symptomatic behavior emerges out of irreconcilable or inexpressible internal contradiction, and this 'unspeakable' affects and overflows on to the *mise en scène*" ("It," 125). Melodrama's visual design includes an emphasis on the symbolic meaning of everyday objects beyond their superficial one. The heightened emotionality of *noir*, however, does tend to result from violence while melodrama's stems more often from pathos; this is most likely why a murder was added to James M. Cain's novel *Mildred Pierce* (1941) in its adaptation into a *film noir* (Curtiz, 1945).

As I have discussed elsewhere, the term melodrama does not have to be restricted to the discussion of classical Hollywood woman's films, but is applicable to male genre films—for example, the cop-action film.[10] Linda Williams has suggested that the idea of melodrama needs revision—that it is not limited to a genre (the woman's film) but is a pervasive mode: "Melodrama should be viewed, then, not as an excess or aberration but in many ways as the typical form of American popular culture narrative in literature, stage, film, and television" ("Melodrama," 50). While I am not sure that I would go so far as to say that melodrama is "the typical form of American culture narrative," I hope that with this chapter I help broaden the category of melodrama through an inclusion of the predominantly male genre of *film noir* whereas other critics have seen it as an either/or debate, for example Stephen Gale and Pam Cook. I argue that melodrama and *film noir* are not so distinct from one other but operate similarly as modes of representation that utilize their visual and aural expression to invite a symbolic interpretation. Unlike the classic realist text in which the *mise en scène*—including sets, costumes, music, and lighting—is expected to perform merely as the backdrop to the story and characters, the *noir* or melodramatic text sees its *mise en scène* highlighted, offering a second level of representation through which to interpret the themes and characters. For example, the television that represents how the consumerist trappings of a suburban lifestyle have all but embalmed widow Cary Scott (Jane Wyman) in *All that Heaven Allows* (Sirk, 1955) functions similarly to the image of the "Spade and Archer" sign cast in shadow (and in reverse) on the office floor between the two detectives in *The Maltese Falcon* (Huston, 1941) that represents the dissolution of their supposed partnership.

The most obvious difference between melodrama and *film noir* is the sex of the protagonist. Certainly, the main thrust of *film noir* seems to be a negotiation of the anxieties of postwar masculinity. In melodrama, on the other hand, men were most often the cause of the female protagonist's problems—from authoritarian patriarchs to lovers who wished to quell her independence and force her to assume her socially prescribed role as wife and mother. Scholars such as Tania Modleski and Diane Waldman suggest that a small group of gothic thrillers centered on a female protagonist, including *Rebecca* (Hitchcock, 1940) and *Gaslight* (Cukor, 1944), can be regarded as *film noir*; however, Neale argues that the position of these films has "always been ambiguous or marginal, as far as proponents of *noir* have been concerned" (*Genre*, 163). Catherine Ross Nickerson argues that detective fiction in general grew out of the gothic tradition, including Edgar Allan Poe's seminal tales of ratiocination (xiii); however, there is an even closer connection between the gothic and women's detective fiction arising from the tradition of the "female gothic" established by Ann Radcliffe's *The Mysteries of Udolpho* (1794) in which a female protagonist is faced with a secret or mystery. However, the female gothic thrillers of the 1940s tend to feature women in period piece settings and in roles typical of the woman's film not, as the three films I discuss, in contemporary urban settings and in the traditionally male and *noir* role of detective.[11]

I would like to suggest that *Phantom Lady*, *Black Angel*, and *Woman on the Run* are not just *noir* but also melodrama—in both the conventional sense and my complication of those definitions. The visual style of the three films is consistent with that traditionally defined as *noir* but all three films have key moments of excess that are more in keeping with conventional notions of melodrama, notably the drum solo in *Phantom Lady*, Marty's amnesia in *Black Angel*, and the rollercoaster ride in *Woman on the Run*. As Neale explains, most critics argue "that desire in *noir* tends to be marked as dangerous or destructive and that it tends to be represented from a male point of view" (*Genre*, 160). And it is in this way that the three films I explore are different from traditional *noir*: Female desire is seen as salvation and is represented from a female point of view. Rather than the exposure of the hero's love interest as a *femme fatale* and his rejection of her as is typical of *noir*, *Phantom Lady* and *Black Angel* begin with a *femme fatale*'s demise and conclude with the creation of a new family order. *Noir* has also been seen as the site of male crisis, as explored by scholars like Krutnik, but these films focus instead on a crisis of female identity in terms of what role these heroines will play to save the men they love—from lounge singer to detective, from adulteress to dutiful wife. Linda Williams suggests that melodrama is "the best example of American culture's (often hypocritical) notion of itself as the locus on innocence and virtue" and that, "In a postsacred world, melodrama represented one of the most significant, and deeply symptomatic, ways we negotiate moral feeling" ("Melodrama," 50 and 61). Indeed, while *noir*-detective films typically feature hardboiled, cynical, and morally ambiguous male heroes, the melodrama-*noirs* offer heroines who embody innocence in the otherwise corrupt universe. The melodrama-*noir* initially presents a world that is morally grey but ultimately polarizes good and evil: in other words, the heroine's investigation facilitates the identification of evil and the relocation of evil and good to their rightful places (the prison or grave, and the home, respectively).

Phantom Lady, *Black Angel*, and *Woman on the Run* offer an interesting hybridization of what are regarded as traditionally either *noir* or melodrama conventions: they offer the female protagonist of the melodrama and a narrative driven by her desires but a protagonist who is simultaneously the problematic independent women of the wartime-era *film noir*. Christian Viviani argues that the Americanization of melodrama made it relevant for the social realties of the 1930s and resulted in the subgenre of the "maternal melodrama," in which a mother makes sacrifices for her child in order to right her social wrong (96). Like the women of the maternal melodrama who had to sacrifice their own desires to see their children thrive, these female protagonists must make sacrifices in order to reinstate their husbands to their patriarchal position—from criminal to head of the household.

The Maritorious Melodrama

Phantom Lady, *Black Angel*, and *Woman on the Run* all suggest that the marriages that begin the films have failed because an imbalance in gender power occurred: the wives became too independent and the husbands too "soft"—to use Carol Richman's description of her boss in *Phantom Lady*. In a reflection of this repolarization of gender, the female detectives of these films are wives (or future wives) attempting to clear their love's name and repair the broken home. Both *Black Angel* and *Phantom Lady* are Woolrich adaptations and, as Phelps says of Woolrich's detective heroines, "The women are fired with devotion, defiance, maternal passion" (66). Just as in the maternal melodrama "the mother's fall from grace was symbolized by a tormented odyssey which marked an opposition to the permanence of the bourgeois household" (Viviani, 86), so too is the descent of these three film heroines into the seedy underbelly of America marked by a tormented odyssey through the public spaces of the city—the courthouse, the night club, the seedy hotel, and the street—in order to return permanence to the bourgeois household.

Phantom Lady finds Scott Henderson (Alan Curtis) in a bar alone: he makes one last attempt to heal the estrangement between himself and his wife with a night out to celebrate their fifth anniversary, but his wife refuses

Fig. 7.1. Fired with Devotion, Defiance, Maternal Passion: Cornell Woolrich (sometimes as William Irish) wrote several stories with female detectives, including *Black Angel* (1946) starring June Vincent and Dan Duryea. Photo from author's collection.

to join him. Scott blames his wife for the collapse of their marriage: she was "too spoiled and too beautiful," he explains to the police. Scott is unaware his wife, Marcella, has been, according to his friend Jack Marlow (Franchot Tone), "amusing herself" with him. When Marcella admits to Jack that she has no intention of leaving her husband for him, he strangles her in a fit of rage. As Scott explains to Inspector Burgess, Marcella refused to be "his wife" (i.e., his lover) but also refused him a divorce (giving him the freedom to pursue another), providing him a motive and making him the prime suspect in her murder. In a melodramatic manner, Marcella haunts the early part of the film but is never shown in person. While the police question Scott about his wife, her full-length portrait dominates the wall behind them (using the same technique that is identified with Otto Preminger's *Laura* released later that year). When the paramedics carry her out, the camera pans somewhat awkwardly past Scott, mirroring her body's passage through the room. Scott exclaims in horror, "Look what they're doing! Her hair . . . along the floor!" but the audience sees nothing but the frozen portrait on the wall behind. Ironically, the "phantom lady" of the film's title is not Marcella but Anne Terry (Fay Helm), the woman with whom Scott spent his anniversary evening but who cannot be found by the police to corroborate his alibi.

The film introduces the heroine, Scott's assistant, Carol Richman (Ella Raines), at work listening to his Dictaphone message until the story in the paper about Marcella's murder catches her eye. Scott calls her "Kansas" after her home state and this highlights that she is a small-town girl now living in the big city. Carol is in love with her boss and, when he is convicted of murder and sentenced to death row, she decides to play detective to clear his name. She pursues people in the case that swore they never saw the phantom lady; as Carol suspects, each has been bribed to remain silent. Her search leads her through the underbelly of the city and, although these shady places are typically *noir*, they are also presented through melodramatic excess. Carol stalks the bartender at work and then on his way home: as they wait alone on the platform for the train, the bartender advances threateningly toward Carol and his implied desire to push her in front of the train is halted only by the arrival of another passenger. The tension of the scene is released by the loud squeal of the train's wheels on the track as it rushes past them. This is echoed in the following scene when the bartender accidentally steps out in front of a car to escape her interrogation and the screams of a woman fuse with the screeching of car tires.

Similarly, the film's most notorious scene—the drum solo—is notable because of its excess. In order to get close to drummer Cliff Milburn (Elisha Cook, Jr.), Carol presents herself as a cheap "dame" and gives him "the eye." He takes her to a basement jam session in which he plays the drums and she dances. Her masquerade of available sexuality is successful at least in his eyes and broken only for a moment when she catches sight of her own image in a mirror while reapplying her lipstick: she shakes her head in disgust at what she sees. Tension in the scene is built through the frenzied music and atypical cinematography—low and canted angles coupled with tight close-ups—and then released with the drummer's orgasmic crescendo. Carol agrees to go back to Cliff's place, knowing that he expects her to have sex with him. When she plays hard to get and he spies the police file in her purse, he turns violent and—it is suggested—decides to rape her. He says menacingly, "Wait until I get you!" but she escapes. When Jack (the man responsible for the murder and bribery) turns up after Carol's sudden departure, he says to Cliff, "She was magnificent! She loathed you but she went with you. She would have humiliated herself to make you talk." Her willingness to "humiliate herself" in order to save the man she loves, sees Carol rewarded. When Jack warns Carol that she is risking her life pursuing what he calls "a man's job" (i.e., playing detective), Carol retorts, "Do you think I'd care? Do you think I'd want to live?"

The film ties the loss of love to madness with two possible outcomes: Anne Terry becomes a reclusive hysteric following her fiancé's death, and Jack Marlow becomes a "homicidal paranoiac" when Marcella rejects him. The former represents Carol's possible future if she does not save Scott from death row. Saving him is, in every way, safeguarding her own future as a woman, given that the film suggests that a woman is nothing unless she marries the man she loves. And it would seem that Carol gets her happy ending. Returning to work after Scott's release, Carol finds a proposal from Scott on the Dictaphone: "You know you're having dinner with me tonight, and tomorrow night, and the next night, and then every night." It is on this last phrase that the Dictaphone skips and continues to do so, ending the film with the image of an ecstatic Carol, holding the horn and listening to Scott's disembodied voice repeating "every night . . . every night . . . every night."

In *Black Angel*, Kirk Bennett (John Phillips) is arrested and later convicted of murdering Mavis Marlowe (Constance Dowling), a singer who is blackmailing him over their affair. Unlike Carol who is a career woman, Cathy Bennett (June Vincent) is a meek and dutiful housewife and she stands by her husband even though, as Marty Blair (Dan Duryea) describes it, Kirk "let her down" (i.e., he was unfaithful). She explains to her husband in prison, "Please, Kirk. You're my husband. I'll always stand by you. You know that." Initially, she pursues the other most likely suspect in the case, Mavis's ex-husband Marty, but, when it appears that he has a solid alibi, she teams up with him to investigate club owner Marko (Peter Lorre). The missing piece of evidence is the heart-shaped ruby brooch that Kirk swears was on Mavis when he first discovered her body and that was later stolen; without the brooch, there is no evidence of a killer other than Kirk.

Marty and Cathy team up not just as investigative partners but also business partners and gain access to Marko's office and his safe (where Cathy assumes the stolen brooch is hidden) by posing as an entertainment duo: he plays piano while she sings. It is never explained why Cathy's husband strayed and who was to blame, but it is clear that they had become estranged. When Marty asks if she plays the piano, she explains that Kirk used to play while she sang—"At least . . . we did when we were first married." One suspects that what attracted Kirk to Mavis was a seductive sexuality and strength of character that Cathy seems to lack. Cathy, however, undergoes a gradual transformation through her experiences as a detective—echoed by her appearance. Cathy initially dresses as a dowdy housewife sporting a checked dress and straw boater; however, while undercover at Marko's club, she masquerades as a glamorous lounge singer in a black, off-the-shoulder gown. Ultimately, Cathy finds an "authentic" middle ground as a well-dressed working woman in tailored suits or shapely dresses. Indeed, through pursuing the investigation, Cathy has discovered that she possesses a masculine strength of character:

Cathy: I was hoping to get closer to that safe.

Marty: That's the *hard* way, isn't it?

Cathy: I have to get into it, Marty . . . no matter how.

The "hard way" is to become Marko's lover and even though Cathy is prepared to "humiliate" herself to save her husband, she is still horrified at the
thought of it—and the cinematography expresses that horror. In the midst of
an otherwise unremarkable scene in terms of film style, there is a melodramatic
medium shot of Cathy teary-eyed, open-mouthed, and swaying with fear that
is almost palpable. The moment is made more dramatic when the camera cuts
to an unperturbed Marko taking out a bottle of champagne that he had "been
saving for a special occasion" and then cuts back to the odd shot of Cathy,
this time showing her trying to force a tearful smile. This moment of visual
excess is followed by one of narrative. Because of the quantity of screen time
that is devoted to this avenue of inquiry and the tense climax that arises when
Marko catches Cathy at his safe, the audience assumes that Cathy's sacrifice
will have been worthwhile—that she will now have the proof to clear her
husband. However, this anticipated resolution is frustrated when it is revealed
that Marko does not have the brooch and was in police custody at the time
of the murder—and therefore *not* the murderer. Cathy, in despair, attempts to
express the ineffable—her realization that her sacrifice has been in vain: "You
mean we . . . All this time, just wasted."

Black Angel is, as many melodramas are, characterized by the return of
the repressed. The essential in *Black Angel* is "whodunit?" (who is responsible
for Mavis's death). The film—just like the killer, it turns out—attempts to
repress the story of the crime but eventually both recall and reveal the truth.
Since he met Cathy, Marty has remained sober; however, her rejection of his
love sends him on a bender, like the one he went on the night that Mavis
was killed. By returning to the same state in which he committed the murder
and confronted with the brooch that he and Cathy had been seeking, Marty
experiences the return of what he had repressed and an oral and visual montage
reveals Marty's actions on the fateful night. As the doctor at the hospital explains,
Marty was suffering from "Korsakoff's psychosis": amnesia brought about by
his excessive consumption of alcohol. Although he remembers committing the
murder and wishes to confess, Marty finds the doctor at the hospital and the
police unwilling to believe him—so he has to escape to tell Cathy the truth.
Alone at her house, Marty begins drinking again. In the film's final moment
of excess, Marty hallucinates that he sees Mavis instead of Cathy: Mavis's head
and body are superimposed over that of Cathy's and eerie music accompanies
her disembodied form.

Ultimately the film, in keeping with the melodramatic tradition, is about
self-sacrifice. Although Cathy gives herself to Marko, the film suggests that this
was an admirable even if futile gesture. However, more importantly, Cathy
refuses the temptation to fall for her partner, Marty, who—as a nice guy—poses
the real threat of replacing Kirk in her affections. Marty professes his love to
Cathy: "I knew from the beginning . . . that you're everything I wanted and
everything I'd missed. It has to be you and me, Cathy." The implication is

that his marriage to Mavis was less than ideal and that she was not a good wife, a fact supported by her blackmailing her lovers, such as Marko and Kirk. However, Cathy refuses to betray Kirk and tells Marty she can never love another man: "Marty, I can't. There's only been one man. There *can* only be one man . . . ever." She is rewarded for her fidelity with Marty's recollection of the truth at the eleventh hour to save Kirk from the gas chamber.

Despite its title, *Woman on the Run* sees Frank Johnson (Ross Elliott) on the run after he witnesses a murder and believes that the police cannot protect him (after all, the victim he saw killed was a witness in police protection). Clear from the start is that Eleanor (Ann Sheridan) and Frank's four-year marriage is a disaster. When Inspector Ferris (Robert Keith) asks Frank if he is married, Frank replies, "In a way." When Ferris asks Eleanor to describe her husband so that the police can find him, she retorts, "I couldn't. I haven't been able to for a long time." Ferris is angered by Eleanor's attitude not befitting of a wife, including encouraging her husband to stay on the run.

> Ferris: If I had a husband I wanted to get rid of, I'd do exactly what you did.
>
> Eleanor: If he wants to run away, that's his business.
>
> Ferris: And your business too, Mrs. Johnson!

Indeed, the film suggests that whatever concerns a husband should concern his wife as well: that is her job. As Frank's doctor tells her, "But naturally, you must know all about his troubles. I'm only his doctor; you're his wife." But she knows nothing of Frank's life, including that he has a heart condition that has been made more serious because of the stress of their failed marriage.

When Ferris inquires about their relationship, Eleanor replies, "If you want to snoop into the remains of our marriage, that's up to you;" however, the film suggests that it is actually up to her. The mystery that Eleanor as detective must solve is not who shot the witness, but rather who killed the marriage. Frank sends her a riddle in a letter that she must solve: "If you think back, you'll know where to find me." As newspaperman Danny Leggett (Dennis O'Keefe) says to her, "He's asking you to admit that your marriage is a failure and that it's your fault. He's saying that he understands you but that you don't understand him." And he is correct: Eleanor must sift through her memories of the marriage and accept some part of the blame for its going wrong in order to track down her husband and give him his lifesaving heart medication. Eleanor neither kept house nor supported her husband's ambitions. Ferris asks why their kitchen contains no food and Eleanor replies, "He's not particular and I'm lazy, so we eat out." Ferris asks her why she didn't get a job if she was so concerned about money and she replies, "Why should I? That's his responsibility not mine." Ferris hits on the truth when he tells Eleanor, "But I don't think you can find him. I

Fig. 7.2. Trusting the Wrong Man: Many wartime and postwar female detectives make this mistake, including Ann Sheridan's in *Woman on the Run* (1950), who investigates alongside the killer played by Dennis O'Keefe (both on the right). Photo from author's collection.

don't think he is running away from us; I think he's running away from you." At the beginning of the film, Eleanor believes that the marriage failed because her husband had let her down by not fulfilling his promise as a successful artist; conversely, through her pursuit of the clues raised in Frank's letter and her resulting investigation of the marriage, Eleanor realizes that she let him down by being too independent. In this film, the repressed that returns is Eleanor's love for her husband and her desire to be a dutiful wife. And for her admission of fault, Eleanor is rewarded with the safe return of her husband—but not before a melodramatic rollercoaster ride.

The melodramatic moments of the film arise from Eleanor's failure in her attempt to subsume male authority and play detective. Despite the fact that Eleanor proves to be successful in figuring out the clues that lead her to her husband's whereabouts, she ultimately fails to keep her husband safe: by trusting Danny, she leads the killer right to his prey. Danny offers them the money to finance Frank's disappearance in exchange for an exclusive story for his paper. The climax of the film is the rollercoaster ride that Danny takes Eleanor on, initially to spot Frank in the crowd and evade the police, but subsequently to keep her out of the way so that he can kill Frank. On the first ride, Danny and Eleanor sit together and the tension builds as they look for Frank from their vantage point. The scene offers a kind of "phantom ride" with the camera mounted on the front of the car to follow their coasting up and down the tracks. This scene is tense, but Eleanor's second ride on the rollercoaster alone is far more melodramatic.

As Danny pays to have her ride once more, he reminds her that the killer may try to kill Frank again. The second ride starts then with Eleanor rehearing both Danny's last comment and Ferris's remark from earlier that day—that the killer is the only other person who knows about the attempt made on Frank's life. This realization starts an emotional rollercoaster represented through the excess of the cinematography of the literal rollercoaster ride. This time the cacophony of noise, laughter, music, and the roar of the rollercoaster is increased in volume and discord and is combined with Eleanor's screams for Frank to run away. Instead of a phantom ride offering the view directly ahead of the car, this time the camera looks down through the tracks and over their edge in a series of spiraling, disorienting, and terrifying shots of Frank as a small figure below. Eleanor is yanked from side to side by the motion of the ride, helpless. The most disturbing sound through the entire scene is the mechanical and repetitive laughter of an animatronic figure from an amusement park stall. Eleanor is finally able to get off the ride but a series of shots with dramatic canted angles maintains a sense of her anxiety as she dashes through the amusement park trying to find Frank. When she hears a shot fired and sees a body in the water, she and the audience assume it is Frank's. Luckily, however, the shot fired was Ferris's and the body is Danny's. The film suggests that Eleanor's problem at the beginning of the film was her resistance to submit to male authority—that of her husband and the police; however, her eventual acceptance of both leads to a happy conclusion. Eleanor must relinquish her "uxorodespotic" role and, instead, allow her husband to run their household *and* marriage.[12]

Sacrificial Women

Phantom Lady, *Black Angel*, and *Woman on the Run* all suggest that a marriage cannot be a successful one if the woman vies for control—either inside or outside the home. That is why *Black Angel* regards Cathy as the superior choice over Mavis for both Kirk and Marty, and why *Phantom Lady* sees the replacement of the original Mrs. Henderson (Marcella) with the new one (Carol) as the key to Scott's happiness. While marriage and family are presented as the ideal in classical Hollywood film, in *film noir* they are presented most often as imprisoning or sterile. Sylvia Harvey argues, "The two most common types of women in film noir are the exciting, childless whores, or the boring, potentially childbearing sweethearts" (38). However, in the case of *Woman on the Run* and *Black Angel*, the threat of death for the husband as an assumed criminal and the working as an independent woman as a detective for the wife—in other words, playing roles outside of those socially sanctioned—facilitate a rejuvenation of the failed marriage and the nurturing wife transformed into an exciting lover figure.

As dutiful wives—in other words, a traditionally female role—these women prove themselves successful; however, as detectives—a traditionally male role—they are exposed ultimately as incompetent. On the one hand, Carol does pursue the bartender doggedly, extract information from the drummer, and locate the phantom lady through her hat and milliner; Cathy does discover that both Marty and Marko could have been Mavis's killer; and Eleanor does figure out her husband's riddle and whereabouts. And, importantly, many of these discoveries are dependent on specifically female knowledge—e.g., of woman's fashion, the seduction of men, and memories of courtship. On the other hand, in each case, these women befriend the real killers—Jack, Marty, and Danny, respectively—and risk either their own lives or that of their loved ones without realizing what they have done until it is too late. The message of these films is that women can be either the downfall (the *femme fatale*) or the savior (the wife as detective) of men. Wives, who pursue independence outside of marriage whether in terms of sex or a career, present a challenge to male dominance. Ironically, however, through attempting to help their men, these women *have* to work outside of the home as detectives and sometimes prostitute themselves to other men—and yet they are never demonized for that, even though the *femme fatale* always is. Each woman's devotion to the man she loves sees her compensated: in other words, each woman is rewarded with the undivided love of her man—something she did not possess at the beginning of the film. The conclusions of these films are then conservative—if read through the lens of *film noir*.

If, however, these endings are read through the lens of melodrama, a reading against the grain is made possible. Indeed, the concluding scenes of each film feel contrived, stemming from a desired narrative conclusion of returning women to the home rather than one that logically fits the film in terms of the actual representation of that narrative. In all three films, the husbands are all but absent and, instead, the relationships that form between their wives and other men (Jack, Marty, and Danny) during the course of the investigation are far more developed and interesting. In *Phantom Lady*, the skipping Dictaphone proposal and addition of a happy-go-lucky score do not convince: Scott was oblivious to Carol's affections for him despite her standing by him through the trial, risking her life to find evidence to exonerate him, and confessing to him that she is in love with him. Indeed, the final shot of the film is not Carol in Scott's arms but of the Dictaphone horn in hers. And this, it would seem, was purposefully done. As Louis Black explains in the *CinemaTexas Program Notes* for the film:

> The film would have maintained its integrity had it ended, as [producer Joan] Harrison and [director Robert] Siodmak evidently wanted, without the romance of Scott and Kansas looking promising. Siodmak was evidently so upset with this idea that he doesn't

even show their meeting but has Scott leave Kansas a message on the Dictaphone. The message getting stuck can be viewed as an overly saccharine touch, but in view of Siodmak's constant portrayal of marital discord (witness the beginning of the film where this is implied), this scene can be read as indicating the monotony and oppression with its repetitive, "every night . . . every night . . . every night." (79–80)

Similarly, in *Black Angel*, the final shot of the film is not the reunion of Kirk and his wife but that of Marty and Cathy on the cover of the sheet music for their hit song "Time Will Tell" and Marty's comment that they were "a good team while it lasted." In *Woman on the Run*, the last shot of the film is not of the couple embracing on the midway of the amusement park but of the disturbing animatronic doll as it continues the mechanical cackle that pervaded the rollercoaster ride.

While I have suggested that they share an expressionistic or excessive impulse at the level of representation, *film noir* and melodrama differ in terms of their ideological motivation. As E. Ann Kaplan suggests,

> It is interesting to compare the *film noir*, with its negative or absent family, with melodrama, a genre in which family and its relations are the focus of ideological representation. While the family melodrama could be seen to deal with the ideological contradictions within patriarchy in terms of sexuality and patriarchal right within the family, the *film noir* as exemplified by *Double Indemnity* stresses precisely the ordering of sexuality and patriarchal right, the containment of sexual drives with patriarchy as Symbolic Order. Thus there is a sense in which *film noir* could be seen to close off the ideological contradictions of patriarchy that the family melodrama opens up. ("Introduction," 18)

Thus, Kaplan sees melodrama as functioning in opposition to *noir*, opening up the possibility of troubling or subverting the film's concession to dominant discourse. However, the focus on a female protagonist and the employ of other conventions of melodrama allow an alternative reading of these *films noirs*. As Tony Williams, reading *Phantom Lady* through a psychoanalytic lens, states,

> At the climax of the film Carol is confined to the office and the offer of monogamy. However, enough remains of the masochistic model in the film to argue that the aesthetic, if not dominant, is there as a fissure, a gap in ideology which permits the partial expression of the female voice. It exists as an alternative operation against patriarchal

> control of the text. Even if subdued at the climax, it is still there,
> attempting to strain against narrative bounds. (134)

The endings of the three films may seem to fall in line with the ideological concerns of *film noir*—that is, the return of the women to appropriate gender roles; however, the focus on the female characters as investigators (rather than the man as typical with *film noir*) and the over-determination of representation (as typical with melodrama) allow for contradictions to resonate past the tacked on endorsement of patriarchal ideology.

In the aftermath of World War II, women had to be returned to their proper place so that men could be returned to theirs—at least that was the general social consensus that Hollywood echoed. Just as the maternal melodrama presented "mother-daughter proximity as dangerous to the daughter's future, and to society" (Whitney, 11), so too does the *film noir* starring a female detective suggest that the wife's appropriation of male power in the marriage is dangerous to the husband's future—and to that of society. Wartime and postwar America needed broken homes mended and gender roles reset to their traditional positions. Whereas the maternal melodrama of the 1930s was "an apologia for total renunciation, total sacrifice, total self-abnegation" (Viviani, 96) in a reflection of the impact of the Depression, *film noir* was similarly a reflection of social attitudes in the 1940s with its recall of women back into the home. *Film noir*, with its darker, more introspective and critical tone, offered a vehicle for the narratives of men struggling with the new roles demanded of them in postwar America. The ubiquitous female detective of the 1930s could be outspoken, independent, and career-minded—with her triumph as both detective and love interest the result of her successful integration of masculinity into femininity. Conversely, the few female detectives of the 1940s had to relinquish their independence (i.e., masculinity) in order to achieve happiness—the only avenue for which was deemed marriage (i.e., femininity). These female detectives, unlike their 1930s counterparts however, seemed happy to submit to marital authority and this is why, in the aftermath of World War II, these women are regarded as meritorious. However, their few successors in the 1950s were not considered so positively.

Part III: Fifties Failures

By 1950, the female detective was rarely seen as positive and, as the decade wore on, her ability to be a reliable authority was questioned—and, ultimately, her sanity too. *Destination Murder* (Cahn, 1950) features Laura Mansfield (Joyce MacKenzie), a murder victim's daughter who begins investigating on her own when the police run out of leads. Although Jackie Wales (Stanley

Clements) feigns ignorance of where the Mansfields live, he confirms Laura's
suspicion of his guilt by hopping over her front gate—just as she saw the
murderer do on the night of her father's shooting. In an attempt to gather
evidence against him, Laura begins dating Jackie and suspects that club owner
Armitage hired Jackie to murder her father. What Laura does not figure out
is that Stretch (Hurd Hatfield), the man she is falling in love with, is the real
head of the business and the man responsible for her father's murder. Worse
than merely being wrong in her attempt to solve "whodunit," Laura is then
compelled to apologize to Lieutenant Brewster for ever doubting his superior
abilities. As the reviewer for the *Hollywood Reporter* suggests, "Inevitably she
gets everything bawled up and only the timely interference of the law saves
her from danger" (7 June 1950). As a detective, Laura is ultimately a failure;
as a woman, she is a poor judge of character, having been seduced by the
man who killed her father.

    In *The Blue Gardenia* (Lang, 1953), Norah Larkin (Anne Baxter) discov-
ers on her birthday that her boyfriend fighting in Korea has fallen in love with
someone else. In retaliation, Norah meets womanizer, Harry Prebble (Raymond
Burr), at "The Blue Gardenia" for a date. Drunk and disoriented, Norah finds
herself back at Prebble's apartment where he tries to force himself on her; in
self-defense, Norah strikes him with a fireplace poker before passing out. In the
morning, Prebble is found dead and Norah, who cannot recall what happened,
worries that she committed the crime. Reporter Casey Mayo (Richard Conte)
explains, "A lot of murderers forget what they don't want to remember. They
call it 'killer amnesia.' " Although initially interested in investigating the crime,
Norah gives up because her being guilty is the only scenario that makes sense
to her, and it is Casey who must play detective to prove her innocence. By
investigating what record Prebble was playing that night, Casey stumbles on
to the real murderess—an employee at the music store—who killed Prebble in
a jealous rage for entertaining another woman, Norah.

    Similar to the melodrama-*noir*, however, *The Blue Gardenia* offers more
than the anticipated male-driven narrative. As Kaplan notes,

> Lang rather turns *noir* conventions upside down in *The Blue Gar-
> denia* by presenting two separate discourses—that is, two modes
> of articulating a vision of reality. There is the usual male discourse
> familiar from *noir* films and represented here by Casey Mayo, a
> journalist playing investigator, and the police; but alongside this,
> [Fritz] Lang has inserted the discourse of Norah, a young telephone
> operator—a discourse that presents the confusion and alienation of
> women in a male world. ("Place," 81)

Kaplan elaborates that the male discourse of the *noir* narrative is undercut in
two ways: first, because Norah possesses more knowledge than the male inves-

tigators about the night of the murder; and, second, because the film offers a perspective on women and female sexuality through the alignment of the audience with Norah rather than Casey (ibid., 85). All along, the film suggests that Norah was not the type of girl who would normally get involved in this kind of situation. When Norah sends her roommate Crystal (Ann Sothern) to meet with Casey, Casey suggests that Crystal is more the type of girl (i.e., a flashy, tough, blonde) who would have gone out with Prebble—and also the type who would have known how to "get rid of him in some other way" (i.e., without having to kill him). The film is a cautionary tale: good girls need to be careful not to get out of control and in a position where bad men can take advantage of them. The film concludes with Casey giving his little black book full of "bad girls" to a photographer as he is determined to have Norah. The film ultimately suggests women during the Korean War remain faithful to their men serving overseas. The film's other conservative discourse—like many other films at the time—is to encourage criminals to turn themselves in and confess their crimes, otherwise the weight of the guilt will cause them to go insane.

It would seem that heroines who attempted to demonstrate masculine intelligence, independence, or control were labeled "unnatural" once again in the 1950s. In the 1930s, it was the woman's sexuality that was questioned if she was demonstratively too masculine; in the 1950s, it was her sanity. In *Witness to Murder* (Rowland, 1954), Cheryl Draper (Barbara Stanwyck) explains to the police that she awoke in the night to see Albert Richter (George Sanders) kill a woman in the apartment across the street; however, the police do not believe her and drop the case after questioning Richter.[13] Cheryl is convinced that she has witnessed a murder and begins to investigate the alleged crime herself. Even Lieutenant Larry Mathews (Gary Merrill), with whom Cheryl begins a romance, does not believe it was anything more than a "realistic" dream. In fact, he worries that Cheryl's "obsession" with Richter is a sign that she is mentally ill:

Larry: I'm worried about you and not just officially. I don't like the *desperate* way you're running after this thing. Turning fantasy into reality. It's . . . it's unhealthy. You're too nice a girl.

Cheryl: You still think I dreamt it.

Larry: I'm positive.

Cheryl: How can you be sure?

Larry: Well, I've been checking. There isn't an iota of evidence that a crime was committed anywhere except in your imagination.

    Cheryl: Either that or Richter is a cleverer murderer than you are
             a detective.

And the film emphasizes this link between thinking, investigation, and masculinity. Larry tells Cheryl to stop thinking about the case and "Think about me instead." He suggests that the only appropriate thing for a woman to be contemplating is romance with the detective—not murder. Even though Larry as the detective and Richter as the murderer operate on opposite sides of the law, they both question Cheryl's psychological state of mind and, in the end, Cheryl is institutionalized. The film, however, supports Cheryl's conclusion that Richter is a cleverer murderer than Larry is a detective as Richter manufactures evidence that leads the official (i.e., male) investigators to erroneous conclusions.

Interestingly, the film begins with Richter removing the body from his apartment. The film thus supports Cheryl's version of the story but does not provide her with any recourse to bring him to justice. When she confronts Richter and asks him if he killed the young woman identified in the papers, he says, "Of course, I admit it. I have nothing to fear from you: you're insane. It's recorded in the police files and in hospital reports. Anything that you might foolishly say concerning my admission would merely corroborate their findings." In fact, Cheryl contemplates suicide while driving home after being rebuffed by Larry and tormented by Richter. At home, she finds Richter in her apartment with a typed suicide note and a plan to throw her out of her window to her death. Cheryl escapes temporarily but Richter corners her in a construction site and throws her over the edge. Luckily, she lands on a scaffolding platform, giving Larry time to dispatch Richter and pull her to safety. Cheryl's career as a detective has proven less than successful: she failed to bring the killer to justice through her discovery of facts and her theory is proven only when the killer attempts to kill her in front of a male witness. The film confirms that, even though Cheryl is a skilled sleuth and absolutely correct in her assumptions, the female detective lacks the respect of the male authorities.

Interestingly, in the 1950s, no longer is the debate for the female detective about careerist ambition, independence, or marriage but about her very sanity. In *Witness to Murder*, the female detective's masculinity (her compulsion to investigate) is regarded not as a nuisance as it often was in the mystery-comedies of the 1940s, but as unnatural and a sign of mental instability. By the 1950s, masculinity and femininity could no longer co-exist in the female detective as a successful combination and, by the end of the decade, the female detective disappears from the screen. In mainstream film, the female detective would not return as a major trend until the 1980s and her only significant outings in the meantime would be in B-level blaxploitation films in the early 1970s. It would be a long time, indeed, before the white female detective would be regarded in Hollywood film as meritorious.

Part III

From Crime-Fighter to
Crime Scene Investigator

1970 to Today

8

Femme Might Makes Right[1]

The 1970s Blaxploitation Vigilante Crime-Fighter

Dalton: I don't know . . . vigilante justice?

Foxy: It's as American as apple pie.

—Terry Carter and Pam Grier in *Foxy Brown* (1974)

Changing Times

The 1960s saw a dearth of detectives—black or white, male or female. While the hardboiled heroes of wartime *film noir* were prolific, detectives had all but disappeared from the screen by the 1960s. Those who did investigate crime during the two decades immediately following the end of World War II were conservative, reliable, and law-abiding procedural detectives—whether police or FBI agents—often fighting international threats. These were not sleuths who used their skills of observation and deduction to solve crimes; nor were they hardboiled private eyes who used their street smarts and fists to see justice served. Instead, the procedural offered an emphasis on the methods of police investigation: tracking and tailing, fingerprints and Photostats, surveillance and forensics were described in great—and often tedious—detail. Whereas the classical detective narrative had foregrounded "whodunit," the procedural—like *The House on 92nd Street* (Hathaway, 1945), *Call Northside 777* (Hathaway, 1948), and *The Naked City* (Dassin, 1948)—was more interested in police procedure—or how the police "dunit." The police detective combated crime by working as part of a team, pounding the pavement, pursuing every lead, and interviewing every witness or suspect until the truth was revealed. In the face of international threats during the Cold War, the procedural police detective or federal agent offered the reassuring message that the U.S. had the science and manpower to combat any threats to national and social security.

191

The stability and assurance that the procedural offered, however, seemed to lose its resonance with audiences and, by the mid-50s, the myth of the perfect police detective was no longer believable. Instead, the heroes of films such as *Rear Window* (Hitchcock, 1954) and *Vertigo* (Hitchcock, 1958)—and the star who played them, Jimmy Stewart—were representative of the fears of 1950s masculinity as feminized, victimized, or neurotic. The 1950s also saw the rise of the violent and corrupt detective from Jim McCleod (Kirk Douglas) in *Detective Story* (Wyler, 1951) to Mike Hammer (Ralph Meeker) in *Kiss Me Deadly* (Aldrich, 1955) and Hank Quinlan (Orson Welles) in *Touch of Evil* (Welles, 1958). It seemed natural that, in the decade following, there would be a shift in focus to the criminal as protagonist—including *Underworld U.S.A.* (Fuller, 1961), *Cape Fear* (Thompson, 1962), *The Killers* (Siegel, 1964), *Point Blank* (Boorman, 1967), *In Cold Blood* (Brooks, 1967), and *The Thomas Crown Affair* (Jewison, 1968). Films that did focus on the efforts of the detective—which were few and include *The Chase* (Penn, 1966) starring Marlon Brando, *Tony Rome* (Douglas, 1967) and its sequel *Lady in Cement* (Douglas, 1968) starring Frank Sinatra, and *Madigan* (Siegel, 1968) starring Richard Widmark—saw the beginning of an increasing focus on action (i.e., pursuing criminals rather than having to identify them).

When 1960s films did offer crime-fighting protagonists, they were most often spies—capitalizing on the success of the "James Bond" films beginning with *Dr. No* (Young, 1962). The detective (i.e., police detective, private investigator, or amateur sleuth) moved to television. A handful of television series focused on the exploits of female detectives: "Decoy" (1957–59) starring Beverly Garland as an undercover cop; "Honey West" (1965–66) a spinoff from "Burke's Law" starring Anne Francis as a private investigator; "The Girl from U.N.C.L.E." (1966–67) as a spinoff from "The Man from U.N.C.L.E." starring Stephanie Powers as female spy; "Police Woman" (1974–78) starring Angie Dickinson as an undercover cop; "Get Christie Love" (1974–75) about a black undercover cop (Teresa Graves); and "Charlie's Angels" (1976–81) the original cast of which included Jaclyn Smith, Kate Jackson, and Farrah Fawcett as private investigators. However, in film, female crime-fighters were all but absent in the 1970s, the exception being a handful of "blaxploitation" films.

The African-American heroes of blaxploitation—a cycle of films produced between 1971 and 1975 that exploited black subculture and black audiences— could not have appeared before the early 1970s. Social changes in the late 1960s coupled with the shifts in the film industry meant that graphic onscreen violence and sexuality became more acceptable and commonplace. As the saying goes, "Necessity is the mother of invention" and, indeed, by the 1960s, Hollywood was in dire need of innovation and change. The studio era had come to an end, beginning in 1948 with "divorcement." The U.S. Supreme Court's ruling in 1948—called the "Paramount Decision" or "Paramount Decree"—found the Majors in violation of U.S. antitrust laws and the Majors were forced to divorce production from exhibition (i.e., to sell off their theaters). The Majors' domination of the industry had been reliant on the guarantee of exhibition for their product; the loss of their theaters was a heavy blow. At the same time as the studios sold off their theaters, they were losing their audiences due to changes in demographics and leisure habits. Americans were moving to the suburbs away from the downtown theaters (and this is before the advent of the suburban mall multiplex) and staying home to watch television. By 1962, box-office admissions had dropped to a quarter of what they had been in 1946 (Maltby, *Hollywood*, 161).

Just as Hollywood had utilized new sound technology in the 1920s to innovate the movie-going experience, so too did Hollywood capitalize on new technologies—from widescreen formats to stereo sound to Technicolor—to differentiate its product from small-screen, black-and-white television. Industry executives, however, proved slow to recognize that big screen spectacle did not guarantee big box-office profits. Many film epics failed to recoup their higher production costs, including *Cleopatra* (Mankiewicz, 1963), *The Fall of the Roman Empire* (Mann, 1964), and *The Battle of Britain* (Hamilton, 1969); similarly, musicals also could not guarantee big returns and *Doctor Doolittle* (Fleischer, 1967), *Star!* (Wise, 1968), and *Paint your Wagon* (Logan, 1969) were all flops. The by-product of the period of instability from the mid-1960s to the mid-70s was an artistic rebirth of film during what critics have labelled the "Hollywood Renaissance." While Hollywood's big "event" films aimed at general audiences were hit or miss, low-budget niche films aimed at target audiences were pulling in profits. For example, *Easy Rider* grossed $19 million in domestic box office but only cost $340,000 to produce.[2] Renaissance films such as *Butch Cassidy and the Sundance Kid* (Hill, 1967), *The Graduate* (Nichols, 1967), *Bonnie and Clyde* (Penn, 1967), *Midnight Cowboy* (Schlesinger, 1969), and *Easy Rider* (Hopper, 1969) were aimed at youth audiences with their popular music soundtracks (vs. traditional orchestral scores) and depictions of drug culture, sexuality, and violence. Producers had pushed the Production Code to its limits from the mid-50s onwards: the influence of European film was being felt; audiences were demanding more realistic portrayals; and federal court decisions (1952–58) extended First Amendment protection to individual motion pictures. In 1968, the Code was abandoned and replaced with the "Ratings System"—under which any film could be released but, depending on its content, could be given a restrictive rating to exclude impressionable minors.

Hollywood's need for profits drove studios to explore niche subjects and audiences; the Civil Rights movement incited an awareness of black culture and subjectivity; and Vietnam and "flower power" created a desire for more realistic depictions of violence and sexuality, respectively. These shifts facilitated the development of a new kind of detective in Hollywood film—one that hit a cultural nerve. Crime-fighting came to be used less in the metaphorical sense—i.e., the detective who investigated the puzzle of a crime to bring a criminal to justice—and more in the literal sense—i.e., detectives engaged in violent physical confrontations with the criminals. Films like *Bullitt* (Yates, 1968), *Coogan's Bluff* (Siegel, 1968), *The French Connection* (Friedkin, 1971), and *Dirty Harry* (Siegel, 1971) offered a tough and often angry hero who—even if it meant breaking the law—could bring about the end of what seemed to be the growing problem of crime. In keeping with President Nixon's hard-line politics on crime and with a widespread loss of confidence in the power of law enforcement, the violent vigilante cop offered a potent fantasy of empowered masculinity. With science and teamwork aligned with bureaucracy, the police detective was a lone hero—not unlike the Western hero—who could win the war against crime because he was as tough, and often as lawless, as the criminals he pursued. The character most readily identified with this kind of hero is Clint Eastwood's Inspector Harry Callahan—nicknamed "Dirty Harry" because he does the dirty jobs that no one else wants to do. Because of his history playing Western heroes through the 1950s and 60s, Eastwood brought to his detective associations of lawlessness, violence, independence, and silent but unwavering resolve. Dirty Harry was, in many ways, a Western hero transplanted to the city streets. As a product of his time, the vigilante hero can be seen as a renovation of traditional models of masculinity to be relevant to a changing social and political landscape. This need and desire for new models of masculinity also meant a redefinition of other kinds of masculinity—including black heroes.

Blaxploitation

This was certainly true during the 1970s: when a group of films did appear centered on black characters and experiences, they were not necessarily the product of the black community but of Hollywood. These films were described as exploiting the black community for the profits of white film producers and thus were dubbed "blaxploitation" films. This group of films was made possible by the success of the independent black-produced film *Sweet Sweetback's Baadas-sss Song* (1971)—starring and written, produced, and directed by Melvin Van Peebles. The exploitative aspect of the genre began when Hollywood attempted to duplicate the film's success with its own "black" film—*Shaft* (Parks, 1971). A notable element of the blaxploitation film was the soundtrack: famous and up-and-coming black artists from Curtis Mayfield to Isaac Hayes produced contemporary rhythm-and-blues tracks for the films, including the Academy Award-winning title track of *Shaft*. While MGM was responsible for *Shaft* and followed it up with a sequel, many other studios hopped on the bandwagon, including major studios like Warner Bros. and Paramount and independents like American International Pictures (AIP), Dimension, General Film Corp, and Moonstone. As Josiah Howard suggests, with *Shaft* and *Sweetback*, "a formula" was established: a cast featuring black actors, black characters who were placed in positions of dominance over whites, a setting in the ghetto, dialogue defined by slang and profanity, and a significant amount of sex and violence were all that was needed for "a sure-fire hit" (11). The idea of blaxploitation as a genre, however, poses a problem in invoking a singular idea of a film. The kinds of films that have been labeled blaxploitation vary greatly from Westerns to prison films to horror flicks. While Howard argues that blaxploitation films maintained popularity from 1971–75 and that the movement's last notable year was 1976, Yvonne Sims suggests that the appeal of the formulaic blaxploitation film had worn thin with audiences by 1974 (140).

Super Fly (Parks, Jr., 1972) was a landmark film. As reported in Variety, Super Fly bumped The Godfather (Coppola, 1971) out of top spot and, for a short time, was the highest grossing film—black or white—in the U.S. (4 October 1972). As Howard explains, the release of Super Fly polarized black filmgoers into two groups: the first who regarded such films positively for giving black actors leading roles on the screen, and the second who regarded them negatively because of their focus on violence, "pornography," and derogatory images of black subculture (12). Pam Grier, the only woman to achieve star status from the movement, defended the violent content of the films at the time. As she explained to Time magazine, "There are a mass of blacks who like action films. They can't release their aggressions on Hollywood soap operas" (Qtd. in Howard, 13). As Chris Holmlund argues, one cannot simply dismiss all blaxploitation films because they may be exploitative; to do so is to overlook the differences in style, political context, and especially the audience's racial constitution ("Wham," 108). Blaxploitation took Hollywood stereotypes of black masculinity as violent, dangerous, and hypersexual (e.g., being attracted, and attractive, to white women) and blew them out of proportion. In doing so, blaxploitation films not only exposed them as stereotypes but also attempted to reclaim and reimagine the mythified conceptions of black masculinity as something determined by the black community—not white. In opposition to Sidney Poitier's Hollywood integrationist hero of the 1950s and 60s, the blaxploitation heroes of the early 1970s embodied the call for equality represented by the Civil Rights movement and for separatism represented by the Black Power movement.

The majority of blaxploitation films focused on the reimagining of black masculinity and black women were often relegated to the minor role of sexual object, present only to highlight the hero's potent masculinity. As Stephane Dunn notes,

> By 1973, black-oriented urban action films demonstrated the precariousness of projecting black empowerment and political radicalism within the context of mainstream perspectives and of Hollywood's commodification of black films. Black power became apoliticized

and largely transformed into a violent and racist phallicization of desire, a desire projected in great part through the spectacle of female bodies. (84)

However, the summer of 1973 did see a dramatic change in the representation of black women onscreen—with the release of both *Coffy* and *Cleopatra Jones*.

Part I: Black Female Vigilantes

Blaxploitation offered several films with female crime-fighting heroes—including *Cleopatra Jones* (Starrett, 1973) starring Tamara Dobson, and *Coffy* (Hill, 1973), *Foxy Brown* (Hill, 1974), and *Sheba, Baby* (Girdler, 1975) all starring Pam Grier.[3] And these films have remarkably similar narrative patterns and common thematic elements: first, the heroine's motivation for getting involved is either because it is her job—e.g., Cleopatra Jones is a government agent and Friday Foster a photojournalist—or, more typically, because a loved one is the victim of criminal violence—e.g., Coffy's sister, Foxy's lover, and Sheba's father. Even Cleopatra's motivation for coming home is personal: the villain organizes a raid on the community's halfway house run by her boyfriend. Second, following the trend set by white cop-action films like *Dirty Harry* and black detective films like *Cotton Comes to Harlem* (Davis, 1970) and *Shaft*, the blaxploitation female crime-fighter films are as much about exciting scenes of action as they are about investigating crime and each film features an array of hand-to-hand combat, shootouts, vehicle chases, explosions, and attempted rapes. And these women are aligned with the white male cop-action heroes of the early 1970s through their use of phallic weapons—for example, Sheba Shayne sports a .44 Magnum and drives a Ford Mustang (just like the hero of *Dirty Harry*). Third, these films, however, also had a social message to offer: they exposed some of the myths about the black community and demonstrated how the white-run drug trade and racism were to blame for the underachievement of black men. Last, like the male detectives in *Cotton Comes to Harlem* and *Shaft*, these female detectives are empowered because of their race; in other words, they investigate crime in a world that white, official law enforcers cannot gain access to, and their intimate knowledge of the black community is one of the blaxploitation detective's special skills. Unlike the male detective, however, these female detectives are also empowered by their sex: as a woman, the blaxploitation heroine can infiltrate a criminal organization unsuspected and fashion weapons out of domestic objects. Indeed, the names of these heroines evoke their race (e.g., Coffy and Brown)—as the lyrics of the theme song for *Coffy* suggest, "Coffy is the color of your skin/Coffy is the color of the world you live in"—or their sex by referencing powerful women of ancient history (e.g., Cleopatra and Sheba).[4]

The earliest of these films—*Cleopatra Jones* and *Coffy*—see the heroine as much more competent; however, by the end of the blaxploitation movement films like *Sheba, Baby* and *Friday Foster* (Marks, 1975) offered—along with their decrease in the level of violence, sex, nudity, and social critique—a diminishment of the level of independence of the heroine. Critics, then and now, have debated the merits of these films, praising the strength of their heroines but condemning their thin plotlines, gratuitous sex and violence, and exploitation of black subculture for white film industry profits. I would argue, however, that this small group of blaxploitation films is significant because these female crime-fighting vigilantes had no white female equivalent during the same period. In fact, these blaxploitation women would be the only group of strong women fighting crime onscreen for more than another decade. As I have explored in previous chapters and will in the ones that follow, Hollywood defines heroism as white, male, and middle-class. The contribution of this handful of blaxploitation films then is to challenge those assumptions through the proffering of black, working-class women as the saviors of their communities.

I have also included *Foxy Brown* (1974) in this section because it was originally intended to be a sequel to *Coffy*—originally entitled *Burn, Coffy, Burn!* According to the film's director Jack Hill, at the last minute the AIP sales department crunched the numbers and said that "Sequels were not making it" (138–39). With little alteration, the same script was used for a new heroine Foxy Brown. As I have explained earlier, the two categories of detective are the sleuth and the undercover crime-fighter/agent: while the former were the dominant type throughout the 1930s and 40s, it is the latter who dominates the 1970s—no doubt capitalizing on the popular "James Bond" and "Dirty Harry" trends. Coffy, Foxy, and Cleo are all effectively the second type (even if Cleopatra does not operate undercover). They investigate a crime racket rather than a specific crime and maneuver in close enough, not to identify the criminal because they already know who it is, but to bring that criminal to justice. Critics tended to dismiss these films for their violence, weak plotlines, and low production values (e.g., *Coffy* had a budget of $500,000 and was completed in 18 days of shooting).[5] The B-level status of these films, however, does not diminish the fact that they struck a cultural nerve with young, black audiences and proved popular. And several of these films do surpass their humble production values or cobbled together scripts. As Sims suggests, Grier's accomplishment was her transcendence of "the one-dimensional roles that focused on her physical attributes and the weak storylines in AIP productions" with her creation of strong heroines (72).

Femme Men

All three of the early films—*Coffy*, *Cleopatra Jones*, and *Foxy Brown*—offer similar characters, tropes, themes, and, especially, heroines. And all three thematize a debate about gender roles—about women being too masculine and men too feminine, with the heroines being presented as the ideal, embodying just the right balance of both. Feminist critics have debated whether or not injecting a woman into a male role—like that of action hero—constitutes a feminist model of womanhood as there is typically little consideration of the hero's sex. The blaxploitation film, however, highlights the issues that arise when the detective is a woman. On the one hand, she has skills afforded by her sex in terms of outwitting the enemy but, on the other, her sex can make her the potential victim of male violence—especially rape. These heroines take on the masculine role of vigilante crime-fighter when they see their loved ones harmed by criminals; they then use a masquerade of excessive femininity to disarm the criminals and get close enough to them to destroy them. In other words, these heroines use the stereotype of femininity against those—especially men—who firmly believe in the stereotype. For example, Coffy (Pam Grier) is introduced undercover: she reclines in a drug dealer's limo in a dress that reveals a lot of leg and cleavage, posing as a junkie willing "to do anything" for a fix. At the time, her conversation with Sugarman (Morris Buchanan) *seems* to be about the exchange of sexual favors for drugs:

> Sugarman: Well honey, you're with friends at last. We're gonna straighten you out for sure.
>
> Coffy: You know just the words that turn me on. And I know what you want too and you're gonna get it. [. . .]
>
> Sugarman: Hey, ain't one man big enough for you, honey?
>
> Coffy: Now, do I look like the kind of girl one man would be enough for?
>
> Sugarman: One big man.
>
> Coffy: One big dealin' man, maybe.

In the end, of course, one man will not be enough to stop the drug ring but it is a start. In the following scene, Coffy sits on the bed with Sugarman with one breast exposed. She asks him to turn out the lights, suggesting she will then take off her clothes; instead, she pulls out a shotgun and explains, "This is the end of your rotten life, you mother fucking dope pusher." Then, in very graphic detail, the film shows her blow his head off as the camera sits unwaveringly behind him. In retrospect, one can reinterpret Coffy's comments to Sugarman in the car as being about revenge for getting her 11-year-old sister hooked on drugs. From a sexy and helpless woman to an empowered killer employing an incredibly phallic weapon, Coffy reveals her "true self:" a nurse-turned-vigilante seeking justice for her community.

Similarly, in *Foxy Brown*, the heroine (Grier) is awakened by a call from her brother, Link (Antonio Fargas) who has been cornered by two white henchmen looking for repayment on his $20,000 loan. Foxy dresses—slipping a gun into her bra as a holster (a masculine use for a feminine object)—and then uses her car as a battering ram against the henchmen to rescue her brother in an interesting twist on the knight-riding-to-the-rescue-of-the-damsel-in-distress trope. Foxy's boyfriend, Dalton Ford (Terry Carter), had been working as an undercover narcotics agent on a case for two years when he was shot; with the villains believing he is dead, Dalton undergoes plastic surgery and an identity change so that he and Foxy can move away and start a new life together. Unfortunately, Link sells Dalton out and Dalton is gunned down on Foxy's doorstep on the day of their planned departure. Rather than fall apart over the death of her lover, Foxy opts for revenge and her first visit is to her brother. She knocks on his door and claims to be a damsel-in-distress needing help; when Link opens the door, Foxy strides in with a gun, trashes his place, and shoots him—demanding information on who Link is working for. When she leaves, Link's girlfriend demands, "Who does she think she is!?" Despite having been shot by her, Link demonstrates his respect for Foxy when he explains, "That's my sister, baby, and she's a whole lotta woman!" From topless in the bedroom to using a car and gun as phallic weapons, Foxy Brown embodies both masculinity and femininity as "a whole lotta woman."

There is something very human and vulnerable about both Coffy and Foxy: they are not invincible superheroes but normal women who end up pursuing the villains out of grief and anger. On the other hand, there is something superhuman about Cleopatra Jones as embodied by former model, Tamara Dobson. As the poster explains "6ft 2in of dynamite explodes into action." Dobson—unusually tall for a Hollywood actress, graceful as a former model, and stylish in flamboyant fur coats and turbans—is presented as an obvious outsider to the spaces she visits in the course of her investigation—from the Turkish desert to a California junkyard. Unlike Coffy and Foxy, Cleo is an official law enforcer and, therefore, is not, by definition, a vigilante. However, I would point out that, while she has the cooperation and respect of the local police (something that Dirty Harry never did), Cleo works alone and does use, perhaps, unnecessary force to defeat the villains—and is, in these ways, similar to Grier's heroines. Despite the respect that she does receive from a variety of different male authority figures, I would note that Captain Crawford (Dan Frazer), along with many men in the film, talk to Cleo in a misogynist tone. For example, after the attack at the airport, Crawford asks her, "Are you okay?" She replies, "My body's okay." Crawford qualifies her reply and comments, "It's magnificent!" Cleo, however, is unfazed by such comments and always remains cool, authoritative, and professional—even if the male authority figures are not.

Unlike Coffy and Foxy who get visibly upset and angry, Cleo never becomes emotional, except for the occasional laugh and smile—usually offered in moments where she performs masculine mastery of martial arts or driving skills.

Although Coffy, Foxy, and Cleo pursue vigilante justice and are effectively action-oriented crime-fighters, they are characterized as highly intelligent and effective sleuths as well. After all, they do pursue clues and leads, interrogate suspects, and discover the truth about who is ultimately responsible for the drug racket plaguing their neighborhood. Cleo employs her skills as an investigator to uncover the truth about the police involvement in the drug and gun trade. Similarly, Coffy extracts information from a prostitute to lead her to a key dealer and pimp, King George (Robert DoQui), and then manipulates King George to lead her to the higher-level mobster Vitroni (Allan Arbus). Lastly, Foxy infiltrates Miss Katherine's prostitution ring and outwits her and her henchmen. The crime-fighting weapons these women rely on are not just their feet, fists, and guns but also their intelligence.

Combating the Problem

At the time, some critics described Cleo as "a black distaff James Bond" (Mebane, 13) with an emphasis on action and, certainly, the film begins—like a Bond film—in an exotic locale: poppy fields in Turkey. The film identifies Cleo as a "wonder woman" (as one of the cops refers to her) and she is—like Bond—an almost cartoon-like hero of exceptional charm and seemingly invincible. And—also like Bond—Cleo drives a fancy car (a Corvette Stingray), has technological gadgets at her disposal (a car phone), is eternally cool and calm in any situation, and is attractive to the opposite sex. Critic Chris Norton argues that Cleo's over-the-top outfits are similarly "analogous with Bond's dinner jackets and playboy wardrobe"—both signify "the height of good taste" (Norton).[6] However—unlike Bond—Cleo's central role is not as a spy fighting international criminals in exotic locales (at least in the first film), but dealing with the real-life issues of drugs at home in the Los Angeles urban black community.

The social problems that all three films identify as plaguing the inner-city black community are the drug trade, political corruption, and the lack of opportunities for the people of that community. In *Foxy Brown*, it is suggested that if there were more opportunities for black men to be successful, they would not turn to illegal rackets.

> Link: Foxy, look baby, I'm a black man, and I don't know how
>   to sing, and I don't know how to dance, and I don't know
>   how to preach to no congregation. I'm too small to be a
>   football hero, and I'm too ugly to be elected mayor. But I
>   watch TV and I see all them people in all them fine homes

Fig. 8.1. A Wonder Woman: Tamara Dobson's Cleopatra Jones has been described as "a black distaff James Bond." As do Bond films, *Cleopatra Jones* (1973) begins in an exotic locale: the poppy fields in Turkey that supply America's drug trade. Photo from author's collection.

>   they live in and all them nice cars they drive, I get all full
>   of ambition. Now you tell me what I'm supposed to do
>   with all this ambition, I got?
>
> Foxy: I don't know, Link, I just don't want to see you end up in
>   jail, or shot down in the streets somewhere.
>
> Link: Baby, jail is where some of the finest people I know are
>   these days.

Similarly, in *Coffy*, the heroine's councilman boyfriend, Howard Brunswick (Booker Bradshaw), talks about youth addiction saying that a young man told him "I would rather be a junkie than be nothing." Brunswick argues that there is a problem with the power structure that would afford no opportunities to "black" (African) and "brown" (Hispanic) Americans. And so many young, ambitious black men turn to the drug trade to make a success of themselves and to realize the American Dream. In *Coffy*, a drug pusher gets Coffy's little sister hooked on dope; in *Cleopatra Jones*, drugs are being smuggled in from Turkey; and in *Foxy Brown*, Link as a drug pusher is responsible for Foxy's boyfriend's murder. However, the overarching problem in each film is not the low-level black pushers or even the mid-level black dealers but the white heads of the organizations or the corrupt officials who benefit from the illegal rackets. In *Coffy*, it is civic leaders like Brunswick, a black councilman, who facilitate the drug trade; in *Cleopatra Jones*, it is an older white woman, "Mommy" (Shelley Winters), who spreads dope to the streets; and in *Foxy Brown*, it is white woman, Miss Katherine (Kathryn Loder), who is a "fixer," using a high-class call girl racket to ensure the protection of her dealers from the judge and grand jury member clientele.

By dispatching the criminals, these women not only avenge the harm done to their loved ones, but they help save their communities. In an article for *The New York Times*, Mary Mebane discusses how films like *Cleopatra Jones* marked a positive shift in the blaxploitation movement to explore the strengths of the black community instead of just exploiting its weaknesses. As Mebane suggests, on the surface *Cleopatra Jones* may appear to be a Bond type of film, "Underneath, however, there is a story of black people loving and helping each other" (13). The final scene of the film is of her community and even Captain Crawford cheering her on as she drives off to ensure a drug-free future for black communities in America. Although critics describe *Cleopatra Jones* as the PG-rated version of the female blaxploitation film, it was actually R-rated (and *Coffy* X-rated) because of the language, violence, and suggested sex (there was, however, no nudity, at Dobson's insistence). While *Cleopatra Jones* does discuss problems in the black community, the white lesbian villain, Mommy, is so over-the-top and the scenes at her lair so campy that it is hard to connect her with the realities of the drug trade. Instead, *Coffy* is more gritty and realistic and certainly more disturbing in its scenes of excessive violence: Coffy shoots a man's head and her boyfriend's private parts off with a shotgun and the villains drag another man behind a car by the neck until dead in a contemporary version of lynching. Cleo does kill a few henchmen in the course of the film but, since her weapon of choice is martial arts, there is not the same level of disturbing violence as in *Coffy*. While *Cleopatra Jones* ends on the happy note that the drug dealers have been dispatched and the heroine is seen off on another mission by her friends and community, *Coffy* ends on a darker note with her maiming/killing her lover and walking off down the beach into the sunrise alone. The song on the soundtrack tries to reassure us that "It's not the end, it's the beginning" but the film has demonstrated that people in power (e.g., Brunswick) are corrupt, that even lovers (e.g., Brunswick) will betray you, and that the good guys (e.g., the cop, Carter) are destroyed. While *Cleopatra Jones* suggests the local law enforcement is on board with attempting to wipe out the drug trade, *Coffy* more pessimistically implies that the only person who is able to bring about the demise of the ring of conspirators is a black woman enacting vigilante justice with a shotgun.

Gender Issues

Rather than blindly insert a female hero into the "Dirty Harry" role, the blaxploitation film highlights the issues that arise when the main protagonist is a
woman. Foxy Brown is the victim of rape at Miss Katherine's ranch: her redneck
captors shoot Foxy full of heroin and then one of them rapes her. Similarly, Coffy
is almost the victim of rape after she and policeman Carter (William Elliott)
are beaten at his apartment. In a related vein, often the blaxploitation heroine
must have sexual relations with a villain—e.g., Coffy with King George and
the gangster Omar (Sid Haig)—in order to achieve her ultimate goals. Interestingly, the punishment for many of these men is a metaphorical, and sometimes
literal, castration. During this period, a cycle of B-grade rape-and-revenge films
appeared in which violence is regarded as the appropriate punishment for the
rapists (Dunn, 126) and the blaxploitation female crime-fighter films echoed
this established theme: while the male villain represents the threat of rape to
the heroine, these films suggest that the heroine represents an equally potent
sexual threat to the male. When men try to have sex with her, Coffy blows off
one man's head (Sugarman), punctures another's neck (Omar), shoots off his
genitalia with a shotgun (Brunswick), and is ultimately responsible for another
being lynched (George). Similarly, Foxy has her revenge on a judge who uses
prostitutes by ridiculing his manhood and, later, presents Miss Katherine with
her lover's genitalia in a pickle jar:

> Katherine: Why didn't you kill me too? Well go on and shoot!
>   I don't want to live anymore!
>
> Foxy: I know. That's the idea. The rest of your boyfriend
>   is still around, and I hope you two live a long time,
>   and then maybe you get to feel what I feel. Death
>   is too easy for you, bitch! I want you to suffer.

Since Miss Katherine took away her happy future with Dalton, Foxy's revenge
is to take away any possibility of one for Miss Katherine with Steve by castrating him. Cleo, as the "PG-rated" version of the genre, is never the victim
of attempted rape and the furthest she goes in castrating a man is to kick a
corrupt cop in the groin.

As in the case of the female detectives of the 1930s, the blaxploitation
heroine is masculinized in some respects (although rarely in terms of physical
appearance) and it is her masculinity that attracts her lovers. For example, Cleo
tracks down the brother of drug dealer Doodlebug's girlfriend at a motocross
race; however, he refuses to talk to her and speeds off onto the course on his
motorbike. Cleo attempts to borrow another man's bike but he does not believe
a beautiful woman like her could drive it without damaging it or herself; her

offering of her Corvette as collateral convinces him. She then removes her fur coat to reveal that she is wearing no bra and a very low-cut blouse: in this hyperfeminine outfit she performs hypermasculine mastery of the bike as she races up and over the hill to catch up to Tiffany's brother. In an extended car chase sequence, Cleo once again shows her mastery of a manly vehicle: this time she drives her Corvette through alleys, streets, and viaducts with the skill of a race car driver and many shots cut from her grinning face to her feminine hand on the phallic gear shift. Similarly, Foxy and Coffy often only gain the respect of men by using strong (i.e., masculine) language, demonstrating their skills performing violence, and proving their ability to kill when necessary. Lastly, all three women demonstrate that they are sexually liberated and pursue sex often with more than one man for their own pleasure. Each woman pursues her lover aggressively—often when he is injured and more vulnerable. For example, Foxy seduces Dalton in his hospital room while he is recovering from surgery and Cleo, her boyfriend Reuben (Bernie Casey) while he is recuperating after being shot.[7]

While these blaxploitation films represent a revision of Hollywood's racial codes by having black heroines at the center of the narrative, they replicate Hollywood's heteronormative codes by aligning criminality with sexual transgression. All of the villains are portrayed as sexually deviant whether because they desire too much sex from too many partners or because their sexual tastes are considered abnormal for their sex. For example, the white female villains are presented as masculine in their behavior and, especially, their sexual appetites. Mommy, despite her name, orders her male minions about and kills them when they do not obey; she also surrounds herself with a stable of pretty, young, female lovers. Likewise, Miss Katherine, despite her feminine looks, proves herself a tough task master and uses her head henchman, Steve (Peter Brown), for sexual gratification (his look as she embraces him suggests that he is not always a willing lover). In opposition to this, many of the male villains are presented as vain (i.e., feminized) and sexually insatiable, demanding multiple lovers. In *Cleopatra Jones*, drug dealer Doodlebug (Antonio Fargas) explains how:

> Hair's like a woman. You treat it good and it treats you good. Ain't that right honey? You hear what I'm saying? Yeah, you got to hold it, caress it, and love it. And if your hair gets out of line you take a scissor and say, "Hair I'm going to cut you."

His last act as he lays in the street dying, the victim of a drive-by ordered by Mommy, is to stroke his afro. Similarly, drug pusher Snake (Christopher Joy) gives up information to Cleo only when she destroys his "double knits" (shirts) and "high heels" (shoes). In *Coffy*, Sugarman strips to matching purple undershirt and boxers just before Coffy blows his head off. These films suggest that women who are too aggressive and men who are too vain are deviant and, thus, evil. In contrast, Coffy, Foxy, and Cleo are not punished for their adoption of masculinity into femininity, but nor do they attempt to rule over their men or men in positions of authority: they are essentially feminine women incited to violence by the violence committed by the gender-bending villains.

Despite her masculine demonstrations of strength, each heroine demonstrates a moment of feminine weakness just before the climax of the film: she is temporarily re-feminized. Although a secret agent, proficient at fighting and shooting, and nicknamed "a wonder woman," Cleo finds herself in need of rescue. Mommy's men successfully entrap Cleo and Doodlebug's girlfriend, Tiffany (Brenda Sykes), in the trunk of a station wagon that is about to be destroyed in the junkyard: rather than being able to free them herself, Cleo must be saved by her male friends—Rueben and karate experts, the Johnson brothers (Albert Popwell and Caro Kenyatta). After the shootouts in which Cleo sports a machine gun, the car chases in which she handled her Corvette like a race car, and the fight scenes in which she defeated every opponent, it seems incongruous that she would be a damsel who needs saving. Yet, she makes no attempt to save herself or Tiffany despite the fact that the car is on a conveyor belt (i.e., she has plenty of time to do so) and the rear window of the car is missing (i.e., she has opportunity to do so). After her rescue by her male friends, Cleo is redeemed as a hero when she triumphs over Mommy in a showdown. Coffy's moment of weakness is an emotional one. Brunswick tries to convince her that he is involved in the racket only so that he can gain the power to change things and put money back into the hands of black people: he says that *together* they can do good things. She is confused and tells him, "I just don't know anymore." He replies, "All you have to know, baby, is that I'm your man. I'm gonna take care of you and I'm gonna steer you straight." She seems capable of forgiving him for his betrayal of the black community as it seems to be working toward a better future; however, she cannot forgive his personal betrayal of her. Whether or not she was about to give in to him, Coffy discovers that he has already replaced her when his white lover appears at the top of the stairs. Coffy is no longer confused and fires a shotgun blast at Brunswick's groin before walking away. Similarly, after the brawl at the lesbian bar, Foxy helps prostitute Claudia (Juanita Brown) escape only to find herself trapped by Miss Katherine's henchman. Steve intervenes, saving her from being killed, but sends her to a more questionable fate at "The Ranch" where she is shot full of heroin and raped. Foxy reasserts herself by killing the henchmen, destroying The Ranch with fire, and castrating Steve.

The purpose of these moments of weakness is twofold: first, likely they are to make the heroines' heroic finales even more satisfying when they reassert their strength and independence; and, second, to re-feminize the heroines—to assure audiences that she is not totally masculine and can still be a woman. After all, as Howard notes in his study, the key demographic for these films was not necessarily a female—but a young male—audience. Indeed, the majority of these films offer a catfight between the heroine and female leader (or the male leader's women) with dresses inevitably torn and breasts exposed, as well as sex scenes in which the heroine is naked. Such visual pleasures were geared for the male audience and so too then, perhaps, is the need to make these heroines re-feminized and vulnerable—even if only for one scene.

Despite these moments of feminine weakness and objectification, the heroines—by and large—are successful *because of* their femininity. The specifically feminine skill demonstrated by all three characters is a MacGyver-like ability to create weapons out of ordinary domestic (i.e., feminine) objects and/or to use their feminine bodies to lull their enemy into a false sense of security.[8] For example, Foxy hides her small firearm, first, in her bra as a holster and, later, in her afro. At The Ranch, she uses her tongue to grab a razor with which to cut her bonds then she turns a handful of coat hangers into a weapon to claw the face of her rapist. Coffy also places razor blades in her hair, anticipating a catfight with King George's girlfriend; she hides a gun in a stuffed animal in her purse when she is sent to have sex with Vitroni; and she turns a hairpin into a knife-like weapon by sharpening it on a stone in the sauna in which she is held prisoner. More importantly, it is their femininity that allows them to infiltrate the villain's racket—often undercover as a prostitute—and also to gain access to male villains when they are at their most vulnerable—in the bedroom. The mistake these men make is underestimating the power, ingenuity, and resolve of a beautiful woman: in other words, these men are guilty of stereotyping women, equating femininity with weakness, and assuming that beauty and brains are mutually exclusive. All three films suggest that what makes these women successful in bringing down the organized crime rackets that the police seem powerless to is their sex.

Part II: Toned Down

Although *Sheba, Baby* and *Friday Foster* follow the same formula as *Coffy*, *Cleopatra Jones*, and *Foxy Brown*, they offer toned-down versions of the earlier films' heroines. *Sheba, Baby* contains several of the elements of the earlier three films: the heroine pursues a ring of criminals because they victimize her loved one; she gains access to the inner circle of the ring by posing as a feminized version of herself, for the leader's sexual pleasure; she engages in a catfight with the leader's girlfriend; she plays MacGyver, extracting a blade from a discarded knife to use as a weapon; and the leader threatens to rape her. And the line for the poster—"Queen of the Private Eyes/Hotter'n 'Coffy'/Meaner'n 'Foxy Brown' "—situates her firmly within their tradition. However, Sheba is a less empowered character than her predecessors, lacking the ability (read: opportunity) to act heroically. By 1975, the blaxploitation heroine is no longer a lone vigilante. Unlike Coffy and Foxy, Sheba Shayne (Pam Grier) is a professional investigator: once a cop in Louisville, Kentucky, she is now a licensed private investigator in Chicago. However, when a hood named Pilot (D'Urville Martin) attempts to scare Sheba's father, Andy (Rudy Challenger), and former boyfriend, Brick (Austin Stoker), into selling their loan business, Sheba returns to Louisville to help. As she explains to her father, "Dad, I know you think I am doing a man's job, but I am not going to sit on the sidelines just because I'm a woman."

Thus, like the earlier blaxploitation films, the heroine's motivation is, initially, to help her father and then, later, to avenge his death and protect his business. Unlike the previous films, however, there is no female frontal nudity (despite one sex scene), the violence is greatly reduced, and the film addresses less hard-hitting social issues. In this film, the problem is no longer drugs in Los Angeles but legitimate black entrepreneurs being forced out of business in the South. As Sheba tells the cops, "I've seen business after business go under. First it was the pawn shops, then the bars, and when I left town it was the employment agencies, now the used car lots." A black man, Pilot, may be the head of the loan shop and car dealership monopoly in the city, but it is a white man, Shark (Dick Merrifield), who is eventually revealed to be the head of the insurance company scam. Sheba goes to the police for protection for her father and to ask them to stop the illegal dealings in town, but they refuse. She explains to Brick that, "Now, I do what the police won't." Brick tries to talk her out of pursuing such dangerous men and to let the official law enforcers deal with it:

> Brick: We're not equipped to fight a bunch like that . . . not on their terms.
>
> Sheba: Well, that's the only way to fight 'em *is* on their terms.
>
> Brick: Not outside the law.
>
> Sheba: Well, we'll just have to bend the law.

Ironically, the film allows her not only to be more successful than the police but also justified in pursuing vigilante justice. She is not punished or even reprimanded by the police for exacting justice on her own and killing several of first Pilot's and later Shark's men in the process.

Unlike her predecessors, however, Sheba is shown as only partly competent. Her investigation takes her to Shark's yacht where she initially gains entry undercover during a party, but she is soon identified by Pilot and jumps overboard. She swims to shore, dons a wetsuit and swims back to the yacht with a machine gun, but one of his men easily disarms her and she is taken captive. While captive she finds a knife, which she then conceals and uses to cut herself loose when they try to drag her behind a speedboat to silence her. She climbs back on board and sneaks up on Shark with a machine gun she has taken from one of his men but is easily disarmed—again. Luckily sirens announce the imminent arrival of the Coast Guard and Shark attempts to get away in a speedboat. Sheba shoots one of his men driving off in another speedboat, uses a jet ski to get to that boat, and then catches up to Shark and dispatches him with a harpoon gun. Although it takes her several attempts to exact justice, in the end, she is successful. When the police arrive on the scene, she informs the lieutenant, "You can have your town back."

Sheba is more reliant on her male interest, Brick, than her predecessors to assist her during her investigation and also to comfort her when the investigation is finally over. She does not, however, stay in Louisville to marry him nor does she take him up on his offer to move to Chicago to be with her. Earlier, he asked her if she was seeing anyone. She replied, "Well, if you're asking if, 'do I sleep alone every night of the week?' I'd have to say 'No.' And then again if you're asking if I am going with someone steady, I'd have to say 'No.' So what are you asking?" Sheba is an independent woman, in charge of her own sexuality and committed to her career. However, the film is uneven or inconsistent in its representation of its heroine: Sheba is sometimes shown to be incompetent even if she is ultimately successful. Similarly, she is mainly shown to be a strong, independent woman and, yet, she is also blatantly objectified—and not in the usual undercover or attempted rape scenes. This schizophrenic representation is perhaps best illustrated in the opening/closing sequence: just as John Shaft does in the famous credit sequence of *Shaft*, Sheba strides purposefully and confidently around the streets of Chicago while her theme song plays. The lyrics suggest an inconsistency in Sheba's construction as a character:

> She's a dangerous lady
> and is well put together
> She's a dangerous lady
> who can change like the weather
> [. . .]
> A sensuous woman playing a man's game
> Chicago fights to Louisville nights
> She's kickin' ass and taking names.

But the ass that is seen on screen is her's: a close-up shows her rear view as she walks away from the camera. As Linda Mizejewski suggests, "Sheba is a heady amalgam of superwoman and centrefold" (*Hardboiled*, 117). While Sheba Shayne may embody a somewhat contradictory representation of the blaxploitation female crime-fighter, *Friday Foster* signifies her extermination.

Friday Foster deviates most from the established pattern despite the fact that the poster tagline—"Wham! Bam! Here comes Pam!"—promises more of the same from its star. Although it offers many of the same elements from the earlier films—the heroine's own theme song, car chases, shootouts, and problems facing the black community—the film abandons several established elements and deviates notably from the themes, plots, and characterizations that had dominated the cycle of film. For example, there is little attempt made to identify whites as being at the top of the conspiracy against the black community; there are no catfights between the heroine and any other women (or men for that matter); there is no prostitution and thus the heroine does not have to work undercover and, relatedly, there is no debate about gender through the heroine's masquerade of hyperfemininity; there is no bad language, no excessive violence, and very little nudity or sex; lastly, there is not really a tough crime-fighting heroine.

Monk Riley (Julius Harris), editor of *Glance Magazine*, asks Friday Foster (Grier) to do a job on New Year's Eve only when he cannot track down his star (white and male) photographer. He needs Friday to take photos of black billionaire, Blake Tarr (Thalmus Rasulala), when he returns to the city. She wonders out loud what brought Tarr back but her editor tells her, "Don't wonder, Friday. Just take your cute little behind out there and get those pictures and, goddamnit, don't get involved!" In other words, don't think just do as you are told; however, she does get involved when an assassination attempt is made on Tarr and when Friday's modeling friend, Clorils (Rosalind Miles) is murdered. Friday and private investigator Colt Hawkins (Yaphet Kotto) decide to investigate and they follow a lead to Washington D.C. There, Friday becomes romantically entwined with Senator David Hart (Paul Benjamin) who

Fig. 8.2. Extermination: Pam Grier's *Friday Foster* (1975) represents the end of the blaxploitation heroine's potency; indeed, the only thing she shoots in the film is her camera. Photo from author's collection.

tells her that billionaire Tarr is the man behind the project nicknamed "Black Widow;" however, then Friday engages in a romance with Tarr who tells her that Hart is the villain she seeks. In the end, it turns out that both men are on the same (good) side and it is the Senator's advisor, Charlie Foley (Jason Bernard) working with white men like Enos Griffith (Jim Backus), who want to assassinate all of the key black community leaders.

Friday is less competent than her predecessors. As a detective, she does not seem capable of discovering the truth on her own and, instead, believes whatever people tell her (e.g., Tarr and Hart). She does figure out on her own that "the walls come tumbling down" refers to biblical Jericho and leads her to the Church of Jericho where the black leaders are congregating; however, she is unable to identify the true enemy behind "Black Widow" until he reveals himself to her. And, as the heroine in an action film, Friday is not capable of fighting her way out of her battles and, instead, is saved usually by someone—a neighbor, the cops, or her sidekick Colt—turning up at the right moment and scaring off her attacker. Lastly, she does not demonstrate any proficiency with weapons and the only thing she shoots is her camera. The film ends with her in her apartment surrounded by gifts and flowers from Tarr and Hart while she heads out the door with Colt for an evening on the town. It is this lack of independence, resourcefulness, and heroism that demonstrates Friday's deviation from the established trend. From Coffy and Cleo's explosive appearance in the summer of 1973 to Friday's lack of independence and competence by the close of 1975, it would seem that in the space of only two and a half years this cycle of blaxploitation female crime-fighter films was introduced, peaked, and become obsolete.

Part III: Model Heroines?

Vigilante Heroism

The three early films—*Coffy*, *Cleopatra Jones*, and *Foxy Brown*—raise the issue of vigilantism as a defensible means to combat criminal organizations since law-enforcement cannot. In *Coffy*, Carter is an honest cop whose partner is on the take. When Carter refuses to be corrupt, he ends up in the hospital with broken bones and brain damage after a severe beating. Later, Brunswick defends his involvement in the racket to Coffy, explaining that, while some money goes to black pushers and distributors, the large part of the profits goes to the white men who import the drugs and the corrupt law enforcement officers who turn a blind eye to the practice. By the end of the film, these motives are questioned when it is revealed that Brunswick, himself, is one of these men on the take and protecting racket powerhouses such as Vitroni. As Brunswick explains, it is not a question of race: "Black, brown, or yellow, I am in it for the green! The green buck." The degree of his corruption is made apparent when he gives permission to Vitroni to kill Coffy, rather than ruin his business relationship with him. In *Cleopatra Jones*, it is revealed in the end that Sergeant Kert (Stafford Morgan) is corrupt and in Mommy's pay. It is because of this paid protection from the inside that Mommy gets away with her crimes, including the raid on the B&S House. In *Foxy Brown*, Dalton is angry that—after two years of undercover work and making a great case against the dope syndicate—he could not get an indictment because "the fix was in" on the grand jury through Miss Katherine's call girl racket.

With officials—from policemen to councilmen to judges—on the take, these films suggest that the only person capable of bringing down the rackets is the lone vigilante. After visiting her sister in rehab, Coffy asks Carter what he thinks about taking the law into one's own hands.

Coffy: Carter, wouldn't you want to kill somebody who had done a thing like that to your little sister?

Carter: Sure would.

Coffy: Then you think it'd be right?

Carter: What? To kill some pusher who's only selling so he can get money to buy for himself? What good would that do, Coffy? I mean, he's only part of a chain that reaches all the way back to some poor farmer in Turkey or Vietnam. What would you do? Kill all of them?

Coffy: Well, why not? Nothing else seems to do any good. You know who they are. Everybody knows who they are. Now, you're a cop. Now, why don't you just arrest them?

Carter: It's not that simple, Coffy. The law can't do that.

Coffy: You bet it can't. And I know why it can't too. Because the law is in for a piece of the action.

Carter: Not all of it. Not yet . . .

Similarly, Foxy Brown tells Dalton that she thinks the only answer for the drug racketeers is to put a bullet in them yourself. They see her friend Oscar (Bob Minor) and the "Neighborhood Committee" deal with a drug dealer in their neighborhood: they beat him up and send him out of town. When Dalton questions Oscar's use of "vigilante justice," Foxy replies, "It's as American as apple pie."

The current conception of the difference between justice and revenge was explored in a 2008 episode of the television series "The Mentalist" (2008–present). In the show, Patrick Jane (Simon Baker), who formerly used his mental acuity as a fraudulent psychic/mind reader, is a consultant for the California Bureau of Investigation, hoping to bring to justice the serial killer, Red John, who murdered Jane's wife and daughter. In the episode "Flame Red," Jane and Agent Teresa Lisbon (Robin Tunney) discuss the case.[9]

> Jane: We've never discussed this, because I thought it went without saying, but, when I catch Red John, I'm going to cut him open and watch him die slowly . . . like he did with my wife and child. Now, if you have a problem with that, we should talk.
>
> Lisbon: Then let's talk. Because when *we* catch Red John, we are going to take him into custody and he's going to be tried in a court of law.
>
> Jane: Not if I'm still breathing.
>
> Lisbon: If you try and do violence to him, I will try and stop you. If you succeed in doing violence to him, I will arrest you.
>
> Jane: I understand.
>
> Lisbon: I hope so.
>
> Jane: Well, I'm glad we talked. I had no idea you were so bourgeois or conventional on the issue.

Although Jane's desire to avenge his wife and child's murder is understandable because he feels somewhat responsible, Lisbon's is the socially acceptable response. In contemporary culture, the Old Testament's "an eye for an eye" is seen as the product of, and morally acceptable only in, a less "progressive" society. In contemporary American culture, such a moral stance is regarded as appropriate only when there is no law to enforce justice—e.g., in the times of the Wild West. However, once the law book can replace the gun in terms of serving justice, vengeance becomes an act that can, in its turn, be judged as unlawful. Jane suggests that, because he is not an official law enforcer, he is not bound by the codes that Lisbon feels compelled to uphold. Their exchange suggests that, while justice can be regarded as impartial and exacted without feeling, vengeance is personal and emotional. Vengeance offers pleasure or at least closure—a kind of catharsis—for the loved one the victim/s left behind.

Similarly, the blaxploitation female crime-fighting films suggest that justice and vengeance are not the same thing; however, since the officials of justice, who are supposed to use the law book to incarcerate criminals and dismantle their rackets, are incapable of doing so (or choose not to do so because they are corrupt), the films put forth vigilante heroes who will see justice served. The films do offer a legitimating motivation: the loved ones of the heroine have been cruelly injured or killed by criminal violence and other members of the community are at risk of being similarly injured. In this sense, the films are somewhat radical (by today's standards) in their attitude toward law and order, sanctioning justice outside of the law. Indeed, Jane is correct when he accuses Lisbon of being "bourgeois" and "conventional" in her attitude toward vengeance: her stance is the socially acceptable one, and his is the dangerous one. If individuals resorted to vigilantism, society would become lawless as Westerns and action films continue to remind us.

Interestingly, later in the same episode of "The Mentalist," Jane confronts the killer, Tommy (Fred Koehler), about his revenge killings—and his favorite novel, *Moby-Dick* (1851).

Jane: I must confess, I never really did get to the end of it. Ahab does die, doesn't he?

Tommy: Yes, but so does the whale.

Jane: That's my point. Revenge doesn't come cheap.

Tommy: Oh, spare me your moralizing! I know what revenge costs. It's worth the price.

Jane acknowledges that he recognizes "the price" of revenge—the avenger's own destruction. The viewer thus realizes that Jane's pursuit of revenge on Red John is not just about alleviating the guilt he feels about his family's murder but also a kind of suicide mission: he knows that his hunt for their killer will destroy him. Similarly, the blaxploitation films suggest that to engage in revenge may destroy the heroine; however, her grief is so profound that she would rather risk her life than do nothing. And that is why the ending of *Coffy* is so much more convincing than those of Grier's later films: just as the Western hero (and Dirty Harry by association) must st/ride off into the sunset alone, so too must Coffy walk off into the sunrise alone. The vigilante has operated outside of society's boundaries of acceptable and lawful behavior; therefore, s/he can no longer live amongst that society. While Foxy Brown, Sheba Shayne, and Friday Foster are all recouped into their social circles—Foxy drives off with Oscar, Friday goes on a date with Colt, and Sheba returns to Chicago—Coffy walks away alone and Cleo departs for another mission. In the contemporary climate, the vigilante hero is incongruous with social values. Viewers know that Patrick Jane cannot be the hero of "The Mentalist" if he kills Red John and, instead, he will most likely hand the killer over to the CBI when he finally catches up with him. Similarly, the television series "24" (2001–10) has not let its hero, Jack Bauer (Kiefer Sutherland), get away with his vigilantism—specifically his use of torture as an interrogation technique. In "24: Redemption," he has to "redeem" himself by saving a school of young African boys from becoming child soldiers and sacrificing his own freedom to ensure their safety.[10] In the sociopolitical climate of the late 1960s and early 70s, however, vigilantism was put forth as a heroic alternative to the perceived impotence of official law enforcement.

Feminist Models?

Feminist film critics have been divided in their assessment of films like *Coffy* and *Cleopatra Jones* in terms of the models of black womanhood they offer: on the one hand, they are strong and central protagonists; on the other, they are hypersexualized/objectified. As Dunn suggests, "These revealing character representations acknowledge the impact of feminism and black feminism and, at the same time, the anxieties they provoked" (4). In an interview with *The New York Times*, Dobson commented on the positive reception of *Cleopatra Jones* among black female audiences:

> I've been on tour for four weeks and I've met so many people who said they were happy I made the film. "It's the first time black women have been shown so positively." They'd say. Before, we were portrayed as maids, mammies or whores. But we're also teachers, doctors, lawyers, mothers, typists. We do everything, and what we don't, we're gonna try. (Qtd. in Klemesrud, 117)

Similarly, Grier regarded her characters as empowered even if others criticized her conception of that power. In an interview for *Essence Magazine* in 1979, Grier explained, "I created a new kind of screen woman, physically strong and active, she was able to look after herself and others. If you think about it, you'll see she was the prototype for the more recent and very popular white Bionic and Wonder Women" (Ebert, 107).[11] Speaking from the 2000s, Grier in retrospect suggests a similar reading of her characters:

> In the '70s, we reaped the rewards of the '50s and '60s—we had lovefests, Woodstock, the power of love was exploding. It was a

time of freedom and women saying that they needed empowerment. There was more empowerment and self-discovery than any other decade I remember. All across the country, a lot of women were Foxy Brown and Coffy. They were independent, fighting to save their families, not accepting rape or being victimized. [. . .] Some people say that Foxy Brown is a castrating character, but the truth is she just doesn't need a man. (53)

Thus, both Dobson and Grier define a feminist model as a woman who does not need a man to take care of her.

On the other hand, in her interview, Dobson was quick to qualify what she meant by a positive feminist model:

I don't think of Cleopatra Jones as being a women's libber. I see her as a very positive, strong lady who knows what she has to do. She's defending an important freedom for her people: the freedom to exist without drugs. (Qtd. in Klemesrud, 117)

Dobson went on to explain that she, herself, was not interested in the Woman's Liberation Movement despite the fact that she was an independent career woman. Thus, while to be a strong and independent woman was seen as positive at the time, to be a politically active supporter of the Women's Movement was not necessarily so since, as Novotny Lawrence notes, the movement was regarded as a white woman's movement (88). More recently, however, on the DVD version of *Jackie Brown* (Tarantino, 1997), Grier was quoted as saying, "Foxy Brown was every woman: able to be assertive, yet feminine, the goal of the women's movement!" It would seem that in evaluating the degree of feminism of a film or character, we must take into consideration the definition of female roles and feminism at the time of the production of the film. Indeed, as Holmlund has suggested, there has been a contemporary rewriting of the importance of blaxploitation heroines, including "Grier's impact as (then) hot action babe and (now) cool action mama" ("Wham," 98) in recent roles like in *Jackie Brown*—itself a reimagining of blaxploitation film. From the position of the present, we are able to reread and rewrite the past through the lens of contemporary culture. Indeed, it has only been recently, with the "cultural turn" in academic criticism that blaxploitation films have even been considered worthy of critical study when—at the time they appeared—they were critically derided.

While early feminist film theorists—such as Laura Mulvey and Mary Ann Doane—had excluded an address of race when considering female spectatorship, black feminists—such as Jacqueline Bobo and bell hooks—began to address black female spectatorship in the 1990s. In Stuart Hall's "preferred reading" model, audiences can "accept," "negotiate," or "oppose" the "preferred" reading implied by dominant ideology. As hooks explains, the black woman must oppose the dominant reading and adopt what hooks terms an "oppositional gaze" when watching mainstream films in order to achieve a "reading against the grain" and to find visual pleasure through the resistance, interrogation, and deconstruction of the dominant meaning (298). While Ed Guerrero agrees with other male critics, including historian Donald Bogle, that "black women could find little in their adolescent-male-fantasy-oriented roles to identify with" (*Framing*, 99), Dunn argues that the "problem with this dismissive reading is that it obscures how black women may negotiate the racial and gender politics underlying the narrative but still find various types of pleasure in viewing [. . .] the rare fantasies of a baad black woman heroine" (16). Bobo has explored, through the response to the film *The Color Purple* (Spielberg, 1985), how black female audiences were able to "read through the text" as a product of mainstream culture and construct for themselves "satisfactory meanings from a mainstream cultural product created by a White male filmmaker" ("Reading," 273). Bobo argues that, even though the film presented caricatures that "made the viewer wince," it offered black women a position of subjectivity with a narrative driven by the desires of a black woman, played by Whoopi Goldberg ("Black"). As Bobo suggests, there is little research on audience reception of films; however, some reviewers, critics, and people involved in the making of blaxploitation films suggest that positive readings of these films were possible for black audiences.

Jack Hill, the white director of *Coffy* and *Foxy Brown*, said that the white producers at AIP had nothing but "contempt" for their black audiences and did not understand "black" pictures; instead, driven by the desire for profits, the studio pushed for more action in their "black" pictures and less of the "humanity" which Hill fought to include (139). Although Hollywood studios may not have understood the black audience as well as the black independent producers like Van Peebles did, it is likely that audiences were able to find progressive meaning in blaxploitation films, ignoring the caricatures and focusing on the empowerment of the films' protagonists. And the recent recuperation of the blaxploitation films with female protagonists by black feminist critics like Dunn and Sims suggests that these films offer a feminist message. I would concur, especially since mainstream film at the time did not even offer strong representations of white women—let alone black. Indeed, mainstream *Ms.* magazine ran a cover story in 1975 in which Jamaica Kincaid suggests that *Coffy, Foxy Brown,* and *Sheba, Baby* are "the only films [. . .] in a long time to show us a woman who is independent, resourceful, self-confident, strong and courageous. Above all, they are the only films to show us a woman who triumphs" (Qtd. in Holmlund, "Wham," 108).

The reading of these heroines was necessarily—using Hall's term—a "negotiated" one. Although it is easy to focus on the meaning of the first part of the portmanteau "blaxploitation"—black—one cannot ignore the second—exploitation. And, in the case of the black female crime-fighter, that exploitation is in part represented by the exploitation of the body of the lead actress. As Howard suggests, "Cleopatra Jones is the embodiment of the liberated '70s woman who can, and does, take care of herself" but that, with the focus on many costume changes in *Cleopatra Jones and the Casino of Gold* (Bail, 1975), the character is also "objectified and overdressed" (115–117). Holmlund argues that the problems in the representation of the blaxploitation heroine go beyond her objectification. She includes three key contradictions in terms of Grier's casting, characters, and performances:

> 1) kick ass and in control, she is nevertheless frequently positioned as beautiful spectacle [. . .] ; 2) articulating Black power and proto- or quasi-feminist positions in the 1970s, she simultaneously functions as exotic "other" [. . .] ; 3) connected to the family and often figuring as an "icon of home." ("Wham," 98)

Certainly, in these ways, Grier's performances are contradictory. I would point out, however, that these scenes of objectification occur usually when Grier's heroines are undercover—that is masquerading as prostitutes—rather than representing themselves as crime-fighters. While this does not perhaps diminish the impact of the objectification in terms of the presentation of Grier's body, it does suggest an acknowledgment on the part of the filmmakers that such representations must be justified in terms of the consistency of the crime-fighting character. Rather than suggest that the female crime-fighter is inherently hyperfeminine (as indicated through her wardrobe), the films present the heroines as everyday women (in everyday clothes) who can perform hyperfemininity to infiltrate the enemy operation. Similarly, hyperfemininity—as aligned with glamorous trappings—represents class ascendancy from the working class (the world of the blaxploitation heroine) to a self-constructed "upper class" (the world of the successful drug lords and pimps). Lastly, just as we saw with silent detective films of the 1920s and into sound film of the 30s, undercover work is a means by which to realign the female investigator with traditional notions of femininity and counteract her foray into masculine work. Despite these moments of objectification in the blaxploitation film, I would argue that the female crime-fighter ultimately represents an empowered model of womanhood as one who successfully fights crime.

Importantly, as Sims notes, these blaxploitation films redefined notions of black female beauty with actors like Grier away from those established by classical Hollywood like the rotund, maternal mammy type (79–81). Not only did Grier project an image of being young, strong, and sexual—all the things that the mammy is not—but she also sported an afro, which had become a powerful embodiment of the "Black is beautiful" mantra of the Black Power movement. Just as the afro represented a rebellion against European standards of beauty with the ideal of long "flowing hair," so too does the concealment of Cleo's hair under hats, turbans, and headscarves function similarly to Grier's

sporting an afro (Dunn, 94). These hats and turbans also function to draw attention to her striking, and specifically, African facial features. At points, as Coffy,
Foxy, and Sheba, Grier dons wigs more in keeping with white aesthetics with a
"coiffed look." Although Sims regards this as problematic and tied to the fact
that Grier wanted to look more glamorous, I would point out again that Grier
wears them only when undercover—e.g., masquerading as a prostitute. These
undercover scenes that present her as more feminized can be read in a variety
of ways: first, as negative, because Grier is objectified and, therefore, her ability
to be empowered is negated to a degree; second, as positive, because she is a
superwoman—intelligent, resourceful, triumphant, and beautiful (i.e., masculine
while retaining her femininity); or, third, as somewhat neutral, because there is
an "excuse" for these moments (e.g., she is working undercover) that can allow
for a narrative justification for these moments. I would like to add, also, that the
action film—from *Dirty Harry* to *Die Hard* (McTiernan, 1988)—implies that
the hero's most effective weapon in the fight against crime, is his body. Thus,
the blaxploitation heroine must also rely on her body as a weapon—from Cleo's
karate kicks at the airport to Foxy's seduction of King George. While potentially
contentious, these scenes, I would suggest, affirm that the blaxploitation heroine
is in control of her body and sexuality and that she reasserts her power on the
rare occasion that control over her body is taken away from her.

    In terms of these women being presented as traditional icons of femininity,
I would argue that they are not presented aligned with domesticity even if they
are presented as heteronormative, especially in comparison to the empowered
white women who are demonized as something "unnatural." Presented as sexually perverse, man-eater Miss Katherine in *Foxy Brown* and lesbians Mommy in
Cleopatra Jones and the Dragon Lady (Stella Stevens) in *Cleopatra Jones and the
Casino of Gold* run criminal empires with great success—that is, until the black
heroine destroys her. Dunn argues that the "sadistic brutality" of these white
women represents the "social dysfunction wrought when white patriarchal power
is transposed onto a white woman" (104). The bigger threat to mainstream
culture is *not* the heterosexual black woman who devotes her energy to ensur-
ing the well-being of her community—but the sex- and power-hungry white
woman. These films suggest that their heroines are tough only because they are
seeking justice for harm done to their loved ones; otherwise they are caring,
nurturing women. In *The Casino of Gold*, Cleo reassures her boss (Norman
Fell) who accuses her of being "a hard woman to deal with," that she is "only
in business, Stanley. Off the job I'm a real pussycat." In terms of Holmlund's
suggestion that Grier is "an icon of the home," I would argue that only Friday
Foster is presented as a traditionally maternal figure and firmly linked with
the space of the home throughout the film. According to Novotny, this was
actually a conscious decision on Grier's part who was trying to distance herself
from roles that exploited her mainly for her sexuality rather than her acting
(91). Certainly, Friday represents a shift for Grier to a more domesticated and

less independent heroine and this is reflected in her more glamorous clothes and her sporting "coiffed" hair rather than an afro. In the case of Coffy, Foxy, and Sheba, Grier's characters may be shown in the home in the early scenes; nevertheless, each woman leaves the home to pursue revenge and is, thereafter, not associated with domestic roles and space again. Indeed, it is in Brunswick's kitchen that Coffy's exacts her revenge for his betrayal of her.

Unquestionably, many critics now regard these blaxploitation women as empowered and, thus, feminist models for the black—if not the white—female audience. For example, black and lesbian filmmaker Cheryl Dunye remarks in a response to *Coffy* that

> Many black feminists might label Grier's work racially and sexually disempowering, an outrage to the image of true black woman-hood. [. . .] To me, though, her characters represent a provocative dismantling of narrow constructions of gender and race. [. . .] Grier successfully pulled off several aggressive roles traditionally tailored for men, all while retaining her femininity. (76)

In *The New York Times* review for *Sheba, Baby*, Grier is described as playing "Sheba in a most unusual way. Although she's no great shakes as an actress, she gives the impression of being as intelligent as she is beautiful" (37). The reviewer implies that it is rare to have a woman portrayed as intelligent as she is good looking: in this sense then, these female detective roles in blaxpoita-tion films were a leap forward. Indeed, if the male blaxploitation hero can be regarded as positive because he represented a reversal of the power struggle between dominant whites and marginalized blacks, then the blaxploitation female crime-fighter should similarly be regarded as positive for inverting the power struggle between dominant men and marginalized women. Even if these women were *fantasies* of black and/or feminist empowerment rather than actu-ally being empowered, at least their presence indicated the inequalities of which they represented the inversion. As Holmlund suggests,

> Grier's blaxploitation vehicles cannot easily be hailed as simply "pro-feminist" or purely "pro-black." By foregrounding femininity and rethinking racism, however, they definitely disrupt conventions common to exploitation action films, whether directed by whites or blacks. ("Wham," 102)

For the early 1970s, these heroines as female crime-fighters were excep-tional characters and represented a challenge not only to patriarchal authority but specifically white patriarchal authority. These blaxploitation women are empowered, self-determining, and intelligent and—even if only a comic-book fantasy—these "wonder women" were at least a fantasy of revolutionary possibilities in terms of *both* gender and race. After all, it is only infrequently that we have seen such tough action women since the 1970s and they have often been dismissed by critics as too masculine—e.g., Ripley (Sigourney Weaver) of *Aliens* (Cameron, 1986) and Sarah Connor (Linda Hamilton) of *Terminator 2: Judgment Day* (Cameron, 1991)—or too feminine—e.g., the Angels (Drew Barrymore, Cameron Diaz, and Lucy Liu) in the *Charlie's Angels* films (McG, 2000 and 2003) and Lara Croft (Angelina Jolie) in the *Tomb Raider* films (West, 2001 and de Bont, 2003). As Holmlund notes,

> . . . when asked in 1997 whether opportunities had improved for women who wanted to play (in Grier's words) "tough, smart, assertive characters who were still feminine, soft and caring," Grier tellingly mentioned only white actresses (including some whom academics have deemed "masculine"). ("Wham," 107)

Instead, these blaxploitation heroines were able to be tough, independent, and intelligent (i.e., masculine) and, simultaneously, sexual and attractive (i.e., feminine) without having to compromise. These women, like the female detectives of the 1930s, were admired for being *both* masculine and feminine and were never faced with the either/or decision that their successors of the 1940s, 50s, 60s, 80s, 90s, and perhaps even today would be. These blaxploitation women could win the affections of the men they loved *and* keep their careers and/or sexual independence. That is why the comment "femme might makes right" is so apt: these women are female and triumphant, and never punished—only celebrated—for it.

9

Detecting the Bounds of the Law

The Female Lawyer Thriller of the 1980s

David: I don't trust her. See, people like us Miriam, we're warm people.
            But she's . . . she's an attorney. [. . .]

Miriam: She's awfully attractive.

David: Not to me she's not. All she cares about is winning, like a
            goddamn machine.

                                    —Don Johnson and Christina Grace in *Guilty as Sin* (1993)

In the 1980s, television offered female cops in "Cagney and Lacey" (1982–88), female private investigators in the comedy-dramas "Hart to Hart" (1979–84) and "Moonlighting" (1985–89), and a female sleuth in "Murder, She Wrote" (1984–96). While television can cater to niche audiences and offer ensemble casts for wider audience appeal, mainstream film must appeal to the broadest audience possible by choosing its one or two central protagonists wisely. This pressure to perform often prevents producers from taking risks and leads to conservative generic formulae. Thus while television offered different kinds of roles for the female detective to embody, mainstream film offered essentially one in the 1980s: the lawyer (the handful of exceptions will be discussed in the next chapter). As Elise Elliot (Goldie Hawn) in *The First Wives Club* (Wilson, 1996) explains, in Hollywood, there are only three things a woman can be: babe, district attorney, or *Driving Miss Daisy*. When Hollywood did offer strong, independent, career women in the 1980s, they were often attorneys—whether publically appointed (e.g., a district attorney) or privately engaged.

The female lawyer film represented a hybridization of the courtroom film and the psychological thriller. The choice of the lawyer as the profession of the female detective in the 1980s was in part due to the growing visibility of women as lawyers in reality: in the 1960s, women comprised 3 percent of the profession; by the 1980s, 20 percent; and, by the 1990s, almost 40 percent (Epstein, et al., 313–14). Similarly, by the mid-80s women comprised over a third of the law student population; nearly half by the 1990s; and more than half by 2001 (Lucia, *Framing*, 14). However, the female lawyer was also the product of Hollywood's attempt to negotiate male anxieties in the 1980s, resulting in a seemingly feminist, while simultaneously reactionary image of feminist empowerment. By the 1980s, women were reaping some of the benefits of second-wave feminism, including moving up the ladder into higher-paid and more professional-level positions; however, this movement of women into a traditionally male sphere was regarded as a challenge to masculine authority and the position of men as familial breadwinners. Social critic Susan Faludi argues the perceived threat of professional women spawned "a powerful counterassault on women's rights, a backlash, an attempt to retract the handful of small and hard-won victories that the feminist movement did manage to win for women" (12)—and this backlash echoed in Hollywood films of the time. A cycle of erotic thrillers—including *Fatal Attraction* (Lyne, 1987), *Shattered* (Petersen, 1991), *Basic Instinct* (Verhoeven, 1992), *The Hand that Rocks the Cradle* (Hanson, 1992), *Final Analysis* (Joanou, 1992), *Single White Female* (Schroeder, 1992), *Jennifer 8* (Robinson, 1992), *Consenting Adults* (Pakula, 1992), *Body of Evidence* (Edel, 1993), *The Crush* (Shapiro, 1993), *Guilty as Sin* (Lumet, 1993), *Disclosure* (Levinson, 1994), *The Last Seduction* (Dahl, 1994), and *Jade* (Friedkin, 1995)—were identified by critics as being *noir*-esque with heroes trying to evade the web of *femmes fatales*. As Linda Ruth Williams suggests, "the erotic thriller is a direct descendent of *film noir*" (28); thus, women were presented as threatening and were criticized for desiring independence from the home and/or equal opportunities in the professional world. With the emphasis on sexual relations, the erotic thriller presented the *femme fatale* as a metaphor for AIDS at a time when the disease was becoming increasingly apparent and a growing threat to heterosexual couples (previously it had been regarded as a disease that only affected intravenous drug users and homosexuals). The *femme fatale*, like AIDS, represented that casual sex (i.e., sex outside the bounds of socially sanctioned marriage) could kill.

Born of the same thematic concerns, another cycle of films appeared concurrently to the erotic thriller—except, rather than offering a male protagonist who must evade the lethal independent woman, the protagonist of the female lawyer thriller *was* the independent woman. The focus of this second cycle of films was on women trying to attain success in the male-dominated world of the law and tended to be played by actors who carried associations of feminist empowerment: Glenn Close in *Jagged Edge* (Marquand, 1985), Cher in *Suspect* (Yates, 1987), Jessica Lange in *Music Box* (Costa-Gavras, 1989), Theresa Russell in *Physical Evidence* (Crichton, 1989), Mary Elizabeth Mastrantonio in *Class Action* (Apted, 1991), Barbara Hershey in *Defenseless* (Campbell, 1991), and Rebecca De Mornay in *Guilty as Sin* (Lumet, 1993). The focus of this section is not on all films of the 1980s and early 90s featuring central female lawyers, but those films in which the female lawyer must play detective (i.e., discover "whodunit") and to which I refer as the female lawyer thriller.[1] Lucia suggests that the female lawyer *appears* to be a feminist model because she is a professional, powerful, central female character; however, at the same time, her authority is always undermined, highlighting the anxieties that the empowered and independent woman incited. Despite her alliance with the law, the female lawyer, like the *femme fatale* of the erotic thriller, is presented as "dangerously ambitious" and her masculine ambition and independence are overturned by her presentation as "personally and professionally deficient" (Lucia, "Women," 33). In terms of their professional lives, these women are proven incompetent as lawyers: they are forced to defer to male authority or proved wrong by a male colleague. In terms of their personal lives, these women are presented as flawed characters, married to their jobs and unfulfilled because they are not wives or mothers. In a commentary for the *Los Angeles Times* at the time of *Jagged Edge*'s release, Katherine Mader—former criminal lawyer, one of the defenders for Angelo Buono, "the Hillside Strangler," and more recently Deputy District Attorney for Los Angeles County—wrote that

> Superficially, the movie does depict a woman as a fierce and competitive gladiator in an exciting courtroom battle. Columbia Pictures must have decided that it would be trendy to place a woman in a role typically dominated by men. However, just below the surface lurks a pervasive and subtle sexism that completely undercuts whatever advantage existed in casting a woman as the starring character. (25)

I would like to stress that these films were the product not of a desire to offer feminist models but to explore the crisis of masculinity ever-present in films of the 1980s. The perceived crisis of masculinity in the 1980s was played out through the retributive male action heroes played by actors such as Arnold Schwarzenegger, Sylvester Stallone, and Steven Seagal. In the detective genre, the detective became a cop action-hero—notably Bruce Willis in *Die Hard* (McTiernan, 1988) and Mel Gibson in *Lethal Weapon* (Donner, 1987). As Susan Jeffords states, the action films of the 1980s were "part of a widespread cultural effort to respond to perceived deterioration in masculine forms of power" ("Can," 246). Feminism attempted to eradicate the differences between men and women, and media images of new masculinities, like "the New Man," offered a redefinition of masculinity as "feminized"—i.e., sensitive, nurturing, and vain. In response to this eradication of difference, mainstream film offered hypermasculine—or as Jeffords terms them, hard-bodied—heroes embodying an increased differentiation between masculinity and femininity (*Hard*). The male cop-action hero was specularized, over-determined, and hypervisible; his body became the site upon which masculine crisis—personal and often national—could be expressed and resolved through beatings, torture, and the performance of action. In a similar way, the body of the female lawyer is the site of crisis—a vessel through which anxieties about the crisis of masculinity could be negotiated and, more importantly, resolved. She is rarely hypersexualized as is the *femme fatale* but she is noticeably "other" in the courtroom despite her masculine-inspired power suit and evidently vulnerable when she must fight the evil male.

Just as other erotic thrillers like *Fatal Attraction* and *The Hand that Rocks the Cradle* concluded with the destruction of the lethal *femme fatale*, so too does the female lawyer thriller end with the neutralization of the threat of empowered and independent women to men. Because the independent woman is the protagonist—rather than the threatened male or the "good woman" wife, as is the case of the erotic thriller—the female lawyer thriller deals with the threat not by killing her but by relegating her to one of two roles: either the victim of male violence in those films in which the male love interest is presented as evil (e.g., *Jagged Edge*); and/or that of submissive to the superior male authority of the love interest in the films in which he is presented as good (e.g., *Defenseless*). These women were born out of the anxieties of masculine crisis with the goal of reassuring male viewers that women could be returned—and/or encouraging female viewers to return—to their "proper" place (just like *film noir*); however, that does not mean that female viewers could not read these films in opposition to this dominant message. Indeed, these women are the central heroes of these films and it is their goals, desires, and struggles that define the narrative and drive the action. Even if these strong, independent, career women are ultimately unsuccessful in some capacity (whether personal or professional), they offer an alternative model of womanhood to the films previous and concurrent with the female lawyer cycle—films that saw women absent from the center in the case of the buddy film or secondary as the love interest of a male protagonist. Her presence at the center of the story meant that these films articulate the debates and anxieties around women moving into the professional sphere and their struggles as they do so. I would argue that the female lawyer is attractive to men, successful in her career, often verging on middle age (at least according to Hollywood), and a person driven to see justice done.[2]

It is this tension in the female lawyer thriller between articulating masculine crisis and offering a feminist model with which previous critical studies of the female lawyer have been preoccupied—and certainly the female lawyer film does focus on issues of sex difference. Nevertheless, I would argue that if we move past the representation of the female lawyer as a *lawyer* and explore instead her accomplishments as a *detective*, it is possible to read these women as empowered. Being an amateur detective—who sleuths to unravel a mystery out of interest or as part of her day job (as opposed to an official criminal investigator)—has always been an acceptable (pre)occupation for women in fiction and film. While these women may ultimately fail in their role as lawyer—i.e., in an attempt to see justice served in the male space of the courtroom—they then engage in a pursuit for the truth *outside* of the courtroom as a detective-figure. As the tagline for the poster for *Suspect* suggests, "Everything is revealed in court . . . but the truth." In this capacity, the female lawyer is *always* successful: in each film she uncovers the truth about the crime committed and is then compelled to see justice served, even if that means exacting it herself as a vigilante crime-fighter.

The female lawyer as a detective sees an evolution from the earlier films—in which she is a successful vigilante crime-fighter who requires the assistance of a male detective—to the later films—in which she is a competent investigator on her own. In a review of *Physical Evidence*, Manohla Dargis comments on the tendency to see the female lawyer turn vigilante:

> Courtroom dramas (*Marie, Suspect, The Accused*)—and especially the subgenre of Woman-Lawyer films—function as a symbolic rite of passage. Gray flannel, briefcases, and legalese are supposed to give actresses (and, by extension, women in general) a veneer of seriousness, as if battling inside the judicial system (like the corporate world) were the ultimate triumph of liberation. Perhaps even more disturbing, however, is the recent spectacle of women wreaking bloody vengeance. The shameless finale of *Physical Evidence* finds Russell with hair flowing and gun blazing. For Hollywood, postfeminism means that women have earned the right to shoot-to-kill as guiltlessly as men; they just get to dress better. (68)

This debate about female appropriation of male violence became a contested topic in the 1980s amongst feminist film critics with action heroines like Ellen Ripley (Sigourney Weaver) in *Aliens* (Cameron, 1986) and I will discuss this further in the next chapter. I would like to put the question of whether the female as violent vigilante is a feminist representation aside and instead note that within Hollywood's own broader codes, this representation is intended to be heroic—in terms of the "preferred" reading model. According to the generic conventions of the detective film at the time, pursuing justice through the legal system (i.e., arrest, trial, and incarceration) is regarded as often impossible—despite the sex of the hero—because the legal system is ineffectual and patriarchal authority most often corrupt. Instead, the hero of the late 1980s and early 1990s—whether male or female—must destroy the villain him- or herself. All of the female lawyer thrillers from the mid-80s to the early-90s explore these key issues: sex difference, the failure of the legal system, and the hero as an investigative and vigilante crime-fighter.

Classical Predecessors

There were predecessors in classical Hollywood film to the female lawyer of the 1980s and 90s but she embodied themes less related to the female detective and more to the career woman in general. Claire Trevor often played the working woman in the 1930s: shop clerks, chorus girls, nightclub singers, and especially girl reporters in *The Mad Game* (Cummings, 1933), *Hold that Girl* (MacFadden, 1931), *Human Cargo* (Dwan, 1936), *One Mile from Heaven* (Dwan, 1937), *Five of a Kind* (Leeds, 1938); however, she also played a lawyer in *Career Woman* (Seiler, 1936). *Career Woman* is concerned with its heroine's desire to make a career out of her passion for seeing justice served. I discuss this film in order to highlight how the courtroom drama centered on a female lawyer has always been concerned with the femininity-achievement conflict even before the genre's hybridization with the psychological thriller in the 1980s. While the 1930s male lawyer—such as Perry Mason—routinely played detective in order to prove the innocence of his client, the female lawyer film was more concerned with the heroine's battle to prove her abilities in a male-dominated profession. The film begins with law student Carroll Aiken (Trevor) at a murder trial where she watches the famous and unscrupulous defense attorney, Barry Conant (Michael Whalen), make a circus out of the courtroom with his faked injuries and shocking revelations. Suave Barry takes a liking to Carroll and, thinking she is a "regular" woman (i.e., not a career woman), asks her to take a vacation with him. When she explains that she is taking her bar exam the following week, Barry is shocked—"Lawyers don't look like you!"—and explains he does not like "brilliant women" (i.e., intelligent and successful women). Later, at her graduation celebration, Barry tries to win her over: he argues that he is a rich lawyer and "That's being great in America, isn't it?" She retorts that it is integrity that equals greatness and, thus, sets up the premise of the film: she will try to win her first court case with integrity, and he will show her that she must resort to questionable tactics to see her client's best interests served.

Back in her hometown of Clarkdale, Carroll defends Gracie Clay (Isabel Jewell) in the accidental death of her abusive father. The case goes badly for Carroll with the judge repeatedly overruling her objections and she proves herself unprofessional by becoming emotional—in other words, behaving like a woman instead of a lawyer. Barry arrives in town just in time to work some of his circus magic (e.g., having Carroll pretend to faint so they can call an adjournment). Carroll eventually wins the case and Barry confesses that his court appearance was all a performance to swing the town's sympathy to her as one of their own. *Career Woman* suggests that Carroll's small-town and/or feminine sensibilities have only limited success in the courtroom and, without the intervention of Barry and his big city "tricks," it is unlikely she would have won her case. Similarly, in *The Law in Her Hands* (Clemens, 1936), the

Assistant District Attorney (Warren Hull) tells the aspiring young female lawyer, Mary Wentworth (Margaret Lindsay), that "The legal profession is full of tricks and technicalities. It's not for a woman." When Mary finds herself defending a racketeer who is responsible for seven deaths, she quits his case and testifies against him—resulting in her disbarment. As in the case of the girl reporter film, classical Hollywood films suggest that ethics are a feminine trait and have little place in the male-dominated world of the courtroom; this would prove to be a theme that reappears with the female lawyer film in the 1980s.

A second theme established in the 1930s is that of the female lawyer being attracted to her rival and/or torn between her desire to have a career and being married. In the final scene of *Career Woman*, when Barry suggests "We'd make a swell team," Carroll asks him to clarify, "Law team?" He answers, "What do you think?" followed by a kiss. It is clear the partnership he desires is romantic but not whether his earlier business offer of "Aiken and Conant" is still on the table. The female lawyers of in *The Law in Her Hands*, former waitresses Dorothy (Glenda Farrell) and Mary (Lindsay), pass the bar and become lawyers. Mary loses her first case when an unscrupulous lawyer plants evidence but she impresses the Assistant D.A. (Hull) who convinces her to quit the law and be his wife. In *Disbarred* (Florey 1939), Assistant D.A., Bradley Kent (Robert Preston), is the rival of Joan Carroll (Gail Patrick) in court but is also attracted to her. Unwittingly, Joan ends up helping the criminals get off with coached witnesses and false testimony and finally, disillusioned, she quits the law and heads to the marriage license bureau with Bradley. Abandoning a courtroom career is not what makes these women failures as lawyers, as the last minute acceptance of a marriage proposal was standard fare in films of this period; rather it is that these women are denied professional success. The one anomaly is *Ann Carver's Profession* (Buzzell, 1933)—and most likely because it was produced in the early 1930s at the same time that very strong and successful female reporters and detectives were in vogue. After graduating from university, Ann (Fay Wray) becomes a dedicated housewife to Bill (Gene Raymond); however, Ann impresses a judge with her legal talents and, after a handful of wins on high profile cases, she becomes a star in the media. Bill's resentment of her success and Ann's jealousy over one of his coworkers causes their marriage to suffer until Bill is accused of murder and Ann must defend him. While she does give up the law after Bill's case to support him in his career ambitions, Ann does achieve unqualified success as a lawyer—a rare accomplishment for the female lawyer in any decade.

Probably the most famous classical Hollywood female lawyer is Katharine Hepburn's in *Adam's Rib* (Cukor, 1949). Like *Career Woman*, *Adam's Rib* highlights issues of female equality. As an Assistant D.A., Adam Bonner (Spencer Tracy) is assigned to prosecute the case of a woman who shoots (but does not kill) her unfaithful husband; his wife, Amanda (Hepburn), decides to defend the wife in order to expose the gender double standard:

Amanda:	What do you think of a man who is unfaithful to his wife?
Grace:	Not nice, but . . .
Amanda:	All right, now what about a woman who is unfaithful to her husband?
Grace:	Something terrible.
Amanda:	Aha!
Grace:	"Aha" what?
Amanda:	Why the difference? Why the difference? Why "not nice" if he does it and "something terrible" if she does it?
Grace:	I don't make the rules.
Amanda:	Sure you do. We *all* do . . . . A boy sows a wild oat or two, the whole world winks. A girl does the same—scandal.

As Amanda explains during the jury selection, at the very heart of the case is the question of whether women should have equal rights to men. However, the battle of the sexes that the case sparks is that between Amanda and Adam in their marriage as Adam says accusingly,

> I've done it all the way I said I would. Sickness, health, richer, poorer, better or worse. But this is *too* worse—this is basic! I'm old-fashioned. I like two sexes! And another thing . . . all of a sudden I don't like being married to what is known as a "New Woman." I want a wife, not a competitor! Competitor! Competitor! If you want to be a big he-woman, go ahead and be it, but not with me!

Amanda proves a strong competitor when she wins the case; however, she loses her husband in the process. Even though Amanda does win the case, the moral victory is—according to the film—Adam's and, when Adam is nominated for a country court judgeship, Amanda's threat to run for the position herself is only in jest. As Cynthia Lucia demonstrates, Amanda, and the threat she represents as competition to the male, "ultimately *is* contained" (*Framing*, 1).[3] Amanda's fate will be the norm for the female lawyer in the 1980s: even if she is successful in winning her case in the courtroom, the female lawyer learns afterwards—and often through a lecture by an authoritative male—that she was wrong in her judgment. Instead, the female lawyer's greatest success in seeing justice served will come from their investigations as detective—outside of the bounds of the law.

Part I: The Female Lawyer Thriller

It Started on a Jagged Edge

Jagged Edge (1985) seems to have been the film that started the female lawyer thriller trend and, perhaps, this can be attributed to the film's writer—Joe Eszterhas—who is also responsible for the scripts of erotic thrillers such as *Basic Instinct, Sliver* (Noyce, 1993), and *Jade*, but also the other female detective thrillers *Betrayed* (Costa-Gavras, 1988) and *Music Box*.[4] In *Jagged Edge*, former-criminal lawyer, Teddy Barnes (Glenn Close), is asked to defend Jack Forrester (Jeff Bridges)—a male gigolo who is accused of murdering his wife to enjoy her money along with his freedom. In a brutal, sex attack, his wife was bound to the bed and then her breasts and genitals mutilated with a hunting knife (a phallic weapon used to eradicate the signs of sexual difference). The rumor is that his wife was intending to divorce him and leave Jack nothing, giving him a solid motive. When asked by his colleague, Al, "You really think he could have done *that* to his own wife?" the District Attorney, Thomas Krasny (Peter Coyote), replies,

> What the hell is *that*, Al? You murder your wife to take all the money. *That* is the oldest crime in the world. Only you're real smart. So you make it look like some fucking Charlie Manson did it. You *want* people to say, "Jesus, you think he could have done that to his own wife?" If I was gonna kill my wife, that's the way I would do it.

The mystery that Teddy must solve is whether Jack killed his wife, and its solution will determine not only whether justice is served but also her personal happiness as she is in love with Jack. Initially, Teddy asks three male authorities for their expert opinions. First, a police detective explains that Jack passed the polygraph test: "He's telling the truth . . . or he's the kind of ice cube even the machine can't melt." Second, a doctor explains the results of his psychological evaluation: "Is he psychopathic? No, but he's manipulative. [. . .] But did he do that bloodbath? I don't know." Last, her private investigator and friend, Sam (Robert Loggia), tells her that, after watching Jack for months, he thinks that he is guilty. Teddy chooses to disregard these warnings: like the other female lawyers who fall in love with their male clients, Teddy is blind—as justice is supposed to be—to her lover's "true" nature.

As Lucia suggests, Teddy is presented as incompetent as a lawyer—past and present. Teddy used to be a prosecutor for the D.A. but quit criminal law after Krasny withheld evidence that resulted in Teddy's successful prosecution of an innocent man—Henry Stiles (who subsequently hanged himself in prison). Obsessed by her past mistake, Teddy sees Jack's case as a chance for redemption. Teddy ignores the evidence in Jack's case that points to his guilt because—in terms of her professional life—she feels guilt over her mishandling of the Stiles case and—in terms of her personal life—she is susceptible to Jack's charms as a late 30-something divorcée with two children. In the end, Teddy proves herself unsuccessful in both aspects of her life: personally, because she begins to neglect her children's needs in favor of Jack's; and, professionally, because she succeeds in attaining a "not guilty" verdict for her very guilty client.

The film suggests that the problem is Teddy's sex; if she were a man, then she would not have been seduced into believing Jack. Teddy is trying to operate in an almost exclusively male world and the sex divide is made evident in this (and in many of the female lawyer films) by the predominance of (hetero)sexualized language used by men: from Krasny saying that Stiles "had a rap sheet as long as my dick" to Sam saying to Teddy in reference to Jack, "Fuck him. He was trash." Teddy tries to prove to Jack that she is his (mas-

Fig. 9.1. The Oldest Crime in the World: Glenn Close's lawyer-heroine defends her lover (Jeff Bridges) who is accused of brutally murdering his wife for her money in *Jagged Edge* (1984). Photo from author's collection.

culine) equal and their romance begins with competition: their first kiss and sexual encounter occur after jumping horses in the woods and playing squash, respectively. However, Teddy's vulnerability due to her sex is proven when the tennis pro from Santa Cruz, Bobby Slade (Marshall Colt), accuses Teddy in the courtroom of being a "fucking bitch" and, later in the parking lot, of being "a cold fuck." He then suggests, "I bet I could warm you up. I bet I could make you real hot." It is at this moment that the audience is reminded that, whoever the killer is, Teddy could end up one of his victims. As the tagline on the film's poster suggests, "When a murder case is this shocking, which do you trust . . . your emotions or the evidence?" Sam, however, suggests that it is not her head or her heart that Teddy is relying on but "another part of [her] anatomy." The most uncomfortable part of the trial is when Bobby explains Jack's seduction techniques—including using his horses as "foreplay." It is at this moment that the audience and Teddy have confirmation of her worst fears: namely, that Jack has been using her to gain his freedom.

And it is here that her incompetence in her personal and private lives intersect: she has been unprofessional by sleeping with her client and now wants to drop his case in the middle of the trial. She visits the judge to get his advice on the situation; the judge, however, explains that unless the client has confessed to the crime, no ethical problem exists . . . legally speaking, that is. Teddy's lack of professionalism is also highlighted when she focuses on Krasny as the villain for withholding evidence in the Stiles case instead of on the murderer of Page Forrester. When the case is over, Teddy tells the press about the Stiles case and likens Krasny's professional betrayal of her to a rape by explaining that when she found out the truth about what had happened, "I didn't do anything; I didn't tell anyone." By clearing Jack's name of murder and by confessing the truth about Stiles, Teddy feels that she has righted all the wrongs that have haunted her but also made the justice system accountable for its corruption. However, after the trail is over, the truth of Jack's guilt finally comes to light.

Throughout the case, Teddy received anonymous letters typed on an old typewriter that gave her information and led her investigation in specific directions. After the trial is over, Teddy discovers the typewriter in Jack's closet. Teddy has again proven herself incompetent and again cannot do anything *legally* about it: the constitutional right of "double jeopardy" states that a person cannot be tried for the same crime twice. Consequently, to right this wrong, Teddy must operate outside of the law. She tells Jack on the phone that she knows about the typewriter and then hangs up: if he is guilty, he will try to kill her; if he is innocent, he will come to explain. Later that evening, a masked killer breaks into her house to kill her as she lies in bed but Teddy shoots him dead with the gun she is concealing beneath the covers. When she hears someone else come into the house, she—and the audience, for her sake—hopes that this is Jack arriving and that the body on the floor belongs to Bobby.[5] However, it is Sam who comes up the stairs and, when he pulls back the mask of her attacker, the face revealed is that of Jack's. In this sense, Teddy's vulnerability as a woman can be regarded as a positive thing: as a woman, her vigilante justice will be justified by her being a potential victim of the male killer. Ironically, although she *appeared* to be a helpless female victim lying in bed, this was a masquerade of traditional femininity in order to conceal her masculine—phallic and deadly—strength. Teddy had the "balls," using the language of her male world, to fix her mistake and see justice served.

While *Jagged Edge* concludes with Teddy's "masculinization" (she uses a phallic weapon to destroy the evil male), the majority of the female lawyer thrillers that followed conclude with a recuperation of their heroines into feminized roles in order to offer the "happy ending" of successful heterosexual coupling. Teddy loses her chance for romance when she identifies her lover as a murderer and then kills him. Rather than being reunited with her children and/or her ex-husband to reconstitute a happy family unit, the film ends with Teddy alone. The "jagged edge" to which the title of the film refers is that of the murderer's hunting knife but it also seems to refer to the precarious position of a woman stepping out of her prescribed role as wife and mother. As a detective, Teddy's success is mixed: as a sleuth, she is somewhat of a failure—after all, her investigation was led by Jack and her discovery of the key piece of evidence against him accidental; as a justice figure, however, she is a success—indeed, she does dispatch the evil villain when the legal system fails. Nevertheless, Teddy discovers that success does come with a price: namely, remaining alone.

Suspect Conduct

The popularity of *Jagged Edge* saw a fully-fledged cycle emerge within a few years.[6] In *Suspect* (1987), Kathleen Riley (Cher) is a public defender who is tired of her job and her lack of a personal life. As she explains to her colleague Morty (Fred Melamed),

> I don't know what I'm doing anymore. I don't have a life. The last time I went to the movies was like a year ago. The only time I listen to music is in my car. I don't date. I'd like to have a child but I don't even have a boyfriend, so how can I have a child. I spend all my time with murderers and rapists. And what's really crazy is I like them.

Kathleen needs a vacation but she is assigned to the case of a homeless man, Carl Wayne Anderson (Liam Neeson), accused of murder. Carl's case, however, ends up being the one that reminds her of why she became a public defender instead of a high-priced defense attorney: as Morty suggests, they do the job "for the one poor bastard who didn't do it"—like Carl. Carl's case brings her satisfaction in her professional life but also her personal life as well by introducing her to juror, Eddie Sanger (Dennis Quaid).

The film suggests that the worlds of the law and politics are corrupt and that everyone must prostitute themselves to find success. For example, Eddie's friend, Marilyn (Lisbeth Bartlett), works for Paul Gray (Philip Bosco), the Deputy Attorney General. Eddie asks her sarcastically, "Type much?" Marilyn laughs and agrees, "The job doesn't require much typing. Anyway, it's temporary. Paul says he wants to groom me for management." She pauses and sighs, "I wish I had a dollar for every promise. Just once, I wish someone would say to me, 'I can't help you out.'" What she implies is that "helping her out" involves sleeping with her bosses to advance her career. While it would be assumed that such exchanges of favors are restricted to women, the film assures the audience that young men seeking their career advancement often need to as well. Eddie is a lobbyist for dairy farmers and needs support for a specific bill; he tries to coerce 50-something Congresswoman Grace Comisky (E. Katherine Kerr) but she informs him that her vote is not for sale. As it turns out, it is—but for sex not money. At a party, Eddie and Grace discuss their sex-specific reactions to tension at work:

> Grace: I know the feeling. There's a vote coming up on a bill I co-sponsored. Gives me a knot in my stomach like a fist. Closer the vote, tighter the fist.
>
> Eddie: Grabs me a little lower.

In the end, so does Grace and his payment is her vote for the bill. However, when Eddie struggles to look her in the eye afterward, the audience knows that he is ashamed of prostituting himself.

When Kathleen runs into resistance from Judge Matthew Helms (John Mahoney) at trial, the audience is led to assume that is due to her sex. Certainly, the prosecutor, Charlie Stella (Joe Mantegna), has issues with her being a woman and uses that to his advantage during the trial. When Kathleen challenges the forensic expert's findings on Carl's knife—i.e., was it wiped clean or wasn't it?—Charlie objects, "Forensic pathology is an exact science. Miss Riley is making this sound like a cooking class." It is revealed, however, that the judge's problem with Kathleen is not her sex but her dogged determination to find out who killed Elizabeth Quinn. While the police assume Carl did, Kathleen—with help from Eddie—eventually proves that the judge did, in order to cover up an old case on which his own and Gray's cooperation were bought. In order to see justice served, however, Kathleen has to circumvent the law—after all, lawyers are not supposed have to any contact with jurors (e.g., Eddie). Kathleen is a good detective, but many of the key clues—i.e., the license plate of the killer's car, the fact that Carl is left-handed, and the Presidential cufflink found at the scene—are Eddie's finds and as much screen-time is given over to his investigation as to hers. Indeed, she almost confesses her suspicions about Gray to Helms without realizing that Helms is the murderer. Ultimately, Eddie is depicted as a competent and driven detective and Kathleen as passable and reluctant. In a review for the *New Yorker*, Pauline Kael comments,

> The screenwriter, Eric Roth, puts a woman lawyer at the center of the movie, as if this were going to be a switch on older courtroom thrillers, and then he provides a man to do all the thinking and to rescue her when she gets into trouble. You can't call this feminist backlash, because there's no hostility in it; it doesn't have the nastiness or the kick that hostility would give it. (16 Nov 1987)

According to Faludi, the year 1987 was the most prolific in terms of demonstrating the backlash against female independence with the top-earning films, for example *Fatal Attraction*, focusing on the danger that the independent woman posed for men (145). While the portrayal of Kathleen in *Suspect* is not necessarily a hostile backlash against feminism as Kael suggests, it is a part of a broader concern with feminism and professional women, and certainly her character's agency as a detective is undermined by Eddie's superior investigative abilities.

Kathleen struggles with the case. In a moment of frustration because Carl is not giving her enough information to win his case easily, Kathleen explains sarcastically,

> Piece of cake! And maybe it won't bother a jury that your fingerprints were all over her body . . . and possibly they won't mind that you carried a big knife . . . and they'll probably understand—I mean, she was dead anyway. What the hell! Why not rob her? And maybe I will play quarterback for the Redskins next season.

Indeed, she will not play quarterback in the NFL next season because she is a woman; and, as a woman, she is revealed to be physically vulnerable to male violence. Early in the film, she is robbed by youths as she sits in her car in a traffic jam; and, later, Eddie has to come to her rescue when a homeless man threatens to cut her throat with a knife. At the courthouse, Kathleen attempts to run and hide from an anonymous pursuer (revealed later to be Helms); she has the wherewithal to arm herself with a knife and defends herself when he attempts to strangle her, but it is Eddie's arrival at the scene that prevents her assailant from attacking her again.

While Kathleen becomes more confident as a lawyer, detective, and at self-defense, she has to break the law to win her case. Not only does she discuss the case with a juror and exchange clues, but she also begins a romantic relationship with him. Helms accuses Kathleen of behavior "bordering on professional misconduct" and he is absolutely correct. Although the title of the film can be interpreted as a noun referring to Carl as a murder suspect or a verb in that Kathleen suspects Gray and later Helms of the crime, it can also be interpreted as an adjective referring to Kathleen: her behavior has been suspect. Kathleen does feel guilt about her actions and confesses her qualms about how she is handling the case to Carl. In response he declares, "I am innocent." The film suggests that illegal or unethical activities on the part of the female lawyer-detective are justifiable when paternal authority is corrupt and it is the only way to see justice served. So, while her handling of her professional life might be suspect, her moral victory sees Kathleen rewarded with the social life that she had complained to Morty was so elusive because of her dedication to her job. In the last scene of the film, Kathleen explains that she has less than an hour before she has to be in court—i.e., to do her job. Rather than reviewing her files for the case, however, she allows Eddie to seduce her in her office.

Following a Similar Tune

Joe Eszterhas who wrote *Jagged Edge* also wrote *Music Box* (1989) but, while the former was sensational because of its thrills, the latter attempts to be so because of its political content. Ann Talbot (Jessica Lange) is horrified when her father, Hungarian émigré Michael J. Laszlo (Armin Mueller-Stahl), is accused of war crimes committed during World War II and is to be extradited to Hungary. Although not an immigration lawyer, Ann decides to defend her father.[7] As with most of the female lawyer films, the system appears corrupt and Ann believes that her father has been misidentified as the war criminal, Mishka; however, by the end of the film, the truth is revealed that the patriarchal authority that has betrayed her is not the legal system but her own father.

The sex of the female lawyer is again a central concern in this film. Ann's brother, Karchy (Michael Rooker), is a rough, working-class man and reminds Ann that their ability to help their father is dependent on their skills and sex:

> Karchy: You're gonna get him out of this, ain't ya? Ain't ya? [. . .] I mean, you'd better. 'Cause, I mean, if this was a bar fight and he needed me, I'd slice some nuts. [. . .] Now, you're gonna have to slice some nuts, here.

> Ann: Karchy, why do you always have to talk so crude?

> Karchy: You know another way of slicing nuts without being crude? Hah? Now, you're gonna have to get crude here.

If their father needed physical help to defeat his enemies, then Karchy could help him; however, since the assistance his father needs is legal, then it is his daughter who can come to his rescue. As Karchy suggests, Ann will have to get tough—and crude—to win this battle in the male dominated arena of the courtroom. Although Ann is a daughter and single mother to her young son, she proves that she can be deceptively tough when she suggests that prosecutor,

Jack Burke (Frederic Forrest), might have been responsible for his wife's death because he was drunk driving. Jack retorts, "You know, I liked you Mrs. Talbot. Now, I think I must have misjudged you. You are your father's daughter. [. . .] You find the soft spot and then you like to turn the knife." And Jack warns her that her relationship with her father will make her lose her case: "If you're trusting your heart, you're going to get it broken. I think maybe you should get another lawyer, Mrs. Talbot. Maybe, a *real* lawyer to defend your father, who isn't emotionally involved." Just as Teddy's judgment was compromised by her emotional (i.e., feminine) involvement with her client in *Jagged Edge*, so too is Ann's. When her father is first accused of the crimes, Ann assures him, "It's not *you*, pop" without even asking him if it was. And she continues to believe in his innocence despite the amount of damning evidence that Ann's assistant, Georgina (Cheryl Lynn Bruce), uncovers: namely, that her father was paying a man called Tibor Zoldan significant sums of money every month until he died. Ann replies angrily, "Stop it! He is not a monster. I'm his daughter, I know him better than anyone."

As a lawyer, Ann is successful in her goal to free her father: the case is dismissed for lack of evidence. As a detective, Ann is ultimately successful in discovering the truth but as in *Jagged Edge*, she does so only after the trial is over. Ann tracks down Tibor's sister in Budapest who gives Ann a pawn ticket that Tibor had sent her. The pawn ticket leads Ann to a music box and, at first, she is overjoyed when it appears to be nothing but a box that plays a charming tune; however, she discovers that the box contains a collection of photos showing her father's killing of innocent people during the war. With the case against her father already dismissed, Ann has failed to see justice served during the trial and so she, like most of Hollywood's female lawyers, must pursue justice outside of the courtroom: she sends the photos and a letter of explanation to Jack who then releases them to a newspaper. Ann wins her case in the courtroom but she does not see justice done until she uncovers the truth as a detective; the same is true for Jenny Hudson in *Physical Evidence* (1989).

Physical Evidence was originally supposed to be the sequel to *Jagged Edge* and to co-star Glenn Close and Robert Loggia once again.[8] The final result, however, starred Theresa Russell as a public defender trying to forge her career as a woman in a department dominated by an "old boys club" mentality. As Jenny (Russell) argues to her superior,

> My problem is my last three cases have been a postman bitten by a poodle, some first time grass smokers, and the derelict knocking quarters out of a parking meter. [. . .] I've been here two years and I want this case. I am better than Kravitz or Sampson. The defendant is entitled to something better than your old thumper pals defending him.

The defendant is a cop on suspension, Joe Paris (Burt Reynolds), who is accused of murder; however, he too is unsure of her abilities as a defender because of her sex—but also, interestingly, because of her class:

> Joe: There's something very strange for a welcome chick like
>   you defending a trickle down case like mine—sounds
>   dangerously like a hobby. A public defender wearing a
>   Rolex. [. . .] Send me someone that works for a living.
>
> Jenny: Fuck you, you arrogant asshole! [. . .] It's my career. [. . .]
>   But *I* can get you off. The minute I don't shine for you,
>   you can fire me but I'll be damned if you're going to pass
>   on me because of the way I dress. That's not me. This is
>   me—guts and brains! You cannot do any better.

Joe does not believe that an upper-middle-class woman can relate to him as a working-class cop and this conflation of class and sex is a debate not necessarily explored in the other female lawyer thrillers.

For example, Jenny's snobbish fiancé, Kyle (Ted McGinley), wants her to be ambitious in her career but hates the effect that being a public defender of "street people" (as he refers to the working class) has on her. He suggests that her job forces her to adopt a masquerade of masculine authority (indicated through her language and wardrobe) and is replacing her "true," more feminine identity:

> Kyle: This case is starting to consume you. I don't like what
>   you're becoming.
>
> Jenny: And what am I becoming that is so intolerable?
>
> Kyle: Mannish.
>
> Jenny: Mannish. Just because I am doing things my way now
>   or is it because I'm involved with something that's more
>   important than your almighty stock swindles.

This shift from domestic femininity to professional masculinity is highlighted in an interesting sequence: Jenny sneaks downstairs at night, dressed in only a silk shirt and wearing her hair long, and practices her opening statement for Joe's trial. She repeats her opening line three times and practices an arm gesture and a turn; the sequence then cuts, in a match-on-action, to her polished completion of the line, gesture, and turn in the courtroom the next morning.

In court, her long hair and revealing silk shirt are replaced with her hair pulled tightly back from her face and a tailored suit. The scene contrasts the insecurity aligned with femininity with masculine mastery of the courtroom and, more importantly, it reveals that her composed deportment in the courtroom is just a performance.

Physical Evidence portrays its protagonist as incompetent as a lawyer and, while she is shown to be competent at detective work, it is the man, as in *Suspect*, who uncovers most of the key leads. Importantly, Joe is able to uncover these leads *because* he is male: he gets the information on the murderer, Norton (Kenneth Welsh), by flirting with Norton's receptionist, and he escapes harm from a handful of goons by using his fighting skills acquired in Vietnam. And, like her predecessors, Jenny is the potential victim of male violence in the climactic showdown with the killer, Norton, because of her sex. Jenny and Joe have laid a trap and now await the killer's arrival; however, rather than remaining vigilant, Jenny—when she fears that Joe has been hurt—lets her guard down. Jenny then demonstrates the "guts and brains" she bragged about possessing at the beginning of the film by convincing Norton that she can lead him to the informant he wishes to silence. Once in the stairwell, Jenny wrestles with Norton for his gun and shoots him accidently. In a somewhat over-the-top conclusion, Jenny marches outside, confidently holding the large gun, and says to Joe, who is lying sprawled on the sidewalk injured, "Jesus, Joe! Can't you do anything right?" From a damsel-in-distress to a cocky gunslinger in only a few moments, Jenny exacts justice outside of the courtroom because she cannot do so inside of it.

Indefensible Conduct

Of all the female lawyer thrillers, *Defenseless* (1991) is the most critical of its heroine (Barbara Hershey). "T.K." (short for Thelma Katwuller) is introduced in her kitchen—the chaos of which confirms that T.K. is single and no domestic goddess. On the radio, an expert for the lovelorn suggests that her caller stop looking for "Mr. Perfect" and T.K. wonders aloud about a "Mr. Okay for the Time Being." Her "Mr. Okay for the Time Being" is her client Steven Seldes (J. T. Walsh), who is married—although he insists "in name only." At lunch, T.K. runs into an old college friend, Ellie (Mary Beth Hurt), who reveals that she is, in fact, Steven's wife. To complicate matters, Steven is subsequently murdered, Ellie is accused of the murder, and T.K. must defend her despite the fact that she is herself a possible suspect. Although released six years after *Jagged Edge*, the key issues in *Defenseless* remain the same, debating the woman's struggle with a career, respect, and love. T.K. is defending Steven because one of his properties has been—unbeknownst (according) to him—used for the production of pornographic films starring underage girls. When T.K. arrives at the office, the mother of one of these girls, Mrs. Bodeck (Sheree North), confronts her:

T.K.:   Mrs. Bodeck, I am Steven Seldes's lawyer. I really don't
            think you should be here.

Bodeck: Neither do I—you're a woman.

T.K.:   Time's change.

Bodeck: They keep saying some things don't change: having
            children, the pain they cause. That doesn't change.

T.K.:   I know.

Bodeck: You have children?

T.K.:   No.

Bodeck: Then how can you say that?

Mrs. Bodeck voices the questions that many female lawyer films pose: why are these women pursuing careers as lawyers instead of as wives/mothers and, as a career woman, how can they understand what it is like to be a "real" woman (i.e., a wife/mother)? Similarly, T.K.'s college friend, Ellie, represents this question by embodying the "other" life—that of suburban homemaker—that T.K. has eschewed in order to become a successful lawyer. T.K.'s indecision in terms of which outfit is appropriate for dinner at the Seldes's should be the stereotypical scene of a woman unable to make up her mind what to wear; however, here the indecision is over which outfit will make her appear innocent of having an affair with her best friend's husband. As T.K. explains as she flips through each dress in her wardrobe:

Yuck! [she comments of the first]
Work. [she declares of the second]
Old Lady. [she claims of the third]
The green—too masculine.
The black—too guilty.
The orange—too flashy.
The brown—why did I ever buy the brown?
The yellow—too yellow.
The print—too young.
The red. . . .
[She returns to the print] Too young? The print's too young.
[She reconsiders the red] Just sign the confession and skip
    dinner!

In the end, she wears a white dress and, later, Ellie explains that it was that dress choice that convinced her that T.K. was sleeping with her husband. Her crime, it seems, is that she is a woman who has sympathy for defending a criminal (Steven) instead of a mother (Mrs. Bodeck), and for poaching the husband (Steven) of a housewife/friend (Ellie).

Although the film begins with a critical view of T.K.'s career-oriented life, the film, interestingly, also offers a biting indictment of the alternative: the American family. T.K.'s investigation into who killed Steven uncovers corruption; however, it is not the legal system that is corrupt but family patriarchs. T.K. is convinced that Mr. Bodeck (George P. Wilbur) killed Steven in revenge for his daughter's exploitation. While the film suggests that it is commendable for Mr. Bodeck to want to protect his daughter, his desire for violent retribution against the filmmaker and Steven is not. Mr. Bodeck is shown to be a deficient husband, physically abusive to his wife, and father, likely having sexually abused his daughter. Steven is presented as similarly deficient: he has affairs while maintaining the pretence of a happy marriage at home; he lies to his lawyer (and lover) when he says that he was not involved with the production of the pornography; and he pursues sexual relations with underage girls—including his own daughter.

While both husbands/fathers represent the corruption of the American family, T.K. is as guilty of corrupting the course of justice. When T.K. discovers Steven's double betrayal, she threatens to send him to prison and he reacts by trying to strangle her. In an attempt to save herself from him, she stabs him in the arm and breaks his nose; however, rather than confessing the truth to Detective Beutel (Sam Shepard), T.K. withholds the fact that she had been having an affair with the victim and that she had struggled with him just minutes before his murder. Instead, she agrees to defend Ellie who is charged with the crime and makes up for her unethical behavior by proving to the jury that the Seldes's daughter, Janna (Kellie Overbey), had means, motive, and opportunity to kill her father. T.K., like Teddy and Kathleen, is successful in getting the case against her client dismissed; however, Ellie is later revealed to be the killer after all and T.K., like her predecessors, is forced to seek justice outside of the courtroom in a violent confrontation. And, in order to see justice served, T.K., like Kathleen and Jenny, requires the assistance of a male detective. Beutel's investigation eventually leads them to Ellie and, here, T.K. is afforded the opportunity to redeem herself. Ellie killed Steven for betraying his family—and, especially, his daughter—but the film is not sympathetic toward her. In fact, the film suggests that Ellie, rather than feeling guilty for allowing the abuse of her daughter to continue, actually resents her daughter for being her husband's lover. As Ellie explains, "She replaced me." And T.K. blames the mother for all that has gone wrong. "There's no one left to blame, just you," T.K. tells her. As Ellie attempts to slit her own throat with a kitchen knife, T.K. intervenes, slapping her until she drops the weapon and can be taken into custody. Although the female lawyer does successfully investigate the murder, it is implied that without Beutel (the official investigator), T.K. herself would have been accused of the crime and/or her extraction of a confession out of Ellie would have been useless without his corroboration. Beutel saves her literally, by helping her uncover the truth and, metaphorically, by becoming her love interest at the end of the film.

Homme Fatal

In terms of being, as Lucia argues, "personally and professionally deficient," T.K. represents a low point in the female lawyer thriller cycle: she is the most dependent on male authority for her emotional happiness and her investigative success. In the same way, Jennifer Haines (Rebecca De Mornay) of *Guilty as Sin* (1993) is the most successful, following in the formula of *Jagged Edge*—a female lawyer hero defends a handsome womanizer against charges of murdering his wife with the assistance of a grizzled private eye father-figure—but offers a far more intrepid and shrewd heroine. *Guilty as Sin*, like *Jagged Edge*, aligns evil with what Linda Ruth Williams calls an "*homme fatal*" (125). David Edgar Greenhill (Don Johnson) is a handsome and charming gigolo who knows how to use women—including manipulating Jennifer into defending him. Unlike the female lawyer thrillers of the 1980s, *Guilty as Sin* is not centrally concerned with the femininity-achievement conflict. Being female and a lawyer is no longer a rare occurrence; indeed, her sex is important only because it allows her womanizing client an opportunity to blackmail her. David, unbeknownst to her, has been planting evidence for a year that will suggest, if discovered, that they have been lovers and planned the murder of his wife together. Instead, the film is concerned with ethics—that lawyers get guilty clients off for the money—and, in this way, the film has much in common with the girl reporter films of the 1930s such as *Back in Circulation* (Enright, 1937) and is as representative of the "Grisham Cycle" of lawyer films in the 1990s (to be discussed in the next section) as the female lawyer thriller of the 1980s. Jennifer's blind ambition as a lawyer is presented as something endemic to the profession and a question of degrees of humanity rather than of sex. David reassures his latest girlfriend Miriam (Christina Grace), who is also paying for his trial, that his only interest in Jennifer is professional:

> David: I don't trust her. See, people like us Miriam, we're warm
>   people. But she's . . . she's an attorney. [. . .]
>
> Miriam: She's awfully attractive.
>
> David: Not to me she's not. All she cares about is winning, like
>   a goddamn machine.

His comments are aimed to appease Miriam, and David, in fact, admires Jennifer for her drive to win at any cost. As he tells her when they first meet, "They tell me you're the best there is. That you're smart and tough." What is admirable in an attorney, however, proves unappealing in a lover and Jennifer's boyfriend, Phil (Stephen Lang)—like Jenny's in *Physical Evidence*—complains that her work is crossing over into her personal life. He ends an argument by telling her, "There's no point in talking, Jennifer. You always have to win."

Jennifer is a very competent lawyer; however, her success stems from her ability to manipulate the system for her criminal clients. Rather than fight the corruption of the system, Jennifer uses it to her fullest advantage: in the opening sequence, she is able to get the case against her client dismissed because convicting him will expose a federal agent working for his organization undercover. Despite the fact that he is guilty, her client (John Kapelos) tells the media in a moment of irony, "This renews my entire faith in the system of American justice." Her new client, David, confirms her suspicions by confessing not only to the murder of his last wife, but also previous lovers. She is unable, however, to leak the information to the police—like Ann in *Music Box*—because it would mean breaking "lawyer-client privilege" and she would risk disbarment. Instead, like her generic predecessors, Jennifer seeks justice outside of the courtroom; interestingly, to enact justice, Jennifer breaks the law, planting evidence from David's apartment that will implicate him in the murder. The film justifies her actions by branding David as pure evil; as Jennifer tells her private investigator (Jack Warden), "I've looked into the face of somebody so . . . evil, I've heard words so vile. Moe, I've gotta destroy him." When the jury cannot agree upon a verdict and David is released, Jennifer vows that she will stop him from killing another woman—even if it means ending her career as a lawyer. Just as *Suspect*'s Kathleen finds a renewed faith in her job through her case, so too does Jennifer experience an ethical turn, recognizing that justice is worth any personal sacrifice. A new sense of humanity replaces her previous single-minded devotion to her career advancement and for this she will be rewarded with a "happy" conclusion with marriage to Phil.

Although Jennifer may follow firmly in the footsteps of her predecessors in terms of her lack of success as a lawyer, she proves infinitely superior as a detective. She uncovers not only that David has likely killed previous lovers in East Coast cities but also the method and means by which he killed his wife. Similarly, she deduces that he must have gone back upstairs after being seen leaving for work and that he must have done so by disguising himself as a painter working on the renovations of the building. The film offers a flashback in which David recalls how he committed the murder and Jennifer's deductions prove accurate in almost every respect; even David is shocked at how accurate she is. Although a better detective than her predecessors and one who does not rely on male assistance, Jennifer must still defeat evil outside of the courtroom in a physical confrontation. David plans to throw her from the upper floor of Phil's office to the foyer below and disguise it as suicide; however, he has misjudged Jennifer's strength of character. She fights back, first, scratching him so that there will be evidence of a struggle and, second, bracing her feet—not to save herself—but to pull David over the edge after her. He hits the ground first and cushions her fall so that she survives and the evil is destroyed. As she explains to Phil in the ambulance afterward, "I beat him, Phil. I beat him." She then laughs and says, "Tough way to win a case."

Doing Something Right

As Nicole Rafter suggests, "*Jagged Edge* set off a debate over whether Teddy Barnes and the women lawyers of subsequent thrillers represent successful professionals or failed females, women who violate their true nature by straying from the kitchen" (106). For example, Carolyn Lisa Miller argues that *Jagged Edge* transforms Teddy "from powerful attorney to powerless woman, resituating her in her 'proper' role" (212). While these films see the female lawyer unable to exact justice inside the courtroom and vulnerable because of their emotional or physical vulnerability (traits attributed to their sex), I would argue that these films judge their heroines less harshly than critics have. After all, these films identify corrupt older men as the threat to society rather than the female lawyer. As Rafter explains, the courtroom film explores the tension between immutable, "natural" law and fallible, "man-made" law and the hero of such films is a "justice figure" that attempts to close the gap between the two—from man-made law to the ideal (93–94). Lucia argues that within the female lawyer film lie two oppositional tendencies:

> One is the popularly held idealized vision of law—that the law is a stable, immutable force beyond the reach of transitory political and cultural influences. This notion becomes complicated by a second factor—the political and cultural context registering a troubled or uneasy acceptance of women in law. Together, these two conditions create some difficulty in resolving the "problem" of women in law. (*Framing*, 3)

While I agree with Lucia that the female lawyer represents an example of feminist empowerment at the same time as a masculine backlash against that empowerment, I disagree with her supposition that these films see the female lawyer as a disruption to the immutability of the idealized popular image of the law. Indeed, I would argue that the female lawyer is the upholder of the idealized vision of the law in the face of the patriarchal corruption of the law. In this sense, the female lawyer thrillers are more concerned with the triumph of "natural" law over "man-made" law—even if the female lawyer must manipulate man-made law to do so—than about repositioning ambitious women into more traditional roles. While all of these films do suggest that women in professional positions struggle to make it in a male-dominated world and also to balance a career with a personal life, *none* of them suggests that these lawyers should give up their careers and return to the kitchen. They may not have the experience to recognize evil immediately and, therefore, do not always see justice served in the courtroom as lawyers; however, their ability to do that job is often complicated by the fact that the evil often occupies a position of power within the legal system—whether as senior partner in a law firm or as a judge on the bench. Whatever the result of their battle in the courtroom, these female lawyers see justice served in the end as vigilante crime-fighters.

Although out of fashion in films of the new millennium, the vigilante execution of evil was a common conclusion to thrillers of the late 1980s and early 90s. This was the legacy of the Dirty Harry generation of detective films of the 1970s—and the assumption that vigilante violence was the only solution to the law made impotent by bureaucracy was only expanded upon in the male cop action films of the 1980s. For example, in *Cobra* (Cosmatos, 1986), the villain taunts the hero, Lieutenant Cobretti (Sylvester Stallone), "Even I have rights . . . don't I, pig? Take me in. They'll say I'm insane, won't they? The court is civilized. Isn't it, pig?" Cobretti replies, "But I'm not. This is where the law stops and I start." The original ending for the erotic thriller *Fatal Attraction* saw the home-wrecker, Alex Forrest (Glenn Close), commit suicide out of despair when her lover, Dan Gallagher (Michael Douglas), rejects her; however, test audiences reportedly did not think that suicide was punishment enough, and the ending was reshot with husband and wife (Anne Archer) united in destroying the monstrous feminine. Similarly, in *The Hand that Rocks the Cradle*, it is the wife (Annabella Sciorra) who outwits her evil usurper (Rebecca De Mornay) and pushes her out of the attic window to fall to her death, ironically, on the family's white picket fence.

The courtroom thriller *Presumed Innocent* (Pakula, 1990) sees the lawyer protagonist (Harrison Ford) discover the awful truth that his wife (Bonnie Bedelia) is the one who murdered his former lover (Greta Scacchi). He does not, however, turn her over to the proper authorities—as the wife (Diane Lane), in a similar situation, does in the millennial thriller *Unfaithful* (Lyne, 2002) when her husband (Richard Gere) kills her lover (Oliver Martinez). While, in *Unfaithful*, the punishment is for the wife to lose her husband by allowing him to turn himself in to the police, in *Presumed Innocent*, the punishment is for husband and wife to remain together, living with the knowledge of the crime. And, as the hero's voice-over explains at the end of the film, "There *is* punishment." Importantly, the husband in *Unfaithful* is guilty only of manslaughter because the lover's death was accidental, while the wife in *Presumed Innocent* is guilty of premeditated murder, having planned the brutal crime down to the last detail and implicating her husband. While, in the new millennium, it seems necessary that all crimes must be reported and punished according to the

Fig. 9.2. Victim of the System: Like Cher's public defender in *Suspect* (1987), many female lawyers discover that paternal authority is corrupt and are forced to circumvent the law to see justice served. Photo from author's collection.

letter of the law, in the late 1980s and early 1990s, vigilante justice was not only acceptable but—as *Fatal Attraction*—proved, popular with audiences. Thus, according to the rules of the genre at the time, I contend that the heroines of the female lawyer thriller cycle are heroic indeed because they take up the slack when the legal system (aligned with masculinity) is circumvented, corrupted, or incapable of delivering justice—through playing detective.

Part II: The Grisham Cycle

The female lawyer all but disappeared from the screen by the early 1990s and instead it was the youth who repeatedly appeared as the lawyer in the courtroom in, what Keith Bartlett dubs, the "Grisham Cycle." In the majority of the films adapted from John Grisham's best-selling novels, the detective-hero is the young lawyer at the start of his career—for example, *The Firm* (Pollack, 1993) starring Tom Cruise, *The Chamber* (Foley, 1996) starring Chris O'Donnell, *A Time to Kill* (Schumacher, 1996) starring Matthew McConaughey, and *The Rainmaker* (Coppola, 1997) starring Matt Damon. The youth can fulfill the role of the lawyer-detective because he is young, inquisitive, and looking to make his mark and, unlike his older and jaded superiors, is more likely to charge headlong in pursuit of an investigation rather than leave it to the police—the official investigators of crime. With the shift from the issue of gender to one of age and experience, so too did the debate of the courtroom film shift from the woman trying to juggle her personal and professional life unsuccessfully, to a focus on American moral and political corruption. These films circulated the conception of lawyers as self-serving—defending wealthy criminals, despite their guilt, for money and glory—and courtroom justice as a three-ring circus for big-time lawyers to sell their version of the truth at the expense of the innocent. A generational debate also arose as older men were portrayed as jaded and the betrayers of justice and the law (as they were in the female lawyer thriller cycle), and the youth as idealistic and determined to bring "natural" (i.e., ideal) law back to the system. Although the cycle was dominated by young men, it did offer a few female lawyers—including *Class Action* (1991) and *The Client* (Schumacher, 1994).[9] These films moved away from the "thriller" model established by *Jagged Edge*, which focused on the female lawyer who is betrayed by patriarchal figures and the potential victim of male violence; instead, the Grisham film sees a shift to, as Bartlett suggests, "a 'David' versus a corporate, criminal or political 'Goliath' " (273). The few female lawyer films that appeared in this cycle, saw their heroine—unlike those of the female lawyer thriller—find ways *within* the system to see justice served rather than being forced to seek vigilante justice outside of the courtroom. In the case of both *Class Action* and *The Client*, the sex of the lawyer is only an issue because the patriarchal figures within the system are corrupt and ethics are identified as belonging to the feminine.

Class Action sees Maggie Ward (Mary Elizabeth Mastrantonio), an up-and-coming lawyer with a high-profile law firm, assigned to a case in which she represents Argo Motors—the Goliath. What complicates the case is that Maggie's father, Jed Ward (Gene Hackman), chooses to represent the people who were injured as a result of the Argo Motor's negligence—the David. Interestingly, in terms of being a detective, Maggie proves to be most proficient—uncovering the truth about Argo Motors's guilt in the case: a Dr. Pavel reported that the circuits of the Meridian car were faulty and would cause an explosion if the car was hit from behind while the driver was indicating left.[10] The cost assessment completed by the company's "bean counter" determined that it would cost the company more to recall and repair the cars than to pay out if any lawsuits arose and so they did nothing about the problem—despite knowing that innocent people were likely to be killed. In terms of being a competent lawyer, however, Maggie is less convincing and the Argo Motors case sees the problems in her professional and personal lives collide.

Maggie's personal issues are twofold: first, she is in a serious relationship with Michael Grazier (Colin Friels), a senior colleague at her firm; and, second, her mother has died recently, leaving her to struggle with her relationship with her overbearing father. Initially, her relationship with Michael seems quite healthy:

he wants her to move in with him but she wants to wait until after she has made partner in the firm. As she explains, "Because it's different for a woman. I don't want them saying I made partner for anything other than my work." And the Argo Motors case is her ticket to "the partnership express." This is one of the few times in the film that Maggie's sex is made an issue: her being female is not a problem, her boss Quinn (Donald Moffat) suggests, if beneath that feminine exterior lies the male instincts of a killer. In order to prove to Quinn that she is capable, Maggie has to "destroy" one of the plaintiffs in the case, Mr. Kellen. Maggie does her job so effectively that Mr. Kellen accuses her of being inhuman. Distraught by what she did to this man, who not only lost his wife in the car accident but also the use of his legs, Maggie drowns her sorrows in a few drinks at a bar and, when asked what she does for a living, Maggie replies, "I'm a professional killer." As the trial continues, Quinn asks her once again to "destroy" a witness, this time Dr. Pavel. Quinn says,

> We have a way of neutralizing him. [. . .] You. I watched your deposition of Mr. Kellen. You discredited him while making it *seem* like if he was doing it to himself. That takes talent. [. . .] The jury accepts this kind of thing much better if a woman does it.

Quinn uses Maggie for trial because he believes that she possesses the perceived masculine ambition to win at any cost while appearing "harmless" because she is a woman. And Maggie is caught between these two father-figures: Jed and Quinn.

Maggie and her father are opposites: she is cool and calm in the court-room while he turns into a circus of emotion; he started up a small (read: left-wing) firm to fight for what he regards as injustice while she wants to have a partnership with a prestigious (read: right-wing) law firm; and he fights for the Davids while she represents the Goliaths. As their mutual friend, Nick (Laurence Fishburne), accuses her,

> Come on, your biggest aspiration is to be his mirror image—exactly the opposite of what he is. The problem is that you don't know what he is. That makes being you impossible. [. . .] You're probably gonna beat him, Maggie. We both know that. You've got the staff and the money to grind us into the ground. But even if he loses he'll know that he went down on the right side. You will have your big success, your partnership . . . and what else?

It is on this last point that the film brings together Maggie's personal and professional lives: professional success is an empty victory without personal fulfillment. Maggie has never forgiven her father for cheating on her mother but, what the film suggests is that she needs to follow in his footsteps if she wishes to be a "good" (i.e., moral as well as successful) lawyer. Like Teddy in *Jagged Edge*, Maggie finds herself on the "wrong side" of the law, defending the "bad guy;" and like Kathleen in *Suspect*, Maggie finds herself confronting systemic corruption. In this case, members of her firm have behaved unethically, destroying evidence (e.g., Pavel's report) that would have proven the plaintiffs' case. In the end, Maggie provides the opposition—her father—with a witness to help them make his case and beat her's. More interesting, perhaps, is that unlike her predecessors, Maggie does not circumvent the law: Jed explains what she did was "not only ethical, legal, but imperative."

In *The Client*, as in *Physical Evidence*, any issue of sex is conflated with class in terms of lawyer Reggie Love (Susan Sarandon). Unlike Jenny with her Rolex and designer clothes, however, Reggie comes from a working-class background, was institutionalized for drug and alcohol abuse, and, with only two years' experience of practicing family law out of her dingy office, Reggie is—as District Attorney, "Reverend" Roy Foltrigg (Tommy Lee Jones) suggests—an amateur. Inexperienced she may be, but after 11-year-old Mark Sway (Brad Renfro) witnesses the suicide of a mafia lawyer, he chooses Reggie to protect his rights (admittedly, he is initially disappointed that she is a woman). In contrast to her polite and soft-spoken Southern manner, however, Reggie proves a force to be reckoned with and challenges a roomful of male lawyers and law enforcers when they attempt to question Mark without the presence of his mother or an attorney. The next day in her office, Mark smiles with glee when Reggie dresses down Foltrigg a second time with a list of the violations of Mark's constitutional rights. It would seem that as a child who struggles for respect in an adult world, Mark appreciates Reggie's David-like triumph in the face of Foltrigg's Goliath-like legal machine. Foltrigg's revelation of Reggie's troubled past sees Mark's smile turn to a frown of consternation, but Reggie wins back Mark's confidence when she confides in him: she started drinking when the husband, whom she had supported through medical school, traded her in for a younger model and took her children away—by hiring expensive lawyers. Reggie put herself through law school in order to safeguard herself against ever being the victim of male paternalist power again. And the film aligns all examples of male paternalist power, drawing parallels between the scheming mafia killers who plot how to kill the young witness and the machinating law enforcers who conspire to have him taken into protective custody.

Just as her thriller predecessors saw their judgment as lawyers clouded by their personal feelings for their client (usually romantic), Judge Roosevelt (Ossie Davis) questions her loss of objectivity: "After all, he is just a client, isn't he?" But Mark is more to Reggie than "just a client:" she has transferred her maternal affection from her own absent children to Mark. Even Reggie's mother, "Momma" Love (Micole Mercurio), is concerned with her daughter's devotion to the case: "He's your client, Regina, he's not your child" but Reggie slams the door before her mother can finish. Rather than her feminine side being her downfall on the case—as it was often for the female lawyer of the decade before—it is her passion that drives her to pull out all of the stops to save her client from a mafia execution. And like a good mother—and as the embodiment of feminine ethics—Reggie encourages Mark to tell the truth when he is forced to take the stand: "You can't lie or you'll be just like them."

On the one hand, rather than manipulate the system in order to get her guilty client off as her 1980s predecessors did, Reggie uses the law to protect her client. On the other hand, like many of her predecessors, Reggie does need saving from the villains. Before the mafia hitman committed suicide at the beginning of the film, he confessed to Mark where he hid the dead body of a senator; at the end of the film, Reggie and Mark attempt to find the body to have evidence supporting their request to place Mark in the witness protection program. When they find the body, they also find Barry "The Blade" Muldano (Anthony LaPaglia). As he threatens to slit Reggie's throat, Mark pulls a gun on him and is tempted to play vigilante by killing him. However, here ethics supplant vigilantism and Reggie insists that Mark allow the law to takes its course. She takes the gun away from Mark but Barry taunts her, "You should have let the kid shoot, bitch. You haven't got the balls." Reggie responds by firing the weapon—not at Barry, however, but at an alarm unit, setting it off and forcing the villains to flee before the police arrive. She proved herself more intelligent than the villains as Mark confirms when he calls her "a genius." And further, she proves herself more intelligent than the D.A. by getting Foltrigg to concede to a long list of demands to ensure the future safety and happiness of Mark and his family. Reggie may not have the opportunity to be a successful single mother to her children, but she sees that Mark's mother (Mary Louise Parker) can be. In the end, Foltrigg admits his respect for Reggie and says, "When I become governor of Louisiana, do you want a job?" But she explains that she has a job—as a lawyer, defending the rights of the innocent. Like *Class Action*, *The Client* assures us that the legal system is ultimately not corrupt and does protect innocent people from the criminal element through female lawyers empowered, like the 1930s girl reporter, with feminine ethics. And, more importantly, by the 1990s they do so from within the bounds of the law.

Part III: The Millennial Lawyer

The female lawyer as the central protagonist has made only a few appearances in the last decade; nevertheless, when she appears, she is presented as a much more competent, intelligent, and successful woman and lawyer than her 1980s predecessors. Perhaps one of the most successful female lawyer films of the last decade has been *Erin Brockovich* (Soderbergh, 2000), except that technically the protagonist is not a lawyer (I will come back to this point). In the 1980s, to have women fight for a right to speak with authority in a space traditionally barred to them was timely and novel. Now it is all but passé and the subgenre has had to find something innovative to rejuvenate it. Without the tension of the femininity-achievement conflict of the 1980s, a film like *High Crimes* (Franklin, 2002) has to rely solely on the corruption of the legal system for interest. And it would seem that the main reason for returning to the formula was to attempt to cash in on star Ashley Judd's previous hits, the serial killer film *Kiss the Girls* (Fleder, 1997) also co-starring Morgan Freeman and the "wrong-(wo)man" thriller *Double Jeopardy* (Beresford, 1999). On the other hand, the *Legally Blonde* comedies and *Erin Brockovich* struck a nerve with audiences because they both resurrect the femininity-achievement conflict, even if their approach and tone differ. In the case of *Legally Blonde* (Luketic, 2001), it is its comedic tone that differs from the thrillers that preceded it even though it follows a typical legal narrative: law-student, Elle Woods (Reese Witherspoon), engages in investigative work of specifically feminine knowledge to prove her female client innocent of the changes against her. *Legally Blonde 2: Red, White and Blonde* (Herman-Wurmfeld, 2003) differs somewhat in that it offers Elle no mystery to solve and is, instead, more of a David-and-Goliath narrative: Elle goes to Washington D.C. to have a bill passed that would end animal testing in the cosmetics industry. *Erin Brockovich* succeeds where *High Crimes* failed because, whereas the latter revived the tired plot of the 1980s legal thriller wholesale including the mystery of whether her lover/client is good or evil, the former did something new. It offered a heroine who was out of her league and not because of her sex but because of her class.

"Criminally Clichéd"

Unlike her twentieth-century predecessors, Claire Kubik (Ashley Judd) in *High Crimes* can have it all. Professionally, she is a highly successful lawyer and about to make partner in the firm; personally, she has a great marriage and is planning to have a baby. When there is a break-in at Kubik's home, the police investigate and find the prints of a Sergeant Ron Chapman wanted for desertion and murder. Unfortunately, the man to whom those prints belong is Claire's husband, Tom (Jim Caviezel). *High Crimes* sees its heroine struggle with the realization that either the system of military justice is corrupt (not unlike *A Few Good Men* [1992]), trying to frame her husband for atrocities committed in El Salvador—or that her husband has lied to her. Initially, like Ann in *Music Box*, Claire refuses to believe that Tom is Ron and, even when she does admit that he was Ron, she refuses to believe that he is guilty of the murder of civilians in El Salvador. Support for Tom's version of the story comes when former military attorney, Charlie Grimes (Morgan Freeman), who is working with Claire, gets a witness to admit on tape that he was coached. By threatening a general that she will go public with the information she has gathered, Claire manages to get the case against her husband dismissed—i.e., going outside of the courtroom to win her case. However, Grimes continues to pursue his investigation, travelling to Mexico to interview the wife of one of the dead witnesses, and uncovers evidence that proves that Tom/Ron is, in fact, guilty of the crimes of which he is accused. As Ann does in *Music Box*, Claire learns that it is not the legal system that is corrupt but the man she loves. And her husband's committing of wartime atrocities leads to the destruction of the American family; Claire can no longer love a man revealed to be a monster and, in the course of the investigation, Claire suffers a miscarriage.

As in the case of the earlier female lawyer thrillers, *High Crimes* accuses Claire of being more concerned with her personal interests (i.e., getting the man she loves off in terms of the murder charges) than with discovering the truth (i.e., being a detective and seeing justice served). While Grimes may chase down leads within the military, Claire does pursue the Salvadoran man (Emilio Rivera) as a witness. She tells him, "I want to know the truth" but he retorts accusingly, "All you care about is saving your husband." And, at this point in the film, he is perhaps right. However, when Grimes reveals that her husband's trips coincided with the murders of the witnesses, Claire cannot overlook the fact that Tom is not only guilty of the murders of which he is accused by the military but the murders of his comrades as well. In keeping with the generic codes of the female lawyer thriller, Claire must exact justice outside of the courtroom and do physical battle with the enemy. When Tom realizes that she knows the truth about him, he attempts to dispose of her. As I explained earlier with the case of *Unfaithful*, however, by the 2000s it was no longer acceptable for the protagonist of the thriller to pursue vigilante justice. Thus, in *High Crimes*, it cannot be Claire who deals the final blow if she is to remain heroic; instead, the Salvadoran comes to her rescue and enacts his revenge for the death of his family at Ron/Tom's hands.

The film concludes with Claire defining her own future independent of the male patriarchs who have controlled her personal life—e.g., Tom—and her professional life—e.g., her firm. Claire leaves behind her successful career and suburban home life to work with Grimes on "skid row" as a business—but not romantic—partner. And when he says that the firm could be renamed "Grimes and Kubik" she replies that it will have to be "Grimes and Grimaldi" because she has returned to her maiden name. *High Crimes* attempts to resurrect the female lawyer thriller almost wholesale from the late 1980s in terms of plot points and themes but, by the 2000s, the female lawyer's battle against corrupt male authority seemed irrelevant and certainly an isolated example. As the title of Rick Groen's review of the film suggests, *High Crimes* is "Criminally clichéd" (5 April 2002). Despite the fact that the female lawyer thriller may have run its course by the 2000s, I would note, however, that *High Crimes* is important for being one of the few films of the detective genre that is not blind to the sex of its heroine. Rather than allowing its heroine to be a schizophrenic combination of masculinity and femininity or to be a woman fulfilling a male role with little consideration of her femininity, *High Crimes* highlights the potential danger for women stepping into an action role: Claire loses her baby during a car chase.

Something New

The heroine and title's namesake, Erin Brockovich (Julia Roberts), is not a lawyer but a victim—literally the victim of a car accident but also a victim in general, especially of men. She has led a tough life as a working-class, single mom with three small children; however, rather than let the car accident ruin her life, she chooses to be a survivor and uses her looks, wiles, and—most importantly—her brains to become a success. She forces her lawyer, Ed (Albert Finney), to give her a job at his office and then pursues a lost-cause case. Her investigative work leads her to the discovery of a cover-up by a large company that has inadvertently poisoned an entire community. By the end of the film, she has cracked the case, helped hundreds of victimized people, and earned two million dollars—and she did so without a law degree or the help of a male investigative assistant (as did the 1980s lawyers). In fact, when the big-time lawyers do step in to help out with the case, they actually hinder it because they are out of touch with the working-class victims. Erin's special skill as a mediator then is her ability to win the trust of the working-class community. When signatures are needed, Erin goes door-to-door to convince all 634 plaintiffs to sign. The hot-shot lawyers are shocked and ask how she managed it; playing with their preconceptions of her in her cheap, revealing clothes, Erin tells them she performed 634 blow jobs.

Presented as hyperfeminine in small, tight, flashy clothes that reveal a lot of leg and cleavage, Erin looks like a woman that invites the wrong kind of attention and has been defined by the men with whom she has had relationships—and, to a point, she has. She was a small-town beauty queen who married young, has two ex-husbands, three kids, and a lot of debt. Despite her appearance of femininity, Erin is tough, independent, and ambitious and jeopardizes her relationship with her kids and her boyfriend, George (Aaron Eckhart), because of her dedication to her new career. A role reversal occurs: George stays at home child-minding while Erin is the career-minded breadwinner of the family. Erin's appearance is deceiving: her hyperfemininity, and the "low class" label it earns her, does mask an intelligent, hard-working, and caring person. The fact that the film is based on a real-life case, and Roberts's character on a real person, complicates the assumption that a woman who *looks* "cheap" is, in fact, worthless. The film plays off the spectacle of Roberts—Hollywood's biggest box-office female star at the time—playing a working-class, single mother with a foul mouth, bad attitude, and poor dress sense. And just as the film plays on the disparity between the star and the role she plays—a disparity that critics and audiences noted and for which she won an Academy Award—so too does it play on that between the protagonist's appearance and her character.

This objectification of the heroine and her identification as lower class was also seen in the blaxploitation films discussed in the last chapter; however, with blaxploitation films, the expectation was that the target audience of black youth would also be working class—namely, that the world of the blaxploitation film was grounded in the realities of black subculture in the 1970s. Mainstream Hollywood films, in contrast, as Giuliana Muscio suggests, have always tended to be predominantly middle class in terms of the social values they proffer (66). Thus, *Erin Brockovich* revived the debate of whether the heroine belonged in the arena of the legal system but not because of her sex but her class. There is no question in the twenty-first century as to whether a woman belongs in a position of authority in the legal system if she is middle-class, well-educated, well-dressed, and well-spoken like Claire in *High Crimes*; however, there is when the woman is a working-class, single mom, with a brash attitude, cheap wardrobe, and only a high-school education. Erin defies her stereotype and proves that intelligence and determination do not have to come in a socially acceptable package. The film also explores the realities of a financially-strapped, single working mother of three and the strain that having a career can effect on a woman's relationships with her lover and children. Rather than a female lawyer thriller, *Erin Brockovich* is, instead, a David-and-Goliath story reminiscent of the Grisham Cycle—except that the battle is twofold: David-like victims fight a corrupt Goliath-like corporation but Erin is also a David-like figure fighting for her right to be recognized by the Goliath-like legal system.

Conclusion: Detecting the Law

In the female lawyer thriller, there is a tension between the protagonists being good lawyers—i.e., defending their clients within the bounds of the law—and being good detectives—i.e., discovering the truth. All of these female lawyers have been competent at their jobs as defense lawyers by getting their guilty clients off on murder charges; however, the criticism these films level at their protagonists is that their main concern *should* have been the revelation of the truth rather than winning their cases. In other words, it is only through being a good detective that these women see justice served.

Lucia begins her investigation of the female lawyer asking, "why is the law the chosen profession for a clear majority of Hollywood's female protagonists of the period?" (*Framing*, 3). I would argue that it is because the role of detective was an acceptable role for women in the 1980s and that, with an emphasis on re-constructing stories, the lawyer film has much in common with the detective film. As David A. Black explains,

> Legal investigators piece together stories. Witnesses tell stories; legal advocates tell and retell stories. Judges and juries evaluate stories [. . .] . [F]ilms about law are stories about the process of story-telling, or *narratives about narrative*. (55)

Tzvetan Todorov argues that the objective of the classical detective story is to create curiosity in the reader with the narrative beginning with an effect (the crime) and looking for the cause (the perpetrator); however, that of the thriller is to create suspense (47). The female lawyer thriller capitalizes on both impulses—curiosity as to "whodunit" and suspense as to whether the killer will strike again, especially when the detective may be the next victim. The protagonist must identify the killer and see him brought to justice; however, to do so, she must reconstruct the story of the crime. With the female lawyer thriller, the ending does not occur with the conclusion of the trial; the protagonist must continue her investigation after the trial is over in order to reconstruct the story of the crime and identify its author (i.e., the killer).

In the cycle of female lawyer thrillers, there is a marked increase in the competence of the female lawyer as a detective. While *Jagged Edge* suggests that Teddy is unsure of the killer's identity even when she shoots him and *Suspect* and *Physical Evidence* present the male detectives (Eddie and Joe, respectively) as more effective than the female ones (Kathleen and Jenny, respectively), later films like *Class Action* and *Guilty as Sin* suggest that their female lawyers are superior detectives. It is not through the legal system that these criminals are identified as such, but by these amateur detectives outside of the bounds of the official law. According to the female lawyer thriller, being a good detective is more important than being a good lawyer because the legal system can be, at best, restrictive and, at worst, corrupt. These films suggest that the pursuit of truth and justice can happen only outside of the system and that is why the female lawyer thriller cycle disappears by the mid-90s. First, the genre of the erotic thriller had run its course, moving into parodies like *Fatal Instinct* (Reiner, 1993) or into the new subgenre in which the female criminals are not punished but celebrated for outwitting or destroying corrupt masculinity, for example *The Last Seduction* (Dahl, 1994), *Bound* (Wachowski Bros., 1996), and *Femme Fatale* (De Palma, 2002). Second, the female detective became increasingly frequent as a "buddy" to a black male detective—beginning with *The Pelican Brief* (Pakula, 1993) and proliferating with *Kiss the Girls* (Fleder, 1997), *Murder at 1600* (Little, 1997), *The Bone Collector* (Noyce, 1999), and *Along Came a Spider* (Tamahori, 2001)—and she is not a lawyer but instead a federal agent or a police detective. It is the woman as an *official* investigator with which the following chapter is concerned. And, while the universe of the legal thriller is decidedly heterosexual, that of the serial killer narrative—established officially with *The Silence of the Lambs* (Demme, 1991) starring Jodie Foster but I would argue beginning with *Black Widow* (Rafelson, 1987) starring Theresa Russell and Debra Winger—complicates and questions the binary of heterosexuality and homosexuality as much as that of masculinity and femininity. Not since the 1930s were Hollywood's female detectives as interesting and challenging as the gender-benders of the early 1990s.

10

Detecting Identity

From Investigative Thrillers to
Crime Scene Investigators

Part 1: Detecting Identity in the 1980s

The 1980s were seen as what Kimberly Dilley calls the "Second Golden Age" of detective fiction (xi) and Sally Munt identifies as the heyday of feminist crime fiction (201) with the publication of fiction by authors such as Sue Grafton, Marcia Muller, and Sarah Paretsky. On the other hand, only a handful of films offered female detectives (other than the lawyer). In the 1980s, heroism was defined by physical action and the detective films of the time were dominated by male heroes who packed big muscles and bigger firepower in the cop-action film (e.g., *Die Hard* [McTiernan, 1988] and *Lethal Weapon* [Donner, 1987]), leaving little space for female/feminine detective-heroes. In the last chapter, I explored the unofficial (i.e., amateur) female investigator of the 1980s in the female lawyer thriller; in this chapter, I will begin with the handful of official female investigators in the 1980s thrillers before I continue on with their more successful criminalist sisters who appeared in the 1990s.

In the 1980s thriller, the female detective—whether FBI agent, private investigator, or police detective—struggles to prove her legitimacy in professions dominated by men. While a mystery surrounding a crime motivates the involvement of the female detective in these films, ultimately the mystery to solve is that of the detective's place—both socially and professionally. In other words, like the female lawyer, these female investigators struggle with balancing their dual roles as women (personally) and detectives (professionally). As Yvonne Tasker notes,

> Women, it seems, are involved in transgression even and to the extent that they are represented as lawmakers or enforcers. Partly this is to do with a working out of issues around women's sexuality which, like women's ambitions and their friendships, is a realm

seemingly in need of almost constant policing in the Hollywood
cinema. (*Working*, 93)

Thus, even when she was a "policeman," the female detective was policed herself.
These thrillers thematized the question of identity, whether the true nature of
the man that the detective loves, her own identity as a woman and detective,
or gender identity in general. In other words, the mystery that the female
detective investigates is often less "whodunit" and more "who are you?"—or
even "who am I?"

Precursor

As I noted in reference to the blaxploitation heroine, the white female detective
was all but absent from Hollywood detective films in the 1960s and 70s. One
notable exception is *Coma* (Crichton, 1978) that offered a preview of the kinds
of female detective films that would appear in the following decade. *Coma* is
centrally concerned with women's social roles and their problematic relationship with male authority as they struggle to ascend the professional ladder. The
sex divide is established in the opening sequence: the women's locker room in
which Dr. Susan Wheeler (Genevieve Bujold) dresses for surgery is contrasted
with that of the men's in which her boyfriend Dr. Mark Bellows (Michael
Douglas) dresses for his. These women are operating in a traditionally male
sphere. Initially, Susan's biggest problem is her relationship with Mark, mainly
because they disagree over their approaches to their careers: Mark's interest is
in hospital politics while Susan's is the care of her patients. And they disagree
over equality in their relationship: she thinks that he does not recognize her,
or her needs, as equal to him, or his needs:

> Mark: Listen, Susan, you want me to heat up the dinner. Is that
>   what you want?
>
> Susan: I want some respect.
>
> Mark: Susan, come on. Don't leave again.
>
> Susan: I don't see why you can't share half the responsibility.
>
> Mark: I share *more* than half the responsibility. [. . .]
>
> Susan: You know what the trouble with you is? All you care
>   about is being chief resident.
>
> Mark: You know what your trouble is? You don't really want a
>   relationship. Look at you . . . you run away from it.

Susan: This is ridiculous.

Mark: You don't want a lover. You want a goddamned wife!

Susan's relationship issues, however, are overshadowed when her married friend Nancy (Lois Chiles), who is pregnant by her lover, dies on the operating table after what should have been a routine abortion. When she sees Nancy lying in a coma, Susan turns away briefly, visibly upset; nevertheless, she quickly composes herself and reviews Nancy's chart to see what happened. Susan does not react in a (stereo)typical fashion and this upsets the men in the film. One of the male doctors comments, "You know, if it had been a friend of mine, I don't know if I would have been that cool." Similarly, Mark thinks that Susan is abnormal when she rejects his attempts to comfort her. She attempts to explain it to him: "I'm not upset. You think because I'm a woman, I'm going to be upset. I'm fine, Mark." Rather than being reduced to tears, Susan's way of coping with her loss is to play detective.

    Her investigation leads Susan to suspect a conspiracy when she discovers that a dozen similar cases of coma have occurred after operations in the past year. Her desire to play "Nancy Drew," however, is curtailed by senior administrator Dr. Harris (Richard Widmark) who warns her to leave the case alone or risk jeopardizing her career as a surgeon. Susan seems willing to concede after she and Mark inspect the operating room where the incidents of coma have occurred and turn up no evidence of foul play. Giving up her male role of detective, Susan embraces her female role of girlfriend and enjoys an idyllic weekend away in the country. The events of the weekend are shown in a montage sequence accompanied by romantic music; the couple—and the soundtrack—come literally to a screeching halt when they drive past the sign for the Jefferson Institute, the place where the coma patients are stored. From the leads that she gathers at the Institute, Susan confirms that there is a conspiracy to place healthy patients into a coma (by substituting carbon monoxide for oxygen fed to the patient during surgery) so that their organs can be harvested for wealthy, terminally ill patients. Back at the hospital, Susan adopts another male role—that of action hero—by shedding her heels and pantyhose (i.e., her femininity) that physically restrict her ability to climb up the shafts behind the operating room. And, when a hired killer comes after her, Susan fights back valiantly using a fire extinguisher and even cadavers (knocking them on top of her pursuer). Later, she snoops around the Jefferson Institute finding evidence to back up her conspiracy theory and then performs a daring escape—riding on the top of a speeding ambulance.

    In a theme that becomes increasingly prevalent in the 1980s and 90s, the male love/authority figure (here Mark) does not believe the female detective's theory and, in fact, begins to question her sanity. Mark comes around only when it is Susan who is slated for a surgery with Dr. Harris in the suspected operating room. Susan made the near fatal mistake of trusting Dr. Harris, who turns out to be the one selling the body parts and the head of the conspiracy. In the end, it is Mark who gets to be the hero and rescue Susan from a coma by racing to the basement and disconnecting the CO supply to the operating room just in time. Although, ultimately, the heroine must be rescued by the male love interest, *Coma* is significant for placing a strong, career-minded woman at the center of the film in a decade that was relatively devoid of such heroines. As the film's star comments in the United Artists's pressbook for the film, "In past years, this role would have gone to a Paul Newman or a Robert Redford. It shows that Hollywood is actually serious about creating important screen roles for women—and I'm delighted to be a part of that trend" (10).[1] And, notably, not only is Bujold a woman but also a physically diminutive one. Most reviewers of the film commented on the novelty of having a woman in the traditionally male role of action hero but also how Bujold's "pixie" or "Peter Pan" looks made her character's strength, determination, and physical abilities even more surprising. And the majority of reviewers commented on Bujold's success in the role; as Robert Martin of *The Globe and Mail* says, "Movie moguls take heed" (14 February 1978). Audiences seemed to like a woman in the role of detective.[2]

Widowed Desire

Debra Winger played the female detective more than any other actress in the 1980s. As Linda Mizejewski explains, "Tellingly, when Hollywood began to portray professional women investigators, the first three were African American, and the next two were Debra Winger" (*Hardboiled*, 114).[3] Winger's first investigative outing was in *Mike's Murder* (Bridges, 1984); however, I will not discuss the film at length here since the heroine does not have much investigative agency here and is an amateur (this chapter is concerned with the professionals only). As Vincent Canby in his *New York Times* review of the film notes, director James Bridges, "who gave Miss Winger her big break in *Urban Cowboy*, leaves her high and dry in this one. [. . .] she has no role to play" (9 March 1984).[4] On the other hand, *Black Widow* (Rafelson, 1987) offers Winger not only a serious role as a detective but also a controversial one as a potential lesbian. The film is not interested in the relationships that either of the female protagonists have with men but that which forms between the two of them—the criminal, Catherine/Mariel/Margaret/Reni (Theresa Russell) and the detective, Alex Barnes (Debra Winger). Alex is an agent in the Justice Department who notices the similarities between the deaths of several middle-aged, wealthy men supposedly of Ondine's Curse (a condition by which apparently healthy middle-aged men die in their sleep) although actually of poisoning. Each dies within a few months of marrying a younger woman and Alex's research suggests that the woman in each case is the same (even if her name is not). Alex's boss, Bruce (Terry

O'Quinn), does not think that a woman is capable of such a complex series of crimes. He tells Alex, "Look, the whole M.O.—a complex series of seductions and murders—that's not something you see a woman do." Alex retorts, "Oh, really? Which part you figure a woman isn't up to—the seduction or the murder?" Her job is data analysis in the office and she longs for the excitement of a field assignment; however, Bruce accuses her of romanticizing field work because her life is devoid of normal romance.

Alex:	Bruce, I've been in this office for six years, this goddamn government office with green windows.
Bruce:	Yeah, I know, you want excitement. Well, a lot of people don't look to get it all from their job.
Alex:	What's that supposed to mean?
Bruce:	Jesus, Alex! What in hell do you think it means? Having a goddamned date for one thing. When was the last time you rolled in here late on a Monday because you had a big weekend?
Alex:	I really can't believe you're saying this to me. I have to listen to this shit from my mother. Who the hell do you think you are, Bruce?
Bruce:	Look, I just . . . . You're not happy. You're not a happy person . . . and you deserve to be, that's all.
Alex:	Bruce, make me happy.

Although Bruce thinks that he could make Alex happy by dating her, she means that he could give her the assignment. When Bruce finally pulls the plug on her investigation after the death of another man in Seattle, Alex decides to leave her job and pursue her "phantom" to Hawaii—as a vigilante. And in this sense the film echoes the structure of the female lawyer thriller in that the heroine must step outside the bounds of the law to see justice pursued and served.[5]

The mystery of the film is not whether or not Reni has committed murder but can Alex stop her from killing again. More importantly, can Alex convince the male authorities that Reni is deadly? Valerie Traub suggests, "No man distrusts Reni; no man believes Alex. From the perspective of the male gaze within the film, Reni is angelic and Alex neurotic" (314). Reni convinces men she is innocent by wearing different masks/identities: as Catherine Petersen, the deadly "black widow" is blonde and aloof; as Mariel, she is a redheaded southern belle; as Margaret, she is a bookish brunette; and as Reni, she is a free-spirited, sandy blonde. In every disguise, Reni is feminine and alluring; in comparison, Alex is masculinized. At the office, she is a frumpy pen-pusher who rejects male suitors and plays poker with her male colleagues; undercover in Seattle as Mrs. Tally, a freelance writer, Alex dresses more professionally; and undercover in Hawaii as Jessie, she is made over by Reni in Reni's image. By the end of the film, Alex has found a middle-ground—somewhere between frumpy office worker and glamorous Hawaiian vacationer—and she leaves Hawaii in a pretty but simple floral dress. While Reni is a chameleon, adapting her looks and behavior to attract each suitor, Alex is the butterfly who finally emerges from her cocoon as beautiful.

This eventual discovery of Alex's "true" sexual self is important because the film highlights the two women's similarities and the danger of Alex's over-identification with her quarry. The danger of over-identifying with the criminal is a theme common to later criminalist/serial killer narratives. For example, *Blood Work* (Eastwood, 2002) and *Insomnia* (Nolan, 2002) see their detectives (played by Clint Eastwood and Al Pacino, respectively) and the killers (played by Jeff Daniels and Robin Williams, respectively) become obsessed with each other. Interestingly, there is no homoerotic tension between hunter and prey in the case of two men; however, in *Black Widow*, this over-identification in played out through the suggestion of lesbian desire. As Alex explains to Bruce, "You want to catch her, you gotta think like she thinks . . . I think." But Bruce is concerned: "All I know is that she is obsessed with killing and you're obsessed with her. What worries me is that you might be as wacky as she is." The film mirrors the two women: Alex compares photos of the different men's wives by projecting them, life-sized, on the wall. The scene concludes with Alex standing in front of the image of Reni and mimicking her graceful stance. In Hawaii, Catherine's newest conquest, Paul (Sami Frey), seems to find the two women somewhat interchangeable too. At his party, he is introduced to Alex made over by Reni. He says, "Oh, I know this dress but who is the woman?" He is obsessed with Reni, in part because she withholds herself sexually from him; he then begins an affair with Alex. In the end, however, he marries Reni. As Alex suggests, "When you put us together, it made him want you all the more. So I guess you could say my wedding gift was the groom." Alex is hurt by Paul's rejection, but he suggests that "Jessie" was the woman he cared about, "not some cop!"—i.e., Alex as herself. Paul asks Alex, "Tell me there is no jealousy. No jealousy at all." Alex does seem to be jealous of Catherine's beauty, sex appeal, lifestyle, confidence, and, perhaps even, her ability to kill men for her own use without any apparent qualms. Ultimately, however, Alex's desire to *be* Reni is conflated with Reni's desire *for* Alex. This is hinted at when the two women perform mouth-to-mouth resuscitation on each other in their scuba diving class and confirmed when Reni kisses Alex fiercely on the lips at her wedding. As

Reni tells her adversary, "You know, of all the relationships I'll look back on in fifty years' time, I'll always remember this one."

1984 signaled the beginning of a trend of, what Alida Moore refers to as, "dyke dicks" with the publication of three important lesbian crime novels: Barbara Wilson's *Murder in the Collective*, Sarah Schulman's *The Sophie Horowitz Story*, and Katherine V. Forrest's *Amateur City* (1).[6] Moore suggests that "By definition alone, lesbian mysteries invert the paradigm, placing sexually suspect women in the role of investigator, freeing them from the stereotypes of victim or fiend, and allowing them to question a society that has long oppressed them" (4). While this is true for mysteries written by lesbians and centered on lesbian detectives, this is not necessarily true for the Hollywood—most often male-directed—versions of lesbians in thrillers. The growing visibility and voice of lesbians in culture in general and through popular culture specifically in the 1980s and 90s encouraged mainstream filmmakers to co-opt lesbians (especially lesbian killers) as a novel kind of heroine in films such as *Basic Instinct* (Verhoeven, 1992), *Heavenly Creatures* (Jackson, 1994) and *Bound* (Wachowski Bros., 1996). As Kelly Kessler notes, the 1990s saw a proliferation of lesbian-focused films and that feminist scholars have generally fallen into two camps in terms of these mainstream attempts at representing lesbian desire:

> Scholars such as Chris Holmlund, Andrea Weiss, Lynda Hart, and Linda Ruth Williams each point to ways in which violent depictions of lesbians empower the heterosexual viewer while marginalizing the lesbian viewer, including equating female sexual agency with deserved heterosexual-on-lesbian violence, reinforcing negative stereotypes, and reaffirming the patriarchal order while providing sexual pleasure for the heterosexual male viewer. Alternately, Clare Whatling and Judith Halberstam have both identified methods of lesbian and/or female empowerment in images of sociopathic lesbians, focusing on the power of the "nostalgia of abjection" and lesbian-on-heterosexual male imagined violence. However, I see the crossover effect identified in Linda Ruth Williams's work on the erotic thriller as most relevant to explaining the cross-market success of *Bound*. (14)

However, Williams suggests that it is "straight-to-video" erotic thrillers that offer space for lesbian identification not mainstream film. As Kessler argues, mainstream films like these "often alienate lesbian viewers by presenting heterosexualized lesbians designed to fulfill a male fantasy" (16).

Certainly, this was a criticism leveled at both *Black Widow* and *Basic Instinct* by some. Indeed, reviewer David Denby commented at the time that Russell's character seems "completely out of place in a movie shaped by bracingly feminist attitudes about the roles of women. *Black Widow* feels like a moldy, leftover male fantasy disguised as a sparkling new woman's fantasy" (16 February 1987). Female protagonists like Reni in *Black Widow* and Catherine Trammell (Sharon Stone) in *Basic Instinct* are not confirmed as lesbians but presented as ambiguously bisexual. The suggestion is that they are so sexually aggressive—i.e., masculine in their sexual appetites—that they are attracted to women as well as men. And this slippage between homosexuality and hyper-heterosexuality reconfigures homosexuality into something "naughty" (i.e., excessive and transgressive) rather than something repulsive (i.e., unnatural). Homosexuality (at least for women and according to Hollywood) then is reconfigured as something along the lines of S&M—as a sexual (and culturally-determined) fetish rather than as a fixed (and biologically-determined) identity. *Black Widow*, I would argue, establishes that Reni desires Alex rather than the lesbian attraction necessarily being mutual. However, although the film may play at offering a lesbian subjectivity, it concludes with homosexuality coded as criminal and Reni safely behind bars and Alex returning home feminized and heterosexual.

While critics tended to see the representation of lesbian desire in the film as an either (for lesbians)/or (for men) debate, Traub suggests that it does both: "By employing multiple transpositions of identity to produce homoerotic tension between the two female leads, *Black Widow* solicits a 'lesbian' gaze at the same time that it invites male heterosexual enjoyment" (308). As Phyllis Betz suggests, lesbians can alter the dominant heterosexual narrative of a text; in doing so, "Traditional narrative strategies are decoded to reveal new possibilities in the relationships presented in the text, what Bonnie Zimmerman calls 'perverse reading' " (10). Rather than suggesting that the heroines of films such as *Black Widow* co-opt masculinity into femininity to be empowered, I argue that the bisexual woman or lesbian can be read as an empowered figure because of her transgression of normative sexual and gender roles. In films of the 1920s and 30s, lesbians were portrayed as "butch"—i.e., masculinized—and repulsive to leading men in *Big News* (La Cava, 1929) and *Front Page Woman* (Curtiz, 1935). In films of the 1980s and 90s, however, lesbianism is recast from being *physically* masculine (i.e., unappealing) to being *psychologically* masculine. The bisexual women and lesbians of *Black Widow*, *Basic Instinct*, and *Bound*, are presented as independent, sexually aggressive, and self-determined enacting a masquerade of femininity to disguise their true and lethal natures to unsuspecting male victims.

In an effort to recover *Black Widow*'s foray into lesbianism from being dismissed as "for male pleasure only," I would argue that the focus on the relationship between the two women—whether the product of lesbian desire, bi-curiosity, or heterosexual aggression—functions to push men out of the center of the narrative. The narrative of *Black Widow* is then driven and determined by the desire of not one woman but two (heroine and criminal)—and, unlike the majority of the erotic thrillers of the 1980s and early 90s, that desire is not seriously directed at men—whether as the criminal of the investigation or as the heroine's partner in detecting (and/or love). In this way *Black Widow* distinguishes itself from both neo-*noirs*—that offer criminal-heroines investigated by male detectives such as *Basic Instinct*—and thrillers—that offer detective-heroines investigating male criminals such as *Jagged Edge* (Marquand, 1985). Neo-*noir* films typically invite, at some level, a sexual attraction between the detective and criminal in order to complicate the detective's desire and/or ability to see justice served—and *Black Widow* follows this pattern even though both protagonists are women. As Jean Noble notes in relation to *Bound*, it is not surprising that we find gender-bending in neo-*noir* thrillers because the genre has a "formal and historical preoccupation with the construction/deconstruction of masculinities, female masculinities included" (2). However, Noble also notes that, as a "Hollywood" film, even *Bound* "foregrounds mainstream or popular discourses about these queer subjectivities" that are often contradictory (2). As Traub argues,

> It is not a matter, therefore, of arguing that Reni or Alex "is" "a" "lesbian" or *Black Widow* is a "lesbian film," but rather that both black widow(s) [Alex and Reni] and *Black Widow* pose the problem of "lesbian" representation within a dominantly heterosexist and patriarchal system. (321)

Black Widow ultimately cannot celebrate a lesbian protagonist but, instead, as Noble suggests, the "strong, sexually expressive female must be closed off, bound, as it were, with the diegetic trajectory and visual strategies for closure" (2). Whatever the motives of the film's producers in including the scenes of lesbian desire, *Black Widow* is a fascinating contribution to the genre for at least posing or "queering" those problems. Certainly, the scenes in question foreground questions of female, if not lesbian, identity and desire in a compelling way, perhaps because the film neither fully confirms nor denies the possibility of lesbian attraction between the heroine and her prey. And, second, *Black Widow* is the only film that has the female *detective* express homosexual desire; all the other films focus on criminal heroines including *Basic Instinct*, *Bound*, and *Femme Fatale* (De Palma, 2002).

Wo/man of Action

Action films grew in popularity and dominance in the 1980s—especially cop-action films featuring male stars like Eddie Murphy, Sylvester Stallone, and Bruce Willis—but audiences did not necessarily seem ready for the woman of action. Two television series that were developed and taken as far as the pilot stage but no further were "Lady Blue" in which Jamie Rose played "Dirty" Harriet—evoking Clint Eastwood's violent vigilante hero—and "Foxfire" in which Joanna Cassidy played a counterspy (Green, 176). By the end of the decade, however, Hollywood offered a couple of cop-action heroines—in what Cora Kaplan calls "Dirty Harriet" films—including Jamie Lee Curtis's cop in *Blue Steel* (Bigelow, 1990), Theresa Russell's undercover cop in *Impulse* (Locke, 1990), and Kathleen Turner's private investigator in *V.I. Warshawski* (Kanew, 1991). The woman as the action hero represented a transgression of generic codes that dictated that women should be passive in Hollywood action films and let men be the heroes. Such a transgression opened up questions about gender identity regarding characters—most famously, Ellen Ripley (Sigourney Weaver) in *Aliens* (Cameron, 1986) and Sarah Connor (Linda Hamilton) in *Terminator 2: Judgement Day* (Cameron, 1991). Through the lens of psychoanalytic theory, feminist film critics saw these women merely as male heroes masquerading as female (Hills 38–9). As Jeffrey A. Brown notes, the reaction to the action woman, both from the public and critics, was mixed: some regarded the action woman as signaling "a growing acceptance of non-traditional roles for women and an awareness of the arbitrariness of gender traits" while others saw her as recycling the same gender politics of the 1980s action film by presenting essentially masculine women (52–3). The 1980s action heroines, like Ripley and Sarah, were masculinized—wielding big guns and sporting the uniform of action men of tank top and combat pants that revealed bulging biceps and deemphasized their breasts, hips, and buttocks. As A. Susan Owen et al. suggest, in the aftermath of Vietnam, "the female body (as memory object) is toughened through necessity by the catastrophe of masculine failure" (41). Just as the failure of masculine power during the Depression inspired the strong, outgoing, and masculinized heroines of the early 1930s, so too did the late 1980s and early 90s see strong women coming to the rescue.

The question of gender identity is central to *Blue Steel*; as Kaplan suggests, *Blue Steel* is "a film which rehearses through its story and through a theoretical metacommentary, the uneasy positioning of women, and by implication feminism, in postfeminist dystopia" (51). Rookie cop, Megan Turner (Jamie Lee Curtis), struggles with her masculine occupation that turns men off; and commodities trader, Eugene Hunt (Ron Silver), struggles with his emasculating life as a "New Man" in the late 1980s. While Eugene is doing his own grocery shopping after work one evening, the store is held up and it is Megan who comes to the rescue to shoot the armed robber. Obsessed with the masculine power that a gun seems to embody, Eugene takes the perpetrator's gun from the scene and commits a series of murders using it. Megan begins a romance with Eugene, unaware that Eugene was present during the robbery and is also obsessed with her. During sexual foreplay, Eugene moves his hand from Megan's breast to her gun and then asks her to hold her gun in both hands and aim it at him: it turns him on. This link between his attraction to her and her ability to wield a deadly weapon (i.e., her possession of the phallus) and the suggestion that female sexuality holds dangers for men are compounded and confirmed when Eugene rapes Megan liked a crazed animal after he sees her being intimate with her police partner, Nick Mann (Clancy Brown). Rape is the only way that Eugene can exert power over the independent woman and this highlights the fact that, despite being a cop, Megan is still vulnerable because of her sex.

Megan's body is the site on which questions of gender are played out. Her uniform as a police officer initially de-genders her and many moments in the film highlight how the uniform is an equalizer. At the beginning of the film, Megan and the other few female cops of her graduating class are shown as almost indistinguishable from the men they stand side by side with in their dress-blues and white caps. However, the film also then highlights the difference between Megan's more feminine body in an elegant dress when on a date with Eugene and her masculinized body in men's shirts and jeans when on duty as a detective. In a nightmare, Megan revisits her date with Eugene in the helicopter ride over the city: this time she falls out of the helicopter and, while he briefly catches hold of her arm, he then lets her fall. As Tasker argues, the motif of the "undercover" operation (e.g., the detective posing as prostitute) "suggests a concern with disguise and exploration in crime fictions and underlines the instability or shifting nature of the female hero;" in opposition to the "undercover" (i.e., hyperfeminine) attire is the "uniform" that highlights the cop identity (*Working*, 107). Thus, Megan can suppress the vulnerability she feels while masquerading as a typical woman when she dons her uniform. Lying in the hospital after being raped, Megan is treated like a victim: her boss pats her awkwardly on the shoulder and a nurse gives her pills to help her sleep. But Megan refuses to play the victim and knocks out her guard and, dressed in his uniform, she heads off in pursuit of Eugene. The uniform makes her a cop rather than just a woman and, as she strides purposefully away, her silhouette and demeanor are contrasted to that of another woman whose hair, dress, and walk mark her as distinctly feminine. Empowered by her uniform and despite (or because of) her ordeal, Megan pursues Eugene, engages him in a shootout, and chooses to kill him even though he is out of ammunition. Megan knows that Eugene will use his money and power to keep himself out of prison and, thus, to kill him is the only way to stop him; however, to do so is to act outside of the bounds of the law and Megan, despite her borrowed uniform, is a vigilante.

Kaplan suggests that the film " 'signifies' simultaneously on the right-wing masculinism of Hollywood encoded in the 'Dirty Harry' genre and on the theories of representation and sexuality that critique it" (53). In some ways, the film does revert back to the signifying system of the very genre it attempts to deconstruct: as a cop-action heroine, Megan must turn violent vigilante to see justice served; however, two decades later, *Blue Steel* is still regarded by feminist critics as one of the few critical meditations on gender in the cop-action genre even if that meditation is somewhat undermined by the ending of the film. *Blue Steel* deviates from the traditional male cop-action film, because as producer Edward Pressman explains, "The end of the film has [Curtis] basically wiped out by her own act of violence. It's not an act of victory, it's an act

of revenge, obsession and fatalism, but it's not a triumph of revenge that this
sort of film generally relishes" (Qtd. in Rev. by Puig, 85). While this ending is
seen as the defeat of the heroine rather than her spectacular triumph, I would
argue that, if *Blue Steel* had concluded with the latter, then the film would have
represented a complete reversion to the tropes of the male-defined genre. By
resisting a triumphant ending, director Kathryn Bigelow retains the question
of how women are to find justice within the system.

At the time of the film's release, many critics derided the film.[7] The issue,
it would seem, was not necessarily that the film starred a female heroine but
that it was directed by a female director with a feminist agenda. In a review
for *The Toronto Star*, Jamie Portman suggests,

> There's a reason why *Blue Steel* is bound to touch sensitive nerves.
> It's not just that it is extremely violent. It's not just the fact that for
> much of its length it deals with male hostility to women, reflected
> both in the attitude of chauvinist male cops to their female coun-
> terpart and also in the psychosis underlying the killer's actions. It's
> not even the shocking rape sequence near the end of the film. No,
> the most controversial aspect of *Blue Steel* is what it symbolizes: it
> has a woman moving into what has previously been regarded as a
> male preserve—the bloody cop action movie. (14 March 1990)

Indeed, reviewers made similar comments about *Impulse* (1990)—a film released
on the heels of *Blue Steel*, also featuring a female cop (Theresa Russell) and
also directed by a woman (Sondra Locke).

In *Impulse*, Lottie Mason (Russell) works nights undercover as a prostitute
for vice. Her female therapist has been asked by Internal Affairs to ascertain
if Lottie should be kept on her current assignment or not because of her
state of mind after shooting a perp. Lottie has had three failed relationships
with three male colleagues and she confesses to the therapist that, "Lately,
sometimes . . . working vice. Strangers. The way they look at you. Feel all that
power over them. Make 'em pay. It excites me. I just . . . I wonder what it'd be
like, just to do it. Lose control." Lottie is affected by her undercover work and
it leaves her unable to commit to a steady relationship with D.A. Stan Harris
(Jeff Fahey). Her "impulse" to "lose control" means that she hates the predictable and does not want her and Stan to become "a habit" (i.e., a committed
heteronormative relationship).

Lottie struggles between her feminine and masculine impulses. Although
she dresses very feminine when undercover as a hooker, in her everyday life
she dresses very masculine in trousers, suit jackets, and tightly buttoned dress
shirts. Lottie has been hardened by her job because she has learned that she can
only rely on herself in a tough situation. This problem is exacerbated when she

alienates her superior, Lieutenant Joe Morgan (George Dzundza), by refusing to sleep with him. He uses her undercover on the case that he and Stan are working together but, when the bust goes wrong and communication is cut off, Lottie is left on her own to deal with the villains. She ends up shooting two of them in a convenience store, blowing one of their heads off with her "out of policy weapon" (i.e., a non-standard issue gun with a lot of firepower). After shooting the two perps, Lottie is too "keyed up" to accept Stan's offer to comfort her and, instead, winds up in a bar with a stranger offering her a lot of money to go back to his place. We know that Lottie is broke and that sometimes her greatest desire is to have a large bankroll; however, it is more likely that she agrees to go home with the stranger for the thrill of crossing the thin blue line between her two identities: Lottie the cop, and Carla the hooker.

The film then offers her a series of choices: to align herself with the law or to be the criminal *femme fatale*. First, at his house, Lottie confronts herself in the mirror and demands, "What am I doing? I'm getting out of here!" Although she makes the "right" decision to go home rather than become a prostitute, she is still punished in the film for her transgression of moral codes: the stranger is murdered while she helplessly looks on. She removes any evidence that she was at the scene and then goes to the airport to inspect the locker for which the man had a key. The second choice Lottie must make is whether to remain a cop and broke or to run off with the million dollars in the airport locker. In some ways, the choice is made for her through Stan. Lottie is re-feminized as she confesses tearfully to him the truth about what she has done and she allows him to use her as bait to lure out the killer. Rather than being concerned about her safety, she tells Stan, "I know this sounds really crazy but, um . . . right now I'm more scared about us than anything." In the end, Stan offers her the choice: run away with the money and gain her freedom, or hand over the money and keep him. Initially, we think that she will do the former, but she returns to him at the airport bar to do the latter. Stan, it turns out, knew that she would change her mind and has a drink ready and waiting for her. She laughs and says, "I hate being predictable" and Stan replies, "You know, Lottie. Not all habits are bad." The female cop is shown to be dangerously transgressive in *Impulse*, willing to break the law more than once, and she is "saved" only through a "healthy" (read: heteronormative) relationship with a man that reasserts her femininity over her "unnatural" masculinity.

V.I. Warshawski (1991) saw the bringing of Sarah Paretsky's popular hardboiled private investigator heroine to the screen but also her makeover. As Mizejewski notes, Paretsky's "gritty, politically tense scenario" was sold to Disney-owned Hollywood Pictures (*Hardboiled*, 138) and the heroine finds herself similarly re-imagined for a more mainstream audience. Vic (Kathleen Turner) is presented as a schizophrenic conflation of a hardboiled detective and a hyperfeminine woman. The opening scene cuts from her athletic (i.e., masculine) legs as she completes her morning run to her attractive (i.e., feminine) legs in a skirt and heels for a meeting with a prospective client. The sausage manufacturer is surprised that this attractive woman is a private "dick;" however, he says that she is perfect for the job as he needs her to go undercover and "penetrate" his competition—and his puns are intended. Her relationship with men is problematic: she finds Murray (Jay O. Sanders), the reporter whom she had been dating, in bed with a redhead. His excuse is that Vic is "too independent." It is in this sense that Vic is schizophrenic: while she demonstrates masculine traits such as emotional and professional independence, she also demonstrates very feminine impulses. She says, "You know, there's something about the right shade of lipstick and a great pair of shoes that just makes a gal feel anything is possible." When, however, her newest love interest hires her to watch his daughter, Kat (Angela Goethals), and is then killed, Vic finds her gender identity tested as her maternal instincts war with professional ones. As Detective Bobby Mallory (Charles Durning) asks her, "Since when do you care about kids." Vic replies, "Since you fished her father out of the lake." As Manina Jones comments, "*V.I. Warshawski* goes through considerable generic contortions [. . .] to portray V.I., a single professional hard-boiled detective, as the 'good mother,' as she must be if she is to occupy the prescribed space available for a female protagonist" (28).

Bobby is an old friend of Vic's father and does not take Vic seriously as a detective when she offers her theories on Bernard's death.

Vic:	Wait a minute! You're saying this was an accident?
Bobby:	When was the last time someone was murdered with a tugboat. Use your head Vicky.
Vic:	Oh, fine! Have it your way.
Bobby:	This is not fun and games. I told you a million times, being a detective is no job for a girl like you.
Vic:	Did my father pass on the torch of guilt to you?
Bobby:	He left it to me in his will. And, while we are on the subject, if your father had turned you over his knee more often instead of spoiling you rotten, you'd be a happy housewife now.
Vic:	Bobby, I'm a *happy* detective. I was a *lousy* housewife.

And the film, at times, seems more preoccupied with women's roles than the murder: Kat must play mother to an egg for a class project; Kat's mother, Paige (Nancy Paul), is an admitted failure who tries to have her daughter killed; and Dr. Lotty Herschel offers a safe space for Kat and advice to Vic on mothering. When Lotty gives Vic a sedative, Vic asks Murray if he thinks she would be a good mother. Murray responds, "Whoa! Lotty, right drug, wrong dose," suggesting that he has been trying to encourage her to settle down in a relationship with him but that is a little more commitment than he was hoping for. On the other hand, the case also forces Vic to embrace her masculine side. She proves physically capable as an expert in aikido, putting up a good fight against two thugs who attack her in her apartment building's dark corridor. And when Earl "Bonehead" Smeissen (Wayne Knight) punches her repeatedly in his office, she answers each blow with a wisecrack.

Unfortunately, the film devolves into parody with several over-the-top and heavy-handed moments and away from believability, especially when Vic takes Kat on the case and trains the preteen to be a detective—training that seems to consist mainly of learning how to deceive men. Kat says, "Men are such suckers" and Vic confirms, "Never underestimate a man's ability to underestimate a woman." The other lesson Vic teaches Kat through her dealings with Murray is, "Basically, the only way to handle men is to treat them like children." The climactic showdown is fittingly between Kat's "bad mother," Paige, and her new "good mother," Vic. The film was intended to be a series for Turner; however, the film's poor performance at the box office saw this film the only adaptation of Paretsky's popular books.[8]

The failure of the female detective as cop action-hero with audiences and critics was not necessarily the result of the sex of the heroine. The genre of the action film was, in general, entering into a phase of self-conscious parody from *Kindergarten Cop* (Reitman, 1990) and *The Last Action Hero* (McTiernan, 1993) with Arnold Schwarzenegger to *Cliffhanger* (Harlin, 1993) and *Demolition Man* (Brambilla, 1993) with Sylvester Stallone. The detective genre moved away from the crime-fighting in the literal sense with an emphasis on action and, instead, embraced the sleuth once more—this time in the form of the criminalist—with a focus on forensics, profiling, and technology as the new weapons for triumphing over the criminal.[9] Suddenly, a new codified language circulated in fiction, film, and television (the crime scene kit, Luminol, partial, hair tag, epithelial, perp, unsub, donor, GSR, M.O., CODIS, and AFIS) and fans of the genre were rewarded for their devotion with—and experienced pleasure in knowing—the ritual of crime scene investigation.[10] With the emphasis on mental/internal rather than physical/external abilities, the detective genre opened up a space where female heroism was regarded as legitimate and could finally thrive—and the film that started the trend was *The Silence of the Lambs* (Demme, 1991), based on the best-selling novel by Thomas Harris.

Fig. 10.1. Redefining the Genre: Jodie Foster's FBI agent-in-training is empowered by her femininity without recuperation or consequence in *The Silence of the Lambs* (1991). Photo from author's collection.

Part II: The Female Criminalist

The Silence of the Lambs, as Barry Keith Grant notes, "brought serial killing squarely into the mainstream" (23). The film captured the popular imagination and created a new trend in the detective film focused on the serial killer as violent, random, and elusive. The serial killer does not kill for the traditional motives of jealousy, greed, and power but because he suffers from a psychosis—often resulting from a traumatic childhood experience related to a mother or other female figure—and cannot refrain from killing until he is stopped by the law. Woody Haut identifies the serial killer as a product of an end-of-the-millennium obsession with personality disorders, sexual deviancy, and AIDS (209). Our reliance on voice mail, e-mail, cell phones, and text messaging instead of face-to-face communications and the isolation of contemporary urban living make us vulnerable to the anonymous serial killer. Hollywood plays on this fear of alienation by suggesting that the greatest threat to the individual is the anonymous "other" who may be a neighbor or a stranger and whose evil is imperceptible to us. And the only kind of detective that is a match for the violent and intelligent serial killer is the criminalist. The contemporary detective film offers reassurance to its audience: the pattern of the killings—the killer's M.O.—is the product of the killer's psychological state of mind and produces a "signature" so that even seemingly motiveless crimes can be understood and resolved. Thus, as Philip Simpson explains, the detective must "read," analyze, and interpret the killer's "work" correctly in "an attempt to appropriate the text's language in order to identify the author" (80). While science and technology may be responsible for our vulnerability to the serial killer, today's detective has mastered the science and technology to track, identify, and stop him. The criminalist can be a forensic psychologist, FBI profiler, or homicide detective; s/he is an expert in analyzing "trace" evidence but, more importantly, an expert in human behavior. S/he uses these skills to track down the serial killer and is—as the title of Michael Mann's 1986 film suggests—a "manhunter." Even though Mann's film was technically the first criminalist film and is based on Harris's first Hannibal Lecter novel *Red Dragon* (1981), it was more of a hit with critics than audiences; instead, it was *The Silence of the Lambs*, based on Harris's second Lecter novel of the same name (1988) that is regarded as starting the criminalist trend.

There has been a proliferation of criminalists in all forms of the detective genre since *Silence*: in films (and TV-movies) including *Just Cause* (Glimcher, 1995), *Citizen X* (Gerolmo, 1995; TV-movie), *Seven* (Fincher, 1995), *Serial Killer* (David, 1995; Video), *American Psycho* (Harron, 2000), *Insomnia* (Nolan, 2002), *Blood Work* (Eastwood, 2002), *Red Dragon* (Ratner, 2002), *Suspect Zero* (Merhige, 2004), *Saw* (Wan, 2004), *Mindhunters* (Harlin, 2005), and *Zodiac* (Fincher, 2007);[11] in the fiction of authors such as Harris, Patricia Cornwell, and Jeffrey Deaver; and on television with the continued popularity of television series such as "CSI: Crime Scene Investigation" (2000–), "Criminal Minds" (2005–), and "Law & Order: Criminal Intent" (2001–). *Silence* was the first film of the criminalist trend, in general, but also the female criminalist, specifically, and many critics would argue that it is still the most compelling and positive image of the female detective to date.

In the Beginning There Was Silence

The professional female detectives of the 1980s, like the female lawyer, were presented as professionally deficient: the vast majority of them were unable to bring the criminals to justice within the bounds of the law and, instead they had to pursue vigilante justice (*Black Widow* and *Blue Steel*). And the future of their professional careers was often jeopardized (*Blue Steel*) or they chose to quit (*Betrayed* [Costa-Gavras, 1988] starring Winger) because of their negative experience with patriarchal authority. *Silence* broke this pattern, however, with a decidedly feminist portrayal of FBI profiler, Clarice Starling (Jodie Foster), who excels at her career. The beginning of the film highlights the audience's assumptions about the diminutive heroine because of her sex. Clarice runs through misty and darkened woods with the camera following her and then alongside her—evoking the sense of the victim running away from her pursuer;

however, Clarice defies these conventions, despite the camera's positioning, and jogs confidently and unperturbed even when a man runs up behind her and calls her name. He is from the FBI Academy and bears a message for Clarice to see Jack Crawford (Scott Glenn). As Clarice returns to the academy, her sex and size are emphasized in this predominantly male world: she jogs in her grey sweatsuit past groups of male agents training in blue sweatsuits and, in the elevator, she is contrasted to a group of male agents in red outfits, towering above her short stature. These opening scenes emphasize the fact that a female presence in the academy in unusual; more importantly, however, it functions to differentiate her from the body of agents-in-training. She is not a run-of-the-mill student, but exemplary; she does not run with the crowd, but is independent; she does not have a muscled, male body, but is petite and unassuming. Her position as a student, an outsider, and a woman will give her the advantage of objectivity, emotional detachment, and a fresh perspective in her pursuit of the serial killer Jame Gumb, referred to by the media as Buffalo Bill. And unlike her female detective predecessors of the 1980s and most of her successors, Clarice is never the sexual victim of a man.

The film is, in many ways, a meditation on gender and sexuality. Christina Lane argues that Jodie Foster's star persona (i.e., the debate over whether or not she is a lesbian) is liminal—resting on the threshold between and encompassing the oppositions of masculine/feminine and heterosexual/homosexual rather than submitting to their binary structure ("Liminal," 149). Certainly, there was much furor in the press in the early 1990s about whether or not Foster was a lesbian. The roles she played as a child and teenager were of tough rather than "girlie" girls, and her publicity as an adult has presented her in a range of images from artificially feminized to gender neutral. Indeed, as Janet Staiger notes in relation to the reception of *Silence*, in the world according to Hollywood a "strong woman must be a lesbian" (144). Mizejewski argues that, in *Silence*, Clarice's lack of opportunities to perform her heterosexuality mark her as a potential lesbian, but that such a reading is displaced onto the body of Gumb as a homosexual man ("Picturing," 18). Rather than being masculinized or lesbianized, I would argue that director Jonathan Demme uses Foster's liminal status to explore issues of gender and sexuality in the film. The film redefines presumed gendered identities: the female detective is not merely a masculinized woman, or the killer an emasculated male killing to assert his manhood. Notably, Gumb does not kill his female victims out of the traditional motives of sexual desire or a troubled childhood; instead, he is a pre-op transsexual for whom murder is merely the by-product of his main intention to remove his victim's skin to sew himself a female "dress."

Clarice is a woman in the male-dominated world of law enforcement and she is tough, self-confident, and ambitious; on the other hand, she uses femininity as an aid in her investigation. Dr. Chilton (Anthony Heald) suggests that Crawford sends Clarice to talk to incarcerated killer, Hannibal "The Cannibal" Lector (Anthony Hopkins), because she is female and Hannibal has not seen a woman in eight years. Clarice does occasionally use her female charms on men when she needs to, for example to placate Dr. Chilton and to procure the help of the entomologist, Dr. Pilchar. She also learns to embrace her emotional connections with the victims, rather than suppress them, and they eventually lead her to the killer. Ultimately, Clarice proves herself a good agent empowered by her ambition, experiences, her skills in behavioral science, psychology, and profiling—and her femininity. As B. Ruby Rich notes in her review of the film, "What's rare is a movie like *Silence*, which shows a woman who, captured, fights back, resists victimization, and gets away with it—because she's rescued by another woman, whose qualities of vulnerability and observation are shown to empower, not endanger, her" (5 March 1991). Just as the female detective films of the 1930s insisted, so too does *Silence* cite female knowledge as the key to unraveling the mystery, and a woman's resolve as a means to bringing the criminal to justice.

In the female detective films of the late 1980s and early 90s from *Black Widow* to *Silence*, it is apparent that the female detective's fear is that through the appropriation of the male position as detective (i.e., "dick") and male weapon of the gun (i.e., phallus), she suffers a loss of femininity—or at least the ability to perform it successfully. In *Black Widow*, Alex's fear is founded when Paul rejects her as "some cop;" in *Blue Steel*, Megan looks uncomfortable and out of place in her evening dress when out on a date compared to the confidence she exudes when in her masculine uniform; and in *Silence*, Hannibal undermines Clarice's self-confidence when he identifies her cheap shoes and perfume. I would also like to suggest that Clarice's fear here is her attempt not only to pass as a woman successfully but also to pass as a middle-class professional. With the shift from the 1980s action cop to the 1990s criminalist, we also see a corresponding shift from a working-class hero to a middle-class professional: becoming a criminalist requires a university education and proficiency with information technology. Megan and Clarice both struggle to leave behind their humble beginnings (both came from working-class homes) and childhood exposure to violence (Megan's father is abusive and Clarice's died). *Silence* is as much about Clarice's transformation as it is about Gumb's attempted one. In the 1980s, for the female detective to be successful as a crime-fighter, she must be masculine; however, by the end of the film she is "re-feminized," typically through her acquiescence to a "healthy" relationship with a male love interest. *Silence*, however, is one of the few films that does not require its heroine's re-feminization at the end of the film. Instead, Clarice enjoys her professional success, graduating from the academy with her career well underway, without any caveat. In her review of the film, Amy Taubin responds to Ron Rosenbaum's scathing commentary (published in *Mademoiselle*, February 1991) on the film,

Unfortunately, his patriarchal self-interest blinds him to what women find so empowering in *The Silence of the Lambs*: the role of Clarice Starling in the narrative. [. . .] Perhaps what bothers Rosenbaum in *The Silence of the Lambs* is not the few seconds of decaying flesh, but the two-hour spectacle of a woman solving the perverse riddles of patriarchy—all by herself. Clarice's heroism renders paternalism superfluous. (5 March 1991)

Or, as Tasker suggests, "The film does not simply allow Clarice Starling her autonomy; it is positively celebrated" (*Silence* 21). Indeed, Clarice is a landmark female detective, essentially breaking the genre's rules: she is an investigator that is empowered by her femininity and without consequence.[12]

Copycatting

Although Clarice's example would spawn an entire cycle of female criminalists in the late 1990s and early 2000s—including *Copycat* (Amiel, 1995), *Kiss the Girls* (Fleder, 1997), *The Bone Collector* (Noyce, 1999), *Murder by Numbers* (Schroeder, 2002), *Taking Lives* (Caruso, 2004), *Twisted* (Kaufman, 2004), and *Untraceable* (Hoblit, 2008)—few would be granted her unqualified success as a detective. Instead, the majority of the female criminalist films that followed—especially those in the 2000s—reverted back to the 1980s legal thriller model of tying her "success" with her acceptance of a heteronormative relationship (most often with a male colleague) at the end of the film. While Taubin lauds *Silence* as "a profoundly feminist movie" ("Grabbing," 129) and Peter Krämer notes that the success of the film was the move to a female hero that was not a marginalized or victimized woman (207–8), in the case of *Copycat* critics were divided. On the one hand, in her review of the film, Lizzie Francke praised the casting of Holly Hunter and Sigourney Weaver as detective and potential victim, respectively—"enhancing its status as an instant post-feminist classic" (52); on the other, in his review of the film, Kenneth Turan argues that the casting led the filmmakers "to believe that they'[d] made a significant feminist statement, the movie's two hours-plus of almost continual sadistic abuse of women notwithstanding" (1).

    Copycat begins with Helen Hudson (Weaver), a psychologist who specializes in studying serial killers, a year after she was attacked by serial killer, Daryll Lee Cullum (Harry Connick, Jr.). The resulting trauma has made her agoraphobic and, unable to leave her apartment, she keeps in touch with the outside world through the newspaper, the Internet, and especially her assistant, Andy (John Rothman). It is Andy who forces Helen to talk to police detectives, M.J. Monahan (Hunter) and Reuben Goetz (Dermot Mulroney), on the trail of a serial killer. Helen proves her expertise when she recognizes the killer's pattern: he is working through the M.O.'s of famous serial killers. The killer, unassuming lab technician Peter Foley (William McNamara), also relies on computers and technology to plan his murders. In the case of his third victim, he watches her jog on video and zooms in on her face as she gasps with exertion, but the close-up is so tight that her face becomes little more than indistinguishable pixels. Later he watches a video of a music festival to pick his next victim; however, rather than let the audience see into the eyes of the killer, the film shows only his glasses reflecting the light from his computer screen. Once he has chosen his victim, Foley taunts Helen by sending her a video file via e-mail in which he shows the crime scene photo from his last murder and then the face of his next victim. Helen is deeply disturbed by this invasion of her computer; as she explains to M.J. and Reuben, it's "the only space that I have in the world."

Copycat's two female detectives are very different women. In the opening scene, Helen is depicted as a strong, professional woman reduced to a quivering, panicked victim after Cullum's attack. In contrast, M.J. is a strong, professional woman who proves herself adept at handling people at the scene of the crime—from withholding information from the media to extracting it from fellow officers. Her coworkers like and respect her, even though Lieutenant Quinn (J. E. Freeman) tells her that she is "one pushy broad," M.J. takes it as a compliment. M.J. meets her match in Helen, however. M.J. attempts to use flattery to win Helen over, but Helen sees through it and asks Reuben, "Does she do this . . . this . . . wide-eyed-little-girl routine often?" Helen is considered unreliable because she pops pills like candy and drinks heavily; indeed, even Helen does not trust herself to distinguish between reality and her nightmares—for example, when the killer sneaks into her apartment to lay out on her bed the red dress she was wearing when Cullum attacked her. When someone breaks in but is scared off by Reuben's arrival, Helen begs the detectives, "Please stop pretending to me that it's a burglar. Stop treating me like I'm some driveling idiot and tell me the truth!" And M.J. respects her enough to give it to her—and to keep Helen on the case when Quinn tells her to keep her off it.

M.J. did not become a detective, like many of her female criminalist successors will, because she suffers from a former trauma—the result of victimization at the hands of a man in her life. Some female detectives struggle with their impulses to break the law (*Impulse* and *Twisted*); others are able to prove themselves competent detectives through their investigations (*Black Widow* and *Silence*); some leave the safety (or boredom) of their desk jobs to work in the field (*Black Widow* and *Untraceable*); however, M.J. in *Copycat* is presented as unequivocally confident and successful. In fact, the only thing suggesting that M.J. is not complete (according to Hollywood convention) is that she is single. She used to date her former partner, Nicoletti (Will Patton), and is attracted to her present partner Reuben; however, on Chinatown detail, Reuben is shot by an armed suspect. Both Nicoletti and M.J. feel responsible for Reuben's death:

Nicoletti because it was his negligence that gave the suspect access to a gun and M.J. because she fired a non-lethal round into the suspect rather than kill him when he was holding Reuben hostage. M.J. comforts Nicoletti after the shooting and he confesses that he loves her: it is implied that M.J. will not necessarily be alone for long. And just as M.J. loses a man dear to her, so too does Helen later that night when the killer chooses a male victim—her assistant Andy. In the end, it is Helen who must prove her abilities as a crime-fighter—not M.J.—and Helen does so by using herself as bait to lure Foley into the open. Foley attempts to recreate Cullum's attack on Helen—hoping he will succeed where Cullum failed. And, just as M.J. defied Quinn's orders regarding Helen, so too does she ignore his command "not to go in there alone" after Foley. M.J. then calls into headquarters to apologize to Quinn that she is "sorry [she] blew it"—by ignoring his orders—but it is in that very act of defiance that she succeeds in saving Helen and bringing the killer to justice.

The two women—Helen and M.J.—work together to defeat the killer in the climactic showdown. Just as the two women worked together in the course of the film to track down and identify the killer (in defiance of male authority), so too do they fight the killer—not to save themselves, but each other. Foley wants to recreate Cullum's attack and so strings Helen up by her neck over one of the toilets in a bathroom so that she can tenuously support her weight with one foot to keep the wire around her neck slack. M.J. comes to Helen's rescue, arriving just in time to prevent Foley from slicing Helen open; however, M.J. then becomes Foley's focus and Helen has to rescue M.J. from being killed; she does so by attempting to hang herself (she lets her feet slip off the toilet). Foley does not want Helen to die by any hand but his own and lets her down to the floor to slacken the noose; she then stabs him with a piece of broken mirror and attempts to blind him with an aerosol. She conquers her agoraphobia by leaving the building to call for help. Just as it looks like he may get his wish to kill Helen, M.J. arrives to shoot him. And she does not make the mistake she made in Reuben's case: this time, she shoots to kill. And Hunter as M.J., like Bujold in *Coma* and Foster in *Silence*, is a compelling heroine with her petite stature and girlish voice (Helen refers to her as "the wee inspector") belying her character's professionalism and strength of character. I would suggest that just as Rich described Gumb's captive in her review of *Silence*, so too is Helen "a woman who, captured, fights back, resists victimization, and gets away with it—because she's rescued by another woman, whose qualities of vulnerability and observation are shown to empower, not endanger, her" (5 March 1991). Like *Silence*, *Copycat* offered a strong and successful female detective but, more interestingly, one that brings the killer to justice by working with a female partner. The film's mediocre performance at the box office may have deterred other filmmakers from producing serial killer narratives centered on two women and, instead, the pattern for the majority of

Fig. 10.2. The Wee Inspector: Holly Hunter's detective in *Copycat* (1995) may be diminutive in size but she possesses an incomparable strength of character in terms of the genre. Photo from author's collection.

female criminalist films for the rest of the 1990s was to pair an inexperienced female sidekick with a central male criminalist.

Buddies to Black Detectives

There is a gap between the success of *Silence* and the subgenre proper of criminalist films featuring female detectives that peaked in the late 1990s and early 2000s. That is because they were actually the product of another subgenre of the detective film: the biracial buddy cop film. The biracial buddy film was a popular subgroup of the cop-action film beginning in the 1980s in which a central white hero was paired with a black sidekick. The black buddy offered his skills to fight the crime that threatened white America in films such as *48 Hrs* (Hill, 1982) starring Nick Nolte and Eddie Murphy, and the *Lethal Weapon* series (Donner, 1987, 1989, 1992, and 1998) starring Mel Gibson and Danny Glover. As buddy narratives, these films focused on the relationship between the two men and the contrast of their often-opposing types of masculinity that is not limited to their racial but also their socioeconomic and educational background. As Ed Guerrero notes, there is a reluctance in mainstream cinema to place a black star in a film without a white co-star and/or a white context to allow a point of identification for the white spectator ("Black," 239). As Christopher Ames notes, the history of the biracial buddy narrative can be traced back to frontier literature, including James Fenimore Cooper's *Leatherstocking Tales* and Mark Twain's *Huckleberry Finn*; however, the biracial buddy film of the 1980s reverses the conventional polarity of the relationship between the two men—namely, in the 1980s it is the racial other who is too civilized and has lost touch with his savage masculinity and the white man who is equipped for survival in the metaphoric wilderness of the urban land-scape (52–53). In the 1990s, the civilized black male was reframed from the position of the white man's sidekick to being the central hero with his own sidekick, typically a white woman, in an effort to maintain biracial—and now unisex—audience appeal. *The Pelican Brief* (Pakula, 1993) and *Murder at 1600* (Little, 1997) offer a central black male hero with a white female sidekick in films firmly rooted in the action genre;[13] however, *Kiss the Girls* (1997) marks the beginning of the shift over to the criminalist detective film that solidified with *The Bone Collector* (1999).

Kiss the Girls was not intended to showcase the talents of the female detective; instead, its production was no doubt inspired by the success of *Seven* (1995) which featured Morgan Freeman as a criminalist detective. Indeed, the central hero of *Kiss the Girls* and *Along Came a Spider* (Tamahori, 2001),[14] is forensic psychologist, Alex Cross (Morgan Freeman)—a black detective work-ing in a predominantly white environment. Although he works with the D.C. police department, his involvement in the "Casanova" case in *Kiss the Girls* is personal: his niece, a Durham University student, has been kidnapped. In both films, Alex ends up working the case alongside a white woman—Dr. Kate McTiernan (Ashley Judd) and Secret Service agent Jezzie Flanagan (Monica Potter), respectively. In a departure from the conventions of the buddy cop film and the erotic thriller of the 1980s, the female body is not put on display in scenes of romance nor is the male body the one of action; instead, Kate's is the body put on display in scenes of action. Kate's physical strength (e.g., her prowess at kickboxing) and strength of character (e.g., her refusing to be a victim) are what prevent her from becoming one of Casanova's permanent captives or one of the women whom he kills for breaking the rules. Not only does Kate choose to jump off a cliff into the raging river below rather than continue to be his prisoner in a plantation dungeon, but she also demonstrates personal strength in her ability to face him again when Detective Nick Ruskin (Cary Elwes) reveals himself to Kate as Casanova. When he attempts to rape her in her kitchen at the end of the film, Kate fights back valiantly, slicing at him with a kitchen knife, kneeing him in the groin, and bringing down a rack of pots onto his head. With him stunned, Kate then drags Nick across the floor and handcuffs him to the stove. As such a strong and admirable character, Kate defies the traditional representation of a woman in this type of film where women tend to be the helpless victims.

The only physical confrontation between the male detective and the villain comes at the last moment when Nick threatens to blow all three of them up by striking his lighter as gas leaks from the stove. Nick assumes that Alex will not fire his weapon because the spark would ignite the leaking gas; however, Alex is cleverer than Nick and fires his weapon through a carton of milk, thus neutralizing the spark. While Alex has the satisfaction of shooting the villain, Kate is the action hero of the film. Kate is not just a woman of action but an intelligent sleuth as well. Although Alex is the primary detective on the case and the official criminalist, Kate does demonstrate skills of observation that not only facilitate her escape from Casanova's dungeon but also her leading Alex back to it. Kate is an amateur sleuth; however, by 1999, Hollywood had resurrected the professional female detective and given her a more significant investigative role in *The Bone Collector*.

The Bone Collector begins with a focus on Lincoln Rhyme (Denzel Washington), a black, male criminalist who is injured on the job and is now a quadriplegic and contemplating what he calls his "final transition" (i.e., suicide). Young beat-patrol cop, Amelia Donaghy (Angelina Jolie)—like Kate in *Kiss the Girls*—is the body of action in the film. Amelia is masculinized: in the film's introduction of her, her lover is shown in bed and a police officer's tools-of-the-trade strewn on the floor—boots, belt, and gun—the implication being that they are his. In the scene that follows, however, it is revealed that Amelia is the cop and her boyfriend the one who complains that she is commitment phobic and that he feels like the night they just spent together was "another slam bam thank you 'mam." This role reversal establishes Amelia's careerist ambitions as her priority rather than romance and, through her stumbling across a dead body, Amelia's career is catapulted upward on Lincoln's forensics team. At the scene, Amelia goes to great lengths to protect and document the evidence; Lincoln is impressed by Amelia's skills of observation and her instincts to preserve the scene at all costs. Working together, Amelia does all the "legwork" while the bed-ridden Lincoln relies on his knowledge and experience to figure out the identity of the serial killer.

Amelia proves that she has the observation skills and strong stomach to excel at forensics, balking from her duty only when Lincoln tells her to cut off the hands of a dead victim for a forensic examination. By her third crime scene, Amelia is more confident, shooting a rat to send the rodents scattering and telling the other officers to clear her space "to walk the grid" of the scene. She is also the hero who must spring to action to save Lincoln from the killer. The killer is revealed to be Richard (Leland Orser), the technician who services Lincoln's heart monitor. Richard was once a cop convicted of an offence based on a report that Lincoln produced while reviewing the case. Although bedridden, Lincoln tries to defend himself valiantly within the limits imposed by his condition when Richard attacks; however, it is Amelia who must arrive in time to shoot Richard and save Lincoln in a reversal of the scenario of *Kiss the Girls*. The film ends with Amelia and Lincoln celebrating Christmas with friends and Lincoln's family. Amelia and Lincoln have healed each other: Lincoln no longer wants to end his life, and Amelia no longer shuts herself off from emotional intimacy. The film signals Lincoln's transformation by showing him in a wheelchair instead of his bed and Amelia re-feminized in a clingy black dress instead of her unisex uniform. Hollywood's reluctance to place the female detective alone at the center of the narrative, in fear of lack of mass appeal, inspired producers to make her the buddy of a more established black star; however, once *Kiss the Girls* and *The Bone Collector* proved the female detective's appeal, more films followed in the early 2000s that tested out her popularity as the central hero herself.

Spectacle of the Gross

While the detective genre has brought women to the center of the narrative with a seemingly greater degree of agency as the protagonists who drive the narrative action forward, this agency is often tempered and contained. In the serial killer film, masculinity is still regarded as the embodiment of strength and heroism and the female body, weakness and victimization. The female detective is portrayed as competent and successful only as a masculinized or de-feminized woman; when she exhibits feminine traits—usually emotional—she is branded as a professional failure. More recent serial killer films offer some of Hollywood's toughest and attractive female stars appearing repeatedly in the genre—for example, Ashley Judd and Angelina Jolie—portraying strong female characters while, simultaneously, undermining their agency through casting them as the former or potential victims of male violence.[15] While the male detective in the contemporary detective film is often empowered through his identification with the serial killer, the female detective often succumbs to an over-identification with the killer's victims and often is a former or potential victim of violence perpetrated by men. The female body—of the detective as well as the victim—thus functions as a site for the working through of masculine anxieties incited by a female presence in the traditionally masculine profession of law enforcement.

   In her discussion of the "body genres" of porn and horror films, Linda Williams argues that there is a "system of excess" with a "gross display of the human body" ("Film," 3). The criminalist film with its focus on crime scene investigation and forensics allows an indulgence in a spectacle that is gross in nature without the guilt of association with the doer of the crimes, as is the case of the horror film. "Gorenography" is a term that has appeared in the popular media to describe films and other visual texts that offer sensationalized and eroticized depictions of violence (Caputi and Russell, 18). While the violence is not necessarily eroticized in the criminalist film and television series, it is, however, sensationalized and can often feel like an onslaught on the senses. In the criminalist film of the last decade, the horrors perpetrated by the killer that were suggested but rarely shown in films like *Silence* are not only exposed but indulged in as cameras offer these extended and hypergraphic scenes of mutilation. In *Murder by Numbers*, the young killers in eerie, astronaut-like suits choke the life out of a panicked victim and blow the brains out of another; in *Twisted*, a victim's face is so viciously battered that the detective only recognizes the corpse by a tattoo on his hand; and in *Taking Lives*, the disfigured faces of the victims, their sawn off wrists, and the photos of the crime scenes are given lingering and detailed close-ups.

As Murray Pomerance suggests, there has been a dramatic increase in the illustration of violence over the past few decades; audiences are now brought "face to face with a vision of conflict and decay that had heretofore been scarcely imaginable in such detail, suggested and implied rather than directly shown" (3). Released in 1999, *The Bone Collector* was one of the first of the cycle of films to draw a lot of criticism from reviewers for the gruesomeness of the violence depicted. Rick Groen of *The Globe and Mail* complained that "There's no compelling or even logical reason for this grisly order" (5 Nov 1999) while Stephen Holden of *The New York Times* was more accepting when he suggests, "Since movies keep pushing the envelope of acceptably gruesome [. . .] [t]hese unsettling moments have become par for the course in a modern horror thriller" (5 Nov 1999). In her review of *The Bone Collector*, Taubin notes that the foregrounding of the investigation "allows director Phillip Noyce to display hideously mutilated corpses and to fetishize the details—skin carved, burnt, or bitten down to the bone—in giant digitized close-up. We've come a long way—technologically speaking—since *Blow-Up*" ("Grabbing," 136). This embodies a kind of pornography of violence, a fetishization of the body in death—rather than sex.

And the cadaver is the key piece of the killer's "work" that must be read by the detective for the "author's" signature. By the turn of the millennium, however, reading those signs became more complicated. In the earlier conceptions of the detective genre, clues were left behind by the killer and could betray the "truth" about the crime—one just had to be able to identify the clues and their importance. In the postmodern shift in the genre, the clues are still readable but there is no single truth. In 1970s *noir*—for example, *The Long Goodbye* (Altman, 1973), *Chinatown* (Polanski, 1974), and *Night Moves* (Penn, 1975)—the detective often "failed" to read the clues correctly but there was still a sense that the truth was located in the clues: it was the detective that was flawed. Todd Davis and Kenneth Womack argue that "postmodernism feigns no assurance than the 'truth' may be founded on the knowledge of providence or science or any other grand narrative that wishes to establish itself as the essence or center on which discourse may be grounded" (xxii). Thus, in the contemporary evocations of the genre, it is the clues themselves that can be read by different readers in multiple ways—and yet each reading can offer a plausible truth. In *Copycat*, the killer does not have his own M.O.; instead he copies that of famous serial killings. Similarly, in *Murder by Numbers*, we see how "signatures" can be faked—that even killers can step outside of their own

M.O. and manufacture one. The detective of postmodernity, therefore, must not only be able to read the clues correctly but to identity the correct version of the truth that the clues can offer.

Victims in a Man's World

Like Clarice, the female criminalist of the new millennium tends to be presented as a masculinized woman. All three detectives in *Murder by Numbers*, *Twisted*, and *Taking Lives* sport the same "uniform": unisex clothes such as jeans and turtleneck sweaters under leather jackets, with natural-looking makeup, and either short hair or long hair tied back for functionality. Importantly, all three women are also shown to be sexually aggressive. In *Murder by Numbers*, the female detective pursues her new partner for casual sex while he is the one who asks, "What about what I want?" In *Twisted*, she roams bars for passionate one-night stands with strangers. In *Taking Lives*, she develops what she describes as a "favorable reaction" to the lead witness, eventually having passionate sex with him.

In *Murder by Numbers*, Cassie Mayweather (Sandra Bullock) is a homicide detective but also a former victim of male violence (her abusive husband stabbed her 17 times) and this attack haunts her life in every aspect. In her private life, she sabotages any relationship that brings any man too close—"That's Cassie's M.O." her ex-boyfriend explains to her new partner. In her professional life, she is pulled off the case because of her close alignment with the victim (betrayed by Cassie's referral to her by her first name, Olivia). As her boss explains, the detective must identify with the killer in order to catch him, not with the victim. Cassie must deal with her own victimization in order to move on with her life, but she avoids it at all costs. When asked by her partner, Sam (Ben Chaplin), why she became a police detective, she lies and says it was because someone she knew was killed. And, later when she recounts her traumatic past, she refers to herself in the third person: she uses a nickname and her maiden name—Cassie Mayweather—to differentiate herself from the victim of the attack—Jessica May Hudson. Her own baggage does cloud her judgment on the case initially: she is convinced Richard (Ryan Gosling)—the boy who reminds her of her ex-husband—is the real villain, and killer, rather than the loner Justin (Michael Pitt), Richard's seeming victim with whom she identifies.

Cassie is able to rewrite her past as victim and enact a psychological cure for her trauma by summoning up the strength (of mind and body) to throw Richard from a balcony to the rocks and sea below instead of letting him kill her. She is not cured as of yet, however. Cassie is able to defeat Richard but she, subsequently, has to be rescued by Justin in order to escape the same fate as Richard. She still believes that Justin is the more innocent of the two killers and it is only when she notices the ring mark left on her neck when Richard choked her that Cassie knows it was Justin who was Olivia's killer. As she tells

Justin, "You get one life and whatever you do with it—and whatever's done to you—you gotta face that. You can't pretend it didn't happen." Thus, she takes her own advice and concludes her rehabilitation by facing her former husband as a witness at his parole hearing and, when called as "Jessica May Hudson," Cassie answers. Whereas Cassie used Sam for sexual gratification at the beginning of the film before literally kicking him out of bed, the film suggests that with her coming to terms with her past as victim and dealing with it, she will now embrace a normal relationship with Sam.

Taking Lives and *Twisted* present a shift from the majority of serial killer films with female detectives that preceded them. Both films present a serial killer that preys on male rather than female victims and this, in turn, *should* present a shift in the representation of the female detective away from being the potential victim of the killer and male violence—but it does not. In *Twisted*, Jessica Shepard (Ashley Judd) is a tough homicide detective who is criticized for being too much like one of the guys. In the opening scene of the film, we see her use excessive force on a male suspect; in the next, we see her hook up with a handsome stranger at a bar and then go home to his place for rough sex. When a killer begins a series of attacks, Jessica's promotion to homicide sees her not as a potential victim but as a suspect since the murder victims are all men with whom she has had sexual relations. As someone asks her, "Why is someone who would normally be considered a prime suspect being allowed to participate in this investigation?" Unlike some of her predecessors who suffered from an unhealthy alignment with the victims—fearing that they may become one, instead Jessica develops an unhealthy alignment with the killer—fearing that she may be the one committing the murders, not unlike her father. Her father—also a police detective—allegedly committed a series of murders that concluded with her mother's murder and his own suicide. It is revealed by the end of the film, however, that it was not her father that committed those atrocities when she was a child, but her seemingly benevolent guardian and Police Commissioner, John Mills (Samuel L. Jackson). John did not like the men that her mother was pursuing affairs with and dispatched them; similarly, he does not like the men that Jessica sleeps with and is killing them.

Once she discovers the truth that it is John and not herself who is the murderer, Jessica is "cured" of her neurosis—and, thus, her related need (at least according to generic convention) to embody masculinity. The film concludes with her re-feminization with the suggestion that Jessica will embark on a meaning-ful—and exclusive—relationship with her police partner, Mike (Andy Garcia). John had attempted to convince Jessica that Mike was the perpetrator because Mike is in love with her. When John threatens to kill Mike, Jessica shoots John and then apologizes to Mike for ever doubting him. As she explains to him, "I'm so sorry, I thought you were the guy"—meaning the killer; however, Mike replies with a smile, "I am the guy"—meaning the guy for her to love. As Geoff Pevere suggests in his review of the film, *Twisted,* "frankly equates a woman's professional and sexual drives with murder" (27 February 2004). In this sense, the female criminalist film of the 2000s has not advanced from the themes of the erotic thriller of the 1980s: those drives are regarded as potentially lethal to the male and must be quelled.

While *Twisted* insists that the personal life of the detective is more important than her professional and, therefore, she must be re-feminized, *Taking Lives* suggests the opposite; namely, that the detective's personal life must be subordinated to her professional life and that she must be masculinized. In *Taking Lives*, the victims are men because the killer wants to be someone else with a life different from his own; he, therefore, kills in order to take their place and live their lives like a hermit crab. Special Agent Illeana Scott (Angelina Jolie) is introduced as a very successful and talented FBI profiler, sent to assist Montreal detectives on a difficult case. Her new colleagues find Illeana lying in the grave where the victim was buried, attempting to assess the scene. One of the problems with the film is that this and other aspects of what the film's official website identify as her "intuitive, unconventional approach" and "unorthodox methods"[16]—like the posting of crime scene photos above her bed, in the bathroom, and on the chair opposite her at dinner—are never developed or explained. The process of lying in the grave, however, would suggest an attempt to align herself with the victim. Similarly, at Martin's childhood home, Illeana discovers a dungeon-like basement room where it is implied Martin as a child was confined—and she lies in his bed. As she tries to identify with Martin as a victim of a cruel mother, Illeana becomes a victim herself—attacked by Martin who is hiding under the bed. Illeana does not suffer from a previous trauma (like Clarice, Cassie, or Jessica) and appears to be confident and stable. Although she wears a wedding ring—suggesting that, unlike the majority of female detectives, she has found a balance between her professional and personal life—she confesses that it is just a prop worn to ward off male advances. Illeana is attracted to the witness in the case, James Costa (Ethan Hawke), who—unfortunately for Illeana—turns out to be the killer she seeks. And here Illeana's investigative skills are called into question: despite being his lover, Illeana does not deduce that Costa is the killer until she finds him crouching over his mother's body in the hospital elevator. And, instead of reacting as a professional and taking him into custody, she reacts emotionally and stands transfixed as the elevator doors close and he escapes.

Despite her gender-neutral choice of clothes and hairstyle, her ability to perform violence, and her masterful handling of her Ford Mustang (Dirty Harry's choice of drive) in a car chase, Illeana is revealed to be a vulnerable woman at heart—and it is her desire for love that could make her the next victim. While she appears self-confident in the first half of the film, her traumatic realization that her lover is the killer sends her into a self-destructive spiral signaled by her increasingly feminized appearance: her long hair lays loose in tangles and her eyes are rimmed red from crying. And Costa confirms her worst fear; namely, that she is just as abnormal as the killer, when he calls her while on the run.

Costa: We are the same. I'm right, aren't I?

Illeana: No.

Costa: No, no. I'm right.

Illeana: Fuck you!

Costa: Fuck you? Yeah, I did fuck you. Remember making love with those pictures of the dead people around us? Let's face it, Illeana, an ordinary person does not love that as much as we did.

Ultimately, Illeana has to face her fears by facing Costa but she does not get the opportunity for several months. In the meantime, after reviewing the case, the Bureau's Office of Professional Responsibility decides to serve Illeana with a letter of termination citing "egregious lack of judgment and conduct unbecoming of a federal agent."

In a seeming return to the themes of the 1980s female lawyer thriller, Illeana *appears* to pursue justice as a vigilante. In the climactic standoff, Illeana embodies hyperfemininity, apparently heavily pregnant with Costa's twins. He confronts her in her farmhouse hideaway and viciously attacks her—beating her, kicking her, strangling her, and ultimately stabbing her in her swollen belly. What was interesting about this scene is the effect it had on the audience. At the screening I attended, the audience—myself included—was visibly and audibly disturbed at the sight of a heavily pregnant woman being beaten so viciously. For Illeana/Jolie to engage in a fight with the killer seems to be acceptable to the audience only when she is masculinized; when she appears hyperfeminized, an incompatibility arises between her role as mother-to-be and "manhunter." However, this image of the detective as a pregnant woman being beaten proves to be only a masquerade. Just as Costa pretended to be other people to evade the law, so too does Illeana pretend to be something she is not (i.e., pregnant) in order to lure Costa out into the open—to exact justice by killing him in "self-defense." The female detective, reduced to feminine vulnerability by her emotional connection with the killer, re-masculinizes herself through the violent destruction of the killer by her own hands. Whether she was actually operating outside of the law or was just pretending to be, the film ends with Illeana's calling her colleagues in Montreal to let them know that *it* is "done."

Conclusions: Sex Impediments

The female criminalist of the early 1990s—such as Clarice in *Silence* and M.J. in *Copycat*—was empowered by her femininity and uses her abilities as a specifically female (i.e., empathetic) detective to rescue another woman from the killer. The millennial female criminalist, on the other hand, is apparently hampered by her sex as it affects her judgment on the case and makes her vulnerable to the killer. Initially, she is presented as extremely successful at her job: she is an intuitive and astute observer and tracker and is either known for her abilities (*Taking Lives*) or gaining recognition for them (*Twisted*). Her failing tends to be in her personal life and she is unable to develop a satisfying and committed relationship with a man because she is married to her job (*Taking Lives*); she was the victim of male violence (*Murder by Numbers*) or her father was the perpetrator of such violence (*Twisted*). However, a shift occurs during the film whereby the female detective's inability to form a normal relationship with a man impedes her ability to perform her job (*Murder by Numbers* and *Twisted*) or she becomes the intended or potential victim of male violence (*Taking Lives*). It is here that her personal and professional lives intersect and see her deficient as a detective. In *Murder by Numbers*, Cassie is pulled off the case because she develops an unhealthy identification with the victim and dislike for Richard; in *Twisted*, Jessica is regarded as the most likely suspect since her father was a killer and she slept with all the victims; and in *Taking Lives*, Illeana embraces the killer as a lover instead of recognizing him for the serial murderer he is.

Like the female lawyer of the 1980s, the millennial criminalist is plagued by the seeming inability to have both a healthy personal life as well as a strong professional one; however, the female lawyer's only crime was to get a personal life. In the 1980s thrillers, the problem came from the outside—whether an evil man (e.g., *Jagged Edge* and *Music Box*) or an evil woman (e.g., *Black Widow* and *Defenseless*)—and is not the result of an earlier moment of victimization; and, if the female detective is the victim of male violence, this occurs during the course of the film and its impact on her is immediate and only temporary. Conversely, in the 2000s, the problem resides within the female detective herself—i.e., Cassie and Jessica are the ones who are damaged—and her victimization at the hands of violent men occurred in her youth and she has *allowed* that violence to continue to haunt her. The result is that the millennial criminalist is less recuperable in terms of being an empowered woman than her 1980s predecessors because she has participated in, to an extent, her own victimization through denial.

While the female criminalist film leaves the heroine at a moment of balance—success in both her professional and personal lives (i.e., a happy ending)—one cannot help but suspect, however, that having dealt with the traumatic past event that drove her to be a detective, our heroine may lose her ambitious (read: masculine) drive in terms of her career. Correspondingly, now that she has found romance and stability with her male partner, the female detective will no longer be able to indulge in the single-minded pursuit of a killer. In films centered on male criminalists (e.g., *Seven* and *Blood Work*), the hero remains unattached at the end of the narrative; like the Western hero, the detective must remain unencumbered by romantic and familial entanglements if he is to remain effective as the detective operating on the margins of society on the thin blue line between crime and the law. The female criminalist, on the other hand, is expected to give up her independence and work as part of a team—with a partner (both professionally and personally). While the female detective may prove her abilities as a manhunter, she is ultimately contained or her success devalued through a reinscribing and containment of her professional ambition and aggressive sexuality.

Part III: The Crime-Fighting Chick Flick

The female detective has appeared increasingly with the proliferation of the criminalist narrative; however, she has also appeared frequently in recent years in female detective comedies and action films that offer crime-fighting chick flick heroines. *Charlie's Angels* (McG, 2000), *Miss Congeniality* (Petrie, 2000), and *Legally Blonde* (Luketic, 2001) offer a less serious approach to law enforcement and crime-fighting and are a testament to the popularity of female detective comedies because, unlike their more serious sister films that I have discussed above, they have all spawned sequels: *Charlie's Angels 2: Full Throttle* (McG, 2003), *Miss Congeniality 2: Armed and Fabulous* (Pasquin, 2005), and *Legally Blonde 2: Red, White and Blonde* (Herman-Wurmfeld, 2003). As I discussed in reference to the mystery-comedies of the 1930s, comedy has traditionally been more popular with audiences than with critics and scholars. Female detective comedies like *Charlie's Angels*, *Miss Congeniality*, and *Legally Blonde* offer, some to a greater extent than the others, a disruption of established gender codes. *Fargo* (Coen, 1996), as a black comedy, is more obviously critical and disruptive than these "lighter," chick flick comedies with its presentation of a highly competent, stable, and successful female detective, Marge (Frances McDormand). Although the contrast between Marge's masculine behavior as a determined, down-to-earth, and effective detective and her overly-determined feminine body as pregnant (i.e., waddling, awkward, and vomiting) generates humor, it also offers a potentially transgressive disruption of assumed sex roles: Marge is the most feminized detective of recent films as a soon-to-be-mother but also one of its least feminine in terms of her dress, manner of speaking, and attitude. Nevertheless, Marge is the exception rather than the rule. As Hilary Radner suggests, Marge "offers not so much a solution, but a fantasy of happiness outside the insanity and delirium that as a rule fuels Hollywood fiction" (260). And that fantasy is possible because of the film's relocation of the female criminalist into the realm of comedy (albeit black comedy).

Although in perhaps a less sophisticated or challenging way, even Natalie (Cameron Diaz), Dylan (Drew Barrymore), and Alex (Lucy Liu) of *Charlie's Angels*—unlike their serious counterparts—seem to manage to embody successfully (if cartoon-like) the contradictory associations of action hero (masculine) and beautiful woman (feminine) or what Marc O'Day has coined the "action babe" (201). The action babe—such as the Angels and Lara Croft (Angelina Jolie) in the *Tomb Raider* films (West, 2001, and de Bont, 2003)—are clad in spectacular outfits that cling to and highlight their femininity (e.g., curvaceous breasts, hips, and buttocks). Even though the 1970s blaxploitation heroine often donned very sexy clothes (or bared her breasts), she did so when "undercover"—masquerading as a prostitute in order to get close enough to the enemy to destroy him. In contrast, her regular choice of clothes—i.e., the one's indicative of her "true" personality—tended to be more masculine-inspired garb (i.e., pantsuits) not unlike the girl reporter of the 1930s. Although lacking the action component, *Legally Blonde* presents its heroine, Elle Woods (Reese Witherspoon), as a disruption of normal expectations for its chick flick audience: here Elle's seeming vacuousness as a fashion student is contrasted to her ability to make it into Harvard law school and then solve a case (albeit through her knowledge of women's beauty routines). As Carol Dole asks,

> Can Elle remain a feminine, sexy blonde and simultaneously become a powerful East Coast lawyer? In the age of third-wave feminism and *Sex and the City* the answer for the film's target audience of young women must be yes. This is a Hollywood comedy, after all.[17] (64)

In *Murder by Numbers*, Sandra Bullock plays your typical female detective—masculine in appearance, manner, and profession and driven to a career in law enforcement because she is haunted by a past in which she was the victim of male violence; conversely, in *Miss Congeniality* and *Armed and Fabulous*, Bullock embodies a parody of that more serious role as both "action babe" (e.g., Lara Croft) and comic chick flick heroine (e.g., Elle Woods). While the *Miss Congeniality* films might appear more superficial than *Murder by Numbers*, they explore the same core issue: a gender-bending heroine who attempts to balance her personal life while hunting a criminal and attempting to succeed professionally in the male dominated world of law enforcement. Although *Miss Congeniality* is comic throughout with jokes, pratfalls, and unexpected outcomes, there is still a threat at the center of the film to investigate—a killer threatens to explode a bomb during the Miss USA pageant. The film begins with Agent Gracie Hart (Bullock) presented as a parody of the female criminalist: unfeminine, unattractive, and lacking in basic social graces in her uniform of a white dress shirt, black blazer and trousers, and, what one woman points out as, "masculine shoes." While these are the pre-established markers of the contemporary female detective, a lone woman working in a man's world, the film takes the stereotype further—and thus into the realm of the comic—by having Gracie walk, talk, and eat "like a man." Her masculinity is highlighted and ridiculed in Victor's (Michael Caine's) attempts to teach her how to be feminine—to transform her from what he calls "Dirty Harriet:" she walks with a manly swagger rather than "glides;" she snorts when she laughs and replies "yah" instead of "yes;" and she talks with her mouth full of burger and/or beer while ketchup drips onto her shirt. Whereas the female criminalist of films like *Copycat* and *The Bone Collector* represents a successful integration of the masculine into the feminine, Gracie embodies the disparity between the two: she is not as cool, competent, or attractive as the female detectives of the criminalist film and is repeatedly shown as awkward, even tripping over her own feet.

Gracie is masculinized at the start of the film and her competence as an agent is called into question when her disobeying of orders gets another agent shot; in the course of the film, she is feminized—although here it is for a job rather than a natural state of events that occurs as she "heals" herself by coming to terms with herself and her past. The result, however, is the same and her feminization attracts the attention of her male colleague, Eric Matthews (Benjamin Bratt), and leads her to a "healthy" relationship with him. Despite this ending, Gracie is shown to be an empowered woman and competent agent as she solves the case no one else can, in part because of her intelligence and ability to read the clues, and in part because of her femininity that allows her to masquerade as a pageant contestant and get behind the scenes of the potential scene of the crime. Gracie proves to be successful in both of these different worlds—the male world of law enforcement and the female world of beauty pageantry. In addition, she proves successful in both her career life of law enforcement having cracked the case and saved lives and her personal life having gained a close female friend, pageant winner Cheryl (Heather Burns), and a caring boyfriend, Eric. At the beginning of the film, Gracie is presented as a feminist who rejects feminine charms (e.g., makeup) and skills (e.g., cooking) in favor of being good at her job. Her criticism at the beginning of the film of the beauty pageant is replaced by an admiration for the women who compete in it. Whether one considers her comment at the end of the film that the beauty pageant was a "liberating" experience as an undermining of any serious comment about gender roles in the twenty-first century is another point altogether. However, the sequel does seem to atone for the "happy"—i.e., hetero-coupling and feminization of the heroine—ending.

The story of *Armed and Fabulous* picks up three weeks after the conclusion of the first film (although the film is released five years after the initial installment). Gracie's success in infiltrating the pageant and cracking of the case has made her a celebrity and, thus, unable to do her job successfully: during her attempt to prevent a bank robbery, adoring fans blow her cover. Her celebrity inhibits her ability to perform in the field but leads her to a new role in the FBI—becoming its "new face" and spokesperson as she makes the talk-show rounds and writes a book. She internalizes her new hyperfeminine identity with her affected manner and speech and is contrasted to the new masculine female detective on the force—Sam Fuller (Regina King)—who is Gracie's bodyguard and echoes how Gracie once was also masculinized. Sam's differentiation from the "new-and-improved" Gracie as African-American, physically larger, socially stunted, and violent—is a running joke within the film. When their assistant from the Nevada office, Jeff (Enrique Murciano), starts to crack under the pressure of their unauthorized covert operation, Sam says to Jeff, "Be a man!" Gracie quips, "Yah, like Fuller!" The film follows the movement of the two women's relationship from combative to supportive through their investigation of the kidnapping of Miss United States, Cheryl (Burns), and the pageant's producer, Stan (William Shatner). While the first film ended with Eric coming to Gracie's rescue, the second has Sam fulfill this masculine role. Rather than end with the successful union of a heterosexual couple, the relationship that is celebrated is the official partnering of its two heroines—Sam and Gracie—in true "chick flick" fashion.

Dole suggests, that "Like girlie feminism, *Legally Blonde* acknowledges and validates the sexual power of feminine masquerade" (67). I would argue that, although in *Legally Blonde* Elle is shown to have to adapt to new environments (i.e., Harvard Law School and the courtroom) by dressing appropriately, the film is not critical of the fact that women must perform a "masquerade;" instead, the film is more critical of Elle for initially being a "Malibu Barbie" and suggests that she did need to evolve into a better person. On the other hand, both "Miss Congeniality" films *are* critical of the femininity that women are expected to perform to be socially acceptable (even if the first film is critical of Gracie's initial masculinity) in that they expose femininity to be a performance. This is especially true of *Armed and Fabulous* in which it is suggested that men and women can perform femininity equally well when the female heroes go "undercover" as drag queens. Ironically, both Gracie and Sam are dressed their most feminine when they infiltrate a gay club as drag performers—women masquerading as men, masquerading as women. And, unlike *Miss Congeniality*, *Armed and Fabulous* does not end with Gracie's acceptance of hyperfemininity and its related social roles (i.e., domesticated and coupled) as the preferred option. Instead, the film ends with her rediscovery of her more masculine self—indicated through her re-adoption of her original FBI uniform (white shirt, dark suit, "masculine" shoes) and her re-embracing of violence as a necessary means to fight crime.

Whether one takes comedy seriously or not, what one must take seriously is that *Armed and Fabulous* is centered on the relationship between two strong female characters who succeed in the male dominated world of law enforcement and who consider the most significant relationship in their personal lives is that with each other. In other words, while the majority of the female criminalist films offer qualified or even reductive messages about female empowerment, the female detective comedy offers strong female characters and their successes to slip under the radar without the need to qualify them. Ultimately, however, the image of empowered women that these detective comedies offer is undermined by the very comic tone that facilitates it.

And certainly critics have debated the feminist possibilities of Hollywood's millennial heroines. Rikke Schubart sees the action babe—with her dual nature "composed from stereotypical feminine traits (beauty, a sexy appearance, empathy) and masculine traits (aggression, stamina, violence)"—as representing an "in-betweenness" rather than uniting the two genders (2). Schubart suggests that while the contemporary action heroine may not be a feminist representation, she represents "the *possibility* for change and empowerment" (ibid., 2).[18] On the other hand, other critics tend to see the contemporary action heroine as less transgressive than this. As Kate Waites suggests, Hollywood's warrior woman (e.g., Lara Croft or Charlie's Angels) is a "strange hybrid of over-determined masculine and feminine qualities, she is the monster-other whose existence challenges, and ever wrestles with, male power. Ultimately, she reveals less about women or femininity and more about the disguise of masculinity" (205). Waites's comment that Lara Croft "*poses* as a tough, intelligent, and resourceful warrior figure" is significant (211);[19] it suggests that Lara's performance of masculinity is a masquerade as well. Critics are still on the fence about the feminist possibilities of these millennial action women. As Karen Hollinger suggests,

> . . . the question of how much progress one can see in all of these new chick flicks remains unresolved. [There] is a sense of the deeply ambivalent messages these films convey to their female viewers. [. . .] As Maureen Turim suggests, the question comes down to whether chick flicks actually offer their female viewers a different desiring female subjectivity than their predecessors. (229)

I would argue that the crime-fighter chick flick resurrects the themes of the *fin-de-siècle* detective dime novel that I explored in Chapter 1. As I discussed earlier, in *film noir* masculinity and femininity are opposed and split between the tough hero and the sultry *femme fatale*, but in the late nineteenth-century dime story both genders are embodied within the single character of the female detective. And, as such, the dime novel heroine is regarded by critics as an escapist fantasy—an impossibility. Just as Kate Edwards of *Lady Kate, The Dashing Female Detective* (1886) is proficient at masquerading in various guises (both male and female/hero and villain) and performing action, so too is the millennial action heroine. Rather than occupying "in-betweenness" as Schubart suggests, I would argue that the chick flick crime-fighter attempts to embody all feminine and masculine traits deemed heroic and, as such, fails to satisfy as a convincing character. As Dole notes, "The tortuous, even tortured endings, of all these chick flicks make clear that we do not currently have a complete cultural consensus on whether women can have it all" (75).

Conclusions: Untraceable

Christina Lane describes the group of female detective films of the late 1980s and early 90s—including *Blue Steel*, *Silence*, and *Copycat*—as "one of the few genres that focus on women's subjectivities, especially women's experience as sexual objects" with "investigative heroines trying to overcome their own powerlessness through their conviction to stop some kind of male villain from preying on women" (*Feminist*, 137–38). This earlier generation of female detective films offered a position of subjectivity to female audiences, a heroine empowered to prevent male violence against other women, and an address of the problems that women faced in a male-dominated profession. The millennial female detective films—criminalist and chick flick—have seen a shift in the debate amongst feminist critics from whether the placement of a woman in the position of the male protagonist of the detective film constitutes a feminist model (as was the debate in the early 1990s), to whether the female detective reflects a feminist (i.e., second-wave) discourse anymore or embodies a postfeminist commodification of feminist discourse. Even if millennial female detective films such as *Twisted* and *Taking Lives* imply that their postfeminist heroines have transcended the "problems" of the female detective as feminist because she is now imbued with "girl power," Mizejewski comments that "the messiness of the crime film—its gendered violence, haunted masculinities, and obsession with the body—resists declaring feminism a closed case" ("Dressed," 126). I concur with Mizejewski who suggests, a "feminist/postfeminist division of the history of the woman detective would foreclose its most interesting questions about gender and genre" (ibid., 122). Similarly, Helen Hanson asserts:

> Questions of agency and choice in the neo-*noir* thriller are played out in the figure of the female investigator and legal agent in ways that show that the crime genre, while it bears traces of post-feminist negotiations, and commodifications of female identity, still advances unresolved questions about women's personal and professional positions. Women's professional and sexual liberation in the crime film frequently clashes with female victimization, showing that second-wave questions of women's agency are still alive in a "post" feminist moment, with no particular purchase on the gender reversals of the crime film. (152)

Whether the millennial female detective film is consciously articulating questions about the clash between personal and professional life or whether those questions are more the by-product of the attempt to generate drama and suspense, these films echo their predecessors in that their heroines struggle to find a balance between being a successful and respected crime-fighter and being a fulfilled woman—the latter still defined by being in a healthy, heterosexual relationship. However, I would suggest that one female criminalist film has broken new ground with a heroine who is represented as unequivocally competent: *Untraceable* (Hoblit, 2008).

In his review of *Twisted*, Pevere argued that the 2004 film was a "so-late-the-party's-over entry in the '90s serial-killer movie sweepstakes—a genre as particular to that period as grunge music and the Clinton administration" (27 Febuary 2004). Although the cycle appeared to have been exhausted by the mid-2000s, the female criminalist made a reappearance in 2008. In *Untraceable*, Agent Jennifer Marsh (Diane Lane) works in the Cybercrimes Division of the FBI in Portland tracking Internet crimes, including child pornography and identity theft. Jennifer represents a significant step in the evolution of the female detective: she is allowed the success in both her personal and professional lives that was denied her predecessors of the last two decades—without the former being defined by a heteronormative relationship. Jennifer is a widow (her husband was killed in the line of duty) and lives with her mother and daughter: together, the three generations of women have a happy home. Jennifer likes her desk job because she can work at night, leaving her free to spend time with her daughter in the mornings and evenings. While her colleague Griffin Dowd (Colin Hanks) searches for love on the Internet through online dating sites, Jennifer is content with her single status and, despite having an attractive and supportive partner, Jennifer does not begin a romance with him. In terms of her job, Jennifer is both liked by her colleagues (they come to her daughter's birthday party) and skilled at her job. She proves her superior abilities when her office is alerted about a Web site called "Kill with Me" on which the dubbed "Internet Killer" posts live videos of his victims. The interactive aspect to the site is that the victim is killed by people visiting the site: the more people who visit, the faster the victim is killed.

Using her skills of observation and logical reasoning, Jennifer deduces that the Internet Killer is Owen Reilly (Joseph Cross). Owen creates "Kill with Me" in retaliation for—and a comment on—the media's exploitation of his father's suicide. In his review of *Untraceable*, Stephen Holden describes the film as "Morally duplicitous torture porn:" he concedes that others "may stand back and see it as a cleverly conceived, slickly executed genre movie that ranks somewhere between *Seven* and the *Saw* movies in sadistic ingenuity" but that he sees the film "as a repugnant example of the voyeurism it pretends to condemn" (25 Jan 2008). I would like to suggest that it is a bit of both: the film criticizes the audience's voyeuristic impulse while, at the same time, com-modifying that criticism and indulging the audience in the very impulse itself. Just as did *Copycat* (and *Mikes' Murder*), so too does *Untraceable* question our reliance on mediated interactions through communication's technology. While criminals use the Internet to circulate child porn or steal people's personal infor-mation, the FBI's Cybercrimes Division has the technology (and the knowledge to use it) to catch them. However, the Internet Killer proves adept at turning technology against its users. Griffin's online dating may have introduced him to some attractive women but it is through that process that Owen lures Griffin to his death online. And while, at the beginning of the film, Jennifer's OnStar system in her SUV helps her to avoid bad traffic on her way home, at the end of the film, it makes her vulnerable to Owen who manages to hack into her car's computer and disable it.[20]

The film ultimately suggests that technology is neutral; it is the person who uses it that is good or evil. The film reminds its audience that humanity must not get lost in our increasingly computerized and mediated society and Jennifer functions as a reminder. Despite Owen's adeptness with technology, Jennifer continually outsmarts him. For example, when he traps her in her own car by manipulating the locking mechanism, she smashes her window to free herself. He may have taken over her car's communications system but she uses the (public) emergency phone on the bridge and contacts her partner, Eric (Billy Burke), to alert him to the situation. And, when Jennifer finds herself Owen's next victim, rather than panicking in a terrifying situation, she keeps a cool head and takes action. Owen has her bound and gagged, suspended from her ankles over her own old-fashioned lawn mower with the exposed blades rotating rapidly just below her head; instead of struggling uselessly (as the stereotypical female victim is want to do), Jennifer swings herself from side, gaining the momentum to grab a pipe at the side of the room. When Owen approaches to force her to let go, she opens a valve and burns him with steam. She then lowers herself to the floor away from the blades and attacks Owen as violently as she can with her hands still bound. Owen frees himself and grabs the lawn mower to kill Jennifer, but she has her gun in hand and does not hesitate to empty the entire contents of her clip into him. The final shot of the film is of Jennifer shoving her badge up into the webcam recording the scene, to remind the Internet audience that the law always wins. Her triumphant gesture is mitigated by the fact that beside the image of her badge appear posts from viewers, one praising Owen and another wondering where he can buy a copy of what he has just witnessed.

Whether the film succeeds in its criticism of the media's exploitation of violence is up for debate; however, what is not, is *Untraceable*'s contribution to the female detective genre. Jennifer is a good mother, a good friend, a good detective, and a woman of action. She is a female detective who is respected and accepted in the law enforcement world—i.e., she does not need to prove herself to male authority; she saves herself from the killer rather than waiting to be rescued by somebody else—i.e., she is not re-feminized; and she has a happy family life defined by female companionship—i.e., she does not need a heterosexual romance. In other words, Jennifer does not seem to embody any of the "problems" of the female detective. *Untraceable* was not a box-office success (although nor was it a disaster either), so perhaps a female detective without personal or professional problems is just not as compelling to audiences as one who does experience the femininity-achievement and personal-professional conflicts. Jennifer represents the end of the evolution of the female detective: rather than being too femininized by her sex to be a successful detective or too masculinized by her job to be a successful woman, Jennifer Marsh has achieved the right balance. The question is where will the genre take the female detective from here?

Appendix I

Appendix I

Type	Status	Skills	Criminal/Crime	Solution
Criminologist (1930s–40s)	Criminologist —amateur —unofficial	Outsider —specialized knowledge e.g., feminine —personal familiarity —deductive reasoning —intelligence —experience	Individual criminal	Arrives after crime is committed
Criminalist (1990s–00s) (aka Sleuth)	Criminalist —official	Criminalist only: —behavioral profiling —forensics analysis —crime scene investigation	Motivation: personal —murder	Goal: to solve "whodunit"
Undercover agent	Undercover agent —official	Insider —specialized knowledge e.g., feminine	Criminal ring	Witnesses crime committed
Crime-fighter	Crime-fighter —amateur —vigilante	—disguises/masquerade —physical action —intelligence	Motivation: greed —vice racket —(drugs, robbery)	Goal: expose crime ring from inside

Appendix II

Girl Reporters[1]

Title (Director, Year) [script only]	Actor (Character) [Series]	Agency as a reporter —Newspaperman, aspiring, sobbie[2] —Sex as impediment or asset	Agency as a detective —Primary, shared, secondary, minor[3] —Sleuth, crime-fighter, scoop only[4]	Conclusions —Resists, partly, upholds[5] —Marriage vs. career[6]
1920s				
The Office Scandal (Stein, 1929)	Phyllis Haver (Jerry)	Aspiring → newspaperman; Sex = impediment → asset	Sleuth; Primary; Very skilled	Resists; Pursues her career
Big News (La Cava, 1929)	Carole Lombard (Margaret)	Supposed newspaperman but never seen working on a story (only her marriage)	Non-investigator; Focus on her husband struggling with marriage, drink, and career	N/A Married & career
1930s				
Dance Fools Dance (Beaumont, 1931)	Joan Crawford (Bonnie)	Cub → newspaperman Career only out of necessity	Crime-fighter; Undercover; Primary	Resists; Chooses marriage
Up for Murder (Bell, 1931)	Genevieve Tobin (Myra)	Sob sister	Non-investigator; Publisher's 'keptie;' Is the cause of a murder	N/A
Sob Sister (Santell, 1931)	Linda Watkins (Jane)	Sob sister Career only out of necessity	Sleuth; Abandons investigating to be domestic for male rival	Upholds; Chooses marriage
Platinum Blonde (Capra, 1931)	Loretta Young (Gallagher)	Sob sister; Pal to male reporter; Class is an issue	No mystery to investigate; Solely female counterpoint to reporter's wealthy wife	N/A Will marry
Anybody's Blonde (Strayer, 1931)	Dorothy Revier (Janet)	Aspiring → newspaperman; Sex = asset	Crime-fighter; Undercover; Primary	Resists; Romance; Career unclear

Film	Actress (Character)	Role / Sex	Investigation	Ending
The Final Edition (Higgin, 1932)	Mae Clarke (Ann)	Aspiring → newspaperman; Sex = impediment → asset	Sleuth; Primary; Very smart	Resists; Marries; Career unclear
Strange Adventure (Del Ruth & Whitman, 1932)	June Clyde (Nosey)	Newspaperman; Sex = asset	Sleuth; Shared/Secondary; Follows the male and draws incorrect conclusions	Resists; Romance; Career unclear
Secrets of Wu Sin (Thorpe, 1932)	Lois Wilson (Nona)	Struggling writer → sob sister → newspaperman	Sleuth; Primary; Very skilled Uncovers smuggling ring	Resists; Marries; Career likely over
Mystery of the Wax Museum (Curtiz, 1933)	Glenda Farrell (Florence)	Aspiring → newspaperman; Sex = asset	Sleuth; Primary	Resists; Will marry but unconvincing
Shriek in the Night (A. Ray, 1933)	Ginger Rogers (Pat)	Aspiring → newspaperman	Sleuth; Primary; Initially undercover as secretary; Trusts killer but saves self	Resists; Chooses marriage
The Spinx (Rosen, 1933)	Sheila Terry (Jerry)	Sob sister; Questions ethics of job	Non-investigator; Love interest for criminal & male detective; Rescued by male	N/A; Chooses marriage
Headline Shooter (Brower, 1933)	Frances Dee (Jane)	Newspaperman but plans to quit because job is unethical	Sleuth; Shared; Plays it cool when kidnapped	Resists; Agrees to marry but chases story
The Mad Game (Cummings, 1933)	Claire Trevor (Jane)	Aspiring → newspaperman; Sex = impediment	Sleuth, but investigation secondary to the activities of the mobster	Resists; Pursues career (lover dies)
Orient Express (Martin, 1934) [script only]	Dorothy Burgess (Mabel)	Newspaperman; Lesbian; Alcoholic	Sleuth; Primary (first half) → absent (second half)	Seems to uphold

Title (Director, Year) [script only]	Actor (Character) [Series]	Agency as a reporter —Newspaperman, aspiring, sobbie[2] —Sex as impediment or asset	Agency as a detective —Primary, shared, secondary, minor[3] —Sleuth, crime-fighter, scoop only[4]	Conclusions —Resists, partly, upholds[5] —Marriage vs. career[6]
1930s (cont'd.)				
Hi, Nellie! (LeRoy, 1934)	Glenda Farrell (Gerry)	Aspiring; Successful but secondary; Hardboiled	Non-investigator; Male is primary focus	N/A No marriage
Hold that Girl (MacFadden, 1934)	Claire Trevor (Tony)	Aspiring → newspaperman Sex = impediment → asset	Sleuth; Shared; Insightful and competent	Resists; Will marry
After Office Hours (Leonard, 1935)	Constance Bennett (Sharon)	Cub; Socialite on uncle's paper; Never seen working on a story	Non-investigator; Witness to crime	N/A Marriage
Death from a Distance (Strayer, 1935)	Lola Lane (Kay)	Newspaperman	Sleuth; Minor; Clever with theories but problematic in action	Partly; Romance; Career unclear
Daring Young Man (Seiter, 1935)	Mae Clarke (Maddy)	Sob sister	Non-investigator; Love interest for male reporter/detective	N/A Chooses marriage
Front Page Woman (Curtiz, 1935)	Bette Davis (Ellen)	Sob sister → to prove to boyfriend Sex = an issue	Sleuth; Shared; Able but allows rival to trick her instead of pursuing her own leads	Upholds; Career failure; Chooses marriage
We're Only Human (Flood, 1935)	Jane Wyatt (Sally)	Newspaperman; Sex = asset (gets her close to cop)	Non-investigator → Crime-fighter; Mainly after scoop only	Partly; Romance; Career unclear

Film	Actress (Character)	Role	Investigation / Competence	Marriage
Big Brown Eyes (Walsh, 1936)	Joan Bennett (Eve)	Cub → to prove to boyfriend	Sleuth; Shared; Competent but quits when she becomes disillusioned	Resists; Will marry
Human Cargo (Dwan, 1936)	Claire Trevor (Bonnie)	Cub; Socialite on uncle's paper; Class = an issue	Crime-fighter; Shared; Smart but confides in real criminal and needs rescuing	Partly; Chooses marriage
36 Hours to Kill (Forde, 1936)	Gloria Stuart (Ann)	Reporter to testify (not on a story)	Non-investigator; Love interest for male detective	N/A Marries
Women are Trouble (Taggart, 1936)	Florence Rice (Ruth)	Aspiring → newspaperman Sex = issue	Sleuth; Shared; Proves successful, but needs rescuing	Resists; Marriage; Career unclear
The Girl on the Front Page (Beaumont, 1936)	Gloria Stuart (Joan)	Cub; Socialite inherits father's paper Class = an issue	Sleuth; Shared; Fails to detect the truth "right under her nose"	Upholds; Career failure; Chooses marriage
Smart Blonde (McDonald, 1937)	Glenda Farrell (Torchy) [Series 1/9]	Newspaperman	Sleuth; Shared, but proves superior to male	Resists; Proposal; Career unclear
Behind the Headlines (Rosson, 1937)	Diana Gibson (Mary)	Newspaperman but her ethics are questionable	Sleuth; Shared with rival reporter; Competent but confides in real criminals	Resists; Chooses marriage
There Goes My Girl (Holmes, 1937)	Ann Sothern (Connie)	Newspaperman	Sleuth; Shared; Competent but is injured in a shooting	Resists; Chooses marriage

Girl Reporters[1]

Title (Director, Year) [script only]	Actor (Character) [Series]	Agency as a reporter —Newspaperman, aspiring, sobbie[2] —Sex as impediment or asset	Agency as a detective —Primary, shared, secondary, minor[3] —Sleuth, crime-fighter, scoop only[4]	Conclusions —Resists, partly, upholds[5] —Marriage vs. career[6]
1930s (cont'd.)				
Fly Away Baby (McDonald, 1937)	Glenda Farrell (Torchy) [Series 2/9]	Newspaperman	Sleuth; Shared, but proves superior	Resists; Romance & pursues career
It Can't Last Forever (MacFadden, 1937)	Betty Furness (Carole)	Newspaperman → quits because business is unethical	Sleuth; Primary but investigation is secondary to male's con exploits	Resists; Chooses marriage
Exclusive (Hall, 1937)	Frances Farmer (Vina)	Cub → quits because she is unethical	Sleuth; Shared; Competent but unethical at first	Upholds; Career failure; Chooses marriage
One Mile from Heaven (Dwan, 1937)	Claire Trevor (Tex)	Newspaperman Chooses ethics over scoop	Sleuth; Primary; Withholds truth to protect innocent	Resists; No romance; New career
My Dear Miss Aldrich (Seitz, 1937)	Margaret Sullivan (Martha)	Cub; Teacher inherits paper Sex = issue & an asset	Sleuth; Primary; Proves more successful than male, but needs rescuing	Resists; Romance; Career unclear
Back in Circulation (Enright, 1937)	Joan Blondell (Timmy)	Newspaperman; Sex = asset & linked to ethics	Sleuth; Primary; Dubious ethics initially; Success when embraces softer/moral side	Resists; Marriage; Career unclear
Adventurous Blonde (McDonald, 1937)	Glenda Farrell (Torchy)	Newspaperman	Sleuth; Primary; Proves more successful than male	Resists; No wedding; Pursues career

Film	Actress (Character)	Career/Work	Detective Role	Romance/Marriage
Blondes at Work (McDonald, 1938)	Glenda Farrell (Torchy) [Series 4/9]	Newspaperman, but jailed for contempt; Male calls in scoop for her	Sleuth; Shared; Proves more successful than male	Resists; Romance & pursues career
International Crime (Lamont, 1938)	Astrid Allwyn (Phoebe)	Cub; Socialite gets job on uncle's paper Class = an issue	Sleuth; Secondary; Assists but makes mistakes	Partly; Appears to pursue career
Torchy Blane in Panama (Clemens, 1938)	Lola Lane (Torchy) [Series 5/9]	Newspaperman	Sleuth and woman of action; Shared, but needs rescuing	Resists; Marriage proposal
Personal Secretary (Garnett, 1938)	Joy Hodges (Gale)	Newspaperman	Sleuth; Shared; Proves more successful than male	Resists; Chooses marriage
Five of a Kind (Leeds, 1938)	Claire Trevor (Chris)	Newspaperman, but career saved by male rival	Non-investigator; Competent but male 'rescues' her	N/A Marriage
Torchy Gets Her Man (Beaudine, 1938)	Glenda Farrell (Torchy) [Series 6/9]	Newspaperman	Sleuth; Primary; Assisted by male comic relief; Needs rescuing	Resists; Romance & pursues career
Off the Record (Flood, 1939)	Joan Blondell (Jane)	Aspiring → homemaker	Non-investigator; Social problem re: children/crime	N/A Wants marriage
Torchy Blane in Chinatown (Beaudine, 1939)	Glenda Farrell (Torchy) [Series 7/9]	Newspaperman	Sleuth; Shared; Ahead of the police	Resists; Romance & pursues career

Girl Reporters[1]

Title (Director, Year) [script only]	Actor (Character) [Series]	Agency as a reporter —Newspaperman, aspiring, sobbie[2] —Sex as impediment or asset	Agency as a detective —Primary, shared, secondary, minor[3] —Sleuth, crime-fighter, scoop only[4]	Conclusions —Resists, partly, upholds[5] —Marriage vs. career[6]
1930s (cont'd.)				
The Adventures of Jane Arden (Morse, 1939)	Rosella Towne (Jane)	Newspaperman	Sleuth; Undercover; Shared; Very intelligent but needs rescuing	Resists; Romance; Career unclear
Torchy Runs for Mayor (McCarey, 1939)	Glenda Farrell (Torchy) [Series 8/9]	Newspaperman; Reputation allows her to run for mayor	Sleuth; Shared; Needs rescuing	Resists; Romance & pursues career
Mr. Wong in Chinatown (Nigh, 1939)	Marjorie Reynolds (Bobbie L.) [Series 1/3][7]	Newspaperman; Smart & competent but screams & interferes	Sleuth; Secondary to two male detectives; saves male's life	Resists mainly; Pursues career
Torchy Blane... Playing with Dynamite (Smith, 1939)	Jane Wyman (Torchy) [Series 9/9]	Newspaperman	Crime-fighter; Undercover; Primary	Resists; Romance & pursues career
The Invisible Killer (Newfield, 1939)	Sue Walker (Grace)	Newspaperman; Skilled w/reputation for scooping the police regularly	Sleuth; Shared; Needs rescuing	Resists; Chooses marriage

1940s

Emergency Squad (Dmytryk, 1940)	Louise Campbell (Betty)	Cub → Newspaperman; Sex = asset	Crime-fighter; Primary; Witnesses the truth, but needs rescuing	Resists; Romance; Career unclear
City of Chance (Cortez, 1940)	Lynn Bari (Julie)	Newspaperman	Crime-fighter; Undercover for DA in casino; Focus on romance vs. mystery	Resists mainly; Chooses marriage
The Fatal Hour (Nigh, 1940)	Marjorie Reynolds (Bobbie L.) [Series 2/3]	Newspaperman; More respected than first outing but faints at key moment	Scoop mainly; Secondary to two male detectives	Resists mainly; Romance & pursues career
His Girl Friday (Hawks, 1940)	Rosalind Russell (Hildy)	Newspaperman; But wants to quit the business for "normal" married life	Non-investigator; Emphasis on her skills as a newsmonger	N/A Marriage & pursues career
Doomed to Die (Nigh, 1940)	Marjorie Reynolds Bobbie L.) [Series 3/3]	Newspaperman	Non-investigation; Scoop only; Will report findings of two male detectives	N/A Romance & pursues career
Double Alibi (Rosen, 1941)	Margaret Lindsay (Sue)	Newspaperman; Sex = impediment	Sleuth; Shared; Works with the falsely-accused killer	Resists; Chooses marriage
Sleepers West (Forde, 1941)	Lynn Bari (Kay)	Newspaperman	Non-investigator; Scoop only; Former fiancée of male series detective	N/A Romance
City of Missing Girls (Clifton, 1941)	Astrid Allwyn (Nora)	Newspaperman; Her scoops make the DA (love interest) look incompetent	Sleuth; Undercover; Secondary	Upholds; Chooses marriage

Girl Reporters[1]

Title (Director, Year) [script only]	Actor (Character) [Series]	Agency as a reporter —Newspaperman, aspiring, sobbie[2] —Sex as impediment or asset	Agency as a detective —Primary, shared, secondary, minor[3] —Sleuth, crime-fighter, scoop only[4]	Conclusions —Resists, partly, upholds[5] —Marriage vs. career[6]
1940s (cont'd.)				
Mr. District Attorney (Morgan, 1941)	Florence Rice (Terry) [Series 1/3]	Newspaperman	Sleuth; Shared	Resists; Romance; Career unclear
The Saint's Vacation (Fenton, 1941)	Sally Gray (Mary)	Aspiring; Love interest for male series detective	Non-investigator; Scoop only	N/A Romance
Bride Wore Crutches (Traube, 1941)	Lynne Roberts (Midge)	Newspaperman	Non-investigator; Merely trains the male cub reporter	N/A Marries
Mystery Ship (Landers, 1941)	Lola Lane (Pat)	Aspiring	Crime-fighter but more scoop than sleuthing; More interference than agency	Partly (but parody); Wants marriage
Man at Large (Forde, 1941)	Marjorie Weaver (Dallas)	Aspiring, but never seen bringing in a story	Sleuth; Shared; Figures out several leads but less competent than male	Partly; Chooses marriage
I Killed that Man (Rosen, 1941)	Joan Woodbury (Geri)	Newspaperman Sex = asset	Sleuth; Shared; Skilled but confides in the real killer	Resists; Chooses marriage
Sealed Lips (Waggner, 1942)	June Clyde (Lois)	Newspaperman	Non-investigator; Scoop only	N/A Chooses marriage

Film	Actress (character)	Career/Role	Sleuth role	Outcome
Corpse Vanishes (Fox, 1942)	Luana Walters (Pat)	Aspiring → newspaperman Gets the scoop but faints	Sleuth; Primary but assisted by male; Potential victim	Resists mainly (but parody); Chooses career
Falcon Takes Over (Reis, 1942)	Lynn Bari (Ann)	Aspiring; Love interest for male series detective	Minor; Sleuthing not shown; Scoop only	N/A Romance
Just off Broadway (Leeds, 1942)	Marjorie Weaver (Judy)	Newspaperman	Sleuth; Secondary; Assists male series detective	Partly; Romance
You Can't Escape Forever (Graham, 1942) [story Hi, Nellie!]	Brenda Marshall (Laurie)	Sob sister → some agency	Sleuth; Shared; Assists male	Upholds; Career failure; Marriage
The Falcon's Brother (Logan, 1942)[8]	Jane Randolph (Marcia)	Aspiring fashion reporter	Sleuth; Minor; Love interest for male series detective	N/A Romance
Boss of Big Town (Dreifuss, 1942)	Florence Rice (Linda)	Newspaperman in name only; Never seen at work	Non-investigator; Scoop only; Mainly love interest	N/A Romance
A Night for Crime (Thurn-Taxis, 1943)	Glenda Farrell (Susan)	Newspaperman Sex = asset	Sleuth; Shared; In second half, demonstrates agency	Resists; Will marry; Career unclear
Criminals Within (Lewis, 1943)	Ann Doran (Linda)	Newspaperman; Successful: keeps apartment & maid	Sleuth; Secondary; Appears halfway through but important character	Resists (but minor role); Romance; Career unclear
Rogues' Gallery (Herman, 1944)	Robin Raymond (Patsy)	Newspaperman	Sleuth; Shared; Very competent	Resists (but parody); No romance; Pursues career

311

Girl Reporters[1]

Title (Director, Year) [script only]	Actor (Character) [Series]	Agency as a reporter —Newspaperman, aspiring, sobbie[2] —Sex as impediment or asset	Agency as a detective —Primary, shared, secondary, minor[3] —Sleuth, crime-fighter, scoop only[4]	Conclusions —Resists, partly, upholds[5] —Marriage vs. career[6]
1940s (cont'd.)				
Midnight Manhunt (Thomas, 1945)	Ann Savage (Gallagher)	Sob sister→ newspaperman but rival gets her job on good paper	Crime-fighter; Shared; More witness than investigator	Partly; Romance & Romance & pursues career
Traffic in Crime (Lesander, 1946)	Anne Nagel (Ann)	Reporter in name only; Does not pursue a story	Non-investigator; Mainly love interest for male detective	N/A
Corpse came C.O.D. (Levin, 1947)	Joan Blondell (Rosemary)	Newspaperman	Sleuth; Secondary; Appears a third of the way in	Resists (but minor role); Will marry
Trouble with Women (Lanfiled, 1947)	Theresa Wright (Kate)	Newspaperman but finds the business unethical	Non-investigator; Undercover as student; Scoop only	N/A Chooses marriage
Whispering City (Otsep, 1947) [Distrib: RKO]	Mary Anderson (Mary)	Newspaperman	Sleuth; Primary; Male takes over when she pretends to be dead to trick the killer	Resists; Romance; Career unclear
Big Town after Dark (Thomas, 1947)	Hillary Brooke (Lorelei) [Series 3/4]	Newspaperman in name only; Never seen at work	Sleuth; Minor; Mainly love interest for male detective	Partly; Romance & pursues career

Film	Actress (Character)	Career trajectory	Role		
Big Town Scandal (Thomas, 1948)	Hillary Brooke (Lorelei) [Series 4/4]	Newspaperman in name only; Never seen at work	Non-investigator; Social problem film re: children & crime	N/A	Romance & pursues career
Behind Locked Doors (Boetticher, 1948)	Lucille Bremer (Kathy)	Newspaperman → quits business because business is unethical	Sleuth; Minor; Assists but male goes undercover	Resists (but minor role);	Chooses marriage
Follow Me Quietly (Fleischer, 1949)	Dorothy Patrick (Ann)	Magazine writer; Will report the male's findings	Non-investigator; Sent home by male investigators; Mainly love interest	Upholds;	Will marry
The Lone Wolf and His Lady (Hoffman, 1949)	June Vincent (Grace)	Promoted: research → police reporter	Non-investigator; Assists love interest in clearing his name and claiming reward	N/A	Romance; Career unclear
House across the Street (Bare, 1949) [story Hi, Nellie]	Janis Paige (Kit)	Aspiring → loss of interest in career	Sleuth; Shared; More competent than male but loses interest in sleuthing	Partly;	Will marry
Crime of Passion (Oswald, 1957)	Barbara Stanwyck (Kathy)	Sob sister → housewife → murderer	Criminal; Her husband investigates the murder she commits	Upholds;	Will be punished

Female Detectives[1]

Title (Director, Year) [script only]	Actor (Character) [Series]	Type of detective —Undercover, official, amateur	Agency as a detective —Primary, shared, secondary, minor[3] —Sleuth, crime-fighter, criminalist[4]	Conclusions —Resists, partly, upholds[5] —Marriage vs. career[6]
1920s				
Girl from Havana (Stoloff, 1929) [script only]	Lola Lane (Joan)	Official; Undercover jewelry detective	Sleuth and Crime-fighter; Primary	Seems to resist
1930s				
Miss Pinkerton (Bacon, 1932) [see Nurse's Secret]	Joan Blondell (Nurse Adams)	Official amateur; Undercover agent; Nurse on a private case	Sleuth; Shared; Investigates with male; Smart & driven	Resists; Chooses job; Might marry
Penguin Pool Murder (Archainbaud, 1932)	Edna May Oliver (Hildegarde) [Series 1/6]	Amateur; Schoolteacher	Sleuth; Shared; Smart & driven; Proves more competent than the male	Resists; Accepts proposal; Career unclear
Woman Unafraid (Cowen, 1934)	Lucile Gleason (Augusta)	Professional; Police woman	Sleuth; Primary; Smart & driven	Resists; Spinster; Pursues career
Woman Condemned (Reid, 1934)	Claudia Dell (Barbara)	Professional; Private detective; Undercover for police	Crime-fighter; Secondary; Fakes confession to smoke out real killer	Resists mainly; Will marry
Murder on the Blackboard (Archainbaud, 1934)	Edna May Oliver (Hildegarde) [Series 2/6]	Amateur; Schoolteacher	Sleuth; Primary; Smart & driven; Proves more competent than the male	Resists; Spinster; Pursues career

Film (Director, Year)	Actress (Character)	Role	Sleuth Role	Marriage/Romance
Murder on a Honeymoon (Corrigan, 1935)	Edna May Oliver (Hildegarde) [Series 3/6]	Amateur; Schoolteacher	Sleuth Primary; Smart & driven; Proves more competent than the male	Resists; Spinster; Pursues career
While the Patient Slept (Enright, 1935)	Aline MacMahon (Sarah K.) [Series 1/6]	Amateur; Nurse on a private case	Sleuth; Minor for first half then secondary to male	Resists; Proposal
Murder of Dr. Harrigan (McDonald, 1936)	Kay Linaker (Sally K.) [Series 2/6]	Amateur; Nurse at a hospital	Sleuth; Minor for first half then secondary to male	Resists; Chooses marriage
The Rogues' Tavern (Hill, 1936)	Barbara Pepper (Marjorie)	Amateur; Store detective	Sleuth; Shared with police detective fiancé	Partly
Moonlight Murder (Marin, 1936)	Madge Adams (Toni)	Amateur; Socialite with a college science degree	Minor; Assists male; Analyzes evidence	Resists (but minor role); Romance; Career unclear
Murder on a Bridle Path (Killy, 1936)	Helen Broderick [Series 4/6]	Amateur; Schoolteacher	Sleuth; Shared; Not as competent as the male	Resists mainly; Spinster; Pursues career
Yellow Cargo (Wilbur, 1936)	Eleanor Hunt (Bobbie R.) [Series 1/4]	Official; Undercover; Dept. of Justice agent posing as girl reporter	Sleuth; Secondary; Assists, and is rescued by the male	Resists; Romance & pursues career
15 Maiden Lane (Dwan, 1936) [script only]	Claire Trevor (Jane)	Amateur; Undercover as jewel thief	Crime-fighter	N/A Abandons career

Female Detectives[1]

Title (Director, Year) [script only]	Actor (Character) [Series]	Type of detective —Undercover, official, amateur	Agency as a detective —Primary, shared, secondary, minor[3] —Sleuth, crime-fighter, criminalist[4]	Conclusions —Resists, partly, upholds[5] —Marriage vs. career[6]
1930s (cont'd.)				
Laughing at Trouble (Strayer, 1936)	Jane Darwell (Glory)	Amateur; Newspaper publisher	Sleuth; Primary; Wise	Resists; Rejects romance
The Plot Thickens (Holmes, 1936)	ZaSu Pitts (Hildegarde) [Series 5/6]	Amateur; Schoolteacher (in name only)	Sleuth; Primary; More competent than the male but is daffy	Resists; Spinster but romance; Pursues career
Girl from Scotland Yard (Vignoli, 1937)	Karen Morley (Linda)	Official; Government agent (UK); Aviatrix	Crime-fighter; Shared; Works with male reporter	Resists; Romance; career likely
Great Hospital Mystery (Tinling, 1937)	Jane Darwell (Miss Keats) [Series 4/6]	Amateur; Nurse at a hospital	Sleuth; Shared; Sets trap for killer; Claims she knew all along	Resists; Spinster; Pursues career
Bank Alarm (Gasnier, 1937)	Eleanor Hunt (Bobbie R.) [Series 4/4]	Official; Dept. of Justice agent but downgraded to male agent's assistant	Sleuth; Shared; Significant investigator; Very strong but rescued by male	Resists; Romance
Forty Naughty Girls (Cline, 1937)	ZaSu Pitts (Hildegarde) [Series 6/6]	Amateur (profession not mentioned)	Sleuth; Primary; More competent than the male but is daffy	Resists; Spinster but romance

Film (Director, Year)	Actress (Character)	Status / Occupation	Role	Outcome
The Patient in Room 18 (Connolly, 1938)	Ann Sheridan (Sara K.) [Series 5/6]	Amateur; Nurse at a hospital	Sleuth; Secondary; Investigates for the male	Resists; Romance; Career unclear
Mystery House (Smith, 1938)	Ann Sheridan (Sarah K.) [Series 6/6]	Amateur; Nurse on a private case	Sleuth; Minor; Assists male detective; Sounding board vs. investigative agency	Partly; Proposal; Career unclear
Mad Miss Manton (Leigh, 1938)	Barbara Stanwyck (Melsa)	Amateur; Socialite Class is an issue	Sleuth; Shared; Works with male and alone (or with socialite friends)	Resists; Proposal; No career to abandon
Nancy Drew, Detective (Clemens, 1938)	Bonita Granville (Nancy) Series 1/4	Amateur; Teenaged socialite	Sleuth; Primary; Enlists assistance of male neighbor	Resists; N/A
Homicide Bureau (Coleman, 1939)	Rita Hayworth (J.G.)	Official; Police forensic scientist; Sex = an issue	Forensics; Minor; Analyzes evidence only	Resists (but minor role); Will marry
Nancy Drew Reporter (Clemens, 1939)	Bonita Granville (Nancy) [Series 2/4]	Amateur; Teenaged socialite	Sleuth; Primary; Enlists assistance of male neighbor	Resists; N/A
Let Us Live (Brahm, 1939)	Margaret O'Sullivan (Mary)	Amateur; Waitress	Sleuth; Shared; Tenacious & driven to clear fiancé's name; Investigates w/police	Resists; Fiancé is freed but broken
They Made Her a Spy (Hively, 1939)	Sally Eilers (Irene)	Official; Undercover for army intelligence	Crime-fighter; Primary	Resists; Will marry

Female Detectives[1]

Title (Director, Year) [script only]	Actor (Character) [Series]	Type of detective —Undercover, official, amateur	Agency as a detective —Primary, shared, secondary, minor[3] —Sleuth, crime-fighter, criminalist[4]	Conclusions —Resists, partly, upholds[5] —Marriage vs. career[6]
1930s (cont'd.)				
Nancy Drew, Trouble Shooter (Clemens, 1939)	Bonita Granville (Nancy) [Series 3/4]	Amateur; Teenaged socialite	Sleuth; Primary; Enlists assistance of male neighbor	Resists; N/A
Nancy Drew and the Hidden Staircase (Clemens, 1939)	Bonita Granville (Nancy) [Series 4/4]	Amateur; Teenaged socialite	Sleuth; Primary; Enlists assistance of male neighbor	Resists; N/A
Private Detective (Smith, 1939) [Torchy script]	Jane Wyman (Jinx)	Professional; Private detective	Sleuth; Shared; Investigates independently but needs rescuing	Resists mainly; Chooses marriage
1940s				
Honeymoon Deferred (Landers, 1940)	Margaret Lindsay (Janet)	Amateur; Socialite marries insurance detective	Sleuth; Shared; Resourceful and intelligent but confides in the real killer	Partly; Dedicates self to marriage
Midnight Limited (Bretherton, 1940)	Marjorie Reynolds (Joan)	Amateur; Undercover for railway police	Sleuth; Minor; Assists the male but no leads of her own; By end he works alone	Resists; Marriage
Girl in 313 (Cortez, 1940)	Florence Rice (Joan)	Official; Jewelry expert; Undercover for police	Crime-fighter; Primary; Falls in love with male thief (but he dies)	Resists; Leaves; Career unclear

318

Film	Actress (Character)	Role 1	Role 2	Outcome
Stranger on the Third Floor (Ingster, 1940)	Margaret Tallichet (Jane)	Amateur; Investigates to clear fiancé of murder	Sleuth; Primary; but only briefly; Focus is on paranoid male	Partly; Dedicates self to marriage
The Nurse's Secret (Smith, 1941) [see *Miss Pinkerton*]	Lee Patrick (Ruth) [Nurse Adams]	Official; Undercover agent; Nurse on a private case	Sleuth; Shared; Investigates in conjunction with male; correct about some ideas	Uneven; Will marry
I Wake up Screaming (Humberstone, 1941)	Betty Grable (Jill)	Amateur; Investigates to clear love interest of her sister's murder	Sleuth; Secondary; Shared; Love interest takes over investigation from her	Initially → Partly
Shadow of a Doubt (Hitchcock, 1943)	Theresa Wright (Charlie)	Amateur; Teenager; Suspects uncle is the "Merry Widow Murderer"	Sleuth; Primary; Continues to pursue murderer after official investigators leave	Resists; Romance
The Leopard Man (Tourneur, 1943)	Jean Brooks (Kiki)	Amateur; Nightclub performer	Sleuth; Minor; Assists love interest but he is main investigator	Partly; Will marry manager
The Seventh Victim (Robson, 1943)	Kim Hunter (Mary)	Amateur; Schoolgirl; Investigates her sister's disappearance	Sleuth; Shared; Needs assistance/encouragement of male to continue	Partly; Will marry brother-in-law
Phantom Lady (Siodmak, 1944)	Ella Raines (Kansas)	Amateur; Secretary to clear boss's name	Sleuth; Primary; Some assistance from real killer	Partly; Dedicates self to marriage
Detective Kitty O'Day (Beaudine, 1944) [Series 1/2]	Jean Parker (Kitty)	Amateur; Secretary Smart but comic and faints	Sleuth; Primary; Assisted by accountant boyfriend; Trusts the killer	Partly; Continued romance and pursuit of work

Female Detectives[1]

Title (Director, Year) [script only]	Actor (Character) [Series]	Type of detective —Undercover, official, amateur	Agency as a detective —Primary, shared, secondary, minor[3] —Sleuth, crime-fighter, criminalist[4]	Conclusions —Resists, partly, upholds[5] —Marriage vs. career[6]
1940s (cont'd.)				
Seven Doors to Death (Clifton, 1944)	June Clyde (Mary)	Amateur; Milliner	Sleuth; Secondary; Assists male	Partly; Chooses marriage; No option for a career
Crime by Night (Clemens, 1944)	Jane Wyman (Robbie)	Amateur; Secretary of a lawyer	Sleuth; Minor; Assists male	Partly; No option for a career
The Adventures of Kitty O'Day (Beaudine, 1945)	Jean Parker (Kitty) [Series 2/2]	Amateur; Hotel receptionist	Sleuth; Primary; Assisted by travel clerk boyfriend	Partly; Continued romance and pursuit of work
Fashion Model (Beaudine, 1945) [script only]	Marjorie Weaver (Peggy) [Kitty series]	Amateur; Model	Sleuth; Primary; Assisted by boyfriend; trusts the killer	N/A; Continued romance and pursuit of work
The Lady Confesses (Newfield, 1945)	Mary Beth Hughes (Vicki)	Amateur; Undercover to clear fiancé's name	Sleuth; Primary, but is assisting the real killer	Partly; New romance
Deadline at Dawn (Clurman, 1946)	Susan Hayward (June)	Amateur; Stranger to help sailor clear his name	Sleuth; Primary, but assisted by the real killer	Partly; Marriage and leaves city for home town

Film	Actress (Character)	Role	Sleuth Role	Outcome
The Dark Corner (Hathaway, 1946)	Lucille Ball (Kathleen)	Amateur; Secretary for private eye	Minor; Assists male love interest but mainly his sounding board/support	N/A Will marry
They Made Me a Killer (Thomas, 1946)	Barbara Britton (June)	Amateur; Schoolteacher; Investigates to clear her brother's name	Sleuth; Secondary to falsely-accused brother	Resists (but little agency); Romance
The Black Angel (Neill, 1946)	June Vincent (Cathy)	Amateur; Housewife to clear husband's name	Sleuth; Shared; Assisted by the real killer; Ideas wrong	Partly; Dedicates self to marriage
Undercurrent (Minnelli, 1946)	Katharine Hepburn (Ann)	Amateur; Newlywed; Investigates husband's past	Sleuth; Primary; Competent detective but believes his lies and then is his captive	Upholds; New romance with brother-in-law
Undercover Maisie (Beaumont, 1947)	Ann Sothern (Maisie)	Official; Undercover police agent	Sleuth; Shared; Mainly competent; Kidnapped but proactive	Resists; Will marry
Shoot to Kill (Berke, 1947)	Luana Walters (Marian)	Amateur; Undercover as secretary to help her criminal husband	Collects evidence but is not seen actively investigating	N/A New romance
I Wouldn't Be in Your Shoes (Nigh, 1948)	Elyse Knox (Ann)	Amateur; Dance instructor trying to clear husband of murder	Sleuth; Minor; Encourages detective to reopen case but does investigate	Resists; Dedicates self to marriage
Sorry, Wrong Number (Litvak, 1948)	Barbara Stanwyck (Leona)	Amateur; Bed-ridden; Discovers murder plot	Passive sleuth; Various callers provide her with info but she does not act	Upholds; But murdered

Female Detectives[1]

Title (Director, Year) [script only]	Actor (Character) [Series]	Type of detective —Undercover, official, amateur	Agency as a detective —Primary, shared, secondary, minor[3] —Sleuth, crime-fighter, criminalist[4]	Conclusions —Resists, partly, upholds[5] —Marriage vs. career[6]
1940s (cont'd.)				
Smart Girls Don't Talk (Bare, 1948)	Virginia Mayo (Linda)	Amateur; Socialite lacking funds	Sleuth; Minor; Assists police last third of film	Partly; New romance
1950s				
Borderline (Seiter, 1950)	Claire Trevor (Madeleine)	Official; Police agent; Undercover dancer sent to Mexico	Sleuth; Shared until last third (male takes over)	Resists
Destination Murder (Cahn, 1950)	Joyce MacKenzie (Laura)	Amateur; Undercover at a club; Investigates father's murder	Sleuth; Primary; Initially competent but confides in the real killer	Upholds; Falls for the killer
The Second Woman (Kern, 1950)	Betsy Drake (Ellen)	Amateur; Secretary on holiday; Investigates male's "accidents"	Sleuth; Secondary; Does some key work but male takes over for climax	Resists (but minor role); Will marry
Woman on the Run (Foster, 1950)	Ann Sheridan (Eleanor)	Amateur; Housewife to help husband	Sleuth; Primary, but assisted by the real killer	Upholds; Dedicates self to marriage
Undercover Girl (Pevney, 1950)	Alexis Smith (Chris)	Official; Police academy trainee; Undercover; Avenging father's death	Crime-fighter; Primary	Resists; Romance; Career unclear
Affair in Trinidad (Sherman, 1952)	Rita Hayworth (Chris)	Amateur; Showgirl; Undercover for UK officials after husband killed	Crime-fighter; Secondary to brother-in-law	Resists (but mainly passive); Will marry brother-in-law

Film	Actress (Character)	Description	Crime Role	Outcome
The Blue Gardenia (Lang, 1953)	Anne Baxter (Norah)	Amateur; Phone operator; Cannot remember if she committed a murder	Passive sleuth; She gives up trying to uncover the truth and male takes over	Upholds; Will likely marry reporter
Witness to Murder (Rowland, 1954)	Barbara Stanwyck (Cheryl)	Amateur; Artist; Witnesses a murder	Sleuth; Primary; Competent but her sanity is questioned by killer & police	Upholds (but not respected); Romance

1970s

Film	Actress (Character)	Description	Crime Role	Outcome
Coffy (Hill, 1973)	Pam Grier (Coffy)	Amateur; Nurse; Vigilante justice	Crime-fighter; Some sleuthing; Primary	Resists; Shoots lover; Leaves
Cleopatra Jones (Starrett, 1973)	Tamara Dobson (Cleopatra) [Series 1/2]	Official; Government agent	Crime-fighter; Primary	Resists; Career over romance
Foxy Brown (Hill, 1974)	Pam Grier (Foxy) [sequel to *Coffy*]	Amateur; (profession unspecified); Vigilante justice	Crime-fighter; Some sleuthing; Primary	Resists; Future unclear
T.N.T. Jackson (Santiago, 1974)	Jeannie Bell (Diana) [Series 2/2]	Official; Government agent	Crime-fighter; Primary	Resists; Career
Sheba, Baby (Girdler, 1975)	Pam Grier (Sheba)	Professional; Private investigator; Vigilante justice	Crime-fighter; Some sleuthing; Primary	Resists; Career over romance
Cleopatra Jones and the Casino of Gold (Bail, 1975)	Tamara Dobson (Cleopatra) [Series 2/2]	Official; Government agent female operative	Crime-fighter; Shared with Asian	Resists; Career

Female Detectives[1]

Title (Director, Year) [script only]	Actor (Character) [Series]	**Type of detective** —Undercover, official, amateur	**Agency as a detective** —Primary, shared, secondary, minor[3] —Sleuth, crime-fighter, criminalist[4]	**Conclusions** —Resists, partly, upholds[5] —Marriage vs. career[6]
1970s (cont'd.)				
Friday Foster (Marks, 1975)	Pam Grier (Friday)	Amateur; Photojournalist	Crime-fighter; Some sleuthing; Shared with detective friend	Partly; Ends with romance
Velvet Smooth (Fink, 1976)	Johnnie Hill (Velvet)	Professional; Private investigator	Crime-fighter; Shared with two female colleagues	Resists; Career
Coma (Crichton, 1978)	Genevieve Bujold (Susan)	Amateur; Medical doctor	Sleuth; Primary and skilled but trusts the villain and needs rescuing	Partly; Unclear career or marriage
1980s				
Eyewitness (Yates, 1981)	Sigourney Weaver (Tony)	Professional; TV reporter	Minor sleuthing; Secondary to male janitor; Absent for key scenes and climax	Partly; Will likely marry
Mike's Murder (Bridges, 1984)	Debra Winger (Betty)	Amateur; Bank teller; Investigated death of lover	Sleuth; Primary but does not bring killers to justice	Partly; Career
Jagged Edge (Marquand, 1985)	Glenn Close (Teddy)	Professional; Defense lawyer; Romance with client	Sleuth; Primary; Assisted by detective friend; Kills guilty lover	Partly; Career (shoots her lover)
Suspect (Yates, 1987)	Cher (Kathleen)	Professional; Public defender; Romance w/juror	Sleuth; Shared with male juror; Trusts the real killer	Resists mainly; Career and romance

Film	Actor (Character)			
Black Widow (Rafelson, 1987)	Debra Winger (Alex)	Professional; Government agent but pursues the case on her own	Sleuth; Primary; Skilled if obsessed; Teams up with local police for final trap	Resists; Career unclear; No romance
Betrayed (Costa-Gavras, 1988)	Debra Winger (Catherine)	Official; FBI agent; Undercover as farm worker	Crime-fighter; Primary; Romance/ kills her target	Resists; Abandons career
Music Box (Costa-Gavras, 1989)	Jessica Lange (Ann)	Professional; Defense lawyer; Defends father	Sleuth; Primary, w/initial assistance; Denies truth about father's past	Resists mainly; Career and family
Physical Evidence (Crichton, 1989)	Theresa Russell (Jenny)	Professional; Public defender; Romance w/client	Sleuth; Secondary to male client (a cop)	Resists mainly; Career and romance
1990s				
Blue Steel (Bigelow, 1990)	Jamie Lee Curtis (Megan)	Official; Police officer Uses unnecessary force	Sleuth and Crime-fighter; Shared with male partner; Romance with killer	Resists mainly; Career unclear
V.I. Warshawski (Kanew, 1991)	Kathleen Turner (Vic)	Professional; Private investigator	Sleuth; Primary; Investigates new lover's death	Resists (but parody); Career
Deceived (Harris, 1991)	Goldie Hawn (Adrienne)	Amateur; Art restorer	Sleuth; Primary; Investigates husband's past	Resists; Career and daughter
Silence of the Lambs (Demme, 1991)	Jodie Foster (Clarice)	Official; FBI agent-in-training	Criminalist; Primary; Proves more skilled than males	Resists; Career

Female Detectives[1]

Title (Director, Year) [script only]	Actor (Character) [Series]	Type of detective —Undercover, official, amateur	Agency as a detective —Primary, shared, secondary, minor[3] —Sleuth, crime-fighter, criminalist[4]	Conclusions —Resists, partly, upholds[5] —Marriage vs. career[6]
1990s (cont'd.)				
Class Action (Apted, 1991)	Mary Elizabeth Mastrantonio (Maggie)	Professional; Defense lawyer; Romance w/superior	Sleuth; Primary and very successful	Resists; Career
Defenseless (Campbell, 1991)	Barbara Hershey (T.K.)	Professional; Defense lawyer; Romance w/client	Sleuth; Shared with official investigator	Upholds; Career and romance
Guilty as Sin (Lumet, 1993)	Rebecca De Mornay (Jennifer)	Professional; Defense lawyer	Sleuth; Primary and very successful	Resists; Career and marriage
The Pelican Brief (Pakula, 1993)	Julia Roberts (Darby)	Amateur; Law student	Sleuth for first half; Then male buddy takes over	Resists mainly; Abandons career
The Client (Schumacher, 1994)	Susan Sarandon (Reggie)	Professional; Defense lawyer	Crime-fighter; Assists young client in bringing down New Orleans mafia	Resists; Career
Copycat (Amiel, 1995)	—Holly Hunter (M.J.)	—Official; Police detective	—Criminalist/Crime-fighter	—Resists; Career
	—Sigourney Weaver (Helen)	—Victim; Assists police	—Criminalist	—Resists; Career

Film	Actress (character)			
Fargo (Coen, 1996)	Frances McDormand (Marge)	Official; Police detective	Sleuth; Primary; Pregnant	Resists (but comic); Career and family
Murder at 1600 (Little, 1997)	Diane Lane (Nina)	Official; Secret Service agent	Sleuth and Crime-fighter; Secondary to male buddy	Resists; Hospital; Probably career
Kiss the Girls (Fleder, 1997)	Ashley Judd (Kate)	Victim/Official; Kidnap victim assists investigator	Sleuth and Crime-fighter; Shared with male buddy	Resists; Career
The Bone Collector (Noyce, 1999)	Angelina Jolie (Amelia)	Official; Police officer	Criminalist; Shared with male buddy	Resists; Career and romance
2000s				
Erin Brockovich (Soderbergh, 2000)	Julia Roberts (Erin)	Official; Assistant at law firm	Sleuth; Primary and very successful; Investigates a large class action suit	Resists; Career and romance
Miss Congeniality (Petrie, 2000)	Sandra Bullock (Gracie) [Series 1/2]	Official; FBI agent	Sleuth and Crime-fighter; Primary	Resists (but comic); Career and romance
Legally Blonde (Luketic, 2001)	Reese Witherspoon (Elle) [Series 1/2]	Amateur; Law student	Sleuth; Primary; Knowledge of female beauty regimes	Resists (but comic); Career and engagement
Murder by Numbers (Schroeder, 2002)	Sandra Bullock (Cassie)	Official; Police detective	Criminalist; Shared with male partner; former victim of male violence	Ultimately resists; Career, perhaps romance

Female Detectives[1]

Title (Director, Year) [script only]	Actor (Character) [Series]	Type of detective —Undercover, official, amateur	Agency as a detective —Primary, shared, secondary, minor[3] —Sleuth, crime-fighter, criminalist[4]	Conclusions —Resists, partly, upholds[5] —Marriage vs. career[6]
2000s (cont'd.)				
High Crimes (Franklin, 2002)	Ashley Judd (Claire)	Professional; Defense lawyer	Sleuth; Secondary to male buddy; Denies truth about her husband	Partly; New career (husband dead)
Insomnia (Nolan, 2002)	Hilary Swank (Ellie)	Official; Police detective	Criminalist; Secondary; Investigates male sleuth	Resists; Career
Taking Lives (Caruso, 2004)	Angelina Jolie (Illeana)	Official; FBI agent	Criminalist; Primary; Romance with witness/killer	Partly; Career
Twisted (Kaufman, 2004)	Ashley Judd (Jessica)	Official; Police detective; Also suspect	Criminalist; Shared; Questions own sanity	Partly; Career and romance
Miss Congeniality, 2 (Pasquin, 2005)	Sandra Bullock (Gracie) [Series 2/2]	Official; FBI agent	Sleuth and Crime-fighter; Shared with female agent	Resists (but comic); Career and friendship
Untraceable (Hoblit, 2008)	Diane Lane (Jennifer)	Official; FBI agent	Criminalist; Primary	Resists; Career & family (no romance)

1. This list includes only films that I have viewed or read the scripts of. Note that "→" indicates a shift from one type of representation to another. I have separated the girl reporters into their own section in order to illustrate the shift in the character's evolution from the 1930s to the 40s.

2. I employ the terms as they are used in 1930s films: a "newspaperman" refers to a girl reporter that has a reputation for being active, driven, and competent as (or more so than) any male on the paper while a "sob sister" writes a society column and is presented in the film as lacking in terms of the drive or skill to be a career reporter. "Aspiring" refers to women who are working as sob sisters but show determination and often conclude the film regarded as successful newspapermen. A "cub" is an inexperienced reporter new to a paper. As women in a male world, their sex can be made an issue by the film either as an impediment (they are not respected by their editors or rivals because they are women) or as an asset (being female can give them advantages). In other films, their sex is a non-issue.

3. I distinguish between the degrees of focus on the female detective's investigation vs. that of the other and/or official investigator (usually the male rival). "Main" refers to the female detective and her investigation as the central focus of the narrative (if there is a male investigator then his investigation is secondary); "shared" to an equal amount of attention paid to the female's as well as the male's investigation (whether or not they investigate together or separately); "secondary" to when the female's investigation takes a back seat to the male's investigation (secondary refers to the amount of narrative focus rather than necessarily the quality of the investigation or the female detective's competence); and "minor" to a female character who investigates alongside a male detective and who uncovers an insignificant amount of information independent of the male.

4. Here I distinguish between the types of detective role: "sleuth" to denote women who investigate a case and/or try to solve the mystery of whodunit; "crime-fighter" to denote women who attempt to bring villains to justice without having a mystery to solve; and "scoop only" to describe girl reporters who do not investigate but merely want the scoop on the sensational story once the male detectives have brought the case to a close. I use "non-investigator" to indicate a female reporter that does not investigate a mystery and/or pursue a scoop. I also include a term "passive sleuth" to indicate a protagonist to whom information is imparted but she is not actively seeking information (i.e., a kind of detective by accident).

5. I use the terms "resists," "partly," "upholds" to explain the prevailing attitude represented by the film toward traditional female roles (i.e., being a wife and mother). In other words, some films "uphold" those traditional roles as the only ones that women should have a desire to fulfill and are critical of heroines who wish to pursue other types of roles (i.e., being a career woman); conversely, other films "resist" that assumption and are sympathetic towards women who wish to pursue non-traditional roles. For example, many films, especially from the 1930s, regard their heroine's engagement in detective work as positive: she is shown to be competent at detective work and she is not punished for her pursuit of a career nor is she expected to give up her career for marriage by the conclusion. Many 1940s films, however, regard the heroine's engagement in detective work as inappropriate work for a woman and her abandonment of it in favor of marriage as the only positive outcome: in these cases, I note that these films "uphold" traditional roles for female characters. I use "partly" to describe films that are ambivalent or divided on their representation of the heroine as a detective: for parts of the film (usually the first part), her desire and abilities to investigate are shown in a positive light and, in other part (usually by the end), negative. I use "N/A" for films that offer a female reporter who does not function as an investigator; typically, she is interested in getting the scoop once the male detective solves the mystery.

6. The female detective is often expected to choose between her career and marriage; however, some films see her embrace romance or marriage but do not indicate whether she will continue with her career: in these cases I use "unclear."

7. There are six films in the "Mr. Wong" series but Bobbie Logan appears in only three of the films.

8. Jane Randolph appears as girl reporter Marcia Brooks in *The Falcon Stikes Back* (Dmytryk, 1943) also and in a role similar to that in the previous film (i.e., minor).

Appendix III

Film	Estimated Budget	Box Office
Mike's Murder (Bridges 1984)	N/A	$1m
Black Widow (Rafelson 1987)	N/A	$25.2m
Jagged Edge (Marquand 1985)	$15m	$40.5m
Suspect (Yates 1987)	N/A	$18.8m
Betrayed (Costa-Gavras 1988)	$19m	$25.8m
Music Box (Costa-Gavras 1989)	N/A	$6.3m
Physical Evidence (Crichton 1989)	$17m	$3.5m
Blue Steel (Bigelow 1990)	N/A	$8.2m
Impulse (Locke 1990)	N/A	$2.5m
V.I. Warshawski (Kanew 1991)	N/A	$11.1m
Deceived (Harris 1991)	N/A	$28.7m
Silence of the Lambs (Demme 1991)	$19m	$130.7m
Defenseless (Campbell 1991)	N/A	$6.4m
Class Action (Apted 1991)	N/A	$24.3m
Guilty as Sin (Lumet 1993)	N/A	$22.9m
The Pelican Brief (Pakula 1993)	N/A	$100.8m
The Client (Schumacher 1994)	$45m	$92.1m
Copycat (Amiel 1995)	$20m	$32.1m
Kiss the Girls (Fleder 1997)	$27m	$60.5m
Double Jeopardy (Beresford 1999)	$40m	$116.7m
The Bone Collector (Noyce 1999)	$48m	$66.5m
Erin Brockovich (Soderbergh 2000)	$51m	$125.5m
Miss Congeniality (Petrie 2000)	$45m	$106.8m
Legally Blonde (Luketic 2001)	$18m	$95.0m
Murder by Numbers (Schroeder 2002)	$50m	$31.9m
High Crimes (Franklin 2002)	$42m	$42.5m
Legally Blonde 2 (Herman-Wurmfeld 2003)	$45m	$89.8m
Charlie's Angels: Full Throttle (McG 2003)	$126m	$100.7m
Taking Lives (Caruso 2004)	$45m	$32.7m
Twisted (Kaufman 2004)	$50m	$25.2m
Miss Congeniality 2 (Pasquin 2005)	$45m	$48.5m
Untraceable (Hoblit 2008)	$35m	$28.7m

Budgets are estimations only and box-office figures are for total domestic gross (see IMDb and/or Boxofficemojo).

Notes

Chapter 1. Introduction: The Case

1. The "Thin Man" series continued with Powell and Loy with *After the Thin Man* (Van Dyke, 1936), *Another Thin Man* (Van Dyke, 1939), *Shadow of the Thin Man* (Van Dyke, 1941), *The Thin Man Goes Home* (Thorpe, 1943), and *Song of the Thin Man* (Buzzell, 1947). The "Joel and Garda Sloane" series consisted of *Fast Company* (Buzzell, 1938) with Melvyn Douglas and Florence Rice, *Fast and Loose* (Marin, 1939) with Robert Montgomery and Rosalind Russell, and *Fast and Furious* (Berkeley, 1939) with Franchot Tone and Ann Sothern.

2. The series consisted of *There's Always a Woman* (1938) with Melvyn Douglas and Joan Blondell, and *There's That Woman Again* (Hall, 1938) with Douglas and Virginia Bruce. There were also a handful of non-series films, including *The Ex-Mrs. Bradford* (Roberts, 1936) with William Powell and Jean Arthur, *Dangerous Lady* (B. Ray, 1941) with Neil Hamilton and Jean Storey, and *Dangerous Blondes* (Jason, 1943) with Allyn Joslyn and Evelyn Keyes.

3. I use the term "detective" to indicate a female protagonist who—for whatever motivation—investigates the commission of a crime. Lisa Dresner prefers the term "female investigator" to "female detective" since the second term implies that the character is a detective by profession (6); however, I would argue that the term "detective" is the more commonly used one and the non-professional is easily differentiated with the term "amateur detective."

4. See Appendix I for a comparison of the two types of detective. The term "criminologist" is one used frequently in classical Hollywood film for someone who undertakes the scientific study of crime, criminals, and criminal behavior; the term "criminalist," on the other hand, is more typical since the early 1990s and refers to a specialist in the collection and examination of the physical evidence of crime.

5. These two character types are related to the two basic kinds of detective story as identified by Tzvetan Todorov: the classical detective story and the thriller (44). The classical detective story consists of two different narratives: (1) the story of the crime is the mystery to be solved, and (2) the story of the investigation leads to the uncovering of the clues that will allow a reconstruction of that past story. There is, therefore, a temporal gap between the events of the crime story and the telling of that story by the detective. Todorov argues that this gap disappears with the advent of the second form

of the detective novel: the thriller or what is now more commonly referred to as the hardboiled detective novel that peaked in America around World War II (47). The thriller sets the story at the time of its occurrence rather than as a retrospective and suppresses the story of the crime while highlighting the story of the investigation. In other words, rather than "whodunit?" the question that generates suspense in the thriller is whether the criminal will get away with his or her crime. Thus in films that focus on "whodunit," the detective-hero is the sleuth and, in the thriller, the crime-fighter.

6. In terms of the 1930s and 40s, many films have been ignored or forgotten by critics and audiences—whether due to availability or because of their secondary status as B-films. My research for this project has included extended visits to the *Margaret Herrick Library* and *UCLA Film and Television Archive* where I have watched hard-to-find films and researched studio files, photos, pressbooks, and contemporaneous reviews of films not available for viewing. *Detecting Women* thus includes original archival research with a significant filmography and analyses of films not previously addressed in scholarly studies; however, my own study has been guided by availability. I have attempted to be objective in choosing the films of which I offer close analyses as ones particularly indicative of the trends of which I have observed. I first searched databases, catalogs, and filmographies to seek out every film that presented a female character in a central role as an investigator into a crime. I hunted far and wide to obtain copies or view these films and was surprised at how many I have been able to track down via the Internet, in archives, and on television channels like *Turner Classic Movies* and *Silver Screen*. However, there were many I could not find—especially the silent films listed in the early chapters. In these cases, I have read the plot synopses provided by film historians such as Michael R. Pitts, Larry Langman, and Daniel Finn and online databases such as the *Internet Movie Database* and the *American Film Institute*'s catalog as well as reading contemporaneous reviews from trade papers (for exhibitors) and newspapers (for audiences) and, when available, plot outlines and scripts, as well as looking at film stills. All pressbooks, photos, and posters referred to were viewed at the *Margaret Herrick Library* in Beverly Hills, California.

Chapter 2. Detecting Criticism: Theorizing Gender and the Detective Genre

1. For more information on the history of women in law enforcement, see Benson, *IAWP*, and NYC.gov.

2. Typically, the gothic plot sees the heroine come to a mysterious house and begin to suspect that her husband/lover has committed murder (often his previous wife) and/or that he will murder the heroine. The heroine struggles with her paranoid fears and her desire to fulfill her role as dutiful wife/lover. In most cases, the man is proven innocent and the real culprit is caught and punished (Modleski, 59). As Diane Waldman explains, this plot structure remains associated with the genre even in Hollywood films such as *Rebecca, Suspicion, Gaslight, Undercurrent,* and *Sleep My Love* (29–30).

3. There is some question about the date of publication of *The Experiences of a Lady Detective* and/or *The Revelations of a Lady Detective*. While Craig and Cadogan suggest the 1861 date is correct, Kestner, Klein, and others support the 1864 date.

4. Emphasis in the original.

5. The Old Sleuth stories began in *Fireside Companion* in 1872 but became its own dime novel series by March of 1885, totalling 101 issues. The series was picked up by another publisher in 1897 for another 146 issues and then another for more exploits from 1908 to 1921.

6. Harry Rockwood's *Clarice Dyke, the Female Detective*, was reprinted in 1883 (the first edition date is not known) but the character is merely an assistant to her detective husband rather than a lone sleuth.

7. Some scholars report a later date for the appearance of Hilda Adams. This is because, although "The Buckled Bag" and "Locked Doors" were serialized in 1914, they were reprinted in an omnibus edition in 1933 no doubt due to the serialization and publication of *Miss Pinkerton* in 1932 (see Freier). *Haunted Lady* was serialized and published in 1942.

8. I have not be able to locate the vast majority of these silent films and rely on the descriptions offered by Langman, Pitts, and the AFI catalog for the information related here.

9. As Langman suggests, many crime films of the silent period did explore the humorous aspects of crime, and parodies and satires of the genre soon followed—including some featuring a female detective (179). *Calamity Anne, Detective* (1913) with Louise Lester and *The Female Detective* (1913) with Mae Hotely were farces; *Kate the Cop* (1913) with Hotely again satirized law breakers and enforcers; and parodies included Edwin S. Porter's *Miss Sherlock Holmes* (1908) with Florence Turner and *Miss Raffles* (1914) with Dorothy Kelly. *Detective Dorothy* (1912) with Sadie Osmond, *Detective Dot* (1913) with Frances Ne Moyer, and three films starring Bess Meredith as *Bess the Detectress* (1914) all featured a female detective for comedic effect. In the comedy *Peggy Does Her Darndest* (1919), a tomboy (May Allison) takes a correspondence course in detective work and then, using jujitsu, stops the robber from stealing the diamond that has been entrusted to her love.

10. Plot synopses for these films are available from the AFI catalog, Pitts, and Langman and Finn (*Silent*). Although the girl reporter also appeared in silent films and serials—including *The Girl Reporter* (1913) with Pearl White, *Adventures of a Girl Reporter* (1914), the serial *Perils of Our Girl Reporters* (1916), *The Girl Reporter's Scoop* (1917), and *The Fourth Face* (1920)—there is not enough information regarding the films to confirm whether or not the girl reporter acted as a detective in these narratives. I did have the opportunity to review the outline (entitled "The Last Chance" by Elaine Sterne) and the Continuity Script (copied for the MGM file 21 June 1930) for the film *The Floor Below* (1918). The outline of the story tells of a young copy girl at a newspaper, Molly O'Rourke, who is sent undercover as a crook. While the film offers a serial queen kind of action heroine, she does not play detective. Similarly, I was able to view *How Molly Made Good* (1915). Although the film follows the attempt of a young Irish immigrant straight off the boat to prove she can be a reporter, she is offered no mystery to solve. For a complete filmography of films featuring female reporters, please see *Image of the Journalist in Popular Culture* <http://ijpc.org/sobsbibliography21900-1920.htm> (accessed 30 July 2008).

11. I was unable to locate copies of the silent films to view nor scripts to read; however, from the photo stills (available at the Margaret Herrick Library), I could

deduce that the heroines go undercover and/or dress up in disguises as part of their investigation. In *The Web of Chance* (Green 1919), Dorothy Hale (Peggy Hyland) wears a flapper gown with pearls when at work at the detective agency; however, she dresses up as a maid to gain entry to a room. In *Wild, Wild Susan* (Sutherland 1925), Susan Van Dusen (Bebe Daniels) is a brunette who typically wears a well-cut tweed suit with a *la cloche* hat; however, at one point in the story, she dresses up as a man in a suit and a rather fake-looking beard.

12. Jane Marple appeared first in the magazine story, "The Tuesday Night Club" (1927), which later became the first chapter of the short story collection, *The Thirteen Problems* (1932). Her first full-length novel was *The Murder at the Vicarage* (1930) and 11 others followed sporadically between 1940 and 1976.

13. Grosset & Dunlap published 56 Nancy Drew novels between 1930 and 1979, and the series and spin-off series have continued since 1979 under the helm of Simon & Schuster.

14. Jane Marple starred in a British film series (1961–65) and two British television series: *Agatha Christie's Miss Marple* starring Joan Hickson was produced by the BBC (1984–92); the new *Marple* series starred Geraldine McEwan (2004–08) and then Julia McKenzie (2008–) is produced by Granada Drama and WGBH Boston. The spinster sleuth inspired America's own version, Jessica Fletcher, in one of the longest-running detective series on television, "Murder, She Wrote" (1984–96), played by Angela Lansbury no doubt because she had once starred as Marple in the British film *The Mirror Crack'd* (Hamilton, 1980).

15. Emphasis in the original.

Chapter 3. Movie Modernization: The Film Industry and Working Women in the Depression

1. Classical Hollywood style is best-known for the many techniques used to maintain continuity and viewer orientation: for example, the establishing shot identifies the axis-of-action; the 180-degree rule involves placing the camera always on the same side of the axis-of-action or center line; match-on-action editing maintains continuity from one shot to another as different camera positions "break up" the space of the establishing shot; and crosscutting creates spatial and temporal relations between different locales.

2. It would later be renamed the Motion Picture Association of America.

3. In terms of advertising, studios utilized an old ploy to drum up box-office business known as "pinking": a film would be advertised as "recommended for adults only!" or "no children under 16 permitted!" (Doherty, 109). Films that benefited from this practice were *Baby Face* (Green, 1933) starring Barbara Stanwyck as a fallen woman who uses sex to facilitate her rise; *She Done Him Wrong* (Sherman, 1933) starring Mae West with the sexually loaded dialogue typical of her pre-Code films; and *Freaks* (Browning, 1932) with its controversial exploitation of people with physical disabilities.

4. Recent scholars have dismissed this aspect of the myth, notably Maltby, Jacobs, and Vasey. The Code was enforced under Jason Joy; however, he may have appeared less stringent in his assessment of films than his successor Joseph Breen because he thought the overall positive message of the film could excuse or justify some of the individual

scenes. In other words, it was less a matter of whether or not the Code was enforced than the manner in which the Code was interpreted. For example, see excerpts of Joy's assessment of *The Sign of the Cross* (De Mille, 1932) (G. Black, 68–9). From my own research in the MPPDA files, it is apparent that Joy felt that as long as those characters who broke the moral laws of the Code were punished by the conclusion of the film, then the Code was being met.

5. I would add that while the popular conception of "Forbidden Hollywood" is that extramarital relations were presented explicitly, they were in fact always presented in a codified manner (e.g., there are no sex scenes) and sexual intimacy was left to the imagination of the filmgoer. Indeed, the suggestion that Joan Crawford's character has sexual relations with Lester Vail's in the pre-Code film *Dance, Fools, Dance* (Beaumont, 1931) is not necessarily more clearly represented than the suggestion that Robert Mitchum and Jane Greer's characters do in the Code-era film *Out of the Past* (Tourneur, 1947). The popular conception is that there is a difference in the degree of the punishment that a woman who engages in extramarital affairs must suffer—i.e., that only the pre-Code film would allow her to "get away with it." I would point out, however, that while Barbara Stanwyck's heroine in *Illicit* (Mayo, 1931) must marry James Rennie's hero to avoid scandal and to have true love, Bette Davis's character remains unpunished for her adulterous affair with Paul Henreid's and unmarried in the Code-Era film *Now, Voyager* (Rapper, 1942).

6. B-films were subdivided into four categories: Major-studio "programmers," Major-studio B's, smaller-company B's, and "quickies" of the Poverty Row companies (Taves, 317).

7. The prohibition of producing, transporting, and selling alcohol in the U.S. began in January 1920, when the Eighteenth Amendment to the Constitution (known as the Volstead Act) became law. The law was repealed in December 1933, with the ratification of the Twenty-First Amendment.

8. It was also a popular subject in feature films in the second half of the 1910s, although some of the films caused controversy with radical feminist messages. See Stamp.

9. For a thorough explanation of modernity, see Singer, *Melodrama*, Ch 1.

10. Similarly, reporter Patsy Clark (Robin Raymond) in *Rogues' Gallery* (Herman, 1944) explains to her editor that her lead "slammed the door right in my kisser!" He asks where her foot was, suggesting it should have been holding the door open. Patsy assures him, "Right where you told me to put it, chum! And it's gonna cost you 15 hunks of lettuce" for a new pair of shoes.

11. Emphasis in the original.

12. In the "Final Script" (17 Oct 1928) of *The Office Scandal*, writers Paul Gangelin and Jack Jungmeyer introduce the heroine as modern:

> Then the camera tilts down to the head and shoulders of Jerry Cullen (Phyllis Haver) as she sits on the edge of her desk, telephoning. She is dressed in rather somber working clothes and has her hat on, tilted at a rakish angle. She is listening to something over the phone. Her face is a dead pan, and she nods laconically, with a cynical "Yeah?". In two fingers of the hand that holds the telephone transmitter she holds a lighted cigaret

[*sic*]. Expertly she twists the phone receiver around to put the cigaret [*sic*] in her lips and blows out an inhalation as she continues to listen and nod. She is a seasoned reporter.

13. Here I use the term "modernistic" associated with Art Deco and not "modernist" associated with the idea of functionalism.

14. Note, that the pteranodon in the film has often been misidentified by critics as a pterodactyl with which the general public is more familiar.

15. The examples Mahdaviani notes are discussed in Goldberger (7 and 38) and Bruno (19).

16. The lyrics for three verses of the song are as follows:

> The rumble of the subway train
> The rattle of the taxies
> The daffy-dills who entertain
> At Angelo's and Maxie's [. . .]

> When Broadway baby says "Good night"
> It's early in the morning
> Manhattan babies don't sleep tight
> Until the dawn [. . .]

> Hush-a-bye, "I'll buy you this and that"
> You'll hear a daddy sayin'
> And baby goes home to her flat
> To sleep all day.

17. This fantasy still appeals to contemporary audiences as indicated by the popularity of films like *Pretty Woman* (Marshall, 1990) and *Maid in Manhattan* (Wang, 2002), in which a prostitute (Julia Roberts) and a chambermaid (Jennifer Lopez), respectively, pass for upper-middle-class women through the donning of new wardrobes.

18. Still # F5-577-579-580 (accessed at the Margaret Herrick Library, June 2006).

19. Still # F5-581 (accessed at the Margaret Herrick Library, June 2006).

20. Dimendberg's use of the term "the walking cure" comes not from psychoanalysis directly but in reference to urbanism in the work of theorists, like Kevin Lynch and especially Guy Debord who wrote about walks through Paris on the verge of redevelopment in the 1950s inspired by the *flânerie* of Baudelaire and the Surrealists.

Chapter 4. Detecting as a Hobby: Amateur and Professional Detectives in the 1930s

1. For further discussion on the 1930s male detective, see Gates, "Softboiled Heroes."

2. Again, I was unable to screen *Are You There?* (MacFadden, 1931) and therefore am relying on the "Continuity taken from the screen" version of the script written by

Harlan Thompson (5 Sept 1930). The film is a musical-comedy and is thus notable as the only musical foregrounding a female detective that I found. The film was set for release near the end of 1930 but then was shelved until early summer 1931—at least in terms of when the trade papers reviewed it. According to the reviewer from *Variety*, the film was "Made so long ago it's too bad Fox could not have forgotten it forever. [. . .] So bad it looks and sounds as though made in England" (14 July 1931). The reviewer for *Exhibitors Herald-World*, on the other hand, described Beatrice Lillie (here Lilly) as "smart-looking, clever and mirth-provoking. [. . .] Her personality and grace are registered superbly upon the screen (6 Dec 1930). Shirley Travis (Lillie) is the owner of London's "Female Detective Agency" and is known for her unorthodox methods. As potential client, Lord Geoffrey Troon (John Garrick) argues, "I grant you that her methods are unusual and a little bit ultra modern perhaps, but you must admit she gets results." Shirley is not just a detective but a detective who instructs future detectives. As she explains to her pupils,

> Girls, what you must learn is how to change your face in less time than it takes to think. This detective game is a fast and furious race. You must act while criminals wink. You must know weeks ahead of the cases that are due—and do every human thing you can—to be armed with facts, situations and a clue. But, remember—always get your man! Now then, girls, to business. Kindly join me in disguise number twenty-three if you please.

Her class then breaks out into song, as expected in a musical-comedy. Because the tone of this film is not serious (as far as I could glean from the script) and because it is a musical, it does not have much in common with the other films I consider. I, therefore, discuss the lyrics of the first verse and the chorus because they highlight the practice of disguises so common in the genre at the time.

> Disguised we creep with eyes that never sleep
> We hide our rosy-cheeks behind the beards of sheiks
> As we slue-foot here—and slue-foot there
> Sh! Sh! Sh! We are detectives.

[Note: "they are made up to represent different characters, Teddy Roosevelt, etc."]

> Eureka! Hallelujah!
> Oh what detectives are we—
> Because we have a [s]hiny badge and gun
> We've got the underworld on the run
> And to accomplish what we do—
> We make the criminal fit the clue—

What the film also suggests is that the genre of the female detective narrative was well established even if mainly through literature to such a degree as to allow this kind of parody of the topic to be produced as early as 1930.

3. In *Murder at the Vanities*, Gail Patrick plays a minor role as female private eye, Sadie Evans, hired by the star of the show "The Vanities" to investigate his ex-girlfriend, Rita. Because of what she uncovers about Rita, Sadie is her first murder victim and, thus, the female private eye is the victim rather than the detective in this early outing.

4. I will discuss *Private Detective* in a subsequent chapter since it was originally intended to be the last in the "Torchy Blane" series.

5. *15 Maiden Lane* (Dwan, 1936) is another film that I could not screen but, instead, my analysis is based on the "Continuity Script" (dialogue taken from the screen) by Lou Breslow, David Silverstein, and John Patrick (screenplay) (18 Sept 1936). Jane Martin (Claire Trevor) poses as a jewel thief but is, in reality, attempting to bring to justice the jewel thieves who have cost her uncle's insurance company so much money. In the end, Jane decides to give up being a detective after she is shot by the villains and a romance appears to be blossoming with Detective Walsh (Lloyd Nolan).

6. Rita Hayworth plays a similar kind of scientist in *Homicide Bureau* (Coleman, 1939). She is a forensic scientist employed by the police to analyze evidence. Her sex is a major issue for many of the men in the police department, including Detective Lieutenant Jim Logan (Bruce Cabot) whom she falls in love with. In the end, she agrees to marry him.

7. It would seem the "young man" comment is a joke. Gleason was actually a year older than Oliver (she was 49 when this film was released), and there is no other suggestion in the series that she is supposed to be older than him.

8. The write-up was entitled "Vital Statistics on *The Patient in Room 18*" (undated).

Chapter 5. Sob Sisters Don't Cry: The Girl Reporter as Detective in the 1930s

1. Yellow journalism is a term that refers to journalism that exploits or sensationalizes the news in order to attract readers.

2. The "fourth estate" refers to the press. The term originates in nineteenth-century writings about eighteenth-century France, referring to the power of the press to influence politics beyond that of the three estates—the clergy, the nobles, and the townsmen.

3. In addition to these city reporter films, there are a number of Westerns that feature girl reporters in the 1930s and 40s, for example *Cimarron* (Ruggles, 1931), *Forbidden Trail* (Hillyer, 1932), *Public Cowboy No 1* (Kane, 1937), *Gangs of Sonara* (English, 1941), *Kansas Cyclone* (Sherman, 1941), *Tonto Basin Outlaws* (Luby, 1941), *Jesse James at Bay* (Kane, 1941), and *Silver Spurs* (Kane, 1943). However, the focus of this book is to explore the female reporter as an example of the career woman and her relationship to the urban environment and also in films in which she functions as a detective.

4. While Good does see Torchy as a positive character, he challenges the assertion of previous critics like Dalton and Zinman that Torchy was "a progressive figure, a kind of proto-feminist" (12). Good argues that Warner Bros. advertised Torchy in posters through romantic and sexually suggestive images and uses the poster for *Torchy Blane . . . Playing with Dynamite* as the example. However, as I explain in the next chapter,

this film (the last in the series) demonstrated a regressive shift from a "proto-feminist" heroine as embodied by Glenda Farrell to a more traditionally feminine character as embodied by Jane Wyman. Although part of Good's project is to highlight Torchy as a fascinating character in the 1930s and in keeping with a broader trend of girl reporters, Good does not consider how the character underwent alteration over nine films, three years, and three different actresses.

5. The term "lady newspaperman" is used in *The Office Scandal*; however, in films of the 1930s, the girl reporter is referred to without the qualifying feminine term.

6. See Brown, 52–53 or Klein, 12n3.

7. Jerry/Gerry/Geri is the most popular name for the girl reporter—short for Geraldine. Timmy is short for Timothea; Tony is short for Antonia; Nosey is her nickname, no doubt, because she is so nosey; Pat is short for Patricia; and Torchy means "pertaining to a torch singer." A torch singer is a woman who sings torch songs: "a popular song concerned with unhappiness or failure in love" (Good, 12). Interestingly, Torchy's real name is revealed only in a few of the films, although, just as she was played by different actresses, so too it seems she is known by different names. In *Fly Away Baby*, she is Teresa, but in *Torchy Blane . . . Playing with Dynamite*, she is Helen.

8. Similarly, when Mabel attempts to visit Dr. Czinner, he protests, "I'm not dressed to receive ladies." Mabel assures him, "I'm no lady." Later, he finds her searching his belongings and threatens to turn her over to the conductor. He says, "If you were only a man . . ." and she replies, "Funny—I've often wished the same thing."

9. The other common implication of the term of the time would have referred to "heterosexually unconstrained lifestyles." See <http://en.wikipedia.org/wiki/Gay#History> or <http://www.etymonline.com/index.php?term=gay> (accessed 1 March 2007).

10. Certainly the girl-reporter-as-kept-woman was a recognizable trope at least by 1938 as a reviewer for *Variety* comments on Joan Blondell's girl reporter in *Off the Record* (Flood, 1939) being "dressed like the publisher's keptie" (22 Feb 1939).

11. Jane Arden was also the protagonist of a radio program starring Broadway actress Ruth Yorke (1938–39) and a film, *The Adventures of Jane Arden* (Morse, 1939) starring Rosella Towne.

12. The film also comes in a sound version but the version I screened was the silent one. From what I could glean from a review in *Variety* (24 July 1929), the sound version had only 1% dialogue and the majority of the sound was for effects like the paper going to print and phones ringing.

13. Here, I have quoted the line from the "Final Script" (17 Oct 1928), continuity by Paul Gangelin and Jack Jungmeyer (Scene 24). In the film, this line is somewhat altered and the words on the intertitle card continued off the screen so I can only reproduce it in part: "Whenever I need a m[an] on a big story, I find [I'm] running a ladies' r[?] room!"

14. Interestingly, both the AFI catalog and *IMDb* cite *Blondes at Work* as based on an original screenplay by Albert DeMond. However, having seen the two films, I have to concur with Dalton that the film is a remake of *Front Page Woman*. The stories are too similar to be coincidence, right down to the trick pulled regarding the jury's verdict. The AFI catalog also suggests that *Front Page Woman* and *Back in Circulation* are similar; however, the former is based on the short story "Women Are Bum Newspapermen" by

Richard Macauley and the latter on a short story "Angle Shooter" by real-life reporter Adela Rogers St. Johns.

15. Roy Chanslor also wrote the story on which *The Final Edition* (1932) was based, perhaps explaining why the editors of both films are both called "Brad" Bradshaw.

16. For example, *Torchy Blane in Chinatown* (1939) begins with a man being shot in a car. The shotgun blast makes his face unrecognizable; Torchy, however, instead of recoiling with horror, sticks her head in the car and inquisitively asks what happened to his head.

17. Farrell's 1932 contract with Warner Bros. expired in 1938; however, the series was very popular so the studio decided to search for a new Torchy. Although Ann Sheridan was rumored to be the replacement for awhile, in the end it was Lola Lane who starred in the next film.

18. Emphasis in the original.

19. Letter from Joseph Breen to Jack Warner at Warner Bros. regarding *Back in Circulation*:

> In addition to all this, the basic story is questionable from the standpoint of the general industry policy. It is a shocking indictment of newspapers and journalistic ethics. There is not the slightest doubt in our minds but that newspaper publishers, everywhere, will deeply resent the production of this picture and, possibly, aggressively oppose it. (5 March 1937)

20. In *Hi, Nellie!* Brad refuses to exploit a coincidence for a big story like the other papers in town do; however, this incurs the wrath of the paper's owner who then demotes Brad. It takes the solution of the mystery that Brad discovers along with the girl reporter's help (i.e., another big story) to get him his job back; in other words, he does not change the paper, its owners, or its readership, and success still equals scandal.

21. Having said that, I would point out that she then hires two "thugs" to prevent Eddie from broadcasting and later steals his broadcasting equipment. This film does not punish the girl reporter for bad behavior and, in fact, the stolen equipment becomes the means by which she can lead the police to the bank robbers.

22. Letter from Joseph Breen to Colonel S. Joy at 20th Century-Fox regarding *One Mile from Heaven*:

> We have been in receipt of a vigorous protest from the Association of Newspaper Editors and Publishers regarding the treatment of editors, reporters, and others in motion pictures. From our conversations on the subject, we take it that this particular scene is just the kind of action which the newspapers resent. Because of this, there is the danger that you may be subjected to severe criticism at the hands of certain newspapers around the country. (3 May 1937)

23. Notably, this interesting shot is not in the "Final Script" (17 Oct 1928), continuity by Paul Gangelin and Jack Jungmeyer. Instead, Scene 110 mentions the use of a mirror to show that Jerry is watching—"she notices that the mirror is so hung that it reflects Lillian and the detective through the half open door into the hall."

24. I viewed a printed copy of the address in the Terry Ramsaye Papers Special Collection, Georgetown University (3 May 2006).

Chapter 6. In Name Only: The Transformation of the Female Detective in the 1940s

1. Girl reporter Bobbie Logan also appeared in *Mr. Wong in Chinatown* (Nigh, 1939). Interestingly, in this film she is an independent sleuth for part of the narrative, even though the male detectives—Mr. Wong (Boris Karloff) and Captain Bill Street (Grant Withers)—complete the majority of the sleuthing. Bobbie's agency as a detective is eliminated by her second and third appearance in the series.

2. For example, as the reviewer for the *Motion Picture Herald* notes, the conclusion of *Bulldog Drummond's Peril* "as usual [leaves] 'Drummond's' long planned and long foiled marriage to 'Phyllis Clavering' about to be arranged anew in the final fadeout" (12 Mar 1938). Similarly, the *Motion Picture Herald* reviewer for *A Date with the Falcon* comments, " 'The Falcon' is again forced to postpone his wedding trip because of crime and the inability of the law to cope with it" (8 Nov 1941).

3. Republic intended to produce a series based on Phillips H. Lord's radio program, *Mr. District Attorney* (NBC and ABC, 1939–52) of which this was the first and *Mr. District Attorney in the Carter Case* (Vorhaus, 1941) was the second with James Ellison and Victoria Gilmore. The third entry was retitled *Secrets of the Underground* (Morgan, 1942) and was not advertised as being part of the series although the two main characters retained their names (played by John Hubbard and Virginia Grey). Although also based on the radio series and starring Dennis O'Keefe in the leading role, Columbia's *Mr. District Attorney* (Sinclair, 1947) changes the hero's name to Steve Bennett and offers him no girl reporter love interest. According to the AFI catalog, various news items at the time indicated that the film was intended to be the first of a series of seven, but no other films followed. I was unable to view the second and third films, but, according to the AFI summary, *Mr. District Attorney in the Carter Case* begins with Terry refusing to give up her career after they marry. Much like a "Torchy Blane" film, the couple's wedding is postponed when a story breaks and, while covering the trial, Terry bribes the bailiff to tip her off on the verdict before it is announced. And like Torchy, Terry investigates the case herself and uncovers the truth but also becomes the captive of the murderer. Lastly, she agrees to marry Jones in the end. Although the review of *Secrets of the Underground* in *Motion Picture Daily* states that Terry "contributes much of the evidence" (13 Feb 1943), the AFI summary of the film, however, suggests that Terry has less agency in this film and seems to be more of an annoyance to Jones than an aid.

4. In a letter from Joseph Breen to Jack Warner (24 June 1939), the film was referred to as *Torchy's Invitation to Murder*. A memo from Walter MacEwan to Wilk in reference to *The Adventurous Blonde* notes that the studio have to pay a $500 royalty to Frederick Nebel every time they make another "Torchy Blane" film (30 June 1937). The first "Torchy Blane" film was based on Nebel's story "No Hard Feelings;" however, Nebel's story featured a male reporter, Pete Kennedy, and girl reporter Torchy Blane is, in effect, the creation of Warner Bros. I cannot help but wonder if the decision to change the last "Torchy Blane" film into *Private Detective* featuring a female private detective was not, in fact, an attempt to avoid paying royalties.

5. I was unable to find copies of *Exposed* and *The Undercover Woman* to view. However, according to the AFI catalog summaries, in *Exposed*, Belinda Prentice (Adele Mara) is a budding protégé but it is her father, Inspector Prentice (Robert Armstrong), who takes over the investigation. In *The Undercover Woman*, Marcia Conroy (Stephanie Bachelor) ends up on a ranch when her car breaks down just before a murder is committed. She investigates alongside (or in a secondary position to) the local Sherriff (Robert Livingstone) and their solution of the case is sealed with a kiss.

6. *Maisie* (Marin, 1939), *Congo Maisie* (Potter, 1940), *Gold Rush Maisie* (Potter, 1940), *Maisie was a Lady* (Marin, 1941), *Ringside Maisie* (Marin, 1941), *Maisie Gets Her Man* (Del Ruth, 1942), *Swing Shift Maisie* (McLeod, 1943), *Maisie Goes to Reno* (Beaumont, 1944), *Up Goes Maisie* (Beaumont, 1946), and *Undercover Maisie* (Beaumont, 1947).

7. The series appears to have been well received by reviewers. For example, the *Variety* reviewer comments, " 'Detective Kitty O'Day,' one of the best films of its kind to come out of Hollywood in recent months, should establish Jean Parker very firmly in the role of comedienne. Her portrayal of a snoopy suspect in the midst of a profusion of murders is comparable with that of better knowns in large budget productions" (22 Mar 1944). See also the review in *Hollywood Reporter*.

8. Similarly Robert Lowery replaced Peter Cookson as her boyfriend and Johnny Jones became Jimmy O'Brien; however, Tim Ryan appeared again as the police detective (although here is called O'Hara).

Chapter 7—The Maritorious Melodrama: The Female Detective in 1940s *Film Noir*

1. Technically, the term "maritorious" is a manufactured one to offer a parallel for the term "uxorious," meaning "excessive devotion to one's wife." See Grandiloquent Dictionary <www.islandnet.com/~egbird/dict/m.htm>; AskOxford <www.askoxford.com/asktheexperts /faq/aboutwords/uxorious?view=uk>; and World Wide Words <www.worldwidewords.org/weirdwords/ww-mar1.htm>

2. For a complete discussion of the history of *film noir* criticism, see Neale, *Genre*, 151–77.

3. Hammett's novel was adapted twice before Huston's film—*The Maltese Falcon* (also known as *Dangerous Female*) directed by Roy Del Ruth (1931) and *Satan Met a Lady* directed by William Dieterle (1936)—however, Huston's was the first *noir* version of the narrative. For more on all the differences of the three adaptations, see Gates, "The Three Sam Spades."

4. As Roscoe Williams for *Motion Picture Daily* writes,

Although a story of today, a double murder mystery with a New York setting, this picture goes back to "The Cabinet of Dr. Caligari" for precedent in the use of camera angles, shadows, distortions, for mystery effects, adding sound tricks, echoes, audible thinking, for present-day touches. (5 Sept 1940)

Similarly, in a review for the *Motion Picture Herald*, W. R. W. notes,

> Producer Lee Marcus, director Boris Ingster and author Frank Partos
> departed from routine in treatment of this melodrama, combining with
> the account of two murders in today's New York City, the techniques of
> suspense and thrill first experienced by American theatergoers in 1921
> when "The Cabinet of Dr. Caligari" made newspaper and magazine copy,
> stirred discussion and drew money into the box offices. Here are employed
> the camera effects, accompanied this time by sound effects, which gave the
> attraction its novelty. (7 Sept 1940)

The casting of Hungarian-born Peter Lorre as the killer in the film also nodded to German Expressionism since the role that brought him international recognition was that of the child killer in Fritz Lang's German film *M* (1931).

5. *Deadline at Dawn* and *Black Angel*, another Woolrich adaptation released later the same year, both feature a hero who cannot remember what happened—and if he committed the murder because of an alcohol-induced blackout.

6. And the reviews at the time noted particularly the heroine's conversion from hard-hearted to nurturing. For example, the reviewer for the *New York Herald Tribune* describes her as "a harsh, plain-speaking but essentially soft-hearted type" (4 April 1946) and the one for *Variety* as "a disillusioned but warm-hearted taxi dancer [. . .] sympathizing with his helplessness and drawn to him despite her outwardly hardboiled attitude towards men" (12 Feb 1946).

7. The film is very conscious of Hitchcock's film: *The Second Woman* begins with a very similar opening scene to *Rebecca* in which the heroine's voice over explains how the story ended and shows an image of the burned down mansion.

8. Although neither *Phantom Lady* nor *Black Angel* was a big-budget film, *Woman on the Run* is noticeably a low-budget film in terms of the quality of the cinematography and sound track. In that sense, it would appear to have more in common with some of the other low-budget *noirs* I have already discussed (e.g., *The Lady Confesses*). However, as reviewers at the time noted, there was something superior about *Woman on the Run* that exceeded its humble origins. For example, in the *New York Times*, A. W. writes,

> Since it never pretends to be more than it is, "Woman on the Run" [. . .]
> is melodrama of solid if not spectacular proportions. Working on what
> obviously was a modest budget, its independent producers may not have
> achieved a superior chase in this yarn about the search by the police and
> the fugitive's wife for a missing witness to a gangland killing. But as a
> combination of sincere characterizations, plausible dialogue, suspense and
> the added documentary attribute of a scenic tour through San Francisco,
> "Woman on the Run" may be set several notches above the usual cops-
> and-corpses contributions from the Coast. (30 Nov 1950)

9. See Bratton et al., Doane, and Gledhill, "Melodramatic."
10. See Gates, "The Man's Film."

11. As Diane Waldman explains,

The plots of films like *Rebecca, Suspicion, Gaslight*, and their lesser-known counterparts like *Undercurrent* and *Sleep My Love* fall under the rubric of the Gothic designation: a young inexperienced woman meets a handsome older man to whom she is alternately attracted and repelled. After a whirlwind courtship (72 hours in Lang's *Secret Beyond the Door*, two weeks is more typical), she marries him. After returning to the ancestral mansion of one of the pair, the heroine experiences a series of bizarre and uncanny incidents, open to ambiguous interpretation, revolving around the question of whether or not the Gothic male really loves her. She begins to suspect that he may be a murderer. (29–30)

12. Uxorodespotic means "tyrannical rule by one's wife." See Babylon: <www.babylon.com/definition /uxorodespotic/English>

13. Stanwyck also played Leona Stevenson in *Sorry, Wrong Number* (Litvak, 1948), another female sleuth who is mentally ill. Unlike her 1930s and 40s predecessors, Leona lacks the strength of character to take action when she is confronted with the fact that she will be murdered that night; instead, she becomes hysterical. Leona fails as a female detective because she reacts emotionally (i.e., like a stereotypical woman) instead of taking physical action (i.e., like a stereotypical man).

Chapter 8. Femme Might Makes Right: The 1970s Blaxploitation Vigilante Crime-Fighter

1. The title of this chapter is taken from a review for *Foxy Brown* in *Variety* in which Beau. comments that "before femme might makes right, Grier and callgirl Juanita Brown have a brawl in a lesbian bar" (17 April 1974).

2. While Hollywood's recession led to the artistic rebirth of American film, the 1970s saw its financial rebirth. First, the industry underwent a restructuring: financial hardship forced the studios to seek the protection of larger conglomerates. For example, MCA took over Universal in 1962, and Gulf + Western took over Paramount in 1966 (Maltby, *Hollywood*, 173–74). The result of these mergers and buy-outs was a new era for the industry, dubbed "New Hollywood." Second, the 1970s saw the birth of the "blockbuster" with the massive success of films such as *The Godfather* (Coppola, 1972), *The Exorcist* (Friedkin, 1973), and especially *Jaws* (Spielberg, 1975). The progressive innovations of the Renaissance were over now that Hollywood had found a "sure fire" way to draw mass audiences, and the period of the blockbuster saw a return to the dominance of the big-budget genre films.

3. Three other films did feature female action crime-fighters: *T.N.T. Jackson* (Santiago, 1974), *Cleopatra Jones and the Casino of Gold* (Bail, 1975), and *Velvet Smooth* (Fink, 1976). Both *T.N.T. Jackson* and *The Casino of Gold* see their heroines fight the drug trade at the source in Asia, while the low-budget *T.N.T. Jackson* sees its heroine (Jeannie Bell) avenge her brother's murder which is related to the drug trade. Like the other films, the heroines are attempting to shut down the operations of the drug suppliers and these

suppliers are white- or black-, not necessarily Asian-operated. They are also there to find their missing "brothers"—for Jackson, it is literally her brother who has gone missing but, for Cleo, it is her two friends and agents from back home (and the first film), the Johnson brothers. Both films offer less of a sense of the drug problem back home and its impact on the black community. Similarly, there is more of a focus on *kung fu* combat (nicknamed "chopsocky" at the time in film reviews). Because these films are more in the James Bond vein of overseas adventure film rather than social commentary, I will not discuss these films in detail in this chapter. In the same vein, *Velvet Smooth* was a low-budget production made by Neshobe Films in an obvious attempt to cash in on the success of the Grier detective films. The film stars Johnnie Hill as private detective, Velvet Smooth, who is hired by local hood King (Owen Watson) to find out who is trying to take over his territory. Velvet is a very competent investigator and employs the help of two other women—Leah, a white woman completing her law degree, and Frankie, an expert at karate. The film's low production values are often a distraction and, overall, the story, dialogue, and acting are not that strong. However, the film is notable as the last of the blaxploitation films featuring a central female detective. Although it only lasted one season, the television series "Get Christy Love" (1974) featured a black, female cop played by Teresa Graves. Graves received a Golden Globe Best Actress nomination for the role, which is notable in itself. Sims suggests that the concept would not have made a successful blaxploitation film: "Graves' bubbly personality as Christie may not have sustained movie-going audiences. In addition, as an action heroine, Christie was not as violent as Grier's Coffy and Foxy Brown or as sophisticated as Dobson's Cleo. She was a 'superhip policewoman' in the words of series executive producer David Wolper" (114).

4. According to Dunn, Foxy Brown's surname was supposed to evoke "brown sugar" and "foxy" was contemporary vernacular for a "fine" woman (114). Sheba Shayne's surname may be a reference to author Brett Halliday's detective, Michael Shayne, played by Lloyd Nolan and Hugh Beaumont in films of the 1940s and Richard Denning in the TV series in the early 1960s. Cleopatra VII was the last pharaoh of ancient Egypt who is remembered for being as great a seductress of powerful leaders (like the emperor of Rome, Julius Caesar) as she was a leader of her nation; and the Queen of Sheba was the tenth-century BCE ruler of a Middle East kingdom—a fitting association since Grier was known as the "Queen of Blackploitation." Foxy Brown has seen the reverse of this naming trend: a female rapper adopted the name in the late 1990s to align herself with the associations that Grier established in 1974 (Dunn, 23–34). I exclude Friday Foster from this discussion since she is a character developed for a comic strip and her name was not determined by blaxploitation film producers or writers.

5. Box-office and budget numbers are elusive for many of these films so it is difficult to estimate the difference in terms of budget between a better production like *Coffy*, which was made for $500,000 and earned $2 million at the box office, and a low-budget film like *Velvet Smooth* or *TNT Jackson*. As Jack Hill explains, AIP allotted $500,000 for its "black" pictures and, although *Foxy Brown* had the same budget as *Coffy*, less money went into the production values because both he as the director and Pam Grier as the star were earning more after the success of the first films (35). *Cleopatra Jones* reportedly grossed over $3.25 million and *Foxy Brown*, $2.46 million (Guerrero, *Framing*, 98). *Cleopatra Jones and the Casino of Gold* proved to be a box-office failure and suffered harsh reviews (Sims, 105).

6. For further discussion of the critical arguments over Cleopatra Jones's similarity to Bond, see Sims (96–100). Interestingly, although Cleo may be a black female Bond, the Bond films were influenced by blaxploitation films—notably *Live and Let Die* (Hamilton, 1973) (see Norton).

7. The heroine's seduction of her injured boyfriend is likely a way to feminize her sexual aggressiveness by casting it in the vein of "sexual healing"—i.e., the heroine is nurturing her injured man through sex.

8. Every week, on the television series, "MacGyver" (1985–92), the titular hero (Richard Dean Anderson) was able to extricate himself out of desperate situations using everyday objects, his Swiss Army knife, and the roll of duct tape that he always seemed to have handy. His name is used today to connote someone who is able to create something useful from seemingly insignificant objects—i.e., "What are you? MacGyver?" or "He was able to macguyver the car and get it running."

9. Season 1, Episode 9: "Flame Red" (aired 2 Dec 2008).

10. "24: Redemption" was a two-hour TV-movie to bridge seasons 6 and 7 (aired 23 Nov 2008). Bauer has been avoiding a subpoena to appear before a Senate hearing back in the U.S. regarding his previous activities. The movie concluded with Bauer having to return to the U.S. and face the hearing if he wanted to see the boys rescued from their war-torn country and taken to the safety of U.S. soil.

11. Grier is referring to the television series "Bionic Woman" (1976–78) starring Lindsay Wagner and "Wonder Woman" (1976–79) starring Lynda Carter.

Chapter 9. Detecting the Bounds of the Law: The Female Lawyer Thriller of the 1980s

1. While Cynthia Lucia includes more female lawyer films in her list—for example, *The Accused* (Kaplan, 1988) and *A Few Good Men* (Reiner, 1992)—neither film follows the thriller plotline in which the female lawyer is, at some point, a potential victim herself. *The Accused* is not a detective film as the criminals' identities are known; instead, it is a film about seeking justice for a rape victim. *A Few Good Men* has more in common with the other male lawyer films of the "Grisham Cycle" as it is primarily concerned with the courtroom success of its male lawyer (Tom Cruise) rather than its female one (Demi Moore). I have also not included *Love Crimes* (Borden, 1992) in my discussion as it is an independently, rather than a Hollywood, produced film and not necessarily representative of the trend.

2. Glenn Close and Jessica Lange were in their late thirties in *Jagged Edge* and *Music Box*, respectively; and Cher and Barbara Hershey were in their early forties in *Suspect* and *Defenseless*, respectively.

3. Emphasis in the original.

4. Lucia suggests that two comedies in the early 1980s—*Seems Like Old Times* (Sandrich, 1980) and *First Monday in October* (Neame, 1981)—established "the codes of theme, structure, and representation" for the female lawyer film, but that *Jagged Edge* set the tone—i.e., as a psychological thriller (*Framing*, 2).

5. The erotic thrillers of the 1980s and early 90s were known for their "surprise" endings—e.g., the audience was left guessing which of the men in the narrative is evil.

Most notoriously the ending of *Sliver*—starring Sharon Stone, William Baldwin, and Tom Berenger—was reshot, changing the killer from one male lead to the other. As Jeff Giles noted in his review of the film,

> . . . it's impossible to ruin *Sliver*'s ending because somebody got there first. [. . .] Eszterhas's new ending short circuits the movie's tenuous logic. It even fingers a different villain, which means that at the eleventh hour somebody finally got around to telling the killer he was the killer. (31 May 1993)

6. See Appendix III for budget and box-office information.

7. For an interesting discussion of the foregrounding of the father-daughter relationship in *Music Box* and *Class Action*, see Lucia, *Framing*.

8. In his review of the film, Leonard Klady explains that Columbia executives were not interested in doing sequels and so kept the script but changed the characters' names (9 August 1987). Instead, the film stars Theresa Russell in the leading role. Although a perfectly adequate actress in other roles, as Manohla Dargis comments in a review for *The Village Voice*, in this role "Russell [. . .] is a disaster. In danger of becoming the Sondra Locke of art-house movies, she's taken on another role meant to prove her versatility" (7 February 1989). This film does looks like a "cheap" version of slicker films like *Jagged Edge*, but it is not the lower production values that this film suffers. Instead it is the often heavy-handed dialogue, over-the-top acting, and poorly conceived plot directions that make this film less thematically cohesive and interesting.

9. *Class Action* is not based on a Grisham novel; however, it does offer similar themes as the Grisham Cycle films. *The Pelican Brief* is based on a Grisham novel and stars Julia Roberts as a law student; however, the film is not a courtroom film and the investigative work is mainly attributed to Denzel Washington's reporter rather than Roberts's law student.

10. The film is loosely based on the case of *Grimshaw vs. Ford Motor Company*, involving a 1972 Ford Pinto that exploded when it was rear-ended (Marcheis, 12).

Chapter 10. Detecting Identity: From Investigative Thrillers to Crime Scene Investigators

1. Pressbook viewed at the *Film Reference Library*, Toronto.

2. Neither <www.boxofficemojo.com> nor <www.imDb.com> list box office for the film; however, Cowie notes that the film was a "big box-office hit, especially in the USA" ("Popular," 59).

3. The three African-American women to which Mizejewski refers are Tamara Dobson and Pam Grier in 1970s blaxploitation films (as discussed in an earlier chapter), and Whoopi Goldberg in *Fatal Beauty* (Holland, 1987). I have not discussed this last film as it is a comedy.

4. Betty (Winger) investigates the drug-related murder of her tennis coach Mike (Mark Keyloun). Betty is not a strong or determined investigator and, rather than bringing the criminals to justice, she merely witnesses their last retaliation. However, the film is ahead of its time in that it explores a theme that will dominate the detective

films in the 1990s: namely, that the complexity of contemporary urban life replaces face-to-face contact with mediated communication. For example, scene after scene sees Betty come home and check messages on her answering machine or leave messages on Mike's. Through her investigation, Betty sees many different sides to Mike through the portraits, surveillance photos, spontaneous Polaroids, and home videos that his male admirers have taken of him.

5. This is the same in the case of *Betrayed* (Costa-Gavras, 1988) in which Winger plays another detective: an FBI agent. Catherine is sent to a rural, mid-west community to investigate whether widower and single-dad Gary Simmons (Tom Berenger) is a member of a white supremacist group. Although the first half of the film is concerned with establishing Gary's true identity as a racist murderer, the second half deals with Catherine's struggle between being in love with a racist and wanting to do her duty as a law enforcer. Gary discovers her true identity and attempts to set her up as the shooter in an assassination; however, Gary has underestimated Catherine and she shoots him. Gary may feel betrayed by Catherine; however, Catherine feels betrayed by the Bureau. Disillusioned, she abandons her career to wander aimlessly around the America that she killed to protect.

6. Perhaps the best known and/or most popular lesbian detectives in fiction are Claire McNab's Inspector Carol Ashton, Penny Micklebury's Lieutenant Gianna Maglione, Barbara Johnson's insurance investigator Colleen Fitzgerald, J. M. Redmann's Micky Knight, Barbara Wilson's Pam Nilsen and Cassandra Reilly, and Katherine Forrest's Kate Delafield. For more discussion, see Betz.

7. For example, see reviews by Jay Scott of *The Globe and Mail* and David Denby of *New York* magazine.

8. For a comparison of the film to Paretsky's original character, see Munt (32 and 41–42).

9. Several reviewers in the 1990s refer to these films as "serial killer," "procedural," or "serial killer procedural" films. I use the term "criminalist" instead to encompass films and especially television shows with a focus on investigative procedure but that do not necessarily focus on serial killers. There have been a handful of other kinds of detectives; however, the criminalist has been the dominant kind of detective since *Silence* started the trend proper. Also often the focus of the other kinds of detectives is not a mystery: for example, both *Out of Sight* (Soderbergh, 1998) and *The Thomas Crown Affair* (McTiernan, 1999) see their detectives—a Federal Agent (Jennifer Lopez) and an insurance investigator (Rene Russo), respectively—fall for their prey—a bank robber (George Clooney) and a playboy-turned-art-thief (Pierce Brosnon), respectively.

10. A "crime scene kit" is the tool box that each crime scene investigator carries, stocked with swabs, baggies, powder, etc.; Luminol is the spray used in conjunction with ultraviolet light to reveal blood; partial refers to a partial fingerprint; hair tag to a hair follicle that has skin still attached to it (that can be used for DNA testing); epithelia are the cells that cover the human body (i.e., skin); perp refers to the perpetrator of the crime; unsub refers to an unknown subject; donor refers to the person who left behind a sample (e.g., semen, saliva, or blood). The others terms are acronyms: GSR for gun shot residue; M.O. for *modus operandi* meaning a habitual method; CODIS for the *Combined DNA Index System*; and AFIS for the *Automated Fingerprint Identification System*.

11. As Rob Salem notes in his review, by some estimates *Copycat* was the eighth film released in 1995 about a serial killer (27 Oct 1995).

12. My discussion does not include the next Lecter film, *Hannibal* (Scott, 2001), despite the presence of Clarice Starling (this time played by Julianne Moore), because she is no longer Demme's intriguing and impressive detective-heroine nor the focus of the film. Rather than being a meditation on gender and a well-crafted thriller like *Silence*, *Hannibal* simply functions to resurrect the cult villain and to let him loose on the world to commit gruesome murders. The film does not focus on Clarice pursuing an investigation but on Hannibal's exploits, and the killer is given no true adversary with which to match wits. In this sense, the film is less a detective film and more a serial killer horror film.

13. As I noted in the previous chapter, *The Pelican Brief*'s focus is on Denzel Washington's reporter as detective rather than Julia Roberts's law student. Similarly, *Murder at 1600* (Little, 1997), is primarily concerned with Detective Harlan Regis (Wesley Snipes) and his attempt to solve a murder at the White House in which the first family seems to be implicated. His Secret Service liaison, Agent Nina Chance (Diane Lane), joins him in his attempt to expose an internal cover-up involving some of the President's most trusted advisors. While *The Pelican Brief* was very successful as a "Grisham Cycle" film and starring two of Hollywood's biggest stars at the time, *Murder at 1600* was a box-office failure, as were many of the late 1990s action films that kept to 80s formulas.

14. *Along Came a Spider* is the first of the Cross novels but is the second Cross film. Spoiler alert: I will not discuss this film here, as the female detective is actually one of the criminals in the case.

15. The reviews for *Taking Lives* identify the film as an "Ashley Judd" film that does not star Judd (see reviews in *The Globe and Mail* and *Entertainment Weekly*) because Judd had dominated similar types of thrillers, including *Kiss the Girls*, *Double Jeopardy* (Beresford, 1999), and *Eye of the Beholder* (Elliott, 1999).

16. Official Web site for the film *Taking Lives* <http://takinglives.warnerbros.com> (accessed 10 April 2004).

17. Critics have used the terms "postfeminism" and "third-wave feminism" somewhat interchangeably. Chris Holmlund identifies "postfeminism" as a broader category that encompasses three distinct trends: (1) "chick" postfeminism "entails a backlash against or dismissal of the desirability for equality between women and men;" (2) "grrrl" postfeminists (aka third-wave feminists) are "happy to acknowledge the diversity among women that 'chick' postfeminism ignores, and they are eager to carry on first- and second-wave feminist struggles;" and (3) "academic" postfeminism "steeped in French, British, and American postmodern, postcolonial, poststructural, queer, (etc.), theory" ("Postfeminism," 116). Other critics like Cristina Lucia Stasia divide the movement into "postfeminism" referring to the social movement that rejects the institutional critique made by second-wave feminism, and "third-wave feminism" as a critical movement that builds upon the second-wave (239).

18. Emphasis in the original.

19. Emphasis added.

20. OnStar is a security, communications, and diagnostics system available in many General Motors vehicles.

Selected Filmography

15 Maiden Lane. Dir. Allan Dwan. Perf. Claire Trevor and Cesar Romero. Twentieth Century-Fox Film Corp., 1936.

Adam's Rib. Dir. George Cukor. Perf. Spencer Tracy and Katharine Hepburn. Metro-Goldwyn-Mayer, 1949.

Adventures of Jane Arden, The. Dir. Terry O. Morse. Perf. Rosella Towne and William Gargan. Warner Bros. Pictures, 1939.

Adventures of Kitty O'Day, The. Dir. William Beaudine. Perf. Jean Parker and Peter Cookson. Monogram Productions, 1944.

Adventurous Blonde, The. Dir. Frank McDonald. Perf. Glenda Farrell and Barton MacLane. Warner Bros. Pictures, 1937.

After Office Hours. Dir. Robert Z. Leonard. Perf. Constance Bennett and Clark Gable. Metro-Goldwyn-Mayer, 1935.

Ann Carver's Profession. Dir. Edward Buzzell. Perf. Fay Wray and Gene Raymond. Columbia Pictures Corp., 1933.

Anybody's Blonde. Dir. Frank R. Strayer. Perf. Dorothy Revier and Reed Howes. Action Pictures, 1931.

Baby Face. Dir. Alfred E. Green. Perf. Barbara Stanwyck and George Brent. Warner Bros. Pictures, 1933.

Back in Circulation. Dir. Ray Enright. Perf. Pat O'Brien, Joan Blondell, and Margaret Lindsay. Warner Bros. Pictures, 1937.

Behind the Headlines. Dir. Richard Rosson. Perf. Lee Tracy and Diana Gibson. RKO Radio Pictures, 1937.

Betrayed. Dir. Costa-Gavras. Perf. Debra Winger and Tom Berenger. United Artists, et al., 1988.

Big News. Dir. Gregory La Cava. Perf. Robert Armstrong and Carole Lombard. Pathé Exchange, 1929.

Black Angel. Dir. Roy William Neill. Perf. Dan Duryea and June Vincent. Universal Pictures, 1946.

Black Widow. Dir. Bob Rafelson. Perf. Debra Winger and Theresa Russell. Twentieth Century Fox, 1987.

Blonde Ice. Dir. Jack Bernhard. Perf. Robert Page and Leslie Brooks. Martin Mooney Productions, 1948.

Blondes at Work. Dir. Frank McDonald. Perf. Glenda Farrell and Barton MacLane. Warner Bros. Pictures, 1938.

Blue Gardenia, The. Dir. Fritz Lang. Perf. Anne Baxter and Richard Conte. Gottlieb Productions and Blue Gardenia Productions, 1953.

Blue Steel. Dir. Kathryn Bigelow. Perf. Jamie Lee Curtis and Ron Silver. Mack-Taylor Productions, 1990.

Bone Collector, The. Dir. Phillip Noyce. Perf. Denzel Washington and Angelina Jolie. Columbia Pictures and Universal Pictures, 1999.

Boss of Big Town, The. Dir. Arthur Dreifuss. Perf. John Litel and Florence Rice. Producers Releasing Corp., 1942.

Bride Wore Crutches, The. Dir. Shepard Traube. Perf. Lynne Roberts and Ted North. Twentieth Century-Fox Film Corp., 1941.

Career Woman. Dir. Lewis Seiler. Perf. Claire Trevor and Michael Whalen. Twentieth Century-Fox Film Corp., 1936.

City of Missing Girls. Dir. Elmer Clifton. Perf. H. B. Warner and Astrid Allwyn. Select Attractions, 1941.

Class Action. Dir. Michael Apted. Perf. Gene Hackman and Mary Elizabeth Mastrantonio. Twentieth Century Fox, 1991.

Cleopatra Jones. Dir. Jack Starrett. Perf. Tamara Dobson and Bernie Casey. Warner Bros. Pictures, 1973.

Client, The. Dir. Joel Schumacher. Perf. Susan Sarandon and Tommy Lee Jones. Warner Bros. Pictures, 1994.

Coffy. Dir. Jack Hill. Perf. Pam Grier and Booker Bradshaw. American International Pictures, 1973.

Coma. Dir. Michael Crichton. Perf. Genevieve Bujold and Michael Douglas. Metro-Goldwyn-Mayer, 1978.

Copycat. Dir. John Amiel. Perf. Sigourney Weaver and Holly Hunter. Regency Enterprises and New Regency Pictures, 1995.

Corpse Came C.O.D., The. Dir. Henry Levin. Perf. George Brent and Joan Blondell. Columbia Pictures, 1947.

Corpse Vanishes, The. Dir. Wallace Fox. Perf. Bela Lugosi and Luana Walters. Banner Productions, 1942.

Crime of Passion. Dir. Gerd Oswald. Perf. Barbara Stanwyck and Sterling Hayden. B.G. Productions, 1957.

Criminals Within. Dir. Joseph Lewis. Perf. Eric Linden and Ann Doran. Producers Releasing Corp., 1943.

Dance, Fools, Dance. Dir. Harry Beaumont. Perf. Joan Crawford and Lester Vail. Metro-Goldwyn-Mayer, 1931.

Daring Young Man, The. Dir. William A. Seiter. Perf. James Dunn and Mae Clarke. Fox Film Corp., 1935.

Deadline at Dawn. Dir. Harold Clurman. Perf. Susan Hayward and Paul Lukas. RKO Radio Pictures, 1946.

Deadline for Murder. Dir. James Tinling. Perf. Paul Kelly and Sheila Ryan. Twentieth Century-Fox Film Corp., 1946.

Death from a Distance. Dir. Frank R. Strayer. Perf. Russell Hopton and Lola Lane. Invincible Pictures Corp., 1935.

Defenseless. Dir. Martin Campbell. Perf. Barbara Hershey and Sam Shepard. New Visions Pictures, 1991.

Destination Murder. Dir. Edward Cahn. Perf. Joyce MacKenzie and Stanley Clements. Prominent Pictures, 1950.

Detective Kitty O'Day. Dir. William Beaudine. Perf. Jean Parker and Peter Cookson. Monogram Productions, 1944.

Disbarred. Dir. Robert Florey. Perf. Gail Patrick and Robert Preston. Paramount Pictures, 1939.

Doomed to Die. Dir. William Nigh. Perf. Boris Karloff, Grant Withers, and Marjorie Reynolds. Monogram Pictures Corp., 1940.

Double Alibi. Dir. Philip Rosen. Perf. Margaret Lindsay and Wayne Morris. Universal Pictures, 1941.

Emergency Squad. Dir. Edward Dmytryk. Perf. William Henry and Louise Campbell. Paramount Pictures, 1940.

Erin Brockovich. Dir. Steven Soderbergh. Perf. Julia Roberts and Albert Finney. Jersey Films, 2000.

Espionage. Dir. Kurt Neumann. Perf. Edmund Lowe and Madge Evans. Metro-Goldwyn-Mayer, 1937.

Exclusive. Dir. Alexander Hall. Perf. Fred MacMurray and Frances Farmer. Paramount Pictures, 1937.

Fashion Model. Dir. William Beaudine. Perf. Robert Lowery and Marjorie Weaver. Monogram Pictures, 1945.

Fatal Hour. Dir. William Nigh. Perf. Boris Karloff, Grant Withers, and Marjorie Reynolds. Monogram Pictures Corp., 1940.

Female. Dir. Michael Curtiz. Perf. Ruth Chatterton and George Brent. First National Pictures, 1933.

Final Edition, The. Dir. Howard Higgin. Perf. Pat O'Brien and Mae Clarke. Columbia Pictures Corp., 1932.

Five of a Kind. Dir. Herbert I. Leeds. Perf. Jean Hersholt and Claire Trevor. Twentieth Century-Fox Film Corp., 1938.

Fly Away Baby. Dir. Frank McDonald. Perf. Glena Farrell and Barton MacLane. Warner Bros. Pictures, 1937.

Follow Me Quietly. Dir. Richard Fleischer. Perf. William Lundigan and Dorothy Patrick. RKO Radio Pictures, 1949.

Forty Naughty Girls. Dir. Edward Cline. James Gleason and ZaSu Pitts. RKO Radio Pictures, 1937.

Foxy Brown. Dir. Jack Hill. Perf. Pam Grier and Antonio Fargas. American International Pictures, 1974.

Friday Foster. Dir. Arthur Marks. Perf. Pam Grier and Yaphet Kotto. American International Pictures, 1975.

Front Page Woman. Dir. Michael Curtiz. Perf. Bette Davis and George Brent. Warner Bros. Pictures, 1935.

Girl from Havana, The. Dr. Benjamin Stoloff. Lola Lane and Paul Page. Fox Film Corp., 1929.

Girl from Scotland Yard, The. Dir. Robert Vignola. Perf. Karen Morley and Robert Baldwin. Major Pictures Corp., 1937.

Girl in 313. Dir. Ricardo Cortez. Perf. Florence Rice and Kent Taylor. Twentieth Century-Fox Film Corp., 1940.

Girl on the Front Page, The. Dir. Harry Beaumont. Perf. Edmund Lowe and Gloria Stuart. Universal Productions, 1936.

Gold Diggers of 1935. Dir. Busby Berkeley. Perf. Dick Powell and Adolphe Mejou. First National Productions Corp., 1935.

Great Hospital Mystery, The. Dir. James Tinling. Perf. Jane Darwell and Sig Rumann. Twentieth Century-Fox Film Corp., 1937.

Guilty as Sin. Dir. Sidney Lumet. Perf. Rebecca De Mornay and Don Johnson. Hollywood Pictures, 1993.

Headline Shooter. Dir. Otto Brower. Perf. William Gargan and Frances Dee. RKO Radio Pictures, 1933.

High Crimes. Dir. Carl Franklin. Perf. Ashley Judd and Morgan Freeman. New Regency Pictures, 2002.

Hi, Nellie! Dir. Mervyn LeRoy. Perf. Paul Muni and Glenda Farrell. Warner Bros. Pictures, 1934.

His Girl Friday. Dir. Howard Hawks. Perf. Cary Grant and Rosalind Russell. Columbia Pictures, 1940.

Hold that Girl. Dir. Hamilton MacFadden. Perf. James Dunn and Claire Trevor. Fox Film Corp., 1934.

House across the Street, The. Dir. Richard L. Bare. Perf. Wayne Morris and Janis Paige. Warner Bros. Pictures, 1949.

Human Cargo. Dir. Allan Dwan. Perf. Claire Trevor and Brian Donlevy. Twentieth Century-Fox Film Corp., 1936.

I Killed that Man. Dir. Phil Rosen. Perf. Ricardo Cortez and Joan Woodbury. King Brothers Productions, 1941.

Impulse. Dir. Sondra Locke. Perf. Theresa Russell and Jeff Fahey. Warner Bros. Pictures, 1990.

Insomnia. Dir. Christopher Nolan. Perf. Al Pacino and Robin Williams. Buena Vista International, 2002.

International Crime. Dir. Charles Lamont. Perf. Rod La Rocque and Astryd Allwyn. Colony Pictures, 1938.

Invisible Killer, The. Dir. Sherman Scott (aka Sam Newfield). Perf. Grace Bradley, Roland Drew, and Jean Brooks. Producers Pictures Corp., 1939.

It Can't Last Forever. Dir. Hamilton MacFadden. Perf. Ralph Bellamy and Betty Furness. Columbia Pictures, 1937.

I Wake up Screaming. Dir. Bruce Humberstone. Perf. Betty Grable and Victor Mature. Twentieth Century-Fox Film Corp., 1941.

I Wouldn't Be in Your Shoes. Dir. William Nigh. Perf. Don Castle and Elyse Knox. Monogram Productions, 1948.

Jagged Edge. Dir. Richard Marquand. Perf. Jeff Bridges and Glenn Close. Columbia Pictures, 1985.

King Kong. Dir. Merian Cooper. Perf. Fay Wray and Robert Armstrong. RKO Radio Pictures, 1933.

Kiss the Girls. Dir. Gary Fleder. Perf. Morgan Freeman and Ashley Judd. Paramount Pictures and Rysher Entertainment, 1997.

Lady Confesses, The. Dir. Sam Newfield. Perf. Mary Beth Hughes and Hugh Beaumont. Alexander-Stern Productions, 1945.

Laughing at Trouble. Dir. Frank Strayer. Perf. Jane Darwell and Sara Hayden. Twentieth Century-Fox Film Corp., 1936.

Law in Her Hands, The. Dir. William Clemens. Perf. Margaret Lindsay and Glenda Farrell. Warner Bros. Pictures, 1936.

Legally Blonde. Dir. Robert Luketic. Perf. Reese Witherspoon and Luke Wilson. Metro-Goldwyn-Mayer, 2001.

Legally Blonde 2: Red, White and Blonde. Dir. Charles Herman-Wurmfeld. Perf. Reese Witherspoon and Sally Field. Metro-Goldwyn-Mayer, 2003.

Mad Game, The. Dir. Irving Cummings. Perf. Spencer Tracy and Claire Trevor. Fox Film Corp., 1933.

Mad Miss Manton, The. Dir. Leigh Jason. Perf. Barbara Stanwyck and Henry Fonda. RKO Radio Pictures, 1938.

Man at Large. Dir. Eugene Forde. Perf. Marjorie Weaver and George Reeves. Twentieth Century-Fox Film Corp., 1941.

Mike's Murder. Dir. James Bridges. Perf. Debra Winger and Mark Keyloun. Skyewiay, 1984.

Miss Congeniality. Dir. Donald Petrie. Perf. Sandra Bullock and Michael Caine. Castle Rock Entertainment, 2000.

Miss Congeniality 2: Armed and Fabulous. Dir. John Pasquin. Perf. Sandra Bullock and Regina King. Castle Rock Entertainment, 2005.

Miss Pinkerton. Dr. Lloyd Bacon. Perf. Joan Blondell and George Brent. First National Pictures, 1932.

Mr. District Attorney. Dir. William Morgan. Perf. Dennis O'Keefe and Florence Rice. Republic Pictures Corp., 1941.

Mr. Wong in Chinatown. Dir. William Nigh. Perf. Boris Karloff, Grant Withers, and Marjorie Reynolds. Monogram Pictures Corp., 1939.

Murder by an Aristocrat. Dir. Frank McDonald. Perf. Lyle Talbot and Marguerite Churchill. Warner Bros. Pictures, 1936.

Murder by Numbers. Dir. Barbet Schroeder. Perf. Sandra Bullock and Ben Chaplin. Warner Bros. Pictures, et al., 2002.

Murder of Dr. Harrigan, The. Dir. Frank McDonald. Perf. Ricardo Cortez and Kay Linaker. Warner Bros. Pictures, 1936.

Murder on a Bridle Path. Dir. Edward Killy. James Gleason and Helen Broderick. RKO Radio Pictures, 1936.

Murder on a Honeymoon. Dir. Lloyd Corrigan. Edna May Oliver and James Gleason. RKO Radio Pictures, 1935.

Murder on the Blackboard. Dir. George Archainbaud. James Gleason and Edna May Oliver. RKO Radio Pictures, 1934.

Music Box. Dir. Costa-Gavras. Perf. Jessica Lange and Armin Mueller-Stahl. Carolco Pictures, 1989.

My Dear Miss Aldrich. Dir. George B. Seitz. Perf. Edna May Oliver, Maureen O'Sullivan, and Walter Pidgeon. Metro-Goldwyn-Mayer, 1937.

Mystery House. Dir. Noel Smith. Perf. Dick Purcell and Ann Sheridan. Warner Bros. Pictures, 1938.

Mystery of the Wax Museum. Dir. Michael Curtiz. Perf. Lionel Atwill, Fay Wray, and Glenda Farrell. Warner Bros. Pictures and Vitaphone Corp., 1933.

Mystery Ship. Dir. Lew Landers. Perf. Lola Lane and Paul Kelly. Columbia Pictures, 1941.

Nancy Drew and the Hidden Staircase. Dir. William Clemens. Perf. Bonita Granville and Frankie Thomas. Warner Bros. Pictures., 1939.

Nancy Drew, Detective. Dir. William Clemens. Perf. Bonita Granville and John Litel. Warner Bros. Pictures., 1938.

Nancy Drew, Reporter. Dir. William Clemens. Perf. Bonita Granville and Frankie Thomas. Warner Bros. Pictures., 1939.

Nancy Drew, Trouble Shooter. Dir. William Clemens. Perf. Bonita Granville and Frankie Thomas. Warner Bros. Pictures., 1939.

Night for Crime, A. Dir. Alexis Thurn-Taxis. Perf. Glenda Farrell and Lyle Talbot. Producers Releasing Corp., 1943.

Nurse's Secret, The. Dir. Noel Smith. Perf. Lee Patrick and Regis Toomey. Warner Bros. Pictures, 1941.

Office Scandal, The. Dir. Paul L. Stein. Perf. Phyllis Haver and Leslie Fenton. Pathé Exchange, 1929.

One Mile from Heaven. Dir. Allan Dwan. Perf. Claire Trevor and Sally Blane. Twentieth Century-Fox Film Corp., 1937.

Orient Express. Dir. Paul Martin. Perf. Heather Angel and Norman Foster. Fox Film Corp., 1934.

Patient in Room 18, The. Dir. Bobby Connolly. Perf. Patric Knowles and Ann Sheridan. Warner Bros. Pictures, 1938.

Pelican Brief, The. Dir. Alan J. Pakula. Perf. Julia Roberts and Denzel Washington. Warner Bros. Pictures, 1993.

Penguin Pool Murder. Dir. George Archainbaud. Edna May Oliver and James Gleason. RKO Radio Pictures, 1932.

Personal Secretary. Dir. Otis Garrett. Perf. William Gargan and Joy Hodges. Universal Pictures, 1938.

Phantom Lady. Dir. Robert Siodmak. Perf. Franchot Tone and Ella Raines. Universal Pictures, 1944.

Physical Evidence. Dir. Michael Crichton. Perf. Burt Reynolds and Theresa Russell. Columbia Pictures, 1989.

Platinum Blonde. Dir. Frank Capra. Perf. Loretta Young and Robert Williams. Columbia Pictures, 1931.

Plot Thickens, The. Dir. Ben Holmes. James Gleason and ZaSu Pitts. RKO Radio Pictures, 1936.

Private Detective. Dir. Noel Smith. Perf. Jane Wyman and Dick Foran. Warner Bros. Pictures, 1939.

Rogues' Gallery. Dir. Albert Herman. Perf. Frank Jenks and Robin Raymond. American Productions, 1944.

Sealed Lips. Dir. George Waggner. Perf. William Gargan and June Clyde. Universal Pictures, 1942.

Second Woman, The. Dir. James V. Kern. Perf. Robert Young and Betsy Drake. Cardinal Pictures, 1950.

Secrets of Wu Sin, The. Dir. Richard Thorpe. Perf. Lois Wilson and Grant Withers. Invincible Pictures Corp., 1932.

Seventh Victim, The. Dir. Mark Robson. Perf. Tom Conway, Jean Brooks, and Kim Hunter. RKO Radio Pictures, 1943.

Shadow of a Doubt. Dir. Alfred Hitchcock. Perf. Teresa Wright and Joseph Cotton. Jack H. Skirball Productions and Universal Pictures, 1943.

Sheba, Baby. Dir. William Girdler. Perf. Pam Grier and Austin Stoker. American International Pictures and Mid-America Pictures, 1975.

Shriek in the Night, A. Dir. Albert Ray. Perf. Ginger Rogers and Lyle Talbot. Allied Pictures, 1933.

Silence of the Lambs, The. Dir. Jonathan Demme. Perf. Anthony Hopkins and Jodie Foster. Orion Pictures, 1991.

Smart Blonde. Dir. Frank McDonald. Perf. Glenda Farrell and Barton MacLane. Warner Bros. Pictures, 1937.

Sob Sister. Dir. Alfred Santell. Perf. James Dunn and Linda Watkins. Fox Film Corp., 1931.

Strange Adventure [Reissued as *The Wayne Murder Case*]. Dir. Hampton Del Ruth and Phil Whitman. Perf. Regis Toomey and June Clyde. I.E. Chadwick Productions, 1932.

Stranger on the Third Floor, The. Dir. Boris Ingster. Peter Lorre, John McGuire, and Margaret Tallichet. RKO Radio Pictures, 1940.

Suspect. Dir. Peter Yates. Perf. Cher and Dennis Quaid. TriStar Pictures, 1987.

Taking Lives. Dir. D. J. Caruso. Perf. Angelina Jolie and Ethan Hawke. Warner Bros. Pictures, et al., 2004.

There Goes My Girl. Dir. Ben Holmes. Perf. Gene Raymond and Ann Sothern. RKO Radio Pictures, 1937.

Torchy Blane in Chinatown. Dir. William Beaudine. Perf. Glenda Farrell and Barton MacLane. Warner Bros. Pictures, 1939.

Torchy Blane in Panama. Dir. William Clemens. Perf. Lola Lane and Paul Kelly. Warner Bros. Pictures, 1938.

Torchy Blane . . . Playing With Dynamite. Dir. Noel M. Smith. Perf. Jane Wyman and Allen Jenkins. Warner Bros. Pictures, 1939.

Torchy Gets Her Man. Dir. William Beaudine. Perf. Glenda Farrell and Barton MacLane. Warner Bros. Pictures, 1938.

Torchy Runs for Mayor. Dir. Ray McCarey. Perf. Glenda Farrell and Barton MacLane. Warner Bros. Pictures, 1939.

Trouble with Women, The. Dir. Sidney Lanfield. Perf. Ray Milland and Teresa Wright. Paramount Pictures, 1947.

Twisted. Dir. Philip Kaufman. Perf. Ashley Judd and Samuel L. Jackson. Paramount Pictures, et al., 2004.

Undercover Girl. Dir. Joseph Pevney. Perf. Alexis Smith and Scott Brady. Universal-International Pictures, 1950.

Undercover Maisie. Dir. Harry Beaumont. Perf. Ann Sothern and Barry Nelson. Metro-Goldwyn-Mayer, 1947.

Undercurrent. Dir. Vincente Minnelli. Perf. Katharine Hepburn and Robert Taylor. Metro-Goldwyn-Mayer, 1946.

Unfaithful. Dir. Adrian Lyne. Perf. Diane Lane and Richard Gere. Fox 2000 Pictures, et al., 2002.

Unknown Woman. Dir. Albert S. Rogell. Perf. Richard Cromwell and Marian Marsh. Columbia Pictures Corp., 1935.

Untraceable. Dir. Gregory Hoblit. Perf. Diane Lane and Billy Burke. Cohen/Pearl Productions and Lakeshore Entertainment, 2008.

Up for Murder. Dir. Monta Bell. Perf. Lew Ayres and Genevieve Tobin. Universal Pictures, 1931.

V.I. Warshawski. Dir. Jeff Kanew. Perf. Kathleen Turner and Jay O. Sanders. Warner Bros. Pictures, 1991.

We're Only Human. Dir. James Flood. Perf. Preston Foster and Jane Wyatt. RKO Radio Pictures, 1935.

While the Patient Slept. Dir. Ray Enright. Perf. Aline MacMahon and Guy Kibbee. First National Pictures, 1935.

Witness to Murder. Dir. Roy Rowland. Perf. Barbara Stanwyck and George Sanders. Chester Erskine Pictures, 1954.

Woman Condemned, The. Dir. Dorothy Davenport (as Mrs. Wallace Reid). Perf. Claudia Dell and Lola Lane. Progressive Pictures and Willis Kent Productions, 1934.

Woman of the Year. Dir. George Stevens. Perf. Spencer Tracy and Katharine Hepburn. Metro-Goldwyn-Mayer, 1942.

Woman on the Run. Dir. Norman Foster. Perf. Ann Sheridan and Dennis O'Keefe. Fidelity Pictures Corp., 1950.

Woman Unafraid. Dir. William Cowan. Perf. Lucile Gleason and Skeets Gallagher. Goldsmith Productions, 1934.

Women are Trouble. Dir. Errol Taggart. Perf. Stuart Erwin, Paul Kelly, and Florence Rice. Metro-Goldwyn-Mayer, 1936.

You Can't Escape Forever. Dir. Jo Graham. Perf. George Brent and Brenda Marshall. Warner Bros. Pictures, 1942.

Works Cited

AFI Catalog <www.afi.com/members/catalog/> (accessed on various dates).

Albrecht, Donald. *Designing Dreams: Modern Architecture in the Movies.* New York: Harper & Row with the Museum of Modern Art, 1986.

Altman, Rick. *Film/Genre.* London: BFI Publishing, 1999.

Ames, Christopher. "Restoring the Black Man's Lethal Weapon: Race and Sexuality in Contemporary Cop Films." *Journal of Popular Film and Television* 20.3 (1992): 52–60.

AskOxford <www.askoxford.com> (accessed 1 March 2007).

Babylon <www.babylon.com/definition/uxorodespotic/English> (accessed 10 April 2007).

Baker, M. Joyce. *Images of Women in Film: The War Years, 1941–1945.* Ann Arbor, MI: UMI Research Press, 1980.

Balio, Tino. *Grand Design: Hollywood as a Modern Business Enterprise, 1930–1939.* Ed. Tino Balio. New York: Charles Scribner's Sons, 1993.

Bartlett, Keith. "Grisham Adaptations and the Legal Thriller." *Genre and Contemporary Hollywood.* Ed. Steve Neale. London: BFI Publishing, 2003. 269–280.

Benson, Bill. "Important Firsts in Women's Law Enforcement." <www.geocities.com/vbenson_2000/firsts.htm> (accessed 18 July 2006).

Bergman, Andrew. *We're in the Money: Depression American and its Films.* New York: New York University Press, 1971.

Berry, Sarah. *Screen Style: Fashion and Femininity in 1930s Hollywood.* Minneapolis: University of Minnesota Press, 2000.

Betz, Phyllis M. *Lesbian Detective Fiction: Woman as Author, Subject and Reader.* Jefferson, NC: McFarland and Company, 2006.

Black, David A. *Film in Law: Resonance and Representation.* Urbana: University of Illinois Press, 1999.

Black, Gregory D. *Hollywood Censored: Morality Codes, Catholics, and the Movies.* Cambridge: Cambridge University Press, 1994.

Black, Louis. "*Phantom Lady* (1944)." *CinemaTexas Program Notes* 14.1 (8 February 1978). 73–81.

Bleiler, Everett Franklin, ed. *Eight Dime Novels.* New York: Dover Publications, Inc. 1974.

Bobo, Jacqueline. "Black Women's Responses to *The Color Purple*." *Jump Cut* 33 (February 1998): 43–51 <http://www.ejumpcut.org/archive/onlinessays/JC33folder/ClPurple-Bobo.html> (accessed 28 November 2008).

———. "Reading through the Text: The Black Woman as Audience." *Black American Cinema*. Ed. Manthia Diawara. New York: Routledge, 1993. 272–87.

Bodnar, John. *Blue-Collar Hollywood: Liberalism, Democracy, and Working People in American Film*. Baltimore, MD: John Hopkins University Press, 2003.

Bogle, Donald. *Toms, Coons, Mulattoes, Mammies and Bucks: An Interpretative History of Blacks in American Films*. New York: The Viking Press, 1973.

Boozer, Jack. *Career Movies: American Business and the Success Mystique*. Austin: University of Texas Press, 2002.

Box Office Mojo <http://boxofficemojo.com> (accessed on various dates).

Bratton, Jacky, Jim Cook, and Christine Gledhill, Eds. *Melodrama: Stage, Picture, Screen*. London: BFI Publishing, 1994.

Broe, Dennis. "Class, Labor, and the Home-Front Detective: Hammett, Chandler, Woolrich, and the Dissident Lawman (and Woman) in 1940s Hollywood and Beyond." *Social Justice* 32.2 (2005): 167–85.

Brown, Jeffrey A. "Gender and the Action Heroine: Hardbodies and the *Point of No Return*." *Cinema Journal* 35.3 (Spring 1996): 52–71.

Browne, Nick. "Preface." *Refiguring American Film Genres: Theory and History*. Ed. Nick Browne. Berkeley, CA: University of California Press, 1998. xi–xiv.

Bruno, Giuliana. *Atlas of Emotion: Journeys in Art, Architecture, and Film*. New York: Verso, 2002.

Butler, Judith. *Bodies that Matter: On the Discursive Limits of Sex*. New York: Routledge, 1993.

———. *Gender Trouble: Feminism and the Subversion of Identity*. London: Routledge, 1990.

Caputi, Jane, and Diana E. H. Russell. "Femicide: Sexist Terrorism against Women." *Femicide: The Politics of Killing Women*. Eds. Jill Radford and Diana E. H. Russell. New York: Twayne Publishers, 1992. 410–26 (e-text).

Chaudhuri, Shohini. *Feminist Film Theorists: Laura Mulvey, Kaja Silverman, Teresa de Lauretis, Barbara Creed*. London: Routledge, 2006.

Chodorow, Nancy. *The Reproduction of Mothering: Psychoanalysis and the Sociology of Gender*. Berkeley: University of California Press, 1978.

Collins, Jim. "Genericity in the Nineties: Eclectic Irony and the New Sincerity." *Film Theory Goes to the Movies*. Eds. Jim Collins, Hilary Radner, and Ava Preacher Collins. New York: Routledge, 1993. 242–63.

Cowan, Ruth Schwartz. (1976) "Two Washes in the Morning and a Bridge Party at Night: The American Housewife between the Wars." *Decades of Discontent: The Women's Movement, 1920–1940*. Eds. Lois Scharf and Joan M. Jensen. Westport, CT: Greenwood Press, 1983. 177–96.

Cowie, Elizabeth. "*Film Noir* and Women." Ed. Joan Copjec. *Shades of Noir: A Reader*. London: Verso, 1993. 121–65.

———. "The Popular Film as a Progressive Text—A Discussion of *Coma*." *m/f* 3 (1979–80): 59–81.

Craig, Patricia and Mary Cadogan. *The Lady Investigates: Women Detectives and Spies in Fiction*. London: Victor Gollancz, 1981.

Dalton, Elizabeth. "Meet Torchy Blane." *Film Fan Monthly* 133/134 (July/Aug 1972): 37–42.

———. (1972) "Women at Work: Warners in the 1930s." *Women and the Cinema: A Critical Anthology.* Eds. Karyn Kay and Gerald Peary. New York: E.P. Dutton, 1977. 267–282.

Davis, Todd F., and Kenneth Womack. *Postmodern Humanism in Contemporary Literature and Culture.* Houndmills, UK: Palgrave Macmillan, 2006.

Day, William Patrick. *In the Circles of Fear and Desire.* Chicago: University of Chicago Press, 1985.

DellaCava, Frances A., and Madeline H. Engel. *Sleuths in Skirts: Analysis and Bibliography of Serialized Female Sleuths.* New York: Routledge, 2002.

DiBattista, Maria. *Fast-Talking Dames.* New Haven, CT: Yale University Press, 2001.

Dilley, Kimberly J. *Busybodies, Meddlers, and Snoops: The Female Hero in Contemporary Women's Mysteries.* Westport, CT: Greenwood Press, 1998.

Dimendberg, Edward. *Film Noir and the Spaces of Modernity.* Cambridge, MA: Harvard University Press, 2004.

Dixon, Wheeler Winston. *The "B" Directors: A Biographical Directory.* Metuchen, NJ: Scarecrow Press, 1985.

Doane, Mary Ann. *Femmes Fatales: Femininism, Film Theory, Psychoanalysis.* New York: Routeledge, 1991.

Doherty, Thomas. *Pre-Code Hollywood: Sex, Immorality, and Insurrection in American Cinema 1930–1934.* New York: Columbia University Press, 1999.

Dole, Carol M. "The Return of Pink: *Legally Blonde*, Third-Wave Feminism, and Having it All." *Chick Flicks: Contemporary Women at the Movies.* Eds. Suzanne Ferriss and Mallory Young. New York: Routledge, 2008. 58–78.

Donnell, Dorothy. "Are You a Screen Shopper?" *Motion Picture* (Sept 1930): 70.

Dooley, Roger. *From Scarface to Scarlett: American Films in the 1930s.* New York: Harcourt Brace Jovanovich, 1981.

Dresner, Lisa M. *The Female Investigator in Literature, Film, and Popular Culture.* Jefferson, NC: McFarland and Company, 2007.

Dunn, Stephane. *"Baad Bitches" and Sassy Supermamas: Black Power Action Films.* Urbana: University of Illinois Press, 2008.

Dunye, Cheryl. "Don't Even Talk to Me till I've had my *Coffy*." *Time Out New York* (Aug 28–Sept 4, 1997): 76.

Dyer, Richard. *Heavenly Bodies: Films Stars and Society.* New York: St. Martin's Press, 1986.

———. *Stars.* London: BFI Publishing, 1979.

Ebert, Alan. "Pam Grier: Coming into Focus." *Essence Magazine* (January 1979): 107.

Eckert, Charles. "The Carole Lombard in Macy's Window." *Quarterly Review of Film Studies* 3.1 (Winter 1978): 1–21.

Epstein, Cynthia Fuchs, Robert Sauté, Bonnie Oglensky, and Martha Gever. "Glass Ceilings and Open Doors: Women's Advancement in the Legal Profession." *Fordham Law Review* 64.2 (November 1995): 291–449.

Esperdy, Gabrielle. "From Instruction to Consumption: Architecture and Design in Hollywood Movies of the 1930s." *The Journal of American Culture* 30.2 (June 2007): 198–211.

Faludi, Susan. *Backlash: The Undeclared War against Women*. London: Vintage, 1992.

Filipcevic, Vojislava. *The Agitated City: Urban Transformations and Cinematic Representations of the American Metropolis, 1929–1950*. PhD Thesis, Columbia University, 2008.

Fischer, Lucy. *Designing Women: Cinema, Art Deco, and the Female Form*. New York: Columbia University Press, 2003.

Freier, Mary P. "The Decline of Hilda Adams." *Women Times Three: Writers, Detectives, Readers*. Ed. Kathleen Gregory Klein. Bowling Green, OH: Bowling Green State University Popular Press, 1995. 129–41.

French, Jack. *Private Eyelashes: Radio's Lady Detectives*. Albany, GA: BearManor Media: 2004.

Friedberg, Anne. *Window Shopping: Cinema and the Postmodern*. Berkeley: University of California Press, 1993.

Gale, Steven H. "*The Maltese Falcon*: Melodrama or Film Noir?" *Literature/Film Quarterly* 24.2 (1996) 145–48.

Gates, Philippa. *Detecting Men: Investigating Masculinity and the Hollywood Detective Film*. Albany, NY: State University of New York Press, 2006.

———."The Man's Film: Woo and the Pleasure of Male Melodrama." *The Journal of Popular Culture* 35.1 (2001): 59–79.

———. "Softboiled Heroes: Investigating Englishness in the Classical Hollywood Detective Film." *Heroines and Heroes: Embodiment, Symbolism, Narratives & Identity*. Ed. Chris Hart. Kingswinford, UK: Midrash Publications (2008). 98–111.

———. "The Three Sam Spades: The Shifting Model of American Masculinity in the Three Films of *The Maltese Falcon*." *Framework* 49.1 (Spring 2008): 7–26.

Gilligan, Carol. *In a Different Voice*. Cambridge, MA: Harvard University Press, 1982.

Gledhill, Christine. "The Melodramatic Field: An Investigation." *Home is Where the Heart is: Studies in Melodrama and the Woman's Film*. Ed. Christine Gledhill. London: BFI Publishing, 1987. 5–39.

———. "Pleasurable Negotiations." *Female Spectators: Looking at Film and Television*. Ed. E. Deirdre Pribram. London: Verso, 1988. 64–89.

Goldberger, Paul. *The Skyscraper*. New York: Alfred A. Knopf, 1982.

Good, Howard. *Girl Reporter: Gender, Journalism, and the Movies*. Lanham, MD: Scarecrow Press, 1998.

Grandiloquent Dictionary <http://www.islandnet.com/~egbird/dict/dict.htm> (accessed 1 March 2007).

Grant, Barry Keith. "American Psycho/sis: The Pure Products of America Go Crazy." *Mythologies of Violence in Postmodern Media*. Ed Christopher Sharrett. Detroit: Wayne State University Press, 1999. 23–40.

Green, Philip. *Cracks in the Pedestal: Ideology and Gender in Hollywood*. Amherst: University of Massachusetts Press, 1998.

Grier, Pam. "Pam Grier." *What it is . . . What it was! The Black Film Explosion of the '70s in Words and Pictures*. Eds. Gerald Martinez, Diana Martinez, and Andres Chavez. New York: Hyperion (Miramax Books), 1998. 46–53.

Guerrero, Ed. "The Black Image in Protective Custody: Hollywood's Biracial Buddy Films of the Eighties." *Black American Cinema*. Ed. Manthia Diawara. New York: Routledge, 1993. 237–46.

———. *Framing Blackness*. Philadelphia: Temple University Press, 1993.

Gunning, Tom. "The Exterior as *Intérieur*: Benjamin's Optical Detective." *Boundary 2* 30.1 (2003): 105–129.

———. "Tracing the Individual: Photography, Detectives, and Early Cinema." Eds. Leo Charney and Vanessa R. Schwartz. *Cinema and the Invention of Modern Life*. Berkeley: University of California Press, 1995. 15–45.

Halberstam, Judith. "Imagined Violence/Queer Violence: Representation, Rage and Resistance." *Social Text* 37 (1993): 187–201.

Hall, Stuart (1973). "Encoding and Decoding in the Television Discourse." *Culture, Media, Language: Working Papers in Cultural Studies, 1972–79*. Eds. Stuart Hall et al. London: Hutchinson, 1980. 128–38.

Hanson, Helen. *Hollywood Heroines: Women in Film Noir and the Female Gothic Film*. London: I.B. Tauris, 2007.

Hanson, Philip. "The Feminine Image in Films of the Great Depression." *The Cambridge Quarterly* 32.2 (2003): 113–41.

———. *This Side of Despair: How the Movies and American Life Intersected during the Great Depression*. Madison, NJ: Fairleigh Dickinson University Press, 2008.

Hapke, Laura. *Daughters of the Great Depression: Women, Work, and Fiction in the American 1930s*. Athens: University of Georgia Press, 1995.

Hart, James D. *The Popular Book: A History of America's Literary Taste*. New York: Oxford University Press, 1950.

Hart, Lynda. *Fatal Women: Lesbian Sexuality and the Mark of Aggression*. Princeton: Princeton University Press, 1994.

Hartmann, Susan M. *The Home Front and Beyond: American Women in the 1940s*. Boston: Twayne Publishers, 1982.

Harvey, Sylvia. "Woman's Place: The Absent Family of Film Noir." *Women in Film Noir*. Ed. E. Ann Kaplan. New Ed. London: BFI Publishing, 2001. 35–46.

Haskell, Molly. *From Reverence to Rape: The Treatment of Women in the Movies*. New York: Holt, Rinehart & Winston, 1973.

Haut, Woody. *Neon Noir: Contemporary American Crime Fiction*. London: Serpent's Tail, 1999.

Hill, Jack. "Jack Hill." *What it is . . . What it was! The Black Film Explosion of the '70s in Words and Pictures*. Eds. Gerald Martinez, Diana Martinez, and Andres Chavez. New York: Hyperion (Miramax Books), 1998. 136–42.

Hills, Elizabeth. "From 'Figurative Males' to Action Heroines: Further Thoughts on Active Women in the Cinema." *Screen* 40.1 (Spring 1999): 38–50.

Hollander, Anne. *Sex and Suits: The Evolution of Modern Dress*. New York: Knopf, 1994.

Hollinger, Karen. "Afterword: Once I Got Beyond the Name Chick Flick." *Chick Flicks: Contemporary Women at the Movies*. Eds. Suzanne Ferriss, and Mallory Young. New York: Routledge, 2008. 221–32.

Holmlund, Chris. "Cruisin' for a Bruisin': Hollywood's Deadly (Lesbian) Dolls." *Cinema Journal* 34.1 (1994): 31–51.

———. "Postfeminism from A to G." *Cinema Journal* 44.5 (Winter 2005): 116–21.

———. "Wham! Bam! Pam! Pam Grier as Hot Action Babe and Cool Action Mama." *Quarterly Review of Film and Video* 22.2 (March 2005): 97–112.

hooks, bell. "The Oppositional Gaze: Black Female Spectators." *Black American Cinema*. Ed. Manthia Diawara. New York: Routledge, 1993. 288–302.

Hopper, Hedda. "Hedda Hopper's Hollywood." *L.A. Times* (31 May 1942).

Howard, Josiah. *Blaxploitation Cinema: The Essential Reference Guide*. Godalming, UK: FAB Press, 2008.

IAWP (*International Association of Women Police*). "History." <www.iawp.org/history/past-present.htm> (accessed 18 July 2006).

Image of the Journalist in Popular Culture <http://ijpc.org> (accessed on various dates).

Internet Movie Database <http://www.imdb.com> (accessed on various dates).

Irons, Glenwood. "New Women Detectives: G is for Gender-Bending." *Gender, Language, and Myth: Essays on Popular Narrative*. Ed. Glenwood Irons. Toronto: University of Toronto Press, 1992. 127–41.

Iskin, Ruth E. "The Pan-European Flâneuse in Fin-de-Siècle Posters: Advertising Modern Women in the City." *Nineteenth-Century Contexts* 25.4 (December 2003): 333–56.

Jacobs, Lea. *The Wages of Sin: Censorship and the Fallen Woman Film, 1928–1942*. Madison: University of Wisconsin Press, 1991.

Jeffords, Susan. "Can Masculinity be Terminated?" *Screening the Male: Exploring Masculinities in Hollywood Cinema*. Eds. Steven Cohan and Ina Rae Hark. London: Routledge, 1993. 245–62.

———. *Hard Bodies: Hollywood Masculinity in the Reagan Era*. New Brunswick, NJ: Rutgers University Press, 1994.

Jones, Manina. "Shot/Reverse/Shot: Dis-solving the Feminist Detective Story in Kanew's Film *V.I. Warshawski*." *Diversity and Detective Fiction*. Ed. Kathleen Gregory Klein. Bowling Green, OH: Bowling Green State University Popular Press, 1999. 22–37.

Kael, Pauline. "Raising Kane." *The Citizen Kane Book*. Eds. Pauline Kael, Herman Mankiewicz, and Orson Welles. Boston: Little, Brown and Co. 1971.

Kaplan, Cora. "Dirty Harriet/*Blue Steel*: Feminist Theory Goes to Hollywood." *Discourse* 16.1 (Fall 1993): 50–70.

Kaplan, E. Ann. "Introduction to 1978 Edition." *Women in Film Noir*. Ed. E. Ann Kaplan. New Ed. London: BFI Publishing, 2001. 15–19.

———. "The Place of Women in Fritz Lang's *The Blue Gardenia*." *Women in Film Noir*. Ed. E. Ann Kaplan. New Ed. London: BFI Publishing, 2001. 81–88.

Kendall, Elizabeth. *The Runaway Bride: Hollywood Romantic Comedies of the 1930s*. New York: Alfred A. Knopf, 1990.

Kessler, Kelly. "Bound Together: Lesbian Film That's Family Fun for Everyone." *Film Quarterly* 56.4 (Summer 2003): 13–22.

Kestner, Joseph A. *Sherlock's Sisters: The British Female Detective, 1864–1913*. Aldershot, UK: Ashgate Publishing Ltd, 2003.

Klein, Kathleen Gregory. *The Woman Detective: Gender and Genre*. 2nd ed. Urbana: University of Illinois Press, 1995.

Klemesrud, Judy. "Tamara Dobson: Not Super Fly but Super Woman." *The New York Times* (19 August 1973): AL117.

Krämer, Peter. " 'A Woman in a Male-Dominated World': Jodie Foster, Stardom and 90s Hollywood. *Contemporary Hollywood Stardom*. Ed. Thomas Austin and Martin Baker. London: Arnold, 2003. 201–14.

Krutnik, Frank. *In a Lonely Street: Film Noir, Genre, Masculinity*. London, Routledge, 1991.

Kuhn, Annette. (1984) "Women's Genres." *The Sexual Subject: A Screen Reader on Sexuality*. Ed. Mandy Merck. London: Routledge, 1992. 301–11.

———. *Women's Pictures: Feminism and Cinema*. London: Routledge and Kegan Paul, 1985.

Kungl, Carla T. *Creating the Fictional Female Detective: The Sleuth Heroines of British Women Writers, 1890–1940*. Jefferson, NC: McFarland & Company, 2006.

Lane, Christina. *Feminist Hollywood: From Born in Flames to Point Break*. Detroit: Wayne State University Press, 2000.

———. "The Liminal Iconography of Jodie Foster." *Journal of Popular Film and Television* 22.4 (Winter 1995): 149–53.

Langman, Larry. *American Film Cycles: The Silent Era*. Westport, CT: Greenwood Press, 1998.

Langman, Larry and Daniel Finn. *A Guide to American Crime Films of the Thirties*. Westport, CT: Greenwood Press, 1995.

———. *A Guide to American Silent Crime Films*. Westport, CT: Greenwood Press, 1994.

LaSalle, Mick. *Complicated Women: Sex and Power in Pre-Code Hollywood*. New York: St. Martin's Griffin, 2000.

Lawrence, Novotny. *Blaxploitation Films of the 1970s: Blackness and Genre*. New York: Routledge, 2008.

Lucia, Cynthia. "Women on Trial: The Female Lawyer in the Hollywood Courtroom." *Cineaste* 19.2-3 (1992): 32–37.

———. *Framing Female Lawyers: Women on Trial in Film*. Austin: University of Texas Press, 2005.

MacQueen, Scott. "*Mystery of the Wax Museum*: A Finale for 2-Strip Technicolor." *American Cinematographer* 71.4 (April 1990): 42–50.

Mader, Katherine. "Commentary." *Los Angeles Times* (20 Oct 1985): 24–25.

Mahdaviani, Bita. "Modern Architecture in the Pre-Code Hollywood Melodrama." Paper presented at the Film Studies Association of Canada Conference (as part of the Annual Congress of the Social Sciences and Humanities Conference), Toronto, May 2006.

Maltby, Richard. *Hollywood Cinema*. 2nd ed. Malden, MA: Blackwell Publishing, 2003.

———. "More Sinned Against than Sinning: The Fabrications of 'Pre-Code Cinema.'" *Senses of Cinema* 29 (Nov–Dec 2003) <http://www.sensesofcinema.com/contents/03/29/pre_code_cinema. html> (accessed 20 July 2007).

———. "Sticks, Hicks and Flaps: Classical Hollywood's Generic Conception of Audiences." *Identifying Hollywood's Audiences: Cultural Identity and the Movies*. Eds. Melvyn Stokes, and Richard Maltby. London: BFI Publishing, 1999. 23–41.

Marcheis, Chiara Besso. "Litigants' duty to disclose." (13 February 2008) <http://www.italianacademy.columbia.edu/publications/working_papers/2007_2008/paper_sp08_Marcheis.pdf> (accessed 10 December 2008).

Martin, Angela. "'Gilda Didn't Do Any of Those Things You've Been Losing Sleep Over!': The Central Women of 40s Films Noirs." *Women in Film Noir*. Ed. E. Ann Kaplan. New Ed. London: BFI Publishing, 2001. 202–28.

McElvaine, Robert S. *The Great Depression: America, 1929–1941*. New York: Times Books, 1984.

Mebane, Mary E. "Brother Caring for Brother." *The New York Times* (23 September 1973): II13.

Miller, Carolyn Lisa. " 'What a Waste. Beautiful, Sexy Gal. Hell of a Lawyer:' Film and the Female Attorney." *Columbia Journal of Gender and Law* 4 (1994): 203–32.

Mizejewski, Linda. "Dressed to Kill: Postfeminist Noir." *Cinema Journal* 44.2 (Winter 2005): 121–27.

———. *Hardboiled and High Heeled: The Woman Detective in Popular Culture*. New York: Routledge, 2004.

———. "Picturing the Female Dick: *The Silence of the Lambs* and *Blue Steel*." *Journal of Film and Video* 45. 2–3 (1993): 6–23.

Modleski, Tania. *Loving with a Vengeance: Mass-Produced Fantasies for Women*. Hamden, CT: Archon Books, 1982.

Moore, Alida M. *Odd Girl Detectives: Investigations in Sexuality, Popular Narrative, and Identity*. Diss. University of Mississippi, 2002.

Mouton, Janice. "From Feminine Masquerade to Flâneuse: Agnès Varda's Cléo in the City." *Cinema Journal* 40.2 (Winter 2001): 3–16.

Mulvey, Laura. " 'It will be a Magnificent Obsession:' The Melodrama's Role in the Development of Contemporary Film Theory." *Melodrama: Stage, Picture, Screen*. Eds. Jacky Bratton, Jim Cook, and Christine Gledhill. London: BFI Publishing, 1994. 121–33.

———. "Visual Pleasure and Narrative Cinema." *Screen* 16.3 (1975): 6–18.

Munt, Sally R. *Murder by the Book? Feminism and the Crime Novel*. London: Routledge, 1994.

Muscio, Giuliana. *Hollywood's New Deal*. Philadelphia: Temple University Press, 1997.

Naremore, James. "American Film Noir: The History of an Idea." *Film Quarterly* 49.2 (1995/1996): 12–28.

Nash, Ilana. *American Sweethearts: Teenaged Girls in Twentieth-Century Popular Culture*. Bloomington: Indiana University Press, 2006.

Neale, Steve. *Genre and Hollywood*. London: Routledge, 2000.

———. "Melo Talk: On the Meaning and Use of the Term 'Melodrama' in the American Trade Press." *Velvet Light Trap* 32 (1993): 66–89.

Nesci, Catherine. "Flora Tristan's Urban Odyssey: Notes on the Missing *Flâneuse* and Her City." *Journal of Urban History* 27.6 (September 2001): 709–22.

Nickerson, Catherine Ross. *The Web of Iniquity: Early Detective Fictions by American Women*. Durham, NC: Duke University Press, 1998.

Noble, Jean. "Bound and Invested: Lesbian Desire and Hollywood Ethnography." *Film Criticism* 22.3 (Spring 1998): 1–21.

Nord, Deborah Epstein. *Walking the Victorian Streets: Women, Representation and the City*. Ithaca: Cornell University Press, 1995.

Norton, Chris. "Cleopatra Jones—007: Blaxploitation, James Bond, and Reciprocal Co-Optation." *Images: A Journal of Film and Popular Culture* 4 (July 1997) <http://www.imagesjournal.com/ issue04/features/blaxploitation.htm> (accessed 27 November 2008)

NYC.gov. "NYPD History." <www.ci.nyc.ny.us/html/nypd/html/3100/retro.html> (accessed 18 July 2006).

O'Day, Marc. "Beauty in Motion: Gender, Spectacle and Action Babe Cinema." *Action and Adventure Cinema*. Ed. Yvonne Tasker. London: Routledge, 2004. 201–18.

Ohmer, Susan. "Speaking for the Audience: Double Features, Public Opinion, and the Struggle for Control in 1930s Hollywood." *Quarterly Review of Film and Video* 24.2 (2007): 143–69.

Online Etymology Dictionary <http://www.etymonline.com > (accessed 1 March 2007).

Owen, A. Susan, Sarah R. Stein, and Leah R. Vande Berg. *Bad Girls: Cultural Politics and Media Representations of Transgressive Women*. New York: Peter Lang, 2007.

Panek, LeRoy Lad. *An Introduction to the Detective Story*. Bowling Green, Ohio: Bowling Green State University Popular Press, 1987.

Parish, James R., and Don E. Stanke. (1975). *The Debonairs*. New Rochelle, NY: Arlington House Publishers.

Parsons, Deborah L. *Streetwalking the Metropolis: Women, the City and Modernity*. Oxford: Oxford University Press, 2000.

Phelps, Donald. "Cinema Gris: Woolrich/Neill's *Black Angel*." *Film Comment* (2000): 64–69.

Pitts, Michael R. *Famous Movie Detectives II*. Metuchen, NJ: The Scarecrow Press, Inc. 1991.

———. *Famous Movie Detectives III*. Lanham, MD: The Scarecrow Press, Inc. 2004.

Place, Janey. "Women in Film Noir." *Women in Film Noir*. Ed. E. Ann Kaplan. New Ed. London: BFI Publishing, 2001. 47–68.

Pollock, Griselda. *Vision and Difference: Femininity, Feminism and the Histories of Art*. New York: Routledge, Chapman & Hall Inc., 1988.

Pomerance, Murray. "Introduction: From Bad to Worse." *Bad: Infamy, Darkness, Evil, and Slime on Screen*. Ed. Murray Pomerance. Albany, NY: State University of New York Press. 2004. 1–18.

Radner, Hilary. "New Hollywood's New Women: Murder in Mind—Sarah and Margie." *Contemporary Hollywood Cinema*. Eds. Steve Neale, and Murray Smith. London: Routledge, 1998. 247–62.

Rafter, Nicole. *Shots in the Mirror: Crime Films and Society*. New York: Oxford University Press, 2000.

Reddy, Maureen T. *Sisters in Crime: Feminism and the Crime Novel*. New York: Continuum Publishing, 1988.

Reiner, Robert. *The Politics of the Police*. Brighton: Wheatsheaf Books Ltd., 1985.

Renov, Michael. *Hollywood's Wartime Women: Representation and Ideology*. Ann Arbor, MI: UMI Research Press, 1988.

Rich, B. Ruby. "The Lady Dicks: Genre Benders Take the Case." *Village Voice Literary Supplement* 75 (June 1989): 24–27.

Richards, Helen. "Sex and the City: A Visible *Flâneuse* for the Postmodern Era." *Continuum: Journal of Media & Cultural Studies* 17.2 (January 2003): 147–57.

Rinehart, Mary Roberts. (1914) "The Buckled Bag." *The Best Mysteries of Mary Roberts Rinehart*. Pleasantville, NY: Reader's Digest, 2002. 525–83.

Roberts, Garyn G., Gary Hoppenstand, and Ray B. Browne. "Introduction: Who was that Androgynous, Angelic, Society Lady Female Detective?" *Old Sleuth's Freaky Female Detectives: From the Dime Novels*. Eds. Garyn G. Roberts, Gary Hoppenstand, and Ray B. Browne. Bowling Green, OH: Bowling Green State University Popular Press, 1990. 1–10.

Roberts, Joan Warthling. "Amelia Butterworth: The Spinster Detective." *Feminism in Women's Detective Fiction.* Ed. Glenwood Irons. Toronto: University of Toronto Press, 1995. 3–11.

Robinson, Bobbie. "Playing Like the Boys: Patricia Cornwell Writes Men." *Journal of Popular Culture* 39.1 (2006): 95–108.

Rosen, Marjorie. *Popcorn Venus: Women, Movies and the American Dream.* New York: Coward, McCann & Geoghegan, 1973.

Ross, Steven J. *Working-Class Hollywood: Silent Film and the Shaping of Class in America.* Princeton, NJ: Princeton University Press, 1998.

Rossell, Deac. "The Fourth Estate and the Seventh Art." *Questioning Media Ethics.* Ed. Bernard Rubin. New York: Praeger, 1978. 232–82.

———. "Hollywood and the Newsroom." *American Film: Journal of the Film and Television Arts* 1.1 (October 1975): 14–18.

Saltzman, Joe. (2003) "Sob Sisters: The Image of the Female Journalist in Popular Culture." <www.ijpc.org/sobsmaster.htm> (accessed 5 July 2005).

Scharf, Lois. *To Work and to Wed: Female Employment, Feminism, and the Great Depression.* Westport, CT: Greenwood Press, 1980.

Schubart, Rikke. *Super Bitches and Action Babes: The Female Hero in Popular Cinema, 1970-2006.* Jefferson, NC: McFarland and Co., 2007.

Silverman, Kaja. *The Acoustic Mirror: The Female Voice in Psychoanalysis and Cinema.* Bloomington: University of Indiana Press, 1988.

Silverman, Sid. "U.S. Film Field for 1930." *Variety* (31 December 1930): 7.

Simpson, Philip L. *Psycho Paths: Tracking the Serial Killer through Contemporary American Film and Fiction.* Carbondale, Illinois: Southern Illinois University Press, 2000.

Sims, Yvonne D. *Woman of Blaxploitation: How the Black Action Film Heroine Changed American Popular Culture.* Jefferson, NC: McFarland & Co., 2006.

Singer, Ben. "Female Power in the Serial-Queen Melodrama: The Etiology of an Anomaly." *Camera Obscura* 22 (1990): 91–129.

———. *Melodrama and Modernity: Early Sensational Cinema and its Contexts.* New York: Columbia University Press, 2001.

Sleuth, Old (pseudonym for Harlan Page Halsey). *Lady Kate, The Dashing Female Detective. Old Sleuth Library* 30.2 (1886). Reprinted in *Old Sleuth's Freaky Female Detectives: From the Dime Novels.* Eds. Garyn G. Roberts, Gary Hoppenstand, and Ray B. Browne. Bowling Green, Ohio: Bowling Green State University Popular Press, 1990. 11–56.

Slung, Michele B. "Introduction." *Crime on Her Mind: Fifteen Stories of Female Sleuths from the Victorian Era to the Forties.* Ed. Michele B. Slung. New York: Pantheon Books, 1975. xv–xxx.

Spinrad, Leonard. "Whodunit First?" *The New York Times* (4 Sept 1948): X5.

Staiger, Janet. "Taboos and Totems: Cultural Meanings of *The Silence of the Lambs.*" *Film Theory Goes to the Movies.* Eds. Jim Collins, Hilary Radner, and Ava Preacher Collins. London: Routledge/AFI, 1993. 142–54.

Stamp, Shelley. "Taking Precautions, or Regulating Early Birth-Control Films." *A Feminist Reader in Early Cinema.* Eds. Jennifer M. Bean, and Diane Negra. Durham, NC: Duke University Press, 2002. 270–97

Stasia, Cristina Lucia. " 'My Guns Are in the Fendi!': The Postfeminist Female Action Hero." *Third Wave Feminism: A Critical Exploration*. Eds. Stacy Gillis, Gillian Howie, and Rebecca Munford. 2nd ed. Houndmills, UK: Palgrave Macmillan, 2007. 237–49.

Stokes, Melvyn. "Female Audiences of the 1920s and Early 1930s." *Identifying Hollywood's Audiences: Cultural Identity and the Movies*. Eds. Melvyn Stokes, and Richard Maltby. London: BFI Publishing, 1999. 42–60.

Stricker, Frank. "Cookbooks and Law Books: The Hidden History of Career Women in 20th Century America." *Journal of Social History* 10 (1976): 1–19.

Strom, Sharon Hartman. *Beyond the Typewriter: Gender, Class, and the Origins of Modern American Office Work, 1900–1930*. Urbana: University of Illinois Press, 1992.

Summers-Bremner, Eluned. "Post-Traumatic Woundings: Sexual Anxiety in Patricia Cornwell's Fiction." *New Formations: A Journal of Culture/Theory/Politics* 43 (Spring 2001): 131–47.

Taking Lives Official Website <http://takinglives.warnerbros.com> (accessed 23 March 2004).

Tasker, Yvonne. *The Silence of the Lambs*. London: BFI Publishing, 2002.

———. *Working Girls: Gender and Sexuality in Popular Cinema*. London: Routledge, 1998.

Taubin, Amy. "Grabbing the Knife: *The Silence of the Lambs* and the History of the Serial Killer Movie." *Women and Film: A Sight and Sound Reader*. Eds. Pam Cook, and Philip Dodd. London: Scarlet Press, 1991. 123–31.

Taves, Brian. "The B Film: Hollywood's Other Half." *Grand Design: Hollywood as a Modern Business Enterprise, 1930–1939*. Ed. Tino Balio. New York: Charles Scribner's Sons, 1993. 313–50.

Thompson, John. "Note on *The Trouble with Women* (1947)." *The Toronto Film Society* (11 Aug 1981).

Todd, Drew. "Decadent Heroes: Dandyism and Masculinity in Art Deco Hollywood." *Journal of Popular Film and Television* 32.4 (Winter 2005): 168–81. (e-text)

Todorov, Tzvetan. *The Poetics of Prose*. Trans. Richard Howard. Ithaca, New York: Cornell University Press, 1977.

Traub, Valerie. "The Ambiguities of 'Lesbian' Viewing Pleasure: The (Dis)articulations of *Black Widow*." *Body Guards: The Cultural Politics of Gender Ambiguity*. Eds. Julia Epstein, and Kristina Straub. New York: Routledge, 1991. 305–28.

Vanacker, Sabine. "V.I. Warshawski, Kinsey Millhone and Kay Scarpetta: Creating a Feminist Detective Hero." *Criminal Proceedings: The Contemporary American Crime Novel*. Ed. Peter Messent. London: Pluto, 1997. 62–88.

Vasey, Ruth. *The World According to Hollywood, 1918–1939*. Madison: The University of Wisconsin Press, 1997.

Viviani, Christian. "Who is Without Sin? The Maternal Melodrama in American Film, 1930–39." *Home is Where the Heart is: Studies in Melodrama and the Woman's Film*. Ed. Christine Gledhill. London: BFI Publishing, 1987. 83–99.

Waites, Kate. "Babes in Boots: Hollywood's Oxymoronic Warrior." *Chick Flicks: Contemporary Women at the Movies*. Eds. Suzanne Ferriss and Mallory Young. New York: Routledge, 2008. 204–20.

Waldman, Diane. " 'At Last I Can Tell It to Someone!' Feminine Point of View and Subjectivity in the Gothic Romance Film of the 1940s." *Cinema Journal* 23.2 (1984): 29–40.

Walker, Janet. "Hollywood, Freud and the Representation of Women: Regulation and Contradiction, 1945–early 60s." *Home is Where the Heart is: Studies in Melodrama and the Woman's Film.* Ed. Christine Gledhill. London: BFI Publishing, 1987. 197–214.

Walsh, Andrea S. *Women's Film and Female Experience: 1940–1950.* New York: Praeger Special Studies, 1984.

Walton, Pricilla L., and Manina Jones. *Detective Agency: Women Rewriting the Hard-Boiled Tradition.* Berkeley: University of California Press, 1999.

Ware, Susan. *Holding their Own: American Women in the 1930s.* Boston: Twayne Publishers, 1982.

Weiss, Andrea. *Vampires and Violets.* New York: Penguin Books, 1992.

Werner, James V. "The Detective Gaze: Edgar A. Poe, the Flaneur, and the Physiognomy of Crime." *The American Transcendental Quarterly* 15.1 (March 2001): 5–21.

Whatling, Clare. *Screen Dreams: Fantasizing Lesbians in Film.* Manchester: Manchester University Press, 1997.

Whitney, Allison. "Race, Class, and the Pressure to Pass in American Maternal Melodrama: The Case of *Stella Dallas.*" *Journal of Film and Video* 59.1 (2007): 3–18.

Wikipedia <http://en.wikipedia.org> (accessed 1 March 2007).

Williams, Linda. "Film Bodies: Gender, Genre, and Excess." *Film Quarterly* 44.4 (1991): 2–13.

———. "Melodrama Revisited." *Refiguring American Film Genres: Theory and History.* Ed. Nick Browne. Berkeley, CA: University of California Press, 1998. 42–88.

Williams, Linda Ruth. *The Erotic Thriller in Contemporary Cinema.* Bloomington: Indiana University Press, 2005.

Williams, Tony. "*Phantom Lady*, Cornell Woolrich, and the Masochistic Aesthetic." *Film Noir Reader.* Eds. Alain Silver and James Ursini. 7th Limelight ed. New York: Limelight Editions, 2003. 129–43.

Wilson, Elizabeth. "The Invisible Flâneur." *Postmodern Cities and Spaces.* Eds. Sophie Watson, and Katherine Gibson. Reprint ed. Cambridge, MA: Blackwell, 1996. 59–79.

———. *The Sphinx in the City: Urban Life, the Control of Disorder, and Women.* Berkeley: University of California Press, 1991.

Wolff, Janet. *Feminine Sentences: Essays on Women and Culture.* Berkeley: University of California Press, 1990.

World Wide Words <www.worldwidewords.org> (accessed 1 March 2007).

Yesil, Bilge. " 'Who Said this is a Man's War?': Propaganda, Advertising Discourse and the Representation of War Worker Women During the Second World War." *Media History* 10.2 (2004): 103–17.

Young, Kimball. Address at the *Motion Picture Conference* (Wisconsin Federation of Women's Clubs). Department of Social Psychology, University of Wisconsin-Madison (10 Oct 1934). 10 pp.

Zinman, David. "Torchy Blane and Glenda Farrell." *Filmograph 3* (1973): 38–43.

Film Reviews

Adventurous Blonde, The [Rev.] Motion Picture Herald (11 Sept 1937): 40, 47.

Anybody's Blonde [Rev. by Mark] Variety (24 Nov 1931): 21.

Are You There? [Rev.] Exhibitors Herald-World (6 Dec 1930).

————. Variety (14 July 1931).

Back in Circulation [Rev.] Variety (27 July 1937): 3.

————. [Rev.] Motion Picture Herald (7 Aug 1937): 52.

Black Widow [Rev. by David Denby] New York (16 February 1987): 72.

Blue Steel [Rev. by Jamie Portman] Toronto Star (14 March 1990): C1+.

————. [Rev. by Jay Scott] Globe and Mail (19 March 1990): C9.

————. [Rev. by David Denby] New York (26 March 1990): 76–77.

————. [Rev. by Claudia Puig] Los Angeles Times (8 April 1990): 5+.

Bone Collector, The [Rev. by Rick Groen] Globe and Mail (5 Nov 1999) <http://www. theglobeandmail. com/servlet/story/MOVIEREVIEWS.19991105.TABONE/ MovieStory/Entertainment/Movies> (accessed 30 March 2009).

————. [Rev. by Stephen Holden] New York Times (5 Nov 1999) <http://movies. nytimes.com/movie /review?res=9D02E4DC1E3BF936A35752C1A96F958260> (accessed 30 March 2009).

————. [Rev. by Amy Taubin] Village Voice (16 November 1999): 136.

Bulldog Drummond's Peril [Rev. by V.K.] Motion Picture Herald (12 Mar 1938): 43.

Cinderella Man [Rev. by Scott Feschuk] National Post (8 June 2005): AL4.

Coma [Rev. by Robert Martin] Globe and Mail (14 February 1978): 14.

Copycat [Rev. by Rob Salem] Toronto Star (27 Oct 1995): C3+.

————. [Rev. by Kenneth Turan] Los Angeles Times (27 October 1995): Calendar 1.

————. [Rev. by Lizzie Francke] Sight and Sound 6.5 (May 1996): 51–2.

Daring Young Man, The [Rev.] Variety (24 July 1935): 56.

Date with the Falcon, A. [Rev.] Motion Picture Herald Product Digest (8 Nov 1941): 350.

Deadline at Dawn [Rev.] Variety (12 Feb 1946): 3+.

————. [Rev. by Otis I. Guernsey Jr.] New York Herald Tribune (4 April 1946).

Deadline for Murder [Rev.] Hollywood Reporter (J.D. Grant 17 June 1946): 3.

Destination Murder [Rev.] Hollywood Reporter (7 June 1950): 3.

Detective Kitty O'Day [Rev.] Hollywood Reporter (22 Mar 1944): 3.

————. [Rev.] Variety (22 Mar 1944): 4.

Fly Away Baby [Rev.] Hollywood Reporter (2 Jun 1937): 3.

Follow Me Quietly [Rev.] Motion Picture Herald Product Digest (16 July 1949): 4681–82.

Forty Naughty Girls [Rev. by Bert.] Variety (8 Sept 1937): 18.

Foxy Brown [Rev. by Beau.] Variety (17 April 1974).

Girl from Havana, The [Rev. by Bige.] Variety (4 September 1929).

Girl on the Front Page, The [Rev. by Edga.] Variety (11 November 1936): 14.

High Crimes [Rev. by Rick Groen] Globe and Mail (5 April 2002) <http://www. theglobeandmail.com/ servlet/story/MOVIEREVIEWS.20020405.RVHIGH/ MovieStory/Entertainment/Movies> (accessed 30 March 2009).

Human Cargo [Rev. by Charles R. Metzger for Joseph Breen] PCA (20 March 1936).

Mike's Murder [Rev. by Vincent Canby] New York Times (9 March 1984): C16.

Mystery of the Wax Museum, The [Rev.] Film Daily (18 Feb 1933): 3.

Office Scandal, The [Rev. by Waly.] Variety (24 July 1929).

Off the Record [Rev. by Hobe.] Variety (22 Feb 1939): 12.

One Mile from Heaven [Rev.] Motion Picture Daily (17 July 1937): 3

———. [Rev.] Motion Picture Herald. (24 July 1937): 47+.

Physical Evidence [Rev. by Leonard Klady] Los Angeles Times (9 August 1987): 30.

———. [Rev. by Manohla Dargis] Village Voice (7 February 1989): 68.

Private Detective [Rev.] Variety (30 Nov 1939): 3.

———. [Rev.] Variety (6 Dec 1939): 14.

———. [Rev. by Doris Arden] Chicago Times (7 Jan 1940): 22.

Secrets of the Underground [Rev.] Motion Picture Daily (13 Feb 1943).

Sheba, Baby [Rev.] New York Times (27 March 1975): 37.

Silence of the Lambs, The [Rev. by B. Ruby Rich] Village Voice (5 March 1991): 59.

———. [Rev. by Amy Taubin] Village Voice (5 March 1991): 56.

Sliver [Rev. by Jeff Giles] Newsweek (31 May 1993): 54

Smart Blonde [Rev. by Shan.] Variety (13 Jan 1937): 13.

Stranger on the Third Floor [Rev. by Roscoe Williams] Motion Picture Daily (5 Sept 1940): 4.

———. [Rev. W.R.W.] Motion Picture Herald (7 Sept 1940): 40.

Suspect [Rev. by Pauline Kael] New Yorker (16 Nov 1987): 145–46.

Taking Lives [Rev. by Stephen Cole] Globe and Mail (19 March 2004) <http://www. theglobeandmail. com/servlet/story/MOVIEREVIEWS.20040319.TAKING19/ MovieStory/Entertainment/Movies> (accessed 30 March 2009).

———. [Rev. by Owen Gleiberman] Entertainment Weekly (26 March 2004) <http:// www.ew.com/ew /article/0,,601908,00.html> (accessed 30 March 2009).

There Goes My Girl [Rev. by Scho.] Variety (16 June 1937): 13.

TNT Jackson [Rev. by Mack.] Variety (19 February 1975).

Twisted [Rev. by Geoff Pevere] Toronto Star (27 February 2004): D8.

Unknown Woman [Rev.] Variety (26 Jun 1935): 26.

Untraceable [Rev. by Stephen Holden] New York Times (25 Jan 2008) <http://movies. nytimes.com/2008/01/25/movies/25untr.html> (accessed 30 March 2009).

Woman on the Run [Rev. by A.W.] New York Times (30 Nov 1950): 24.

Index

Abbott, Laurie, 152

Adams, Amy, 44

Adams, Hilda, 23, 29

Adams, Madge, 315

Adams, Ruth, 158

Adam's Rib (1949), 227–229

Adventures of a GIrl Reporter (1914), 335*n10*

The Adventures of Jane Arden (1939), 95, 129, 308, 341*n11*

The Adventures of Judith Lee (Marsh), 20

The Adventures of Kitty O'Day (1944), 159, 320

The Adventurous Blonde (1937), 72, 95, 122, 126, 146

"The Affairs of Ann Scotland" (radio), 71

After Office Hours (1935), 95, 304

After the Thin Man (1936), 333*n1*

Ainsworth, Cupid, 99

Albrecht, Donald, 61

Aldrich, Martha, 124, 125, 129

Aliens (1986), 225, 266

All About Eve (1950), 3

Allen, Diana, 25

Allen, Grant, 20

Allingham, Margery, 28

Allison, May, 335*n9*

All that Heaven Allows (1955), 174

Allwyn, Astrid, 80, 131, 147, 307, 309

Along Came a Spider (2001), 254, 280

Altman, Rick, 6, 7

Amateur City (Forrest), 263

Amazing Lovers (1921), 25

American International Pictures, 194, 216

American Psycho (2000), 273

Ames, Christopher, 279

Anderson, Mary, 312

An Hour before Dawn (1913), 24, 73

Ann Carver's Profession (1933), 227

Another Thin Man (1939), 333*n1*

Antifeminism, 30

Anybody's Blonde (1931), 95, 103, 302

Arbus, Allan, 200

Archer, Anne, 244

Archer, John, 147

Arden, Doris, 151

Arden, Jane, 129

Are You There? (1931), 73

Arlen, Michael, 70

Armchair detective, 5

Armstrong, Robert, 99, *100*

Arson Gang Busters (1938), 95

Art Deco, 59–63, 338*n13*

Arthur, Jean, 58

Astaire, Fred, 61

Atherton, "Lou," 124

Atwill, Lionel, 111, 116, 131

Austin, Rose, 25

Ayres, Lew, 104

Baby Face (1933), 61, 336*n3*

Bachelor, Stephanie, 154, 344*n5*

Back in Circulation (1937), 95, 98, 111, 126, 127, 128, 241, 306, 341*n14*, 342*n19*

Back Page (1934), 95, 98

Backus, Jim, 210

Baker, M. Joyce, 137

Baker, Simon, 212

Bakewell, William, 102

Balio, Tino, 38, 47, 55, 60

Ball, Lucille, 167, 321

Bank Alarm (1937), 75, 316

Banks, Margaret, 99

Bardéhe, Maurice, 24

Bari, Lynn, 309, 311

Barnes, Alex, 260

Barrymore, Drew, 220, 290

Bartlett, Keith, 245

Bartlett, Lisbeth, 233

Basic Instinct (1992), 222, 229, 263, 264, 265

Baxter, Anne, 186, 323

Beaumont, Hugh, 168, 169

Beauvoir, Simone de, 30

Bedelia, Bonnie, 244

Bedford, Barbara, 26

The Bedroom Window (1924), 25

Beecher, Janet, 129

Before Midnight (1925), 26

Behind Locked Doors (1948), 139, 146, 313

Behind the Headlines (1937), 95, 110, 126, 127, 305

Bell, Jeannie, 323

Bell, Monta, 104

Bellamy, Ralph, 128, 140

Bellamy, Tony, 112

Bendix, William, 56

Benjamin, Paul, 209

Bennett, Bruce, 153

Bennett, Constance, 304

Bennett, Joan, 305

Bergman, Andrew, 49, 53, 67

Bernard, Jason, 210

Berry, Sarah, 63

Bess the Detectress (1914), 335*n9*

The Best Years of Our Lives (1946), 166

Betrayed (1988), 229, 273, 325, 332

Betz, Phyllis, 264

Beware of Blondes (1928), 26

Beware of Ladies (1936), 95

Big, Brown Eyes (1936), 95, 305

Bigelow, Kathryn, 268

Biggers, Earl Derr, 70

Big News (1929), 93, 95, 98, 99, 100, 264, 302

Big Town (1947), 138, 146

Big Town after Dark (1947), 139, 146, 312

"Big Town" (radio), 71

Big Town Scandal (1948), 139, 146, 313

Birmingham School of Cultural Studies, 12, 31

Blaché, Alice Guy, 25

Black, David, 254

Black, Louis, 183

Black Angel (1946), 167, 172, 174, 175, 178–180, 182–185, 321, 345*n8*

Black Power Movement, 195, 217

Black Widow (1987), 255, 260–263, 264, 265, 273, 277, 325, 332

Blake, Timmy, 111, 127

Blane, Sally, 128

Blane, Torchy, 71, 72, 73, 79, 81, 90, 93, 94, 96, 107–111, 114–124, *120*, 126, 129, 130, 133, 136, 143, 150–153, 340*n4*, 343*n4*

Bleiler, E.F., 21

Blockade (1928), 26

Blonde Ice (1948), 149

Blondell, Joan, 64, 71, 75, 76, 92, 127, 147, 158, 306, 307, 312, 314, 333*n2*, 341*n10*

Blondes at Work (1938), 95, 107, 114, 115, 120, 129, 307, 341*n14*

Blood Work (2002), 262, 273

The Blue Gardenia (1953), 186, 187, 323

Blue Steel (1990), 266–268, 273, 294, 325, 332

Bobo, Jacqueline, 215

Bodnar, John, 52

Body of Evidence (1993), 222

Bogart, Humphrey, 56
Bogle, Donald, 216
Bond, James, 192, 197
The Bone Collector (1999), 254, 276, 280, 281–282, 283, 327, 332
Boozer, Jack, 138
Borrowed Hearts (1941), 138
Bosco, Philip, 233
The Boss of Big Town (1942), 138, 144, 145, 146, 311
Boston Blackie, 70
Bound (1996), 254, 263, 265
B-pictures, 46–49; blaxploitation films as, 11; categories of, 337*n6*; classical detective stories in, 48; during Depression, 46–49; disappearance of, 70; girl reporter, 111; importance to studios, 48; move to television, 70; mysteries, 11; realism of, 48; representations of femininity in, 12; transgressive figure of female detective in, 48, 49
Braddon, Mary Elizabeth, 19
Bradford, Glory, 89
Bradley, Mary, 110, 127
Bradshaw, Booker, 201
Brady, Scott, 157
Brando, Marlon, 192
Brasillach, Robert, 24
Bratt, Benjamin, 291
Breen, Joseph, 46, 114, 126, 132, 133, 336*n4*, 342*n17*, 342*n22*, 343*n4*
Bremer, Lucy, 146, 313
Brent, George, 76, 100, 107, 147, 153, 158
Breslin, Abigail, 44
Brewster, Amy, 27
Brewster, Bonnie, 112, 113
The Bride Wore Crutches (1941), 138, 144, 147, 310
Bridges, Jeff, 229–232
Britton, Barbara, 321
Broderick, Helen, 86, 315
Broe, Dennis, 55
Brooke, Hillary, 146, 312, 313
Brooke, Loveday, 81

Brooks, Jean, 167, 169, 319
Brooks, Leslie, 149
Brown, Clancy, 267
Brown, Jeffrey, 266
Brown, Juanita, 205
Brown, Peter, 204
Browne, Nick, 15
Bruce, Cheryl Lynn, 236
Bruce, Nigel, 69
Bruce, Virginia, 333*n2*
Bryant, Betty, 144
Buchanan, Morris, 198
Bujold, Genevieve, 258–260, 324
Bullitt (1968), 194
Bullock, Sandra, 284–285, 290–292, 327, 328
Burgess, Dorothy, 99, 303
Burke, Billy, 296
Burke, Edwin, 73
Burns, Heather, 291
Burr, Raymond, 161, 186
Butler, Judith, 13
Butterworth, Amelia, 18, 22, 28, 81

The Cabinet of Dr. Caligari (1920), 166, 344*n4*
Cabot, Bruce, 340*n6*
Cadogan, Mary, 32, 81
"Cagney and Lacey" (television), 9, 221
Cain, James, 173
Caine, Michael, 291
Calamtiy Anne, Detective (1913), 335*n9*
Call Northside 777 (1948), 144, 191
Camera Obscura (journal), 31
Campbell, Louise, 144, 309
Canby, Vincent, 260
"Candy Matson, Yukon" (radio), 71
Cape Fear (1962), 192
Career Woman (1936), *65*, 226, 227
Carey, MacDonald, 170
Carey, Sue, 147
Carlon, Fran, 71
Carlson, Richard, 146
Carroll, Joan, 227
Carter, Grace, 25
Carter, Nick, 21, 24

Carter, Terry, 191, 199
Casey, Bernie, 204
Cassidy, Joanna, 265
Castle, Don, 167
Castle, Irene, 25
Caviezel, Jim, 250
The Cell (2000), 13
Challenger, Rudy, 207
The Chamber (1996), 245
Chan, Charlie, 11, 70
Chandler, Raymond, 55, 164
Changeling (2008), 44
Channing, Margo, 6
Chanslor, Roy, 152, 342*n15*
Chaplin, Ben, 284
Charles, Nick and Nora, 7, 70
Charlie's Angels 2: Full Throttle (2003), 289, 332
Charlie's Angels (2000), 289, 290
"Charlie's Angels" (television), 8
Charteris, Leslie, 69
The Chase (1966), 192
Chatterton, Ruth, 101
Cheating Cheaters (1919), 25, 26
Chelsea 7750 (1913), 24, 73
Cher, 222, 225, 232–235, *245,* 324
Chick-flicks, 15; crime-fighting, 15, 289–294
Chiles, Lois, 259
China Passage (1937), 75
Chinatown (1974), 283
Chodorow, Nancy, 32
Christie, Agatha, 17, 20, 28, 130
Churchill, Marguerite, 89
Cigarettes, 62
Cinderella Man (2005), 43
Cinema *gris,* 172
The Circular Staircase (Rinehart), 23
Citizen X (1995), 273
City of Chance (1940), 138, 309
City of Missing Girls (1941), 138, 139, 148, 309
Civil Rights Movement, 11
Clarice Dyke, the Female Detective (Rockwood), 335*n6*
Clark, Cliff, 90

Clarke, Ann, 126, 130
Clarke, Mae, 62, 104, 303, 304
Class: adoption of language of lower, 56; identity, 56; middle, 72; mobility of, 56; shaping national culture and, 55; upper, 72; working, 64, 72, 252–253
Class Action (1991), 222, 246–248, 254, 326, 332, 349*n9*
Clements, Stanley, 186
Cleopatra Jones (1973), 196–220, 323
Cleopatra Jones and the Casino of Gold (1975), 217, 218, 323, 346*n3*
The Client (1995), 246, 248–249, 326, 332
Cliffhangar (1993), 271
Clifford, Ruth, 25
Clooney, George, 44
Close, Glenn, 222, 229–232, 236, 244, 324, 348*n2*
Clyde, June, 145, 303, 310, 320
Cobra (1986), 244
Coffin, Estelle, 25
Coffin, Tris, 143
Coffy (1973), 196–206, 347*n5*
Collins, Jim, 97
Collins, Wilkie, 19
The Color Purple (1985), 216
Colt, Marshall, 231
Columbia Pictures, 7, 44, 223
Coma (1978), 34, 258–260, 324
Comedy films, 7, 46–49, 55; screwball, 57, 58, 81
Compson, Betty, 26
Connick, Harry Jr., 276
Conselman, William, 99
Consenting Adults (1992), 222
Constance Dunlap: Woman Detective (Reeves), 23
Conte, Richard, 186
Conway, Tom, 70
Coogan's Bluff (1968), 194
Cook, Elisha Jr., 168, 177
Cook, Pam, 31, 175
Cookson, Peter, 158
Cool, Bertha, 27
Cooper, Susan, 130, 150

Copycat (1995), 14, 276–279, 283, 294, 326, 332

Cornwell, Patricia, 14, 273

The Corpse Came C.O.D. (1947), 139, 148, 312

The Corpse Vanishes (1942), 97, 98, 129, 138, 139, 143, 149, 311

Cortez, Ricardo, 56, 88, 147

Cotten, Joseph, 170

Cotton Comes to Harlem (1970), 196

Counterfeit (1919), 25

Cowan, Ruth Schwartz, 30, 50

Cowie, Elizabeth, 34, 163

Coyote, Peter, 229

Craig, Patricia, 32, 81

Cranston, Lamont, 131

Crawford, Joan, 57, 60, 64, 102, 302, 337*n5*

Cregar, Laird, 168

Crehan, Joseph, 119

Crime Club, 79

The Crime Doctor, 70

Crime of Passion (1957), 135, 160, 162, 313

Criminalists, 7, 15, 272–289, 333*n4*

Criminals Within (1943), 138, 139, 145, 311

Criminologists, 7, 333*n4*

Croft, Lara, 290

Cross, Joseph, 295

Cruise, Tom, 245

The Crush (1993), 222

"CSI" (television), 273

Cullen, Jerry, 108, 109

Cultural identity, 56

Culture: high, 12; lesbian, 13; mass, 12; popular, 12

Cummings, Claire, 149

Curtis, Alan, 175

Curtis, Jamie Lee, 266–268, 325

Dalton, Elizabeth, 57, 81, 114, 132, 150, 340*n4*

Damon, Matt, 245

Dance, Fool, Dance (1931), 46, 57, 95, 102, 302, 337*n5*

The Danger Girl (1926), 26

Daniels, Bebe, 26

Daniels, Jeff, 262

Dano, Royal, 160

Dargis, Manohla, 225, 349*n8*

The Daring Young Man (1935), 52, 95, 146

The Dark Corner (1946), 55321

Darwell, Jane, 89, 316

Davis, Bette, 3, 64, 107, 304, 337*n5*

Davis, Joan, 89

Davis, Ossie, 248

Davis, Todd, 34, 283

Day, William Patrick, 18

The Dazzling Miss Davison (1917), 25

The Dead Letter (Victor), 18–20

Deadline at Dawn (1946), 167, 168, 320

Deadline for Murder (1946), 139, 144

Dean, Priscilla, 26

Deane, Myra, 103

Death From a Distance (1935), 95, 120, 304

Deaver, Jeffrey, 273

"Decoy" (television), 8, 192

Dee, Frances, 110, 303

The Deep End of the Ocean (1999), 13

Defenseless (1991), 222, 224, 238–241, 326, 332, 348*n2*

Dell, Claudia, 74, 314

DellaCava, Frances, 28

Del Ruth, Roy, 56

Demolition Man (1993), 271

De Mornay, Rebecca, 16, *16,* 223, 241–243, 244, 326

Dempsey, Florence, 95, 98, 111, 115, 116, 118, 131, 132

Denby, David, 254, 263

Dench, Judi, 44

Destination Murder (1950), 185, 186, 322

Detective Dorothy (1912), 335*n9*

Detective Dot (1913), 335*n9*

Detective-hero: criminologist, 7, 333*n4*; softboiled, 69–72; specialized knowledge and, 7, 8, 252–253; undercover agents, 7

Detective Kitty O'Day (1944), 158, 319

Detectives, classical: threats to social order and, 17; upper class anxieties and, 17

Detectives, female: ability to wield deadly weapons, 266; absence from 1950's films, 159–162; acceptance of heteronormative relationships by, 276; acts of defiance by, 278; adolescent, 169–172; black, 9, 13, 15; in B-pictures, 48, 49; as buddy to black male detective, 254, 279–282; cast as sidekick, 136, 139, 158; challenging sex roles, 13; concern with proving abilities, 5; criminalists, 272–289, 333*n*4; defies prescribed gender role, 36; degree of feminism represented by characters in, 32–33; "dyke dicks," 13, 14, 263; early, 17, 18; embodiment of things American and modern, 54; failure with audiences as cop-action hero, 271; feminine intuition and, 127, 128; feminine/masculine traits and, 3, 13, 21, 22, 97–111; femininity-achievement conflict for, 71; feminist criticism on, 30–39; femme fatales, 9, 13; in fiction, 17–23; fighting back, 275; as figure of parody, 15, 271; in *film noir,* 163–172; financial necessity and, 101, 102, 117; former victims of male violence, 284–285; as "gender-benders," 6, 12; hardboiled, 10, 27, 70, 71, 97, 98, 100, 102, 103, 110, 111, 112, 115, 117, 269; hyperfeminine, 269, 287; importance of type of clothing, 63, 64; justification for masculine activities of, 23, 24; Latina, 13; lawyers, 9, 15; lesbian, 263 (*See also* Lesbian(s)); love interests, 76, 85, 86, 87, 88, 91, 94, 114; "lust of investigation" of, 6, 105; marriage/career dilemma and, 4, 5, 6, 10, 102, 105, 106, 107; in melodrama-noir, 172–185; need for rescue, 39; negative experience with patriarchy, 273; as official investigators, 257–297; oppositional to socially accepted female behavior, 36; physical action by, 120; police officers, 7, 154, 155; possession of female knowledge by, 129–133, 250, 276; private investigators, 7, 8, 17, 18, 27; problems with male authority, 258; professional, 7, 154–157; professional/personal balance and, 3, 4, 10; question of identity in, 258; on radio, 71; as reader of clues, 35; "reading" crime scene differently, 32–33; refeminization of, 102, 281, 282, 285–286; regarded as problematic, 36; sharing investigation with love interest, 136; in silent films, 23–27; softboiled, 69–72; spinsters, 18, 28; status unrevealed until end of film, 36, 77; struggle to prove professional legitimacy, 257; struggle to pursue career in male world, 7; on television, 192; trust in wrong person, 39, 149, 183, 250–252; undercover, 9, 36, 71, 75–77, 154–157; willingness to abandon career for marriage, 3

Detectives, female (amateur), 5, 7, 9, 15, 65, 77–92, 157–159; nurses, 87–91; socialites, 78–81, 113; spinsters, 81–87; temporary interest by, 80

Detectives, female (black): ability to fashion weapons from ordinary objects, 196, 206; competence of, 197, 207; empowerment because of race and sex, 196; as hypersexualized and objectified, 214; infiltration of criminal organizations by, 196; masculinity of, 203, 204; moments of feminine weakness by, 205, 206; sexual threat to males of, 203; sole existing strong female film figures, 197; as strong, central protagonist, 214; use of phallic weapons, 196, 199; vigilante roles of, 197–200

Detectives, female (film noir), 164–172; nurturer/femme fatale bifurcation

of roles in, 165, 166; as sexualized
mother figure for hero, 166
Detectives, female (girl reporter), 9,
15, 56, 58, 59, 65–68, 93–133, 99,
138–153, 302–313; alterations in
roles for, 150–153; appearance and
dress, 98–99; case studies, 111–124,
150–153; diminishing agency of,
139; empowered gaze of, 131, 132;
feminine ethics and, 124–129;
feminine intuition and, 127, 128;
as feminist hero, 96–97; as *flâneuse,*
65–68; hardboiled, 128; independence
of, 67; interfering, 143; marriage/
career dilemma and, 121, 122, 123,
124, 133, 146–148; parodic decline
in, 139–144; pitted against male
competitor, 98; possession of female
knowledge by, 129–133; possession
of the gaze herself, 65; rescued by
male protagonist, 98; saving loved
one, 9, 99; secondary role to male
investigator, 144–146; self-parody
in, 98; as sidekick, 139; as signifier
detached from Depression origins,
144; sob sisters, 101–107; treated as
colleague, 65; well-meaning, 143
Detectives, male: consistent appearance in
film, 8; in fiction, 17–23; hardboiled,
17, 27, 55; private investigators, 17
Detective Story (1951), 192
Devil's Mate (1933), 95
Diaz, Cameron, 220, 290
DiBattista, Maria, 55, 57, 58
Dickinson, Angie, 192
Die Hard (1988), 223, 257
Dietrich, Marlene, 49
Dietrichson, Phyllis, 165
Digges, Dudley, 56
Dilley, Kimberly, 35, 257
Dimendberg, Edward, 67
Dirty Harriet, 265, 291
Dirty Harry, 11, 197
Dirty Harry (1971), 194
Disbarred (1939), 227
Disclosure (1994), 222

Dixon, Wheeler Winston, 48
Doane, Mary Ann, 36, 215
Dobson, Tamara, 196, 199, *201,* 214,
215, 323, 349*n1*
Dr. No (1962), 192
Doherty, Thomas, 45, 46
Dole, Carol, 290, 292
Donlevy, Brian, 113
Doomed to DIe (1940), 94, 110, 139,
309
DoQui, Robert, 200
Doran, Ann, 145, 311
Double Alibi (1941), 94, 110, 147, 309
Double Indemnity (1944), 165
Double Jeopardy (1999), 250, 332
Douglas, Kirk, 192
Douglas, Melvyn, 333*n1,* 333*n2*
Douglas, Michael, 244, 258–260
Dowling, Constance, 178
Doyle, Arthur Conan, 17, 130
Drake, Betsy, 169, 322
Draper, Cheryl, 187
Dreier, Hans, 60
Dresner, Lisa, 20, 333*n3*
Drew, Nancy, 4, 15, 28, 57, 65, 71, 77,
78, 79, 81, 169, 317, 318
Drummond, Bulldog, 143
Dunn, James, 103, 112
Dunn, Stephane, 195
Dunne, Irene, 64
Dunye, Cheryl, 219
Dupin, Auguste, 17, 130
Durant, Rosemary, 147
Duryea, Dan, *176,* 178
Dyer, Richard, 111
Dzundza, George, 269

Eastwood, Clint, 194, 262, 265
Eberhart, Mignon, 15, 87, 89
Eckert, Charles, 46, 63
Eckhart, Aaron, 252
Edwards, Alan, 112
Edwards, Kate, 22, 293
Egan, Richard, 157
Eilers, Sally, 317
Elliot, George, 19

Elliott, Dick, 152
Elliott, Ross, 180
Elliott, William, 203
Ellison, James, 343*n3*
Elwes, Cary, 280
Emergency Squad (1940), 138, 144, 309
Empowerment, female: of bisexual
    female figure, 264; lesbian, 254,
    263; post-war downturn in attitude
    toward female independence,
    135–139; realistic advancement of,
    4; by specifically female appoach to
    homicide investigation, 14
Engel, Madeline, 28
Erin Brockovich (2000), 250, 252–253,
    327, 332
Erwin, Stuart, 131
Espionage (1937), 95, 98
Eszterhas, Joe, 229, 235
Ethics, film, 124–129, 227
Ethnicity, 13
Evans, Madge, 80
Exclusive (1937), 95, 306
The Experiences of a Lady Detective
    (Hayward), 20
*The Experiences of Loveday Brooke, Lady
    Detective* (Pirkis), 20
Exposed (1947), 154, 344*n5*

Fahey, Jeff, 268
Fair, A.A., 27
Fair Plan (1925), 26
The Falcon, 70
The Falcon's Brother (1942), 70, 139, 311
The Falcon Strikes Back (1943), 139
The Falcon Takes Over (1942), 139, 144,
    311
Faludi, Susan, 222, 234
The Famous Ferguson Case (1932), 95
Fargas, Antonio, 204
Fargo (1996), 289, 327
Farmer, Frances, 306
Farrell, Glenda, 57, *58,* 64, 92, 93, 94,
    111, 114–124, *120,* 129, 130, 131,
    132, 150, 152, 227, 303, 304, 305,
    306, 307, 308, 311, 340*n4, 342n17*

Fashion Model (1945), 159, 320
Fast and Furious (1939), 333*n1*
Fast Company (1938), 333*n1*
Fatal Attraction (1987), 222, 224, 234,
    245
Fatal Beauty (1987), 13
The Fatal Hour (1940), 138, 139, 309
Fatal Instinct (1993), 254
Fawcett, Farrah, 8
Fein, I.A., 90
Fell, Norman, 218
Female (1933), 101
The Female Detective (1913), 335*n9*
The Female Detective (Junior), 20
The Female Eunuch (Greer), 30
The Feminine Mystique (Friedan), 30
Femininity: alternative models of, 24;
    associated traits, 13; in blaxploitation
    films, 12; constructing, 14; ethics and,
    124–129, 227; in girl reporter films,
    124–129; as guise for undercover
    work, 154–157; as masquerade,
    198; proper roles and, 71; used by
    undercover agents, 8, 36; as weakness
    and victimization, 282
Feminism: defining, 19, 35, 39; effect of
    Great Depression on, 50, 51; screen
    theory, 31; second wave, 30, 31, 222;
    seen as unfashionable by younger
    generation in 1920s, 51; theory, 31;
    traditional notions reconciled with
    "masculine" demands of detecting, 21
Feminist: criticism, 4, 30–39; critique of
    texts, 31; degree of in texts, 34–35;
    film theory, 4; first wave, 30; militant,
    30; reflection theory, 31
Femme Fatale (2002), 254, 265
Femme fatales, 9, 13, 133, 138, 269; as
    dangerous femininity, 163; in erotic
    thrillers, 222; in fiction, 27
Fenton, Leslie, 108
Ferguson, Elsie, 25
Ferguson, Kathy, 160
Feschuk, Scott, 43
Fiction: anti-feminist, 19; armchair
    detecting, 29; British detective, 4, 19,

20–21, 43, 55; critique of paternalist
power in, 19; dime novels, 21,
22; domestic novels, 18–20; early
American, 21–23; early detective, 14,
17–23; effect of World War I on, 27,
28; feminine/masculine traits and, 14;
feminist crime, 257; femme fatales
in, 27; golden age of, 27–29; gothic,
18–20, 334n2; "had-I-but-known,"
18, 20, 23; lesbian mystery, 14, 263;
limitations on heroines in, 20; *Old
Sleuth* series, 21, 22; periodical, 20;
sensation novels, 19
15 Maiden Lane (1936), 75, 80, 315
Filipcevic, Vojislava, 61
Film noir, 19, 43, 69, 136, 158, 162,
293; anxieties of postwar masculinity
and, 174; challenge to restrictions of
Production Code by, 164; changed
images of women in, 165; changing
gender roles in, 165; chiaroscuro visual
style in, 173; dark vision of society
in, 166; "fallen women" in, 4; female
detectives in, 162–172; hardboiled
private eye in, 8; hybridization of
generic conventions in, 15; male
paranoid fears in, 165; problems
of returning veterans and, 165;
psychoanalytic frameworks in, 164,
165; representation of marriage and
family in, 182; scarcity of female
detectives in, 9; sex and violence in,
164; shift in conception of city in, 67
Film(s). *See also* specific types: appeal
to broadest audience possible, 56;
assault on women's rights in, 222;
biracial buddy cop, 254, 279–282;
B-picture, 10, 11, 46–49; chick flick,
15, 289–294; comedy, 46–49, 55, 57;
conspiracy theories in, 259; couple-
detective, 7; cross-class fantasy in,
56; cultural relevance of, 32; defining
American national identity through,
56; demand for realistic portrayals
in, 193; double feature, 10, 11;
empowered representations of women

in, 4; encoded meanings in, 31, 32;
entertainment function, 5; erotic
thrillers, 222, 223, 254, 263, 348n5;
as escape from realities of Depression,
47; ethnography of audiences, 32;
European, 193; failure to recoup
production costs, 193; female detective
comedies, 15, 289–294; glamorization
of gangsters in, 46; "good girls"
in, 10; horror, 19; house style, 59;
increase in illustration of violence in,
282, 283; inter-war period, 43; male
action, 223, 224; *mise en scène* in,
60, 166, 173; modern style, 59–63,
338n13; mystery-comedy, 7, 11, 15,
46–49, 55; newspaper-crime, 71, 76;
niche subjects for, 193; parody in, 7;
popularity of, 6; postclassical, 15; pre-
Code, 4; Production Code and, 44–
46; as products of their time, 33–38;
profitability of low-budget films, 193;
scrutiny of law enforcement agencies,
72; as social and economic institution,
32; social issue, 71; socioeconomic
change and, 16; specificity of, 33–38;
studio era of, 44–46; studio look, 59;
studio system and, 111; theorizing
gender and, 17–39; use of new
technology to bring in audiences, 193
Films, blaxploitation, 9, 15, 258;
alternative representations of
masculinity in, 11; B-level status of,
197; blurred gender lines in, 13;
as B-pictures, 11; calls for equality
and, 195; derogatory images of black
subculture in, 195; dialogue, 195;
empowered models of womanhood in,
217; exploitation of black community
by, 194; exploration of strengths of
black community in, 202; female
vigilantes in, 191–220; formula for,
194–195; gender issues in, 203–206;
gender roles in, 197–200; heroines as
everyday women in, 217; heroines as
role models, 210–220; polarization of
black filmgoers by, 195; popularity

Films *(continued)*
  of, 197; redefinition of black female
  beauty in, 217; reimaging of black
  masculinity in, 195; representations
  of femininity in, 12; revision of
  Hollywood racial codes by, 204; scenes
  of action in, 196; social messages in,
  196; social problems as subject matter,
  200–202; specialized knowledge of
  black community in, 13; stereotypes of
  black masculinity in, 195; women of
  action in, 11
Films, classical, 44–46, 333*n*5, 336*n*1;
  continuity editing style, 44–45; moral
  endings in, 45; old-fashioned gender
  roles in, 4; studio era and, 44–46
Films, female lawyer, 221–255; attempt
  to resolve male anxieties regarding
  feminist empowerment, 222, 223;
  betrayals in, 229–245; class issues in,
  252–253; competence in, 249–253;
  continuation of investigation after
  trial, 254; creation of suspense
  in, 254; demise of, 245; female
  viewers reading of, 224; feminine/
  masculine traits and, 252–253;
  femininity-achievement conflict and,
  226; feminist empowerment in,
  243–244; growing visibility of female
  lawyers and, 222; hybridization of
  courtroom/psychological thriller, 221;
  impossibility of justice through legal
  system in, 225; increase in competence
  of women as detectives in, 254; lawyer
  as detective, 223, 224, 225; marriage/
  career dilemma and, 227, 242;
  predecessors to, 226–229; protagonist
  as "other" in, 224; protagonists shown
  as professionally incompetent, 223,
  229, 230, 231, 238; pursuit of truth
  outside courtroom, 225, 231, 251,
  252; tension between "good lawyers"
  and "good detectives," 253–255
Films, melodrama-noir, 172–185; as
  cautionary tales, 187; defining, 172,
  173; emotional effect of, 172; female
  desire in, 174; innocent heroines in

corrupt universe in, 175; men as cause
  of female protagonist's problems, 174;
  moments of excess in, 174, 177, 179;
  symbolic meaning of everyday objects
  in, 173; visual and aural rhetoric in,
  173
Films, mystery-comedy, 7, 11, 15,
  46–49, 55
Films, silent, 23–27; acceptable roles for
  women in, 23, 24; action as solution
  to mystery in, 24; crime types in, 26,
  27; feminine/masculine traits and, 26,
  27; gender roles in, 26, 27; happy
  endings in, 26; identity in, 26, 27;
  romance in, 26
Films (1930s): amateur detectives in,
  77–92; apparel styles in, 63–64;
  association between upper-class and
  effeminacy, 57, 58; backing away
  from feminist messages, 132–133;
  concentration on American urban
  settings, 54–68; disparity between
  Hollywood representation of women
  and reality, 52; domination by female
  stars, 4; economic circumstances
  determine roles for women in, 52, 53;
  exploration of changing women's roles
  in, 4; "fallen women" in, 4, 52, 53,
  60, 61, 63, 64, 67; female detective,
  9, 314–318; gangster, 54; gender-
  benders, 53; gender of audiences, 38;
  girl reporter, 53, 93–133, 302–308;
  glamorization of gangsters in, 46;
  illusions of reality in, 61; independent
  women in, 5; marriage/career dilemma
  and, 102, 105, 106, 107, 121, 122,
  123, 124, 133; masquerade as strategy
  in, 36; modern style, 59–64; more
  masculinized roles for women in,
  52, 58, 97–124; mystery-comedy,
  11, 46–49, 55; nurse detectives,
  87–91; period of modernity, 54;
  police matrons in, 75; postponement
  of marriage depicted in, 53; private
  detectives in, 73–75; professional
  detectives in, 69–77; refashioning
  of America's image through, 55;

reflection of change in marital roles in, 53; rejection of marriage in, 5, 6; representation of female detectives in, 10; sob sister, 101–107; social context in, 133; socialite sleuths in, 78–81, 113; softboiled detectives in, 69–72; sound, 54–59; spinster sleuths, 81–87; success and freedom for female detectives in, 15; undercover detectives in, 75–77; upholding of law by G-men, 46; urban images in, 61–62; use of cigarettes to signify modernity in, 62; use of modern language in, 55; women's ability to compete with men in, 59

Films (1940s), 135–162; with adolescent detectives, 169–172; amateur detectives in, 157–159; antifeminist messages in, 135–138; demise of girl reporter in, 15; "fallen women" in, 4; female detective, 318–322; femme fatales in, 138, 163; *film noir,* 136, 158, 162–172; girl reporter, 138–153, 309–313; hardboiled detectives in, 8; marriage/career dilemma and, 142, 146–148, 154–157, 159; melodrama-noir, 172–185; mysogynist satire in, 137; parodic decline in girl reporter films, 139–144; positive image of police force in, 144; positive portrayals of women returning to traditional roles, 138; professional detectives in, 154–157; representation of "positive" female role models in, 136; saving loved one in, 9, 99; secondary role of girl reporter to male investigator, 144–146; symbolic meaning of everyday objects in, 173; transformation of female detectives in, 135–162; "weepies," 173; women cast as sidekicks in, 136, 139, 158

Films (1950s), 185–188; absence of female detective, 159–162; corrupt detectives in, 8, 192; female detective, 322–323; negative image of female detectives in, 185–188

Films (1960s): absence of police detectives in, 8; criminals as protagonists in, 192; dearth of detectives in, 191; increased focus on action, 192; police procedurals in, 191; spies in, 192

Films (1970s): blaxploitation, 15, 191–220; female detective, 323–324; masquerade as strategy in, 36, 37; vigilantes in, 8

Films (1980s): action, 265; actors associated with feminist empowerment, 222, 223; appearance of feminist models in, 223; biracial buddy cop, 254, 279–282; black female investigators in, 9; cop-action, 265, 266; dominance of police detectives in, 8–9; dominated by male heroes, 257; ethics as feminine trait in, 227; exploration of crisis of masculinity in, 223; female appropriation of male violence in, 225; female detective, 324–325; female lawyer, 221–255; feminine/masculine traits and, 229–245, 260–263, 266, 268, 269; feminist empowerment in, 243–244; hardboiled private detective in, 8; lesbian roles in, 263; male action heroes in, 223, 224; male love/authority figure in, 259; official female investigators in, 257–297; predecessors to female lawyer roles, 226–229; professional/personal balance and, 229–245; protagonists pesented as dangerously ambitious, 223; toughening of female body in, 266; uniforms as equalizers in, 267; women trying to attain professional success in, 222, 223

Films (1990s): cop-action, 266; crime scene investigation in, 271; criminalist in, 9, 271–289; "David/Goliath" stories, 248, 249, 252, 253; ethics in, 246–248; ethics v. vigilantism in, 249; female detective, 325–327; female lawyers, 9, 245–249; feminine/masculine traits and, 246–248, 268, 269; gender-benders, 255; "Grisham Cycle," 241, 245–249, 348*n1,* 349*n9;*

Films (1990s) *(continued)*
  issues of gender and sexuality in, 274;
  lesbian roles in, 263; male love/
  authority figure in, 259; professional/
  personal balance and, 248–249, 251,
  252; redefinition of gender identity in,
  274; serial killers and, 272, 273
Films (2000s): competent female
  lawyers in, 249–253; dominance of
  criminalists in, 9; female detective,
  327–328
Final Analysis (1992), 222
The Final Edition (1932), 95, 104, 126,
  130, 303, 342*n15*
Finn, Daniel, 24, 25, 71, 94
Finney, Albert, 252
The Firm (1993), 245–249
The First Wives Club (1996), 221
Fischer, Lucy, 63
Fishburne, Laurence, 247
Fitton, Amanda, 28
Fitzgerald, F. Scott, 55
Five of a Kind (1938), 95, 112, 114,
  226, 307
Five Star Final (1931), 93, 126
Flanagan, Jezzie, 280
Flânerie, 65–68
Fletcher, Jessica, 4, 5, *5,* 9, 82, 336*n14*
The Floor Above (1914), 25
The Floor Below (1918), 335*n10*
Fly Away Baby (1937), 95, 96, 122, 146,
  306
Follow Me Quietly (1949), 139, 148, 313
Fonda, Henry, 80, 136
Foran, Dick, 154
Ford, Harrison, 244
Forrest, Frederic, 236
Forrest, Katherine, 263, 350*n6*
Forty Naughty Girls (1937), 86, 87, 316
Foster, Ellen, 169
Foster, Jodie, 255, 272–276, 325
Four's a Crowd (1938), 95
The Fourth Face (1920), 335*n10*
"Foxfire" (television), 265
Fox Studios, 44, 47
Foxy Brown (1974), 37, *37,* 196,
  199–220, 323

Francis, Anne, 192
Francis, Arlene, 71
Francke, Lizzie, 276
Frankfurt School, 12
Frazer, Dan, 199
Freeman, J.E., 280
Freeman, Morgan, 250–252, 280
French, Jack, 71
The French Connection (1971), 194
Freud, Sigmund, 135
Frey, Sami, 262
Friday Foster (1975), 197, 208–210, 324
Friedan, Betty, 30, 160
Friedberg, Anne, 66, 67, 68
Friels, Colin, 246
From Reverence to Rape (Haskell), 31
The Front Page (1931), 140
Front Page Woman (1935), 95, 99,
  100, 107, 114, 115, 125, 264, 304,
  341*n14*
Furness, Betty, 128, 306

Gable, Clark, 57, 102
Gale, Stephen, 175
Gangsters, 54, 55
Garbo, Greta, 49, 64
Garcia, Andy, 285–286
Gardner, Erle Stanley, 27
Garfield, Ellen, 107
Gargan, William, 110, 145, 147
Garland, Beverly, 8, 192
Garrick, John, 338*n2*
Gaslight (1944), 174, 346*n11*
Gaze: deflecting, 65; empowered, 67;
  female body as object of, 35; lesbian,
  264; male, 56, 66; oppositional, 216;
  utilization to identify criminals, 66
Gender: blurred lines of, 13; change
  in social conception of, 15–16;
  contingent dimensions of, 36;
  dichotomy, 10; double standard,
  227; in girl reporter films, 124–129;
  hierarchy, 30; identity, 13, 14,
  36, 258; performative, 13, 14,
  36; polarities, 136; relations, 132;
  repolarization of, 175; roles, 4, 10, 13,
  15, 20, 21, 22, 23, 26, 27, 33, 35,

36, 64, 91, 165, 264; social anxiety
and, 16; studies, 4; theorizing, 17–39
Generation of Vipers (Wylie), 135
Genres: change within, 6, 7; defining,
6; hybridity, 7; as products of
socioeconomic moments, 15
Gere, Richard, 244
"Get Christie Love" (television), 8
Gibbons, Cedric, 60
Gibson, Diana, 110, 305
Gibson, Mary, 169
Gibson, Mel, 223
Gilligan, Carol, 32
Gilmartin, "Dallas," 149
Gilmore, Victoria, 343*n3*
The Girl Detective (1914), 25
The Girl from Chicago (1927), 26
The Girl from Havana (1929), 73, 91,
314
The Girl from Scotland Yard (1937), 75,
316
Girl in 313 (1940), 154, 318
The Girl on the Front Page (1936), 95,
106, 132, 305
The Girl Reporter (1913), 335*n10*
Girl Reporter (Good), 96
Girl reporters, 9, 15, 53, 58, 59, 65–68,
93–133, 138–153, 302–313. *See also*
Detectives, female (girl reporter);
alterations in roles for, 150–153;
demise of, 15; diminishing agency
of, 139; as fast-talking dame, 57;
feminine ethics in, 124–129; as
feminist hero, 96–97; as kept women,
341*n10*; marriage/career dilemma and,
146–148; parodic decline in, 139–144;
quick wits of, 56; as sidekick, 139;
sob sisters, 101–107
The Girl Reporter's Scoop (1917), 335*n10*
The Girls on the Front Page (1936), 80
Gladden, Mrs., 20
Gleason, James, 69, 82, *83,* 86, 130
Gleason, Lucile, 75, 314
Gledhill, Christine, 31
Glenn, Scott, 274
The Godfather (1971), 195
Godwin, Frank, 108

Goethals, Angela, 270
Goldberg, Whoopi, 13, 216, 349*n1*
Gold Diggers of 1935 (1935), 62
The Golden Slipper (Green), 23
The Gold Racket (1937), 75
Good, Howard, 94, 96, 340*n4*
Goodwin, Isabella, 18
Gordon, Gavin, 116
Gorenography, 282
Gosling, Ryan, 284
Goth, June, 168
Gould, Nona, 105, 106
Grable, Betty, 167, 319
Grace, Christina, 221, 241
Grafton, Sue, 27, 257
Grand Hotel (1932), 60
Grant, Barry Keith, 272
Grant, Cary, 140, *141*
Grant, Jack, 144
Granville, Bonita, 28, *28,* 78, 317,
318
Graves, Teresa, 8
Gray, Sally, 310
Great Depression, 135; creation of social
climate amenable to transgressive
women, 11; decline in film studio
earnings during, 47; effect on
emergence of detective film, 14; effect
on working women, 49–54; feminist
movement and, 50; film as escape
from realities of, 47; film fascination
with period of, 43, 44; impact on
film attendance, 45; nostalgia for era
of, 43, 44; popularity of detective
fiction in, 27–29; shift in gender roles
during, 10; women in film during, 5;
World War II recovery from, 51
The Great Hospital Mystery (1937), 87,
89, 90, 316
The Great Jewel Robbery (1925), 26
Green, Anna Katharine, 17, 18, 19, 23,
66, 81
The Green Jacket (Lee), 23
Greenstreet, Sydney, 56
Greer, Germaine, 30
Greer, Jane, 165, 337*n5*
Gregory, Linda, 145

Grier, Pam, 13, 37, *37,* 191, 198, 206, 208, 209, *209,* 214, 215, 217, 218, 220, 323, 324, 346*n1,* 348*n11,* 349*n1*

Grisham, John, 245–249

Groen, Rick, 251, 283

Groves, Ernest, 102

Guerrero, Ed, 216, 279

Guilty as Sin (1993), 16, *16,* 221, 222, 223, 241–243, *254, 326, 332*

Gunning, Tom, 57, 66

Hackman, Gene, 246–248

Haines, Jennifer, 241

Halberstam, Judith, 254, 263

Hall, Stuart, 31, 215

Halsey, Harlan, 21

Hamilton, Ann, 168

Hamilton, Linda, 220, 266

Hammett, Dashiell, 17, 55, 70, 164, 344*n3*

The Hand That Rocks the Cradle (1992), 222, 224, 244

Hanson, Helen, 167, 294

Hanson, Philip, 52

Hapke, Laura, 93, 136

Harding, Tess, 58, 136, 137

Hardy, Thomas, 19

Harlow, Jean, 56, 64, 104

Harolde, Ralf, 145

Harris, Julius, 209

Harris, Thomas, 272, 273

Hart, Gracie, 290–292

Hart, James, 27

Hart, Lynda, 254, 263

Hartmann, Susan, 137

"Hart to Hart" (television), 221

Harvey, Sylvia, 182

Haskell, Molly, 31

Hatfield, Hurd, 186

Hatton, Raymond, 108, 122

The Haunted Lady (Rinehart), 23

Haut, Woody, 272

Haver, Phyllis, 59, 108, 131, 302, 337*n12*

Hawke, Ethan, 286

Hawks, Howard, 140, 143

Hawn, Goldie, 221, 325

Hayden, Sterling, 135, 160

Hayes, Isaac, 194

Hayle, Grace, 100

Hays, Will, 45

Hayward, Susan, 168, 320

Hayward, W. Stephen, 20

Hayworth, Rita, 113, 317, 322, 340*n6*

Headline Shooter (1933), 95, 110, 125, 140, 146, 303

Heald, Anthony, 274

Heather, Jean, 165

Heavenly Creatures (1994), 254, 263

Hecht, Ben, 140

Helm, Fay, 176

Hemingway, Richard, 74

Henreid, Paul, 337*n5*

Henshaw, Gail, 71

Hepburn, Katharine, 58, 136, 137, 168, 227–229, 321

Here Come the Waves (1945), 137

Hershey, Barbara, 222, 238–241, 326

Heterosexuality, 254–255; enforcing, 13; equality in relations of, 53; hegemonic, 36

Hi, Nellie! (1934), 95, 98, 115, 119, 150, 152, 153, 304

Hickson, Joan, 336*n14*

High Crimes (2002), 250–252, 328, 332

High Gear (1933), 95

Hilda Wade (Allen), 20

Hill, Johnnie, 324

His Girl Friday (1940), 58, 94, 110, 139, 140, 141, *142,* 143

Hodges, Joy, 110, 307

Holden, Stephen, 283

Hold That Girl (1934), 57, 95, 98, 112, 114, 226, 304

Hollinger, Karen, 293

Holmes, Sherlock, 17, 20, 43, 69, 130

Holmlund, Chris, 195, 217, 218, 219, 254, 263

Homans, Bob, 143

Homicide Bureau (1939), 340*n6*

Homosexuality, 255. *See also* Lesbian(s); coded as criminal, 264; determining,

264; overtones in early characters, 70; use of term "gay," 99–100
"Honey West" (television), 192
hooks, bell, 215, 216
Hoover, Herbert, 47
Hopkins, Anthony, 275
Hopper, Hedda, 24
Hotely, Mae, 335*n9*
The House Across the Street (1949), 139, 150, 152, 153, 313
House of Horror (1929), 95
The House on 92nd Street (1945), 144, 191
Hovey, Carl, 99
Howard, Josiah, 194, 195
Howes, Reed, 103
How Molly Made Good (1915), 335*n10*
Hughes, Mary Beth, 168, 320
Hull, Warren, 227
Human Cargo (1936), 64, 80, 95, 107, 112, 113, 114, 226, 305
Hunt, Eleanor, 75, 96, 315, 316
Hunt, Marsha, 155
Hunter, Holly, 276–279, *279,* 326
Hunter, Kim, 169, 319
Hunter, Pat, 130, 143
Hurt, Mary Beth, 238
Huston, John, 56, 164, 344*n3*
Huston, Virginia, 155, 165
Hyland, Peggy, 25
Hymer, Warren, 74

I Cover the Big Town (1947), 139, 146
Identity: class, 56; cultural, 56; gender, 13, 14, 36, 258; mobile transformation of, 66; national, 56, 61; purchased, 63; sexual, 166; social, 50; urban, 59
I Killed that Man (1941), 138, 147, 148, 310
Illicit (1931), 337*n5*
Immigration, 54
Impulse (1990), 266, 268–269, 277, 332
In Cold Blood (1967), 192
Innes, Rachel, 23
Insomnia (2002), 262, 273, 328

International Crime (1938), 80, 95, 131, 133, 148, 307
In the Headlines (1929), 95
The Invisible Killer (1939), 96, 308
The Invisible Web (1921), 25
Irish, William, 167, 176
Irons, Glenwood, 14
It Cant Last Forever (1937), 95, 128, 306
I Wouldnt Be in Your Shoes (1948), 167, 321

Jackie Brown (1997), 215
Jackson, Kate, 8
Jackson, Peter, 43
Jackson, Samuel L., 285
Jackson, Selmar, 154
Jacobs, Lea, 61, 63
Jade (1995), 222, 229
Jagged Edge (1985), 222, 223, 224, 229–232, 243, 248, 254, 265, 324, 332, 348*n2*
Jameson, Fredric, 34
The Jazz Girl (1926), 26
Jeffords, Susan, 223
Jenkins, Allen, 88
Jenks, Frank, 143
Jennifer 8 (1992), 222
Jewell, Isabel, 226
Johnson, Barbara, 350*n6*
Johnson, Don, 16, *16,* 221, 241
Johnson, Hildy, 58, 140, 141, 142
Johnston, Claire, 31
Jolie, Angelina, 44, 220, 281, 282, 286–287, 290, 327
Jones, Manina, 14, 270
Jones, Tommy Lee, 248
Jordan, Bonnie, 102, 103
Joy, Christopher, 204
Judd, Ashley, 250–252, 280, 282, 285–286, 327, 328
Judith Lee, Some Pages from Her Life (Marsh), 20
Julie, Angelina, 328
Jump Cut (journal), 31
Junior, Andrew Forrester, 20

Just Cause (1995), 273
Just Off Broadway (1942), 138, 311

Kael, Pauline, 94, 234
Kapelos, John, 242
Kaplan, Cora, 266, 267
Kaplan, E. Ann, 184, 186
Karloff, Boris, 343*n1*
Kate the Cop (1913), 335*n9*
Keate, Sarah, 29, 65, 71, 77, 81, 87, 88, 89, 90, 158
Keating, Sally, 87, 89
Keene, Carolyn, 28
Keep Your Powder Dry (1945), 137
Keith, Robert, 162, 180
Kelly, Dorothy, 335*n9*
Kelly, Paul, 120, 131, 143
Kendall, Elizabeth, 49
Kenyatta, Caro, 205
Kerr, E. Katherine, 233
Kessler, Kelly, 254, 263
Kibbee, Guy, 88, 90
Kilbourne, Lorelei, 71, 146
Kilgallen, Dorothy, 96
The Killers (1964), 192
Kindergarten Cop (1990), 271
King, Geoff, 49
King, Regina, 292
King Kong (1933), 62
King Kong (2005), 43
Kinkaid, Gambler (1916), 25
Kirby, Kate, 24, 73
Kiss Me Deadly (1955), 192
Kiss the Girls (1997), 250, 254, 276, 280–281, 327, 332
Kit Kittredge: An American Girl (2008), 44
"Kitty Keene, Inc." (radio), 71
Klein, Kathleen Gregory, 4, 19, 32, 33, 35, 53, 136
Knight, Wayne, 271
Knowles, Patric, 90
Knox, Elyse, 167, 321
Koehler, Fred, 213
Kotto, Yaphet, 209
Krale, Gerry, 119, 152
Krutnik, Frank, 163, 166, 167, 174

Kuhn, Anna, 32
Kuhn, Annette, 30
Kungl, Carla, 33, 34, 81, 97

"Lady Blue" (television), 265
The Lady Confesses (1945), 168, 320
Lady in Cement (1968), 192
Lady Kate, The Dashing Female Detective, 22, 293
Lady Raffles (1928), 26
Lady Scarface (1941), 138
La Font, Phyllis, 84
Lambert, Midge, 144
Lambert, William, 64
Landis, Carole, 167
Lane, Allen, 89
Lane, Christina, 294
Lane, Diane, 244, 295–297, 327, 328
Lane, Lola, 73, 74, *74*, 84, 91, 93, 119, 120, 121, 143, 168, 304, 307, 310, 314
Lane, Phoebe, 131, 147
Lang, Stephen, 242
Lange, Jessica, 222, 235–236, 325, 348*n2*
Langford, Joan, 106
Langman, Larry, 24, 25, 71, 94
Lansbury, Angela, 5, *5*, 336*n14*
LaPaglia, Anthony, 249
Larkin, Norah, 186
La Rocque, Rod, 80, 131
LaSalle, Mick, 4, 38
The Last Action Hero (1993), 271
The Last Seduction (1994), 222, 254
Laughing at Trouble (1936), 89, 316
Laura (1944), 163, 166, 176
Lauretis, Teresa de, 31
The Law in Her Hands (1936), 226, 227
"Law & Order" (television), 273
Lawrence, Kathy, 146
Lawyers, 9, 15
Leatherheads (2008), 44
The Leavenworth Case (Green), 17, 18–20
Lecter, Hannibal, 273
Lee, Jane, 112
Lee, Jeanette, 23

Legally Blonde: Red, White and Blonde (2003), 250, 289, 332
Legally Blonde (2001), 250, 289, 290, 292, 327, 332
Legion of Decency, 46
Leisure revolution, 10
The Leopard Man (1943), 167, 319
Lesbian(s), 81, 99, 260–263, 346*n1*; black, 13; criticism, 31; growing visibility of, 13; heterosexualized, 254, 263; "masculinized" portrayals of, 264; pushing men from center of narratives, 264; representation in patriarchal system, 265; sociopathic, 254, 263; violent depictions of, 254, 263
Lester, Louise, 335*n9*
Lethal Weapon (1987), 223, 257, 279
Levant, Oscar, 99
Lillie, Beatrice, 338*n2*
Linaker, Kay, 88, 110, 315
Linden, Eric, 145
Lindsay, Margaret, 95, 98, 111, 127, 147, 227, 309, 318
Litel, John, 78, 127
Liu, Lucy, 220, 290
Livingston, Margaret, 109, 131
Locke, Sondra, 268
Loder, Kathryn, 202
Logan, Bobbie, 143
Logan, Jacqueline, 26
Loggia, Robert, 229, 236
Lombard, Carole, 99, *100,* 302
The Lone Wolf and His Lady (1949), 139, 313
The Long Goodbye (1973), 283
Lopez, Jennifer, 13
Lord, Phillips, 343*n3*
Lorre, Peter, 178
Love, Reggie, 248–249
Love is on the Air (1937), 152
Lowe, Edmund, 106
Loy, Myrna, 7, 26, 333*n1*
Lubitsch, Ernst, 49
Lucia, Cynthia, 223, 228, 241, 243, 253, 348*n1,* 348*n4*
Lugosi, Bela, 130, 149
Lyotard, Jean-François, 34

MacArthur, Charles, 140
MacDonald, Edmund, 168
MacKenzie, Joyce, 185, 322
MacLane, Barton, 93, 115, 119, *120,* 129
MacMahon, Aline, 87, 89, 315
MacQueen, Scott, 59
Madame Sphinx (1918), 25
Mader, Katherine, 223
The Mad Game (1933), 95, 112, 114, 226, 303
Madigan (1968), 192
The Mad Miss Manton (1938), 80, 107, 136, 317
Mahdaviani, Bita, 62
Mahoney, John, 233
Maiden Lane (19363), 340*n5*
Mallory, Jane, 110
Maltby, Richard, 5, 11, 37, 45, 46
The Maltese Falcon (1941), 56, 164, 174, 344*n3*
Man, Woman and Sin (1927), 104
Man at Large (1941), 138, 149, 3310
Mann, Michael, 273
Mansfield, Laura, 185
Mantegna, Joe, 233
Mara, Adele, 154
Marlowe, Ann, 145
Marlowe, Mavis, 178
Marple, Jane, 4, 20, 28, 29, 82, 336*n12,* 336*n14*
Marquand, John, 70
Marsh, Marian, 75
Marsh, Richard, 20
Marshall, Brenda, 152, 311
Marshall, Pat, 143
Martin, Angela, 163, 166
Martin, D'Urville, 207
Martin, Robert, 260
Martinez, Oliver, 244
Mary Ryan, Detective (1950), 155
Masculinity: action defined in, 130; associated traits, 13; in blaxploitation films, 11; as embodiment of strength, 282; feminized, 70, 100, 223, 224; penetrating gaze of, 131, 132; social attitudes on, 9; stereotypes of black,

Masculinity *(continued)*
195; threat to from professional women, 222
Mason, Bobbie Ann, 79
Mason, Perry, 70, 79, 91, 226
Mastrantonio, Mary Elizabeth, 222, 246–248, 326
Matthews, Joan, 154
Mature, Victor, 167
Mayfield, Curtis, 194
Mayo, Virginia, 322
Mayweather, Cassie, 284–285
McBride, Steve, 73
McConaughey, Matthew, 245
McDormand, Frances, 289, 327
McElvaine, Robert, 52, 106, 128
McEwan, Geraldine, *336n14*
McGinley, Ted, 237237
McGuire, John, 167
McGuire, Vicki, 168
McHugh, Frank, 115
McKenzie, Julia, *336n14*
McNab, Claire, *350n6*
McNamara, William, 280
McTiernan, Kate, 280
Mebane, Mary, 202
Meet John Doe (1941), 58, 138, 139
Melamed, Fred, 232
Mellen, Joan, 31
Melodrama-noir, 172–185
Mencken, H.L., 55
Mercurio, Micole, 248
Meredith, Bess, *335n9*
Merrifield, Dick, 207
Merrill, Gary, 187
Merwin, Sam, 27
Metzger, Charles, 73, 114
MGM Studios, 7, 44, 86, 156
Micklebury, Penny, *350n6*
Midnight Manhunt (1945), 138, 144, 312
Mike's Murder (1984), 260, 324, 332
Mildred Pierce (1945), 144, 173
Miles, Rosalind, 209
Miller, Ann, 165
Miller, Carolyn Lisa, 243

Miller, Chris, 157
Millet, Kate, 30
Mindhunters (2005), 273
Minor, Bob, 211
Miss Cayley's Adventures (Allen), 20
Miss Congeniality 2: Armed and Fabulous (2005), 289, 290–292, 328, 332
Miss Congeniality (2000), 289, 290–292, 327, 332
Miss Madelyn Mack, Detective (Weir), 23
Miss Pettigrew Lives for a Day (2008), 44
Miss Pinkerton (1932), 75, 76, 158, 314, 335*n7*
"Miss Pinkerton" (radio), 71
Miss Pinkerton (Rinehart), 23
Miss Raffles (1914), 335*n9*
Miss Sherlock Holmes (1908), 335*n9*
Mr. Deeds Goes to Town (1936), 58, 95
Mr. District Attorney (1941), 138, 145, 310, 343*n3*
Mr. Wong in Chinatown (1939), 96, 143, 308, 343*n1*
Mitchell, Ann, 58
Mitchell, Grant, 80
Mitchum, Robert, 168, 337*n5*
Mizejewski, Linda, 33, 35, 208, 260, 269, 294
Mobility: class, 56; possibility of, 63; social, 54
Modleski, Tania, 19, 34, 165, 174
Moffat, Donald, 247
Moffet, Kathie, 165
"Momism," 135–136
The Monogrammed Cigarette (1910), 25
Monogram Studios, 44, 47
"Moonlighting" (television), 221
Moonlight Murder (1936), 80, 315
Moore, Alida, 263
Morgan, Pat, 109
Morgan, Ralph, 99
Morgan, Stafford, 211
Morley, Karen, 75, 316
Morris, Chester, 80
Morris, Wayne, 147, 153
Motion Picture Association, 126
Motion Picture Conference, 132

Moto, Kentaro, 70
Mueller-Stahl, Armin, 235–236
Muller, Marcia, 257
Mulroney, Dermot, 276
Mulvey, Laura, 31, 35, 56, 67, 173, 215
Muni, Paul, 119
Munro's Publishing House, 21
Munson, Ona, 71
Munt, Sally, 257
Murciano, Enrique, 292
"Murder, She Wrote" (television), 5, 221
Murder at 1600 (1997), 254, 280, 327
Murder at the Vanities (1934), 73
Murder by an Aristocrat (1936), 87, 89
Murder by Numbers (2002), 276, 283,
  284–285, 327, 332
Murder in the Collective (Wilson), 263
Murder in the Vanities, 340n3
The Murder of Dr. Harrigan (1936), 87,
  88, 90, 315
Murder on a Bridle Path (1936), 86,
  315
Murder on a Honeymoon (1935), 83, 83,
  84, 85, 120, 315
Murder on the Blackboard (1932), 84,
  314
"Murders in the Rue Morgue" (Poe), 17
Murphy, Eddie, 265, 279
Muscio, Giuliana, 253
Music Box (1987), 222, 229, 235–236,
  251, 325, 332, 348n2
Mutual Film Corporation vs. Ohio
  Industrial Commission, 45
My Dear Miss Aldrich (1937), 95, 124,
  129, 306
The Mysteries of Udolpho (Radcliffe), 19,
  174
The Mysterious Mr. Tiller (1917), 25
Mystery House (1938), 87, 89, 90, 158,
  317
The Mystery of Richmond Castle (1914),
  25, 73
Mystery of the Wax Museum (1933), 19,
  57, 58, 59, 61, 95, 111, 115, 131,
  132, 150, 303
Mystery Ship (1941), 138, 143, 310

Nagel, Anne, 146, 312
Nagel, Conrad, 75
Naish, J. Carrol, 112
The Naked City (1948), 144, 191
Naremore, James, 172
Narratives: about narrative, 254;
  beginning with effect, 254;
  clarification of, 45; detective, 12;
  mainstream, 35; social reality of, 5
Nash, Ilana, 79
Navy Spy (1937), 75
Nebel, Frederick, 115, 152
Neeson, Liam, 232
Nelson, Barry, 156
Nelson, Christine, 112
Ne Moyer, Frances, 335n9
Newberry, Millicent, 23
New Historicism, 32
News is Made at Night (1939), 96
Nickerson, Catherine Ross, 18, 19, 20,
  23, 81, 174
A Night for Crime (1943), 124, 130,
  138, 139, 150, 311
Night Moves (1975), 283
Nilsson, Anna, 26
Noble, Jean, 265
Nolan, Lloyd, 80
Nolan, Ruth, 131
Nolte, Nick, 279
Nord, Deborah Epstein, 68
North, Sheree, 238
North, Ted, 144
Norton, Chris, 200
No Time to Marry (1938), 95
Novotny, Lawrence, 215, 218
The Nurse's Secret (1941), 158, 319

O'Brien, Pat, 95, 98, 104, 111, 127,
  130
O'Day, Kitty, 71, 344n7
O'Day, Marc, 290
O'Donnell, Chris, 245
The Office Scandal (1929), 59, 93, 95,
  98, 106, 108, 125, 131, 133, 302,
  341n5
Off the Record (1939), 95, 307, 341n10

O'Keefe, Dennis, 145, 167, 180, *181, 343n3*
Oland, Warner, 70
O'Leary, Lance, 89, 90, 91, 158
Oliver, Edna May, 69, 82, 86, 124, 314, 315
One Mile From Heaven (1937), 95, 97, 98, 112, 114, 128, 133, 149, 226, 306
One Wild Night (1938), 95
O'Quinn, Terry, 260–261
Orient Express (1934), 95, 98, 303
Orser, Leland, 281
Orth, Frank, 78
Osborne, Robert, 136
Osmond, Saide, 335n9
O'Sullivan, Margaret, 317
O'Sullivan, Maureen, 124
Our Blushing Brides (1930), 61
Our Dancing Daughters (1928), 61
Our Modern Maidens (1929), 61
Out of Sight (1998), 13
Out of the Past (1947), 165, 337n5
Overbey, Kellie, 240
Owen, A. Susan, 266
Owens, Mary, 18

Pacino, Al, 262
Page, Bradley, 105
Page, Nora, 147
Page, Paul, 73, *74*
Paige, Janis, 153, 313
Paige, Robert, 149
Palmer, Kay, 120
Palmer, Stuart, 15, 28
Paramount Decision/Decree, 192
Paramount Pictures, 44, 45, 47, 194
Pardoe, Janet, 99
Pardon My Stripes (1942), 138
Paretsky, Sarah, 27, 257, 269
Parish, James, 70
Parker, Jean, 159, 319, 320
Parker, Mary Louise, 249
Parker, Terry, 145
Parkhurst, Genevieve, 50
Parks-Masters, Natalie, 71

Parody, 7, 15, 98, 139–144, 271, 335n7
Parole Racket (1937), 95
Parsons, Deborah, 66, 68
Paschal, Mrs., 20
The Patient in Room 18 (1938), 87, 89, 90, 317
Patriarchy, 31, 265, 273
Patrick, Dorothy, 313
Patrick, Gail, 227, 340n3
Patrick, Lee, 319
Patterson, Elizabeth, 76
Patton, Will, 277
Paul, Nancy, 271
Pearl as a Detective (1913), 25
Peggy Does Her Darndest (1919), 335n9
The Pelican Brief (1993), 254, 280, 326, 332, 349n9
Penguin Pool Murder (1932), 69, 83, 84, 85`, 314
Pepper, Barbara, 315
Perils of Our Girl Reporters (1916), 335n10
Personal Secretary (1938), 95, 110, 307
Pevere, Geoff, 285
The Phantom Creeps (1939), 95
Phantom Lady (1944), 166, 167, 172, 174, 175–178, 182–185, 319, 345n8
Phantom Submarine (1940), 94, 110
Phelps, Donald, 172
Phillips, John, 178
Physical Evidence (1989), 222, 225, 236–238, 248, 254, 325, 332
Pidgeon, Walter, 124
Pinkerton National Detective Agency, 18
Piper, Oscar, 82, 83, *83,* 84, 85, 86, 87, 90, 130
Pirkis, Catherine Louisa, 20, 81
Pitts, Michael, 24, 158, 284
Pitts, ZaSu, 86, 87, 316
Place, Janey, 165
Platinum Blonde (1931), 95, 98, 104, 302
Playing with Dynamite, 151
The Plot Thickens (1936), 86, 87, 130, 316
Poe, Edgar Allan, 17, 18, 66, 130, 174

Point Blank (1967), 192
Poirot, Hercule, 82, 130
Poitier, Sidney, 195
Polglase, Van Nest, 60
Police officers: conservatism of, 8;
    corruption and, 8, 233; female, 7, 18,
    154, 155; matrons, 75; positive image
    of, 144
"Police Woman" (television), 192
Pollock, Griselda, 67
Popcorn Venus1 (Rosen), 31
Popwell, Albert, 205
Porter, Edwin, 335*n9*
Portman, Jamie, 268
The Port of Doom (1913), 24, 73
Potter, Monica, 280
Powell, William, 7, 70, 71, 333*n1*
Powers, Stephanie, 192
Pratt, Purnell, 104, 109
Preston, Robert, 227
Presumed Innocent (1990), 244
Private Detective (1939), 73, 150, 151,
    152, 154, 318
Private investigators, 7, 8, 17, 18, 27
Producers Releasing Corporation (PCR),
    48
Production Code, 14, 193, 336*n4*;
    classical Hollywood film and, 44–46;
    impact in representation of women,
    10; implementation of, 132, 133;
    initial lack of enforcement, 45;
    Legion of Decency and, 46; limits
    on sexuality by, 10; replacement of,
    11; as response to suggestive/violent
    films during Depression, 45; strict
    enforcement of, 96; Studio Relations
    Committee and, 45
Production Code Administration (PCA),
    46, 97, 114
Prohibition, 54
Purcell, Dick, 90

Quaid, Dennis, 232
Quinn, Ann, 167

Radcliffe, Ann, 19

Radner, Hilary, 289
Rafter, Nicole, 243
Raines, Ella, 177, 319
The Rainmaker (1997), 245
Rambeau, Marjorie, 25
Randolph, Jane, 311
Rasulala, Thalmus, 209
Rathbone, Basil, 69
Ratings system, 11, 193
Ratiocination, 17, 18, 29, 130
Ray, Jane, 103
Raymond, Gene, 227
Raymond, Robin, 311, 337*n10*
Reardon, Sally, 7
Rear Window (1954), 192
Rebecca (1940), 174, 345*n7*, 346*n11*
Red Dragon (1981), 273
Reddy, Maureen, 19, 35, 39
Redmann, J.M., 350*n6*
Reed, Philip, 146
Reeves, Arthur, 23
Reeves, George, 149
Regester, Seeley, 18–20
Reiner, Robert, 17
Renfro, Brad, 248
Renov, Michael, 166
Republic Studios, 44, 47
Revier, Dorothy, 103, 302
Reynolds, Bobbie, 75, 96
Reynolds, Burt, 237
Reynolds, Craig, 127
Reynolds, Geri, 147
Reynolds, Marjorie, 308, 309, 318
Rice, Florence, 131, 145, 154, *155,* 305,
    310, 311, 318
Rich, B. Ruby, 14, 275
Richman, Carol, 175, 177
Richmond, Kane, 145
Rinehart, Mary Roberts, 6, 15, 19, 23,
    29, 76, 98, 157
Ripley, Ellen, 225, 266
Rivera, Emilio, 251
Rivier, Maisie, 156
RKO Studios, 44, 47, 61, 82, 86, 87
Roberts, Edith, 26
Roberts, Garyn, 21

Roberts, Julia, 252–253, 326, 327,
    349*n9*
Roberts, Lynne, 310
Robinson, Bobbie, 14
Rodgers, Gale, 110
Rogers, Ginger, 49, 61, 109, 303
Rogues' Gallery (1944), 138, 139, 143,
    311, 337*n11*
Roland, Ruth, 25
Rooker, Michael, 235
Rooney, Peggy, 159
Roosevelt, Franklin, 46, 51, 135
Rose, Jamie, 265
Rosen, Marjorie, 31
Rosenbaum, Ron, 276, 277
Ross, Steven, 10, 56
Rossell, Deac, 53, 94
Roth, Eric, 234
Rothman, John, 276
Rubens, Alma, 25
Russell, Rosalind, 94, *141,* 309, 333*n1*
Russell, Theresa, 222, 255, 260, 266,
    268–269, 325, 349*n8*
Ryan, Tim, 158, 159

The Saint, 43, 69
St. John, Adela Rogers, 94, 341*n14*
The Saint's Vacation (1941), 138, 139,
    144, 310
Sanders, George, 69, 70
Sanders, Jay, 270
Sanford, Ralph, 150
Sarandon, Susan, 248–249, 326
Savage, Ann, 312
Saw (2004), 273
Sawyer, Laura, 24, 73
Sayers, Dorothy, 17, 28
Scacchi, Greta, 244
Scarpetta, Kay, 14
Scharf, Lois, 50, 51, 138
Schubart, Rikke, 293
Schulman, Sarah, 263
Schwarzenegger, Arnold, 223, 271
Sciorra, Annabella, 244
Scott, Cary, 175
Screen (journal), 31

Seabiscuit (2003), 43
Seagal, Steven, 223
Sealed Lips (1942), 73, 138, 145, 146,
    310
The Second Woman (1950), 169, 322,
    345*n7*
Secrets of the Underground (1942), 138
The Secrets of Wu Sin (1932), 95, 105,
    303
Sellon, Charles, 99
Serial Killer (1995), 273
Series, film: Blane, Torchy, 71, 79, 81,
    94, 96, 107–111, 114–124, 133, 143,
    150–153; Carter, Nick, 24; Chan,
    Charlie, 11; Charles, Nick and Nora,
    7; Crime Club, 79; Dirty Harry, 11,
    194, 197; Drew, Nancy, 4, 28, *28,* 57,
    65, 78, 79, 81, 317, 318; The Falcon,
    70; Federal Agent, 75; Joel and Garda
    Sloane, 333*n1*; Keate, Sarah, 81,
    87, 89, 90; The Saint, 43, 69; The
    Shadow, 80, 131; Sloane, Joel and
    Garda, 7; The Thin Man, 136, 333*n1*;
    Withers, Hildegarde, 71, 81, 82, 83,
    83, 84, 85, 86, 87, 89
Seven (1995), 273
The Seventh Victim (1943), 169–170, 319
Sexual Politics (Millet), 30
The Shadow, 80, 131
Shadow of a Doubt (1943), 170–172,
    319
Shadow of theThin Man (1941), 333*n1*
Shaft (1971), 11, 194, 196
Shannon, Frank, 122
Shatner, William, 292
Shattered (1991), 222
Shayne, Michael, 70
Shearer, Norma, 38, 64
Sheba, Baby (1975), 196, 206–208, 323
She Done HIm Wrong (1933), 336*n3*
Shepard, Sam, 240
Sheridan, Ann, 162, 180, *181,* 317, 322,
    342*n17*
A Shot in the Dark (1941), 152
A Shriek in the Night (1933), 95, 109,
    303

The Silence of the Lambs (1991), 14, 255, 271–276, 277, 294, 325, 332
Silver, Ron, 266
Silverman, Kaja, 56
Silverman, Sid, 45
Simpson, Philip, 273
Sinatra, Frank, 192
Singer, Ben, 4, 26, 27, 172
Single White Female (1992), 222
Sklar, Robert, 45
Skyscraper Souls (1932), 62
Sleepers (1941), 138, 139
Sliver (1993), 229
Sloane, Joel and Garda, 7
Slung, Michele, 20, 21
Smart Blonde (1937), 93, 94, 95, 115, 119, 120, 122, 130, 152, 305
Smith, Alexis, 155, 157, 322
Smith, Jaclyn, 8
Sob Sister (1931), 95, 98, 103, 107, 302
Sob sisters. *See* Girl reporters
Social: acceptability, 33, 35, 36; anxieties, 16; assumptions, 102; attitudes, 9, 61; change, 31, 137, 192; connections, 161; conventions, 35; identity, 50; issues, 71, 114; mobility, 54; order, 17, 57; reality, 5, 34; roles, 35, 52, 258; upheavals, 11
Solomon, Barbara Miller, 81
Song of the Thin Man (1947), 333n1
The Sophie Horowitz Story (Schulman), 263
So Proudly We Hail! (1943), 137
Sothern, Ann, 91, 92, 155, 156, 157, 187, 305, 321
Spade, Sam, 56
The Sphinx (1933), 95, 98, 303
Spinrad, Leonard, 11
Spinster detectives, 18, 28, 81–87
Stagecoach (1939), 112
Stallone, Sylvester, 223, 244, 265, 271
Stanke, Don, 70
Stanwyck, Barbara, 49, 58, 61, 80, 135, 136, 160, 165, 187, 313, 317, 321, 323, 336n3, 337n5, 346n13
Starling, Clarice, 9, 14, 273–276

Stevens, Mark, 55–56, 167
Stevens, Stella, 218
Stewart, Jimmy, 192
Stoker, Austin, 207
Stokes, Melvyn, 38
Stone, John, 73
Stone, Sharon, 264
Stonehouse, Ruth, 25
Strange, Violet, 23
Strange Adventure (1932), 95, 145
Stranger on the Third Floor (1940), 166, 319
Stricker, Frank, 51
Strom, Sharon Hartman, 52
Stuart, Gloria, 106, 305
Stuart, Kathleen, 167
Studio era, 44–46; control of all aspects of business, 44
Studio Relations Committee, 45
"A Study in Scarlet" (Doyle), 17
Style Moderne, 59–63
Sullivan, Margaret, 306
Sullivan, Mary, 18
Summers-Bremner, Eluned, 14
Super Fly (1972), 195
Suspect (1987), 222, 225, 232–235, 245, 248, 254, 324, 332, 348n2
Suspect Zero (2004), 273
Swank, Hilary, 328
Sweet Sweetback's Baadasss Song (1971), 194
Swing Shift Maisie (1943), 137
Sykes, Brenda, 205
Sylvia of the Secret Service (1917), 25

Taking Lives (2004), 276, 283, 286–287, 294, 328, 332
Talbot, Lyle, 89, 109, 150
Tallicher, Margaret, 167, 319
Tasker, Yvonne, 257, 267, 277
Taubin, Amy, 276, 277, 283
Taves, Brian, 46, 48
Taylor, Estelle, 26
Taylor, Kent, 155
Taylor, Robert, 168
Teasdale, Verree, 62

Television. *See also* individual programs: "Cagney and Lacey," 221; "CSI," 273; detective series, 192; explosion of female detectives on, 9; "Foxfire," 265; "Hart to Hart," 221; "Lady Blue," 265; "Law & Order," 273; "Moonlighting," 221; "Murder, She Wrote," 221

Terminator 2: Judgement Day (1991), 266

Terry, Anne, 177

Terry, Sheila, 303

Thalberg, Irving, 60

That Affair Next Door (Green), 23

"The Girl from U.N.C.L.E." (television), 192

Theory: psychoanalytic film, 31, 32; queer, 31; reflection, 31; screen, 31

There Goes My Girl (1937), 91, 95, 305

There's Always a Woman (1938), 333n2

There's That Woman Again (1938), 333n2

The Thin Man (1934), 7, 70, 136, 333n1

The Thin Man Goes Home (1943), 333n1

The Thirteen Problems (Christie), 336n12

Thomas, Frankie, 78

The Thomas Crown Affair (1968, 1999), 13, 192

Thompson, Dorothy, 94, 136

Thompson, John, 12

Thornton, Edith, 26

Three Wise Girls (1932), 62

A Time to Kill (1996), 245

Tobin, Genevieve, 103, 302

Todd, Drew, 70

Todorov, Tzvetan, 254, 333n5

Toluboff, Alexander, 60

Tomb Raider (2001), 290

Tone, Franchot, 176

Tony Rome (1967), 192

Toomey, Regis, 158

Too Tough to Kill (1935), 95

Top Hat (1935), 61

Torchy Blane in Chinatown (1939), 95, 121, 307, 342n15

Torchy Blane in Panama (1938), 95, 119, 120, 121, 122, 143, 307

Torchy Blane...Playing with Dynamite (1939), 96, 124, 150, 308

Torchy Gets Her Man (1938), 95, 123, 307

Torchy Runs for Mayor (1939), 95, 123, 308

Touch of Evil (1958), 164, 192

Towne, Rosella, 129, 308, 341n11

Tracy, Dick, 70

Tracy, Lee, 110

Tracy, Spencer, 112, 227–229

Traffic in Crime (1946), 138, 312

Trapped in the Great Metropolis (1914), 25

Traub, Valerie, 261, 264

Trevor, Claire, 57, 64, 65, 71, 75, 80, 92, 112–114, 128, 149, 303, 304, 305, 306, 307, 315, 322, 340n5

The Trouble with Women (1947), 12, 139, 312

Tunney, Robin, 212

Turner, Florence, 335n9

Turner, Kathleen, 266, 269–271, 325

Twisted (2004), 276, 277, 283, 285–286, 328, 332

Ulmer, Edgar, 48

Undercover detectives, 7, 8, 9, 36, 71, 72–77, 102, 103, 106

Undercover Girl (1950), 155, 157, 322

Undercover Maisie (1947), 155, 156, 321

Undercover Woman (1946), 154, 344n5

Undercurrent (1946), 168, 321

Underworld U.S.A. (1961), 192

Unfaithful (2002), 244251

United Artists, 44, 47, 93, 260

Universal Studios, 44, 47, 48

Unknown Woman (1935), 75, 91

Untraceable (2008), 276, 277, 295–297, 328, 332

Up for Murder (1931), 95, 98, 103, 302

Vail, Lester, 337n5

Vanacker, Sabine, 14

Van Alen, William, 61

Vance, Philo, 70, 79, 91

Van Dine, S.S., 70, 79
Vane, Harriet, 28
Vertigo (1958), 192
V.I. Warshawski (1991), 266, 269–271, 325, 332
Victor, Metta, 18–20, *19*
Vincent, Allen, 117
Vincent, June, *176*, 178, 313, 321

Waites, Kate, 293
Waldman, Diane, 174, 334*n2*, 346*n11*
Wales, Ethel, 25
Walker, Kiki, 167
Walker, Sue, 308
Wallace, Morgan, 114
Walsh, Andrea, 10, 33, 71, 96, 137
Walsh, J.T., 238
Walters, Luana, 130, 143, 311, 321
Walters, Pat, 149
Walthall, Henry, 25
Walton, Pricilla, 14
Ward, Maggie, 246–248
Warden, Jack, 242
Ware, Irene, 99
Ware, Susan, 81
Warne, Kate, 18
Warner Bros. Studios, 44, 47, 59, 60, 79, 81, 82, 87, 88, 89, 90, 126, 151, 194
Warren, Lucy "Tex," 112
Warshawski, V.I., 9, 266, 269–271, 325, 332
Washington, Denzel, 281, 282, 349*n9*
Watkins, Linda, 103, 302
Weaver, Marjorie, 149, 159, 310, 311, 320
Weaver, Sigourney, 220, 225, 276–279, 324, 326
Webb, Clifton, 55
The Web of Chance (1919), 25
Wedding Present (1936), 95
Weir, Hugh, 23
Weiss, Andrea, 254, 263
Welles, Orson, 192
Wells, Alice Stebbin, 18
Wentworth, Mary, 227

We're Only Human (1935), 95, 304
Werner, James, 66
West, Mae, 38, 45, 56, 336*n3*
Whalen, Michael, 226
Whatling, Claire, 254, 263
While the Patient Slept (935), 87, 315
White, Pearl, 24, 25, 335*n10*
Whitlock, Lloyd, 103
Who is Hope Schuyler? (1942), 138
Widmark, Richard, 192, 259
Wilbur, George, 240
Wild, Wild Susan (1925), 26
Williams, Bill, 168
Williams, Kit, 153
Williams, Linda, 173, 174, 282
Williams, Linda Ruth, 241, 254, 263
Williams, Raymond, 31
Williams, Robert, 104
Williams, Robin, 262
Williams, Tony, 184
Willis, Bruce, 223, 265
Wilson, Barbara, 263, 350*n6*
Wilson, Dorothy, 52
Wilson, Edmund, 55
Wilson, Elizabeth, 66, 67
Wilson, Lois, 101, 105, 303
Wimsey, Lord Peter, 28
Wingate, James, 99
Winger, Debra, 255, 260–263, 273, 324, 325, 349*n2*
Winslow, Myrna "Jinx," 151, 154
Winters, Shelley, 202
Withers, Grant, 105, 343*n1*
Withers, Hildegarde, 15, 28, 29, 65, 69, 71, 77, 81, 82, 83, *83*, 84, 85, 86, 87, 89, 120
Witherspoon, Reese, 250, 290, 327
Witness to Murder (1954), 187, 188, 323
Wolff, Janet, 67, 323
Wollstonecraft, Mary, 30
Womack, Kenneth, 34, 283
A Woman Against the World (1928), 95
The Woman Condemned, 74, 314
Woman in Distress (1937), 95
Woman of the Year (1942), 58, 136, 139

Woman on the Run (1950), 163, 172, 174, 175, 180–185, 322, 345*n8*

Woman Unafraid (1934), 75, 314

Women: abandonment of feminine traits by, 3; backlash against working, 51, 52; divorce from traditional life-giving roles, 14; as domestic goddesses, 160; effect of Great Depression on, 49–54; feminine motivations for willingness to join workforce, 137; lack of authoritative film voice, 56; masculine, 97–111; on police forces, 7, 18, 154, 155; recast from producer to consumer, 50; replacements for men in workforce in wartime, 137; social backlash against female independence, 135–138, 234

Women Are Trouble (1936), 95, 131, 145, 305

The Women Condemned (1934), 36, 73

Women from Headquarters (1950), 155

Women's Liberation Movement, 4, 11, 31, 215

The Women Who Dared (1911), 25

Wong, James Lee, 70

Wood, Mrs. Henry, 19

Woodbury, Joan, 147, 310

Woodman, Anne, 104

Woods, Elle, 250

Woolf, Virginia, 55

Woolrich, Cornell, 164, 167, 168, 172, 176

World War II: downturn in popular attitudes toward working women, 135; effect on Great Depression, 51; gender role shift during, 10; progressive female roles prior to, 5

Worth, Constance, 75

Wray, Fay, *58*, 111, 117, 131, 161, 227

Wright, Teresa, 170

Wright, Theresa, 312, 319

Wyatt, Jane, 304

Wylie, Philip, 135

Wyman, Jane, 92, 122, 124, 150, 151, 152, 154, 175, 308, 318, 320, 340*n4*

Yankee Film Company, 25

Yellow Cargo (1936), 75, 96, 315

Yesil, Bilge, 137

Yorke, Ruth, 341*n11*

You Cant Escape Forever (1942), 138, 150, 152, 311

Young, Clara Kimball, 25

Young, Kimball, 132

Young, Loretta, 104, 302

Young, Robert, 169

Younger, Beverly, 71

Zanuck, Darryl, 60

Zellweger, Renée, 44

Zimmerman, Bonnie, 264

Zinman, David, 115, 340*n4*

Zodiac (2007), 273